# Operational Code Analysis and Foreign Policy Roles

In this book, senior scholars and a new generation of analysts present different applications of recent advances linking beliefs and decision-making in the area of foreign policy analysis with strategic interactions in world politics.

Divided into five parts, Part 1 identifies how the beliefs in the cognitive operational codes of individual leaders explain the political decisions of states. In Part 2, five chapters illustrate progress in comparing the operational codes of individual leaders, including Vladimir Putin of Russia, three US presidents, Bolivian President Evo Morales, Sri Lanka's President Chandrika Kumaratunga, and various leaders of terrorist organizations operating in the Middle East and North Africa. Part 3 introduces a new Psychological Characteristics of Leaders (PsyCL) data set containing the operational codes of US presidents from the early 1800s to the present. In Part 4, the focus is on strategic interactions among dyads and evolutionary patterns among states in different regional and world systems. Part 5 revisits whether the contents of the preceding chapters support the claims about the links between beliefs and foreign policy roles in world politics.

Richly illustrated and with comprehensive analysis *Operational Code Analysis and Foreign Policy Roles* will be of interest to specialists in foreign policy analysis, international relations theorists, graduate students, and national security analysts in the policy-making and intelligence communities.

**Mark Schafer** is a Professor of Political Psychology in the School of Politics, Security, and International Affairs at the University of Central Florida working primarily in the field of international relations. His research interests include groupthink, the operational code, and psychological correlates of foreign policy behavior. He has published his research in major journals such as *Journal of Politics, International Studies Quarterly,* and *Journal of Conflict Resolution.* He received the Erik Erikson Award for Early Career Achievement from the International Society of Political Psychology in

2003 and was honored with the Distinguished Scholar Award from the Foreign Policy Analysis Section of the International Studies Association in 2021.

**Stephen G. Walker** is Professor Emeritus in the School of Politics and Global Studies at Arizona State University. His research interests focus on conflict management and resolution, foreign policy analysis, and political psychology. His research articles have appeared in *Political Psychology, Journal of Conflict Resolution,* and *International Studies Quarterly.* He received the Foreign Policy Section's Distinguished Scholar Award from the International Studies Association in 2003.

Routledge Advances in International Relations and Global Politics

For information about the series: https://www.routledge.com/Routledge-Advances-in-International-Relations-and-Global-Politics/book-series/IRGP

# Operational Code Analysis and Foreign Policy Roles

## Crossing Simon's Bridge

**Edited by Mark Schafer**
**Stephen G. Walker**

Routledge
Taylor & Francis Group

NEW YORK AND LONDON

First published 2021
by Routledge
52 Vanderbilt Avenue, New York, NY 10017

and by Routledge
2 Park Square, Milton Park, Abingdon, Oxon, OX14 4RN

*Routledge is an imprint of the Taylor & Francis Group, an Informa business*

*British Library Cataloguing-in-Publication Data*
A catalogue record for this book is available from the British Library

*Library of Congress Cataloging-in-Publication Data*
A catalog record for this title has been requested

ISBN: 978-0-367-65090-2 (hbk)
ISBN: 978-0-367-67363-5 (pbk)
ISBN: 978-1-003-13102-1 (ebk)

Typeset in Times New Roman
by KnowledgeWorks Global Ltd.

## Dedication

We dedicate this book to the two most
important people in our lives, our partners
Joey and Jackie. They have been by our side
for many years and it is impossible for us
to say how much we cherish their support,
companionship, encouragement, patience,
friendship, and love.

# Contents

xii   *Contents*

# Preface

The operational code research program is almost 70 years old, dating back to the study of the operational code of the Soviet Politburo by Nathan Leites and evolving over the years as an approach to studying the beliefs of political leaders about the effective exercise of power in the conduct of politics. The focus in this volume is on the results of efforts to expand the horizons of the research program in two directions from a focus on beliefs and actions regarding the exercise of power to include the origins of those beliefs and the consequences of those actions. In doing so, this book represents the current efforts by members of the operational code research program to "cross Simon's bridge." Herbert Simon had discussed bridging the gap between the sciences of the mind (psychology) and one of the social sciences (politics) as president of the American Political Science Association in his 1985 inaugural address, "Human Nature and Politics: The Dialogue of Psychology with Political Science."

This volume is an example of subsequent research in the emerging trans-discipline of political psychology as the study of the interface between psychology and politics, which has evolved as both an area of inquiry and in the form of the International Society of Political Psychology as a professional organization of scholars from the disciplines of psychology and political science. Our efforts have been inspired and supported by membership in ISPP and by several individuals and other institutions over the past decade and a half. Psychologist Margaret Hermann's NSF research training grant at Ohio State University investigated the links between individual cognitions and collective decisions and funded talented doctoral students from the disciplines of psychology and political science. A dissertation grant from this program helped train one of us and catalyzed the other one to focus more directly on this area of research into the cognitions of leaders and their foreign policy decisions.

We are inspired as well by the example and support of political scientists Alexander George and Ole Holsti, who led during their lives and careers by example with pioneering investigations into the psychology of crisis decision-making, coercive diplomacy, and statecraft. These two scholars rescued the Leites concept of an operational code from relative obscurity and created the operational code research program as a "thing." Michael Young and Robert Woyach at Social Science Automation developed the software for an automated version of the Verbs In Context System (VICS) in collaboration with the editors of this volume, which has been the primary instrument developed for the metrics used by authors in this volume (and many others elsewhere) to measure a leader's cognitive operational code. We owe a large intellectual debt as well to Steven Brams for the game models from his *Theory of Moves* (Oxford, 1994), which we deploy as a binary role theory of world politics to specify different types of social operational codes.

Our own efforts to emulate the success of these pioneers have been supplemented by generations of our graduate students at Arizona State University, Louisiana State University, and the University of Central Florida who have become faculty members and researchers at various institutions around the country and around the world. In turn, they continue with their own scholarship to stimulate their students and build Simon's bridge. Several of them are represented in this volume along with other younger scholars who employ these models and metrics. Our current role as editors has been to organize a sample of this research into a more or less coherent argument about the significance of the results and suggest how this research program may evolve into the future.

We are grateful to several institutional sources of support in getting this volume into print. They include the School of Politics and Global Studies at Arizona State University and the School of Politics, Security, and International Affairs at the University of Central Florida where many of the contributors were trained as researchers. We thank these institutions for travel and computer support in the pursuit of our research projects. Also crucial is the enthusiastic support of the editors at Routledge Press, especially Senior Editor for Politics Natalja Mortensen and Editorial Assistant Charlie Baker, who saw our vision of this project, provided guidance, and answered many questions along the path to completion.

Finally, we would be remiss if we did not recognize the role that our respective spouses have played in bringing this project across the finish line. They have endured (with a minimum of eye-rolling) arcane conversations between the editors in various venues about getting this volume organized and into print, ranging from car rides across New England to plane rides across the country and professional meetings around the world. They have also been good humored about our efforts to put the volume together while still carrying on the responsibilities of family life in a time of the COVID-19 virus. We have dedicated this volume to them, because we recognize that the project would probably not seem worth doing without their confident affirmation of us and the value of our work.

*Mark Schafer*
*Orlando, Florida*
*August 28, 2020*

*Stephen G. Walker*
*Flagstaff, Arizona*
*August 28, 2020*

# List of Contributors

**Femke E. Bakker** is an Assistant Professor at the Institute of Political Science of Leiden University. Her research interests focus on microfoundations of IR theories, decision-making behavior, and political psychology. Her research articles have appeared in *Acta Politica, Perspectives on Political Science*, and *Political Research Exchange*. Her dissertation, *Hawks and Doves: Democratic Peace Theory Revisited*, received the *ECPR Jean Blondel Ph.D. Prize (2019)*, and an Honorary Mention from the *ISPP Dissertation Prize (2019)*.

**Clayton Besaw** is a Research Associate at the One Earth Future Foundation. His research interests focus on political violence, natural language processing, rare event forecasting, and machine learning development. His research articles have appeared in *Journal of Conflict Resolution, Conflict Management and Peace Science*, and the *Journal of Quantitative Criminology*.

**Sercan Canbolat** is a Ph.D. Candidate in Political Science at the University of Connecticut. His doctoral dissertation is on patterns of learning and political survival by beleaguered Middle Eastern leaders in the face of the post-2011 Arab Uprisings. His research articles have appeared in *International Studies Review, Political Research Quarterly, and Polity*. He and his coauthors received the *Polity* Prize in 2018 for the best research article published in the journal's previous volume.

**Huiyun Feng** is a Senior Lecturer in the School of Government and International Relations and Deputy Director of the Centre for Governance and Public Policy at Griffith University, Australia. Her publications have appeared in the *European Journal of International Relations, Security Studies, The Pacific Review, International Politics, Chinese Journal of International Politics*, and *Asian Perspective*. She is the author of *Chinese Strategic Culture and Foreign Policy Decision-making: Confucianism, Leadership and War* (2007), the coauthor of *Prospect Theory and Foreign Policy Analysis in the Asia–Pacific, How China Sees the World: Insights from China's International Relations*

*Scholars,* and a coeditor of *China's Challenges and International Order Transition: Beyond Thucydides's Trap.*

**Paul Gill** recently earned his M.A. at Georgetown University's Security Studies Program. His research interests focus on conflict studies, diplomacy, economics, and political psychology. Previously, he served as a research assistant for the University of Central Florida's Intelligence Community Center for Academic Excellence.

**Kai He** is a Professor of International Relations, Griffith Asia Institute and Center for Governance and Public Policy, Griffith University, Australia and a Visiting Chair Professor of International Relations at the Zhou Enlai School of Government, Nankai University, China. He is currently an Australian Research Council (ARC) Future Fellow (2017–2020). He is the author of *Institutional Balancing in the Asia Pacific: Economic Interdependence and China's Rise* and *China's Crisis Behavior: Political Survival and Foreign Policy; How China Sees the World: Insights from Chinese International Relations Scholars* (coauthored with Huiyun Feng and Xiaojun Li); and *China's Challenges and International Order Transition: Beyond "Thucydides's Trap"* (co-edited with Huiyun Feng).

**Collin J. Kazazis** is a recent graduate from the School of Politics, Security, and International Affairs at the University of Central Florida. His research interests focus on threat perception and political psychology. His honors thesis investigated the effect of leadership traits on cognitive constructions of threat perception.

**Joshua E. Lambert** is the NLP/Machine Learning Researcher for the University of Central Florida's National Center for Coastal Research. His research interests include leveraging GIS and machine learning tools to better understand environmental security, civil-military relations, conflict outcomes, and political psychology. His research has been published in *Small Wars and Insurgencies*, the nonprofit *One Earth Future*, as well as the popular commentary outlet *The Conversation.*

**Akan Malici** is a Professor of Political Science at Furman University. His scholarly interests are in the areas of foreign policy analysis and international security. Akan is the author of *When Leaders Learn and When They Don't* and *The Search for a Common European Foreign and Security Policy;* coauthor of *U.S. Presidents and Foreign Policy Mistakes,* and *Role Theory and Role Conflict in U.S.-Iran Relations: Enemies of Our Own Making;* coeditor of *Re-thinking Foreign Policy Analysis* and *Political Science Research in Practice.*

**B. Gregory Marfleet** is the Dorothy H. and Edward C. Congdon Professor of Political Science at Carleton College. His research interests are in the areas of foreign policy analysis, elite foreign policy decision-making, complex systems, and agent-based modeling in politics. He has published articles in *Political Psychology* and *Foreign Policy Analysis*. His research awards include a Harry Frank Guggenheim Foundation Fellowship.

**Didara Nurmanova** is a Research Fellow in the School of Politics, Security, and International Affairs at the University of Central Florida. Her research interests primarily center on comparative political behavior, including protests, public opinion, and voting with a regional focus on Russia and post-Soviet Eurasia. Her broader research interests include ethnic politics, political psychology, and foreign policy analysis.

**Mark Schafer** is a Professor of Political Psychology in the School of Politics, Security, and International Affairs at the University of Central Florida working primarily in the field of international relations. His research interests include groupthink, the operational code, and psychological correlates of foreign policy behavior. He has published his research in major journals such as *Journal of Politics*, *International Studies Quarterly*, and *Journal of Conflict Resolution*. He received the Erik Erikson Award for Early Career Achievement from the International Society of Political Psychology in 2003 and was honored with the Distinguished Scholar Award from the Foreign Policy Analysis Section of the International Studies Association in 2021.

**Seyed Hamidreza Serri** is an Assistant Professor of Security Studies at the University of North Georgia. His research interests focus on American foreign policy, foreign policy analysis, and international security. His two upcoming works include "League of Nations: Strategic Preferences of the United States at the End of WWI," in *America and World War I*, edited by Craig B. Greathouse and Austin Riede and "Security and Military Power," in *Prospectus for The Basics of World Politics: Theory and Practice*, edited by Dlynn A. Williams and Raluca Viman Miller.

**Gary E. Smith** is a Research Fellow at the University of Central Florida where he also serves as an Academic Advisor for Undergraduate Advising Services in the School of Politics, Security, and International Affairs. Additionally, he is an Adjunct Professor of Political Science at Valencia College. His research interests focus on civil conflict studies, elite decision-making, and political psychology. His research articles have appeared in *African Affairs, Politics*, and *PS: Political Science & Politics*. He has also coauthored contributions to the *Oxford Encyclopedia of Foreign Policy Analysis* and the *Oxford Handbook of Behavioral Political Science*) and received the Roberta Siegel Award for Best Paper by an Early Career Scholar from the International

Society of Political Psychology in 2016 for his research coauthored with Rebecca Schiel.

**Consuelo Thiers** is a Ph.D. Candidate in Politics and International Relations at the University of Edinburgh. Her research interests focus on political psychology, foreign policy analysis, enduring rivalries, and Latin America. She has coauthored "Coding in tongues: Developing non-English coding schemes for leadership profiling" in the *International Studies Review* and received the Politics and International Relations Career development Ph.D. scholarship granted by the University of Edinburgh (2016–2019) plus the Santander kick-start research funding granted by the Centre for Contemporary Latin American Studies, University of Edinburgh (2018).

**Niels van Willigen** is an Associate Professor of International Relations in the Institute of Political Science at Leiden University. His research interests focus on foreign policy analysis, security studies (more in particular peace operations, arms control, and European security) and international organizations. His research articles have appeared in *International Peacekeeping, East European Politics,* and *Evaluation: The International Journal of Theory, Research and Practice,* and he has published a monograph *Peacebuilding and International Administration.* He received a NATO/EAPC Fellowship for a research project on European security and defense and participated in the ERASMUS + Network on Research and Teaching in EU foreign affairs (NORTIA).

**Stephen G. Walker** is a Professor Emeritus in the School of Politics and Global Studies at Arizona State University. His research interests focus on conflict management and resolution, foreign policy analysis, and political psychology. His research articles have appeared in *Political Psychology, Journal of Conflict Resolution,* and *International Studies Quarterly,* and he has published *U.S. Presidents and Foreign Policy Mistakes* coauthored with Akan Malici; *Role Theory and the Cognitive Architecture of British Appeasement Decisions,* and *Role Theory and Role Conflict in U.S.-Iran Relations* coauthored with Akan Malici. He received the Foreign Policy Section's Distinguished Scholar Award from the International Studies Association in 2003.

# Part I

# Beliefs and Roles in World Politics

# 1 The Interface between Beliefs and Roles in World Politics

*Stephen G. Walker and Mark Schafer*

## Introduction

Nobel Laureate Herbert Simon proposed over 30 years ago the desirability of bridging the sciences of the mind (psychology) and the social sciences (political science) with the concept of bounded rationality (Simon 1985; see also Simon 1957, 1969). Lupia, McCubbins, and Popkin (2000, 12) commented 15 years later that "the scientific advances of the last four decades give us an opportunity that Simon did not have when he forged the concept of bounded rationality—the opportunity to build Simon's bridge." They identified advances in computer simulations of human information processing and new game theory models of decision-making under uncertainty as analytical tools that were not available to Simon when he first advocated this bridge. We began to apply those tools in the operational code research program over the next 5 years and presented the initial results in an edited volume (Schafer and Walker 2006).

We employ those same tools in this volume and report further progress toward Simon's goal in the form of results from the research of a mix of senior scholars and a new generation of analysts over the past decade and a half. The results show that advances in the metrics of operational code analysis together with advances in the models of binary role theory "cross Simon's bridge." These advances synthesize the psychological beliefs of leaders and the social roles of states in world politics via statistical indices of bounded rationality and computational models of role theory dynamics to explain collective interaction patterns of cooperation and conflict by agents in world politics. The chapters in this volume report the results of different applications linking personality traits, operational code beliefs, and foreign policy roles in the subfield of foreign policy analysis (FPA) within the field of international relations (IR).

In this chapter, we present an outline of our main argument that an alliance of operational code metrics and role theory models can provide the actor-specific, situation-generic, and abstract-theoretical levels of knowledge necessary to link the individual cognitions of leaders and the collective decisions of states within an agent-based theory of strategic interactions in world politics (George 1993). The details that provide the context for our argument are elaborated in Chapter 2 along with a brief conceptual history and two possible future trajectories for the research program in operational code analysis. The subsequent chapters in Parts II, III, and IV of the volume contain studies of the different levels of foreign policy knowledge identified by George (1993). A concluding chapter in Part V provides an appraisal of our argument with various criteria for assessing progress in scientific research programs (Kuhn 1962; Lakatos 1970; Laudan 1977; Walker 2003; Jackson 2011).

## Main Argument

Our main argument is made possible because of recent advances in operational code analysis and binary role theory (Walker, Malici, and Schafer 2011; Walker 2013, 2016; Malici and Walker 2017). The theoretical advances show how personality traits and operational code beliefs steer foreign policy decisions and evolve as larger patterns of foreign policy roles enacted by states as complex adaptive systems (CAS) in world politics. The methodological advances include the expansion of automated content analysis capabilities for retrieving operational code beliefs to include dictionaries in Spanish and Arabic as well as in English, the construction of new indices to measure operational code beliefs, and the disaggregation of belief indices to allow the targeted operational code analyses of strategic interaction patterns within different issue areas between role dyads plus facilitate the longitudinal analysis of belief changes (learning) and the evolution of roles in world politics.

The methodological advances accompany the collection, archiving, and coding of bigger data sets covering years, decades, and generations of statements and documents attributed to US leaders and presidential administrations, as well as other states and agents in world politics. The effects of these developments in instrumentation and data sets join with theoretical advances to extend the substantive advances in operational code analysis beyond the analysis of decisions by individual leaders. The scope of analysis extends to larger decision units such as single groups, bureaucratic organizations, and institutions within states plus the strategic interactions among dyads, triads, and larger ensembles of states, including other agents such as alliances, rivalries, terrorist networks, and international organizations in world politics.

The shift from the study of the belief systems of leaders as decision units to include states and other agents as decision units has led to a focus on role theory to organize and illuminate this expansion in the levels of analysis. Accompanying this expansion is a move to unify the study of FPA and IR as a hierarchy of CAS inspired by the earlier work of Simon (1969), Axelrod (1984), Jervis (1997), and Axelrod and Cohen (1999). FPA in this account focuses on subsystems of states as agents who interact within an overarching regional, functional, or global system and which are themselves constituted internally as subsystems of institutions, organizations, groups, and leaders. While recognizing that these agents are entangled as a single overarching system, the nature of their hierarchical organization also makes them "nearly decomposable," i.e., the interactions within agents as subsystems are stronger than the interactions between those agents as members of the larger system (Simon 1969, 99–103).

The implications of this feature as an organizing principle for unifying FPA and IR are illustrated below with the following brief examples from the study of American domestic politics and US foreign policy. The US political system's three main branches of government, Executive, Congress, and Judiciary, have stronger interactions among organizations within each branch than between each branch. Each branch constitutes a subsystem within the larger US political system. Their horizontal organization as coequal branches is based on the separation of powers between them and locates them at the apex of the vertical organization defined by the federal division of power in the US political system between Washington, DC, and the 50 state political systems. These separation and division patterns in the "span of control" (Simon 1969, 89) characterize different subsystems as levels of analysis in American politics. Nevertheless, they are also levels in a hierarchical political system that is "nearly decomposable" while remaining connected as a larger complex system by the exercise of social power both within and between the agents that compose it.

Similarly, the organizational features of "near decomposability" and "complex connectivity" enable FPA and IR to retain their identities as a subfield and field, respectively, while communicating and coordinating research efforts across levels of analysis in the study of US foreign policy. FPA scholars can analyze interactions among American institutions of government that make US foreign policy decisions to exercise social power in world politics, while IR scholars can study the United States as a member of regional or functional subsystems as agents within the larger global system of world politics.

### Role Theory

Is it possible to move beyond this division of labor between FPA and IR to communicate and coordinate research efforts within the context of an effective theory of foreign policy that also interfaces with a unifying theory of world politics (Hudson and Day 2020, 209–215)? Role theory offers the promise of fulfilling this possibility in the study of world politics (Walker 1987, 241–259; Thies 2010; Walker, Malici, and Schafer 2011, 245–282; Walker 2013, 186–194; Walker 2016). Role theory is both a psychological and a social theory of human behavior. These two features make it especially suitable for the task of analyzing and synthesizing different levels of world politics ranging from the psychological characteristics and actions of individual world leaders to the social exercise of power among leaders, single groups, and coalitions of agents that constitute the states and subsystems in the global system of world politics.

Role theory as an empirical theory of IR has an underlying logical structure with the ability to generate different models of cooperation and conflict in world politics at multiple levels of analysis: system-oriented models of incentives and role demands, actor-centered models of role conceptions and expectations, and action-focused models of cues and role enactment. An emphasis at each of these levels of analysis on strategic interaction positions role theory as a theory of IR between Ego and Alter as well as a theory of their respective foreign policy decisions (Walker 2016; Malici and Walker 2017). However, previous assessments of role theory applications to FPA and IR have characterized the first and second waves of role theory studies as conceptually rich but methodologically poor (Walker 1987, 2016, 2; Thies 2010; Breuning 2011).

With some significant exceptions, the concepts of role theory were used initially for framing historical narratives that provided "thick descriptions" (Geertz 1973) of single cases to identify the role conceptions of leaders in the first wave or the role demands on states in the second wave. These applications of role theory focused on agent-centered foreign policy decisions rather than on the interactions within and among agents. Therefore, they did not employ or emphasize the concepts of role conflict, role competition, role contestation, role transition, and role evolution in role theory, which could have expanded the application of role theory from FPA to the analysis of IR. More recently, a third wave of role theory applications to world politics has begun to address the social dynamics of IR as well as the psychological dynamics of foreign policy decision-making (Walker 2016; see also Thies 2013; Walker 2013; Cantir and Kaarbo 2016; Malici and Walker 2017; Thies and Nieman 2017).

We position the binary role theory in our edited volume within this third wave of role theory scholarship. An alliance of operational code metrics and role theory concepts offers a way for role theory to analyze systematically the complex connections linking the microlevel, individual cognitions of leaders with the meso-level, collective decisions by states and ultimately to the macro-level, systemic outcomes generated by their strategic interactions. The metrics of operational code beliefs provide role theory with the building blocks for "crossing Simon's bridge," the project advocated by Nobel Laureate Herbert Simon to link "the sciences of the mind and the social sciences such as economics and political science" (Lupia, McCubbins, and Popkin 2000, 12; see also Simon 1969).

### *Bounded Rationality*

Simon (1985) suggested "bounded rationality" as the basic concept for bridging the gap between individual cognitions that are the focus of the sciences of the mind and collective decisions that are the focus of political science. Operational code analysis employs several mechanisms in the elaboration of bounded rationality as the basis for a psychological explanation of human decision-making. Cognitive, emotional, and motivational elements of human nature interact as psychological mechanisms that receive and process information. They limit an organism's response to the environment by functioning "as *internal* boundaries on the organism's ability to make rational choices within the *external* boundaries that constrain the possibilities for taking actions to protect or achieve goals" (Walker 2013, 117).

The architecture for how these elements interact to generate decisions by individual leaders as a state's decision unit in a social system is diagrammed in Figure 1.1. Neuroscientists have identified the neural networks of cognition, emotion, and motivation, respectively, which influence an individual's decisions (Ledoux 2002). They specify information about what the individual knows (cognition), feels (emotion), and wants (motivation) regarding the exercise of power by the self toward others in a social environment (Schafer and Walker 2006, 27–30). Simon (1985) distinguishes decisions based on feelings unmediated by cognitions or motivations as instances of "radical irrationality," which are relatively rare unless the decision maker is under considerable stress or surprised (M. Hermann 1979; C. Hermann, 1969; Walker and Watson 1992). Nevertheless, the emotion network reacts to stimuli from the environment faster than the other two networks and influences the responses and interactions of cognitions and motivations as the more rational processes for making decisions (Zajonc 1980; Neumann 2007).

The interaction among these three neural networks represents a model of bounded rationality: positive or negative feelings from the emotional network, motivated biases from the motivational network, and limits on the ability to store and retrieve information from the cognitive network

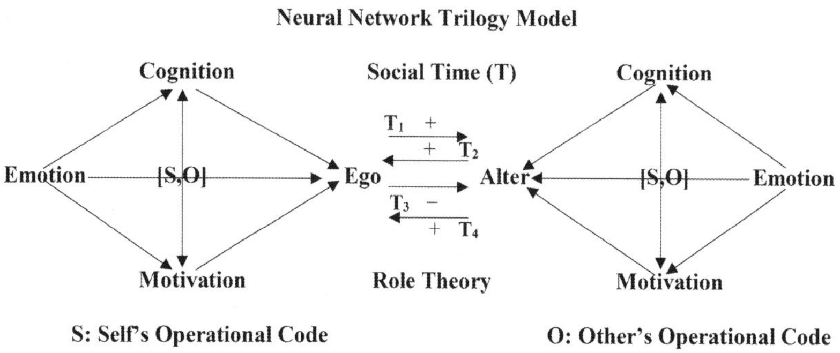

*Figure 1.1* Neural Network Trilogy Model of Role Theory[*]

[*]Ego: Crusoe; Alter: Friday. T: Time; S: Self (Crusoe); O: Other (Friday).
Positive sanction: (+); negative sanction (−).

interact to generate an imperfect response that does not meet the optimal standards of a decision-making model of "substantive rationality" governed by exact cost-benefit calculations and goal maximization (Simon 1985; Lau 2003). Instead, the interactions among these three networks are a satisficing rather than optimizing process of reaching goals and estimating rather than calculating the costs and benefits of ends/means relationships (Simon 1957, 1985; Mintz 1997, 2002; Lau 2003; Walker 2009).

The bounded rationality model in Figure 1.1 also depicts an example of the exercise of social power by two individuals in the simplest version of a political system, namely, when politics begins as Crusoe meets Friday in Daniel Defoe's famous novel about a shipwrecked sailor (Robinson Crusoe) who encounters a native on an isolated desert island (Walker, Malici, and Schafer 2011, 45). Crusoe names the native "Friday" after the day in the week when they had their first encounter. The novel can be read as a parable about English colonialism in the 17th century when the British Empire expanded across the globe, and more broadly, about the logic of Western imperialism's expansion of world politics into what is today the Global South (Shinagel 1994). Friday becomes Crusoe's "man Friday" in the novel, as their relations evolve from their initial interactions into a master–servant role dyad. This evolution in their social relations is defined in Figure 1.1 by the exercise of social power between them as they exchange positive (+) sanctions (appeal/promise/reward) or negative (–) sanctions (oppose/threaten/punish).

The evolutionary pattern of relations between Crusoe and Friday over time in Figure 1.1 is shown by the arrows connecting Ego and Alter at successive time periods ($T_1$ $T_2$ $T_3$ $T_4$), which depict the following sequential pattern in the exchange of cues (signals) between Crusoe (Ego) and Friday (Alter): {+ + − +}. This pattern defines their respective roles as Patron (+ + −) and Client (+ − +), respectively, as Crusoe and Friday exchange positive cues (+ +) at $T_1$ $T_2$ and then mixed signals (− +) at $T_3$ $T_4$. The first pair of signals defines their relations as friendly (+), hostile (–), or mixed (±), while the second pair of signals defines their power relations as either symmetrical (=) or asymmetrical (< or >), depending on whether the pair is identical (+ + or − −) or not (+ − or − +). The inferences about roles are drawn from binary role theory, which employs metrics from operational code analysis to infer the roles of Patron and Client for Self and Other in Figure 1.1 from their exchange of cues as Ego and Alter (Walker 2013).

The sources of the roles attributed to Ego and Alter in Figure 1.1 are the respective operational code beliefs emanating from the interaction between their respective cognitions and motivations, which are extracted from texts (fictional in this example) either authored as first-party accounts by the two members of the role dyad or extracted from third-party accounts by an audience of contemporary observers (other agents and journalists) or subsequently by historians and political scientists.

These sources rely on the logic of a language network to retrieve and analyze this information. The logic may be either a grammatical system or a mathematical system, which can be translated from one system to another. A common example is Morse code, which can translate sequences of letters for words into sequences of dots and dashes for the same words. In turn, dots and dashes can be translated into 0s and 1s and the information coded in the binary language of a computer program with mathematical operators and formulas as the grammar (Lloyd 2007).

These steps for translating letters of the alphabet into mathematical symbols are similar to the grammar of the Verbs in Context System (VICS) of content analysis, which is the language system for retrieving operational code beliefs as the basis for the roles in Figure 1.1. VICS provides a common language of mathematical symbols to retrieve both mental events (cognitions, emotions, and motivations) and social events (positive and negative sanctions) from different alphabetical languages, e.g., English, Spanish, Arabic, so long as dictionaries are available to match the relevant vocabularies of words from each language with each other (Brummer and Young 2020). The recursive logic of the language network that connects operational code beliefs and social roles is represented in Figure 1.2.

The belief and role networks in Figure 1.2 are linked by a language network along with the formulas for calculating the key VICS indices that define the belief networks of Self and Other and the corresponding roles for Ego and Alter. The logical steps in constructing the key VICS indices from observations in the language network at the center of Figure 1.2 are given in the formulas for the Self and Other indices at the bottom of the figure. The transitive verbs containing images of the exercise of power attributed to Self (S) and Other (O) are represented in the a, b, c, d cells of the language network. The respective percentage differences in these observations are the elements of positive (+) or negative (−) sanctions attributed to Self $(a - b)/(a + b)$ and Other $(c - d)/(c + d)$ in the text

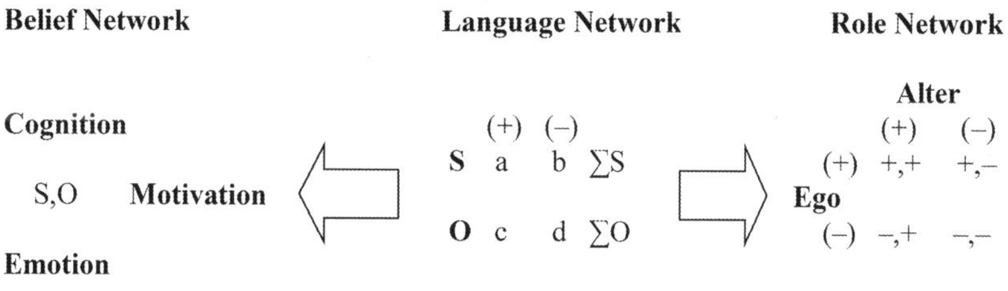

| Belief Network | Language Network | Role Network |
|---|---|---|

*Figure 1.2* Belief, Language, and Role Networks for Constructing Key VICS Indices[*]

[*]Self VICS indices: approach to strategy: $S = [(a - b)/(a + b)]$; historical control: $S = [\Sigma S - \Sigma O] / [\Sigma S + \Sigma O]$.
Other VICS indices: political universe: $O = [(c - d)/(c + d)]$; historical control: $O = [\Sigma O - \Sigma S] / [\Sigma S + \Sigma O]$.

under analysis, and the percentage differences in their respective sums are the historical control indices for Self $[\Sigma S - \Sigma O] / [\Sigma S + \Sigma O]$ and Other $[\Sigma O - \Sigma S] / [\Sigma S + \Sigma O]$.

The VICS rules for retrieving the information for these indices from a text include the following steps: (1) identify the relevant transitive verbs from a language attributed to the speaker and other agents of interest to the analyst; (2) count the number of transitive verbs attributed to each agent; (3) calculate the percentages for different kinds of transitive verbs attributed to each agent; (4) combine these percentages into different indices of the exercise of power by different agents; and (5) infer from these attribution patterns the diagnostic, choice, and shift propensities of relevant agents to exercise positive (+) or negative (–) sanctions toward one another (Schafer and Walker 2006).

Finally, use the rules of binary role theory (not shown in Figure 1.2) to identify the sequential patterns of behavior attributed as roles to different agents, which emerge from the analysis of their different propensities to exercise positive (+) and negative (–) sanctions. Then construct as mathematical game matrices the role network of their social interactions from the intersection of these roles. Binary role theory employs the rules of sequential game theory developed by Brams (1994) to solve these games and assess the fit between these models for the strategies and outcomes that define the relations between Ego and Alter. Conversely, if strategies and outcomes are known, it is possible to infer from the game between them the operational code beliefs that specified the roles of the agents (players). These possibilities make binary role theory a recursive hierarchical model of IR specified by the mathematical logic of game theory and the statistical metrics of operational code analysis (Walker 2013; Malici and Walker 2017).

## Beliefs and Roles: Alliance Benefits

An alliance of beliefs and roles to specify games of strategic interaction goes beyond the separate study of FPA and IR toward integration with a common set of concepts, models, and metrics. The "nearly decomposable" relationship between the decisions of agents as subsystems and their roles as members of a larger system allows scholars of FPA and IR theory to pursue separate research agendas with middle-range theories of beliefs and foreign policy decisions that are nonetheless guided by models that are isomorphic (share consistent logics) and commensurable (share identical metrics) within a general role theory of world politics. Moreover, the products of these efforts at different levels of aggregation and analysis yield conceptual insights and empirical results that answer questions raised by both scholars and practitioners, thereby "bridging the gap" regarding foreign policy in theory and practice between the academic and policy communities (George 1993).

This volume contains only studies that have employed statistical indices and computer algorithms from the VICS of content analysis (Walker, Schafer, and Young 1998; Young 2001; Schafer and Walker 2006). This methodological focus provides more coherence to the collection of papers at the risk of losing "the idiosyncrasies of the case which, at times, may be critical to understanding why a leader is acting in a specific manner. Much of this richness is lost in a number-based approach" (Young and Schafer 1998, 72, cited by Malici 2017, 28–29). Offsetting this risk is the ability of categories to allow counterfactual analysis from a comparative perspective and thereby minimize committing "the fallacy of misplaced concreteness," which is to mistake a particular interpretation of a case as the only one (Whitehead 1948, 52; see also Hedstrom and Swedberg 1998, 15; Post and Walker 2003, 403; Walker and Malici 2011, 297 and 317, n. 2).

The authors of the chapters in this volume strike a balance in managing these risks by including a discussion of the qualitative features of their cases and embedding the quantitative results within the context of a relevant analytical narrative (Bates et al. 1998). Scholars and practitioners who are interested in actor-specific models of particular leaders or states can employ the metrics of operational code analysis to identify the roles and corresponding strategies that those leaders attribute to themselves and others in the political universe. As George (1993, xvii) points out, policymakers also need generic knowledge about actors in situations, i.e., generalizable knowledge about leaders who occupy roles in the same state or other institutions over time or who face similar situations or challenges. Finally, both scholars and policymakers need abstract-theoretical knowledge about the conceptualization of strategies, "a conceptual framework for each of the many different strategies and instruments available for … attempting to influence other states" (George 1993, xvii; see also Aron 1967). The book's organization reflects the demand for these different kinds of knowledge by scholars and practitioners.

In Part II, *The Operational Codes of World Leaders*, five chapters provide *actor-specific knowledge* of leaders for practitioners and geographic area experts, including Vladimir Putin of Russia; US presidents Bush 43, Obama, and Trump; Bolivian president Morales; Sri Lankan president Kumaratunga; and leaders of various terrorist groups operating in the Middle East and North Africa (MENA). They employ single-case and small-N research designs with structured-focused comparison methods to understand changes in a leader's belief system over time or to highlight differences across leaders and between their respective organizations. This actor-specific knowledge is valuable information for practitioners, in order to avoid or remedy foreign policy mistakes (Walker and Malici 2011). Some chapters extend the analytical focus to include the agreement between a leader's beliefs and the beliefs embodied in a state's policy documents or to link beliefs and domestic or foreign conflict behavior. Others employ new methodological tools, such as VICS dictionaries in the native languages of the speakers, e.g., Spanish or Arabic, instead of English.

In Part III, *The Psychological Characteristics of US Presidents*, the contributors focus on *situation-generic knowledge* about situations and generalizations about a sample of leaders rather than on actor-specific models of particular US presidents. The samples of leaders shared by these studies are occupants of the White House from James Monroe to Barack Obama. The authors employ sampling and large-N research designs to introduce a new Psychological Characteristics of Leaders (PsyCL) data set containing the operational code beliefs of US presidents from the early 1800s to the present. Also coded are other psychological characteristics from the Leadership Trait Analysis (LTA) research program, such as distrust, belief in ability to control events (BACE), and self-confidence, which permit the investigation of the origins of operational code beliefs in the personalities of leaders (M. Hermann 2003).

One chapter links composite models of LTA and operational code analysis (OCA) variables to the conduct of foreign conflict behavior by US presidents, such as the initiation or escalation of militarized interstate disputes (MIDS) while controlling for various systemic-level variables, e.g., power level, contiguity, and joint democracy. Three other chapters address the evolution of US conflict behavior in the 20th century as the product of the interaction between presidential leadership and international norms, probe more deeply into the link between LTA personality variables and cognitive threat perceptions measured with OCA belief variables, and investigate learning effects and the electoral success exhibited by US presidents over time. Collectively, the analyses in these four chapters offer evidence on behalf of generic knowledge of the US presidency rather than a detailed analysis of specific US presidents.

In Part IV, *Computational Models of Foreign Policy Roles*, the focus is on *abstract-theoretical knowledge* of strategies and modeling strategic interactions among dyads and the evolutionary patterns among states in different regional and world systems. The emphasis is explicitly on the task of aggregation from the actor-specific level of operational code analysis to the general-systemic level of role theory. Two chapters employ VICS indices to link agent-based, decision-making variables such as strategic culture, social identities, and national interests with strategic outcomes of settlement, deadlock, domination, or submission between state dyads in world politics. In particular, the link between different VICS belief indices about the nature of the political universe, the optimal strategies for exercising social power in the form of positive and negative sanctions, and control over historical development are linked to the emergence of variants within families of the foreign policy roles of friend, partner, rival, and enemy in world politics.

Two other chapters employ computational modeling to demonstrate that, depending on the mix of foreign policy roles across states, simulations of their interactions generate different distributions of the strategies of appeasement, bandwagoning, balancing, and hegemony. The analysis of the ensuing strategic interaction games suggests a solution to the empirical historical puzzle of how and why balancing strategies are relatively rare and often unsuccessful in the histories of international systems outside the European international system covering over 2000 years of world politics (Wohlforth et al. 2007; Kaufman et al. 2007).

In Part V, *Beyond Beliefs in World Politics*, we revisit whether the chapters in this volume support the main argument about the synergistic effects of an alliance between the metrics of the research program in operational code analysis and the models of binary role theory. As a "theory complex," do they make progress in crossing Simon's bridge between FPA and IR while bridging the gap between theory and practice in FPA (George 1993; Hudson and Day 2020)? We also assess the results of the analyses in the preceding chapters with criteria for identifying scientific progress in IR theory from philosophers of science (Kuhn 1962; Lakatos 1970; Laudan 1977; Jackson 2011; see also Walker 2003; Elman and Elman 2003; Walker and Schafer 2010). We contextualize these assessments further with the criteria suggested by Greenstein (1987) and Smith (1968) for evaluating progress in solving problems of evidence, inference, and conceptualization in psychological explanations of politics.

## Conclusion

We turn now to Chapter 2 to present a more detailed and contextualized version of the main argument outlined in this chapter regarding belief metrics and role theory in the development of foreign policy roles as complex adaptive social systems. The details include conceptualizing the operational code construct as a set of key philosophical and instrumental beliefs constituting the operational code as a political belief system and a code of conduct for the exercise of social power in world politics (George 1969; Haas 2020). We also demonstrate in more detail how operational codes are the building blocks for drawing inferences about an agent's strategies in making foreign policy decisions and enacting roles in world politics. We discuss as well solutions to the problem of identifying patterns of decision-making and role enactment by the different kinds of agents (individual leaders, single groups, coalitions, and states) that are focal actors in subsequent chapters of this book.

This analysis will support our claim that aggregations of these agents interacting in world politics constitute CAS, which can be modeled and measured with the analytical tools provided by sequential game theory and binary role theory (Holland 2012; Brams 1994; Walker, Malici, and Schafer 2011; Malici and Walker 2017). We demonstrate in subsequent chapters that substantive, methodological, and theoretical progress over the past decade and a half has extended well beyond beliefs as the central focus of the operational code research program. The patterns of progress extend in the two directions foreshadowed in the prototypical operational code study of the Bolsheviks by Leites (1951, 1953) at the Rand Corporation during the early years of the Cold War. He focused on the psychological origins of Soviet beliefs about the distribution and exercise of political power embedded in the personalities of leaders and extended his analysis as well to focus beyond the beliefs shared by leaders in the Soviet Politburo to the cultural origins of their beliefs and their impact on groups, institutions, and states as agents and ultimately to the dynamics of regional and global systems in world politics.

## References

Aron, R. 1967. *Peace and war: A theory of international relations.* New York, NY: Praeger.

Axelrod, R. 1984. *The evolution of cooperation.* New York, NY: Basic Books.

Axelrod, R., M. Cohen 1999. *Harnessing complexity.* New York, NY: Free Press.

Bates, R., A. Greif, M. Levi, J. Rosenthal, B. Weingast. 1998. *Analytic narratives.* Princeton, NJ: Princeton University Press.

Brams, S. 1994. *Theory of moves.* Cambridge: Cambridge University Press.

Breuning, M. 2011. Role theory research in international relations: State of the art and blind spots. In *Role theory in international relations: Approaches and analysis*, eds. S. Harnisch, C. Frank, and H. Maull, 16–35. New York, NY: Routledge.

Brummer, K., M. Young, O. Özdamar, S. Canbolat, C. Thiers, C. Rabini, and A. Mehvar. 2020. Coding in Tongues: Developing Non-English Coding Schemes for Leadership Profiling. *International Studies Review, 22*(4): 1039–1067.

Cantir, C., J. Kaarbo. 2016. *Domestic role contestation, foreign policy, and international relations.* New York, NY: Routledge.

Elman, C., M. Elman. 2003. *Progress in international relations theory.* Cambridge: MIT Press.

Geertz, C. 1973. Thick description: Toward an interpretive theory of culture." In *The interpretation of cultures*, 13–30. New York, NY: Basic Books.

George, A. 1969. The operational code: A neglected approach to the study of political leaders and decision making. *International Studies Quarterly* 23: 190–222.

George, A. 1993. *Bridging the gap: Theory and practice in foreign policy.* Washington, DC: United States Institute of Peace Press.

Greenstein, F. 1987. *Personality and politics.* 2nd Edition. Princeton, NJ: Princeton University Press.

Haas, M. 2020. Operational codes in foreign policy: A deconstruction." In *The Oxford research encyclopedia of international studies.* DOI: 10.1093/acrefore/9780190846626.013.539.

Hedstrom, P., R. Swedberg. 1998. *Social mechanisms.* Cambridge: Cambridge University Press.

Hermann, C. 1969. *Crises in foreign policy.* Indianapolis, IN: Bobbs-Merrill.

Hermann, M. 1979. Indicators of stress in policymakers during foreign policy crises. *Political Psychology* 1(1): 27–46.

Hermann, M. 2003. Assessing leadership style. In *The psychological assessment of political leaders*, ed. J. Post, 178–212. Ann Arbor, MI: University of Michigan Press.

Holland, J. 2012. *Signals and boundaries: Building blocks for complex adaptive systems*. Cambridge: MIT Press.

Hudson, V., B. Day. 2020. *Foreign policy analysis: Classical and contemporary theory*. 3rd Edition. Lanham: Rowman and Littlefield.

Jackson, P. 2011. *The conduct of inquiry in international relations*. New York, NY: Routledge.

Jervis, R. 1997. *System effects*. Princeton, NJ: Princeton University Press.

Kaufman, S., R. Little, W. Wohlforth. Eds. 2007. *The balance of power in world history*. New York, NY: Palgrave-Macmillan.

Kuhn, T. 1962. *The structure of scientific revolutions*. Chicago, IL: University of Chicago Press.

Lakatos, I. 1970. Falsification and the methodology of scientific research programs. In *Criticism and the growth of scientific knowledge*, eds. I. Lakatos, A. Musgrave, 91–196. Cambridge: Cambridge University Press.

Lau, R. 2003. Models of decision-making.". In *The Oxford handbook of political psychology*, eds. D. Sears, L. Huddy, R. Jervis, 19–59. New York, NY: Oxford University Press.

Laudan, L. 1977. *Progress and its problems*. Berkeley, CA: University of California Press.

Ledoux, J. 2002. *Synaptic self: How our brains become who we are*. New York, NY: Viking Press.

Leites, N. 1951. *The operational code of the politburo*. New York, NY: McGraw-Hill.

Leites, N. 1953. *A study of bolshevism*. New York, NY: Free Press.

Lloyd, S. 2007. *Programming the universe*. London: Vintage Books.

Lupia, A., M. McCubbins, and S. Popkin. Eds. 2000. *Elements of reason: Cognition, choice, and the boundaries of rationality*. New York, NY: Cambridge University Press.

Malici, A. 2017. Foreign policy belief systems and operational code analysis. In *The Oxford research encyclopedia of politics*, 1–38. Oxford University Press. Online Publication Date: Oct 2017. DOI: 10.1093/acrefore/9780190228637.013.459.

Malici, A., S. Walker. 2017. *Role theory and role conflict in U.S.-Iran relations*. New York, NY: Routledge.

Mintz, A. 1997. The poliheuristic theory of decision making.". In *Decision making on war and peace*, eds. N. Geva, A. Mintz, 81–102. Boulder: Westview.

Mintz, A. 2002. *Integrating cognitive and rational theories of foreign policy decision making*. New York, NY: Palgrave.

Neumann, W. Ed. 2007. *The affect effect*. Chicago, IL: University of Chicago Press.

Post, J., S. Walker. 2003. Assessing leaders in theory and practice. In *The psychological assessment of political leaders*, ed. J. Post, 399–412. Ann Arbor, MI: University of Michigan Press.

Schafer, M., and S. Walker. Eds. 2006. *Beliefs and leadership in world politics*. New York, NY: Palgrave.

Shinagel, M. Ed. 1994. *Robinson Crusoe*. New York, NY: W.W. Norton.

Simon, H. 1969. *Sciences of the artificial*. Cambridge: MIT Press.

Simon, H. 1985. Human nature in politics. *American Political Science Review* 79(2): 293–304.

Smith, M. B. 1968. A map for the analysis of personality and politics. *Journal of Social Issues* 24: 15–28.

Thies, C. 2010. Role theory and foreign policy. In *The international studies encyclopedia*, ed. R. Denemark, 6335–56. Vol. X. Oxford: Blackwell.

Thies, C. 2013. *The United States, Israel, and the search for international order*. New York, NY: Routledge.

Thies, C., M. Nieman. 2017. *Rising powers and foreign policy revisionism*. Ann Arbor, MI: University of Michigan Press.

Walker, S. 1987. *Role theory and foreign policy analysis*. Durham, NC: Duke University Press.

Walker, S. 2003. Operational code analysis as a scientific research program. In *Progress in international relations theory*, eds. C. Elman, M. Elman, 245–276. Cambridge: MIT Press.

Walker, S. 2009. The psychology of presidential decision making.". In *The Oxford handbook of the American presidency*, eds. G. Edwards, W. Howell, 550–576. New York, NY: Oxford University Press.

Walker, S. 2013. *Role theory and the cognitive architecture of British appeasement decisions*. New York, NY: Routledge.

Walker, S. 2016. Role theory as an empirical theory of international relations. In *The Oxford research encyclopedia of empirical international relations theory*, ed. W. Thompson. New York, NY: Oxford University Press.

Walker, S., A. Malici. 2011. *U.S. Presidents and foreign policy mistakes*. Stanford, CA: Stanford University Press.

Walker, S., M. Schafer. 2010. Operational code theory: Beliefs and foreign policy decisions. In *The international studies encyclopedia*, ed. R. Denemark, 5493–5514. Vol. VIII. Chichester: Wiley-Blackwell.

Walker, S., G. G. Watson. 1992. The cognitive maps of British leaders, 1938–39. In *Political psychology and foreign policy*, eds. E. Singer, V. Hudson, 31–58. Boulder, CO: Westview.

Walker, S., A. Malici, M. Schafer. 2011. *Rethinking foreign policy analysis: States, leaders, and the microfoundations of behavioral international relations*. New York, NY: Routledge.

Walker, S., M. Schafer, M. Young. 1998. Systematic procedures for operational code analysis. *International Studies Quarterly* 42: 175–190.

Whitehead, A. 1948. *Science and the modern world*. New York, NY: New American Library.

Wohlforth, W., R. Little, S. Kaufman, D. Kang, C. Jones, V. Tin-Bor Hui, A. Eckstein, D. Deudney, W. Brenner. 2007. Testing balance-of-power theory in world history. *European Journal of International Relations* 13: 155–185.

Young, M. 2001. Building world views with profiler+. In *Progress in communication sciences*, ed. M. West, 17–32. Vol. 17. Westport: Ablex Publishing.

Young, M., M. Schafer. 1998. Is there method in our madness? *Mershon International Studies Review 43*: 63–96.

Zajonc, R. 1980. Feeling and thinking: Preferences need no inferences. *American Psychologist* 39(2): 151–175.

# 2 The Development of Foreign Policy Roles

## Beliefs and Complex Adaptive Systems

*Stephen G. Walker*

## Introduction

The goal in this chapter is to demonstrate in detail the main argument in this volume that the theoretical and methodological logics governing the formation and identification of a leader's operational code as a system of *beliefs* also govern a state's operational code as a system of *roles*. Similar aggregation processes apply in both the organization of the *cognitive* operational code of an individual and the *social* operational code of a state. Both the individual and the state are agents in subsystems within larger systems, in which the logic of complex adaptive systems (CAS) can account for regularities in the exchange of information as the exercise of social power between agents as members of systems in a dynamic environment (Simon 1969; Gell-Mann 1994; Holland 2012). Beliefs define an individual's operational code of instrumental and philosophical beliefs about the exercise of social power (acts of cooperation and conflict) by Self and Other; those beliefs can also define a state's operational code regarding the exercise of social power between states as agents (Ego and Alter) enacting roles in world politics.

Social roles are defined and beliefs are attributed to an agent in the form of role conceptions (RC) for Ego (Self) and role expectations (RX) for Alter (Other) regarding role enactments (REs) as the exercise of social power between Ego and Alter (Holsti 1970; Walker 1987; Malici and Walker 2017). In this account RC and RX at the state level of analysis perform the prescriptive and diagnostic functions of instrumental and philosophical beliefs at the individual level of analysis. Beliefs at both levels of analysis follow the same organizational logic. Beliefs aggregate to display an individual's diagnostic and choice propensities regarding interactions with the environment, which also includes other agents. Their subsequent interactions generate social patterns of behavior between them, which are hypothesized to be congruent (match up) with the cognitive patterns of their beliefs.

The sources of beliefs in an individual include relevant personality traits, which reflect inherited genes that interact in different combinations to produce them (Nowak 2006). All beliefs are "learned" from interaction by agents with the environment, in which some are transmitted directly as memes from cultural sources while others are generated by the reactions of agents and interactions with the individual's personality traits. The individual's environment may also enhance or depress the influence of some genes, which makes the causal story of the sources of beliefs even more complex (Dawkins 1999, 1996; Edey and Johanson 1989; Nowak 2011).

The following propositions summarize a general model of the origins of operational code beliefs, which incorporate genetic and environmental sources (Walker 1983, 2003; Walker and Falkowski 1985; Walker, Malici, and Schafer 2011, 54–55):

> Prop. 1. As a result of inherited personality traits interacting with childhood and early adult socialization experiences in family and society, an individual acquires the dominant motivational needs for power, affiliation, and achievement in his personality and the instrumental and philosophical beliefs regarding the exercise and distribution of social power in his operational code.
>
> Prop. 2. An individual tends to adopt an operational code that is compatible with the constellation of the needs for power, affiliation, and achievement in his personality.
>
> Prop. 3. Although an individual's operational code may develop a consistency that is independent from random fluctuations in immediate personal needs, the activation of these beliefs by environmental stimuli may arouse personal needs embedded in the belief system as the individual uses the various elements of his operational code to interpret and act in a decision-making situation.
>
> Prop. 4. Once aroused, these motivational needs may contribute to the cognitive rigidity of an individual's belief system and account for the intensity of cognitive dissonance and behavioral intransigence in the face of new information from the environment or other stimuli from the environment.
>
> Prop. 5. Conversely, vivid stimuli or changes in context, respectively, may lead to behavioral change in the form of social learning or structural adaptation and even cognitive change in the form of experiential learning (changes in beliefs).

Can this model of the origins of an individual's operational code beliefs be extended to include the origins of foreign policy roles attributed to groups, institutions, and states, along with the trace effects of inherited personality traits? The short answer is "yes," but with some important qualifications.

## The Origins of Beliefs and Roles

Individuals, groups, institutions, and states are all agents, which are also members of systems. However, they are "nearly decomposable," which means that the coherence and intensity of interactions within each of them as smaller *subsystems* are more intense than the relatively weak interactions among them that aggregate and constitute a larger *system* (Simon 1969, 99–103). That is, the boundaries for each of these subsystems make them semi-independent from one another as agents unless one level of organization absorbs one or more of the others. The two extremes that illustrate this possibility are (1) a political system in which a leader absorbs the other units so that "L'état, cest moi" (I am the state), to quote the French king Louis XIV (Tucker 1965) and (2) a totalitarian system in which the state as an institution penetrates the lives of its groups and individuals so that they lose their autonomy of thought and action (Tucker 1963). This aspiration to control the thoughts and beliefs of individuals is attributed to Communist and Nazi political systems in the 20th century, often headed by a supreme leader, making the distinction between (1) and (2) somewhat moot (Tucker 1965).

### *Predominant Leader Model*

The personality-and-culture sources in Propositions 1–5 of an individual's operational code as a psychocultural construct are modeled in Figure 2.1 in the simplest case of a predominant leader. The psychological and social sources of the key beliefs in an agent's operational code in this figure are personality traits and cultural norms, respectively, inherited from parents or acquired from agents of socialization that define a society's social structure and the individual's niche within it. The acquired socialization experiences come from "distal social antecedents" in the form of big historical events, such as wars, famines, or depressions, or the social norms acquired from them indirectly and transmitted to the individual by family, group, or societal institutions. In addition, "immediate social antecedents" transmit cultural social norms to individuals through personal life experiences in situations as members of families or broader reference groups such as socioeconomic classes within a society (Smith 1968).

Reading from left to right and following the arrows in Figure 2.1, individuals with different personality traits are socialized into their societies and acquire key beliefs about I-1 Approach to Strategy, P-1 Nature of the Political Universe, and P-4 Control over Historical Development (see Appendix) regarding the exercise and distribution of social power in families, reference groups, and the society's government. These key beliefs

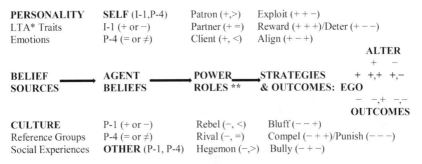

| **PERSONALITY** | **SELF** (1-1,P-4) | Patron (+,>) | Exploit (+ + −) |
| **LTA\* Traits** | I-1 (+ or −) | Partner (+ =) | Reward (+ + +)/Deter (+ − −) |
| Emotions | P-4 (= or ≠) | Client (+, <) | Align (+ − +) |

| | | | | **ALTER** | |
| | | | | + | − |
| **BELIEF** ⟶ | **AGENT** ⟶ | **POWER**⟶ | **STRATEGIES** | + +,+ | +,− |
| **SOURCES** | **BELIEFS** | **ROLES \*\*** | **& OUTCOMES: EGO** | | |
| | | | | − −,+ | −,− |
| | | | | **OUTCOMES** | |

| **CULTURE** | P-1 (+ or −) | Rebel (−, <) | Bluff (− − +) |
| Reference Groups | P-4 (= or ≠) | Rival (−, =) | Compel (− + +)/Punish (− − −) |
| Social Experiences | **OTHER** (P-1, P-4) | Hegemon (−,>) | Bully (− + −) |

*Figure 2.1* Origins of Operational Code Beliefs and Power Roles for Predominant
Leaders

\*Leadership Personality Analysis traits are identified by Hermann (2003, 181) to be related
to leadership style, defined as "the ways in which leaders relate to those around them—
whether constituents, advisers, or other leaders—and how they structure interactions and
the norms, rules, and principles they use to guide such interactions." LTA traits include
(1) a belief in ability to control events, (2) need for power, (3) self-confidence, (4) conceptual complexity, (5) task focus, (6) in-group bias, (7) distrust of others, which combine
in pairs to define different dimensions of leadership style: (1) and (2) dispose leaders to
respect or challenge political constraints in the environment, (3) and (4) incline them to be
open or closed to incoming information, (5) provides motivations for seeking leadership
positions, and (6) and (7) motivate leaders on how to respond to threats and problems by
dealing and solving versus eliminating them (Hermann 2003, 184–203). \*\*I-1 or P-1 belief
index specifies cooperation (+) or conflict (−) role; P-4 index specifies equal (=) or unequal
(≠), i.e., weak (<) or strong (>) role for Self or Other.

become the core of an individual's operational code and collectively
interact to locate the individual's *power roles* assigned to Self and Other
within the context of different institutions and social situations. The six
possible power roles for Self and Other shown in Figure 2.1 are the three
cooperation (+) roles of client (+, <), partner (+, =), and patron (+, >) in
the top half of this figure versus the three conflict (−) roles of rebel (−, <),
rival (−, =), and hegemon (−, >) in the bottom half of the figure. They are
defined by the intersection of the I-1 and P-4 beliefs for Self and the intersection of the P-1 and P-4 beliefs for Other (Walker 2013).

In turn, these power roles are associated with different RE strategies,
which intersect to answer Lenin's *kto-kovo* (who-controls-whom) question
identified by Leites (1951, 1953) about the mediation of Self-Other relations
in politics and locate the outcome as a pattern of *social power relations*
between Ego (Self) and Alter (Other) in one of the cells in the Ego, Alter
matrix of outcomes at the right-hand edge of the figure. The four cells of
the (Ego, Alter) matrix show their power relations at a given point in time
as mutual cooperation (+, +) in the upper left cell, submission/domination
(+, −) in the upper right cell, mutual conflict (−, −) in the lower right cell, or
domination/submission (−, +) in the lower left cell.

For example, if Ego's role is Patron and Alter's role is Client, then Ego's strategy is Exploit (+ + –) and Alter's strategy is Align (+ – +) in Figure 2.1. The intersection of their respective strategies is {+ + – +}, which is the sequence of alternating decisions to choose cooperation (+) by Ego, cooperation (+) by Alter, conflict (–) by Ego, and cooperation (+) by Alter. The enactment of their respective roles is a role location process with an outcome that both defines their roles {E,A: Patron, Client}and specifies their power relations (– +) in the lower left cell, in which Ego dominates and Alter submits.

This example illustrates the potential of the operational code analysis (OCA) model in Figure 2.1 to explain the outcomes of social power relations under the restricted condition when Self and Other as agents are the predominant leaders of states in the model. This version of the agents in the model assumes that the belief systems of leaders steer the actions of states in world politics, which makes the personalities of leaders and the matrix of their cultural experiences both the sources of their belief systems and the bases for their strategies in world politics. In turn, the intersection of their respective strategies generates the patterns of international power relations between them. The key assumption is that the leadership style and pattern of instrumental and philosophical beliefs in the predominant leader's operational code matches the pattern of actions by the state as an agent in world politics. The strong version of the argument in this model is that the leader's actions are indispensable to account for political outcomes, and the leader's personality is indispensable to account for the leader's actions (Greenstein 1987; see also Etheredge 1978; Walker 1982).

### *Focal Actor Model*

However, this argument weakens when Self and Other in this model are not individuals and are instead single groups or multiple coalitions of groups (Achen 1988; Hermann and Hermann 1989). If the agent who makes decisions and enacts roles in world politics is conceptualized and measured as a state constituted by groups or institutions, it becomes more difficult (but not impossible) to apply the logic of the model in Figure 2.1. One possibility is to identify a "focal actor" within the state, which can be a group or institution and the channel through which foreign policy decisions are generated (Achen 1988). The beliefs and actions attributed to the focal actor define the state's operational code and power role in world politics. This approach makes the state's operational code primarily a social rather than a psychological construct. Its macro-level, social regularities "supervene," i.e., are generated and rely ontologically on micro-level, psychological processes but do not directly represent any particular individual's traits and beliefs. Instead, the macro-level construct is an emergent property of a social system rather than an attribute of an individual (Walker, Malici, and Schafer 2011, 25–29).

An example of the two constructs is the distinction in studies of the US presidency between the occupant and the office, i.e., the "personal" and the "institutional" presidencies (Walker 2009, 550; see also Neustadt 1960; Greenstein 2004; Burke 2000, 1–25; Cameron 2000, 106–110; Preston 2001, 253–254). The puzzle of the connection between the macro-level patterns of regularity attributed to the institutional presidency and the micro-level patterns of decision-making exhibited by the personal presidency is solved by the invocation of the rationality theorem in some form (Dennett 1989; Little 1991, 195–199; Walker 2009, 28):

Once we accept the point that macroexplanations require microfoundations, we must next ask what types of individual-level processes we should look for. And here there are two broad families of answers: rational choice models and social-psychology models. The first approach attempts to explain a given social process as the aggregate result of large numbers of individuals pursuing individually rational strategies. The second approach attempts to explain the social phenomenon as the complex outcome of a variety of motives, rational and nonrational, that propel individual action (Little 1991, 198).

The theoretical and methodological logic of OCA as an information-processing approach shares some characteristics of both rational choice and social psychology models. It employs an adaptive model of bounded rationality associated with complex adaptive system analysis and evolutionary biology, in which agent characteristics and environmental conditions interact as sources of rational choice (Simon 1957, 1969, 1985; George 1969; Axelrod and Cohen 1999; Gigerenzer and Selten 2001; Nowak 2011; Walker, Schafer, and Smith 2018). This model can also be applied to groups and states as well as leaders.

Theoretically, a leader's operational code in Figure 2.1 is assumed to be the aggregate result of large numbers of interactions with others pursuing individually rational strategies with a variety of motives, rational and nonrational, which make the leader's beliefs the product of a model of bounded rationality. The boundaries include incomplete or imperfect information and motivated biases plus the environmental setting in which decisions occur and the limits of human capacities to process information in that environment (George 1969; Simon 1969, 23–55, 1985; Walker and Malici 2011, 16–25, 193–198). Methodologically, the predominant leader model of OCA in Figure 2.1 represents the decision-making process of a single agent (the individual leader) in a single period (the time interval necessary to construct the outcome matrix in the leader's mind), which specifies the initial conditions from which the leader's subsequent decisions occur to enact a power role in the political universe.

These theoretical and methodological features exhibit two information processes by individuals accessible to outside observers, however, which also apply to decision-making by groups, institutions, and states as aggregations of individuals. One information process is the sampling and encoding of fine-grained, "statistical and time-varying patterns of low-level components... [N]o individual component of the system can perceive and communicate the 'big picture' of the state of the system. Instead, information must be communicated via spatial and temporal sampling" (Mitchell 2009, 180). The system in Figure 2.1 is the "Self" (leader, group, or coalition); the low-level components are particular personality traits and valenced cognitions. The other information process that applies to the analysis of different decision units is the coarse-grained properties of the system, which aggregate into operational codes, roles, strategies, and outcomes that represent the "big picture" or the state of the agent (leader, group, or coalition) as a system.

The methods of measuring and modeling these two types of information processes apply to individuals, groups, coalitions, and institutions as hierarchical levels (subsystems) of analysis within a complex adaptive system such as the state. The relatively unfocused analysis of fine-grained patterns is the statistical sampling of large numbers of low-level components, which constructs information that "is not, as in a traditional computer, precisely statically located in any particular place in the system. Instead, it takes the form of statistics and dynamics of patterns over the system's components" (Mitchell 2009, 179–180). These configurations may be random or only probabilistic patterns producing a statistical model of the system's dynamics, e.g., the modal, median, or mean "state" of the system or correlations between components of the system (Mitchell 2009, 180–185).

The more focused analysis of coarse-grained patterns measures the "big picture" of the system. They are constructed from low-level components and constitute single cases that are successive "states" of the system with particular locations rather than abstract averages from a sample of locations in time and space (Dennett 1989, 43–68; Cioffi-Revilla 1998). These "states" of the system are represented by computational models, which employ rules rather than calculations to display the dynamics of the system as sequential rather than statistical patterns (Mitchell 2009, 169–185; Nowak 2006, 27–30). Examples of such coarse-grained patterns are the specific roles of Self and Other for a particular time period computed by the logical rules in Figure 2.1 for inferring power roles, strategies, and outcomes from Self's I-1, P-1, and P-4 master beliefs, which were previously calculated as statistics specified by the Verbs in Context System (VICS) indices.

OCA in this context is the analysis of the relatively unfocused stage of exploration by individuals, groups, and states as they interact to design and operate larger social systems. Role theory analyzes the relatively focused stage of direction that follows exploration at various levels of aggregation from individuals to groups to institutions to states in world politics. Both OCA and role theory address how the exercise of social power as a process of adaptation via the exchange of information between agents accounts for the processes of role evolution and role transition in world politics (Walker and Malici 2011; Malici and Walker 2017).

The two approaches to the same phenomena at different stages suggest that a balanced relationship between these two modes of information processing constitute complementary ways of understanding the hierarchical relations between subsystems and larger systems, in which subsystems become agents in the larger systems. The wholes of the smaller subsystems become parts in the larger system, e.g., the power roles attributed to various states in an international system become parts of the operational code of the international system. It follows that maybe the calculations used to measure the cognitive operational code of an individual can be used to calculate the social operational code of an aggregation of individuals, such as the state (Feng 2007; He and Feng 2015). In turn, the social operational codes of states may be used to calculate the operational codes of larger aggregations of systems in world politics, e.g., alliances and other international organizations at the regional and global levels of world politics (Malici 2005; Thies 2006; Stevenson 2006).

These possibilities are the topics of the papers in this volume, which follow collectively the logic of the building blocks approach to the understanding of complex adaptive systems pioneered by Simon (1969) and Holland (1995, 1998, 2012), an approach that is compatible with complex adaptive systems designed by nature in the evolution of natural systems and in the design and evolution of artificial systems by humans and computers (Dawkins 1996; Mitchell 2009; Bejan and Zane 2012; Dennett 2017). The building blocks approach specifies that our reality is characterized by signals and boundaries, which are the building blocks of natural and artificial systems in the universe. Building blocks are the smaller particles that form larger wholes, and both are best understood as systems, i.e., sets of elements that interact and are sufficiently interdependent so that it is possible to identify their boundaries even though these systems may also be subsystems, i.e., the parts that are the building blocks for larger systems.

The logic of this approach appears in Figure 2.2, which employs the building blocks logic from Figure 2.1 to other decision units than an individual. The patterns in Figure 2.2 show how the operational codes of individuals are aggregated as an additive statistical model with the VICS indices for I-1, P-1, and P-4, based on the assumption that groups have a relatively linear pattern of "groupthink," in which the operational code beliefs of individual members are the smaller components of the statistical information about the group's operational code communicated by the VICS indices (Janis 1972; Kowert 2002; Schafer and Crichlow 2010).

In contrast, the operational code of a coalition (defined as a collection of individuals and/or groups) does not have a pattern that aggregates and sums to the operational codes of its members. Instead, these multiple autonomous members of a coalition have a non-linear "polythink" pattern of computational interactions to form alliances, bargain to

The Operational Codes of Individuals, Groups, Coalitions, and States

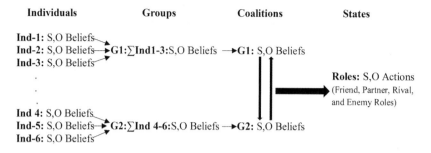

*Figure 2.2* The Aggregation Process of a State's Operational Code from Building Blocks*

*S,O beliefs for Individuals are VICS indices I-1, P-4 = S and P-1, P-4 = O. S,O beliefs for Groups are calculated as VICS indices from the aggregation of self and other attributions by individual members of the group. S,O beliefs for coalitions are the product of communication between members of the coalition, which may be either individuals or groups. S,O operational code actions for the state are different strategies (role enactment patterns), which emerge from different patterns of interaction between coalitions of groups that are the building blocks of the state.

reach consensus, or compete to achieve domination of the State's decisions and actions (Allison 1971; Hermann and Hermann 1989; Hermann 2002; Mintz and Wayne 2016). The outcomes of these processes generate the state's operational code, which emerges as the enactment of different families of foreign policy roles (friend, partner, rival, enemy) that entail the power roles of leaders listed in Figure 2.1 (Malici and Walker 2017).

The foreign policy roles for states as agents are outcomes of the interactions between and among the groups and organizations that constitute the state. While these emergent role identities are directed outward toward other agents outside the state as constitutive elements of the interactions between Ego and Alter as states in world politics, they also define collective identities for the individuals, groups, and institutions inside the states. In turn, the interactions between states may evolve from Self-and-Other relations as Ego and Alter into a collective identity as a union of states in world politics (Wendt 1999, 225–232). Macro-level regularities of the system of states may generate the emergence of new agents, e.g., the European Union or NATO, which "supervene" to guide the collective actions of Self and Other or Ego and Alter as "nearly decomposable" subsystems within this hierarchical system (Simon 1969; Wendt 2003).

## Beyond Beliefs: Crossing Simon's Bridge

Bridging the gap between the sciences of the mind and the social sciences requires building blocks to connect them and a general model to frame the construction project. The metrics of operational code beliefs provide the building blocks while the models of binary role theory supply the framework for constructing the bridge between psychology and political science. A brief conceptual history of this effort is in the Appendix to this chapter, which also contains the details of the metrics of OCA supplied by the VICS of content analysis. This construction project has emanated from the operational code research program (Walker 1990, 2003; Walker and Schafer 2010), which began with the efforts of George (1969) and (Holsti 1977) to transform the "operational code" (Leites 1951, 1953) from a concept into a construct:

> A *concept* expresses an abstraction formed by generalization from particulars.... A *construct* is a concept. It has the added meaning, however, of having been deliberately and consciously invented or adopted for a special scientific purpose .... One, it enters into theoretical schemes and is related in various ways to other constructs.... Two...it is so defined and specified that it can be observed and measured (Kerlinger 1986, 26–27; cited in Walker and Schafer 2010, 5493).

The decision by George and Holsti to adopt a narrow focus on the beliefs of leaders to launch the research program in OCA carried opportunity costs with it in the form of emphasizing the study of cognitive processes at the expense of affective, motivational, and social phenomena. What if a leader's political decisions are driven as much by the affective processes of ego defense and the motivational processes of mediating Self-Other relations as by the cognitive processes of object appraisal (Smith 1968)? Then to investigate these processes implies, "the operational code construct becomes an analytical conduit through which these processes flow and by which an analyst observes their interactions" (Walker 1990, 415). The affective, motivational, and social contents of beliefs would serve as the building blocks for crossing Simon's bridge.

If future operational code research should proceed along these psychological and social paths, it would "return to the characterological feature which George and Holsti excluded as they extracted and developed its cognitive aspect" (Walker 1990, 415). The effect would be to anchor the cognitive processes of object appraisal with both the processes of ego defense associated with the study of personality and politics and the social processes of mediating Self-Other relations and thereby cross Simon's bridge (Smith 1968). How much progress has occurred along either of these paths of future research? The chapters in the remainder of this volume offer evidence of progress in both directions.

George (1969, 195–196) also addressed these very possibilities: "[I]t is one of the attractive features of the operational code construct for behaviorally-inclined political scientists that it can serve as a useful 'bridge' or 'link' to psychodynamic interpretations of unconscious dimensions of belief systems and their role in behavior under different conditions." He concluded, "a knowledge of beliefs facilitates the task of assessing the extent to which behavior is based on reality-testing or reflects the influence of latent motives and ego defenses" (Walker 1990, 415). Although not highlighted in the brief conceptual history of OCA in the Appendix to this chapter, there are some studies that have explored this possibility and influenced the reconceptualization of operational code beliefs within different theoretical contexts (Walker 1983, 1995; Walker and Falkowski 1985).

### Beliefs and Personalities

Successive conceptualizations of OCA have employed cognitive consistency, motivational biases, and valenced attributions, respectively, as contextual descriptors to emphasize different aspects of beliefs as the cognitive products of object appraisal processes, the externalization of ego defense processes, and "hot" rather than "cold" cognitions with valenced tags of positive and negative affect (Walker 2003, 265–273; Schafer and Walker 2006b, 3–22). The VICS indices of master beliefs reflect these conceptual developments by scaling transitive verbs with positive and negative affect valences of friendliness (+) or hostility (–) regarding Other's (P-1) philosophical beliefs, positive and negative valences of motivational biases for cooperation (+) or conflict (–) to Self's (I-1) beliefs in pursuing strategies and scaling the valences for the (P-4) beliefs of Self and Other regarding historical control as positive (+) incentives or negative (–) constraints in the mediation of Self-Other relations.

In sum, a full definition of the operational code approach represented by the VICS system "asks what the individual knows, feels, and wants regarding the exercise of power in human affairs.... Operational code analysis addresses this trilogy by focusing on beliefs (cognitions) with valences of positive and negative affect (emotion) associated with needs (motivations) for power, achievement, and affiliation" (Schafer and Walker 2006b, 29 and n. 2; see also LeDoux 2002, LeDoux and Hirst 1986). However, endogenizing the effects of personality traits on a leader's beliefs within the belief indices is not the same as measuring the sources of these effects, which may also have direct effects on a leader's decisions as well as indirect effects by virtue of their impact on operational code beliefs.

A leader's personality traits may act separately or interact with one another to affect a leader's beliefs or behavior (Hermann 2002, 2003). These traits may also have selective effects, i.e., different traits may impact different beliefs or kinds of beliefs. For example, some may influence philosophical beliefs that constrain the process of object appraisal while others may act on instrumental beliefs that drive the process of ego defense. These possibilities suggest an avenue for research *before* beliefs, which focuses on the psychological origins of operational code beliefs in the personality traits that define and explain extra-cognitive aspects of leadership style exhibited by predominant leaders such as US presidents (Walker 2009).

In fact, the research program in OCA is proceeding along this path with a major effort to collect and analyze both the operational codes of US presidents and their extra-cognitive personality traits. The Psychological Characteristics of Leaders (PsyCL) project at the University of Central Florida has collected data on the personality traits and operational code beliefs of all US presidents from the early 1800s to the present. The data collection methods employ Profiler Plus, the automated computer software and dictionaries developed at Social Science Automation, Inc. for OCA and Leadership Trait Analysis (LTA), two research programs in elite political psychology (Young 2001). The Profiler Plus software retrieves transitive verbs to calculate VICS indices for the philosophical and instrumental beliefs in the OCA program and retrieves other parts of speech to calculate indices for various personality traits in the LTA program (Walker, Schafer, and Young 1998, 2003; Hermann 2002, 2003; Schafer and Walker 2006b). The results of this effort are reported in Part III of this volume.

### Beliefs and Roles

Another avenue for future progress in the operational code research program is to proceed systematically *after* beliefs along the social path from the beliefs of individuals to the roles and actions of states as social entities. Many states do not have a leader like the US president with a relatively direct link between a predominant leader's beliefs and the state's roles in world politics. Single groups like the British Cabinet in a two-party system and multiple autonomous actors who form coalition governments in a multiparty system like Israel present obvious puzzles regarding how the beliefs of different individuals or the shared beliefs of group members combine to make state decisions and enact roles in domestic, regional, or global politics (Schafer and Crichlow 2010; see also Kowert 2002; Mintz and Wayne 2016; Hagan 1993; Hermann and Hermann 1989; Hermann 2001; Kaarbo 2012; Walker 2013). Do the functional equivalents of operational code belief systems for states emerge from these aggregation processes? Do they constitute a common strategic culture or bureaucratic operational code consisting of a common worldview, norms of behavior, and standard operating procedures? Do they compete and cooperate as strategic subcultures located within the organizations and institutions of the state (Merton 1940; Janowitz 1960; Allison 1971; Johnston 1995)?

The Leites (1951, 1953) studies of the Bolsheviks actually attributed a common set of shared operational code beliefs to the members of the Soviet Politburo, which they acquired from Lenin's writings by a process of socialization and character formation (George 1969). Similar dynamics characterized four generations of Chinese communist leadership demarcated by Mao's writings and their interpretations by his successors (Feng 2007). In both the Russian and Chinese cases, there were also other sources of political culture. Leites (1953) emphasized themes from Russian culture that resonated with Lenin's revolutionary generation while Feng (2007) notes the influence of Confucian and Parabellum schools of thought regarding political strategy that helped shape the strategic culture of Chairman Mao and his successors.

US presidents have also not been immune to cultural influences on their operational codes. The operational codes of Theodore Roosevelt and Woodrow Wilson are identified by historians as cultural archetypes of realist and idealist strategic subcultures in American politics (Walker and Schafer 2007). More broadly, different strategic cultures have been attributed to democracies versus dictatorships and presidential versus parliamentary democracies (Russett 1993; Schafer and Walker 2001, 2006a). The point is that culture may be an important source of operational code beliefs even in political systems with a predominant leader no matter whether the state's institutions are democratic or autocratic. Individual leaders are subject in principle to broad cultural socialization processes that may or may not reenforce idiosyncratic personality traits and beliefs. They may also be socialized into different roles with particular bureaucratic codes embedded in institutions such as the military or diplomatic corps and other organizations within the state. Some results of research efforts along this path are reported in Part IV of this volume.

## Conclusion

The organization of the remaining chapters in this volume begins with individuals as the building blocks of world politics in Part II, which themselves are systems organized according to the logic of the model in Figure 2.1. Two strategies of aggregation from the operational codes of leaders to the foreign policy roles of states are pursued in Parts III and IV. The chapters in Part III employ the fine-grained, inductive logic of *statistical exploration* to link personality traits of individuals as predominant leaders with their cognitive operational codes and relate both characteristics as well with various statistical characteristics of domestic and world politics. Also examined are different patterns of dyadic relations between states ranging from severe conflict rivalries to security communities of cooperation.

Part IV employs the coarse-grained, deductive logic of *computational direction* to link the roles and strategies of states as aggregations of individuals with the strategic cultures and the historical settings of their environments. Formal game theory models of strategic rationality based on the distributions of the roles in Figure 2.1 among dyads in both historical international systems and simulated systems of world politics guide the analyses in the papers in this part of the book. In Part V, we assess in a final chapter the results of the analyses in the preceding chapters along the dimensions of substantive, theoretical, and methodological progress identified below in the Appendix to this chapter.

## Appendix: A Brief History of Operational Code Analysis from Concept to Construct

The conceptual history of OCA is demarcated by its invention (Leites 1951, 1953), its initial specification as a cognitive construct by the first generation of operational code scholars (George 1969, 1979; Holsti 1976, 1977; Walker 1990, 2003), and adaptation as a social construct by later generations of operational code analysts (Barnet 1973; Yergin 1977; Bobrow et al. 1979; Kegley 1987; Johnson 1995; Bennett 1999; Walker 2004; Feng 2007; Walker and Schafer 2007; Malici 2008; Walker and Schafer 2010; Walker 2013; Malici and Walker 2017). The term, "operational code," initially referred to the "conceptions of political strategy" in Bolshevik ideology (Leites 1953, 15), which were expressed in the texts of public statements by Lenin and Stalin and originated more broadly from themes in the cultural milieu of Russian society occupied by revolutionaries in Tsarist Russia prior to World War I.

At the core of Bolshevik strategic conceptions was the question that Lenin posed, "kto-kovo" or "who-whom," which translates as "who (controls) whom?" (Leites 1953, 27–29; 1951, 78–81). The answer to this question specified the Bolshevik operational code as "a mix of different kinds of conceptions—ontological statements, causal attributions, and prescriptive norms—labeled generically as 'beliefs,' with overtones of positive and negative 'affect' (the feelings and emotions associated with them), and focused on the exercise of power" (Walker 2003, 247–248).

Collectively, these conceptions portrayed the Bolshevik operational code as a code of conduct "with a drive for power that was unusually high by Western standards" (Walker 2003, 246). It was the product of both the characterological personality traits of Lenin and his successors plus themes in the Russian cultural environment undergoing the stresses of late industrialization and modernization by Western standards at the turn of the 20th century. The subsequent evolution of OCA as a research program focused primarily on the psychological dimensions of a leader's operational code, conceptualizing it as a political belief system. This focus was the product of efforts by George (1969) and Holsti (1977) who extracted and developed the cognitive-strategic elements of the operational code concept, which was the primary focus of Leites' first book, *The Operational Code of the Politiburo* (1951), and also the focus in Part II of this volume.

George intended to "factor out the psychoanalytically based, characterological aspect of operational code analysis and focus upon the 'maxims of political strategy' solely as beliefs. Viewed as cognitive rather than affective phenomena, he argued that these premises would be more susceptible to investigation and analysis by political scientists" (Walker 1990, 404; see also George 1969, 195). This move was designed to address a question that George raised in a reexamination of Leites' pioneering, two-volume analysis of the Bolsheviks. He asked why this study had not generated similar analyses of other leadership groups. He noted "the unusually complex nature of Leites' work, which is not one but several interrelated studies that are subtly interwoven....[and concluded]....while the complexity of the work adds to its richness and intellectual appeal, it has also made it unusually difficult for readers to grasp its structure or to describe its research mode" (George 1969, 193; cited in Walker 1990, 404).

### Theoretical Progress

George's solution was to conceptualize the cognitive elements of the Bolshevik operational code reported by Leites (1951) as "answers" to a set of questions about the nature of the political universe and the optimum means to achieve political goals. George distinguished in the Leites (1951) study diagnostic philosophical beliefs about (P-1) the nature of the political universe, (P-2) the prospects of realizing fundamental political values, (P-3) the predictability of the political future, (P-4) the degree of control over historical development, and (P-5) the role of chance in human affairs and historical development. He also identified prescriptive instrumental beliefs about (I-1) the best approach for selecting goals for political action; (I-2) how political goals are pursued most effectively; (I-3) how to calculate, control, and accept the risks of political action; (I-4) the best "timing" of action to advance one's interests; and (I-5) the utility and role of different means for advancing one's interests. George (1969, 199-216) then reformulated these 10 Bolshevik beliefs as a series of questions about any leader's beliefs.

Holsti (1977) developed a typology of six operational code belief systems in the form of different sets of alternative answers to the questions identified by George's (1969) reanalysis of the Bolshevik operational code in the Leites (1951) study. Holsti's typology of operational codes identified types that are internally consistent, interdependent, and organized hierarchically as a belief system derived from (P-1) as a master belief about the nature of the political universe. The results of subsequent research by others qualified this assumption of the Holsti typology and promoted two other beliefs to the status of master beliefs so that P-1, I-1, and P-4 identify hybrid belief systems of philosophical and instrumental beliefs that remain internally consistent within each category of beliefs; however, they are not necessarily consistent, interdependent, and hierarchical across the two categories of philosophical and instrumental beliefs (Walker 1983, 1990, 1995, 2003).

**Political Universe***

| | | Friendly (+) | | | Hostile (−) | | |
|---|---|---|---|---|---|---|---|
| | | +, < | +, = | +, > | −, < | −, = | −, > |
| | +, < | *** | *** | 1 | *** | *** | 2 |
| CO (+) | +, = | *** | 3 | *** | *** | 4 | *** |
| | +, > | 5 | *** | *** | 6 | *** | *** |

**Political Strategy****

| | | | | | | | |
|---|---|---|---|---|---|---|---|
| | −, < | *** | *** | 7 | *** | *** | 8 |
| CF(−) | −, = | *** | 9 | *** | *** | 10 | *** |
| | −, > | 11 | *** | *** | 12 | *** | *** |

*Figure 2.3* Expanded Operational Code Typology

*Friendly (+) or hostile (−) political universe with equal (=) or unequal (> or >) power distribution.

**Cooperation (CO+) or conflict (CF−) strategy with equal (=) or unequal (< or >) power distribution.

The relationship between the master beliefs of P-1 Nature of Political Universe and I-1 Approach to Strategy is conditioned in Figure 2.3 by P-4 Historical Control as a third master belief. The P-1 and I-1 beliefs specify the exercise of power by others (P-1) and self (I-1), respectively, while the P-4 belief specifies the distribution of power between self and others in the political universe. Collectively, they answer Lenin's *kto-kovo* question at the core of the Bolshevik operational code belief system. Depending on P-4's answer as to who controls whom, the remaining philosophical beliefs are a function of interaction between P-1 and P-4 while the remaining instrumental beliefs are a function of interaction between I-1 and P-4.

The logically possible relationships among the three P-1, I-1, and P-4 master beliefs are shown in Figure 2.3 and revise the belief systems in the original Holsti typology from 6 to 12 types (four symmetrical types in which the power distribution [control over historical development] is equal [=] and eight asymmetrical types with a power distribution [control over historical development] that is unequal [≠]). In all 12 types, the exercise of power in the political universe is friendly (+) or hostile (−), and the exercise of power by the leader is cooperative (+) or conflictual (−). The asterisked cells within the typology in Figure 2.3 are logically impossible power distributions (<,<; >,>; <,=; >,=) in which the power distribution is not complementary, i.e., the control over historical development (P-4) attributed to a leader, and the political universe contradict one another.

*Methodological Progress*

The development and refinement of the operational code typology in Figure 2.3 were accompanied by the development of quantitative indices for each belief identified by George's ten questions. The VICS of content analysis identified beliefs about the exercise of social power (Baldwin 1989) attributed to Self (a particular agent) versus Others in the political universe by retrieving the transitive verbs in the public statements of political leaders. The distribution of these codable verbs attributed to the speaker is the basis for measuring (I-1) the political strategy of the agent as cooperative (CO) or conflict (CF) while the codable verbs attributed to others as cooperative or conflict measure (P-1) the nature of the political universe as friendly or hostile. The attribution of all codable verbs to the speaker and others measures the distribution of control over historical development (P-4) between the speaker and others, which reflects the leader's beliefs about the distribution of the exercise of social power in the political universe.

The VICS index for I-1 is calculated by coding transitive verbs attributed to Self (S) as either CO or CF, then subtracting CF from CO and dividing this number by the sum of CO and CF attributed to Self. The same formula applies to the VICS index for P-1, which is to subtract the verbs attributed to Other agents (O) and coded as CF from the verbs attributed to Others and coded as CO, followed by dividing this number by the sum of CO and CF verbs attributed to others. The VICS index for the P-4 belief regarding historical control attributed to Self is to subtract the sum of all codable verbs attributed to Others (O) from the sum of all codable verbs attributed to Self (S) and then divide by the sum of all codable verbs attributed to both Self and Others. The formulas for calculating the VICS indices of the three master beliefs are as follows:

- I-1. Approach to Strategy (Self): $S = [(CO - CF)/(CO + CF)]$
- P-1. Nature of the Political Universe (Others): $O = [(CO - CF)/(CO + CF)]$
- P-4. Historical Control (Self vs. Other): $S = [(S - O)/(S + O)]$ vs. $O = [(O - S)/(S + O)]$

The VICS indices for I-1, P-1, and P-4 all vary between $-1.0$ and $+1.0$ and measure the balance between the exercise of social power in the form of positive sanctions (acts of cooperation) versus negative sanctions (acts of conflict) by Self (I-1) and Others (P-1) or the balance between the exercise of both positive and negative sanctions (P-4) between Self and Others (Schafer and Walker 2006b, 25–51; Walker and Schafer 2010). These VICS indices provide a map (P-1) and a compass (I-1), respectively, to locate and navigate the balance of social power exercised by Self and Others and distributed between Self and Others in the political universe

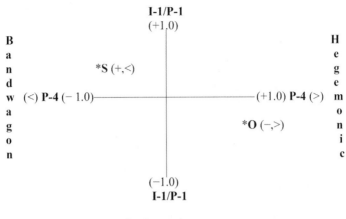

*Figure 2.4* Self and Other Power Dynamics in the Political Universe*

*Positive (+) and Negative (–) sanctions. Less (<) and More (>) powerful position

represented by the political field diagram of power relations in Figure 2.4. The examples in Figure 2.4 show Self's location (S) in the upper left quadrant with a positive (+) VICS index of greater than zero for I-1 and a VICS index of less than zero (<) for P-4. The VICS indices for a generalized Other (O) in the political universe is less than zero for P-1 (–) and greater than zero (>) for P-4.

The exercise of social power by Self and Other in Figure 2.4 is conceptualized as the exchange of positive (+) and negative (–) sanctions (Baldwin 1989, 2016) between agents (S and O) and communicated in the form of words (support/oppose or promise/threaten statements) and deeds (reward or punish actions), which aggregate as building blocks to calculate the I-1, P-1, and P-4 VICS indices. Depending on their respective locations, the location of S and relations with O are likely to exhibit different strategies of interaction. The strategies at the edges of Figure 2.4 are bandwagoning (unconditional cooperation), appeasement (conditional cooperation), hegemonic (unconditional conflict), and balancing (conditional conflict) strategies, which describe and explain decisions by Self and Other based on combinations of the I-1 or P-1 indices and the corresponding P-4 index.

The I-1, P-4 indices of (+, <) define Self's location in Figure 2.4 in a relatively weak power position, prescribing and predicting a bandwagoning strategy of unconditional cooperation rather than an appeasement strategy of conditional cooperation in the political universe. Other's P-1, P-4 indices map a relatively strong power configuration in Self's strategic environment, which diagnoses the relative likelihood of a hegemonic strategy of unconditional conflict by others rather than a balancing strategy of conditional conflict in the political universe. If the power positions of Self or Other had been more symmetrical (=), the prescriptions, diagnoses, and predictions would be the pursuit of conditional strategies of reciprocation in the form of appeasement (conditional cooperation) for Self (+, =) and balancing (conditional conflict) for Other (–, =) in the political universe.

In sum, the predictions of Self's foreign policy decisions that follow from the master beliefs are about the *direction* of Self's decisions (either cooperative or conflictual) in the form of exercising positive (+) or negative (–) sanction as a function of the interaction between the I-1 or P-1 and P-4 operational code indices for Self and Other in Figure 2.4. Together they provide a navigational compass for Self and a cognitive map of Other in the political universe. The individual transitive verbs are aggregated by their valences to calculate the I-1, P-1, and P-4 indices. They also fall into words and deeds categories, which are scaled for intensity (deeds speak louder than words) as well as direction (cooperation or conflict) in Figure 2.5, which contains formulas to calculate VICS indices for the remaining philosophical and instrumental beliefs identified by George (1969).

The indices in Figure 2.5 contain additional information about the exchange of positive and negative sanctions between Self and Other. They describe important features of *how* the strategies predicted by the interaction of I-1, P-1, and P-4 are likely to be enacted: the intensity (P-2 and I-2) of cooperative or conflictual tactics associated with the strategies, the risk-acceptant or risk-averse orientations (P-3 and I-3) associated with the strategies, the role of chance (P-5) and the shift propensities describing the "timing" between words and deeds (I-4a) or between cooperation and conflict (I-4b) associated with Self's strategy, and the variety and relative frequency (I-5) of the exercise of different types of social power by Self. The accuracy of these predictions depends on two assumptions.

First, the VICS indices of an operational code are estimates of a system's various macrostates, e.g., the strategy of a belief system represented by I-1 or its risk orientation represented by I-3, which are statistical properties of the belief system aggregated and inferred from microstates (verbs) that constitute the belief system. The formulas for the VICS indices are statistical mechanics (calculations) to identify global statistical properties of the belief system. They are information about the belief system as a whole and can only identify the probable future behavior of the system based on its past behavior (Mitchell 2009, 47–50; Cioffi-Revilla 1998). Second, the information from this cognitive system of beliefs about the social system of behavioral interactions between an agent (Self) and its environment (Other) converge, i.e., one system's properties are or become congruent (match up) with the other system. The cognitive and social systems at least tend toward convergence as the agent and its environment interact over time (Walker, Malici, and Schafer 2011, 10–19; see also Malici and Walker 2017, 9–20).

## PHILOSOPHICAL BELIEFS

| Elements | Index* | Interpretation |
|---|---|---|
| **P-1.** **NATURE OF THE POLITICAL** **UNIVERSE (Image of Others)** | **%Positive minus %Negative** **Transitive Other Attributions** | **+1.0 friendly to** **-1.0 hostile.** |
| P-2. REALIZATION OF POLITICAL VALUES (Optimism/Pessimism) | Mean Intensity of Transitive Other Attributions divided by 3 | +1.0 optimistic to −1.0 pessimistic. |
| P-3. POLITICAL FUTURE (Predict-ability of Others Tactics) | 1 minus Index** of Qualitative Variation for Other Attributions | 1.0 predictable to 0.0 uncertain. |
| **P-4.** **HISTORICAL CONTROL** **(Locus of Control)** | ***Diff. Self & Other Attributions** **÷ (Self plus Other Attributions)** | **-1.0 low control to** **+1.0 high control.** |
| a.   **Self Control** | ***Self minus Other Attributions** | Index numerator. |
| b.   **Other Control** | ***Other minus Self Attributions** | Index numerator. |
| P-5. ROLE OF CHANCE (Absence of Control) | 1.0 − Political Future x Self Attri-butions÷(Self + Other Attributions) | + 1.0 high role to 0.0 low role. |

## INSTRUMENTAL BELIEFS

| Elements | Index* | Interpretation |
|---|---|---|
| **I-1.** **APPROACH TO GOALS** **(Direction of Strategy)** | **%Positive minus %Negative** **Transitive Self Attributions** | **+1.0 high cooperation** **−1.0 high conflict.** |
| I-2. PURSUIT OF GOALS (Intensity of Tactics) | Mean Intensity of Transitive Self Attributions divided by 3 | +1.0 high cooperation to −1.0 high conflict. |
| I-3. RISK ORIENTATION (Predictability of Tactics) | 1 minus Index of Qualitative Variation for Self Attributions | 1.0 risk acceptant to 0.0 risk averse. |
| I-4. TIMING OF ACTION ((Flexibility of Tactics) | 1 minus Absolute Value [%X minus %Y Self Attributions] | 1.0 high to 0.0 low shift propensity. |
| a. Coop v. Conf Tactics | Where X = Coop and Y = Conf | |
| b. Word v. Deed Tactics | Where X = Word and Y = Deed | |
| I-5. UTILITY OF MEANS (Exercise of Power) | Percentages of Self Attributions for Power Categories a through f | +1.0 very frequent to 0.0 infrequent. |
| a. Reward.   b. Promise.   c. Appeal/Support.   d. Oppose/Resist.   e. Threaten.   f. Punish. | | |

*Figure 2.5* Verbs in Context (VICS) Indices for Operational Code Beliefs

*All indices vary between 0 and 1.0 except for P-1, P-2, P-4, I-1, and I-2, which vary between −1.0 and +1.0. P-2 and I-2 are divided by 3 to standardize the range (Walker, Schafer, and Young 1998).

**"The Index of Qualitative Variation is a ratio of the number of different pairs of obser-vations in a distribution to the maximum possible number of different pairs for a distribu-tion with the same N [number of cases] and the same number of variable classifications" (Watson and McGaw, 1980, p. 88).

***Diff. is difference between Self and Other Attributions. Master beliefs are in bold.

## Substantive Progress

OCA tests these two assumptions by focusing on three mechanisms (pro-cesses) associated with the study of relations between beliefs and behav-ior: (1) the mirroring effects of behavior on beliefs; (2) the steering effects of beliefs on behavior; (3) the learning effects of changes over time in beliefs and behavior (Walker 2002; Walker and Schafer 2010, 5504–5509). Most of the operational code studies employing VICS as an instrument for identifying and analyzing the operational codes of political leaders since its invention in 1998 have focused on one or more of these mech-anisms (Walker, Schafer, and Young 1998; Walker and Schafer 2010).

Subjects for investigation include the domains of leader-adviser relations, international security relations, and international political economy (Schafer and Walker 2006b).

While there have been several conceptual and methodological innovations, including the evolution of new models of these mechanisms and additional indices of belief system properties, they have taken place largely within the context of a focus on individual leaders as agents. New models include the use of schemas, analogies, and algorithms to describe beliefs in the operational codes of leaders (George 1979; Bennett 1999; Khong 1992; Marfleet and Walker 2006); games and simulations to describe and explain links between operational code beliefs and decisions (Schafer and Walker 2006b; Walker and Schafer 2011); and role theory and signed graph theory to map relations between agents with different operational code beliefs as complex adaptive systems (Walker, Malici, and Schafer 2011; Walker and Malici 2011; Malici and Walker 2017). In each of these studies, the analytical focus is primarily on the operational code beliefs of individual leaders as they engage in cognitive efforts to (1) mirror the political environment with philosophical beliefs, (2) navigate the political environment with instrumental beliefs, and (3) monitor feedback from the political environment to maintain or alter both kinds of beliefs (Walker 2002; Walker and Schafer 2010, 5505).

## References

Achen, C. 1988. A state with bureaucratic politics is responsible as a unitary actor. In *Presented at the annual meeting of the American Political Science Association*, September 1–4, Washington, DC.

Allison, G. 1971. *Essence of decision*. Boston, MA: Little, Brown.

Axelrod, R., M. Cohen. 1999. *Harnessing complexity*. New York, NY: Free Press.

Baldwin, D. 1989. *Paradoxes of power*. New York, NY: Blackwell.

Baldwin, D. 2016. *Power and international relations*. Princeton, NJ: Princeton University Press.

Barnet, M. 1973. *Roots of war*. New York, NY: Atheneum.

Bejan, A., J. Zane. 2012. *Design in nature*. New York, NY: Doubleday.

Bennett, A. 1999. *Condemned to repetition: The rise, fall, and reprise of Soviet-Russian military interventionism, 1973–1996*. Cambridge, MA: MIT Press.

Bobrow, D., S. S. Chan, J. Kringen. 1979. *Understanding foreign policy decisions: The Chinese case*. New York, NY: Free Press.

Burke, J. 2000. *The institutional presidency*. 2nd Edition. Baltimore, MD: John Hopkins University Press.

Cameron, C. 2000. *Veto bargaining*. Cambridge, MA: Cambridge University Press.

Cioffi-Revilla, C. 1998. *Politics and uncertainty*. New York, NY: Cambridge University Press.

Dawkins, R. 1996. *Climbing mount improbable*. New York, NY: W.W. Norton.

Dawkins, R. 1999. *The extended phenotype: The long reach of the gene*. Oxford: Oxford University Press.

Dennett, D. 1989. *The intentional stance*. Cambridge, MA: MIT Press.

Dennett, D. 2017. *From bacteria to Bach and back: The evolution of minds*. New York, NY: W.W. Norton.

Edey, M., D. Johanson. 1989. *Blueprints: Solving the mystery of evolution*. Boston, MA: Little, Brown.

Etheredge, L. 1978. *A world of men: The private sources of American foreign policy*. Cambridge, MA: MIT Press.

Feng, H. 2007. *Chinese strategic culture and foreign policy decision-making*. New York, NY: Routledge.

Gell-Mann, M. 1994. *The quark and the jaguar*. New York, NY: Henry Holt & Company.

George, A. 1969. The operational code. *International Studies Quarterly* 13: 190–222.

George, A. 1979. The causal nexus between cognitive beliefs and decision-making behavior. In *Psychological models of international politics*, ed. L. Falkowski, 95–124. Boulder, CO: Westview Press.

Gigerenzer, G., R. Selten. 2001. *Bounded rationality*. Cambridge, MA: MIT Press.

Greenstein, F. 1987. *Personality and politics*. 2nd Edition. Princeton, NJ: Princeton University Press.

Greenstein, F. 2004. *The presidential difference*. 2nd Edition. Princeton, NJ: Princeton University Press.

Hagan, J. 1993. *Political opposition and foreign policy in comparative perspective*. Boulder, CO: Lynn Rienner Press.

He, K., H. H. Feng. 2015. Transcending rationalism and constructivism: Chinese leaders' operational codes, socialization processes, and multilateralism after the cold war. *European Political Science Review* 7: 401–406.

Hermann, M. 2001. How decision units shape foreign policy. *International Studies Review* 3: 47–81.

Hermann, M. 2002. *Leadership style*. Hilliard, OH: Social Science Automation.

Hermann, M. 2003. Assessing leadership style: A trait analysis. In *The psychological assessment of political leaders*, ed. J. Post, 178–214. Ann Arbor, MI: University of Michigan Press.

Hermann, M., C. Hermann. 1989. Who makes foreign policy decisions and how? *International Studies Quarterly* 33: 361–388.

Holland, J. 1995. *Hidden order: How adaptation builds complexity*. Reading: Addison-Wesley.

Holland, J. 1998. *Emergence: From chaos to order*. Reading: Addison-Wesley.

Holland, J. 2012. *Signals and boundaries: Building blocks for complex adaptive systems*. Cambridge, MA: MIT Press.

Holsti, K. 1970. National role conceptions in the study of foreign policy. *International Studies Quarterly* 14: 233–309.

Holsti, O. 1976. Foreign policy viewed cognitively. In *The structure of decision*, ed. R. Axelrod, 18–54. Princeton, NJ: Princeton University Press.

Holsti, O. 1977. The 'operational Code' as an approach to the analysis of political belief systems. In *Report to the national science foundation*. Grant SOC 75-15368. Durham, NC: Duke University.

Janis, I. 1972. *Victims of groupthink*. Boston, MA: Houghton-Mifflin.

Janowitz, M. 1960. *The professional soldier*. Glencoe: Free Press.

Johnston, A. 1995. *Cultural realism: Strategic culture and grand strategy in Chinese history*. Princeton, NJ: Princeton University Press.

Kaarbo, J. 2012. *Coalition politics and cabinet decision making*. Ann Arbor, MI: University of Michigan Press.

Kegley, C. 1987. Decision regimes and the comparative study of foreign policy. In *New directions in the study of foreign policy*, eds. C. Hermann, J. Rosenau, C. Kegley, 247–268. Boston, MA: Allen and Unwin.

Kerlinger, F. 1986. *Foundations of behavioral research*. 3rd Edition. New York, NY: Holt, Rinehart, & Winston.

Khong, H. 1992. *Analogies at war*. Princeton, NJ: Princeton University Press.

Kowert, P. 2002. *Groupthink or deadlock?* Albany, NY: SUNY Press.

LeDoux, J. 2002. *Synaptic self: How our brains become who we are*. New York, NY: Viking Penguin.

Ledoux, J., W. Hirst. 1986. *Mind and brain: Dialogues in cognitive neuroscience*. Cambridge, MA: Cambridge University Press.

Leites, N. 1951. *The operational code of the politburo*. New York, NY: McGraw-Hill.

Leites, N. 1953. *A study of Bolshevism*. New York, NY: Free Press.

Little, D. 1991. *Varieties of social explanation*. Boulder, CO: Westview.

Malici, A. 2005. Discord and collaboration between allies. *Journal of Conflict Resolution* 49: 90–119.

Malici, A. 2008. *When leaders learn and when they don't*. Albany, NY: SUNY Press.

Malici, A., S. Walker. 2017. *Role theory and role conflict in U.S.-Iran relations*. New York, NY: Routledge.

Marfleet, G., S. Walker. 2006. A world of beliefs. In *Beliefs and leadership in world politics*, eds. M. Schafer, S. Walker, 53–76. New York, NY: Palgrave.

Merton, R. 1940. Bureaucratic structure and personality. In *Reader in bureaucracy*, ed. R. Merton, 195–206. New York, NY: Free Press.

Mintz, A., C. C. Wayne, 2016. *The polythink syndrome*. Stanford: Stanford University Press.

Mitchell, M. 2009. *Complexity: A guided tour*. New York, NY: *Oxford University Press*.

Neustadt, R. 1960. *Presidential power*. New York, NY: Macmillan.

Nowak, M. 2006. *Evolutionary dynamics: Exploring the equations of life*. Cambridge, MA: Harvard University Press.

Nowak, M. 2011. *Super cooperators*. New York, NY: Free Press.

Preston, T. 2001. *The president and his inner circle*. New York, NY: Columbia University Press.

Russett, B. 1993. *Grasping the democratic peace*. Princeton, NJ: Princeton University Press.

Schafer, M., S. Crichlow. 2010. *Groupthink vs. high-quality decision making in international relations*. New York, NY: Columbia University Press.

Schafer, M., S. Walker. 2001. Political leadership and the democratic peace: The operational code of prime minister tony Blair. In *Profiling leaders and the analysis of political leadership*, eds. O. Feldman, L. Valenty, 21–35. Westport, CT: Greenwood Press.

Schafer, M., S. Walker. 2006a. Democratic leaders and the democratic peace: The operational codes of Tony Blair and Bill Clinton. *International Studies Quarterly* 50: 561–584.

Schafer, M., S. Walker, eds. 2006b. *Beliefs and leadership in world politics*. New York, NY: Palgrave.

Simon, H. 1957. *Models of man*. New York, NY: John Wiley.

Simon, H. 1969. *The sciences of the artificial*. Cambridge, MA: MIT Press.

Simon, H. 1985. Human nature in politics. *American Political Science Review* 79: 293–304.

Smith., M. 1968. A map for the study of personality and politics. *Journal of Social Issues* 24: 15–28.

Stevenson, M. 2006. Economic liberalism and the operational code beliefs of U.S. Presidents: The initiation of NAFTA disputes. In *1989-2002. In beliefs and political leadership in world politics*, eds. M. Schafer, S. Walker, 201–218. New York, NY: Palgrave.

Thies, C. 2006. Bankers and beliefs: The political psychology of the Asian financial crisis. In *Beliefs and political leadership in world politics*, eds. M. Schafer, S. Walker, 219–236. New York, NY: Palgrave.

Tucker, R. C. 1963. *The Soviet political mind.* New York, NY: Praeger.

Tucker, R. C. 1965. The dictator and totalitarianism. *World Politics* 17: 555–583.

Walker, S. 1982. Psychological explanations of international politics: Problems of aggregation, measurement, and theory construction. In *Biopolitics, political psychology, and international politics*, ed. G. Hoppel, 114–150. London: Frances Pinter.

Walker, S. 1983. The motivational foundations of political belief systems: A re-analysis of the operational code construct. *International Studies Quarterly* 27: 179–201.

Walker, S. 1987. *Role theory and foreign policy analysis.* Durham, NC: Duke University Press.

Walker, S. 1990. The evolution of operational code analysis. *Political Psychology* 11: 403–418.

Walker, S. 1995. Psychodynamic processes and framing effects in foreign policy decision making. *Political Psychology* 16: 697–717.

Walker, S. 2002. Beliefs and foreign policy analysis in the new millennium. In *Conflict, security, foreign policy, and international political economy*, eds. M. Brecher, F. Harvey, 56–71. Ann Arbor, MI: University of Michigan Press.

Walker, S. 2003. Operational code analysis as a scientific research program. In *Progress in international relations theory*, eds. C. Elman, M. Elman, 245–276. Cambridge, MA: MIT Press.

Walker, S. 2004. Role identities and the operational codes of political leaders. In *Advances in political psychology*, ed. M. Hermann, 71–106. Vol. I. Amsterdam: Elsevier.

Walker, S. 2009. The psychology of presidential decision making. In *The Oxford handbook of the American presidency*, eds. G. Edwards, W. Howell, 550–576. New York, NY: Oxford University Press.

Walker, S. 2013. *The cognitive architecture of British appeasement decisions.* New York, NY: Routledge.

Walker, S., L. Falkowski. 1985. The operational codes of U.S. Presidents and secretaries of state. *Political Psychology* 5: 237–266.

Walker, S., A. Malici. 2011. *U.S. Presidents and foreign policy mistakes.* Stanford: Stanford University Press.

Walker, S., M. Schafer. 2007. Theodore Roosevelt and Woodrow Wilson as cultural icons of U.S. foreign policy. *Political Psychology* 28: 747–776.

Walker, S., M. Schafer. 2010. Operational code theory: Beliefs and foreign policy decisions. In *The international studies encyclopedia*, ed. R. Denemark, 5493–5514. Vol. VIII. Chichester, UK: Wiley-Blackwell.

Walker, S., A. Malici, M. Schafer. 2011. *Rethinking foreign policy analysis: States, leaders, and the microfoundations of behavioral international relations.* New York, NY: Routledge.

Walker, S., M. Schafer, M. Young. 1998. Systematic procedures for operational code analysis. *International Studies Quarterly* 42: 175–190.

Walker, S., M. Schafer, M. Young. 2003. Profiling the operational codes of political leaders. In *The psychological assessment of political leaders*, ed. J. Post, 215–245. Ann Arbor, MI: University of Michigan Press.

Walker, S., M. Schafer. 2011. Dueling with dictators: Explaining the strategic interaction patterns of U.S. Presidents and rogue leaders. In *Rethinking foreign policy analysis*, eds. S. Walker, A. Malici, M. Schafer, 223–244. New York, NY: Routledge.

Walker, S., M. Schafer, G. Smith. 2018. The operational codes of Hillary Clinton and Donald Trump. In *The Oxford handbook of behavioral political science*, eds. A. Mintz, L. Terris. New York, NY: Oxford University Press. DOI: 10.1093/oxf ordhb/9780190634131.013.4.

Watson, G., D. McGaw, D. 1980. *Statistical inquiry*. New York, NY: John Wiley & Sons.

Wendt, A. 1999. *Social theory of international politics*. Cambridge, MA: Cambridge University Press.

Wendt, A. 2003. Why a world state is inevitable. *European Journal of International Relations* 9(4): 491–542.

Yergin, D. 1977. *Shattered peace*. Boston, MA: Houghton-Mifflin.

Young, M. 2001. Building world views with profiler. In *Progress in communication sciences*, ed. M. West, 17–32. Vol. 17. Westport, CT: Ablex Publishing.

# Part II
# The Operational Codes of World Leaders

# 3 Revisiting the Operational Code of Vladimir Putin

*Mark Schafer, Didara Nurmanova,
and Stephen G. Walker*

## Introduction

Twenty years ago, Vladimir Putin replaced the ailing Boris Yeltsin as the president of Russia. A year later, two of us conducted an operational code analysis of Putin's early interviews with three Russian journalists (Schafer and Walker 2014 [2001]; Putin et al. 2000). In the meantime, much has changed since the beginning of the first Putin presidency. Given that Putin has arguably become and appears likely to remain an even more powerful global presence, revisiting his operational code seems highly appropriate. We found in our earlier study some indications that Putin might well become an assertive leader who was more prone toward conflict than cooperation. Behavioral historical evidence indicates that Russia has become less cooperative and more conflictual in recent times, and we wonder if and how Putin's cognitive operational code changed consistently with these behavioral changes in Russian foreign policy (Sakwa 2004; Hill and Gaddy 2015).

Therefore, in this paper we revisit Putin's operational code and conduct a statistical analysis of the differences in his belief system between his initial two terms (2000–2008) as Russia's president and during his third term between 2012 and 2015 after an interlude serving as the Russian prime minister (2008–2012). We also compare and contrast his operational code with the US presidents George W. Bush and Barack Obama who had to deal with Russia as an increasingly difficult partner and potential rival during Putin's tenure in office. These comparisons are facilitated by the use of formal game theory models of the respective operational codes of the three leaders, in order to develop simulations of the strategic interactions between Russia and the United States that may capture patterns in the belief systems of each leader associated with the pattern of worsening relations between the two nuclear powers.

## Operational Code Analysis

An agent's "operational code" generally refers to the diagnostic, choice, and shift propensities in the exercise of social power between Self and Other as agents in the form of positive or negative sanctions (stating support or opposition, making promises or threats, implementing rewards or punishments). The propensities may be exhibited as cognitive or social patterns, depending on whether they refer to patterns of thoughts (beliefs) exhibited in public statements or patterns of social behaviors (actions) directed at other(s). An operational code analysis of a particular agent may also be either general or targeted, i.e., focused on general patterns of thoughts or behaviors regarding a generalized Self and Other or targeted on patterns of beliefs and actions referring to the exercise of power between a particular self and other. The agent itself may be defined at different levels of aggregation as an individual leader, a single group, a coalition of groups, an organization, or an institution (Schafer and Walker 2006; Walker and Schafer 2010).

The spatial focus of our operational code analysis is first on Mr. Putin's general beliefs about the nature of the political universe (P-1), the most effective strategies for the exercise of power to realize fundamental political values (I-1), and the level of historical control over political events (P-4). Then we aggregate our focus to examine the implications of this analysis for the conduct of general relations between Russia and the United States as friends, partners, rivals, or enemies. These spatial patterns of aggregation may vary temporally as well, aggregated over time periods of different lengths in terms of days, weeks, months, and years or terms in office. Therefore, our temporal focus is also on "experiential learning" in the form of changes in the key philosophical and instrumental beliefs in Putin's operational code, by comparing the average values for these beliefs during different periods of his presidency (Levy 1994; see also Walker, Schafer, and Marfleet 2012).

We employ a research design that compares these values in a repeated measures panel study that includes as well a change in the identity of the US president from Bush to Obama. Our basic research questions are as follows: did Putin change his key operational code beliefs over time and what were the implications of continuity and change in his beliefs for strategic interactions between Russia and the United States guided by the operational codes of the two US presidents whose key beliefs may be the same or differ from the beliefs of the Russian president?

There are three key operational code beliefs, which have indices that summarize the exercise of power by self and others in a leader's cognitive representation of the political universe. The nature of the political universe belief (P-1) summarizes self's beliefs about the exercise of power by Other as positive sanctions (cooperation) or negative sanctions (conflict) in the political universe. The Approach to Goals belief (I-1) summarizes self's beliefs about Self's exercise of power in the form of positive sanctions (cooperation behavior) or negative sanctions (conflict behavior). The historical control belief (P-4) summarizes self's beliefs about the distribution of historical control between Self and Other in the political universe. The entire set of beliefs in the operational code construct plus the indices for calculating their values are in the Appendix of this chapter. In the following analysis of Putin's operational code, we focus only on the key I-1, P-1, and P-4 beliefs (Schafer and Walker 2006; Walker and Schafer 2010).

Collectively, the information from the indices for these three key beliefs in Putin's operational code constitute his definition of the situation and power position *vis-a-vis* others in the political universe. The instances of significant change and continuity among these three key beliefs across time identify changes in his power position with potentially important strategic implications for changes in Russia's behavior and interactions with others in the political universe. We have developed a typology of *general roles* or different definitions of the self-in-situation, which model the interactions between a generalized self as Ego and a generalized Other as Alter in the political universe, based on the indices for these three beliefs. The steps in constructing the typology are shown in Figure 3.1. Each of the definitions of self-in-situation constructed from the modeling rules in Figure 3.1 are associated with different rank orders for Self and Others regarding the goals of domination, deadlock, settlement, and submission in the exercise of power between them.

We can hypothesize from information about I-1, P-1, and P-4 beliefs the likely general patterns of strategic interaction and the outcomes between Russia and significant others in the political universe, e.g., the United States, within a given time period bounded by continuity in the belief systems of their respective leaders. By extension we can also hypothesize general changes in their strategic interaction patterns when the indices for the key beliefs (I-1, P-1, P-4) change for Putin or his US counterpart (Bush or Obama). We use TOM, a Theory of Moves, developed by Brams (1994) for ordinal games with sequential rules of play, to model formally the emergent patterns among changes in beliefs, foreign policy strategies, and international outcomes as dyadic systems models of strategic interactions.

These formal models are based on our empirical analysis of different levels of learning by leaders in the form of changes in I-1 beliefs (simple learning) and changes in P-1 beliefs (diagnostic learning). Changes in all three key operational code beliefs of I-1, P-1, and P-4 (complex learning) reframe the respective subjective games of leaders (Levy 1994; Walker, Schafer, and Marfleet 2012; Walker 2013). We hypothesize from our game theory models that complex learning leads to changes in the preferences for domination, deadlock, settlement, or submission as strategic outcomes between self and others and corresponding changes in the strategic interaction games of world politics. In turn, these hypotheses provide a potential explanation for continuity and change in Russian-American relations between 2000 when Putin came to power in Moscow and the post-2012 period of rising tensions in their relations.

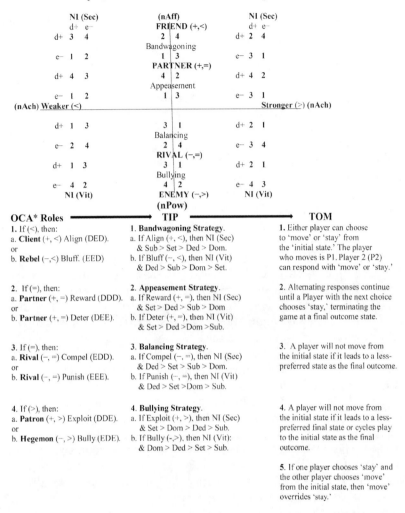

**OCA\* Roles** ⟶ **TIP** ⟶ **TOM**

1. If (<), then:
a. **Client** (+, <) Align (DED).
or
b. **Rebel** (−,<) Bluff. (EED)

1. **Bandwagoning Strategy.**
a. If Align (+, <), then NI (Sec)
& Sub > Set > Ded > Dom.
b. If Bluff (−, <), then NI (Vit)
& Ded > Sub > Dom > Set.

1. Either player can choose
to 'move' or 'stay' from
the 'initial state.' The player
who moves is P1. Player 2 (P2)
can respond with 'move' or 'stay.'

2. If (=), then:
a. **Partner** (+, =) Reward (DDD).
or
b. **Partner** (+, =) Deter (DEE).

2. **Appeasement Strategy.**
a. If Reward (+, =), then NI (Sec)
& Set > Ded > Sub > Dom
b. If Deter (+, =), then NI (Vit)
& Set > Ded >Dom >Sub.

2. Alternating responses continue
until a Player with the next choice
chooses 'stay,' terminating the
game at a final outcome state.

3. If (=), then:
a. **Rival** (−, =) Compel (EDD).
or
b. **Rival** (−, =) Punish (EEE).

3. **Balancing Strategy.**
a. If Compel (−, =), then NI (Sec)
& Ded > Set > Sub > Dom.
b. If Punish (−, =), then NI (Vit)
& Ded > Set >Dom > Sub.

3. A player will not move from
the initial state if it leads to a less-
preferred state as the final outcome.

4. If (>), then:
a. **Patron** (+, >) Exploit (DDE).
or
b. **Hegemon** (−, >) Bully (EDE).

4. **Bullying Strategy.**
a. If Exploit (+, >), then NI (Sec)
& Set > Dom > Ded > Sub.
b. If Bully (-,>), then NI (Vit):
& Dom > Ded > Set > Sub.

4. A player will not move from
the initial state if it leads to a less-
preferred final state or cycles play
to the initial state as the final
outcome.

5. If one player chooses 'stay' and
the other player chooses 'move'
from the initial state, then 'move'
overrides 'stay.'

*Figure 3.1* Role Models of Mechanisms Linking Beliefs, Behavior, and Strategic
Interactions

\*OCA: Operational Code Analysis (Walker 2013); TIP: Theory of Inferences about
Preferences (Walker, Malici, and Schafer 2011); TOM: Theory of Moves (Brams 1994); E:
Escalate (e−); D: De-escalate (d+). NI: National Interest; Sec: Secondary; Vit: Vital; Set:
Settlement Outcome; Ded: Deadlock Outcome; Dom: Domination Outcome; Sub: Submission
Outcome. I-1/P-1: (+ or −); P-4: (< = >). Ego's Ranked Outcomes: (4) high …. (1) low

We begin our analysis with the beliefs of the agents, which define roles
in Figure 3.1 under the OCA Types column as combinations of values
for their respective key operational code beliefs (I-1, P-1, P-4). The values
of these three beliefs are positive (+) and negative (−) for I-1 or P-1 and
greater (>), equal (=), or lesser (<) for P-4. Together they locate an agent
in one of the four quadrants formed by the intersection of the vertical
axis for I-1 or P-1 and the horizontal axis for P-4. In turn, this location is

associated with one of the four roles and corresponding strategies of role enactment on the vertical axis. Each strategy is specified by the combination of P-4 values and I-1 or P-1 values expressed by the four pairs of "If/Then" statements in the OCA column.

In the TIP (theory of inferences about preferences) column of Figure 3.1, we infer from these roles and strategies what combinations of power and interest distributions are likely to constrain the enactment of the respective roles and counter roles attributed to self and other according to the different rank orders for the outcomes of domination, deadlock, settlement, and submission specified by TIP for self and other. Examples of these rank-ordered outcomes from (4) highest to lowest (1) for Self as Ego are listed for each strategy and plotted as $2 \times 2$ games of deescalation (d+) and escalation (e–) at different locations in the four quadrants of Figure 3.1 (Walker 2013; Malici and Walker 2017).

Finally, we can construct a $2 \times 2$ subjective game from these TIP inferences and solve for the nonmyopic equilibrium (NME) solutions emerging from the interaction between self and others as they play their respective subjective games according to the rules specified by TOM (Walker, Malici, and Schafer 2011, 283–288). The rules of TOM are summarized under the TOM column as alternating moves of Escalation (E) or Deescalation (D) by Ego as the row player and Alter as the column player in the possible $2 \times 2$ ordinal games formed by the intersection of their respective strategies. Play begins from one of the four cells as an "initial state" and ends in a nonmyopic equilibrium when both players choose "stay" in a particular cell as a "final state," which may be the "initial state" or one of the other cells reached by alternating decisions to choose "move" from the initial state.

Collectively, OCA roles, TIP preferences, and TOM moves constitute a theory complex of beliefs, preferences, and strategic interactions, which binary role theory unifies as mechanisms in a complex adaptive system of foreign policy roles defined by strategic interactions between Self as Ego and Other as Alter (Walker, Malici, and Schafer 2011; Walker 2013; Malici and Walker 2017). The motivational foundations of the operational code beliefs that interact to generate this social system in Figure 3.1 are the needs for power (nPow), affiliation (nAff), and achievement (nAch). They are extra-cognitive elements of the agent's personality formed by the interaction between genetic personality and cultural socialization mechanisms, which are also mapped along the axes in Figure 3.1 (Walker 1983; Walker and Falkowski 1985). The need for power is associated with conflictual beliefs and behavior while the need for affiliation is associated with cooperative beliefs and behavior and the need for achievement is associated with beliefs and behavior regarding control over outcomes in the environment (Winter 2003).

## Putin's Operational Code

Our initial analysis in 2000 gave some indications that Putin had the potential to be an assertive leader in global politics, and since that time, indeed there have been some specific situations where it is easy to perceive him as escalating beyond what others might have done. Two specific violent international conflicts are of particular interest: the 2008 war with Georgia over South Ossetia during Putin's second term and the escalation with Ukraine over Crimea in 2014 during his third term. These two conflicts took place during the presidential terms of US presidents George W. Bush and Barack Obama, respectively, who both generally opposed Russia's actions in these conflicts. This configuration of events and players on the world stage sets up a multipart set of specific research questions:

- First, was our very early analysis of Putin typical or atypical of how his general operational code developed as he began to govern during his first term?
- Second, did Putin's operational code beliefs change in any telling ways late in his second term during the run-up to the Georgian conflict?
- Third, were there key changes in his operational code in his third term as president, following 4 years when the Russian presidency was held by Dmitry Medvedev?
- Fourth, if so, do those changes provide some insights about Putin's behavior following the Ukrainian conflict?
- Fifth, might Putin's conflict behavior be understood more fully as a result of his operational code relative to the operational codes of his US counterparts?

Collectively, these research questions address whether Putin experienced changes in his operational code beliefs over time in the form of simple learning about the best strategy (I-1), diagnostic learning about the nature of the political universe (P-1), and complex learning with respect to controlling the mediation of relations between Self and Other (P-4). Operational code analysis investigates the beliefs of leaders with the assumption that those beliefs have an effect on their policy choices. There is little doubt about Putin's authority over Russian foreign policy since 2000, which makes us wonder if a shift toward more conflictual actions by Russia can be explained by either critical changes in his operational code or from significant differences in his operational code compared to the operational codes of relevant US leaders.

## Research Design

All of the research questions identified above involve either comparisons of Putin's beliefs over time or comparisons of Putin's beliefs with the beliefs of US presidents. We gathered verbal material for each of the three leaders in our design (Putin, Bush, and Obama). For Putin, we included verbal material during his first two terms as president (2000–2008) and during his third term (2012–2015). For each of the US presidents, we used a sample that matched the period of investigation we used for Putin. For all three leaders we gathered all of their verbal material during the times identified, including both prepared and spontaneous remarks. We aggregated their verbal material temporally by quarter-year and then ran that material through Profiler Plus (Young 2001). This procedure gave us unique operational code scores for each leader for each quarter-year under analysis.

The verbal material for Putin came from the English language version of the official website of the president of Russia (http://eng.kremlin.ru/). The verbal material for the two US presidents came from the website: http://www.presidency.ucsb.edu/ (see Peters and Woolley n.d.). All verbal material was reviewed before processing, and any material not spoken by the president was removed from each file. In the ANOVA (analysis of variance) statistical models that we discuss below, the unit of analysis is the leader-quarter-year. The dependent variables in all models are the three different operational code indices identified by bold font in the Appendix: the first Philosophical Belief (P-1), which is the leader's beliefs about the nature of the political environment and other actors in that environment (conflictual to cooperative); the first Instrumental Belief (I-1), which is the leader's beliefs about the best direction (conflictual to cooperative) for his own strategies; and the fourth Philosophical Belief (P-4), which is the leader's beliefs about his own level of control (low to high) over political events.

The initial independent variable in our models is a grouping variable (or factor), which means that different values on the dependent variable are grouped together, and a mean score is calculated from them for comparison to another group. The grouping variables vary by model, depending upon the question we are investigating in that model. Some models compare Putin to himself at a later point in time, in which case the grouping variable designates two different sets of years of Putin's scores. Other models compare Putin to his US counterpart during a specified period, in which case the grouping variable designates a separate set of scores for each president during the time period specified. In turn, these statistical models are the basis for constructing formal game models of the interactions between Putin and the US presidents in different time periods during his tenure as the principal Russian leader.

## Results

Our initial analysis in 2000 of Putin's belief system was based on a series of interviews with the new leader conducted by journalists when he first came to office as the new president of Russia (Putin et al. 2000). We analyzed 15 interview segments taken from this source with the automated VICS software and have since found that his key operational code beliefs in comparison to public statements (n = 168) by a norming group of world leaders were very close to the norming group for P-1 nature of the political universe (+0.26 vs. +0.27, SD = 0.28), equal to the norming group average for I-1 approach to strategy (+0.33 vs. +0.35, SD = 0.34), and clearly above the norming group average for P-4 control over historical development (0.35 vs. 0.21, SD = 0.11). Together these scores indicate a leader whose language is no more likely than the language from our norming group of world leaders from different geographical areas and historical eras to favor escalatory strategies (I-1) but who is quite confident in his ability to control events (P-4), indicating a high need for achievement (Walker 1983; Walker and Falkowski 1985; Schafer and Walker 2006, 170, fn. 13).

It is important to keep in mind that these scores came from a former officer of the KGB and a new leader who had just taken office after a rather quick rise through the ranks to become the chief of state (Hill and Gaddy 2015). Confidence and assertiveness may not have been much of a surprise. But what happens after he begins to govern initially? Our first analysis compares these early Putin operational code scores to his scores a few years later, but still early during his first term of office. Because the unit of analysis is different in our earlier research compared to our present, we were not able to conduct ANOVA models for these comparisons. Instead we report his mean scores in each period, along with the Z-score change in his indexes, using the standard deviation from our sample of world leaders. The results are in Table 3.1.

As seen in the table, Putin's operational code made notable changes in a short period of time. His P-1 score increases somewhat (Z = +0.52) and his I-1 score increases significantly (Z = +1.10). These two indices suggest that Putin became more cooperative – not less – during his early stages of governing. And his P-4 score declined (Z = −0.88), indicating that he sensed he had somewhat less control over events in the political world. The assertive and confident former KGB officer appears to have found himself not only in a world where he learned that he was less in control, where others called the shots more than he earlier anticipated, but also a world that was somewhat friendlier (P-1) than anticipated. His beliefs in a strategy in that kind of world became more cooperative. In sum, Putin exhibited significant learning in his instrumental beliefs (I-1) and

*Table 3.1* Putin's Operational Code Indices Early in His First Term[a]

| Index | Putin et al. 2000 | Putin 01–03 | Z-Score Change |
|-------|-------------------|-------------|----------------|
| P-1 | 0.26 | 0.41 | +0.52 |
| I-1 | 0.33 | 0.70 | +1.10 |
| P-4 | 0.35 | 0.25 | −0.88 |

[a] Z-scores are calculated using the standard deviation for each index from a sample of world leaders (n = 168). Z-score change indicates the number of standard deviations, up (+) or down (−), that Putin's index changed across the two-time periods.

his beliefs about control over historical development (P-4) as well as some adaptation in his diagnostic (P-1) beliefs.

It is possible to imagine a version of cognitive dissonance experienced by Putin; the changes we found were quick and notable and certainly may have resulted in some frustration for Russia's chief who was earlier so confident and assertive. Indeed, some previous research has found that decreasing P-4 scores, indicating less control, is tied to rising levels of frustration and even aggression (Schafer, Robison, and Aldrich 2006). Nonetheless, there is not a corresponding turn to conflict in his operational code indicators in his first presidential term, either in the way he viewed others in the political universe (P-1) or in his preferred strategies in the political universe (I-1); indeed, these scores actually became more positive, i.e., more cooperative – perhaps reflecting a high need for achievement but with a cooperative rather than a conflictual strategy.

The Georgian conflict, however, came later in his second term. Is it possible that his operational code changed in the run-up to that conflict, perhaps as his frustration increased? That possibility is the subject of our next analysis, which we present in Table 3.2. Here we report three ANOVA models that focus on change in Putin's operational code in the run-up to the Georgian conflict in 2008. We selected the six quarters prior to the war and compared them to a similar sample of Putin's from earlier in his term of office. The results show that Putin's view of the political universe (P-1) remains high, i.e., he tends to see others as more cooperative than conflictual.

Putin also continues to have a lower score on P-4, meaning that he sees others as much in control as himself, a sign perhaps of ongoing frustration since this is somewhat lower than his pre-presidency score. There are no statistically significant changes in these two indexes (P-1 and P-4) from early Putin to pre-Georgia Putin. The dramatic change in his operational code is in the I-1 index, his beliefs about his own best approach to strategies in the political world. His mean I-1 score drops to .55, a change that is highly statistically significant ($F (10, 1) = 7.834$, $p < 0.02$). The shift indicates a from a strategy of unconditional cooperation to conditional cooperation, as Putin leaves office in May, 2008, immediately preceding the escalation of the Georgian conflict to war in August, 2008.

We infer that Putin's operational code in the run-up to the Georgian conflict manifested a mild version of the frustration-aggression

*Table 3.2* Early Putin Compared to the Pre-Georgian-War Putin

| Index | Putin Early[a] | Putin Pre-Georgia | F(10,1)= | p= |
|---|---|---|---|---|
| P-1 | 0.39 | 0.52 | 1.58 | 0.24 |
| I-1 | 0.77 | 0.55 | 7.83 | 0.02 |
| P-4 | 0.24 | 0.27 | 0.63 | 0.45 |

[a]n = 6 quarters to match the number of pre-Georgia quarters.

*Table 3.3* Early First-Term Putin Compared to Third-Term Putin

| Index | First Term[a] | Third Term | $F(22,1)=$ | $p=$ |
|-------|-----------|------------|-----------|------|
| P-1   | 0.40      | 0.52       | 3.51      | 0.07 |
| I-1   | 0.70      | 0.69       | 0.01      | 0.93 |
| P-4   | 0.25      | 0.22       | 2.07      | 0.16 |

[a]n = 12 quarters in this table to match the number of quarters in Putin's third term.

syndrome: a perceived low level of control and a strategic orientation that shifted notably in the direction of conflict (Schafer, Robison, and Aldrich 2006; Walker 2011). While Putin continued to see a world with cooperative others in it, he may have been frustrated that he was less in control of events than he would like in Georgia, and so his (I-1) beliefs about strategy turned in the direction of conflict.

What about the Ukrainian conflict in 2014? Do we see similar patterns for Putin? In this analysis we first compare Putin's operational code in his third term to the early period of his first term. The results in Table 3.3 show that after Putin returns to office in 2012, he once again had a cooperative view of others in the political universe (P-1). Indeed, compared to early in his first term, his score on P-1 is actually higher, indicating an even more cooperative view of others than he held in the early period, and the difference between those two scores is significant, $F(22,1) = 3.514$, $p = 0.074$. This time, however, his I-1 score is indistinguishable from the earlier period.

However, we see that his P-4 score is slightly lower than it was in the early part of his first term, indicating that he perceives himself as having less control over events, though this difference only approaches statistical significance ($F(22,1) = 2.07$, $p = 0.16$). It appears that after Putin had been out of the presidency for 4 years, he came back to it with a renewed optimism about cooperative politics, but he still had a lowered belief in his ability to control events. This latter point, his lower control orientation, seems to be a common thread for Putin, and it would seem to point to a sense of frustration on his part given his early and continued propensity toward high cooperation.

In sum, our analysis in Figure 3.2 of Mr. Putin's operational code and general role in world politics between his accession to the Russian presidency in 2000 and the Georgian conflict in 2008 indicate that he experienced some experiential learning, in which his I-1 and P-4 indices changed significantly from a new leader in 2000 whose strong belief in historical control (P-4) was not accompanied by a clear sense of strategic direction regarding the roles of Partner vs. Rival regarding the exercise of power (I-1) as a great power. By 2003, he had experienced a clear decrease in his belief in historical control (P-4) and a sharp increase in his belief in a strategy of unconditional cooperation (I-1) and the role of Friend during his first presidential term.

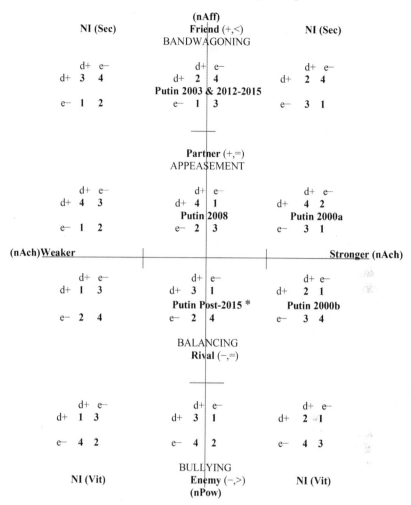

*Figure 3.2* Putin's Learning Patterns and General Roles for Three Presidential Terms**

*Predicted Russian role from frustration-aggression syndrome and motivational analysis by Semenova and Winter (2020; see also Winter 2010).

**Escalate: (e–); De-escalate: (d+). NI: National Interest; Sec: Secondary; Vit: Vital. I-1/P-1: (+ or –); P-4: (< = >). Ego's Ranked Outcomes: (4) high.... (1) low. Need for Affiliation: nAff; need for Achievement: nAch; need for Power: nPow.

The latter belief decreased from a strategy of unconditional cooperation as a Friend to a strategy of conditional cooperation as a Partner in the run-up to war with Georgia in 2008 near the end of his second presidential term. He did not show much evidence of diagnostic learning regarding the nature of the political universe (P-1), which remained relatively friendly throughout his first two terms as the president of Russia.

He defined Russia's general foreign policy role as a Friend in his first term and as a Partner in his second as Russian president.

During his third term as the Russian president between 2012 and 2015, his pattern of experiential learning in Figure 3.2 followed a telescoped version of the temporal pattern exhibited during his first two terms between 2000 and 2008. Putin's belief in cooperation as a strategy (I-1) early in his third term (2012) resembled his strong belief early in his first term as president (2000–2003). The Russian president's belief in the friendly nature of the political universe (P-1) significantly increased while his belief in the ability to control historical development (P-4) continued to be relatively modest compared to his initial appearance on the world stage. He defined the general Russian foreign policy role as a Friend in world politics prior to the Russian seizure of the Crimea region in 2014.

When Ukrainian president Yanukovych was removed from power early in 2014 and impeached by the Ukrainian parliament after refusing to sign an association agreement with the European Union, Russian soldiers occupied Crimea and annexed the region. US economic sanctions and Russia suspension from the G8 followed, which foreshadowed a long-term deterioration of relations between Russia and the United States that has continued into the present (Hill and Gaddy 2015, 406). Thus, Putin's actions in the Ukraine almost certainly signaled a post-2015 change in Putin's role as a Friend with a belief in unconditional cooperation as a strategy. Our hypothesis specified in Figure 3.2 is that if it manifested as well the frustration-aggression syndrome, Putin's post-2015 strategic beliefs (I-1) probably shifted even beyond the conditional cooperation as a Partner manifested in the run-up to the Georgia War to conditional conflict and the role of Rival following the Crimean conflict.

## Putin and the Presidents

Another important factor during Putin's terms in office is that two different US presidents were leading a hegemonic state under a terrorist threat in a unipolar world; they pursued policies, perhaps unintentionally, that contributed to Russia's isolation and possible frustration (Sakwa 2004; Covington 2015; Hill and Gaddy 2015; Mandelbaum 2016). For example, both US presidents took strong positions that were opposite to Putin's in the Georgian and Ukrainian conflicts. Were the general operational codes of the two US presidents significantly different from Putin's general operational code? In order to answer this question, we shall compare and contrast the operational codes of Putin with George W. Bush and Barack Obama.

We begin with Putin vs. Bush; the results of the ANOVA tests can be found in Table 3.4. Here we compare Putin's early operational code (2001–2003) to Bush's operational code in the same time period. Both Putin and Bush have similar, cooperative views of others in the political universe, as seen in their P-1 scores (0.40 and 0.42, respectively), and

*Table 3.4* Early Putin Compared to Bush

| Index | Putin 01–03 | Bush 01–03 | F(22,1)= | p= |
|---|---|---|---|---|
| P-1 | 0.40 | 0.42 | 0.15 | 0.7 |
| I-1 | 0.70 | 0.59 | 3.14 | 0.09 |
| P-4 | 0.25 | 0.30 | 8.26 | 0.01 |

indeed those scores are statistically indistinguishable (F (22,1) = 0.15, p = 0.703). The two do differ, however, on the other two indices. Bush's I-1 score is lower than Putin's, indicating that Bush's strategic approach to politics is less cooperative than Putin's, and the difference between the two is statistically significant, F(22,1) = 3.14, p = 0.09. In addition, Putin's control orientation is statistically lower than Bush's, F (22,1) = 8.26, p = 0.01. Taken together, both leaders see cooperative opportunities in the world out there, but Bush's own strategic orientation is much less cooperative than Putin's, and Putin's belief in control over historical events in the political universe is significantly lower than the US president.

We turn now to the comparison of Putin to Obama. Here we compare Putin's operational code early during his third term in office (2012–2015) to Obama's during the same time period. The results of these ANOVA tests can be seen in Table 3.5. In this case, there are differences between Putin and his US counterpart for all three indices, perhaps in surprising ways. On both P-1 and I-1, Obama has the more conflictual orientation. Obama sees the world in less friendly terms than Putin does (P-1), and the differences between the two are statistically significant, F (24,1) = 5.47, p = 0.03. Likewise, in terms of their own strategic orientations (I-1), Obama is much more conflictual than Putin, and those results are highly statistically significant, F (24,1) = 23.41, p < 0.001. Obama sees a more conflictual world than Putin does and is strategically inclined to act more conflictual in that world.

As in the comparison with Bush, Putin also perceives himself as having less control than Obama, and that difference is statistically significant F(24,1) = 4.32, p = 0.05. Although US actors, the media, and the public may be loath to recognize it, the data clearly show that Putin's operational code was more cooperative than his US counterparts between 2000 and 2015. Combining this result with Putin's evolving belief that he has less control over events than others, it is not difficult

*Table 3.5* Third-Term Putin Compared to Obama

| Index | Putin 12–15 | Obama 12–15 | F(24,1)= | p= |
|---|---|---|---|---|
| P-1 | 0.52 | 0.39 | 5.47 | 0.03 |
| I-1 | 0.69 | 0.45 | 23.41 | 0.001 |
| P-4 | 0.22 | 0.25 | 4.32 | 0.05 |

to imagine a rising frustration level in Russia's leader, a theme that we revisit in the conclusion.

## Strategic Interaction Hypotheses

Can we infer some hypotheses from these comparisons regarding the likely patterns of strategic interaction between Russia and the United States? Each leader's I-1, P-1, and P-4 beliefs define cognitively their respective power positions and corresponding roles in the political universe. Based on these three beliefs and the rules for the OCA, TIP, and TOM role models in Figure 3.1, we can represent each leader's general cognitive model of the "self-in-situation" as a strategic interaction game, in which self and other enact roles defined by their OCA master beliefs (P-1, I-1, P-4) to generate the pattern of international relations between their respective states. The subjective game models of strategic interaction for Putin and the two US presidents are produced for analysis in the top half of Figure 3.3 for Putin and Bush. These roles in Figure 3.2 are differentiated with TIP by different preference rankings for the strategic outcomes of domination, deadlock, settlement, and submission between self and other (Walker, Malici, and Schafer 2011) and enacted according to the rules of TOM.

Based on the significantly higher I-1 score (0.01 short of one standard deviation above the norming group) and lower P-4 score for Putin compared to Bush, the Russian leader's definition of self is likely to be a Friend role (+, =) while Bush's lower I-1 score and higher P-4 score indicate leaning toward a strong Partner role (+, >) for the United States. Both leaders assign a relatively friendly role to other, based on the lack of a significant difference in their respective P-1 scores: Putin assigns a role of Partner (+, =) to the United States based on other's similar P-4 score in his operational code while Bush assigns a role of weaker Partner (+, <) role to Russia based on other's lower P-4 score in his operational code. The subjective interaction games for Putin and Obama are in the bottom half of Figure 3.3. The significant differences in their respective I-1 scores lead them to rank differently their preferences for strategic outcomes in their respective roles. Putin assigns a role of Friend (+, =) to Russia and a role of Partner (+, =) to the United States; Obama assigns the role of Partner (+, =) to Russia and to the United States.

Mr. Putin's subjective game with three nonmyopic equilibria and one myopic equilibrium remained the same in Figure 3.3 during the presidential terms of both US presidents. His highest ranked outcome was consistent with a strategy of alignment with the West as a Friend. However, this equilibrium was not the solution as a "final state" unless it was also the "initial state" in his subjective game, which would be a source of frustration and an incentive to choose aggression in the form of moving to deadlock (3,3) from mutual cooperation (2,4) as the other two nonmyopic

**General Role Enactment Games***

|  | Alter d+ | Alter e− |
|---|---|---|
| d+ | 2,4* | 4,2 |
| **Putin** | | |
| e− | 1,1 | 3,3 |

(Game 56)
**Putin's Subjective Game**
Putin: Friend (+,=)
(0,2/2, 1/1, & 3/0)
Alter: Partner (+,=)
(0,2/0, 1/1 & 3/2)

|  | Alter d+ | Alter e− |
|---|---|---|
| d+ | 4,4* | 1,1 |
| **Bush** | | |
| e− | 3,3 | 2,2 |

(No-Conflict Game)
**Bush's Subjective Game**
Bush: Stronger Partner (+,>)
(0,1,2,3/0)
Alter: Weaker Partner (+,<)
(0,1,2,3/0)

|  | USA d+ | USA e− |
|---|---|---|
| d+ | 2,4* | 4,3 |
| **Rus** | | |
| e− | 1,1 | 3,2 |

(Game 50)
**Objective Game**
Rus: Friend (+,=)
(0/2, 1,2/1 & 3/0)
USA: Stronger Partner (+,>)
(0,2/0, 1/1 & 3/2)

**Column Player**

|  | d+ | e− |
|---|---|---|
| d+ | Row and Column Settle | Row Submits/ Column Dominates |
| **Row Player** | | |
| e− | Row Dominates/ Column Submits | Row and Column Deadlock |

0 | 1
3 | 2

**Outcome Quadrants for Games**

|  | Alter d+ | Alter e− |
|---|---|---|
| d+ | 2,4 | 4,2 |
| **Putin** | | |
| e− | 1,1 | 3,3 |

(Game 56)
**Putin's Subjective Game**
Putin: Friend (+,=)
(0,2,/2, 1/1, & 3/0)
Alter: Partner (+,=)
(0,2/0, 1/1 & 3/2)

|  | Alter d+ | Alter e− |
|---|---|---|
| d+ | 4,4* | 1,2 |
| **Obama** | | |
| e− | 2,1 | 3,3 |

(No-Conflict Game)
**Obama's Subjective Game**
Obama: Partner (+,=)
(0,1,2,3/0)
Alter: Partner (+,=)
(0,1,2,3/0)

|  | USA d+ | USA e− |
|---|---|---|
| d+ | 2,4* | 4,2 |
| **Rus** | | |
| e− | 1,1 | 3,3 |

(Game 56)
**Objective Game**
Rus: Friend (+, =)
(0,2/2, 1/1 & 3/0)
USA: Partner (+,=)
(0,2/0, 1/1 & 3/2)

*Figure 3.3* Early Role Enactment Games between Putin and US presidents

*Nonmyopic solutions for each game are in bold. Outcomes are ranked for each player from highest (4) ... to lowest (1) for Row, Column in each cell; d+: de-escalate; e−: escalate. The possible initial state and outcome quadrants for each game are numbered clockwise from 0 (upper left) to 3 (lower left) cells. The paths across cells from initial states to final outcomes for each player are in parentheses. Dominant strategies are underlined. Game ID numbers are from Brams (1994, 215–219).

equilibrium solutions to his game. This pattern continues for the "objective games" in Figure 3.3, which are formed by the intersection of Putin's strategy with the strategies of Bush and Obama. It is rare for the highest ranked Russian outcome of alignment as a Friend to be a nonmyopic equilibrium solution to these objective games unless it is also the "initial state" in each game.

In other words, the (4,3) outcome can be bestowed magnanimously as a status for Russia by the United States, but it cannot be easily achieved by Russia. In each case, an aggressive move by Putin to (3,3) deadlock from an initial state of mutual cooperation (2,4) is an incentive that improves the ranked final outcome for Russia from (2) to (3), and it is a potential path to alignment (4) as a final outcome in successive repetitions of the objective Putin-Bush game but not in the Putin-Obama game. This frustration-aggression analysis is also consistent with the diagnosis of social identity theory (SIT) regarding Russian and Chinese foreign policy toward the United States by Larson and Shevchenko (2010); see also Larson, Paul, and Wohlforth (2014). They suggest further that in order to reduce tensions, instead of emulating others or directly competing with higher status others in a particular domain or issue area, status seekers should identify (and others should help them) to find another area of social and political life in which they can achieve higher status.

## Conclusion

In this chapter, we have investigated the evolution of Russian leader Vladimir Putin's operational code during his three terms in office as the president of the Russian Federation. We found a high level of continuity in his key operational code beliefs marked by a somewhat surprising level of friendliness and cooperation regarding Russian relations with others in the political universe. His view of the political universe (P-1) was as friendly as President Bush's and friendlier than Obama's. His approach to goals (I-1) exhibits a higher propensity for cooperation than either of his US counterparts. Finally, his belief about self's relative control over historical events was also significantly lower than the corresponding beliefs exhibited by the two US leaders.

We inferred from an analysis of this information that strategic interaction patterns based on the relative differences in the operational codes of Putin and the two US presidents were likely to generate some conflict between Russia and the United States even though all three leaders have general belief systems that dispose them toward cooperation in a friendly political universe. We have hypothesized that the differences in their respective beliefs about cooperation and historical control disposed them toward the assignment of different general roles to self and other in Russian-American relations. In turn, these roles may have led them to overlook opportunities for mutual cooperation in Russian-US relations and actually reflected the emergence in Putin of a frustration-aggression syndrome leading to a transition in Russia's general role from Friend to Partner to Rival in world politics over the 20 years spanning his first three terms as the president of Russia.

Perhaps the most telling part of Putin's operational code is his low control orientation (P-4), and perhaps this should not be much of a surprise after all (Dyson 2001; Dyson and Parent 2017). Putin's experience prior to becoming the president of Russia in 2000 no doubt included high levels of control: he was an officer with the KGB and climbed the political ladder very quickly (he became president after being in politics for only 9 years). Indeed, our analysis of Putin very early in his term as president demonstrates his initial belief that he had lots of control over politics. Playing the game of international rather than domestic politics is an entirely different matter, however, and even a couple of years later in 2003, our data show that his control orientation (P-4) dropped significantly. Putin learned that he could no longer so easily control political events, and that others played a bigger role in "doing the doing."

Moreover, changes in a leader's (P-4) control orientation have been associated with changes in conflict patterns in previous research. Schafer, Robison, and Aldrich (2006) have demonstrated that Patrick Pearse's control orientation dropped notably immediately prior to his agreement to join the coalition that conducted the Easter Rising in Ireland in 1916. Prior to that point, Pearse and his organization had been content to negotiate with the British and work on a cooperative outcome. These researchers argue that Pearse's lower control orientation was part of his rising level of frustration and thus connected to his decision to pursue aggression: as he felt less and less in control of political events, he turned toward armed conflict.

Other research has shown the other side of the same coin regarding a leader's control orientation. Schafer and Gassler (2000) have demonstrated that Anwar Sadat's control orientation increased in a very big way following the October 1973 war with Israel. Prior to the war, Sadat's P-4 score was extremely low compared to a sample of world leaders, but after the war, his score was way above average. Although one cannot argue Egypt won that war, of course, it most certainly is the case that it was Egypt's best showing, by far, against Israel. It certainly changed the landscape of the relations between the two antagonists. Sadat claimed victory and was hailed as a hero. His rising control orientation demonstrates that, finally, Sadat felt like he had more control and that he was "doing more of the doing." These researchers argue that it was this change in his control orientation that allowed him from a position of strength to travel to Israel and address the Knesset, thus opening up the door to the famous peace pact between the two former adversaries.

As the stronger member in the Russian-US dyad, it may have been easier for the United States to alter the assignment of roles to Russia and the United States so that opportunities for strategic cooperation between them were enhanced. In the absence of realistic empathy from the United States (Malici and Buckner 2008), however, Putin's operational code beliefs became more prone to change toward a more hostile role for Russia in local conflicts such as in Georgia or over Crimea in the Ukraine where the power asymmetry between Russia and the United States is equalized or reversed in favor of Russia. A frustration-aggression syndrome appears to have germinated in Putin's belief system regarding the Georgian conflict in his first term and actually blossomed regarding the Ukraine conflict during his third term in office (Sakwa 2004; Hill and Gaddy 2015).

The reality for Putin, of course, is that Russia was not as powerful in 2015; he likely did not believe in as much control over political events then as during his career as a KGB agent in the heyday of the Soviet Empire. No matter how much Putin escalates or rearms as a president, another reality is that Russia is not likely to regain its old strength and influence as a superpower any time soon. But those realities may mask the psychological imperatives that Putin feels. For a person who, prior to becoming president, was affiliated to an organization (the KGB) with so much control based upon so much power and influence, the sense of lower control now must be frustrating (Winter 2013; Hill and Gaddy 2015; Semenova and Winter 2020). Many of his actions since 2015 seem geared to increasing power, influence, and control: invading Georgia, taking the Crimea, escalating against Ukraine, and building more ICBMs.

The world was moving around Putin, seemingly against him, and he could not stop it between 2000 and 2015. He had wanted NATO *not* to build an ABM in Eastern Europe, yet the project continued; Putin had wanted NATO *not* to expand eastward, yet that happened; Putin had wanted to increase the size and power of Russia's economic circle, yet many countries in Eastern Europe turned more and more to the EU and the West and away from Russia. As he was unable to control these and other events, his frustration and subsequent conflict policies were likely to escalate, culminating in the seizure of Crimea in response to the ouster of Putin's ally as the leader of Ukraine (Hill and Gaddy 2015).

The solutions for the West to growing estrangement with Russia were not obvious at the time. NATO wanted an ABM for reasons beyond Russia; states wanted to join NATO in an alliance expansion not targeted anymore toward Russia in the absence of an overt Russian threat. States turning to the EU and away from Russia also seemed reasonable, because the opportunities for economic growth were much higher. Perhaps at the time, other elements of Putin's operational code held out some hope against an estrangement between Russia and the West. His default sense of others (P-1) and his preferred strategic orientation (I-1) were both positive and cooperative; there were opportunities to work with Putin, based upon our reading of his cooperative propensities as late as 2015. Perhaps the United States and the West might have made improvements in relations with Russia simply by knowing about Putin's lower (P-4) control orientation and adopting some policies intended to ease that frustration.

Maybe there were confidence-building measures or cooperative ventures that could have reassured Putin, brought him to the table, given him a role, and increased his sense of control.

Putin appeared in 2015 to have had an orientation toward cooperation that held out some hope for a brighter future. However, Putin in 2020 does not appear to be the same leader. Instead, he may have succumbed completely to the frustration-aggression syndrome's dynamics. Winter's (2010) analysis of leaders with a high need for achievement and an average need for power (personal control) also leads to the same conclusion as ours with an additional warning: if a leader with a high need for achievement motivation and a low need for power motivation does not satisfy this need for achievement, then the leader out of frustration may turn to extraordinary and even illicit means to satisfy it. His subsequent analysis of Putin's motivational profile reveals that the Russian leader had a dramatic shift in his motivational profile from his first two terms (2000–2008) to his third term beginning in 2012 (Semenova and Winter 2020).

Specifically, the relationship between Putin's need for achievement and his need for power shifted from nAch imagery being higher than nPow imagery in his public statements to the reverse: his expressed motives changed from frustrated achievement to power and control (Semenova and Winter 2020). This shift was accompanied by a significant increase in his need for affiliation imagery directed toward a domestic audience and away from an international audience. These changes are consistent with an escalation of Russian involvement in regional conflicts with the EU and the United States over the Ukraine and Russian intervention in the Syrian civil war on Russia's southern border (Semenova and Winter 2020; see also Covington 2015; Hill and Gaddy 2015).

The explanation for these shifts in motivational and behavioral patterns offered both by Winter (2010; see also Semenova and Winter 2020) and by Dyson and Parent (2017) is ironically Putin's increasing preoccupation with the question of "kto-kovo?," i.e. "who (controls) whom?" at the core of the old Bolshevik operational code (Leites 1951, 78–81; Leites 1953, 27–29). Dyson and Parent's (2017) analysis of Putin's operational code identifies a bifurcation in Putin's (P-1) beliefs about the nature of the political universe, in which he distinguishes between others who conform to his conception of an appropriate political order and rogues who do not follow the rules and pose threats either to his personal or political survival. If the former threaten his belief in the ability to exert historical control (P-4), his strategic (P-1) beliefs shift from cooperation to conflict in defining their roles in the political universe dealing with them. This cognitive analysis by Dyson and Parent of Putin's beliefs is consistent with Winter's extra-cognitive analysis of Putin's shift in motivations from exhibiting a higher need for achievement to manifesting a higher need for power.

Future research on Putin's general operational code should investigate whether the general subjective game in his public statements shifted Russia's general foreign policy role from Friend and Partner to Rival or even Enemy following the Ukraine crisis and Russian invasion of Crimea in 2014. The complex learning that Putin likely experienced in the form of substantial changes in his key operational code beliefs since 2015 is juxtaposed in Figure 3.4 with the subjective games of US presidents

**General Role Enactment Games***

| | Alter | | | Alter | | | USA | |
|---|---|---|---|---|---|---|---|---|
| | d+ | e− | | d+ | e− | | d+ | e− |
| d+ | **3,4*** | 1,3 | d+ | **4,4*** | 1,2 | d+ | **3,4*** | 1,2 |
| **Putin** | | | **Obama** | | | **Rus** | | |
| e− | 2,1 | **4,2*** | e− | 2,1 | 3,3 | e− | 2,1 | **4,3*** |
| | (Game 52) | | | (No-Conflict Game) | | | (Game 51) | |

**Putin's Subjective Game** / **Obama's Subjective Game** / **Objective Game**

Putin: Rival (−,=) / Obama: Partner (+, =) / Rus: Rival (−, =)
(0,2/2 & 1,3/0) / (0,1,2,3/0) / (1,3/0 & 0,2/2)
Alter: Stronger Partner (+, >) / Alter: Partner (+, =) / USA: Partner (+,=)
(0,2/0 &1/1 & 3/2) / (0,1,2,3/0) / (0,2/0 & 1,3/2)

| | Alter | | | Alter | | | USA | |
|---|---|---|---|---|---|---|---|---|
| | d+ | e− | | d+ | e− | | d+ | e− |
| d+ | **3,4*** | 1,2 | d+ | **3,4*** | 1,2 | d+ | 3,3* | 1,2 |
| **Putin** | | | **Trump** | | | **Rus** | | |
| e− | 2,1 | **4,3*** | e− | 2,1 | **4,3*** | e− | 2,1 | **4,4*** |
| | (Game 51) | | | (Game 55) | | | (No-Conflict Game) | |

**Putin's Subjective Game** / **Trump's Subjective Game** / **Objective Game**

Putin: Rival (−,=) / Trump: Rival (−,=) / Rus: Rival (−,=)
(1,3/0 & 0,2/2) / (1,3/0 & 0,2/2) / (0,1,2,3/2)
Alter: Partner: (+,=) / Alter: Partner (+,=) / USA: Rival (−,=)
(0,2/0 & 1,3/2) / (0,2/0 & 1,3/2) / (0,1,2,3/2)

| | Alter | | | Alter | | | USA | |
|---|---|---|---|---|---|---|---|---|
| | d+ | e− | | d+ | e− | | d+ | e− |
| d+ | 3,3* | 1,2 | d+ | **4,3*** | 1,2 | d+ | **3,4*** | 1,3 |
| **Putin** | | | **Biden** | | | **Rus** | | |
| e− | 2,1 | **4,4*** | e− | 3,1 | **2,4*** | e− | 2,1 | **4,2*** |
| | (No-Conflict Game) | | | (Game 52) | | | (Game 52) | |

**Putin's Subjective Game** / **Biden's Subjective Game** / **Objective Game**

Putin: Rival (−,=) / Biden: Stronger Partner (+,>) / Rus: Rival (−,=)
(0,1,2,3/2) / (0,2,3/0 &1/2) / (1,3/0 & 0,2/2)
Alter: Rival (−,=) / Alter: Rival (−,=) / Alter: Stronger Partner (+,>)
(0,1,2,3/2) / (1,3/0 & 0,2/2) / (0,2/0 & 1/1 & 3/2)

*Figure 3.4* Post-2015 Role Enactment Games Projected for Putin and US presidents

*Nonmyopic solutions for each game are in bold. Outcomes are ranked for each player from highest (4) … to lowest (1) for Row, Column in each cell; d+: de-escalate; e−: escalate. The possible initial state and outcome quadrants for each game are numbered clockwise from 0 (upper left) to 3 (lower left) cells. The paths across cells from initial states to final outcomes for each player are in parentheses. Dominant strategies are underlined.

Barack Obama in Figure 3.3 and then Donald Trump (Walker, Schafer, and Smith 2018). This figure also projects a possible general foreign policy role of Strong Partner for the United States should Joe Biden replace Donald Trump as the US president.

Neither Putin nor the US leaders have a dominant (unconditional) strategy of cooperation or conflict in these models. The objective games constructed from these possibilities suggest that when Obama or Biden is projected as the US president, Russian-American relations should oscillate erratically between mutual cooperation and mutual conflict. When Trump is projected as the US leader, however, a more stable pattern of mutual conflict as mutual rivals is predicted along with the opportunity for occasional conditional cooperation. In order to test the predictions of these general operational code models, it will be necessary to collect systematic behavioral observations regarding the social operational codes of the foreign policy roles enacted directly between Russia and the United States (Malici and Walker 2017).

## Appendix: VICS Operational Code Indices

| Elements | Index[a] | Interpretation |
|---|---|---|
| **Philosophical Beliefs** | | |
| **P-1. NATURE OF THE POLITICAL UNIVERSE (Image of Others)**[c] | **%Positive minus %Negative Other Attributions** | **+1.0 friendly to −1.0 hostile** |
| P-2. REALIZATION OF POLITICAL VALUES (Optimism/Pessimism) | Mean Intensity of Transitive Other Attributions divided by 3 | +1.0 optimistic to −1.0 pessimistic |
| P-3. POLITICAL FUTURE (Predictability of Other Tactics) | 1 minus Index of Qualitative Variation[b] for Other Attributions | 1.0 predictable to 0.0 uncertain |
| **P-4. HISTORICAL DEVELOPMENT (Locus of Control)**[c] **a. Self Control b. Other Control** | **Self or Other Attributions divided by Total Attributions** **Self Attributions/Total Attributions** **Other Attributions/Total Attributions** | **1.0 high to 0.0 low control** |
| P-5. ROLE OF CHANCE (Absence of Control) | 1 minus [Political Future × Historical Development Index] | 1.0 high role to 0.0 low role |
| **Instrumental Beliefs** | | |
| **I-1. APPROACH TO GOALS (Direction of Strategy)**[c] | **%Positive minus %Negative Self Attributions** | **+1.0 high cooperation to −1.0 high conflict** |
| I-2. PURSUIT OF GOALS (Intensity of Tactics) | Mean Intensity of Transitive Self Attributions divided by 3 | +1.0 high cooperation to −1.0 high conflict |

(*continued*)

| Elements | Index[a] | Interpretation |
|---|---|---|
| I-3. RISK ORIENTATION (Predictability of Tactics) | 1 minus Index of Qualitative Variation for Self Attributions | 1.0 risk acceptant to 0.0 risk averse |
| I-4. TIMING OF ACTION (Flexibility of Tactics) | 1 minus Absolute Value [%X minus %Y Self Attributions] | 1.0 high to 0.0 low shift propensity |
| a. Coop vs. Conf Tactics b. Word vs. Deed Tactics | Where X = Coop and Y = Conf Where X = Word and Y = Deed | |
| I-5. UTILITY OF MEANS (Exercise) | Percentages for Exercise of Power Categories a through f | +1.0 very frequent of Power to 0.0 infrequent |
| a. Reward | a's frequency divided by total | |
| b. Promise | b's frequency divided by total | |
| c. Appeal/Support | c's frequency divided by total | |
| d. Oppose/Resist | d's frequency divided by total | |
| e. Threaten | e's frequency divided by total | |
| f. Punish | f's frequency divided by total | |

[a]All indices vary between 0 and 1.0 except for P-1, P-2, I-1, and I-2, which vary between –1.0 and +1.0. P-2 and I-2 are divided by 3 to standardize the range (Walker, Schafer, and Young 1998).
[b]"The Index of Qualitative Variation is a ratio of the number of different pairs of observations in a distribution to the maximum possible number of different pairs for a distribution with the same N [number of cases] and the same number of variable classifications" (Watson and McGaw 1980: 88).
[c] Master beliefs are in bold

## References

Brams, S. 1994. *Theory of moves*. Cambridge: Cambridge University.

Covington, S. 2015. *Putin's choice for Russia*. Digital Edition. Cambridge, MA: Belfer Center for Science and International Affairs at the Harvard Kennedy School.

Dyson, S. 2001. Drawing policy implications from the operational code of a new political actor: Russian president Vladimir Putin.". *Policy Sciences* 34: 329–346.

Dyson, S., M. Parent. 2017. The operational code approach to profiling political leaders: Understanding Vladimir Putin. *Intelligence and National Security*, DOI: 10.1080/02684527. 2017.1313523.

Hill, F., C. Gaddy. 2015. *Mr. Putin: Operative in the kremlin*. New and Expanded Paperback Edition. Washington, DC: Brookings.

Larson, D., A. Shevchenko. 2010. Status seekers: Chinese and Russian responses to U.S. Primacy. *International Security* 34: 63–95.

Larson, D., T. V. Paul, W. Wohlforth. 2014. *World status in politics*. Cambridge: Cambridge University.

Leites, N. 1951. *The operational code of the politburo.* New York, NY: McGraw-Hill.

Leites, N. 1953. *A study of bolshevism.* New York, NY: Free Press.

Levy, J. 1994. Learning and foreign policy. *International Organization* 48: 279–312.

Malici, A., A. Buckner. 2008. Empathizing with rogue leaders. *Journal of Peace Research* 45: 783–800.

Malici, A., S. Walker. 2017. *Role theory and role conflict in U.S.-Iran relations.* New York, NY: Routledge.

Mandelbaum, M. 2016. *Mission failure: America and the world in the post-cold war era.* New York, NY: Oxford University Press.

Peters, G., J. T. Woolley. n.d. *The American Presidency Project.* http://www.presidency.ucsb.edu/ws/?pid=2583.

Putin, V., N. Gevorkyan, N. Timakova, A. Kolesnikov. 2000. *First person: An astonishingly frank self portrait.* Translated by C. Fitzpatrick. New York, NY: Public Affairs Press.

Sakwa, R. 2004. *Putin: Russia's choice.* New York, NY: Routledge.

Schafer, M., A. Gassler. 2000. Sadat takes control: A quantitative analysis of Anwar Sadat's operational code before and after the October war of 1973. *Political Psychologist* 5(Spring): 10–16.

Schafer, M., S. Robison, B. Aldrich. 2006. Operational codes and the 1916 Easter rising in Ireland. *Foreign Policy Analysis* 2(1): 65–84.

Schafer, M., and S. Walker, eds.2006. *Beliefs and leadership in world politics.* New York, NY: Palgrave-Macmillan.

Schafer, M., S. Walker. 2014. The operational code of Vladimir Putin: Analyzing a New global leader with a New automated coding system. (Japanese translation). In *Language politics,* ed. Yoshi Araki, 293–330. Buren Shupan. This chapter is a revised version of a paper presented at the Annual Meeting of the International Studies Association, Chicago, IL, February 21-24, 2001.

Semenova, E., D. Winter 2020. A motivational analysis of Russian presidents, 1994-2018. *Political Psychology* 41: 813–834.

Walker, S. 1983. The motivational foundations of political belief systems: A re-analysis of the operational code construct. *International Studies Quarterly* 27: 179–202.

Walker, S. 2011. Anticipating attacks from the operational codes of terrorist groups. In *Dynamics of asymmetric conflict,* DOI: 10.1080/17467586.2011.6279376. Reprinted in *The relationship between rhetoric and violence,* ed. A. Smith. New York, NY: Routledge, 2013.

Walker, S. 2013. *The cognitive architecture of British appeasement decisions.* New York, NY: Routledge.

Walker, S., L. Falkowski 1985. The operational codes of U.S. Presidents and secretaries of state: Motivational foundations and behavioral consequences. *Political Psychology* 5: 237–266.

Walker, S., M. Schafer. 2010. Operational code theory: Beliefs and foreign policy decisions. In *The international studies encyclopedia,* ed. R. Denemark, 5492–5514. Vol. VIII. Chichester, West Sussex: Blackwell, Ltd.

Walker, S., A. Malici, and M. Schafer, eds. 2011. *Rethinking foreign policy analysis.* New York, NY: Routledge.

Walker, S., M. Schafer, G. Marfleet. 2012. The British strategy of appeasement: Why Britain persisted in the face of negative feedback. In *When things go wrong,* ed. C. Hermann, 111–141. New York, NY: Routledge.

Walker, S., M. Schafer, G. Smith. 2018. The operational codes of Hillary Clinton and Donald Trump. In *The Oxford handbook of behavioral political science*, eds. A. Mintz and L. Terris. New York, NY: Oxford University Press.

Walker, S., M. Schafer, M. M. Young 1998. Systematic procedures for operational code analysis. *International Studies Quarterly* 42: 175–190.

Watson, G., D. McGaw, 1980. *Statistical inquiry*. New York, NY: John Wiley & Sons.

Winter, D. 2003. Measuring the motives of political actors at a distance. In *The psychological assessment of political leaders*, ed. J. Post, 153–177. Ann Arbor, MI: University of Michigan Press.

Winter, D. 2010. Why achievement motivation predicts success in business but failure in politics: The importance of personal control. *Journal of Personality* 78(6): 2–31.

Young, M. 2001. Building worldviews with profiler+. In *Progress in communications sciences*, ed. G. Barnett, 17–32. Vol. 17. Westport, CT: Ablex Publishing.

# 4 Deciphering Deadly Minds in Their Native Language

## The Operational Codes and Formation Patterns of Militant Organizations in the Middle East and North Africa

*Sercan Canbolat*

## Introduction

There is no firm scholarly consensus over the definition of terrorism within the literature on terrorist violence. Some scholars have argued that terrorism has a random and/or indiscriminate nature, in order to cause fear in individual members of a target audience (Kalyvas 2004). Others have noted that terrorism might be of a highly discriminate nature or a mixture of both discriminate and random violence (Crenshaw 1981). Another issue with a comprehensive definition of terrorism is the identity of the terrorist actor and/or perpetrator. Terrorism is aptly identified as a tactic that can be utilized by both states and a variety of nonstate actors (Hoffman 2006). The focus here is on the latter, violent nonstate actors (VNSAs) who employ terrorism for political purposes, such as the intimidation of a public audience (Sandler and Enders 2007) by the strategic targeting of civilians and/or governmental actors (Stanton 2013).

This definition comports with Crenshaw's (1981) assertion that terrorism can have both a discriminate and indiscriminate outcome, with special emphasis on the conditions of intentional and strategic violence. However, the study of terrorist violence necessitates not only the study of specific acts of terrorism but also the study of the social context or milieu in which such acts are made. Research on terrorist violence should consequently be familiar with general psychological principles of terrorism to account for both its causes and effects, and also with the psychological backgrounds of influential terrorist leaders such as the ISIS ringleader Abu Bakr al-Baghdadi. The social context and leadership dynamics include the tendency for VNSAs usually to break down and/or split apart, with new groups emerging from the ranks of existing organizations.

Many terrorist groups afflicting the Middle East and North Africa (MENA) region from Syria to Iraq and from Afghanistan to Palestine have splintered and proliferated in the face of altering political and strategic conditions. These emergent "radical flanks" further complicate the landscape of the conflict-ridden MENA region (Haines 2013). For example, in their study on the Palestinian radical flanks' response to the Israeli settlement movement, Krause and Eiran (2018) argue that some radical flanks succeed in turning the state-centric norms/constrains on territorial revisionism and war into advantages on the ground. These novel splinter groups and their leaders often have very different trajectories than their parent organizations such as Al-Qaeda (AQ). Some last for a long time such as AQ in Yemen; others quickly fall apart or sometimes morph into a more radicalized character, e.g., AQ in Iraq. In their counter-terrorism strategies, states generally pursue a divide and conquer strategy against VNSAs, aiming to splinter terrorist groups, hamper their organizational networks, and compel existing members to relinquish terrorist violence.

Strikingly, there has been a dearth of systematic analysis of how in-group fragmentation impacts the trajectories of terrorist organizations and how to deal with the subsequent splinter groups that devolve in different ways (Perkoski 2019). This chapter analyzes the variation among certain parent organizations versus radical flanks in the MENA, which reasserted themselves in the political realm in the aftermath of Arab uprisings. I focus on the following militant groups: (1) AQ central led by Zawahiri and the Muslim Brotherhood (MB) under Badie's leadership in Egypt as parent groups; (2) ISIS in Syria and Iraq plus al-Nusra (also known as Hayat Tahrir al-Sham or simply HTS) in Syria as AQ's splinter groups; (3) Hamas and Islamic Jihad in the Gaza Strip as the MB's radical flanks. This study focuses on the role of individual leaders of certain VNSAs in the MENA region and poses the following research question: How do the operational codes of terrorist leaders of parent groups and radical flanks affect the lethality of terrorist-group violence?

This chapter is composed of five sections plus an Appendix. First, an overview of the literature on VNSA's formation and propensities for violent behavior with special emphasis on leadership factors is presented. The second part expounds upon the theoretical and methodological framework of this research and introduces operational code analysis (OCA) as an at-a-distance leadership assessment tool. Third, this study's proposed research design to study the belief systems of Islamist terrorism in the MENA is put forward. The fourth section presents the findings of an automated at-a-distance leadership analysis with a detailed interpretation and discussion. The fifth section ends the chapter by stressing the significance and overall contribution of this research project. The Appendix highlights the technical mechanics of constructing the Arabic coding scheme and identifies the data and language limitations of applying the novel Arabic scheme on a well-established research topic within the terrorism scholarship (Canbolat 2020a).

## Literature Review

The collective identity of a group becomes an integral part of an individual militant's perception through which the values are dictated by the leadership of a terrorist organization (Crenshaw 2013; Post 1998). There is a burgeoning debate within terrorism scholarship about the actual utility of studying the leader within these organizations (Crenshaw 2013). The caveats about studying leaders are as follows: (1) groups may tend to follow the paradigm of leaderless resistance; (2) an individual's own goal or inclination is the most important motivator of becoming active in political violence (Rapoport 2001). Many groups do follow a leaderless or incentive-based organization structure, yet this does not mean all collectivities are organized this way. More recent scholarship has focused on how and why terrorist leaders are indispensable factors of group behavior and outcomes (Hermann and Sakiev 2011; Price 2012; Walker 2011).

It is safe to argue that the magnitude of terrorist violence committed by different terrorist organizations has a considerable degree of variance (Asal and Rethemeyer 2008). Earlier studies in the terrorist violence literature have focused mostly on organizational mechanisms that cause specific groups to be more violent than others (Asal and Rethemeyer 2008). The bulk of the scholarship has focused on structural and/or material mechanisms that influence terrorist violence levels, but there are few studies focusing on the political psychology of individual terrorist leaders as an alternative explanatory variable. These studies deal with certain questions such as what provokes individuals to pursue political violence (Crenshaw 1986), and whether psychology can predict when terrorists will use violence (Hermann and Sakiev 2011; Walker 2011). Other studies argue that terrorist leaders' verbal outputs (or rhetoric) are radically different in their operational codes from average political leaders (Lazarevska et al. 2006).

The literature on terrorist violence shows that capabilities and ideology are empirically important predictors of lethality among terrorist organizations (Hoffman 2006). This study does not adjudicate previous hypotheses concerning the lethality of terrorist-group behavior. It instead places individual-level, actor-specific variables at the center of analysis when studying terrorist-group behavior. While a few proponents of leadership analysis looked at the political psychology of certain terrorist leaders (Picucci 2008; Walker 2011; Hermann and Sakiev 2011), they did not take issue with the research questions about the direction and magnitude or lethality of terrorist violence.

This study posits that political speeches, both scripted and spontaneous variants, of predominant terrorist leaders can be used to explain and forecast their propensities for the direction and magnitude of terrorist violence.

The analysis, therefore, is not only germane to theories of terrorism and leadership studies in the field of international relations. It is also politically relevant to the tools and strategies for countering terrorism in the world. This study employs OCA, a prominent actor-specific approach to leader psychology rooted in the field of foreign policy analysis (FPA), to assess the top leadership profiles of several militant groups in the MENA region.

## Theory and Method

How should we study terrorist leaders presiding over VNSAs and their impact on political behavior? Although early leadership studies were psycho-biographical and anecdotal (see Dyson 2015 for a history), the state-of-the-art for some time now has involved quantitative content analysis (Hudson 2005). Some examples are the works of Axelrod (1976) and Bonham et al. (1978) on cognitive maps; Tetlock (1998) and Suedfeld et al (2005) on integrative complexity; Leites (1951), George (1969; 1979), and Walker et al. (1998) on OCA; Hermann (1980, 2005) on leadership trait analysis; Boulding (1956), Hermann (1976), and Cottam (1985, 1992) on image theory; Walker (1987), Thies (2010), Harnisch et al. (2011), and Thies and Breuning (2012) on role theory. OCA focuses on the beliefs of political leaders as causal mechanisms in explaining foreign policy decisions (Leites 1951; George 1969, 1979; Walker 1983, 1990; Walker and Schafer 2007).

OCA was originally developed by Leites (1951) to analyze the decision-making style of the Soviet Politburo and was later developed and refined by George (1969; 1979), Holsti (1977), and Walker (1983, 1990). According to OCA, a leader's cognitive schemata or belief system has two components. The first set is the five philosophical beliefs about the political universe in which the leader finds himself and the nature of the "other" he faces in this environment. Second, there are five instrumental beliefs that represent the image of "self" in this political universe and the best strategies and tactics one could employ to achieve one's ends (George 1979; Walker 1990). Taken together operational code beliefs explain "what the individual knows, feels, and wants regarding the exercise of power in human affairs." (Schafer and Walker 2006, 29).

The "automation turn" in political psychology has addressed many challenges associated with the study of political leaders from a distance such as the paucity and low quality of text materials as data (Walker et al. 1998). Automated at-a-distance analysis of verbal statements by political leaders to create leadership profiles has remained largely confined to English-language texts (Brummer et al. 2020). To overcome this limitation, a novel Arabic language coding scheme is employed, which is compatible with the Profiler Plus software and the OCA research program in FPA (Walker, Schafer, and Young 1998; Young 2001; Canbolat 2020a). For the main terrorist leaders in the MENA, three key variables from OCA are generated by utilizing this Arabic coding scheme[1]: P-1, Nature of the Political Universe; I-1, Approach to Goals (direction of strategy); P-4, Control over Historical Development. According to Walker et al. (1998), there are three master beliefs shaping a leader's operational code construct, namely, the P-1, I-1, and P-4 beliefs (see also George 1969).

P-1, Nature of the Political Universe, is a measure of the hostility or friendliness Self as an actor sees in the political environment. Lower scores indicate a more hostile worldview by a generalized Other. The score is calculated as the balance of verbs referring to other actors indicating hostile action versus verbs referring to other actors taking cooperative action. I-1, Approach to Goals, is the counterpart for Self to P-1: how conflictual or cooperative is Self's exercise of political power? The index is calculated as the balance of verbs referring to Self that indicate hostile action versus verbs referring to one's Self taking cooperative action. The index for P-4, Control over Historical Development, evaluates the perceived degree of control by the actor over the political environment. The measure is a ratio of all verbs indicating action attributed to Self rather than Other as a proportion of the total verbs in a speech sample.

## Research Design and Hypotheses

To execute the coding of the leadership psychology variables from OCA, this study employs an automated version of the Arabic content analysis scheme via the Verbs in Context System (VICS) and its software application Profiler Plus (Walker et al. 1998; Canbolat 2020a). Automated coding has significant advantages over human coding. The computer codes the same piece of text the same way over indefinite runs, guaranteeing replicability of results, and does not make mistakes in coding decisions due to human fatigue or bias. Locating and compiling enough speeches of MENA's terrorist leaders in Arabic proved quite challenging. So far, a total of 45 public statements of six leaders have been compiled, which comport with the speech selection criteria set by the pioneers of the Profiler Plus school (Young 2001; Schafer and Walker 2006).

Table 4.1 lists the MENA's high-profile, jihadist leaders included in this study's data set. The databases utilized in this study to obtain verbal material for these leaders include LexisNexis, the Foreign Broadcast Information Service (FBIS), Al Jazeera Online Achieve, the official websites of the MB and Hamas, al-Mayadeen News, al-Masdar News, and other sundry websites and blogs. For coding the leaders' public speeches and following the criteria for creating eligible data (see Schafer and Walker 2006), a minimum of five (for Badie) and a maximum of ten (for Meshal) public statements in Arabic are compiled in Arabic and their official English translations, the content analysis of which results are used as a robustness check. There were no statistically significant differences among the operational code scores in the Arabic and English speech data sets. Each public speech contains more than 1000 words and a minimum of 15 transitive verbs.

*Table 4.1* The Main Islamist Terrorist Leaders and Organizations Included in This Study

| Leader | Militant Organization(s) | Leadership Period | | |
|---|---|---|---|---|
| Ayman al-Zawahiri[2] | Al-Qaeda Central | 2011–Present | | |
| Mohammad al-Jolani[3] | Al-Nusra/Fateh al-Sham | 2012–Present | | |
| Abu Bakr al-Baghdadi[4] | ISIS (or ISIL, IS, DAESH) | 2014–2019 | | |
| Mohamed Badie[5] | Muslim Brotherhood (in Egypt) | 2010–2013 | | |
| Khaled Mashal[6] | Hamas (Gaza Strip) | 2004–2017 | | |
| Ramadan Shalah[7] | Palestinian Islamic Jihad (PIJ) | 1995–2017 | | |
| **Number of Files** | **Min.** | **Max.** | **Tot. Words** | **Mean** **STDEV** |
| 45 | 1126 | 2768 | 79,200 | 1760    460 |

Three hypotheses are drawn from the terrorism literature on parent versus radical flank organizations within the subfield of international security. According to Kydd and Walter (2006), "outbidding" is one of the five main strategic logics of terrorism – along with attrition, intimidation, provocation, and spoiling. Outbidding refers to a situation where a terrorist group shows greater resolve to attack the enemy targets than rival terrorist groups to gain more public support and recruits for their cause (Kydd and Walter 2006, 51). Bloom (2004, 61) argues that while multiple terrorist organizations compete with other groups to increase their prestige, the extreme tactics of radical (or outlier) militant groups, e.g., suicide bombings, give such groups an upper hand in outbidding more mainstream groups and gaining constituents' support.

There is a latent assumption in the literature on the outbidding theory about group decision-making regarding the use and lethality of terrorist violence, which can be observed and tested at the individual level as an actor-specific analysis. If a militant leader decides that outbidding behavior is the best way to pursue political goals, then the group's lethal behavior is likely to escalate (Pape 2003; Kydd and Walter 2006). This assumption in the literature leads to the first two hypotheses given below, which relate to the beliefs of terrorist leaders about the strategic approach to goals (Hypothesis 1) and nature of the political universe (Hypothesis 2).

H1: When a fragmentation of a parent organization transpires, the beliefs of leaders of the radical flanks will be prone toward more violent strategies (I-1) than the beliefs of leaders of the parent organization to gain recognition and recruit more members from the latter (Outbidding theory).

H2: When a parent terrorist organization splinters into smaller groups, the new flanks will be presided over by leaders with more conflictual beliefs about the political universe (P-1) than the beliefs of the leaders of the parent organization (Outbidding theory).

Individual leaders with a higher sense of control over events accept the political environment around them and are generally more satisfied with the status quo. Individuals with a lower sense of this personal capacity are more reactive to and frustrated by the status quo within their surrounding environment. Some empirical research ties lower P-4 scores to the frustration–aggression hypothesis (Schafer et al. 2006). Thus, it is hypothesized that radical flank leaders should have a belief in lower historical control than parent group leaders, which will incite the former to use highly indiscriminate and lethal violent action against their enemy (Greenberg et al. 1997; Bar-Tal 2001; Schafer et al. 2006; Besaw 2014).

*H3:* When a parent terrorist organization splinters into smaller groups, the leaders of the new flanks will have a belief (P-4) in a lower level of control over historical development (Capacity Hypothesis).

## Results and Discussion

An automated content analysis of the studied terrorist leaders' speeches reveals consequential insights regarding the general patterns of militant leadership in MENA and the effects of group fragmentation on the lethality of radical flanks' strategies. This section presents the results of disparate tests for each pair of leaders to answer four basic questions: are the three master belief scores significantly different (1) between each leader and a norming group? (2) between parent and radical flanks within each terrorist group? (3) between parent groups across different terrorist organizations and between radical flanks across different terrorist organizations?

### *Individual Leaders versus Average World Leader*

Table 4.2 presents the scores of the militant leaders' master beliefs compared with those of the world leadership norming sample via two-tailed difference of means tests. This table presents the three belief variables (on the left vertically), leaders and norming group (on the top horizontally), and the belief scores in a comparative format. The average world leadership group has the highest P-1 score while MB leader Badie's score comes a close second and is followed by those of MB radical flank leaders Meshal and Shalah. The parent AQ leader Zawahiri's P-1 is lower than all MB leaders but higher than radical AQ leaders Jolani and Baghdadi. In other words, the MB-affiliated militant leaders view the political universe as more conflictual than the average world leader but as more peaceful than the AQ-affiliated leaders.

One of the unexpected findings is that Badie's I-1 score is even higher than the norming sample score, which is followed by those of Zawahiri, Meshal, Shalah, Jolani, and Baghdadi. The most statistically significant differences between the MENA leaders and the norming group are between the I-1 scores of AQ's outlier leaders Baghdadi followed by those of Jolani compared with the other militant leaders. The MENA leader who is most like the norming group is Badie, who does not have statistically significant, different beliefs barring a more cooperative approach to strategy (I-1) than the average world leader. The belief in historical

*Table 4.2* Master Operational Code Beliefs of Main Militant Leaders in MENA Compared with Average World Leadership Norming Group[*]

| Leader | Zawahiri | Jolani | Baghdadi | Badie | Meshal | Shalah | Norm. Grp. |
|---|---|---|---|---|---|---|---|
| **Org. Type** | P-AQ | R-AQ | R-AQ | P-MB | R-MB | R-MB | N/A |
| **P-1** | 0.099** | −0.095*** | −0.146*** | 0.239 | 0.157** | 0.104** | 0.25 |
| **I-1** | 0.267* | −0.101** | −0.292*** | 0.569* | 0.235* | 0.118** | 0.334 |
| **P-4a** | 0.133** | 0.207 | 0.218 | 0.229 | 0.099** | 0.068*** | 0.212 |
| **Speech N** | 8 | 8 | 7 | 5 | 10 | 7 | 255 |

| | |
|---|---|
| **Leader** | **Zawahiri** |
| **Org. Type** | P-AQ |
| **P-1** | 0.099** |
| **I-1** | 0.267* |
| **P-4a** | 0.133** |
| **Speech N** | 8 |

[*]*Abbreviations*: (1) Org: organization; (2) P: parent organization; (3) R: radical flank organization; (4) AQ: Al-Qaeda; (5) MB: Muslim Brotherhood; (6) Norm. Grp: norming group; (7) Asterisks indicate significant differences are at the following levels (two-tailed test): $^*p \leq 0.10$, $^{**}p \leq 0.05$, $^{***}p \leq 0.01$. The scores for the norming group sample (N = 255) of average world leaders are courtesy of Schafer and Walker (2006, 170, n.13).

control over events (P-4a) for Jolani, Baghdadi, and Badie is also not significantly different from the norming group's average belief.

Regarding the P-4a distribution, Badie and Baghdadi's belief about Self's level of control is slightly higher than the average leader and Jolani comes a close third, which are all within one standard deviation from the norming group score. While Zawahiri and Meshal's P-4a scores are lower than Baghdadi and Jolani and the differences are statistically significant from the norming group score, their scores exceed Shalah's control score, the statistical difference of which stands out as the most significant from the norming group. In contrast to the P-1 and I-1 distributions, there is no clear-cut pattern for the P-4 beliefs of the studied leaders whose individual idiosyncrasies might have made more difference than their organization types. For example, while the radical flank leaders of AQ have higher P-4 scores than the parent AQ leader, the other way around is true for the MB-affiliated militant leaders. An emerging, yet under-tested, pattern could be that the AQ-affiliated leaders perceive more control over political events than the MB leaders, who operate in drastically different political and socioeconomic contexts than the former.

### *Parent Groups versus Radical Flank Groups*

Table 4.3 shows the results of an additional statistical analysis in the form of a difference of means t-test to further investigate similarities or differences between parent VNSA and radical flank leaders. The t-test results

*Table 4.3* Mean Operational Code Beliefs of Generic Terrorist Groups in MENA Region*

| Org. Type | Parent AQ (N = 8) | Parent MB (N = 5) | Difference of Means |
|---|---|---|---|
| **P-1** | 0.099 | 0.239 | 0.140*** |
| **I-1** | 0.267 | 0.569 | 0.302*** |
| **P-4a** | 0.133 | 0.229 | 0.096** |

| Org. Type | Radical AQ (N = 15) | Radical MB (N = 17) | Difference of Means |
|---|---|---|---|
| **P-1** | −0.121 | 0.131 | 0.252*** |
| **I-1** | −0.197 | 0.177 | 0.374*** |
| **P-4a** | 0.213 | 0.084 | 0.129*** |

| Org. Type | Parent AQ (N = 8) | Radical AQ (N = 15) | Difference of Means |
|---|---|---|---|
| **P-1** | 0.099 | −0.121 | 0.220*** |
| **I-1** | 0.267 | −0.197 | 0.464*** |
| **P-4a** | 0.133 | 0.213 | 0.080** |

| Org. Type | Parent MB (N = 5) | Radical MB (N = 17) | Difference of Means |
|---|---|---|---|
| **P-1** | 0.239 | 0.131 | 0.108*** |
| **I-1** | 0.569 | 0.177 | 0.392*** |
| **P-4a** | 0.229 | 0.084 | 0.145*** |

| Org. Type | Parent Group (N = 13) | Radical Flank (N = 32) | Difference of Means |
|---|---|---|---|
| **P-1** | 0.169 | 0.005 | 0.164*** |
| **I-1** | 0.418 | −0.01 | 0.428*** |
| **P-4a** | 0.181 | 0.148 | 0.033** |

*Significant differences are at the following levels (two-tailed test): *$p \leq 0.10$, **$p \leq 0.05$, ***$p \leq 0.01$.

show that there are significant differences between the scores of parent group leaders and those of the radical flanks. Key leadership style distinctions between the parent VNSA and radical flank leadership styles can be seen in all three OCA variables: P-1, I-1, P-4. In contrast to the parent group leaders, the radical flank leaders believe the political universe (P-1) is significantly less friendly, and they are significantly more conflict oriented in both their strategy (I-1). While both parent group and radical flank leaders' mean self-control (P-4a) belief scores are lower than the norming group score (0.212), the radical flank leaders have a notably lower score for their beliefs in controlling historical events (0.148).

### Within-group Differences

Tables 4.4 and 4.5 break down the aggregated operational code scores of parent VNSA and radical flank leaders and compare the master belief scores of the two groups: (1) parent AQ to radical AQ (Table 4.4) and

*Table 4.4* Differences in Master Operational Code Beliefs of Parent Group and Radical Flanks Leaders of Al-Qaeda[*]

| Org. Type | Parent AQ (N = 8) | Parent MB (N = 5) | Difference of Means |
|---|---|---|---|
| **P-1** | 0.099 | 0.239 | 0.140*** |
| **I-1** | 0.267 | 0.569 | 0.302*** |
| **P-4a** | 0.133 | 0.229 | 0.096** |

| Org. Type | Radical AQ (N = 15) | Radical MB (N = 17) | Difference of Means |
|---|---|---|---|
| **P-1** | −0.121 | 0.131 | 0.252*** |
| **I-1** | −0.197 | 0.177 | 0.374*** |
| **P-4a** | 0.213 | 0.084 | 0.129*** |

| Org. Type | Parent AQ (N = 8) | Radical AQ (N = 15) | Difference of Means |
|---|---|---|---|
| **P-1** | 0.099 | −0.121 | 0.220*** |
| **I-1** | 0.267 | −0.197 | 0.464*** |
| **P-4a** | 0.133 | 0.213 | 0.080** |

| Org. Type | Parent MB (N = 5) | Radical MB (N = 17) | Difference of Means |
|---|---|---|---|
| **P-1** | 0.239 | 0.131 | 0.108*** |
| **I-1** | 0.569 | 0.177 | 0.392*** |
| **P-4a** | 0.229 | 0.084 | 0.145*** |

[*]Significant differences are at the following levels (two-tailed test): [*]$p \leq 0.10$, [**]$p \leq 0.05$, [***]$p \leq 0.01$.

*Table 4.5* Differences in Master Operational Code Beliefs of Parent Group and Radical Flanks Leaders of the Muslim Brotherhood[*]

| Org. Type | Parent AQ (N = 8) | Parent MB (N = 5) | Difference of Means |
|---|---|---|---|
| **P-1** | 0.099 | 0.239 | 0.140*** |
| **I-1** | 0.267 | 0.569 | 0.302*** |
| **P-4a** | 0.133 | 0.229 | 0.096** |

| Org. Type | Radical AQ (N = 15) | Radical MB (N = 17) | Difference of Means |
|---|---|---|---|
| **P-1** | −0.121 | 0.131 | 0.252*** |
| **I-1** | −0.197 | 0.177 | 0.374*** |
| **P-4a** | 0.213 | 0.084 | 0.129*** |

| Org. Type | Parent AQ (N = 8) | Radical AQ (N = 15) | Difference of Means |
|---|---|---|---|
| **P-1** | 0.099 | −0.121 | 0.220*** |
| **I-1** | 0.267 | −0.197 | 0.464*** |
| **P-4a** | 0.133 | 0.213 | 0.080** |

| Org. Type | Parent MB (N = 5) | Radical MB (N = 17) | Difference of Means |
|---|---|---|---|
| **P-1** | 0.239 | 0.131 | 0.108*** |
| **I-1** | 0.569 | 0.177 | 0.392*** |
| **P-4a** | 0.229 | 0.084 | 0.145*** |

[*]Significant differences are at the following levels (two-tailed test): [*]$p \leq 0.10$, [**]$p \leq 0.05$, [***]$p \leq 0.01$.

(2) parent MB to radical MB (Table 4.5). While the MB's parent group leader Badie's I-1 score stands out across all the comparison groups, of both parent organization leaders' instrumental belief scores are more positive and higher than the radical flank leaders' scores. Likewise, there is a statistically significant difference between the P-1 scores of parent group leaders Zawahiri (parent AQ) and Badie (parent MB) on the one hand, and radical flank leaders Jolani, Baghdadi (radical AQ), and Meshal, Shalah (radical MB) on the other.

As for the P-4a scores, while both parent group leaders' scores are significantly different from those of their respective radical flank leaders, the directions of P-4a scores of parent and radical flank leaders are different. Interestingly, radical AQ leaders' mean P-4a score (0.213) is higher than both parent group leaders' mean (0.133), and the norming group score (0.212), however slightly. In marked contrast to the AQ leaders, the mean P-4a score of radical MB leaders (0.084) is significantly lower than those of their parent group leaders (0.229) and those of average world leaders (0.212). In other words, the relationship between the P-4a scores of parent and radical MB leaders is compatible with the Capacity hypothesis, while the direction of two AQ-affiliated group leaders' P-4a scores of contravenes the hypothesized relationship between parent groups and radical flanks. In sum, the results presented in Tables 4.4 and 4.5 substantiate that the three master belief scores significantly differ between parent and radical flanks for each terrorist group, but the direction of the P-4 score is qualified by differences between the main terrorist organizations.

### Between Group Differences

Tables 4.6 and 4.7 present the results of difference of means tests comparing master belief scores of parent groups (Table 4.6) and radical flanks (Table 4.7) across different terrorist organizations. First, all the master belief mean scores of parent MB are higher and more positive than those of parent AQ. In other words, Badie perceives the political universe (Other) in more peaceful terms and believes in more cooperative tools in his strategic approach than the AQ chief Zawahiri. Likewise, Badie's sense of political control (0.229) is stronger than both Zawahiri's (0.133) and the average world leader (0.212). Second, the MB-affiliated radical leaders have higher and more positive P-1, I-1, and P-4a operational code scores than those of radical AQ leaders. While radical AQ leaders attribute more control to themselves (P-4a) than radical MB leaders, the former's view of the Other (political universe) is more conflictual than the latter. The hostility perceived by radical AQ leaders is compounded with their salient propensity for more conflictual strategies compared with their MB counterparts. In brief, the operational codes of both parent organizations and radical flank leadership are markedly different between the two terrorist groups.

*Table 4.6* Differences in Master Operational Code Beliefs of Parent Group Leaders Across Different Militant Organizations[*]

| Org. Type | Parent AQ ( N = 8 ) | Parent MB ( N = 5 ) | Difference of Means |
|---|---|---|---|
| **P-1** | 0.099 | 0.239 | 0.140*** |
| **I-1** | 0.267 | 0.569 | 0.302*** |
| **P-4a** | 0.133 | 0.229 | 0.096** |

| Org. Type | Radical AQ ( N = 15 ) | Radical MB ( N = 17 ) | Difference of Means |
|---|---|---|---|
| **P-1** | −0.121 | 0.131 | 0.252*** |
| **I-1** | −0.197 | 0.177 | 0.374*** |
| **P-4a** | 0.213 | 0.084 | 0.129*** |

| Org. Type | Parent AQ ( N = 8 ) | Radical AQ ( N = 15 ) | Difference of Means |
|---|---|---|---|
| **P-1** | 0.099 | −0.121 | 0.220*** |
| **I-1** | 0.267 | −0.197 | 0.464*** |
| **P-4a** | 0.133 | 0.213 | 0.080** |

| Org. Type | Parent MB ( N = 5 ) | Radical MB ( N = 17 ) | Difference of Means |
|---|---|---|---|
| **P-1** | 0.239 | 0.131 | 0.108*** |
| **I-1** | 0.569 | 0.177 | 0.392*** |
| **P-4a** | 0.229 | 0.084 | 0.145*** |

[*]Significant differences are at the following levels (two-tailed test): [*]$p \leq 0.10$, [**]$p \leq 0.05$, [***]$p \leq 0.01$.

*Table 4.7* Differences in Master Operational Code Beliefs of Radical Flank Leaders across Different Militant Organizations[*]

| Org. Type | Radical AQ ( N = 15 ) | Radical MB ( N = 17 ) | Difference of Means |
|---|---|---|---|
| **P-1** | −0.121 | 0.131 | 0.252*** |
| **I-1** | −0.197 | 0.177 | 0.374*** |
| **P-4a** | 0.213 | 0.084 | 0.129*** |

| Org. Type | Parent AQ ( N = 8 ) | Radical AQ ( N = 15 ) | Difference of Means |
|---|---|---|---|
| **P-1** | 0.099 | −0.121 | 0.220*** |
| **I-1** | 0.267 | −0.197 | 0.464*** |
| **P-4a** | 0.133 | 0.213 | 0.080** |

| Org. Type | Parent MB ( N = 5 ) | Radical MB ( N = 17 ) | Difference of Means |
|---|---|---|---|
| **P-1** | 0.239 | 0.131 | 0.108*** |
| **I-1** | 0.569 | 0.177 | 0.392*** |
| **P-4a** | 0.229 | 0.084 | 0.145*** |

[*]Significant differences are at the following levels (two-tailed test): [*]$p \leq 0.10$, [**]$p \leq 0.05$, [***]$p \leq 0.01$.

Collectively, the results in Tables 4.2–4.7 corroborate the first two hypotheses concerning the militant leaders' view of the political universe (P-1) and their strategic orientation (I-1), with robust empirical evidence. Tables 4.2, 4.4, and 4.5 cast some doubt on the third (capacity) hypothesis as the control over historical development (P-4) scores of the AQ and the MB radical flank leaders show reverse directions compared with their respective parent groups leaders. While the radical flank leaders of the AQ (Jolani and Baghdadi) assign higher Self's control to themselves compared with the parent group leader (Zawahiri), the MB-affiliated radical flanks leaders' (Meshal and Shalah) control scores are significantly lower than those of the parent organization leader (Badie). Table 4.3 supports the capacity hypothesis at the group level of analysis, showing statistically significant differences between the parent and radical flank groups' the P-4a scores ($p \leq 0.05$); these results are qualified by differences in direction of the P-4 scores within each terrorist group.

Thus, it can be argued that when a parent organization splinters, the emerging leaders of the radical flanks are likely to have more violent beliefs (I-1) about strategy than the beliefs of the parent organization leaders. Likewise, once a parent terrorist organization fragments into smaller groups, the new flanks will be led by individuals with more conflictual beliefs about the other policy actors (P-1) within the political universe. This study hypothesized that the shifts in I-1 and P-1 toward conflict are likely to be more lethal when accompanied by radical flank leaders' lower capacity to control historical development (P-4a) compared with their parent group leaders. The exceptions are the AQ's outliers: Baghdadi's and Jolani's propensities for using more lethal and cruel militant tactics to compete with other terrorist groups in the MENA are accompanied by their belief in historical control similar to the norming group (Friis 2015; Abrahms 2018).

Figure 4.1 classifies all the militant decision makers and their respective groups in terms of leadership styles and roles. These are classified as operational code types A, B, C, or DEF (Holsti 1977; Walker 1990), which correspond to the four quadrants in this figure. The VICS indices for the master beliefs, P-1 (nature of the political universe), I-1 (strategic approach to goals), and P-4 (ability to control historical development), are mapped on intersecting vertical (P-1/I-1) and horizontal (P-4) axes to locate the leader's image of the Self and Other in one of the four quadrants. The coordinates for Self (I-1, P-4a) and Other (P-1, P-4b) lead to predictions regarding strategic preferences over the goals of settle, submit, dominate, and deadlock (Walker and Schafer 2006).

Leaders who fall into the same zones within each quadrant share the similar roles and relations of friend and alignment, partner and cooperation, rival and conflict, or enemy and domination attributed to Self and Other (Malici and Walker 2017). These locations with corresponding roles and relations are inferred from comparing the scores for the MENA terrorist leaders to the mean P-1, I-1, and P-4 indices of the norming

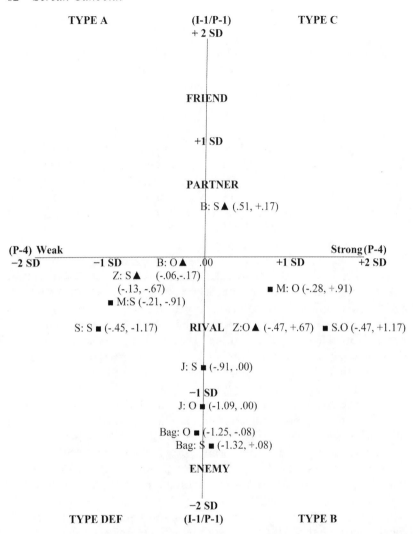

TYPE A                    (I-1/P-1)                    TYPE C
                          + 2 SD

                          FRIEND

                          +1 SD

                          PARTNER
                          B: S▲ (.51, +.17)

(P-4) Weak                                          Strong (P-4)
−2 SD          −1 SD        B: O▲  .00        +1 SD              +2 SD
               Z: S▲   (-.06,-.17)
               (-.13, -.67)
               ■ M:S (-.21, -.91)                ■ M: O (-.28, +.91)

S: S ■ (-.45, -1.17)     RIVAL  Z:O▲ (-.47, +.67)   ■ S.O (-.47, +1.17)

                         J: S ■ (-.91, .00)

                         −1 SD
                         J: O ■ (-1.09, .00)

                    Bag: O ■ (-1.25, -.08)
                    Bag: S ■ (-1.32, +.08)

                         ENEMY

                         −2 SD
TYPE DEF                 (I-1/P-1)                    TYPE B

*Figure 4.1* Operational Code Types and Roles of Terrorist Leaders and Groups
    in the MENA Region

Sources: Holsti (1977); Walker (1990); Malici and Walker (2017). Abbreviations: SD =
Standard deviation; Bag = Baghdadi; B = Badie; J = Jolani; M = Meshal; S = Shalah; Z =
Zawahiri. S = Self; O = Other; Triangle Symbol = Parent Group; Square Symbol = Radical
Flank Group

group of world leaders from a variety of geographical leaders and historical eras (Schafer and Walker 2006; Malici and Walker 2017). To render
the comparisons more robust, the norming group scores are used as the
reference points (origin) of the coordinate system in Figure 4.1. A Z-score
measurement is used to plot all the militant leaders on Figure 4.1. Table 4.8

*Table 4.8* Standard Deviation Z-Scores for Deviations in Beliefs from Norming Group for Militant MENA Leaders[a]

| Leader | Z | J | Bag | B | M | S | Norm. Grp. |
|--------|-----|-----|-----|-----|-----|-----|------------|
| Org. Type: | P | R | R | P | R | R | Ave. (SD) |
| P-1 | −0.47 | −1.09 | −1.25 | −0.06 | −0.28 | −0.47 | 0.25 (0.32) |
| I-1 | −0.13 | −0.91 | −1.32 | +0.51 | −0.21 | −0.45 | 0.33 (0.47) |
| P-4a | −0.67 | 0.00 | +0.08 | +0.17 | −0.91 | −1.17 | 0.21 (0.12) |
| P-4b | +0.67 | 0.00 | −0.08 | −0.17 | +0.91 | +1.17 | 0.79 (0.12) |

[a]Z score = (observed score minus sample mean) divided by standard deviation of sample. Org. = Organization; Z = Zawahiri; J = Jolani; Bag = Baghdadi; B = Badie; M = Meshal; S = Shalah; P = Parent Group; R = Radical Flank Group; Norm. Grp. = Norming Group (N = 255).

*Source:* Schafer and Walker (2006, 170, n. 13).

presents the Z-scores for the standard deviations, respectively, from the norming group means for I-1, P-1, and P-4 (N = 255).

Strikingly, only the MB leader Badie's image of Self falls under the Type C operational code system, who attributes himself a partner role of cooperation in the foreign policy realm with somewhat strong control over events. Nevertheless, Badie views Other as enacting a rival role of conflict with a Type DEF leadership style. The other parent leader Zawahiri sees both Self and Other as rivals in a conflictual political universe, yet he perceives Other as the stronger rival (Type B), while he wields less power (Type DEF) in any strategic interaction between Self and Other.

The difference between the MB leader Mohamed Badie and the AQ's Zawahiri speaks volumes about the distinct characters of parent VNSAs. While the AQ views itself as an armed group fighting the West and secular Muslim regimes in MENA and elicits a similar image in the Western countries, the MB has a more convoluted modus operandi in which the organization claims to wear two hats: (1) a democratic player in electoral regimes (such as in Egypt and in the Gaza Strip) which operates within the parameters of democratic politics; (2) maintaining a military wing and resorting to terrorist violence via the radicalized cells when necessary. Thus, wearing two hats at the same time, the MB leader Badie has both a democratic and a militant ringleader image, which manifest themselves in his public speeches. These distinctions in the organizational structures of the MB and AQ account for the dissimilarity between al-Zawahiri and Badie's operational code types and different role attributions to Self and Other.

Figure 4.1 indicates that the studied radical flank leaders have a high propensity to waver between the leadership types B and DEF regarding both their conceptualizations of Self and Other, which influence their preference rankings for different political outcomes. All the radical flank leaders are situated on the lower half of Figure 4.1, which means that both their Self and Other images are more conflictual (I-1) and hostile (P-1); they see Self and/or Other in rival or enemy roles. Nonetheless, the MB-affiliated, radical flank leaders project less conflictual and hostile leadership styles than the AQ's radical wing leaders. Shalah assigns rival foreign policy roles to both Self and Other, yet views himself as the weaker rival (Type DEF) with a tendency to pursue more conflictual strategies than Other (Type B), who has stronger control over events. While Meshal has less conflictual and hostile beliefs about the political universe and a strategic approach to foreign policy than those of Shalah, his leadership style and role attributions are the same as those of Shalah.

The AQ-affiliated radical flank leaders' operational code types and roles dwell in the lowest zones of Figure 4.1, which correspond to their extremely negative P-1 and I-1 belief scores compared with the rest of the militant leaders. Jolani attributes a very hostile rival role of conflict to Self and an enemy role of domination to Other; his perception of hostility is stronger for Other (within the −2 standard deviation zone) compared with those of his self-assigned, "almost enemy" role (just within the −1 standard deviation zone). Because of the Z-scores distribution of his P-4 beliefs, Jolani's leadership style dwells on the vertical axis, which could shift between the Type DEF and Type B quadrants and render his operational code type less predictable compared with other militant leaders. Baghdadi overtops all the studied militant leaders in having the most negative I-1 and P-1 scores; his role assignments to both Self and Other correspond to enemy roles (both within the −2 standard deviation zone) in a struggle for domination.

Intriguingly, Baghdadi construes Other as a (however marginally) weaker enemy with Type DEF leadership particularities, while he attributes a stronger "enemy" role and a Type B leadership style to Self in dealing with others in the political realm. Put differently, the ISIS chief stands out as the most conflictual individual in the entire group, and he has the second highest self-control (P-4a) score after Badie. While this finding is not surprising because ISIS is viewed as "one of the most lethal terrorist organizations in today's world," it is still interesting to confirm that argument by a systematic analysis of speeches (Friis 2015: 745). This research also bears out a scholarly argument that very lethal terrorist organizations, e.g., ISIS, sow the seeds of their own destruction by using extremely vitriolic rhetoric and resorting to cruel terrorist violence (Abrahms 2013, 2018).

## Conclusion

Analyzing the splinter groups that break away from AQ and the MB, i.e., ISIS, al-Nusra (currently known as HTS), Hamas, and Islamic Jihad, is integral to explaining and forecasting their terrorist behavior. The results of this study concur with the argument that the formation of militant splinter groups influences their organizational evolution and future behavior (Perkoski 2019). The results lend a nuanced support to the hypotheses in this chapter that there are consequential differences even among leaders who hail from the same Islamic creed and ideological training. In addition to their idiosyncratic beliefs, the type of their militant organizations also influences an individual leader's inclinations for making strategic choices and their lethality in dealing with others in the political universe.

Using OCA to construct psychological profiles of key terrorist leaders from a content analysis of their written statements reveals a set of master political beliefs, which are hypothesized to motivate their terrorist behavior. These political beliefs are instrumental in understanding the VNSAs' strategies because many terrorist leaders in the MENA region encounter very few institutional/structural constraints within their organizations. These MENA terrorist groups perceive the political world through religious and ideological lenses, and therefore, their political behavior rests on the specific formation (or fragmentation) patterns of these movements.

Put differently, top decision makers of these jihadist radical flanks – e.g., Baghdadi of ISIS, Jolani of al-Nusra, and Shalah of Islamic Jihad – interact with the political world solely based on their judgment of the capabilities of the jihadist movement rather than more concrete structural and material conditions. What terrorist leaders say about others in their respective environment does matter. When terrorist leaders say they view violent strategies as the only way toward gaining political objectives, their organization's violent behavior, by and large, reflects that strategic belief. Moreover, militant leaders who show more hostility in their utterances will be more likely to promote increased lethality in their group's violence.

Evidence to support this argument is in the comparison of relevant political beliefs about the political universe and political strategies across parent and splinter terrorist organizations and with the operational codes of reference groups, e.g., average world leaders. Preliminary results suggest that OCA provides a set of scientific tools for linking differences in terrorist behavior to differences in belief systems. Finally, by comparing observed operational code variables to expected findings informed by commonly held assumptions within the field of terrorism studies, OCA provides a rigorous analytical means of testing the validity of such assumptions.

While automated at-a-distance leadership assessment research programs have made steady progress since the late 1990s (Walker et al. 1998), there is still a gap in the leadership research program concerning the study of non-Western decision makers using languages beyond English (Brummer and Hudson 2015). Hinnebusch (2015) argues that while the leaders operating in Western liberal democracies have been studied extensively and in a comparative fashion, non-Western leadership cases including terrorist leaders have received less attention in the FPA field (for exceptions, see Malici 2008; Malici and Buckner 2008; Duelfer and Dyson 2011; Ozdamar and Canbolat 2018; Canbolat 2020a, 2020b; Ozdamar et al. 2020). This chapter has aimed to address this gap by expanding the North America–bounded FPA approach toward the Global South by studying in their native language a MENA "brand" of terrorism from the vantage point of at-a-distance leadership assessment tools.

In that sense, future avenues of research in this area include the following: (1) tracking political beliefs of key decision makers over time within the same terrorist organization; (2) assessing the internal belief system differences within the same parent and/or splinter groups (Perkoski 2019); (3) developing an actor-specific framework to anticipate the timing and lethality of terrorist attacks from the operational codes of individual terrorist leaders (Walker 2011); (4) analyzing the "audience effect" on the militant leaders' strategic rhetoric and operational codes, which might differ depending on the type of audience including domestic versus regional versus international (Canbolat 2020a, 2020b).

In a nutshell, this research aims at helping both the scholars of FPA with more rigorous theoretical advancement and MENA specialists with more far-sighted policy recommendations. Providing them with an inroad into the mindsets of key terrorist groups and drawing inferences on the future trajectory of terrorist groups' behavior and lethality in the MENA region, this study avoids making sweeping or normative statements about possible solutions to the vicious circle of terrorist violence in MENA. This chapter also casts doubt on key assumptions that are central to counterinsurgency policies of regional and international players in MENA such as the United States, Russia, and Israel.

Accordingly, the foremost policy recommendation in this chapter is that regional and world leaders should give heed to the *leaders* of terrorist organizations. By and large, most of what terrorist leaders say has been censored or overlooked. Eliminating terrorist violence and hampering terrorist movements are by nature convoluted issues, the solutions of which are dependent on a variety of factors. Nevertheless, putting White's (1991) notion of realistic empathy, not a naïvely construed sympathy or tolerance, into practice to understand certain militant actors – who mostly make group decisions singlehandedly in the MENA region – should be part and parcel of regional and global counterterrorism efforts.

## Appendix: Challenges of Coding in Native Tongues: Data and Language Limitations

Studying non-mainstream leaders, who mostly speak in their native languages and who run rather clandestine organizations, from a distance has proved onerous. Major methodological hurdles include, (1) the availability of text, (2) the veracity of authorship problem, (3) the lost-in-translation issue, and (4) the danger of the individualistic fallacy.

First, the availability of text – transcripts of words spoken by the subject of study – determines the shape of the research. The ideal is an online archive of carefully curated text, sortable by date, topic, and audience, maintained on behalf of a leader who spoke regularly. Occasionally, research will be driven by the appearance of an enticing text corpus: the availability of new tapes from the Nixon presidency, for example, or the discovery that Saddam Hussein kept his own taping system to track his meetings and phone calls (Dyson and Raleigh 2014). In this research, the most pressing problem was finding sufficient speech data to establish foreign policy profiles for the terrorist leaders. Particularly, ISIS leader Al-Baghdadi's and Nusra leader Al-Jolani's public speeches on politics and foreign policy have been elusive and so locating and retrieving them was the most time-consuming part of the research. This is because such militant leaders' public appearances are rather scant and so their speeches often lack confirmation and reliability and such leaders' speeches are subject to broad censorship in both their countries and in the world media.

Second, the common question about using a leader's public speeches is whether a leader pens their own speeches or just reads a speechwriter's script from the prompter. This study's rejoinder to this criticism is twofold: (1) all leaders, even the terrorist leaders under investigation, are accountable for what they say in front of the public, and this constrains their policy behaviors later on; and (2) no leader will publicly utter a political statement without approving it.

Third, there is the "automation problem": missing the particular contextual meanings of speech due to the context-free nature of automated coding in all the languages including Arabic. This is an undeniable challenge to content analysis methods, but I still opt for an "at-a-distance" text analysis since it is more feasible than doing hand coding in Arabic or traveling to war-torn MENA countries to conduct field research and interviews with the militant groups.

Fourth, any agent-centered approach runs the risk of reductionism – explaining the behavior of a complex phenomenon like terrorist behavior and militants' motives for resorting to violence through a simple recourse to the idiosyncratic will of its leaders. At some level, this possibility is methodologically impossible to eliminate because of lacking access to an alternate reality in which terrorist organizations have other leaders. One cannot definitively test the impact of the selected group of militant leaders on policy outcomes. In FPA research programs, counterfactual analyses based upon assuming leaders with different measured characteristics are usually the best available remedy.

At this early stage, the author merely signals an awareness of the need to perform this in-depth analysis in future iterations of this project. That said, using "at-a-distance" leadership analysis tools powered through the Arabic scheme to unveil terrorist leaders' psychological profiles mitigates the financial and logistical costs associated with studying leaders, i.e., a lack of direct access to the leader, the potential security risks of visiting worn-torn countries such as Syria and Iraq, and the linguistic and cultural problems associated with conducting field research.

## Developing an Arabic Coding Scheme for OCA

Creating automated content analysis coding schemes for texts in English and Arabic requires particular attention to each language. While the basic strategic task is similar for each language, the linguistic details prompt the adoption of different tactics.

The similarities are as follows:

1  Content words in both languages are set off by spaces in texts. This is nontrivial, since some languages do not (e.g., Chinese).
2  The basic task is to identify the distinguishable content forms in the most efficient way. This involves a robust grammatical analysis for both languages, so that purely (or partially) grammatical indicators may be separated from content forms.
3  The scheme design is similar for both languages. Grammatical analysis is done first, isolating the content forms but preserving the grammatical context. Content forms are assigned values, which are turned into data. Each analyzed text (called a "token") has a text form, a lemma form, and various values associated with it (part-of-speech, truth-value, etc.). One can use these values in the analysis, change them, create new ones, etc.
4  Particular content values are determined by native reader judgments, for both languages.

The differences are,

1  English tends to have consistent stem content forms (which are called "lemmas"), with endings attached for grammatical differences. There are some exceptions, such as "man/men." Arabic makes much more use of internal consonant and vowel pattern distinctions than English.
2  English grammatical function words (prepositions, pronouns, particles, auxiliary verbs, etc.) are separate words. In Arabic, some of these are attached either at the beginnings or ends of words (such as bi-, li-, wa-, and -kum).
3  English has a predominantly subject–verb–object (SVO) declarative word order. The normal Arabic Order is verb–subject–object (VSO).
4  The English lexical grammatical analysis (called "tagging") primarily involves recognition of word forms, grammatical endings, and labeling of parts of speech. It proceeds from word matches in dictionaries. The content form (stem form without endings) is cited as the "lemma" in the scheme. These forms, labels, or other values are then available for later parts of the scheme to access.
5  The Arabic scheme is different because there are so many different morphemes, clitics, and word-internal distinctions.[8] The procedure here is to treat unanalyzed Arabic words as strings of individual characters set off by spaces.

6  Clitic strings (mostly prepositions and pronouns) can be recognized, separated, and collapsed, treating them as separate words, but in the same order. Then the content word can be recognized, grammatically and lexically analyzed, and a lemma form can be created. The result is collapsed into a single analyzed word ("token"). So, for example, للامم المتحدة ("to the United Nations") in Arabic is separated into 5 separate forms: متحدة, ال, امم, ال, ل by this process.

## Notes

1. Courtesy of Michael D. Young and Doug Fuller of Social Science Automation, who graciously helped me develop the Arabic coding scheme and generate the three OCA variables via the scheme. The Arabic coding scheme's mechanics are detailed in the Appendix (see also Canbolat 2020a).
2. Most of the Al-Zawahiri speeches are retrieved from the AQ's primary media platform (al-Sahab): https://archive.org (accessed 12/15/2019).
3. There is a dearth of speeches associated with al-Jolani. The author had to rely on a few long interviews with the Al-Nusra leader, many of which are broadcasted by Al-Jazeera, available at https://www.aljazeera.com/ (accessed 05/15/2020).
4. Like al-Jolani, the ISIS leader al-Baghdadi's speeches are retrieved from various clandestine illicit jihadi blogs and/or the ISIS's media platform, called Dabiq, on Twitter (accessed 04/15/2020).
5. Badie's speeches can be accessed at the MB's official website: https://www.ikhwanonline.com/ (accessed 12/15/2019).
6. Mashal's speeches and interviews are available at Al Jazeera: https://www.aljazeera.com/ and at Al Hadath (a local newspaper in Gaza Strip): https://www.alhadath.ps/ (accessed 12/15/2019).
7. Shalah's speeches are retrieved from the website of Saraya al-Quds (the military wing of Islamic jihad movement in Palestinian territories): https://saraya.ps/ and from the Al Mayadeen (a well-known Lebanese media platform): http://almayadeen.net (accessed 12/15/2019).
8. In linguistics, the difference between morpheme and clitic is as follows: morpheme is the smallest linguistic unit within a word that can carry a meaning, such as "in-," "escape," and "-able" in the word "inescapable" while clitic is a morpheme that is always attached to following or preceding words instead of an independent word.

## References

Abrahms, M. 2013. The credibility paradox: Violence as a double-edged sword in international politics. *International Studies Quarterly* 57(4): 660–671.

Abrahms, M. 2018. *Rules for rebels: The science of victory in militant history.* New York, NY: Oxford University Press.

Asal, V., R. Rethemeyer. 2008. The nature of the beast: Organizational structures and the lethality of terrorist attacks. *The Journal of Politics* 70(2): 437–449.

Axelrod, R. 1976. *Structure of decision: The cognitive maps of political elites.* Princeton, NJ: Princeton University Press.

Besaw, C. 2014. *Deadly premonition: Does terrorist-leader psychology influence violence lethality?* (Unpublished M.A. Thesis). Retrieved from http://stars.library.ucf.edu/etd/4494

Bar-Tal, D. 2001. Why does fear override hope in societies engulfed by intractable conflict, as it does in the Israeli society? *Political Psychology* 22(3): 601–627.

Bloom, M. 2004. Palestinian suicide bombing: Public support, market share, and outbidding. *Political Science Quarterly* 119(1): 61–88.

Bonham, G., D. Heradstveit, O. Narvesen, M. Shapiro. 1978. A cognitive model of decision-making: Application to Norwegian oil policy. *Cooperation and Conflict* 13(2): 93–108.

Boulding, K. 1956. *The image: Knowledge in life and society.* Ann Arbor, MI: University of Michigan Press.

Brummer, K., and V. Hudson. Eds. 2015. *Foreign policy analysis beyond North America.* Boulder, CO: Lynne Rienner Publishers, Incorporated.

Brummer, K., M. Young, O. Özdamar, S. Canbolat, C. Thiers, C. Rabini, A. Mehvar. 2020. Coding in tongues: Developing non-English coding schemes for leadership profiling. *International Studies Review.* 22: 1051–1055. Online first: https://doi.org/10.1093/isr/viaa001.

Canbolat, S. 2020a. Profiling leaders in Arabic. In Forum *Coding in Tongues: Developing Non-English Coding Schemes for Leadership Profiling. International Studies Review.* Online first: https://doi.org/10.1093/isr/viaa001.

Canbolat, S. 2020b. Understanding political Islamists' foreign policy rhetoric in their native language: A Turkish operational code analysis approach. *APSA-MENA Politics Newsletter* 3(1): 13–16.

Cottam, M. 1985. The impact of psychological images on international bargaining: The case of Mexican natural gas. *Political Psychology* 6: 413–440.

Cottam, M. 1992. The Carter Administration's policy toward Nicaragua: Images, goals, and tactics. *Political Science Quarterly* 107(1): 123–146.

Crenshaw, M. 1981. The causes of terrorism. *Comparative Politics* 13(4): 379–399.

Crenshaw, M. 1986. The psychology of political terrorism. *Political Psychology* 21(2): 379–413.

Crenshaw, M. 2013. Decisions to use terrorism: Psychological constraints on instrumental reasoning. In *Terrorism studies*, 272–281. New York, NY: Routledge.

Duelfer, C. and S. Dyson. 2011. Chronic misperception and international conflict: The US-Iraq experience. *International Security*, 36(1): 73–100.

Dyson, S. 2015. *Leaders in conflict: Bush and Rumsfeld in Iraq.* Manchester: Manchester University Press.

Dyson, S., A. Raleigh. 2014. Public and private beliefs of political leaders: Saddam Hussein in front of a crowd and behind closed doors. *Research & Politics* 1(1): 1–7.

Friis, S. 2015. 'Beyond anything we have ever seen': Beheading videos and the visibility of violence in the war against ISIS. *International Affairs* 91(4): 725–746.

George, A. 1969. The "operational code": A neglected approach to the study of political leaders and decision-making. *International Studies Quarterly* 13(2): 190–222.

George, A. 1979. The causal nexus between beliefs and behavior and the operational code belief system. In *Psychological models in international politics*, 95–124. Boulder: Westview Press.

Greenstein, F. 1967. The impact of personality on politics: An attempt to clear away underbrush. *The American Political Science Review*, 61(3): 629–641.

Greenberg, J., S. Solomon, T. Pyszczynski. 1997. Terror management theory of self-esteem and cultural worldviews: Empirical assessments and conceptual refinements. In *Advances in experimental social psychology*, 61–139. Cambridge, MA: Elsevier Academic Press.

Harnisch, S., C. Frank, and H. Maull. Eds. 2011. *Role theory in international relations*. New York, NY: Routledge.

Haines, H. 2013. Radical flank effects. In *The Wiley-Blackwell encyclopedia of social and political movements*. Chichester: John Wiley & Sons.

Hermann, M. 1976. Circumstances under which leader personality will affect foreign policy: Some propositions. In *Search of global patterns*, 326–332. New York: Free Press.

Hermann, M. 1980. Explaining foreign policy behavior using the personal characteristics of political leaders. *International Studies Quarterly* 24(1): 7–46.

Hermann, M. 2005. Assessing leadership style: A trait analysis. In *The psychological assessment of political leaders*, 178–212. Ann Arbor, MI: University of Michigan Press.

Hermann, M., A. Sakiev. 2011. Leadership, terrorism, and the use of violence. *Dynamics of Asymmetric Conflict* 4(2): 126–134.

Hinnebusch, R. 2015. Foreign policy analysis and the Arab world. In *Foreign policy analysis beyond North America*, eds. K. Brummer, V. Hudson, 77–100. Boulder, CO: Lynne Rienner.

Hoffman, B. 2006. *Inside terrorism*. New York, NY: Columbia University Press.

Holsti, O. 1977. *The "operational code" as an approach to the analysis of belief systems*. Durham, NC: Duke University.

Hudson, V. 2005. Foreign policy analysis: Actor-specific theory and the ground of international relations. *Foreign Policy Analysis* 1: 1–30.

Kalyvas, S. 2004. The paradox of terrorism in civil war. *The Journal of Ethics* 8(1): 97–138.

Krause, P., E. Eiran. 2018. How human boundaries become state borders: Radical flanks and territorial control in the modern era. *Comparative Politics* 50(4): 479–499.

Kydd, A., B. Walter.,. 2006. The strategies of terrorism. *International Security* 31(1): 49–80.

Lazarevska, E., J. J. Sholl, M. Young. 2006. Links among beliefs and personality traits: The distinctive language of terrorists. In *Beliefs and leadership in world politics*, 171–184. New York, NY: Palgrave Macmillan.

Leites, N. 1951. *The operational code of the politburo*. New York, NY: McGraw-Hill.

Malici, A. 2008. *When leaders learn and when they don't: Mikhail Gorbachev and Kim Il Sung at the end of the cold war*. Albany, NY: SUNY Press.

Malici, A., A. Buckner. 2008. Empathizing with rogue leaders: Mahmoud Ahmadinejad and Bashar Al-Asad. *Journal of Peace Research* 45(6): 783–800.

Malici, A., S. Walker. 2017. *Role theory and role conflict in US-Iran relations: Enemies of our own making*. New York, NY: Routledge.

Ozdamar, O., S. Canbolat. 2018. Understanding new Middle Eastern leadership: An operational code approach. *Political Research Quarterly* 71(1): 19–31.

Ozdamar, O., S. Canbolat, and M. Young. 2020. Profiling leaders in Turkish. In Forum *Coding in Tongues: Developing Non-English Coding Schemes for Leadership Profiling. International Studies Review*. online first: https://doi.org/10.1093/isr/viaa001.

Pape, R. 2003. The strategic logic of suicide terrorism. *American Political Science Review* 97(3): 343–361.

Perkoski, E. 2019. Internal politics and the fragmentation of armed groups. *International Studies Quarterly* 63(4): 876–889.

Picucci, P. 2008. *Terrorism's operational code: An examination of the belief systems of al-Qaeda and Hamas* (Doctoral dissertation, University of Kansas).

Post, J. 1998. Terrorist psycho-logic: Terrorist behavior as a product of psychological forces. In *Origins of terrorism: Psychologies, ideologies, theologies, states of mind*, ed. W. Reich, 25–42. Washington, DC: Woodrow Wilson Center Press.

Price, B. 2012. Targeting top terrorists: How leadership decapitation contributes to counterterrorism. *International Security* 36(4): 9–46.

Rapoport, D. Ed. 2001. *Inside terrorist organizations*. New York, NY: Routledge.

Sandler, T., W. W. Enders. 2007. Applying analytical methods to study terrorism. *International Studies Perspectives* 8(3): 287–302.

Schafer, M., and S. Walker. Eds. 2006. *Beliefs and leadership in world politics: Methods and applications of operational code analysis*. New York, NY: Palgrave Macmillan.

Schafer, M., S. Robison, B. Aldrich. 2006. Operational codes and the 1916 Easter Rising in Ireland: A test of the frustration–aggression hypothesis. *Foreign Policy Analysis* 2(1): 63–82.

Stanton, J. 2013. Terrorism in the context of civil war. *The Journal of Politics* 75(4): 1009–1022.

Suedfeld, P., K. Guttieri, P. Tetlock. 2005. Assessing integrative complexity at a distance: Archival analyses of thinking and decision making. In *The psychological assessment of political leader*, 246–270. Ann Arbor, MI: University of Michigan Press.

Thies, C. 2010. Role theory and foreign policy. In *Oxford research encyclopedia of international studies*. DOI: 10.1093/acrefore/9780190846626.013.291.

Thies, C., M. Breuning. 2012. Integrating foreign policy analysis and international relations through role theory. *Foreign Policy Analysis* 8(1): 1–4.

Tetlock, P. 1998. Social psychology and world politics. In *Handbook of social psychology* 868–912. New York, NY: McGraw-Hill.

Walker, S. 1983. The motivational foundations of political belief systems: A re-analysis of the operational code construct. *International Studies Quarterly*, 27(2): 179–202.

Walker, S. Ed. 1987. *Role theory and foreign policy analysis*. Durham, NC: Duke University Press.

Walker, S. 1990. The evolution of operational code analysis. *Political Psychology* 11: 403–418.

Walker, S., M. Schafer, M. Young. 1998. Systematic procedures for operational code analysis: Measuring and modeling Jimmy Carter's operational code. *International Studies Quarterly* 42(1): 175–189.

Walker, S., M. Schafer. 2007. Theodore Roosevelt and Woodrow Wilson as cultural icons of US foreign policy. Political Psychology 28(6): 747–776.

Walker, S. and M. Schafer. 2007. Theodore Roosevelt and Woodrow Wilson as cultural icons of US foreign policy. *Political Psychology*, 28(6): 747–776.

Walker, S. 2011. Anticipating attacks from the operational codes of terrorist groups. *Dynamics of Asymmetric Conflict* 4(2): 135–143.

White, R. 1991. Empathizing with Saddam Hussein. *Political Psychology* 12(2): 291–308.

Young, M. 2001. Building worldview(s) with Profiler+. In *Progress in communication sciences: Applications of computer content analysis*, ed. M. West, 17–32. Westport, CT: Ablex Publishing.

# 5 Operational Code Analysis and Civil Conflict Severity

*Gary E. Smith*

## Introduction

How can a leader's operational code affect the severity of civil conflicts? As multiple chapters in this volume demonstrate, operational code analysis continues to provide valuable insights for scholars seeking to explain the foreign policy preferences and behaviors of world leaders. Individual political leaders play a significant role in shaping a state's foreign policy and, as a result, have a significant effect on the outcome of those related events. However, much less research has focused on the effect that leaders have on the origins and conduct of civil conflicts. This is particularly important given the sustained scholarly emphasis on understanding the dynamics of civil conflicts following the end of the Cold War (Walter 2017). Despite the increased emphasis on the study of civil conflicts, one particular dynamic that remains understudied is conflict severity (Chaudoin, Peskowitz, and Stanton 2017, 57). The fact that civil conflict severity is understudied is particularly perplexing given that civil conflicts tend to have greater variation in the number of battle-related fatalities both *within* and *between* conflicts than interstate conflicts (Chaudoin, Peskowitz, and Stanton 2017, 57).

While civil conflict severity is understudied relative to the factors that affect the likelihood of civil conflict onset, the majority of the research that does seek to explain the variation in civil conflict severity suffers from shortcomings that are common to most conflict-studies research. These shortcomings are a reliance on the rational actor model of decision-making and the consistent use of independent variables that capture situational or structural dynamics that are related to more severe or less severe civil conflicts. The result is that the theories, and subsequent empirical inferences, dilute or outright assume away individual, leader-specific variables.

For example, some researchers have used economic development as a proxy for a state's capacity to respond to armed rebel groups. Such research links economic development to more severe civil conflict (e.g., Lacina 2006; Chaudoin, Peskowitz, and Stanton 2017). Others have found that shocks to export prices lead to shorter, more severe civil conflicts

(Bazzi and Blattman 2014). Still others have linked the selective distribution of economic goods to an increase in political stability and a decrease in the geographic spread of civil violence (Levi 2006; Gerschweski 2013; DeJuan and Banks 2015). In general, inclusion of variables measuring economic dynamics are meant to indirectly measure things like a state's capacity to respond to rebellion or the incentives that rebel groups have to control a state. Studies of this nature have provided valuable insights into the situational factors that can help one to explain why some civil conflicts are more violent than others.

However, the studies that permeate the literature on civil conflict severity – and conflict studies more broadly – tend to ignore the effects of individual political actors on those political dynamics and the tactical or strategic choices used to respond to armed opposition. Such individual political actors, particularly political elites, have a marked impact on how civil conflicts play out. Therefore, adding variables that capture the individual beliefs of leaders would help in painting a more complete picture explaining the variation in civil conflicts.

This chapter seeks to address two general shortcomings in both the operational code and civil conflict literatures. In the latter, the role of political leaders and their individual beliefs and preferences are almost entirely ignored. In the former, research has focused heavily on the study of foreign policy preferences and behaviors and has, as yet, not turned attention to the dynamics of *intra*state conflict. The goal of this chapter is to provide insights into what operational code analysis can tell scholars about the wide variation in conflict severity both within and between civil conflicts.

This chapter attempts to address the shortcomings in both literatures by including operational code variables in quantitative models alongside more common conflict-studies control variables. Beyond simply including operational code variables in conflict severity models, this chapter will also construct theories that propose the ways that individual beliefs can affect individual preferences, as well as a leader's ability to process incoming information that results from the conflict.

## Literature Review

The intuition that individual leaders play a significant role in shaping foreign policy has found routine empirical support (e.g., Etheredge 1978; Hermann and Hagan 1998; Keller 2005; Schafer and Walker 2006a; Foster and Keller 2014). However, the link between a leader's operational code and the dynamics of a civil conflict is not as clear. Those scholars who have purported to include leaders in their civil models have not actually done so. For example, Kim (2010) asks when leaders will be incentivized to utilize mass killing as a tactic during civil war, and the literature review makes explicit reference to psychological factors that can affect individual preferences and decision-making. However, the theory and research design treated the individual as a constant that simply responds to a situational variable (in this case, popular grievance). The following sections explore some of the structural variables that have been found to affect civil conflict severity.

### Structural Explanations for Civil War Severity

There are few cross-national studies of civil war severity relative to the studies of civil war onset (Chaudoin, Peskowitz, and Stanton 2017, 61). Scholars who emphasize the role of economic factors using cross-national data build their theories on the logic applied to theories of civil war onset. Lacina (2006) argues that economic development may serve proxy for a state's capacity to develop strong counter-insurgency abilities and thus be related to a more severe civil war. Instead, she finds that state capacity is unrelated to the severity of civil wars (Lacina 2006, 287). Rather, she finds that democratic regimes are related to less severe civil wars, while foreign assistance (military or economic) to either rebels or the state results in more severe civil wars (Lacina 2006, 287).

Instead of focusing on narrow definitions of economic growth, Bazzi and Blattman (2014) explore the effect of export price shocks on civil war severity. They find that export price shocks are unrelated to the emergence new civil wars, but steadily rising export prices lead to shorter and less severe civil wars (2014). This finding indicates support for the argument that a strengthening economy is often associated with the strengthening of counter-insurgency capabilities of a state[1]. Moreover, the findings challenge the assumption that an increased desire to take control of an economically growing state should make civil wars more severe (Bazzi and Blattman 2014). Similarly, using instrumental variables for a variety of indicators of economic development, Chaudoin, Peskowitz, and Stanton (2017) find that economic growth is negatively related to both the duration and severity of civil wars.

Others have explored factors other than economic growth when trying to explain variance in civil war violence. De Juan and Banks (2015) consider how the selective allocations in public goods can influence political violence during civil war. They argue that, when the allocation of electricity is selectively distributed, there was increased political violence in certain subdistricts during the Syrian civil war (De Juan and Banks 2015). Their theory states that an authoritarian government facing dissatisfaction from the broader population cannot rely on repression alone; rather, they need to allocate certain public goods to loyal sectors of the population to encourage compliance (De Juan and Banks 2015, 93–94). Using satellite data and geospatial methods, De Juan and Banks find that subdistricts in Syria that experienced positive relative and absolute changes in nighttime light distribution were less likely to experience political violence during the first 18 months of the Syrian conflict. This provides unique empirical support for the broader theory that the selective distribution of goods contributes to political stability (e.g., Levi 2006; Gerschweski 2013).

### Ethnicity and Civil War Severity

While most research finds that ethnic divisions have a limited effect on civil war onset (Fearon and Laitin 2003), scholars of civil war severity have argued that the ethnic makeup of a country experiencing civil war can play a meaningful role in explaining the level of civil violence (Costalli and Moro 2012). Scholars who argue that civil war severity can be informed by the division of ethnic power approach the research by focusing on subnational units of analysis (Slack and Doyon 2001; Costalli and Moro 2012). Investigating the variance in violence between municipalities during the Bosnian civil war, Costalli and Moro (2012) argue that the balance of ethnic groups within a municipality can explain the level of violence observed in them. They find that when there is a high level of ethnic polarization in a municipality, there are higher degrees of observed violence. Additionally, they find that ethnic dominance in a municipality decreases the severity of violence in the municipality (Costalli and Moro 2012, 807–809).

Other scholars have investigated how the makeup of governing coalitions influences the severity of ongoing civil conflicts. Heger and Salehyan (2007) argue that the size of a governing coalition can help one to explain some of the observed variance in conflict severity. They argue that countries with larger governing coalitions – especially democratic ones – should be much more constrained in the methods that they use to fight an armed domestic opponent. When using the ethnic affiliation of heads of state as a proxy for coalition size, the evidence suggests that smaller ruling coalitions present fewer constraints for leaders, thus leading to more severe civil conflicts (Heger and Salehyan 2007).

As with the study of civil war onset, there is a strong reliance on using structural proxy variables to explain variance in civil war severity. However, there is ample room for the inclusion of leadership psychology in the study of civil war severity. Once a civil war has begun, the head of state exercises a great deal of control over the strategies and tactics the state uses to conduct the war. The number of battle-deaths that occur during a civil war can be directly informed by these strategic choices made by these heads of state. Moreover, there should be a great deal of variation in relevant psychological characteristics of leaders in civil wars. As discussed in Chapter 1, there is evidence that the psychological characteristics of leaders can affect their decisions to rely on violence as a policy tool, but there is a lack of such research attempting to explain civil conflict severity.

## Leaders and Severity of Civil Conflicts

The most basic starting point for any theory arguing that political executives can influence the conduct of civil conflicts is political leaders matter. While foreign policy outcomes are easier to link directly to individual political executives, the link is not as clear in the arena of domestic security issues. In autocratic societies, the task of linking individuals to domestic policy outcomes is slightly easier, as these leaders face fewer checks on their exercise of power. While more checks exist in democratic societies, officials like presidents and prime ministers still exert a great deal of influence in domestic policy. This is particularly true in the area of security policy. Therefore, it is prudent to include certain factors about leaders in models of civil conflict severity.

In addition to establishing that leaders are important for understanding the variation of civil conflict severity, it is important to highlight that it is unlikely that two different leaders would respond to the same situation in the same way. For example, there is some conflict studies research that purports to include leaders and their individual motivations in their models (e.g., Kim 2010). However, such research often anchors theories about leaders' willingness to use violence in the rational actor model of decision-making. At the most basic level, the rational actor model of decision-making assumes that individuals will seek out as much information about a given situation as possible and use that information to calculate the potential costs and benefits of a potential course of action. In the end, these calculations will conclude with the decision-maker maximizing benefits and minimizing costs.

Scholars of economics, psychology, and political science have noted that such assumptions may not accurately reflect the cognitive limitations that most individuals bring to the decision-making process (see Simon 1972). These limitations are even more evident during periods of great uncertainty and stress (Greenstein 1969). There are few situations that create greater uncertainty than the instability of civil war. Therefore, the assumption that individuals – regardless of individual idiosyncrasies – process information and make calculations in the same way seems fundamentally flawed. Therefore, a more evolved theory of decision-making should include variables that capture the heterogeneity of leader beliefs, preferences, and/or experiences.

This theory focuses on how a leader's beliefs about others in the political universe, as well as beliefs about how he or she should exercise power in that political universe, affect policy choices during civil conflicts. In the universe of policy choices available to leaders during a civil conflict, most can range between policies that escalate and those that deescalate conflict. For example, when faced with domestic opposition, a leader can choose to allow officials closer to the unrest (such as local law enforcement) to respond to the unrest, or he or she can delegate law enforcement or law enforcement support to a national military. In this hypothetical, the latter is more likely to escalate the severity of a conflict than the former. The policy that the national leader advocates is not only the result of information from the conflict or political constraints, but also the result of his or her individual beliefs.

Operational code analysis provides two general categories of beliefs that can affect policy preferences and resultant outcomes. The first category is philosophical beliefs; these are beliefs that the individual self holds about other actors in the political universe. The specific beliefs within this category are understood as the leader's diagnosis of the nature of the actors and the political universe in which they operate (Walker 2011, 136). The second category is instrumental beliefs; these are the ones that a leader holds about himself or herself and the strategies he or she should pursue to achieve political goals (Walker 2011, 136–137). This section will consider certain individual beliefs from each category and derive hypotheses for each to highlight how they may affect the severity of civil conflict.

### *Philosophical Beliefs and Conflict Severity*

Many of the beliefs that leaders hold about the nature of the political universe are potentially instructive for understanding variation in civil conflict severity. The first philosophical belief (P-1) relates to whether or not the leader believes that the fundamental nature of the political universe is one of conflict or cooperation. This belief also captures how a leader perceives the fundamental nature of his or her political opponents (Walker, Schafer, and Young 2005, 218). Individuals who believe that the fundamental nature of the political universe is one of conflict are far less likely to believe that their opponents have cooperative aims. In the context of civil war, this should result in political leaders discounting signs that the opponent would prefer a nonviolent resolution or a lessening of overall hostility. As a result, such leaders should tend to prefer policies that are conflictual to those who are cooperative when responding to domestic unrest and should implement such policies, thereby increasing the severity of civil conflict. Such logic yields the first hypothesis:

> *H1:* Leaders who believe the political universe is one of cooperation will preside over less severe civil conflicts.

The second philosophical belief (P-2) is also potentially relevant for understanding civil conflict severity. P-2 captures whether a leader is optimistic or pessimistic about achieving his or her political goals. In a robust portion of the interstate war literature, mutual optimism is often associated with miscalculation leading to the onset of war (Morrow 1985; Werner 1998; Wagner 2000; Wittman 2001). While this particular approach to optimism and conflict decision-making is generally limited to *ex ante* conflict bargaining, the logic is also applicable to intra-conflict decision-making. Just as leaders need to process information before a conflict begins, leaders need to process information that is generated by that conflict. However, the way the information generated by the conflict is interpreted and processed can be influenced by a leader's optimism or pessimism.

Leaders vary in their degree of baseline optimism or pessimism and, therefore, are likely to respond to information differently. While greater degrees of optimism can make a leader more likely to start a conflict, greater degrees of optimism will likely make a civil conflict *less* severe. Optimistic leaders inherently believe that they are going to achieve their political goals. This implies that such leaders should be better suited to weather setbacks on the battlefield and meet those setbacks with strategic and tactical flexibility. Rather than becoming frustrated in the face of potentially negative battlefield information, the optimistic leader is more likely to see such information as an opportunity to learn and change strategy. Put another way, optimistic leaders are undaunted by setbacks. Contrarily, pessimistic leaders are more susceptible to respond to set-backs with aggression because they see such developments as a confirmation of their negative outlook about the likelihood of achieving political goals. Therefore, pessimistic leaders are more likely to become frustrated at this confirmation and respond aggressively.

> *H2:* A more optimistic leader will preside over a less severe civil conflict.

The final philosophical belief is a leader's belief in about the amount of control he or she can have over historical development (P-4). This belief is similar to a leader's belief in his or her ability to control events in the Leadership Trait Analysis framework. Leaders who have a higher belief in their ability to control events tend to be impulsive and willing to challenge perceived or actual constraints (Hermann 2005). Therefore, any perceived constraints of norms prohibiting violent politics may be more easily challenged. However, belief in ability to control events may also decrease the severity of civil war. When a leader has a weak belief in his or her ability to control events, he or she may become frustrated and desperate when choosing tactics. This may lead them to choose more aggressive and possibly foolish tactics in response to armed opposition. Whether or not the tactics are "successful," a frustration-driven overre-action may result in a greater number of battle-deaths and, therefore, a more severe civil war. This leads to two rival hypotheses.

> *H3a:* A leader's belief in ability to control events should be negatively related to civil war severity.
> *H3b:* A leader's belief in ability to control events should be positively related to civil war severity.

## *Instrumental Beliefs and Civil Conflict Severity*

The key instrumental variable of interest to the understanding of civil conflict severity is a leader's belief regarding the most effective strategy for achieving his or her political goals (I-1). Recall that instrumental beliefs are an individual's beliefs about how and when he or she should exercise power and achieve political goals (Walker 2011). This particular belief is most intuitively linked to the way a leader opts to respond to and generally conduct civil conflicts. If a leader believes that cooperation is a more effective strategy for achieving his or her political goals, he or she is more likely to use more cooperative tactics to resolve the conflict such as engaging in negotiation rather than committing more military forces. Conversely, a leader who believes that conflictual tactics are more effective for achieving their goals is likely to see negotiation as futile and commit to a strategy that places greater emphasis on the use of the armed forces of the state to respond to armed domestic opposition.

*H4:* A leader who believes that cooperative tactics are more effective for achieving political goals will preside over less severe civil conflicts.

## Research Design

### *Sampling Criteria and Unit of Analysis*

Because the dependent variable – discussed in greater detail below – is the severity of a civil war, the appropriate unit of analysis is the civil conflict-year. This is appropriate because severity is often measured using annual battle-deaths and those can only occur *during* a civil conflict. Therefore, including non-civil conflict-years within the data set would create far too many false negatives. A state is considered to be experiencing a civil war in any year that there is contestation between the government and some internal group in which there are more than 25 battle-related deaths per year (Gleditsch et al. 2002). The baseline population is all civil conflict-years worldwide from 1989 to 2015. This creates a population of 615 civil conflict-years. However, the nature of my key-independent variables greatly limits this sample.

To generate scores for the psychological characteristics of interest, I rely on open-source speech transcripts of world leaders. Furthermore, to generate accurate scores for world leaders, I have to code 4000–5000 spoken words. This limits the sample size to 52 potential civil conflict-years. Finally, missing data points on certain economic control variables results in a final *N* of 33 civil conflict-years. Despite the smaller sample size, my sample looks similar to the population in terms of economic development. My sample has a slightly higher average GDP per capita (Mean: 8.46, SD: 1.63) than the population (Mean: 6.43, SD: 2.15).

*Variables, Sources, and Procedures*

The dependent variable for this chapter is the severity of a civil war. Severity is measured as the number of total battle-deaths during an active conflict-year. These battle-death counts are generated by the Uppsala Conflict Data Program (UCDP) Battle-Related Deaths Dataset (Allansson and Croicu 2017). I utilize the "best" battle-death estimate provided in the data set instead of the high or low estimates. My sample has an annual battle-death range between 26 and 4755. These numbers capture the total number of battle-deaths experienced by both actors in the civil conflict-year.

The specific process of the Verbs in Context System is discussed in detail in elsewhere (Schafer and Walker 2006b); therefore, I will limit my discussion of the operational code variables to their numerical ranges and what they imply. P-1 measures whether a leader believes that the political universe and the actors in it are inherently conflictual or cooperative. The theoretical range for this variable is −1 (indicating that the leader believes the political universe is extremely hostile) to +1 (indicating that the leader believes that the political universe is extremely friendly) (Walker, Schafer, and Young 2005, 227). In my sample, the realized range is 0–0.8.

P-2 measures a leader's optimism or pessimism about the likelihood of achieving his or her eventual political goals. Similar to P-1, P-2 can theoretically range from −1 (indicating that a leader is extremely pessimistic about the likelihood of achieving his or her goals) to +1 (indicating that a leader is extremely optimistic about the likelihood of achieving his or her goals) (Walker, Schafer, and Young 2005, 227). The range of my sample for P-2 is −0.11 to 0.51. P-4 is a measure of how much influence a leader believes he or she can have over the development of historical events. This variable theoretically ranges from 0 (indicating that a leader believes that he or she has very little control) to 1 (indicating that he or she believes that they have a high degree of control). My sample data range from 0.06 to 0.36. Finally, I-1 measures the degree to which a leader believes that he or she should use cooperative tactics or conflictual tactics to achieve political goals. Like P-1 and P-2, I-1 can range between −1 (indicating a belief that conflict is the most effective strategy for achieving political goals) and +1 (indicating a belief that cooperation is the most effective strategy for achieving political goals). The range for I-1 in my sample is 0.07 and 0.85.

*Control Variables*

To avoid omitting potentially influential political and economic factors that influence civil conflict severity, I include a variety of control variables that capture these factors. The first economic indicator of potential interest is a state's GDP growth from the previous year. I utilize a logged version of GDP growth – measured in 2005 constant US dollars – to control for the possibility that the severity of a civil war is informed by the amount of economic growth a state experienced. Additionally, I control for GDP per capita (in constant US dollars). This variable is associated with two possible outcomes. Some research indicates that GDP per capita serves as a proxy for state capacity and an incentive for rebels to more vigorously pursue control of the state, thereby increasing civil conflict severity (i.e., Fearon and Laitin 2003; Bazzi and Blattman 2014).

Alternatively, others have argued that a stronger economy results in less severe civil conflicts. The predominant argument for this assertion is that an economically growing and well-off state creates incentives for individuals to pursue economic opportunities other than rebelling against the state (Lacina 2006). Additionally, I control for a state's dependence on fuel exports (as a percentage of total merchandise exports) in a given year. A state that is more dependent on fuel exports should experience more severe civil conflicts, because there is greater incentive, for both the opposition and the government, to seek to acquire or to protect the available rents generated by these exports (Fearon and Laitin 2003; Bazzi and Blattman 2014).

Finally, I include three controls meant to capture societal and regime dynamics that may be relevant to civil conflict severity. I control for one demographic factor and one key political variable. I control for a state's (logged) population in a given year. These data are provided by the World Bank. I expect population to be positively related to civil conflict severity. Additionally, I generate a binary indicator for the presence or absence of a democratic government. To generate this measure, I utilize the Polity IV score (Marshall and Jaggers 2016) for each state and code any state with a score of 6 or higher as a democracy; all other states are coded as non-democracies. I expect democracy to be negatively related to civil war severity.

I also include a binary control variable that captures whether or not a country is a personalist dictatorship. Interstate conflict literature finds that pairs of states where at least one country is a personalist dictatorship are more likely to experience a conflict (Weeks 2008). This finding is driven by the belief that these specific types of dictators face fewer constraints on their power and are less vulnerable to domestic reprisals for failure (Weeks 2008). In the context of civil conflicts, I expect this theorized lack of constraint to increase the severity of civil conflict in a given country.

### Statistical Methods

Because the dependent variable is a count of the number of battle-deaths in a given year, the appropriate statistical technique is some version of nonlinear maximum likelihood method. For count variables, there are generally two principal techniques used: a poisson regression or a negative binomial regression. In order to determine which method is appropriate, one has to determine whether or not the dependent variable exhibits signs of over-dispersion. If the variable does not show signs of this (i.e., mean and variance are roughly equal), then the poisson regression is appropriate. However, the dependent variable in this sample is clearly over-dispersed (mean: 917.13, variance: 1262,074). Therefore, this model will use a panel-correct negative binomial regression with a random effects estimator to capture any potential, unit-specific heterogeneity.

## Findings

### Statistical Analysis

Table 5.1 presents the findings of the statistical tests of the hypotheses. Model 1 is a fully specified model, which includes all independent and control variables without regard to any potential multicollinearity. In the

*Table 5.1* Statistical Results

| Variables | Constant | | |
| --- | --- | --- | --- |
| | *Model 1* | *Model 2* | *Model 3* |
| P-1 | −11.53** | −1.728* | |
| | (3.542) | (0.871) | |
| P-2 | 14.17** | | −1.395 |
| | (5.250) | | (1.584) |
| P-4 | 4.330* | 3.183 | 1.856 |
| | (1.881) | (2.708) | (3.195) |
| I-1 | −0.988 | −2.198** | −2.289* |
| | (0.680) | (0.832) | (1.111) |
| Democracy$_{(t-1)}$ | 1.164 | 1.201 | 1.097 |
| | (1.077) | (0.881) | (0.872) |
| GDP growth$_{(\log, t-1)}$ | −0.270+ | −0.357+ | −0.320 |
| | (0.152) | (0.203) | (0.241) |
| Personalist dictatorship$_{(t-1)}$ | −14.95* | −7.809 | −6.955 |
| | (6.525) | (5.821) | (6.073) |
| Population$_{(\log, t-1)}$ | 0.442+ | 0.0837 | −0.0439 |
| | (0.266) | (0.225) | (0.240) |
| GDP per capita$_{(\log, t-1)}$ | −1.101** | −0.548* | −0.365 |
| | (0.357) | (0.279) | (0.306) |
| Fuel exports$_{(t-1)}$ | 0.286* | 0.171 | 0.158 |
| | (0.124) | (0.117) | (0.121) |
| Constant | 3.322 | 4.271 | 4.778 |
| | (3.042) | (2.961) | (3.021) |
| Observations | 33 | 33 | 33 |
| Number of countries | 8 | 8 | 8 |

Standard errors in parentheses.

*** p < 0.001, ** p < 0.01, * p < 0.05, + p < 0.10

first model, all three philosophical variables are statistically significant. A leader who believes that the political universe is more cooperative (P-1) will preside over a less severe civil conflict. Additionally, P-2 is statistically significant; however, the relationship is contrary to hypothesis two. In Model 1, a more optimistic leader presides over more severe civil conflicts than a pessimistic one. Inferences from this result should be derived carefully, however. P-1 and P-2 are highly collinear variables ($r = 0.94$); this means that both the significance and direction of the relationship should not be viewed as reliable without additional models. Model 1 also indicates that a leader who believes that individuals can shape historical events (P-4) is more likely to preside over more violent civil conflicts. However, in Model 1, a leader's belief about which strategy is most effective for achieving political goals is not statistically related to civil conflict severity. Nevertheless, the sign of the coefficient is consistent with hypothesis four.

Models 2 and 3 address the collinearity between P-1 and P-2. In Model 2, P-1 is statistically significant in the expected direction. Leaders who believe that the political universe is more cooperative than conflictual will preside over less violent civil conflicts. However, P-4 is not statistically related to civil conflict severity in Model 2, though the coefficient remains positive. With the multicollinearity addressed, Model 2 shows that I-1 is statistically significant and negatively related to conflict severity as hypothesized. This means that a leader who believes cooperation is the best method for achieving political goals will preside over less violent civil conflicts. Model 3 removes P-1 and replaces it with P-2. Though P-2 is not statistically significant in Model 3, the sign is in the expected direction, unlike in the full model with the collinearity problem. This indicates that more optimistic leaders may pursue policies that are less conflictual than more pessimistic leaders, but our confidence in this pattern is low. Finally, in Model 3, I-1 remains statistically significant and negatively related to civil conflict severity: leaders who believe in the utility of more cooperative policies preside over civil conflicts that are less severe.

In all three models, the effect of the control variables is somewhat mixed. The two economic variables (growth and GDP per capita) have the same sign in all three models and are significant or approach significance more often than not: the better the economic conditions, the lower the level of severity in the civil conflict. This is consistent with the argument that positive economic conditions disincentivize taking part in armed rebellion (Lacina 2006). In Model 1, personalist dictatorships significantly decrease civil conflict severity. While the variable is not significant in Models 2 and 3, the coefficient remains negative. This result is contrary to the theoretical expectation derived from the international conflict literature (Weeks 2008). This may be the result of personalist dictatorships having a stronger hold on the domestic political situation, thus not allowing the conflict to over-escalate. Alternatively, it could also result from a general lack of diverse political constituencies associated with personalist dictatorships. When there are fewer political actors to please, the incentive to demonstrate resolve and respond forcefully to armed challengers may be lower. Finally, in Model 1, fuel exports and population are significantly related to more severe civil conflicts as anticipated.

In sum, the statistical analysis provides interesting and valuable findings that can inform the way that scholars think about the factors that influence civil conflict severity. A leader's beliefs about the nature of the political universe (P-1) and about the appropriate strategy for achieving political goals (I-1) are significantly related to civil conflict severity. The coefficients are consistent with the hypotheses. Leaders who believe that the political universe is inherently one of cooperation (P-1) will preside over less severe civil conflicts. Additionally, leaders who think their best strategy for achieving political goals (I-1) is a cooperative one will preside over less severe civil conflicts. However, a leader's optimism about the likelihood of achieving political goals (P-2) and belief about his or her ability to shape historical events (P-4) are not consistently related to civil conflict severity. Nevertheless, the consistency of the relationship between P-1, I-1, and conflict severity provides valuable information about the effect that individual leaders can have on the conduct of civil conflicts.

### The Sri Lankan Civil War in 1995

In this section, I will evaluate the case of a single conflict and the way that a political leader shaped the dynamics of that conflict. The most violent civil conflict-year in my sample is 1995 in Sri Lanka. This is the same year that Chandrika Kumaratunga came to office as president. In order to illustrate the process of the relationship between leader beliefs and civil war severity, I will briefly review how Sri Lankan President Chandrika Kumaratunga responded to the violence of the civil conflict in her country. Some of the components of her operational code beliefs are statistically significantly more cooperative than average in this study, and, although she inherited a highly violent civil conflict, she led her country consistently and effectively in the direction of conflict de-escalation.

From independence until the 1970s, politicians affiliated with the Tamil minority group routinely found themselves excluded from the political decision-making process. As a result, multiple governments implemented policies that left the Tamil minority feeling excluded from education and employment opportunities. By 1976, moderate Tamil politicians had begun to lose hope that they would ever achieve the relative autonomy of a federal system using traditional channels. In 1983, the LTTE took up the banner of the Tamil cause and launched an armed rebellion against the state (Bullion 2005). Eleven years later, Chandrika Kumaratunga won a landslide election on a campaign of pursuing a peaceful resolution of the civil conflict, as well as accountability for the abuses of previous governments (Schaffer 1995; Human Rights Watch 1996).

At the beginning of her term in 1995, Kumaratunga's government announced that they had reached a ceasefire with the LTTE. This ceasefire was short-lived, as the LTTE continued to launch attacks on the government and civilians. Despite the ongoing development of a lasting peace plan, it was not the LTTE alone violating the ceasefire. The annual country report of the Human Rights Watch in 1996 noted that there continued to be reports of disappearances, extrajudicial executions, and torture conducted by the Sri Lankan security forces. Members of the security forces were also implicated in death-squad like incidents that targeted young Tamil individuals around the capitol city (Human Rights Watch 1996).

Moreover, as the ceasefire broke down, Kumaratunga came to rely more and more on the military for advice on how to respond to the LTTE. Generally, while both sides of the conflict were at least paying lip-service to the ceasefire process, both sides continued to engage in atrocities that were the hallmark of the war. While the first full-year of her term in office was, by far, the most violent of my sample, the overall trajectory of her presidency resulted in a notable decrease in the year-to-year severity of the Sri Lankan conflict. Therefore, comparing some aspects of her operational code to other leaders in the sample is worthwhile.

Chandrika Kumaratunga's operational code has a few notable features. In 1995, she believed that the political universe was perhaps somewhat conflictual, though she does not vary significantly from the sample mean ($z$-score: $-0.71242$). However, she believed that cooperation was the most effective strategy for achieving her political goals, scoring significantly above the sample mean ($z$-score: $1.54275$). She was also optimistic about the likelihood of achieving her political goals ($z$-score: $1.64717$) and was slightly below the sample mean on her belief that individuals can shape historical outcomes ($z$-score: $-0.56138$).

While no one leader can perfectly embody the general quantitative findings of cross-sectional time-series data, Kumaratunga's behavior and resultant policy during her first year in office appear generally consistent with some of the expectations derived from the theory. First, her government did actively pursue negotiated settlement to the conflict. The weak ceasefire began in January 1995, and by August the government unveiled a peace proposal that included a devolution of power to special regional councils that were determined partially along ethnic lines (Human Rights Watch 1996). This was a rather sizeable concession, given that every government since independence had generally refused any sort of regional autonomy for the Tamil minority (Wayland 2004). Additionally, the government she led actively pursued policies that sought to address and curb previous government human rights abuses, albeit with mixed success (Human Rights Watch 1996).

While the civil conflict continued throughout her term in office, President Kumaratunga is the only Sri Lankan President who presided over 2 (nonconsecutive) years of relative peace. From 2002 until the last year of her presidency, the intensity of the Sri Lankan civil conflict plummeted. In 2002 and 2004, the total number of battle-related deaths fell below the 25-death threshold required by UCDP/ACD (Armed Conflict Dataset) to be considered an active conflict. In 2003, there were only 29 total deaths and in 2005 there were 88. In all, the case of President Kumaratunga captures the principal challenge of studying leadership in civil conflict: civil wars are messy conflicts. Civil conflicts have a large number of actors, and those ones play roles by different rules than most states who engage in conflicts with other states. Cross-national time-series data are good for identifying patterns that can generally explain variation in civil conflict severity, but each conflict has its own unique dynamics. Additionally, these dynamics transcend leadership, economic structure, and regime type. These dynamics can include lasting social anger and other grievances generated by the war itself.

Leadership can be an important factor for navigating resolutions to these problems, but leadership cannot necessarily implement these policies or build the good faith necessary just by coming to office with the promise of pursuing a different approach to civil conflict. Moreover, in most countries, leaders do not stay in power indefinitely. President Kumaratunga, over the totality of her tenure, did preside over a notable decrease in the severity of the civil conflict. However, when her term ended, she was replaced by someone who abandoned any political process and brought an end to the Sri Lankan conflict through the complete military annihilation of the LTTE in 2009.

## Conclusions and Directions for Future Research

This chapter began with a simple question: how can leaders influence the severity of civil conflicts? Operational code analysis and other at-a-distance approaches to the study of leadership have provided valuable insights into the dynamics of foreign policy decision-making and other aspects of leadership style. However, they had not previously entered the domain of civil conflict dynamics. Conversely, scholars who do conduct research of civil conflict dynamics assume away the effect of political leadership. By assuming that all leaders will follow a mechanical decision-making process necessarily implies that every leader will respond the same way in a given situation. Intuitively, most people know that this is not true.

Using cross-sectional time-series data, I demonstrate that variables that capture an individual leader's beliefs can result in more or less severe civil conflicts. The findings of the quantitative model indicate that leaders who believe that the political universe and the actors in it are more cooperative than conflictual will preside over less violent civil conflicts in a given year. Additionally, a leader who believes that individuals can shape the path of historical events is likely to preside over more violent conflicts. However, this finding is sensitive to model specification. In all, a leader's belief about the "other" is consistently related to the severity of civil conflict, even when controlling for important economic and regime dynamics identified by the civil conflict severity literature. Additionally, a leader's belief about the "self" and the most appropriate strategy to achieve political goals is significantly related to civil conflict severity. Regardless of the presence of economic and situational controls, a leader who believes that cooperation is a more effective strategy for achieving political goals will preside over a less violent civil conflict.

The case analysis of President Chandrika Kumaratunga provides some valuable insights into the potential value and potential challenges of including leader-specific variables in civil conflict severity models. The case helps one to demonstrate that President Kumaratunga did make a meaningful difference in terms of the severity of the civil conflict during her term in office. Nevertheless, she faced many dynamic obstacles that made the achievement of her political solution to the conflict very, very difficult to achieve. These challenges provide useful prescriptions for future research into the relationship between leadership and civil conflict dynamics.

First, the Sri Lanka case highlights that focusing on state leaders alone in civil conflict research omits the important role of the opposition leadership. It can be difficult to find reliable speech sources for the leadership of armed opposition groups like the LTTE. Armed rebellion and the associated tactics often lead the outside world to be wary of the legitimacy of such groups. Also, the fact that rebel groups are acting outside the bounds of a state's law makes it difficult to safely and reliably host websites that would grant open-source outlets. Even if they could, the true accuracy of "verbatim" materials should be suspect to scholars seeking to accurately measure key psychological characteristics. In Sri Lanka, despite general good faith efforts at negotiation, the leader of the LTTE continued to wage war against the government and Sinhalese civilians in Sri Lanka. Therefore, the leadership of the LTTE is clearly important in explaining conflict severity.

Another vein of future research is the role of time in explaining variation in civil conflict severity. While her first year in office was one of the most violent in the civil conflict, President Kumaratunga's term ended on much more peaceful note. Clearly, leadership can have a generalizable effect on civil conflict severity, but it is less clear whether the effect is immediate, or if there is a lag period. If there is a lag period, the next step would be to identify just how long that lag period is. These factors can significantly influence the development and trajectory of a civil conflict, as well as the scholarly understanding of such dynamics.

Overall, this chapter represents a significant step forward in the study of both political leadership and civil conflict. Leaders can, and do, shape the trajectory of civil violence, and the findings of this chapter provide some insights into how. These findings also identify the potential limitations of including political leadership in models of civil conflict dynamics. Most importantly, however, these findings provide further justification for the continued application of leadership to the study of civil conflicts. Civil conflicts can ravage multiple aspects of the lives of the individuals who experience them, and expanding our understanding of their dynamics is important to understanding how they can finally end. Adding leadership to that understanding is an essential next step in expanding just such understanding.

## Note

1. However, the counter-insurgency techniques of a state may not be adequately measured by economic development alone. Others have pointed out that the introduction of private military and security companies can greatly increase the counter-insurgency capabilities of a weak state and lead to a more severe civil war (Petersohn 2017).

## References

Allansson, M., M. Croicu. 2017. UCDP battle-related deaths dataset codebook. Uppsala Conflict Data Program.

Bazzi, S., C. Blattman. 2014. Economic shocks and conflict: Evidence from commodity prices. *American Economics Journal: Macroeconomics* 6: 1–38.

Bullion, A. 2005. Civil society and the peace process in Sri Lanka. *Civil Wars* 7: 117–119.

Chaudoin, S., Z. Peskowitz, C. Stanton. 2017. Beyond zeroes and ones: The intensity and duration of civil conflict. *Journal of Conflict Resolution* 61: 56–83.

Costalli, S., F. N. Moro. 2012. Ethnicity and strategy in the Bosnian civil war: Explanations for the severity of violence in Bosnian municipalities. *Journal of Peace Research* 49: 801–815.

De Juan, A., A. Banks. 2015. The Ba'athist blackout? Selective good provision and political violence in the Syrian civil war. *Journal of Peace Research* 52: 91–104.

Etheredge, L. 1978. *A world of men: The private sources of American foreign policy.* Cambridge, MA: The MIT University Press.

Fearon, J. D., D. L. Laitin. 2003. Ethnicity, insurgency, and civil war. *American Political Science Review* 97: 75–90.

Foster, D. M., J. W. Keller. 2014. Leaders' cognitive complexity, distrust, and the diversionary use of force. *Foreign Policy Analysis* 10: 205–223.

Greenstein, F. I. 1969. *Personality and politics: Problems of evidence, inference, and conceptualization.* Princeton, NJ: Princeton University Press.

Gledisch, N. P., P. Wallenstein, M. Eriksson, M. Sollenberg, and H. Strand. 2002. Armed conflict, 1946-2001: A new data set. Journal of Peace Research 39: 615–637.

Heger, L., I. Salehyan. 2007. Ruthless rulers: Coalition size and the severity of civil conflict. *International Studies Quarterly* 51: 385–403.

Hermann, M. G., J. Hagan. 1998. International decision-making: Leadership matters. *Foreign Policy* 110: 124–137.

Hermann, M. G. 2005. Assessing leadership style: Trait analysis. In *The psychological assessment of political leaders*, ed. J. M. Post, 178–214. Ann Arbor, MI: University of Michigan Press.

Human Rights Watch. 1996. Annual report. Sri Lanka: Human Rights Watch.

Keller, J. W. 2005. Leadership style, regime type, and foreign policy crisis behavior: A contingent monadic peace? *International Studies Quarterly* 49: 205–231.

Kim, D. 2010. What makes state leaders brutal? Examining grievances and mass killing during civil war. *Civil Wars* 12: 237–260.

Lacina, B. 2006. Explaining the severity of civil war. *Journal of Conflict Resolution* 50: 276–289.

Levi, M. 2006. Why we need a new theory of government. *Perspectives on Politics* 4: 5–19.

Marshall, M. G. T. R., K. Jaggers. 2016. Polity IV project: Political regime characteristics and transitions, 1800-2016 data set users' manual. Center for Systemic Peace.

Morrow, J. D. 1985. Capabilities, uncertainty, and resolve: A limited information model of crisis bargaining. *American Journal of Political Science* 33: 941–972.

Petersohn, U. 2017. Private military security companies (PMSCs), military effectiveness, and conflict severity in weak states, 1990-2007. Journal of Conflict Resolution 61: 1046–1072.

Schafer, M., S. G. Walker. 2006a. Democratic leaders and the democratic peace: The operational codes of Tony Blair and Bill Clinton. *International Studies Quarterly* 50: 561–583.

Schafer, M., S. G. Walker. Eds. 2006b. *Beliefs and leadership in world politics: Methods and applications of operational code analysis.* New York, NY: Palgrave.

Schaffer, H. 1995. The Sri Lankan elections of 1994. *Asian Survey* 35: 409–425.

Simon, H. 1972. Theories of bounded rationality. In *Decision and organization*, eds. C. B. McGuire, R. Radner, 161–176. Amsterdam: North-Holland Publishing.

Slack, A., R. Doyon. 2001. Population dynamics and susceptibility for ethnic conflict: The case of Bosnia and Herzegovina. *Journal of Peace Research* 38: 139–161.

Wagner, R. H. 2000. Bargaining and war. *American Journal of Political Science* 44: 469–484.

Walker, S. G. 2011. Anticipating attacks from the operational codes of terrorist groups. *Dynamics of Asymmetric Conflict* 4: 135–143.

Walker, S. G., M. Schafer, M. Young. 2005. Profiling the operational codes of political leaders. In *The psychological assessment of political leaders*, ed. J. M. Post, 215–245. Ann Arbor, MI: University of Michigan Press.

Walter, B. F. 2017. The new civil wars. *Annual Review of Political Science* 20: 469–486.

Wayland, S. 2004. Ethnonationalist networks and transnational opportunities: The Sri Lankan Tamil diaspora. Review of Iinternational Studies 30: 405–426.

Weeks, J. 2008. Autocratic audience costs: Regime type and signaling resolve. *International Organization* 62: 35–64.

Werner, S. 1998. Negotiating the terms of settlement: War aims and bargaining leverage. *Journal of Conflict Resolution* 42: 321–343.

Wittman, D. 2001. *War or peace.* Typescript. University of California–Santa Cruz.

Winter, D. 1973. The Power Motive. New York: The Free Press.

# 6 Policy Documents and the Beliefs of Foreign Policy Decision-Makers

## A Next Step in Operational Code Analysis

*Femke E. Bakker and Niels van Willigen*

## Introduction

As a psychological approach to foreign policy analysis, operational code analysis (OCA) has traditionally focused on individual leaders. In this exploratory study, we aim to expand the scope of OCA to the analysis of foreign policy documents and thus to collective operational codes. Foreign policy documents are considered to be important sources of information for students of international relations and foreign policy analysis. They are either analyzed using qualitative or quantitative content analysis approaches. The objective of scholars executing a content analysis is to discover and test "generalizations about political behavior and policy-making which are revealed in human communications" (Winham 1969, 192; also see e.g., Hermann 2008; Grimmer and Stewart 2013). This comes very close to what analysts try to do with OCA, which is to discover and test generalizations about political behavior and policy-making that are rooted in cognitive belief systems. We argue, therefore, that OCA can enrich quantitative and qualitative content analysis by adding a cognitive dimension to the analysis of foreign policy documents.

OCA was developed to analyze the political belief systems (the operational codes) of individual leaders. The underlying assumption of OCA is that leaders matter and that their beliefs about the world influence decision-making processes and thus (foreign) policies. In particular, when leaders are the predominant decision-makers or the leaders of a decision-making unit (Hermann 2001), it can logically be expected that their beliefs are reflected in the policy documents that are written during their terms in office. However, even when leaders have such influential positions, there are many others involved in the policy-making process.

Knowing whether or not the beliefs of leaders are co-opted by the policy makers, including civil servants implementing the decisions, and understanding how that works can inform us about the cognitive dimension of decision-making processes.

The overall objective of this chapter is to contribute to more complete and better explanations of foreign policy-making by exploring the opportunities and limits of collective OCA. More specifically, we explore the value of applying OCA to foreign policy documents by asking whether the beliefs of decision-makers are reflected in foreign policy documents. By this exploration, we hope to offer some insights into the extent to which US foreign policy papers are affected by the US president. By posing this question, we add OCA as an analytical tool for content analysis of policy documents. Moreover, we also expand the scope of OCA and hence contribute to the substantive progress of OCA as a research program as it is defined in Chapter 1 of this edited volume. OCA has primarily been used on oral materials (speeches, press statements, interviews) with few exceptions (Marfleet 2000; Walker and Schafer 2000; Yang, Keller, and Molnar 2018). Policy papers are written to be read, not spoken. Studying these documents with a tool for speech analysis can unearth the opportunities and limitations of such an approach.

To discover the possible value of our argument, we offer a comparative analysis of the operational codes and key foreign policy documents of four US presidents: Bill Clinton (1993–2001), George W. Bush (2001–2009), Barack Obama (2009–2017), and Donald Trump (2017–present). The objective is to discover whether similar patterns exist between the individual operational codes of the US presidents on the one hand and the collective operational codes in their respective foreign policy documents on the other hand. The choice of these four US presidents is motivated by the following reasons.

First, US presidents are chosen because they represent a most likely case for their beliefs to affect policy documents. The foreign policy architecture of the United States allows its presidents to be predominate in the decision-making process (Hermann 2001). The White House has a key role in US foreign policy. However, that does not automatically mean it has a large impact on the content of the foreign policy papers as well. Although important foreign policy decisions are made by the White House, most foreign policy papers are primarily drafted by other decision-makers than the US president. Studying the influence of US presidents' beliefs on their foreign policy papers is therefore a crucial element of our exploration.

Second, already many OCAs of US presidents exist, including Clinton, Bush, and Trump. However, these analyses have not yet been connected to foreign policy documents. This endeavor thus enables us to contribute to already existing knowledge (Schafer and Crichlow 2000; Schafer, Young, and Walker 2002; Robison 2006; Renshon 2008; Dyson 2010;

Walker, Schafer, and Smith 2018) about the foreign policy behavior of US leaders. There is no full OCA of Obama yet, but there do exist limited OCAs and leadership profiles (Walker, Malici, and Schafer 2011; Winter 2011). Our chapter adds to this body of knowledge by not only presenting an original OCA in a traditional way (analyzing speeches, press conferences, or interviews of individual decision-makers), but also by analyzing foreign policy documents and thus presenting a collective OCA.

Lastly, a choice for US presidents is a practical one. We need sufficient data in English in order to use the Verbs in Context System (VICS) to analyze the beliefs in speeches and policy documents. VICS is a quantitative content analysis system that retrieves and analyzes operational codes, based on attributions from sources such as speeches, press conferences and interviews, and other publicly spoken statements. The VICS method analyzes verbs used by a political leader within the context these verbs are used. The coding of the verbs is based on an analysis of the other words in the sentence. The four most recent US presidents are of substantive interest and there is ample verbal material available for both their personal operational codes and their administrations' policy documents.

The remainder of this chapter is structured as follows. The second section of this chapter elaborates on US foreign policy documents. We explain their function in the US foreign policy decision-making process and elaborate on the extent to which they are interrelated. In the third section, we explain what we mean by collective operational codes and how they relate to individual operational codes. The fourth section contains the methodology. As is common in OCA, we use VICS to measure the beliefs – both the individual beliefs in the speeches of the presidents and the collective beliefs in the policy papers. The fifth section presents the results and they are discussed in the sixth section. We end this chapter with a reflection on the limits and opportunities of extending OCA to policy documents and some concluding remarks on how the OCA of foreign policy documents can advance OCA in general.

## US Foreign Policy Documents

OCA assumes that beliefs have an impact on foreign policy-making. Given the traditional grip of US presidents on US foreign policy-making, we expect that there is a large degree of agreement between the beliefs found in the speeches of US presidents and the patterns in the policy documents. The predominant position of the US president in foreign policy-making is assured by the US Constitution, which gives the president the authority and the means to significantly shape foreign policy (Fink 1983; Siniver 2008, 22). As head of state and as commander in chief, for example, the US president executes two key functions in the foreign policy domain. Also, the names that US presidents have given to foreign policy doctrines (e.g., the Monroe Doctrine, the Nixon Doctrine, and the Bush Doctrine) show the dominance of the White House in US foreign policy-making. Moreover, in recent years, the influence of the White House on foreign policy-making has increased; especially at the expense of Congress (Masters 2017).

Whereas the role of the president in US foreign policy-making has been studied extensively, that is not the case with foreign policy documents. Obviously, the documents themselves are used for foreign policy analysis, but reflections on what role these policy documents play in the formulation and implementation of US foreign policy are rare. We aim to address this gap in the literature by making an OCA of a selection of key foreign policy documents. We choose to focus on foreign policy documents that are related to national and international security issues, because, other things equal, the role of the US president in security policy is the largest in the security domain. Including national security documents, such as the National Security Strategy (NSS), is necessary because national and international security are strongly interrelated. That is aptly illustrated by the first sentence of Trump's NSS of 2017: "An America that is safe, prosperous, and free at home is an America with the strength, confidence, and will to lead abroad" (Trump 2017).

Key foreign policy documents are important for defining the objectives and the policy priorities for several years. That being said, international and/or domestic political developments can make key foreign policy documents quickly outdated. The COVID-19 pandemic that erupted in the Spring of 2020 is a case in point; although there is some limited mention of pandemics, none of the selected documents include analyses or policy options to the same extent as were taken as a result of the outbreak of the virus. Despite these and other limits, policy documents are important for identifying, proposing, explaining, and/or legitimizing foreign policy options. Our selection includes four key foreign policy documents: the abovementioned NSS, the Quadrennial Defense Review (QDR, replaced by the National Defense Strategy [NDS] as of 2018), the Nuclear Posture Review (NPR), and the National Strategy for Counterterrorism (NSCT). This is not an exhaustive list, but it does include some of the most important topics of foreign policy to serve this first exploration of the value of applying OCA to policy documents.

The US government releases a large number of foreign policy papers and these vary according to scope and government level. First, the scope of a foreign policy document concerns the width of a paper's content. A broad scope implies that a paper's content applies to many (or all) issues or cases that the paper's *topic* could concern. For example, the NSS covers a broad range of domestic and international security topics relevant to the United States. The NSS can therefore be considered as the overarching policy document with the largest scope. Looking at the most recent NSS (2017), it is a document that formulates a security policy resting on four pillars: protecting the US homeland, promoting American

*Table 6.1* Overview of Policy Documents

| Topic | Paper | Scope Width | Government Level |
|---|---|---|---|
| Security | NSS | Large | White House (NSC) |
| Defense | QDR | Medium | DoD |
| Nuclear strategy | NPR | Small | DoD |
| Terrorism | NSCT | Medium | NSC + "independent" agency (by way of DNI → CIA) |

prosperity, preserving peace through strength, and advancing American influence in the world. Effectively, this comes down to a grand strategy, which not only includes military means but also mobilizes "all the resources of a nation," including political and economic means (Liddell Hart 1967, 336). The QDR is an example of a document with a narrower scope; it describes the military strategy of the United States and does not elaborate so much on civilian aspects of security.

Second, the governmental level denotes where in the executive branch a paper originates from. The policy paper output of the executive branch can be hierarchically ordered. We distinguish five levels, starting with the US president, and subsequently followed by the National Security Council (NSC), secretaries (of State, Defense, Homeland Security, etc.), departments, and finally, agencies that fall under departments. These categories are not entirely clear-cut (for instance, the Joint Chiefs of Staff who are responsible for some papers can be placed both on the departmental level under the Secretary of Defense, but also on the NSC, to which they are advisers), but generally, policy papers can be hierarchically ordered based on these levels. Moreover, the NSS is the only foreign policy document that is directly written under the leadership of the president (through the NSC). With this document, the president communicates his ideas about national security and a grand strategy to the US Congress. Table 6.1 shows an overview of the policy documents included in the analysis.

## Exploring Collective Operational Codes

OCA is used to study individual operational codes, but here we explore to what extent it can be used to study collective operational codes as well. Doing so, we relate to (the rather limited) existing research on collective operational codes. Our research comes closest to the studies of Walker and Schafer (2000), Robison (2006), and Yang, Keller, and Molnar (2018). Yang, Keller, and Molnar analyzed China's national defense white papers that were published between 1998 and 2015. Their aim was to find the "core collective beliefs of three generations of Chinese leadership" (Yang, Keller, and Molnar 2018, 586). They found some important cross generational changes of beliefs in the white papers. Walker and

Schafer (2000) and Robison (2006) studied leader-advisor relations of the Lyndon B. Johnson administration and the George W. Bush administration, respectively. Both studies present a classical OCA by analyzing the speeches of the president on the one hand and the advisory team on the other. Walker and Schafer find some differences and some similarities between the public OCA of Johnson and the OCA of his advisory team in regard to the Vietnam War, making it unclear the extent to which one set of beliefs influenced the other set. In Robison's study, the OCA of Bush and seven of his main advisors are compared. Subsequently, Robison makes a comparative analysis between the president and his advisors and between different groups of advisors (Hawks and Doves).

Our approach differs from Walker and Schafer's, and Robison's analyses in the sense that we take policy documents as the unit of analysis rather than speech materials. But just like all of these three studies, we aim to analyze the operational code of a decision-unit, or "an extensive array of different entities" being involved in foreign policy-making (Hermann 2001, 47). A final study that should be mentioned is the research done by Lazarevska, Sholl, and Young (2006). Using indicators from Leadership Trait Analysis and OCA, they analyzed the difference between the verbal behavior of terrorists and the verbal behavior of non-terrorist political leaders. Thus, they too aimed to get insight into a collective operational code, namely, the "terrorist." Based on the above, we define the collective operational code as the sum of the individual operational codes of the entities that are involved in the decision-making unit. In our study, we not only analyze the collective operational code, but also try to link the collective operational code to the individual US presidents.

Investigating policy documents is not the same as investigating the beliefs of US presidents. After all, the US president is not the only official who is involved in the drafting of the document. The OCA data drawn from a policy document can therefore be better qualified as the beliefs of a decision-unit rather than the personal beliefs of a US president. That makes it interesting to see what the extent of agreement is between the president's beliefs and the decision-unit's beliefs. A high level of agreement would point toward high levels of influence on the process by the US president, whereas a low level of agreement would indicate that policy documents are influenced by a broader set of diffuse inputs.

**Method**

Beliefs are measured through the operational code indices from the VICS and quantitatively measured by the software program Profiler Plus[1] (Levine and Young 2014). For all four presidents, we collected foreign policy documents and speeches on a selection of relevant security topics. Since this is an explorative study, and since there are many policy papers produced, we decided to limit our data collection to four main foreign policy topics: national security, nuclear strategy, terrorism, and defense. Policy papers needed to be valid for at least 2 years and preferably repetitive across administrations. With the exception of the NSS, most of the policy papers were gathered from the Department of Defense (DoD), the NSC, and the Department of Homeland Security (DHS). Some others were collected from military archives.[2] Since we wanted to include policy papers that we could plausibly assume the president had a say in, we decided to limit the selection of papers to those that were no more than one step away from the president. For instance, among the policy papers released by the DoD, we selected only those the Office of the Secretary of Defense had been involved in. Being politically appointed by the president and being one of his important advisors, the Secretary of Defense is institutionally close to the White House. Also, the policy papers we gathered at the DHS were created in close cooperation with the White House and signed by the president.

We ran into some limitations during the collection of relevant policy papers. Several documents are classified and can therefore not be used. The NDS (which replaced the QDR as of 2018), for instance, is unavailable besides a brief executive summary, which was – based on the criteria for text as dictated by the VICS – too short to include. Because of a too low number of transitive verbs, we could neither include the National Military Strategy nor the China Military Posture Review in our selection. In short, the gathered data regarding the four foreign policy topics include all publicly accessible policy papers at the highest governmental levels that meet the methodological criteria of the VICS. More policy papers can be found at lower levels of government (different agencies that fall under DoD, NSC, or DHS). We have deliberately chosen to not use these because the drafters stand further away from the president. The number of policy papers per administration is, due to all reasons mentioned above, limited to a range from 5 (Trump) to 16 (Bush). The speeches were gathered for each president from the duration of their respective administrations, by focusing on speeches that dealt with the same security topics as the policy papers, and which were delivered in the same year the policy papers were published.

## Results

To explore the collected data and detect whether we can find a link between the beliefs of the presidents and the collective beliefs in the policy documents, we conduct three analyses. The first compares, for every president, the level of agreement between the beliefs of the president (measured through speeches) and the beliefs found in the policy papers. The second analysis investigates whether there are any differences in the collective beliefs of the policy papers related to political party affiliation

(Democrat and Republican). Third, we analyze whether there are differences in policy papers created by the four different administrations.

### Analysis 1: Comparative Analysis of Beliefs by US Presidents and Beliefs in Policy Papers

Table 6.2 shows for all four presidents whether there are significant differences in beliefs when measured through speeches (and thus assumed to be the beliefs the president holds) and measured through policy papers. An eyeball comparison of the significant differences leads to two observations. First of all, there are more similarities between the beliefs of the presidents and the collective beliefs underlying the policy papers than there are differences. Overall, it therefore seems to be the case that the policy documents reflect the individual beliefs of the presidents. Second, there are some significant differences between a few of the presidents' beliefs and the collective beliefs found in the policy papers. However, these differences do not show a clear pattern. In other words, there are differences, but it is unclear what they tell us.

There are two notable generalizations that we can identify based on the comparative analysis. First, there is a difference in P4 (the belief in control over historical outcomes). The data show that all the presidents scored significantly higher on P4 than the collective beliefs found in their policy papers. These results indicate that all four presidents felt significantly more in control of historical development than their policy papers indicate. The second generalization concerns P5 and we identify that (with the exception of Clinton) the policy papers assign the influence of chance on political life a significantly higher probability than the presidents show in their speeches. The differences are, on a scale of 0–1, very small. However, the differences are statistically significant and thus indicate that the presidents overall assign a smaller role to chance than their papers show.

The differences in both beliefs can be explained by the differences of the used materials. It has been argued that one of the potential difficulties for studying speeches is that verbal actions by leaders might be led by attempts to create an impression for a more general audience (Tetlock and Manstead 1985, 62–64; Dille 2000, 538). That might be the reason why the personal beliefs of leaders differ partially from those underlying the policy papers, which have been written with the intent to inform rather than to impress and are targeted at a more specific audience, namely, other policy makers. It might thus be that the found differences in P4 and P5 are an artifact of the materials used.

As mentioned, other differences exist but do not point to a clear pattern. Clinton differs in P1 (the belief about the nature of the political world). In his speeches he believes the world to be significantly less friendly than the beliefs of the papers of his administration, and with a substantial

*Table 6.2* Differences in Beliefs in Speeches and Foreign Policy Documents per US President

| | | Clinton | | Bush | | Obama | | Trump | |
|---|---|---|---|---|---|---|---|---|---|
| | | Speeches (n = 7) | Papers (n = 10) | Speeches (n = 12) | Papers (n = 16) | Speeches (n = 18) | Papers (n = 14) | Speeches (n = 7) | Papers (n = 5) |
| P1 | Nature political universe | .17 | **.41 (3.23\*)** | .19 | .26 (1.42) | .23 | .32 (1.40) | .24 | .32 (.64) |
| P2 | Realization political values | .04 | **.26 (3.05\*)** | .08 | .15 (1.61) | .08 | **.20 (2.57\*)** | .04 | .19 (1.49) |
| P3 | Predictability political future | .11 | .09 (−.67) | .09 | .09 (−1.40) | .12 | **.09 (−2.58\*)** | .16 | **.09 (−2.69\*)** |
| P4 | Control historical development | .28 | **.17 (−2.52\*)** | .30 | **.07 (−4.95\*\*\*)** | .40 | **.12 (−5.13\*\*\*)** | .49 | **.15 (−2.72\*)** |
| P5 | Role of chance | .97 | .98 (1.58) | .97 | **.99 (5.43\*\*\*)** | .95 | **.99 (4.47\*\*\*)** | .92 | **.99 (2.97\*)** |
| I1 | Strategic approach to goals | .23 | .46 (1.68) | .53 | **.15 (−2.31\*)** | .19 | .32 (.98) | .14 | .50 (2.12) |
| I2 | Tactical pursuit of goals | .11 | .28 (1.89) | .28 | .05 (−1.82) | .04 | .15 (1.28) | −.01 | **.26 (3.23\*\*)** |
| I3 | Risk orientation | .14 | .11 (−1.32) | .24 | .35 (.98) | .15 | .21 (.82) | .22 | .12 (−.99) |
| I4a | Timing of action: Cooperation/Conflict | .64 | .54 (−1.30) | .47 | .48 (.12) | .76 | **.53 (−2.53\*)** | .73 | .50 (−1.67) |
| I4b | Timing of action: Words/deeds | .64 | .73 (.93) | .47 | .37 (−.95) | .70 | .65 (−.44) | .40 | .40 (−.00) |
| I5a | Utility means: Reward | .18 | **.26 (2.08\*)** | .19 | .14 (−.83) | .17 | .18 (.06) | .07 | .11 (.83) |
| I5b | Utility means: Promise | .06 | **.10 (2.00\*)** | .12 | .11 (−.22) | .04 | **.15 (2.65\*)** | .03 | **.31 (5.59\*\*)** |
| I5c | Utility means: Appeal/support | .37 | .37 (−.02) | .45 | .32 (−1.64) | .38 | .34 (−.55) | .46 | .33 (−1.75) |
| I5d | Utility means: Oppose/resist | .21 | .14 (−1.74) | .12 | .20 (1.21) | .15 | .12 (−.89) | .20 | .09 (−2.55) |
| I5e | Utility means: Threaten | .04 | .04 (−.43) | .05 | .06 (.57) | .05 | .06 (.22) | .10 | .07 (−.72) |
| I5f | Utility means: Punish | .14 | .11 (−.76) | .07 | .17 (1.14) | .20 | .16 (−.93) | .13 | .09 (−.73) |

Values are means, Welch-values of t-tests in parentheses.

Bold denotes significant differences between speeches and papers of a president.

\*\*\* p < .001; \*\* p < .01; \* p < .05.

effect. Clinton also differs in P2, where he shows a significantly weaker belief in his ability to realize his political values within his speeches than within his policy papers. Clinton shares this tendency with Obama, who also shows a significant difference between his speeches and his policy papers on P2.

Strikingly, Obama and Trump, generally not known for their similarities, show more mutual differences between speech and policy papers than Bush and Clinton. Besides the already discussed P4 and P5 beliefs, Bush's beliefs only differ significantly from the beliefs in his policy papers, on his I1 belief about his strategic approach to goals in which he scores much higher in his speeches than policy papers. But Obama and Trump differ on several beliefs: P3, the belief that the political future can be predicted, where they both score significantly higher in their speeches than in their policy papers. Obama's beliefs also differ from the beliefs in the policy papers on the I4a belief about the timing of action, in which he shows a significantly higher belief in cooperation in the speeches compared to the policy papers where he leans more toward conflict. No other presidents show this difference. And when we compare Trump's beliefs with those underlying his policy papers, these show to differ significantly on the I2 belief. Trump's speeches show that Trump believes that hostile tactics are needed to get what he wants, while his administration's policy papers lean more toward cooperative tactics.

Summarizing, there seems to be no clear patterns of differences between the beliefs of presidents and the policy papers. Moreover, Table 6.2 suggests that there is quite some consistency in policy-making over the years, irrespective of the different administrations. To investigate this question, we ran another test to see if there are any differences between the policy papers created by Democrats and by Republicans.

### *Analysis 2: Differences between Individual and Collective Beliefs Related to Party Affiliation*

Table 6.3 shows the results of a comparison of the collective beliefs found in policy documents between Democratic administrations and Republican administrations, as well as a comparison between the beliefs derived from speeches made by Republican presidents and Democratic presidents. As could be expected, there are some significant differences between the policy papers of Democratic and Republican administrations. P1 (the belief about the nature of the political world) shows that Democrats have a significantly higher belief in the friendliness of the political world than Republicans. For P2, Democratic policy papers show a significantly stronger belief that they can realize their political values than Republicans. And for P5, there is a very subtle but statistically significant difference between the Democrats' policy papers and the Republicans' in the belief in the role of chance. For the instrumental

*Table 6.3* Difference in Beliefs between Speeches and Foreign Policy Documents by Party Affiliation

|  |  | Speeches | | Foreign Policy Documents | |
|---|---|---|---|---|---|
|  |  | *Democrats* (n = 25) | *Republicans* (n = 19) | *Democrats* (n = 24) | *Republicans* (n = 21) |
| **P1** | Nature political universe | .21 | .21 (.08) | .35 | **.28 (2.74\*\*)** |
| **P2** | Realization political values | .07 | .06 (.06) | .22 | **.16 (2.93\*\*)** |
| **P3** | Predictability political future | .12 | .12 (.11) | .09 | .09 (.1.17) |
| **P4** | Control historical development | .37 | .37 (.01) | .14 | .09 (1.54) |
| **P5** | Role of chance | .95 | .95 (.13) | .99 | **.99 (−2.17\*)** |
| **I1** | Strategic approach to goals | .20 | **.39 (−2.07\*)** | .38 | .23 (1.03) |
| **I2** | Tactical pursuit of goals | .06 | .18 (−1.69) | .20 | .10 (1.03) |
| **I3** | Risk orientation | .15 | .23 (−2.02) | .17 | .29 (−1.41) |
| **I4a** | *Timing of action:* Cooperation/conflict | .72 | **.56 (2.35\*)** | .54 | .48 (.67) |
| **I4b** | *Timing of action:* Words/deeds | .68 | **.44 (2.83\*\*)** | .69 | **.38 (4.05\*\*\*)** |
| **I5a** | *Utility means:* Reward | .18 | .15 (.67) | .21 | **.14 (2.30\*)** |
| **I5b** | *Utility means:* Promise | .05 | .09 (−1.61) | .13 | .16 (−.91) |
| **I5c** | *Utility means:* Appeal/support | .38 | .46 (−1.64) | .35 | .32 (.51) |
| **I5d** | *Utility means:* Oppose/resist | .17 | .15 (.79) | .13 | .18 (−.92) |
| **I5e** | *Utility means:* Threaten | .05 | .07 (−.79) | .05 | .06 (−.50) |
| **I5f** | *Utility means:* Punish | .18 | **.09 (3.05\*\*)** | .14 | .15 (−.15) |

Values are means, Welch-values of t-tests in parentheses.

Bold denotes significant differences between Democrats and Republicans.

\*\*\* p < .001; \*\*p < .01; \*p < .05.

beliefs, I4b, the Democrats use significantly more diversity in mixing words and deeds in policy papers, compared with Republicans. Also, the score on I5aReward shows that Democrats' policy papers use significantly more words of reward than Republicans.

The results for the comparison between the speeches of Democratic and Republican presidents, however, show a different picture. As it turns out, the only differences between the Democratic and Republican presidents are to be found in the instrumental beliefs. For the I1 belief, the Republicans believe more in cooperation as a strategic action than the

Democrats. Both I4 beliefs, about the timing of actions, show significant differences between Republican and Democratic beliefs. For the I4a belief, Democrats use more diversity in cooperative and conflictual tactics than Republicans. For the I4b belief, Democrats diversify more between words and deeds than Republicans. Lastly, for the I5Punish belief, Democrats use significantly more words about punishing than Republicans.

Taken all together, there are more similarities between the beliefs of Democrats and Republicans than there are differences. Interestingly, we see that the beliefs of presidents differ only in the instrumental beliefs, which are the beliefs about how we should approach the other, whereas the differences in beliefs in the policy papers are mainly found in the philosophical beliefs, which says something about the lens through which the world outside is seen.

### Analysis 3: Differences in Policy Papers Created by the Four Different Administrations

In order to make sense of these differences, we ran an ANOVA to see if there are significant differences between the policy papers of the different administrations. Table 6.4 shows the means and standard deviations of the beliefs underlying the policy documents of different administrations. As could be expected, based on these results, ANOVA comparisons show that there are again more similarities between administrations than differences. There are some significant differences, however, in three of the philosophical beliefs: P1 (the nature of the political universe), P2 (belief in the realization of political values), and P5 (the belief in the role of chance) and in three of the instrumental beliefs: I4b (timing of action) and two of I5 (utility of means) when it comes to the use of promises and rewards.

Interestingly, post hoc tests[3] show that all differences in the philosophical beliefs, and almost all differences in the instrumental beliefs are explained solely by differences between the beliefs of the Clinton administration on the one hand and the Bush administration on the other hand; all post hoc tests confirm these differences at the .05 level. In other words, there are no significant differences between the collective beliefs of different administrations, except between Clinton and Bush. Bush's administration shows to have the least optimistic view of the nature of the political universe, and the least optimistic view about his potential to realize his political values, when compared with Clinton, who scores most optimistic on both P1 and P2. In the timing of action in regard to the flexibility to switch between words and deeds (I4b), Clinton's administration is most flexible, whereas Bush's shows to be most rigid.

One exception is the instrumental belief I5 (promise), for which Trump's policy documents differ significantly from all three other administrations. Trump's documents use significantly less words of promise than the other

*Table 6.4* Differences in Beliefs Underlying Foreign Policy Documents of Different Administrations

|  |  | Clinton | Bush | Obama | Trump | ANOVA |
|---|---|---|---|---|---|---|
|  |  | Mean (sd) | Mean (sd) | Mean | Mean | F (3,41) |
| **P1** | Nature political universe | **.41 (.09)** | **.26 (.09)** | .32 (.08) | .32 (.13) | 5.28** |
| **P2** | Realization political values | **.26 (.07)** | **.15 (.06)** | .20 (.07) | .19 (.11) | 4.77** |
| **P3** | Predictability political future | .09 (.02) | .08 (.02) | .09 (.02) | .09 (.03) | .62 |
| **P4** | Control historical development | .17 (.05) | .07 (.09) | .12 (.13) | .15 (.13) | 1.90 |
| **P5** | Role of chance | **.98 (.01)** | **.99 (.01)** | .99 (.01) | .99 (.01) | 3.41* |
| **I1** | Strategic approach to goals | .46 (.11) | .15 (.61) | .32 (.44) | .50 (.29) | 1.32 |
| **I2** | Tactical pursuit of goals | .28 (.04) | .05 (.45) | .15 (.26) | .26 (.14) | 1.32 |
| **I3** | Risk orientation | .11 (.02) | .35 (.40) | .21 (.26) | .12 (.16) | 1.76 |
| **I4a** | *Timing of action:* Cooperation/conflict | .54 (.11) | .48 (.33) | .54 (.27) | .50 (.29) | .16 |
| **I4b** | *Timing of action:* Words/deeds | **.73 (.13)** | **.37 (.27)** | .65 (.32) | .40 (.26) | 5.50** |
| **I5a** | *Utility means:* Reward | .26 (.04) | .14 (.12) | .17 (.13) | **.11 (.07)** | 3.12* |
| **I5b** | *Utility means:* Promise | **.10 (.04)** | **.11 (.10)** | .15 (.14) | **.31 (.11)** | 5.18** |
| **I5c** | *Utility means:* Appeal/support | .37 (.06) | .32 (.25) | .34 (.23) | .33 (.11) | .14 |
| **I5d** | *Utility means:* Oppose/resist | .14 (.04) | .20 (.25) | .12 (.13) | .09 (.07) | .84 |
| **I5e** | *Utility means:* Threaten | .04 (.02) | .06 (.09) | .06 (.13) | .07 (.04) | .22 |
| **I5f** | *Utility means:* Punish | .11 (.03) | .17 (.33) | .16 (.13) | .09 (.06) | .31 |

Values are means, standard deviations in parentheses.

Bold denotes significant differences between the beliefs of presidents, derived from post hoc analyses using Hochberg's GT2, Bonferroni, and Games-Howell.

\*\*\* p < .001; \*\*p < .01; \*p < .05.

three administrations. Another exception is the instrumental belief I5 (reward), which shows a significant difference between Clinton and Bush and between Clinton and Trump. This difference is, however, somewhat weaker than the others since only one post hoc test (Games-Howell) supports these differences at the .5 level, while the others (Bonferroni and Hochberg's GT2) confirm this difference at .1 level.

Thus, it seems that the beliefs underlying the foreign policy documents of the last three administrations are fairly similar, which might be an indication that despite the different presidents, foreign policy is built on similar beliefs. Moreover, these results explain the differences found between Republicans and Democrats, since we can now see that these differences are almost all driven by differences between two specific administrations: the Clinton administration and the Bush administration, rather than by party ideology.

**Discussion**

We have explored the applicability of OCA on policy documents. We wanted to know (1) if we can use OCA as a tool to investigate beliefs in foreign policy documents and (2) whether the beliefs of presidents are reflected in these documents. To answer the latter question, we explored the beliefs of presidents based on speeches as is common within OCA and compared these with the collective beliefs of the administration in foreign policy documents. Moreover, we explored the differences between the collective beliefs across administrations. The results are not straightforward and raise several new questions to think about. For now, the main conclusion is that OCA can be applied to study beliefs in policy papers, but with the important caveat that the collective beliefs of policy papers do not perfectly reflect the beliefs of the presidents. Interestingly, however, the policy papers do show rather consistent foreign policy beliefs across administrations. Applying OCA to policy documents led further to three more specific conclusions.

First, applying the OCA on policy papers seems a valid and reliable tool for analysis. As Yang, Keller, and Molnar (2018) already showed in their study of Chinese white papers, there is an added value in analyzing the collective beliefs found in policy documents. Although we had a limited data collection, for all selected documents, we could determine the collective operational code using VICS and Profiler Plus. Second, regarding the comparison of the individual beliefs of the presidents and the beliefs underlying the policy papers, the main conclusion is that we cannot detect a clear pattern of similarities or differences. There are more similarities than differences, which might be an indication that the beliefs of presidents are *grosso modo* underlying the policy papers. The existing differences suggested a pattern related to P4 (belief in control over historical development) and P5 (belief in the role of chance), which indicate that presidents show significantly more confidence in their ability to control events and give chance a smaller role in the outcome of political events. The fact that all presidents showed this difference (besides Clinton for P5) might be an artifact of the nature of the different types of documents, rather than a gap between the underlying beliefs.

We think the reason for this is twofold. First, speeches are orally transmitted materials, and policy papers are written materials. Although beliefs are also expected to underlay written language, written language is different from speech language. In particular, when leaders give speeches, they aim to transmit a certain message that is connected to their role as leader. Subsequently, it is imaginable that their speeches will contain more references to themselves. Speeches are, after all, also a tool for leaders to show leadership. Leaders want to assure their audience they are in control of situations and outcomes, at least more than might be evident in the written language of policy papers. Second, the policy papers are drafted, commented on, and revised by multiple people who each might have clear ideas about the policies. Where speeches are aiming to speak the language of leaders, we can assume that policy papers are trying to express a more consensual outcome of a policy process. And this might show more clearly in P4 and P5 because these deal with uncertainty.

Our third conclusion is related to the comparison between Democratic and Republican administrations. We found that the beliefs underlying the foreign policy documents did not differ so much across administrations. In other words, it seems that the foreign policies of the different administrations are built on similar beliefs. When we investigated the few existing differences, the analysis showed that it was mainly a difference in beliefs between the Clinton and the Bush administrations. All other administrations shared similar beliefs. The significant difference might be explained by the fact that the Bush administration scored much lower on the P1 and P2 beliefs, which can be explained by real-world events. Since the Bush administration experienced the traumatic terrorist attack of 9/11, which changed the beliefs of President Bush (Renshon 2008), it might well be that this event has also altered some of the beliefs underlying the policies of his administration.

These results support our analysis above: policy papers are written by several bureaucrats and although expressing the decisions made by presidents (and assumingly based on the beliefs of these presidents) in the policy-making process, it seems that a broad consensual process that is based on an overarching perspective of the United States within the world is leading the drafting of the policy papers. There are some differences based on party affiliation, but we found that this was primarily limited to the differences between the Clinton and Bush administration. And for that difference, the influence of the 9/11 attacks might be the explanatory factor.

## Conclusion

Our explorative study shows that OCA can have an added value to content analysis of policy documents. That makes it an advancement because OCA was developed to analyze speech language rather than written language. The results led to three main conclusions: it is worthwhile to apply OCA on foreign policy documents, there are more similarities than differences between the presidential beliefs found in speeches and the collective beliefs in foreign policy documents, and there are no significant differences between Democratic and Republican administrations when it comes to collective operational codes. Obviously, there are limitations to our research design as well.

First, we only studied a selection of foreign policy documents, which are mainly about security issues. A more complete analysis would include also topics like trade, human rights, and environmental policies, including an analysis of possible differences depending on different topics (as Walker and Schafer (2000) found). Also, future research should expand to foreign policy documents that are written at lower levels of the administration's hierarchy. Is there a match between the beliefs found in speeches, the collective beliefs in the overarching policy document and the collective beliefs found in the lower ranked policy documents? And of course, the analysis should be expanded to the foreign policy documents of other countries than the United States.

Second, OCA is an indirect way of analyzing foreign policy decision-making and that remains the case when one includes content analysis. Nonetheless, an important finding is that beliefs underlying foreign policy papers seem to be fairly stable, across time, administrations, and, interestingly, also across party affiliation. In other words, there is more consistency in American foreign policy than there is divergence. This finding feeds into more general analyses of continuity in US foreign policy (Glassman 2005; Burgos 2008; Jackson 2011). It would be interesting to further investigate to what extent there exists a general collective US foreign policy operational code, relatively stable across time and administrations. Moreover, since the beliefs of presidents seem to be reflected in the policy papers, it seems worthwhile to investigate whether the presidents' beliefs shaped foreign policy, or that the collective beliefs underscoring the foreign policies have shaped the presidents' beliefs.

Third, although we now know that we can use OCA to study foreign policy documents, we remain still in the dark about the process of how these beliefs are leading the foreign policy-making process. Future research questions could include as follows: what do these beliefs express exactly: reflections of the bureaucrats who remain stable in their beliefs over time, or do these beliefs rather express the consensus of advisory teams of the president? How do the beliefs of advisors, departments, the NSC, and the president meld together into the collective beliefs underlying the foreign policy documents?

All in all, many intriguing questions are raised by the results of this explorative study and we believe that these can lead to promising new research avenues.

## Acknowledgments

We would like to thank our research assistants Annabel de Wit and Ferdi van Ingen for their valuable efforts to collect the data for us.

# Notes

1. Provided by Social Science Automated at www.profilerplus.org.
2. For an overview of all policy documents and speeches, see Table 6.1.
3. Due to the differences in sample size, we used Hochberg's GT2 post hoc test, and we also ran a Bonferroni, which is a conservative test that controls strongly for possible type I errors. As an additional post hoc test, we ran Games-Howell.

# References

Burgos, R. A. 2008. Origins of regime change: "Ideapolitik" on the long road to Baghdad, 1993–2000. *Security Studies* 17(2): 221–256.

Dille, B. 2000. The prepared and spontaneous remarks of presidents Reagan and Bush: A validity comparison for at-a-distance measurements. *Political Psychology* 21(3): 573–585.

Dyson, S. B. 2010. George W. Bush, the surge, and presidential leadership. *Political Science Quarterly* 125(4): 557–585.

Fink, J. S. 1983. The foreign policy role of the president: Origins and limitations. *Hofstra Law Review* 11(2): 773–804.

Glassman, J. 2005. The new imperialism? On continuity and change in US foreign policy. *Environment and Planning A* 37(9): 1527–1544.

Grimmer, J., B. M. Stewart. 2013. Text as data: The promise and pitfalls of automatic content analysis methods for political texts. *Political Analysis* 21(3): 267–297.

Hermann, M. G. 2001. How decision units shape foreign policy: A theoretical framework. *International Studies Review* 3(2): 47–81.

Hermann, M. G. 2008. Content analysis. In *Qualitative methods in international relations*, eds. A. Klotz, D. Prakash, 151–167. London: Palgrave Macmillan.

Jackson, R. 2011. Culture, identity and hegemony: Continuity and (the lack of) change in US counterterrorism policy from Bush to Obama. *International Politics* 48(2–3): 390–411.

Lazarevska, E., J. M. Sholl, M. D. Young. 2006. Links among beliefs and personality traits: The distinctive language of terrorists. In *Beliefs and leadership in world politics: Methods and applications of operational code analysis*, eds. M. Schafer, S. G. Walker, 171–184. New York, NY: Palgrave MacMillan.

Levine, N., M. D. Young. 2014. Leadership trait analysis and threat assessment with Profiler Plus. *Proceedings of ILC 2014 on 8th International Lisp Conference*, Montreal, QC, Canada – August 14–17, 2014. Association for Computing Machinery.

Liddell Hart, B. H. 1967. *Strategy: Second revised edition*. New York, NY: Fredrick A. Praeger Publishers.

Marfleet, B. G. 2000. The operational code of John F. Kennedy during the Cuban missile crisis: A comparison of public and private rhetoric. *Political Psychology* 21(3): 545–558.

Masters, J. 2017. US Foreign policy powers: Congress and the president. Council on Foreign Relations. https://www.cfr.org/backgrounder/us-foreign-policy-powers-congress-and-president.

Renshon, J. 2008. Stability and change in belief systems: The operational code of George W. Bush. *Journal of Conflict Resolution* 52(6): 820–849.

Robison, S. 2006. George W. Bush and the Vulcans: Leader-Advisor Relations and America's Response to the 9/11 Attacks. In Beliefs and Leadership in World Politics, eds. M. Schafer, S.G. Walker, 101–126. New York: Palgrave.

Schafer, M., S. Crichlow. 2000. Bill Clinton's operational code: Assessing source material bias. *Political Psychology* 21(3): 559–571.

Schafer, M., M. D. Young, S. G. Walker. 2002. US presidents as conflict managers: The operational codes of George H. W. Bush and Bill Clinton. In *Political leadership for the new century: Lessons from the study of personality and behavior among American leaders*, eds. O. L. Valenty, O. Feldman, 51–63. Westport, CT: Praeger.

Siniver, A. 2008. *Nixon, Kissinger, and US foreign policy making: The machinery of crisis*. Cambridge: Cambridge University Press.

Tetlock, P. E., A. S. R. Manstead. 1985. Impression management versus intrapsychic explanations in social psychology. A useful dichotomy? *Psychological Review* 92(1): 59–77.

Trump, D. J. 2017. National security strategy of the United States. Available at: https://www.whitehouse.gov/wp-content/uploads/2017/12/NSS-Final-12-18-2017-0905.pdf (accessed 17 March 2020).

Walker, S. G., M. Schafer. 2000. The political universe of Lyndon B. Johnson and his advisors: Diagnostic and strategic propensities in their operational codes. *Political Psychology* 21(3): 529–543.

Walker, S. G., A. Malici, M. Schafer. 2011. *Rethinking foreign policy analysis. States, leaders, and the microfoundations of behavioral international relations*. New York, NY: Routledge.

Walker, S. G., M. Schafer, G. E. Smith. 2018. The operational codes of Donald Trump and Hillary Clinton. In *The Oxford handbook of behavioral political science*, eds. A. Mintz, L. Terris. Oxford: Oxford University Press. DOI: 10.1093/oxfordhb/9780190634131.013.4.

Winham, G. 1969. Quantitative methods in foreign policy analysis. *Canadian Journal of Political Science* 2(2): 187–199.

Winter, D. G. 2011. Philosopher-king or polarizing politician? A personality profile of Barack Obama. *Political Psychology* 32(6): 1059–1081.

Yang, Y. E., J. W. Keller, J. Molnar. 2018. An operational code analysis of China's national defense white papers: 1998–2015. *Journal of Chinese Political Science* 23(4): 585–602.

# 7 One Step Forward, Two Steps Back

## The Steering Effects of Operational Code Beliefs in the Chilean-Bolivian Rivalry

*Consuelo Thiers*

## Introduction

In 2007, after a year in office the Bolivian president Evo Morales included in his speech delivered at the UN General Assembly some optimistic words directed toward Chile. During this address to the international community, he referred to the building of trust between both countries and expressed his hope for a prompt solution to Bolivia's historical claims (see Morales 2007). In 2011, at the beginning of his second term in office and during the commemoration of the Day of the Sea, Morales had changed his positive tone and announced the filing of a lawsuit against Chile at the International Court of Justice (ICJ) to demand sovereign access to the Pacific Ocean. On that occasion, he stressed the severe damage that Chile had inflicted on Bolivia by being responsible for Bolivia's landlocked condition. He emphasized how the loss of the sea had limited the country's development and had created a feeling of isolation and disadvantage among Bolivians. In that speech, he addressed the international community and explained that after 132 years of struggle, it was finally time to "close this immense wound" (see Morales 2011).

Morales's approach toward Chile not only changed rhetorically but also shifted in terms of his handling of the bilateral relation. Morales's decision to file a lawsuit against Chile marked a new period of escalation in the rivalry between these states. Why did Evo Morales change his behavior? Drawing on the foreign policy analysis (FPA) literature, I shall argue that the change in Evo Morales's foreign policy behavior can be associated with a process of learning that resulted in a change in his beliefs regarding the bilateral relations with Chile. To conduct this analysis, I utilize the operational code analysis (OCA) framework and the concept of learning in foreign policy.

The remainder of this article proceeds in five parts. The first section provides a brief background on the development of the rivalry between Bolivia and Chile, including Evo Morales's approach to the rivalry. The second section reviews the literature on the role of leaders in rivalries. The third section introduces the OCA approach to assessing political leaders as well as learning approaches to understanding foreign policy change. Thereafter, I present the method and data utilized in the analysis, followed by a discussion of the results. The chapter concludes by summarizing the main findings and proposing avenues for future research.

## Brief Historical Background

It is not possible to understand the complexity of the bilateral relations between Bolivia and Chile without referring to their belligerent past. In the War of the Pacific (or Saltpeter War), Chile confronted the alliance between Peru and Bolivia from 1879 to 1883. This War ended with victory for Chile, which resulted in significant territorial expansion. Peru lost land that was rich in natural resources, while Bolivia lost access to the Pacific Ocean and became a landlocked country. The War of the Pacific engendered tensions that persist today, which are reflected in constant diplomatic impasses, hostile rhetoric, threats, and two lawsuits filed before the ICJ. Scholars have identified the War of the Pacific as the event that initiated the Chilean-Bolivian rivalry, shaping these countries' bilateral relations (see Gutiérrez 2007; Rodríguez 2014, 2016; Rivera 2016).

Some analyses have stressed the impact that the outcomes of the War had on the identity formation of these states as well as on the creation of negative images of the Other that have hindered their capacity to overcome the conflict (see Wehner 2011; González and Ovando 2016). The origin of this War is still a contentious matter between these states as they have different interpretations of the reasons why the armed conflict was initiated. Due to this disagreement, the following is a brief chronology that only indicates some relevant dates and the main contents of treaties and negotiations that are necessary to have a better understanding of the past of the rivalry.

- Before the War of the Pacific, in *1873*, Peru and Bolivia signed the "Treaty of Defensive Alliance" *(Tratado de Alianza Defensiva, 1873)*, a pact that compelled both the states to guarantee each other their independence, sovereignty, and integrity over their respective territories, obliging them to defend themselves against any external aggression.
- In *1874*, Bolivia and Chile signed a Treaty *(Tratado de Límites, 1874)* that established the boundary between both the states at parallel 24°. It was also agreed that Bolivia would not raise taxes to Chilean enterprises for 25 years. In *1878*, owing to Bolivia's economic

hardship, Bolivia established a ten cent tax per quintal.[1] of saltpeter to a Chilean company, which violated the Treaty. As a response, in February *1879*, Chile occupied the Bolivian port of Antofagasta and later in April 1879 declared War on both Peru and Bolivia.

- In *1884*, Chile and Bolivia signed an indefinite truce that stated that during the term of the truce, Chile would continue to govern the territories from the 23° parallel to the mouth of the Loa River *(Pacto de Tregua Bolivia-Chile 1884)*.

- In *1904*, Chile and Bolivia signed the "Treaty of Peace and Friendship" *(Tratado de Paz y Amistad entre Chile y Bolivia, 1904)*. The Treaty defined the boundaries between the two states and recognized the absolute and perpetual dominion of Chile over the territories indicated in the Truce Pact of 1884. The parties also agreed to build a railway between Arica and La Paz. Additionally, Bolivia was granted the perpetual right of free transit through Chilean ports. The signing of this Treaty converted Bolivia into a landlocked country.

- In *1929*, Peru and Chile signed the Treaty of Lima *(Tratado de Lima Entre Chile y Perú* 1929), which established the final status of the provinces of Tacna (Peru) and Arica (Chile). Additionally, they signed a supplementary protocol, which stipulated that neither Chile nor Peru could cede to a third party any of the territories over which they were granted sovereignty in the Treaty without the previous agreement of the cosigner. Although this Treaty was signed between Chile and Peru, this last clause severely affected and continues to affect the relationship between Bolivia and Chile. The territory to which the Treaty refers is precisely the area that could be ceded to Bolivia to access the Pacific Ocean without having to split Chilean territory in two.

### The Claim for Sovereign Access to the Pacific Ocean

Over the years, Bolivian decision-makers have sought to recover part of the maritime domain lost as a result of the War and the Treaty of 1904. The demand for sovereign access to the Pacific Ocean stems from the negative implications that being a landlocked country has brought to Bolivia. Bolivia justifies its demand based on the claim that the Treaty of 1904 took place in a context where Bolivia was overpowered by Chile, and hence, left with no choice but to sign an unfair and detrimental agreement.

The claim for sovereign access to the Pacific Ocean appears as central in the dispute between both countries. From the Chilean perspective, despite the context in which the Treaty was signed, the result is a legally binding agreement that for the most part, Chile does not wish to alter. From the Bolivian perspective, regaining access to the sea is a fair request and a matter of historical justice that Chile needs to acknowledge and collaborate with Bolivia in finding a suitable solution. While the main objective of the Bolivian position has remained mostly unaltered, the strategy and arguments to justify the claim have to some extent varied. Before Bolivia filed a lawsuit against Chile at the ICJ in 2013, Bolivia's stance was mainly concerned with the contestation of the Treaty of 1904 due to the unfairness of the terms and its alleged invalidity as it was supposedly procured by the use of force.[2] The later argument presented in the Bolivian lawsuit was grounded on Chile's alleged obligation to negotiate with Bolivia sovereign access to the sea.

Bolivia's lawsuit invoked different legal bases upon which Chile's obligation to negotiate rested, i.e., bilateral agreements or declarations, unilateral acts, acquiescence, estoppel, and legitimate expectations. In a nutshell, Bolivia's general argument was grounded in the idea that Chile's previous behavior and promises to negotiate with Bolivia constituted a legal obligation at present. In October 2018, the ICJ ruled that Chile did not undertake a legal obligation to negotiate sovereign access to the Pacific Ocean for Bolivia which put an end to that legal dispute.

### Evo Morales and His Struggle for the Sea

The election of Evo Morales in 2005 as president of Bolivia is a milestone in Bolivia's political history as he was the first president who belonged to the Indigenous population of the country. Morales, a descendant of an Aymara family, was born in a small and impoverished community in Bolivia (Estado Plurinacional de Bolivia 2010). In his early political life, he was an active member of the coca growers' union of which he later became the General Secretary. Morales was the first Indigenous leader to obtain more than the absolute majority of the votes (53.7%) since the transition to democracy in 1982 (Deheza 2007, 43).

This election was relevant not only because a representative of a historically underrepresented group came into power in a country where, according to the last census (2012), 41% of the population is of Indigenous origin, but also because the 2005 presidential election completely changed the correlation of political forces in Bolivia, affecting the three largest parties that dominated the scene since 1982 (Deheza 2007, 44). Evo Morales, as the leader of the "Movement for Socialism–Political Instrument for the Sovereignty of the Peoples" (MAS-IPSP), was reelected president for three consecutive terms from 2006 to 2019.

Evo Morales's victory coincided with the election of Michelle Bachelet as the president of Chile in 2005. This election is also a milestone in Chile's political history as Bachelet was the first woman to occupy this position. Both leaders not only epitomized two underrepresented groups now in power but also shared a left-leaning political stance. These common features, as well as the alleged good personal relationship between these leaders, were widely recognized by the media and political analysts, who augured an improvement in the bilateral relations. These predictions proved to be rather accurate, as the relationship between these states took a positive turn.

Evo Morales was invited to Bachelet's inauguration ceremony, and both presidents expressed their willingness to cooperate and work toward a common agenda to improve the bilateral relation. During his visit to Santiago, Morales attended a demonstration in his honor where the Chilean audience cheered "sea for Bolivia," which he took as a meaningful sign as well as a source of hope. He continued to refer to this episode in subsequent interviews and speeches portraying it as a confirmation that the Chilean people agreed with Bolivia's claim.

Morales began to speak about "the diplomacy of the people," which mainly referred to direct communication between the people to guarantee a solution to the long-lasting problem between Chile and Bolivia. It also stressed the idea that the issues between both countries in the past were mainly due to individual neoliberal interests that did not relate to the real feeling present in the population.

Gestures and expressions of trust marked the positive turn in the bilateral relations between both countries. In June 2006, Chile and Bolivia agreed on a working plan known as the "13 points agenda," which intended to prompt negotiations on 13 relevant bilateral issues, including controversial matters such as the maritime dispute. Both the states portrayed this milestone as an example of the development of trust. A few years later, it was revealed that during Morales's first term, both administrations were close to reaching an agreement that entailed granting a coastal enclave to Bolivia in the Tiviliche Bay. The details of this negotiation are unknown, but press reports indicate that while negotiations had been an unprecedented improvement, granting sovereignty to Bolivia was off the table (see Cooperativa.cl 2015; Quiroz 2016).

During Evo Morales's second term from 2010 to 2015, the positive tone of the bilateral relations took a drastic negative turn, which culminated with the filing of a lawsuit against Chile at the ICJ. Evo Morales's rhetoric shifted and became aggressive and confrontational, marking an increase in tensions. This negative turn coincided with a change in the Chilean administration direction of which went from a left-leaning charismatic president (Michelle Bachelet) to a right-wing businessman (Sebastián Piñera). While at the beginning of Sebastián Piñera's term, Morales's rhetoric still showed some elements of hope, by 2011, this changed dramatically.

In 2011, during the commemoration of the Day of the Sea, the change in Morales's tone was quite evident. In this speech, Morales announced the filing of a lawsuit against Chile at the ICJ. Politicians and analysts have acknowledged this transformation in Morales's foreign policy behavior regarding the bilateral relations with Chile. For instance, former president of Bolivia Carlos Mesa indicates in one of his books,

Evo Morales approach to the maritime issue had two distinct stages - his first and second term. In his first administration, he was driven by a positive attitude and overlooked historical prejudices. He believed that the ideological affinities with his Chilean colleague Michelle Bachelet would allow us to find a definitive solution to our forced landlocked condition. In January 2010, Evo Morales began his second term and in March Sebastián Piñera took office in Chile. In December, the presidents of Bolivia and Chile decided to form a committee to put the 13-point agenda into effect. But what actually happened was a turning point in the history of the Bolivian maritime claim. The meetings that the committee held in early 2011 in Santiago and La Paz were not fruitful. That was the breaking point (Mesa 2016, 212).[3]

After the announcement of the lawsuit, a round of antagonizing declarations took place. Morales accused the Chilean authorities of being a danger to the region (Morales 2012) and of preferring to see Bolivia "geographically amputated, economically weak and socially dependent" (Morales 2013a). Morales blamed Chile for preventing integration in Latin American and "denying peace, security, brotherhood and destroying the people's desire to live in peace and harmony" (Morales 2013b). Later, he accused President Piñera of "lying to his country and the world" (Morales 2013c).

## Interstate Rivalries and the Roles of Political Leaders

The confrontational feature of the bilateral relations between Bolivia and Chile differs from the usual competition between states. What is particularly puzzling about this rivalry is its longevity and resistance to change. The maintenance of this rivalry over time, the facility with which tensions tend to escalate, and the capacity that the rivalry narratives have to pass down from generation to generation are features that have made this dyadic interaction unique and worth studying from a FPA approach. The particular features that have characterized the bilateral relations between these states can be placed conceptually within the description of interstate rivalries.

Much scholarly work has been done on the study of rivalries in the last 30 years, giving birth to different conceptualizations and definitions. Broadly speaking, the study of rivalries has been approached in two different ways. On the one hand, there is a body of research focused on the quantitative features of these conflicts, and on the other, there is an approach mostly centered on the qualitative analysis of their characteristics. Within quantitative approaches, Diehl and Goertz (2000) propose the concept of enduring rivalries to describe a relationship between two states, in which both use military threats and force regularly as well as one in which both states formulate foreign policy in military terms. They define three main components of enduring rivalries, i.e., competitiveness (tangible and intangible), time (whether or not it persists over time), and spatial consistency (a consistent set of dyads) (Goertz and Diehl 1992). In this context, enduring rivalries between two states should involve at least five militarized disputes in a period lasting at least 10 years, which terminates after 10 years without the occurrence of a militarized interstate dispute (MIDs) (Goertz and Diehl 1992).

This quantitative classification excludes a group of rivalries, such as Chile-Bolivia, that have not engaged in recent militarized disputes but dynamics of which remain conflictual and enduring. This exclusion is acknowledged by qualitative approaches that have relied on nonmilitarized elements to better understand rival interactions. These qualitative conceptualizations have pinpointed psychological factors that intervene in rivalries between states. For instance, Vasquez (1996) stresses extreme competition and psychological hostilities as main characteristics of rivalries. The particularity of the competitive dynamic between rival states relies on the fact that as the conflict recurs, "contenders become more concerned with hurting or denying their competitor than with their own immediate value satisfaction, and with this, hostility deepens and goes beyond that associated with normal conflict" (Vasquez 1996, 532). In this sense, Vasquez (1996) argues that contenders are mainly driven by their attitude toward each other rather than by the stakes at hand.

The relevance attributed to psychological factors in explaining rivalries is also present in the work of Thompson (1995), who introduces the notion of strategic rivalries to differentiate them from other interstate conflicts. He argues that the study of rivalries requires a focus on key decision-makers' perceptions of whom they consider to be their primary opponents and enemies. Rivals need to identify and recognize each other as such (Thompson 1995). In later work, Thompson (2001) differentiates rivalries from conflicts that take place in neutral contexts, stressing that rivals "deal with each other in a psychologically charged context of path-dependent hostility" (Thompson 2001, 558). He claims that to create a rivalry, decision-makers must consider each other as competitors, enemies, and possible sources of actual or latent threats that pose some risk of becoming militarized. This categorization is considered by Thompson (2001) as a social-psychological process, for it requires the interpretation of others' intentions.

The acknowledgement of the role of sociopsychological elements present in rivalries is extensively developed by Bar-Tal (2007, 2013), who focuses specifically on intractable conflicts. These sorts of conflicts are considered more meaningful than tractable ones due to their severity, durability, and the serious implications for the societies involved (Bar-Tal 2013). Bar-Tal (1998, 2013) contends that a central element present in societies implicated in intractable conflicts is the perception of their goals as being indispensable for the group survival and at the same time incompatible with the ones kept by the rival. The centrality attributed to perception has relevant implications for the study of these sorts of conflicts, as it shows that the incompatibility, and the conflict itself, are not necessarily objective in nature.

As Bar-Tal puts it "conflicts always begin in our heads" (Bar-Tal 2013, 7). This observation is central as it reveals that sociopsychological factors play a major role in the inception, escalation, maintenance of the conflict, as well as in peace-making and reconciliation processes (Bar-Tal 2013). Bar-Tal (2013) posits that people act upon their ideas and that both their rational and irrational acts are steered by what they think, believe, and anticipate. While these qualitative approaches have shed light on the psychological factors that can help one to explain the characteristics of rivalries, they have not delved into the specific role of the psychology of key decision-makers in shaping rival interactions. For instance, although Vasquez (1996) mentions the psychological angle of rivalries and points out the actor dimension in explaining the hostility between the contenders, it is not clear what the specific actors' views that underlie this hostility are.

Thompson's (2001) categorization of 174 strategic rivalries based on actors' identification of which states qualify as enemies is a significant advance in the inclusion of a cognitive dimension to the study of rivalries. However, the focus needs to be expanded beyond the identification of rivalries toward understanding the dynamics involved in the development of these interactions. While I concur with Thompson's (2001) contention about the importance of decision-makers' perceptions of whom they consider to be their main opponents, it is not clear which cognitive elements underlie this perception.

Bar-Tal's (2013) more comprehensive approach recognizes what he defines as a sociopsychological repertoire composed of beliefs, attitudes, emotions, and behaviors, among others, present in both leaders and followers that lead to conflicts. However, his work is mostly centered in explaining collective psychological phenomena present in societies involved in intractable conflicts, rather than evaluating individual psychological characteristics of decision-makers. This approach leaves aside the difference that powerful individuals can make in shaping rivalries. While decision-makers as members of a society involved in intractable conflicts may share similar views than the rest of the society, individual differences in the type of beliefs and emotions or even in the intensity of these elements can make a relevant difference in the life cycle of the conflict.

More importantly, one limitation of these approaches to rivalries is the insufficient focus on the variability of these conflicts over time. The hostile interaction between rival states is not static as they undergo periods of cooperation, escalation, and de-escalation of hostilities. This variation plays a relevant role in understanding the life cycle of a rivalry. In fact, one of the main concerns that made researchers pay attention to the study of rivalries in the field of International Relations is their greater propensity to escalate compared to other conflicts between states (e.g., Goertz and Diehl 1992; Thompson, 1995, 2001; Maoz and Mor 1996). In this sense, understanding the specific perceptions and beliefs of individuals that have the power to mobilize state resources and, therefore, increase and decrease tensions is particularly relevant.

In the specific case of the rivalry between Bolivia and Chile, scholarly literature that has addressed the development of this rivalry shows general references to the role of political leaders. Milet (2002) and Van Klaveren (2011) describe Chile's foreign policy toward its neighboring states during the transition to democracy stressing the role of Chilean presidents in shaping the bilateral relations. Quiroga and Guerrero (2016) point out the importance of elites' narratives in the maintenance of the rivalry between these states. Ovando and González (2012) stress the relevance of beliefs in the dynamic of this rivalry. They emphasize the influential role of key decision-makers of both states in the improvement and deterioration of the bilateral relations.

There is also evidence in the literature of the variation that these rivalries have experienced, which are associated to some extent with the role of presidents. Wehner (2011) refers to the positive shift that bilateral relations between Chile and Bolivia took during Morales's and Bachelet's presidencies, and the role they had in the creation of mutual trust. González and Ovando (2016) mention Morales's shift from a pragmatic stance toward Chile during the presidency of Bachelet to an "emotivist" attitude as a result of Piñera's decision to reject Morales's proposal of trading gas for access to the sea. Rodríguez (2014) refers extensively to the history of the relationship between Peru, Bolivia, and Chile after the War of the Pacific, stressing the role of presidents, diplomats, and foreign affairs ministers in the trajectories of these rivalries.

While these studies clearly acknowledge the role of foreign policy elites, especially presidents, in shaping the bilateral relations between these states, the reference to individual characteristics that may help one to explain foreign policy decision-making processes is rather anecdotal. In this sense, political leaders' specific characteristics or beliefs about this rivalry and how they might influence decision-making processes have not been thoroughly explored.

## Operational Code Analysis and Learning in Foreign Policy

As mentioned earlier, a more nuanced understanding of the psychological factors that explain rivalries must include the analysis of the variation of the conflict across time considering the periods of cooperation and escalation of tensions in the rivalry. This gap in the study of rivalries has been recognized by Thompson (1995, 220–221), who indicates that "the processes that characterize the emergence, the escalation, and the de-escalation, and the endings of rivalries need theoretical explication and empirical examination. We know very little about the 'life cycles' of rivalries of any kind." Similarly, Thies (2001) criticizes the inductive nature of the different approaches to understanding rivalries. He indicates that they have not explained why the levels of intensity vary during the course of a rivalry's life cycle.

The non-static nature of rivalries raises the question of what can help one to explain the variation they undergo over time. Given the cognitive characteristics of rivalries and how their definition and development rely on people's worldviews, examining leaders' beliefs stands as a suitable approach to analyzing their life cycles. I argue that the variation of these rivalries in terms of cooperation and escalation should be reflected in decision-makers' beliefs regarding the conflict. In this sense, changes in the trajectory of rivalries should also be reflected in a change of beliefs in political leaders in charge of making decisions. This process of changing beliefs falls within the concept of learning in foreign policy.

The analysis of learning in foreign policy, understood by Levy (1994, 283) as "a change of beliefs (or degree of confidence in one's beliefs) or the development of new beliefs, skills, or procedures as a result of the observation and interpretation of experiences" may be a contribution to the study of the dynamics that rivalries undergo over time. The potential that learning approaches have to shed light on rivalries' dynamics is pointed out by Thies (2003), who argues that the few studies that have focused on learning in the context of rivalries have taken an adaptive or structural approach to it, in which states learn by rationally adapting their policies depending on the rewards or punishments imposed by the international system. He contends that a thorough understanding of learning in rivalries must elucidate how main decision-makers, acting on behalf of the state, learn from their experience with the rival.

The case of the Bolivian-Chilean rivalry during Evo Morales's presidency provides a very good case to test the learning hypothesis. On the one hand, Morales's extended time in office (13 years) not only gave him enough time to acquire specific knowledge about the rivalry and the rival's characteristics but also to learn about the consequences of his own behavior. On the other hand, the noticeable change in his foreign policy behavior regarding Chile allows for comparisons of his beliefs in two distinct periods of the bilateral relations. In order to examine leaders' beliefs and the variation that can be associated to learning processes, I utilize the OCA framework (see Leites 1951; George 1969; Holsti 1970; Walker 1983, 1990).

The operational code is an analytical tool initially developed by Nathan Leites (1951) for evaluating leaders' worldviews concerning international politics. This framework was later developed by George (1969), who identified ten questions about politics that together attempted to assess two groups of beliefs. The first group consisted of philosophical beliefs about the fundamental nature of politics. The second group, i.e., instrumental beliefs, are those concerned with ends-means relationships in the context of political action. George (1969) suggests that the responses that political actors provide to these questions could help one to define their fundamental orientations toward the problem of leadership and action. In a nutshell, the operational code approach to the study of beliefs asks what the individual knows, feels, and wants concerning the exercise of power (Schafer and Walker 2006). This information can be accessed through what leaders say in their public addresses by using content analysis tools.

The use of the OCA framework not only provides tools to assess leaders' behaviors in light of their beliefs but also allows for a comparison of beliefs across time or subjects. Moreover, the use of this framework helps one to distinguish between different types of learning. Levy (1994) differentiates between causal, diagnostic, simple, and complex learning. Causal learning refers to a change of beliefs about the laws of cause and effect, the consequences of actions, and the best strategies under different conditions. Diagnostic learning refers to changes in beliefs about the definition of the situation or the preferences and intentions of others or others' capabilities. In terms of levels of learning Levy (1994) differentiates simple from complex learning; the former corresponds to a type learning that leads to a change in means but not in ends, the latter leads to a modification of goals as well as means.

Malici and Malici (2005) utilize OCA to hypothesize these different types of learning so as to help one to explain Cuban and North Korean foreign policy behavior in the post-Cold War era. In this study, simple learning is defined as changes in instrumental beliefs about the best means to realize goals, and diagnostic learning is defined as changes in philosophical beliefs about the political universe. Complex learning takes place when an actor's key philosophical beliefs about political goals and key instrumental beliefs about the most effective means to achieve them are altered to modify the leader's strategic preferences. Based on Walker, Schafer, and Young (2003), key beliefs take into consideration both the disposition of the leader (I-1 Approach to Strategy and P-4a Self's Historical Control) and relevant features of the context (P-1 Nature of the Political Universe and P-4b Other's Historical Control) to achieve a definition of the "self-in-situation." If their learning hypotheses hold true in the case of Evo Morales, there should be changes in his operational code beliefs between his first and second term. Depending on the potential changes in his beliefs, it will also be possible to distinguish between different levels of learning and assess what he learned from the rivalry.

## Methods and Data

To assess leaders' operational codes, I utilize the Verbs in Context System (VICS) developed by Walker, Schafer, and Young (1998). This system builds indicators for the philosophical and instrumental propensities proposed by George (1969). VICS first identifies positive and negative attributions for the beliefs that the leader expresses in the context of self-other relations. Subsequently, the self-other valences are characterized as propensities to diagnose and employ cooperative or conflictive behaviors that represent the exercise of power. These procedures allow one for the construction of VICS indices to answer each question in George's (1969) inventory of philosophical and instrumental operational code beliefs.

To conduct the analysis, I considered two recent milestones in the bilateral relations between Bolivia and Chile during Evo Morales's presidency, one of them marking a period of cooperation and the other one a period of escalation in tensions. I considered Morales's first presidential term from 2006 to 2010 as a period of cooperation, which was characterized by the development of trust between both countries and the creation of a new cooperation plan (the 13-points agenda). The period of escalation in tensions corresponds to Morales's second period in office from 2010 to 2014, marked by a negative shift in the bilateral relations and the filing of a lawsuit against Chile at the ICJ.

Considering that the main objective of this analysis pertains to Evo Morales's beliefs regarding the rivalry, the verbal material utilized for the analysis was explicitly targeted at the bilateral relations with Chile. I used speeches and more spontaneous material such as interviews or press conferences responses, where he referred to Chile or its policymakers. In this sense, instead of using one speech act as the unit of analysis, my work required the aggregation of data. This decision was grounded in two considerations, i.e., the specificity of the analysis and data availability. This is in line with Schafer and Walker's (2006) guidelines on research design using the OCA framework; they indicate that sometimes the research design favors a larger unit of analysis.

On the other hand, the decision also considered the availability of verbal material. In many Latin American countries, access to decision-makers' verbal material presents some difficulties due to the lack of archives or databases that compile this information (Brummer et al. 2020). Source texts are usually disorganized and scattered around different governmental websites, presidential libraries, and ministerial archives (Brummer et al. 2020). Additionally, given the specificity of the verbal material required for this analysis, the data is itself limited. While presidents refer to the rivalry in their interviews and speeches, they do not talk about it extensively or very often. In this sense, the number of utterances concerning the topic is restricted. The disadvantage of this method is that it is no longer possible to run some statistical analyses (t-tests or ANOVA) as the aggregation results in one score for each period (Schafer and Walker 2006). However, these data can still be interpreted by using a norming group as the basis for temporal comparisons in a quasi-experimental research design (Schafer and Walker 2006; Walker, Malici, and Schafer 2011, 62–66; see also Gerring 2012, 272–275, 285–290).

The verbal material was retrieved from different sources. I mostly used official websites belonging to the Bolivian Presidency and the Ministry of Communication. From 2009 to 2019, Morales's public addresses were easily accessible through the official newspaper *El Cambio*. However, the information from previous years was more difficult to obtain. In the cases where the information was no longer available online, I utilized the WayBack Machine digital archive to access old contents in the official websites. In order to have access to as much of Morales's utterances as possible, I also employed the LexisNexis database, which facilitated the search of newspaper interviews or recorded videos of Morales's interventions.

Evo Morales's utterances were collected and analyzed in their original Spanish language. These statements were aggregated totaling 14,228 words for his first term (2006–2010) and 17,612 words for his second term (2010–2014)[4] (530 and 641 coded verbs, respectively). The verbal material was processed using the Profiler Plus automated content analysis system. This is the first published research that utilizes the Spanish version of the OCA scheme to analyze and compare leaders' beliefs. Until the beginning of 2020, leadership profiling through automated at-a-distance assessment techniques, such as OCA, was limited to the assessment of English verbal statements. The Spanish version of the operational code scheme has been recently developed and made available for the use of scholars and institutions interested in the assessment of political leaders (see Brummer et al. 2020).

## Evo Morales's Operational Code: Results and Discussion

### *Evo Morales First Term (2006–2010)*

To put Evo Morales's first term results into perspective, I compared his scores to the average of VICS scores for a norming group of 15 Latin American leaders (see Table 7.1). Compared to other leaders in the region, none of Evo Morales's philosophical beliefs differed significantly from the average of the norming group. However, major differences were found in his instrumental beliefs. His beliefs regarding the best strategic approach to achieve his goals were more cooperative than the average leader ($Z = 1.5$). Morales's risk orientation was much higher than other leaders in the norming group ($Z = 2.4$). His flexibility in shifting between cooperation and conflict as well as between words and deeds was lower than other leaders from the region ($Z = -1.5$ and $-1.7$, respectively). Regarding the utility of means, his preference for expression of appeal as a way to exercise political power was much higher than the average Latin American leader ($Z = 2.0$). On the contrary, expressions of punishment and threat were more than two standard deviations below the average regional leader ($Z = -2.0$ and $-2.1$, respectively).

*Table 7.1* Evo Morales's Operational Code (2006–2010)

| | OpCode | Mean Norming Group | Z-score | Comparison to the Norming Group |
|---|---|---|---|---|
| P-1 | 0.51 | 0.46 | 0.4 | Average |
| P-2 | 0.32 | 0.30 | 0.3 | Average |
| P-3 | 0.15 | 0.13 | 0.8 | Lean high |
| P-4 | 0.63 | 0.59 | 0.3 | Average |
| P-5 | 0.91 | 0.92 | −0.7 | Lean low |
| I-1 | 0.77 | 0.65 | 1.5 | High |
| I-2 | 0.39 | 0.36 | 0.4 | Average |
| I-3 | 0.37 | 0.23 | 2.4 | Very high |
| I-4a | 0.23 | 0.35 | −1.5 | Low |
| I-4b | 0.50 | 0.68 | −1.7 | Low |
| I-5 Punish | 0.03 | 0.07 | −2.0 | Very low |
| I-5 Threaten | 0.00 | 0.01 | −2.1 | Very low |
| I-5 Oppose | 0.08 | 0.09 | −0.5 | Average |
| I-5 Appeal | 0.65 | 0.51 | 2.0 | Very high |
| I-5 Promise | 0.02 | 0.04 | −1.5 | Low |
| I-5 Reward | 0.22 | 0.27 | −0.8 | Lean low |

## Evo Morales's Second Term (2010–2014)

To put Evo Morales's results during his second term into perspective, I compared his scores to the average of VICS scores for a norming group of 15 Latin American leaders (see Table 7.2). Compared to other Latin American leaders, Evo Morales's philosophical beliefs showed noticeable differences. He perceived the nature of the political universe as less

*Table 7.2* Evo Morales's Operational Code (2010–2014)

| | OpCode | Mean Norming Group | Z-Score | Comparison to the Norming Group |
|---|---|---|---|---|
| P-1 | 0.17 | 0.46 | −2.3 | Very low |
| P-2 | 0.05 | 0.30 | −2.6 | Very low |
| P-3 | 0.10 | 0.13 | −1.4 | Low |
| P-4 | 0.31 | 0.59 | −2.4 | Very low |
| P-5 | 0.97 | 0.92 | 2.4 | Very high |
| I-1 | 0.53 | 0.65 | −1.6 | Low |
| I-2 | 0.23 | 0.36 | −2.0 | Very low |
| I-3 | 0.19 | 0.23 | −0.7 | Lean low |
| I-4a | 0.47 | 0.35 | 1.6 | High |
| I-4b | 0.75 | 0.68 | 0.7 | Lean high |
| I-5 Punish | 0.15 | 0.07 | 3.5 | Very high |
| I-5 Threaten | 0.03 | 0.01 | 3.2 | Very high |
| I-5 Oppose | 0.06 | 0.09 | −1.3 | Low |
| I-5 Appeal | 0.50 | 0.51 | −0.2 | Average |
| I-5 Promise | 0.05 | 0.04 | 0.3 | Average |
| I-5 Reward | 0.22 | 0.27 | −0.8 | Lean low |

friendly and more hostile than the average leader in the region ($Z = -2.3$). Likewise, the prospect for realizing his fundamental political goals was much more pessimistic than the average leader ($Z = -2.6$). Morales perceived the political future as less predictable than other leaders in the norming group ($Z = -1.4$). Moreover, his perception of his capacity to control historical developments was over two standard deviations below other Latin American leaders ($Z = -2.4$). The role attributed to chance in political outcomes is greater than two standard deviations above the average leader ($Z = 2.4$).

Concerning Morales's second-terms instrumental beliefs, his strategic approach to achieve his political goals was less cooperative than other leaders in the region ($Z = -1.6$). The tactics to pursue his goals were also more conflictual than the average leader ($Z = -2.0$). His flexibility in shifting between cooperation and conflict was higher than other leaders in the norming group ($Z = 1.6$). Regarding the utility of means, his preferences for expressions of punishment and threat to exercise political power were greater than three standard deviations above the average Latin American leader ($Z = 3.5$ and $3.2$, respectively). Expressions of opposition were more than one standard deviation lower than the average regional leader ($Z = -1.3$).

### Comparing Evo Morales's First and Second Terms

The results of the OCA of Evo Morales showed some noticeable differences in Morales's beliefs concerning the rivalry with Chile between his first and second term (Table 7.3). His philosophical beliefs shifted to a less friendly perception of the political universe ($Z = -2.7$) and a less optimistic

*Table 7.3* Comparison Morales's Operational Code First and Second Terms

|  | First term Z-score | Second term Z-score | Z-score difference (degree of learning) | Direction |
|---|---|---|---|---|
| P-1 | 0.4 | −2.3 | −2.7 | Weakened |
| P-2 | 0.3 | −2.6 | −2.9 | Weakened |
| P-3 | 0.8 | −1.4 | −2.2 | Weakened |
| P-4 | 0.3 | −2.4 | −2.7 | Weakened |
| P-5 | −0.7 | 2.4 | 3.1 | Strengthened |
| I-1 | 1.5 | −1.6 | −3.1 | Weakened |
| I-2 | 0.4 | −2.0 | −2.4 | Weakened |
| I-3 | 2.4 | −0.7 | −3.1 | Weakened |
| I-4a | −1.5 | 1.6 | 3.1 | Strengthened |
| I-4b | −1.7 | 0.7 | 2.4 | Strengthened |
| I-5 Punish | −2.0 | 3.5 | 5.5 | Strengthened |
| I-5 Threaten | −2.1 | 3.2 | 5.3 | Strengthened |
| I-5 Oppose | −0.5 | −1.3 | −0.8 | Weakened |
| I-5 Appeal | 2.0 | −0.2 | −2.2 | Weakened |
| I-5 Promise | −1.5 | 0.3 | 1.8 | Strengthened |
| I-5 Reward | −0.8 | −0.8 | 0 | Unchanged |

prospect of achieving his political values (Z = –2.9). The political future became less predictable (Z = –2.2), and his perception of control over historical events also decreased during his second term (Z = –2.7). The role attributed to chance increased during his second term (Z = 3.1). Morales's instrumental beliefs also showed differences between his two presidential terms. His beliefs about the best strategy and tactics to achieve his goals became less cooperative (Z = –3.1 and –2.4, respectively). He was also less prone to accept risks (Z = –3.1). Overall, he also became more flexible in shifting between cooperation and conflict (Z = 3.1) as well as between words and deeds (Z = 2.4). Concerning the utility of means, his preferences remained similar, except for expressions of punishment, where he shifted from well-below average to way above average (Z = 5.5), and expressions of promise, which shifted from below average to about average (Z = 1.8).

The differences observed in Evo Morales's belief system in Table 7.3 support the learning hypothesis. Morales's noticeable change in the majority of his philosophical and instrumental beliefs pertaining to the rivalry, including those considered as key beliefs, indicate that the learning process occurred in all three levels: simple, diagnostic, and complex. His shift to a more negative stance toward the rivalry can help one to explain the negative turn that the bilateral relations took during his second term, which was marked by the escalation of the conflict. In a nutshell, Morales learned from his first term to his second term to be less optimistic and friendly about the rivalry with Chile. The future of the rivalry became less predictable and his perception of control decreased. Likewise, Morales learned that less cooperative strategies and tactics were a better way to achieve his goals, which can help one to explain his more aggressive approach toward Chile in his second term. Morales's new belief system can contribute to the explanation of his confrontational stance, his decision to file a lawsuit at the ICJ as well as the series of diplomatic impasses.

## Conclusions

Drawing on the FPA literature, this chapter explored the role of political leaders in shaping periods of cooperation and escalation of tensions in interstate rivalries. More specifically, I analyzed the role of the former president of Bolivia, Evo Morales, in two pivotal moments of the bilateral relations with Chile. These milestones correspond to a period of improvement of the bilateral relations during Morales's first administration, and a period of increasing tensions during his second mandate. I argued that the change in Evo Morales's foreign policy behavior was the consequence of a process of learning that can be observed in the change of his belief system regarding the rivalry and the bilateral relations with Chile.

This study used a cognitive approach to understanding decision-making processes in the context of interstate rivalries. Specifically, I utilized the OCA approach as a tool to assess Morales's change in beliefs. The results showed a noticeable difference in Morales's beliefs from his first to his second term, which supports the general learning hypothesis proposed at the beginning of this chapter. This finding fills a gap in the scholarly literature on rivalries, as it helps one to shed light on the reasons for the variation of rivalries between states across time. This finding also supports the idea that the mechanism of cooperation and escalation of hostilities can be located in leaders' beliefs concerning the self and the other in the context of a rivalry.

While the learning hypothesis sheds light on the individual mechanisms that might help one to explain leaders' behavior, it is also relevant to highlight the dyadic nature of rivalries as a source of learning. In this study, the source of learning for Evo Morales appears to be a change in the situation between Bolivia and Chile in the form of a change in Chile's leader from Bachelet to Piñera. This change was the environmental stimulus or treatment that likely evoked a change across presidential terms in the Bolivian leader's instrumental and philosophical beliefs. In future studies, it would be relevant and desirable to consider how leaders' beliefs from both sides interact in periods of cooperation and escalation of the rivalry, in order to gain a deeper understanding of their cognitive and behavioral dynamics. Another aspect that could help one to shed light on the variation of rivalries is concerned with leaders' personality traits. Due to their personal characteristics, some leaders may be more prone to escalate conflicts or engage in cooperation. This aspect is worth further analysis.

This study also showed a methodological advance in the application of the OCA approach, as it is the first time that a Spanish-speaking leader has been assessed using the Spanish-language version of the automated content analysis software. This step stands as a relevant advance in the study of political leaders in the Latin American context where presidents have a strong influence in shaping foreign policy decision-making processes due to the characteristics of presidential regimes in the region. Future work could include the expansion of the norming group and the OCA of other leaders in the context of interstate rivalries to develop a more robust body of research.

## Notes

1. Quintal is a unit of weight.
2. This justification is in line with the Article 52 of the Vienna Convention on the Law of Treaties (1969) which states that "A treaty is void if its conclusion has been procured by the threat or use of force in violation of the principles of international law embodied in the Charter of the United Nations." However, this Treaty does not apply to the case of Chile and Bolivia due to its nonretroactivity.
3. Own translation.
4. While Morales's second term spanned 5 years, I employed verbal material from 2010 to 2014. I made this decision to prevent the change in the Chilean administration in 2014 from affecting the results.

# References

Bar-Tal, D. 1998. Societal beliefs in times of intractable conflict: The Israeli case. *International Journal of Conflict Management* 9(1): 22–50.

Bar-Tal, D. 2007. Sociopsychological foundations of intractable conflicts. *American Behavioral Scientist* 50(11): 1430–1453.

Bar-Tal, D. 2013. *Intractable conflicts: Socio-psychological foundations and dynamics*. Cambridge: Cambridge University Press.

Brummer, K., M. Young, Ö Özdamar, S. Canbolat, C. Thiers, C. Rabini, K. Dimmroth, M. Hansel, A. Mehvar. 2020. Forum: Coding in tongues: Developing non-English coding schemes for leadership profiling. *International Studies Review*, 22(4): 1039–1067

Deheza, I. 2007. Bolivia 2006: reforma estatal y construcción del poder. *Revista de ciencia política* 27: 43–57.

Diehl, P. F., G. Goertz. 2000. *War and peace in international rivalry*. Ann Arbor, MI: University of Michigan Press.

Estado Plurinacional de Bolivia 2010. February 4, 2010. https://web.archive.org/web/20100204065550/http://www.presidencia.gob.bo/perfil.htm.

Cooperativa.cl. 2015. "Evo Morales Reveló Supuesta Negociación Marítima Durante El Primer Gobierno de Bachelet," March 20, 2015. https://www.cooperativa.cl/noticias/pais/relaciones-exteriores/bolivia/evo-morales-revelo-supuesta-negociacion-maritima-durante-el-primer/2015-03-20/130746.html.

George, A. 1969. The operational code: A neglected approach to the study of political leaders and decision-making. *International Studies Quarterly* 13(2): 190–222.

Goertz, G., P. Diehl. 1992. The empirical importance of enduring rivalries. *International Interactions* 18(2): 151–163.

González, S., C. Ovando. 2016. Emotivistas bolivianos en la relación diplomática entre Bolivia y Chile en torno a la mediterraneidad. *Estudios Internacionales* 183: 39–65.

Gerring, J. 2012. *Social science methodology*. 2nd Edition. New York, NY: Cambridge University Press.

Gutiérrez, C. 2007. Chile, Perú y Bolivia: entre el conflicto y la cooperación. In *Seguridad humana y nuevas políticas de defensa en Iberoamérica*, ed. I. Sepúlveda, 291–322. Madrid: Instituto Universitario General Gutiérrez Mellado-UNED.

Holsti, O. 1970. The operational code approach to the study of political leaders: John Foster Dulles' philosophical and instrumental beliefs. *Canadian Journal of Political Science/Revue Canadienne de Science Politique*, 3(1): 123–157.

Leites, N. 1951. *The operational code of the politburo*. 1st Edition. New York: McGraw-Hill Book Co.

Levy, J. 1994. Learning and foreign policy: Sweeping a conceptual minefield. *International Organization* 48(2): 279–312.

Malici, A., J. Malici. 2005. The operational codes of Fidel Castro and Kim Il Sung: The last cold warriors? *Political Psychology* 26(3): 387–412.

Maoz, Z., B. Mor. 1996. Enduring rivalries: The early years. *International Political Science Review* 17(2): 141–160.

Mesa, C. 2016. *La historia del mar boliviano*. La Paz, Bolivia: Editorial Gisbert.

Milet, P. 2002. La política exterior de los gobiernos de la concertación. *Colombia Internacional* (56–57): 46–63.

Morales, E. 2007. General assembly official records, 62nd session: 7th plenary meeting. https://digitallibrary.un.org/record/607840?ln=es.

Morales, E. 2011. Discurso del Presidente de Bolivia en el acto de recordación de 132 años de enclaustramiento. *Bolpress.Com*, March 23, 2011. https://www.bolpress.com/?Cod=2011032304.

Morales, E. 2012. Evo Morales afirma que 'Chile es un peligro para la región' *La Razón*, October 2, 2012. https://web.archive.org/web/20121228115306/ http://www.la-razon.com:80/nacional/Evo-Morales-Chile-peligro-region_0_1698430185.html.

Morales, E. 2013a. Carta del Presidente Evo Morales a los soldados Choque, Fernández y Cárdenas presos injustamente en Chile. Ministerio de Comunicación - Bolivia. https://www.comunicacion.gob.bo/?q=20130224/carta-del-presidente-evo-morales-los-soldados-choque-fern%C3%A1ndcz-y-cardenas-presos.

Morales, E. 2013b. Haremos valer nuestro derecho a tener un acceso soberano al mar. *América Latina en movimiento*, March 23, 2013. https://www.alainet.org/es/active/62790.

Morales, E. 2013c. Evo Morales: 'Chile tiene una deuda no solo con Bolivia sino con Latinoamérica.' *CNN Español*, June 5, 2013. https://cnnespanol.cnn.com/2013/06/05/evo-morales-chile-tiene-una-deuda-no-solo-con-bolivia-sino-con-latinoamerica/.

Ovando, C., S. González. 2012. La política exterior chileno-boliviana en la década de 1950 mirada desde la región de Tarapacá. *Polis: Revista Latinoamericana* (32): 1–22.

Quiroga, M., N. Guerrero. 2016. ¿Qué se esconde tras La Haya?: análisis de los discursos presidenciales y cobertura mediática en los conflictos Chile-Perú/Chile-Bolivia. *Si Somos Americanos* 16(1): 147–180.

Quiroz, M. 2016. Historia secreta del último diálogo fallido entre Bolivia y Chile. *La Razón*, March 26, 2016. https://web.archive.org/web/20191226110254/http://www.la-razon.com:80/suplementos/especiales/Historia-dialogo-fallido-Bolivia-Chile_0_2459154116.html.

Rivera, P. 2016. Fantasmas de rojo y azul. Los saqueos de las tropas chilenas en la Guerra del Pacífico. *Anuario Colombiano de Historia Social y de La Cultura* 43(1): 263–293.

Rodríguez, J. 2014. *Historia de dos demandas: Perú y Bolivia contra Chile*. Santiago, Chile. Aguilar Chilena de Ediciones.

Rodríguez, J. 2016. *Todo sobre Bolivia*. Santiago, Chile. Ediciones El Mercurio.

Schafer, M., Walker S. 2006. Operational code analysis at a distance: The verbs in context system of content analysis. In *Beliefs and leadership in world politics: Methods and applications of operational code analysis*, eds. M. Schafer, S. Walker, 25–51. Advances in foreign policy analysis. New York, NY: Palgrave Macmillan.

Thies, C. 2001. A social psychological approach to enduring rivalries. *Political Psychology* 22(4): 693–725.

Thies, C. 2003. The political psychology of interstate rivalry. In *Advances in psychology research*, ed. Shohov, S., 155–170. Vol. 22. New York, NY: Nova Science Publishers, Inc.

Thompson, W. 1995. Principal rivalries. *Journal of Conflict Resolution* 39(2): 195–223.

Thompson, W. 2001. Identifying rivals and rivalries in world politics. *International Studies Quarterly* 45(4): 557–586.

Van Klaveren, A. 2011. La política exterior de Chile durante los gobiernos de la Concertación (1990-2010). *Estudios Internacionales* 44(169): 155–170.

Vasquez, J. 1996. Distinguishing rivals that go to war from those that do not: A quantitative comparative case study of the two paths to war. *International Studies Quarterly* 40(4): 531.

Walker, S. G. 1983. The motivational foundations of political belief systems: A re-analysis of the operational code construct. *International Studies Quarterly* 27(2): 179–202.

Walker, S. G. 1990. "The evolution of operational code analysis. *Political Psychology* 11 (2): 403.

Walker, S. G., M. Schafer, M. Young. 1998. Systematic procedures for operational code analysis: Measuring and modeling Jimmy Carter's operational code. *International Studies Quarterly* 42: 175–190.

Walker, S., A. Malici, M. Schafer. Eds. 2011. *Rethinking foreign policy analysis.* New York, NY: Routledge

Walker, S. G., M. Schafer, M. Young. 2003. Profiling the operational codes of political leaders. In *The psychological assessment of political leaders*, ed. J. M. Post, 215–245. Ann Arbor, MI: The University of Michigan Press.

Wehner, L. 2011. Developing mutual trust: The othering process between Bolivia and Chile. *Canadian Journal of Latin American and Caribbean Studies* 36(71): 109–138.

# Part III

# The Psychological Characteristics of US Presidents

# 8 Psychological Correlates and US Conflict Behavior

## The PsyCL Data Set

*Mark Schafer, Stephen G. Walker, Clayton Besaw, Paul Gill, and Gary E. Smith*

## Introduction

The idea that psychology can have an effect on politics has a long history in academic research (see, for example, Lasswell 1930). And the relationship between psychology and foreign policy behavior in particular has been well studied over the years (for example, Leites 1951; Holsti 1967; George 1969; Cottam 1977). However, we rarely see psychological variables included in any of the best scientific studies of international conflict behavior. Most of that work instead focuses on state- or system-level variables – the structures and situational factors in place in any given situation. And yet, theoretically speaking, it is impossible to divorce the actor from the action: human beings – with all of their psychological parts and pieces – make decisions. Think for a moment about any major foreign policy case throughout history: both World Wars, Vietnam, the Berlin Crisis, wars in the Middle East, Iran-Contra, 9/11, and many more; which of them were devoid of major personalities? For which of them can we really leave the individuals out and still understand the unfolding of the case?

How then can we justify our best scientific models of conflict behavior without including psychology? We do not think we can, and it is time that we more routinely and systematically investigate the effects of psychological characteristics of individual actors on foreign policy behavior and include those characteristics in our best models. In order to do so, we need data. Today we have the computing technology to more effectively gather and process such data than we had in the past. This chapter explores the current status of a major research project that intends to gather and make publicly available the psychological characteristics of a very large number of foreign policy actors throughout history. We call this data set the Psychological Characteristics of Leaders (PsyCL).[1]

In this chapter, we will first discuss the two most prolific research programs using psychological characteristics: Leadership Trait Analysis

(LTA) (Hermann 2003) and Operational Code Analysis (OCA) (Walker, Schafer, and Young 1998). These two programs provide the basis for the initial set of psychological characteristics in PsyCL. We then turn to a description of PsyCL, describe the research design strategies in building it and making it functional for other scholars, and present some descriptive statistics and examples coming out of the data set. Then we present the first empirical investigation using our new data set: a study of the psychological characteristics of US presidents and their effects on US conflict behavior. We present a brief literature review and theory section, a research-design section, and the results of our analysis of the effects of psychological characteristics on US behavior in Militarized Interstate Disputes (MIDs).

## Psychological Assessment At-A-Distance

### *Leadership Trait Analysis*

Margaret Hermann is one of the most important and earliest contributors to "at-a-distance" methods that make it possible to measure psychological characteristics of foreign policy makers, and she refers to her approach as LTA (Hermann 1999, 2003). We do not generally have direct access to leaders, past and present so that we can use traditional methods of psychological assessment, such as paper-pencil responses or clinical observation. As a result, early researchers in this area developed the idea that the verbal behavior of actors can tell us certain things about leaders' psychological characteristics. And, since most leaders conduct public speeches and interviews, we can with these methods ascertain psychological characteristics for many different actors, both present and past.

Hermann's work in this area began in the 1970s (Hermann and Milburn 1977), when she began to identify several psychological characteristics that are politically relevant and could be identified by patterns in a speaker's verbal behavior. The methods required the specification of words or phrases in a subject's rhetoric that indicate positive or negative manifestations of a psychological characteristic. For instance, conceptual complexity is a characteristic that shows a leader's propensity to "differentiate things and people in one's environment," that is, to see the world in complex terms versus simple, black-and-white terms (Hermann 1999, 10).

To operationalize this variable, Hermann constructed two sets of words and phrases: those marking more differentiation, more shades of gray in the environment, such as *sometimes*, *perhaps*, and *possibly*, and those marking less differentiation, more black-and-white thinking, such as *always*, *forever*, and *absolutely*. A leader's verbal material is then content analyzed to count these two sets of words. A ratio between the two separate counts tells us whether the subject is more complex (higher use of differentiating words) or less complex (lower use of differentiating words). Besides conceptual complexity, Hermann's LTA also includes the following psychological characteristics: need for power, belief in ability to control events (BACE), distrust, in-group bias, self-confidence, and task orientation.

### *Operational Code Analysis*

While OCA has a long history in the field of political psychology (Leites 1951; George 1969; Holsti 1970; Walker 1977), the development of at-a-distance measurement methods for the construct is more recent (Walker, Schafer, and Young 1998). Leites (1951) was the first major contribution to the operational code literature when he conducted a study to try to understand the unusual bargaining behavior of those in the Soviet Politburo. Using complex depth psychology constructs with qualitative methods, he found that those in the Politburo had a particular mindset – an operational code – that was at once fairly uniform in the Politburo and yet very different from those in the West; it was derived largely from the impacts of Lenin and Stalin and their own individual-level psychology. Because of its complexity and its idiosyncratic nature, few scholars built on the initial work of Leites.

George (1969) revisited the operational code and laid the groundwork to convert it into a more functional research program. Writing at the time of the cognitive revolution in psychology, George argued that the operational code needed to be a cognitive construct, focusing on the beliefs of actors. George then posited ten questions that he said comprised a subject's operational code belief system. Five of the questions are called "philosophical" and assess the subject's beliefs about external factors, such as other actors, human nature, and international politics. The other five questions are called "instrumental" and pertain to the subject's beliefs about his or her own approach to politics, strategies, and tactics. Answers to the ten questions comprise a leader's operational code, which is likely to have an effect on that actor's behavior.

For many years, OCA was marked by qualitative research on one or a small number of actors at a time (for example, McLellan 1971; Johnson 1977; Walker 1977; Stuart and Starr 1981; Walker and Falkowski 1984). In the late 1990s, however, Stephen Walker and his colleagues developed an approach for quantitatively assessing actors' operational codes by using at-a-distance methods (Walker, Schafer, and Young 1998). The approach, called the Verbs in Context System, identifies the verbs in a subject's verbal material, codes them on a continuum from conflictual (e.g., *attack*) to cooperative (e.g., *help*), differentiates the grammatical subject of the clause as *self* or *other*, then uses various aggregations to determine index scores that quantitatively answer each of George's philosophical and instrumental questions. The result is that the system generally provides indicators of a subject's conflict versus cooperation orientation in terms of his or her perceptions of others (philosophical beliefs) and self (instrumental beliefs).

### From Hand Coding to Automation

When Hermann and later Walker started their at-a-distance research programs, all of the content analysis of verbal material was done by hand, a highly laborious and slow task that also introduced such potential problems as coder bias and fatigue. The result was a limited number of projects that investigated a fairly small number of leaders (for example, Hermann 1980; Walker, Schafer, and Young 1998). More recent times have brought about various technological breakthroughs that are now letting us move past this coding bottleneck. First, a full-language, coding software program called Profiler Plus was developed at the company Social Science Automation (http://socialscience.net/). Profiler Plus first parses the verbal material into manageable language components, and then codes the material based upon the specified phrase books and coding rules for each of the different psychological characteristics. This means that once a speech act is digitized and prepped, it can be coded almost instantaneously.

The second important breakthrough with modern technology revolves around the new digital age. Many past and present speech acts for many foreign policy actors are now digitally available. In addition, software engineers have developed programs that can (1) scrape the Internet for verbal material of interest and (2) pre-clean the material to make it ready for coding by Profiler Plus. In the past, it would have taken a small team of coders working by hand many months to code 1 year's worth of verbal material from one US president. The current project, which has coded all verbal material for all US presidents, was done in a few months from start to finish.

### The Psychological Characteristics of Leaders (PsyCL) Data Set

There are some steps to go through to get to the point of having coded data by Profiler Plus. First, each speech act must be identified. For this stage of the project, focusing only on US presidents, we used the American Presidency Project website (www.presidency.ucsb.edu/) as our source for verbal material of the presidents. The data set includes every single available speech act delivered verbally by every US president. Speech-act documents must then be prepped before running through Profiler Plus. For example, many speech acts begin with perfunctory comments by the president, introductory comments by someone else, or questions or comments by others, and these irrelevant comments need to be "ignored" by Profiler Plus (which is done by inputting ignore tags around the irrelevant verbal material). Second, we record a variety of secondary information for each speech act, such as date, type of audience, and type of speech act. Then each speech act is coded by Profiler Plus, which gives us relevant data for our psychological characteristics.

The output from Profiler Plus can take the form of raw counts for each psychological characteristic (which then needs to be converted to index scores) or already calculated index scores. PsyCL is set up with the former so that researchers can specify and aggregate their own units of analysis. The unit of analysis in PsyCL is always the individual speech act (typically these are individual speeches, interviews, or press conferences), though, typically speaking, one should not use the speech act as the unit of analysis for statistical research projects. This is the case because not all speech acts are long enough to provide meaningful measurements once the raw data are converted to indexes.

For example, with some of the OCA indexes, if there are not enough verbs coded in the speech act, then errors will be reported for index scores. This means that researchers will typically need to specify an aggregated unit of analysis (this could be such things as the president, president-term, president-year, or even in most cases the president-quarter year). Our empirical analysis in this chapter uses the president-year as the unit of analysis for statistical purposes. Once the unit of analysis is specified, the researcher needs to aggregate all of the raw scores for each psychological characteristic to the level of the unit of analysis. Once that step is done, then the indexes can be calculated, resulting in the psychological measurements for the unit of analysis.

## Descriptive Data and Anecdotal Applications of PsyCL

The initial version of the PsyCL data set contains interesting variations concerning presidential beliefs and personality. While the base data set contains individual speech acts as the unit of analysis (N = 2349), this chapter demonstrates some basic descriptive information and basic relationships for two types of unit aggregations. Two such aggregations that can be explored are cross-sectional (president, N = 43) and time series cross-sectional (president-year, N = 242). Table 8.1 displays the means, standard deviations, minimum values, and maximum values for both aggregation types.

Moving beyond basic descriptive statistics, there are a variety of ways to demonstrate the potential for interesting variation within the presidential data set. Figure 8.1 displays time-series plots for four psychological traits (distrust, BACE, self-confidence, and control over historical development).[2] These four plots demonstrate not only interesting temporal patterns, but also show potential substantive relationships between presidential psychology and temporal progression. Distrust shows a decreasing trend over time, with the greatest drop taking place after the

*Table 8.1* Descriptive Statistics

| Variable | Mean | SD | Min | Max |
|---|---|---|---|---|
| President year data N = 242 | | | | |
| Distrust of others | 0.194 | 0.096 | 0.027 | 0.572 |
| Task orientation | 0.644 | 0.082 | 0.354 | 0.823 |
| Belief in ability to control events | 0.274 | 0.081 | 0 | 0.418 |
| In-group bias | 0.139 | 0.051 | 0 | 0.34 |
| Self-confidence | 0.378 | 0.131 | 0 | 0.708 |
| Conceptual complexity | 0.597 | 0.043 | 0.472 | 0.733 |
| Need for power and influence | 0.269 | 0.059 | 0 | 0.482 |
| Nature of the political universe | 0.413 | 0.111 | 0.04 | 0.77 |
| Control over historical development | 0.144 | 0.08 | 0.017 | 0.313 |
| Strategy | 0.593 | 0.202 | −0.333 | 1 |
| President data N = 44 | | | | |
| Distrust of others | 0.196 | 0.078 | 0.064 | 0.401 |
| Task orientation | 0.643 | 0.08 | 0.43 | 0.75 |
| Belief in ability to control events | 0.259 | 0.065 | 0.154 | 0.375 |
| In-group bias | 0.14 | 0.027 | 0.088 | 0.207 |
| Self-confidence | 0.365 | 0.11 | 0.17 | 0.655 |
| Conceptual complexity | 0.596 | 0.038 | 0.472 | 0.66 |
| Need for power and influence | 0.276 | 0.041 | 0.195 | 0.424 |
| Nature of the political universe | 0.407 | 0.084 | 0.203 | 0.553 |
| Control over historical development | 0.137 | 0.077 | 0.045 | 0.293 |
| Strategy | 0.606 | 0.106 | 0.406 | 0.801 |

turn of the 20th century. Additionally, there is a slight upward bump after the year 2000.

Both belief in one's ability to control events and beliefs over control of historical development show similar temporal patterns. Both traits indicate upward trends that correspond to around the start of the 20th century, with slight decreases in this trend after 2000. Similar in substance to the previous two traits, self-confidence shows a steady upward trend during the whole of US history, with an eventual plateau and decrease starting in the 1980s. It is clear that each of these trends shares some interesting changes that correspond to two major events. First, each trait seems to see substantial changes near the 1900 mark, a date that nearly corresponds to the COW project's date (1898) for the transition to great power status for the United States (Correlates of War Project 2011). Finally, downward or upward trends that deviate from historical patterns seem to occur at the time of the September 11th attacks.

Focusing on a purely cross-sectional analysis, Tables 8.2 and 8.3 show presidents with statistically significant z-scores for each psychological trait.[3] The results are interesting in that they show a wide degree of variation across both traits and presidents. Note, for instance, that James Madison was the most distrusting president, while James Garfield had an extremely high need for Power. George Washington had low self-confidence,

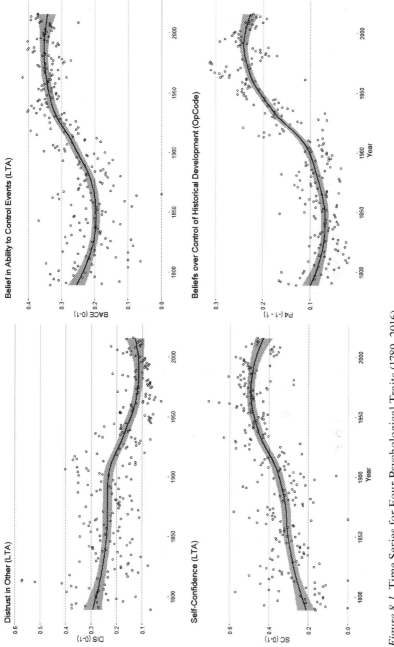

*Figure 8.1* Time Series for Four Psychological Traits (1789–2016)

*Table 8.2* Significant Deviations (z-Score) on LTA Traits

| *Distrust of Others* | |
| --- | --- |
| James Madison | 2.59 |

| Task orientation | |
| --- | --- |
| George Washington | −1.87 |
| James Garfield | −2.65 |
| John Adams | −2.22 |
| Warren Harding | −1.96 |

| Belief in ability to control events | |
| --- | --- |
| Ronald Reagan | 1.76 |
| Barack Obama | 1.74 |

| In-group bias | |
| --- | --- |
| George Washington | 1.92 |
| Franklin Pierce | −1.74 |
| James Garfield | −1.89 |
| John Tyler | 1.99 |
| William Harrison | 2.46 |
| Franklin D. Roosevelt | −1.86 |

| Conceptual complexity | |
| --- | --- |
| Warren Harding | −3.24 |

| Self-confidence | |
| --- | --- |
| George Washington | −1.77 |
| John Kennedy | 2.62 |

| Need for power and influence | |
| --- | --- |
| James Garfield | 3.59 |
| William Harrison | 2.02 |
| Martin Van Buren | −1.95 |

*Table 8.3* Significant Deviations (z-Score) on OpCode Traits

| *Nature of the Political Universe (P-1)* | |
| --- | --- |
| Andrew Johnson | −1.83 |
| James Buchanan | −2.19 |
| James Garfield | −2.41 |
| James Polk | −1.78 |
| John Quincy Adams | 1.72 |

| Control over historical development (P-4) | |
| --- | --- |
| Lyndon Johnson | 1.98 |
| Gerald Ford | 2.01 |

| Strategy (I-1) | |
| --- | --- |
| Chester Arthur | 1.83 |
| Millard Fillmore | 1.82 |
| Ronald Reagan | −1.88 |

while John F. Kennedy's was very high. Both Ronald Reagan and Barack Obama had high control orientations, demonstrating that psychological characteristics are typically not a partisan matter.

The data set is useful for exploring these differences for all presidents, but it is perhaps more helpful to focus on influential and well-studied presidents to illustrate the power of this data. Woodrow Wilson has been extensively studied within the psychoanalytic and political psychology literature (George and George 1964, 1998; Post 1983; Weinstein 2014). These studies tend to focus on either Wilson's troubles with his father or his disconnect with the reality of the world around him (George and George 1964; Freud and Bullitt 1999). Examining Wilson in depth using the data set, one finds that he had a relatively high need for power ($z = 1.31$), low conceptual complexity ($z = -1.52$), and a conflictual strategic orientation ($z = -1.26$). These scores are consistent with other at-a-distance findings as well as some of the less statistical psychoanalytic conjectures. His high scores on the need for power and more conflictual strategic orientation are consistent with findings that question his idealist tendencies (Walker and Schafer 2007). His low scores on conceptual complexity are in line with arguments concerning his inability to acknowledge complex facts about the world, and a dependence on simplistic beliefs concerning right and wrong (Freud and Bullitt 1999).

Moving forward in time, Ronald Reagan is an important presidential figure in that he oversaw the end of the Cold War. With actions such as the famous "evil empire" speech, Reagan represented an ideological and instrumental shift in how the United States would approach the Soviet Union. There is some suggestive psychological evidence that predicts his shift toward more military-oriented approaches; this can be seen in his more conflictual strategic orientation (I-1, $z = -1.88$). There is also some construct validity between our score showing Reagan as high in self-confidence ($z = 1.54$) and Weintraub (1986), who described Reagan as being confident and humorous as a result of his background as an actor.

While examining cross-sectional differences and the building of psychological profiles serves as a useful tool, there is no doubt that additional interesting variation exists across both president and time. Here we pick two presidents who served through times of conflict and show how their psychological scores varied over time. First, James Madison oversaw the first major war since the American Revolution. By declaring war on Britain, the War of 1812 sought to address political issues concerning the policies of trade restriction, naval impressment, and domestic interference as practiced by the British. Figure 8.2 shows time-series plots for James Madison's scores on distrust, beliefs concerning the nature of the political universe (P-1), and strategy (I-1). Madison's distrust steadily increases during the buildup to war while peaking midway through the conflict. During the latter half of the war, and postwar,

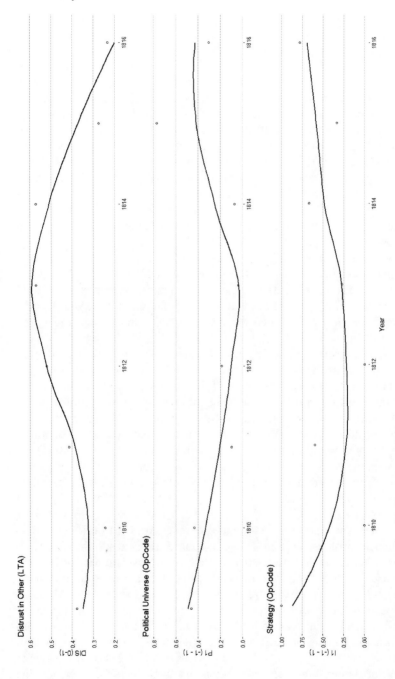

*Figure 8.2* James Madison Psych Traits (1809–1817)

Madison's distrust decreases substantially. Similar patterns appear for both beliefs concerning the political universe and strategic orientation. Both beliefs fall during the buildup to the conflict (meaning his beliefs became more conflictual) and increase during the late- and post-conflict periods.

While the United States' involvement in World War I would not take place until roughly 3 years after the initial onset of the conflict, Woodrow Wilson had been heavily involved in both attempting to promote a peaceful resolution and aiding the Allied powers. The buildup to the conflict included consecutive U-boat attacks on American merchant ships and the infamous Zimmerman telegram. As a result of these actions, Wilson formally asked for a declaration of war in April of 1917. Figure 8.3 shows how Wilson's scores on conceptual complexity, need for power, and strategy changed during his tenure. Wilson's conceptual complexity remained somewhat stable during the prewar period, but shows a sharp decline after 1916 with the lowest point coming in 1917, the year that the United States formally entered the war.

Interestingly, Wilson's need for power score began to increase sharply in the aftermath of the war. This is perhaps due to his dissatisfaction with his influence on postwar issues such as the Treaty of Versailles and the League of Nations.[4] Finally, Wilson's changes concerning strategy seem to have been heavily dependent on the war. Wilson's cooperative idealism shows a greater shift toward a more competitive/conflictual orientation as the United States enters the war, with this trend roughly continuing into the postwar years of his tenure. Interestingly, this is almost analogous to the findings of Walker and Schafer (2007), who found that Wilson perhaps became more of a realist as a result of the war.

## Psychological Characteristics and US Conflict Behavior

### Introduction and Hypotheses

In this section, we present a research project that empirically examines the effect of some psychological characteristics of US presidents on US foreign policy behaviors in terms of MIDs. While PsyCL provides us measurements for all LTA and OCA variables, here we investigate the effects of two different subsets of the variables that we believe are theoretically linked to US conflict behavior.

The first subset of variables is those dealing with the president's general perception of the nature and intentions of others. Some presidents will have a rosier outlook on who other actors are and what they might do, while other presidents will have a more negative outlook. We anticipate that those who have more negative views of others and their intentions are more likely to escalate a conflict situation. There are two variables among our psychological characteristics that assess this concept: *distrust*

162  *Schafer et al.*

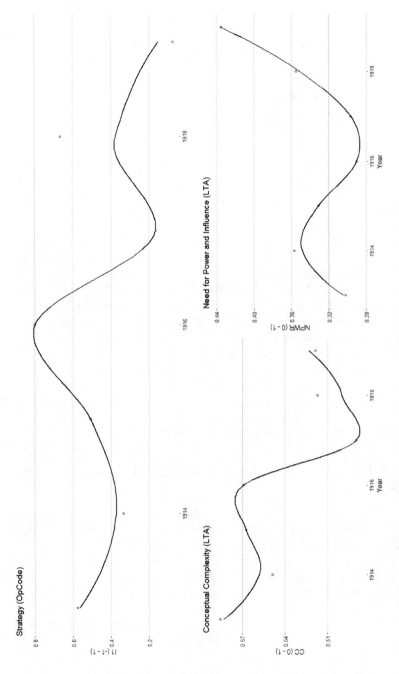

*Figure 8.3*  Woodrow Wilson Psych Traits (1913–1919)

(from LTA) and *nature of the political universe* (P-1 from OCA). *Distrust* measures a subject's general level of wariness and suspiciousness of others (Hermann 1999). When a leader scores higher on this characteristic, she or he is more likely to perceive escalating conflict behavior in others (whether it is there or not) and respond in kind. *Nature of the political universe* (P-1) assesses the subject's views of international politics and other actors in international politics in terms of harmony versus conflict. Similarly to *distrust*, those who view human nature and other actors as inherently hostile are more likely to escalate a situation, all other factors being equal.[5]

*H1:* Presidents scoring higher on *distrust* are more likely to engage in escalatory conflict behavior.

*H2:* Presidents scoring higher on *nature of the political universe* (friendlier perceptions) are less likely to engage in escalatory conflict behavior.

The second subset of variables is those dealing with the president's confidence, assuredness, and sense of control. Similar to the concept of self-esteem, these tap into a president's perceptions about self's capabilities, efficacy, and self-reliance. More confidence in one's abilities to defend and enhance one's interests means there is less of a need to demonstrate or escalate conflict. The connection between negative perceptions of self's efficacy and conflict behavior has a long history in clinical psychology (e.g., Korman 1970; Brown 1993; Ferris, Brown, and Heller 2009), and it also has theoretical support in the intergroup conflict literature (e.g., Tajfel and Turner 2001). We investigate three different psychological characteristics that relate to this concept: *self-confidence* (from LTA), *BACE* (from LTA), and *control over historical development* (P-4 from OCA). We anticipate that those scoring higher on these characteristics, indicating higher levels of self-confidence, efficacy, and control, will be less likely to escalate a conflict situation.[6]

*H3:* Presidents scoring higher on *self-confidence* are less likely to engage in escalatory conflict behavior.

*H4:* Presidents scoring higher on *BACE* are less likely to engage in escalatory conflict behavior.

*H5:* Presidents scoring higher on *control over historical development* are less likely to engage in escalatory conflict behavior.

### Research Design

We are interested in the effect of the psychological characteristics of a leader on his state's international conflict behavior. Much of the most important research published in the area of international conflict focuses on MIDs and derives much of its data from the data set by the same name (MID) (Gochman and Maoz 1984; Jones, Bremer, and Singer 1996;

Ghosn, Palmer, and Bremer 2004; Palmer, D'Orazio, and Kenwick 2015). Our project uses two different dependent variables from the MID data set: MID initiation and MID hostility level. MID initiation is a dichotomous variable indicating whether the United States initiated a MID in the dyad year. MID hostility level is a five-point ordinal variable indicating the highest level of hostile activity conducted by the United States in the dyad year; it ranges from no MID activity to war.

Following the lead of the best MID research that focuses on the behavior of one actor, our unit of analysis is the directed-dyad year. This means that the focus is on the state behavior of one side of a dyad ("Side A"), and that the key explanatory variables pertain to that side. Essentially we are asking if the psychological characteristics of the leader of one state in a dyad affect the MID behavior of that state toward the other member of the dyad. Nonetheless, it is theoretically possible (and empirically supported) that certain characteristics of the dyad itself (such as whether both states are democracies) may also affect the behavior of the Side A actor (Maoz and Russett 1993; Bueno De Mesquita, Morrow, and Siverson 1999).

Thus, directed-dyad research allows us to focus on one state's characteristics and behavior toward another state while controlling for characteristics that exist between the two states in the dyad (control variables are discussed below). Finally, each unit of analysis has variables that pertain to 1 single year: the psychological characteristics of the president are aggregated for the full year, the MID variables assess US behavior in the dyad during that year, and control variables describe characteristics of the dyad during that year as well.

The sample in our study includes all politically relevant US dyads from 1815 to 2007. Politically relevant dyads are those dyads that have some possibility of significant political interaction over the year in question (if there is no real chance of political action between two actors, then there is also no real chance of a MID occurring between them). It is defined and operationalized in the MID data set as a pair of states that is close to one another geographically or includes at least one major power in the dyad (Lemke and Reed 2001). We define close geographic proximity as two states being separated by less than 450 miles of water. Our statistical models generally include three classic control variables for large-n quantitative conflict research in general and MID-directed-dyad research in particular.

First, we control for joint democracy. This is a dichotomous variable that indicates whether both actors in the dyad were democracies. Following the logic of the democratic peace, we anticipate that the United States is less likely to engage in escalatory conflict when the other member of the dyad is also a democracy. A state is considered democratic if it has a Polity score of 6 or higher. Second, we control for geographic proximity, with the expectation that states that are closer will be more likely to engage in escalatory conflict behavior than states that are more distant. The variable is operationalized as an ordinal variable in the MID data set, with increasing values indicating that the states are geographically farther apart. Third, we control for the power differential between the two states in the dyad year. This is operationalized as a ratio of Side A's to Side B's capabilities. MID research has shown that when the ratio increases, meaning there is a bigger power gap between actors' power levels in the dyad, then escalatory conflict behavior is less likely to occur (Weede 1976; Bremer 1992; De Dreu 1995; Russett and O'neal 2001).

To test our hypothesized relationships, we use two different modeling techniques. The initiation dependent variable is a binary outcome; therefore, a panel logistic regression is the appropriate method to test the relationship between the independent variables and MID initiation. To model the effect of the independent variables on the level of hostility, we use a panel-ordered logistic regression. This technique is chosen because the dependent variable in these models is rank ordered. With panel data, there is always the risk of unit heterogeneity. In these models, the unit of interest is the dyad in question. More precisely, there may be something about a dyad that goes unmeasured that may cause these states to be more or less prone to conflict. A Hausman specification test is used to test for differences between the coefficients in a random effects model and the coefficients in a fixed effects model. The results indicate that there is no significant difference between the coefficients in the models. Therefore, the random effects estimator is appropriate to control for unit heterogeneity.

## MID Initiation Findings

### *Wariness About Others and the Political Universe*

To test our hypotheses regarding the initiation of militarized disputes, we first focus on the variables that capture a president's wariness about the intentions of others and the political universe. These can be found in Table 8.4. Findings for *distrust* appear in models one and three in the table. In model one, *distrust* increases the likelihood that a president will initiate a MID. However, in model three, *distrust* only approaches statistical significance. This provides preliminary support for the role of *distrust* as an explanatory variable for US conflict behavior. Models two, four, and six test the effect that a president's belief about the *nature of the political universe* has on his willingness to initiate a conflict. The direction of the coefficient for this variable is as anticipated in all three models: presidents who see others in more cooperative terms are less likely to initiate a MID. However, the variable is significant only in model two.

*Table 8.4* Initiation Models

| Variables | One Initiation | Two Initiation | Three Initiation | Four Initiation | Five Initiation | Six Initiation |
|---|---|---|---|---|---|---|
| Distrust | 3.138* (1.413) | | 2.790+ (1.508) | | 2.136 (1.647) | |
| P-1 | | -2.124+ (1.267) | | -1.915 (1.231) | | -1.030 (1.300) |
| Belief in ability to control events | -5.724** (2.055) | -6.454** (2.024) | | | | |
| Self-confidence | | | -1.819 (1.228) | -2.681* (1.117) | | |
| P-4 | | | | | -3.774+ (2.043) | -4.723** (1.812) |
| Jointdem × distrust | 2.754 (3.755) | | 7.149 (4.403) | | 8.037+ (4.157) | |
| Jointdem × P-1 | | -0.755 (3.461) | | -0.466 (3.546) | | -2.732 (3.740) |
| Jointdem × belief in ability to control events | -1.685 (6.741) | -3.113 (6.745) | | | | |
| Jointdem × self-confidence | | | 9.147* (4.529) | 6.444 (4.086) | | |
| Jointdem × P-4 | | | | | 16.18* (7.647) | 11.66+ (6.989) |
| Joint democracy | -0.809 (2.395) | 0.365 (2.798) | -6.525* (2.683) | -3.974 (2.582) | -5.771** (2.187) | -2.401 (1.817) |
| Capability ratio | -0.451*** (0.114) | -0.429*** (0.109) | -0.460*** (0.112) | -0.447*** (0.109) | -0.461*** (0.113) | -0.450*** (0.110) |
| Direct contiguity | -0.856*** (0.187) | -0.829*** (0.184) | -0.846*** (0.184) | -0.826*** (0.183) | -0.857*** (0.186) | -0.845*** (0.185) |
| Constant | 2.735* (1.302) | 4.140** (1.380) | 1.790 (1.285) | 3.281* (1.314) | 1.854 (1.244) | 2.701* (1.234) |
| Observations | 9998 | 9998 | 9998 | 9998 | 9998 | 9998 |
| Number of dyads | 198 | 198 | 198 | 198 | 198 | 198 |

Standard errors in parentheses.

* $p < 0.05$, ** $p < 0.01$, *** $p < 0.001$, + $p < 0.10$.

### Sense of Confidence, Control, and Efficacy

We turn now to the effect of a president's sense of confidence, control, and efficacy. These are tested using the variables: *self-confidence*, *BACE*, and *control over historical development (P-4)*. Models one and two mentioned below test the effect of *BACE* on the likelihood that a president will initiate militarized disputes. The findings are consistent and robust: *BACE* has a significant and negative effect on the likelihood that a president will initiate a MID. This indicates that a president with a higher score on *belief in his ability to control events* is less likely to initiate a MID than counterparts with a lower score on *BACE*.

Models three and four test the effect of *self-confidence*. Model four finds that there is a significant and negative relationship between *self-confidence* and the likelihood that a president will initiate a MID. A president with a higher score for *self-confidence* will be less likely to initiate a MID than his counterpart with lower *self-confidence*. Models five and six test the effect of a president's belief that he has some *control over historical development (P-4)*. There is a significant and negative relationship between beliefs about *control over historical development and MID initiation*. This means that a president who believes that he has *control over historical development* is less likely to initiate a MID than a president who believes that he has less *control over historical development*.

### Interaction Terms

In this section, we explore the effect of these psychological traits in interaction with the pacifying effect of shared democratic institutions. The idea here is that these psychological characteristics may have more or less of an effect depending upon the regime type of the other dyad member. We first consider *distrust* and the belief about the *nature of the political universe* as interacted with joint democracy. Models one, three, and five test the interaction between *distrust* and joint democracy. The findings do not indicate there is a significant relationship between these interactions and the likelihood that a leader will initiate a MID. Models two, four, and six test the interaction between a president's belief about the *nature of the political universe* and joint democracy. These findings also indicate that there is no relationship between the interaction term and the willingness of a president to initiate a MID. Taken together, these models indicate that regime type of the other dyad member does not alter the effect of *distrust* or a president's belief about the *nature of the political universe* on MID initiation by the United States.

We next test interaction terms that capture the connection between joint democracy and the variables pertaining to a president's sense of confidence and control. The interaction between a president's *belief in his ability to control events* and joint democracy does not achieve statistical significance. This result means that leaders with a high *BACE* do not have a significantly higher or lower chance of initiating a MID against democratic actors. Models three and four test the interaction between joint democracy and *self-confidence*. Self-confidence on its own has the expected negative effect on MID initiation (confident presidents are less likely to initiate a MID). When interacted with joint democracy, however, the direction of the effect is opposite: as a president's self-confidence goes up in a dyad that is a joint democracy, MID initiation becomes more likely.

Those results do not mean that self-confident presidents will rush into conflict with democracies. Instead, they mean that of the subset of democratic dyads where the United States initiates a MID,[7] a self-confident president is more likely to do so than a non-self-confident president. Finally, we interact a president's belief that he can *control historical development* with joint democracy. We find that there is a significant and positive relationship between this interaction and the willingness of a president to initiate a MID. This result means that, when faced with a potential democratic target, of those rare times when the United States initiates a MID, it is more likely to happen when the president perceives himself as having a high level of control.

## MID Hostility Findings

### Wariness About Others and the Political Universe

Now we explore the effect of these psychological characteristics on MID level of hostility. As with the initiation models, we consider the effect of measures of a president's wariness about others and the political universe on MID's five-point hostility level. These results can be seen in Table 8.5. Models one, three, and five test the effect of *distrust* on level of MID hostility. The sign for *distrust* in all three models is the same and is as expected: more distrusting presidents are likely to pursue higher levels of hostility than more trusting presidents. However, only in model one is the relationship significant. A similar pattern shows the *nature of the political universe*: the direction is as anticipated – presidents who see others as friendlier tend to pursue lower levels of hostility – but none of the models are statistically significant.

### Sense of Confidence, Control, and Efficacy

We next explore a leader's sense of confidence and control. Models one and two test the effect of a president's *BACE* on the level of hostility chosen by the United States. The results indicate that presidents with a strong belief in their *ability to control events* are likely to be significantly *less* hostile than those scoring lower scores on this characteristic. This effect is consistent in both models and fits our hypothesis. We turn to the effect of *self-confidence* on the hostility level of the United States. Model three finds no significant relationship, though the direction of the coefficient is as hypothesized, while model four finds a significant and negative effect, as anticipated, on the level of hostility chosen by the presidents. Finally, models five and six test how a president's belief about his ability to *control historical development* can affect the level of hostility chosen in

*Table 8.5* Hostility Level Models

| | One | Two | Three | Four | Five | Six |
|---|---|---|---|---|---|---|
| Variables | Hostility | Hostility | Hostility | Hostility | Hostility | Hostility |
| Distrust | 2.613+ | | 2.286 | | 1.735 | |
| | (1.397) | | (1.491) | | (1.624) | |
| P-1 | | −1.704 | | −1.523 | | −0.739 |
| | | (1.237) | | (1.212) | | (1.277) |
| Belief in ability to control events | −5.207** | −5.832** | | | | |
| | (2.015) | (1.984) | | | | |
| Self-confidence | | | −1.722 | −2.439* | | |
| | | | (1.221) | (1.111) | | |
| P-4 | | | | | −3.424+ | −4.237* |
| | | | | | (2.022) | (1.794) |
| Jointdem × distrust | 3.244 | | 7.628+ | | 8.513* | |
| | (3.770) | | (4.437) | | (4.173) | |
| Jointdem × P-1 | | −1.104 | | −0.742 | | −2.988 |
| | | (3.465) | | (3.549) | | (3.749) |
| Jointdem × belief in ability to control | −2.384 | −3.845 | | | | |
| | (6.707) | (6.722) | | | | |
| Jointdem × self-confidence | | | 9.060* | 6.234 | | |
| | | | (4.539) | (4.098) | | |
| Jointdem × P-4 | | | | | 16.16* | 11.44 |
| | | | | | (7.675) | (7.026) |
| Joint democracy | −0.677 | 0.730 | −6.578* | −3.782 | −5.866** | −2.276 |
| | (2.383) | (2.801) | (2.691) | (2.594) | (2.194) | (1.821) |
| Capability ratio | −0.476*** | −0.456*** | −0.484*** | −0.473*** | −0.485*** | −0.476*** |
| | (0.115) | (0.110) | (0.113) | (0.110) | (0.114) | (0.112) |
| Contiguity | −0.844*** | −0.821*** | −0.833*** | −0.815*** | −0.843*** | −0.832*** |
| | (0.188) | (0.185) | (0.186) | (0.184) | (0.187) | (0.186) |
| Observations | 9998 | 9998 | 9998 | 9998 | 9998 | 9998 |
| Number of dyads | 198 | 198 | 198 | 198 | 198 | 198 |

Standard errors in parentheses.

* $p < 0.05$, **$p < 0.01$, ***$p < 0.001$, +$p < 0.10$.

a MID. These findings provide robust support for the effect of a leader's sense of control. If a president believes that he has a strong level of control, he is less likely to be hostile in international politics. The following section explores the effect of the psychological characteristics in interaction with joint democracy.

### Interaction Terms

As before, the findings here reflect the behavior of US presidents when in dyads with other democratic states. Though *distrust* did not have a consistent direct effect on hostility level, as seen in models three and five below, it appears to have at least a small effect in interaction with joint democracy. When a president is in a dyad with another democracy, a distrustful president is likely to pursue higher conflict levels than a trusting president. However, the interaction between joint democracy and a leader's belief about the *nature of the political universe* does not affect the hostility level of American presidents in dyads with other democratic states as seen in models two and four.

Next, we explore the interactions between joint democracy and the variables measuring a president's sense of confidence and control. First, we look at how *BACE* affect presidential behavior toward other democracies. Models one and two show that a president's *belief in his ability to control events* does not affect hostility levels toward other democracies. The results are mixed for *self-confidence*. One model (three) finds that presidents with higher self-confidence scores are likely to be more hostile in their interactions with other democracies. However, model four finds no significant relationship, though the direction remains the same. Models five and six explore how a president's belief about his *control over historical development* can affect US MID behavior against other democracies. As with *self-confidence*, the effect of this interaction term is mixed. Model five shows that a president with a stronger belief in his *control over historical development* is likely to be more hostile in his conduct with other democracies. However, model six, though the coefficient has the same sign, is not significant.

Broadly speaking, it is evident that the effects of a president's wariness about the intentions of others and the political universe have at most only a modest effect on hostility levels by the United States, even in interaction with other democracies. The same is true for leaders' sense of control as an explanatory variable; the models have mixed significance levels, though they provide some support. There is, however, a strong relationship between these traits and the MID behavior of the United States toward democratic actors, with more confident and controlling presidents more likely to escalate.

### Control Variables

The direction and significance of the control variables in the models do not change for either dependent variable. Joint democracy behaves as expected in models three and five. This means that when the United States is facing a democratic opponent, it is less likely to initiate a MID, and it is likely to be *less* hostile toward that opponent. The capability ratio is the log of the ratio of power between the United States and its potential target. As expected, it has a negative effect on both hostility and initiation. The greater the power preponderance the United States has over its potential target, the less likely the president is to choose force, and the less hostile they are toward the target.

Finally, the effect of geographic distance also behaves as expected. Presidents are more likely to initiate MIDs and conduct more hostile policies with states that are closer to them than states that are farther away from them.

## Conclusion and Discussion

Although each psychological characteristic is not significant in every model presented, the direction of all five characteristics is always in the hypothesized direction, and each one is significant in enough models to warrant support for the general argument that the psychological characteristics of US presidents have an effect on US dyadic conflict behavior. *BACE* is the most consistent and strongest predictor of conflict behavior among the psychological characteristics. As a president's sense of control increases, the United States is less likely to initiate a MID and tends to choose less hostile activity toward the dyadic target. Similar patterns are seen for our other variables pertaining to our concept of a leader's sense of confidence and efficacy. The president's *self-confidence, BACE,* and his *control over historical development* generally predict fewer MID initiations and lower hostility levels. These three variables provide support for our general theory that presidents who are more self-assured, confident, and believe they are more in control have less of a psychological need to escalate a situation.

We also investigated the general concept of the president's wariness of others and the nature of the political universe, though the results were somewhat weaker in this area. For this concept, we included two psychological characteristics. First, a higher level of *distrust* is directionally correlated with a higher likelihood of MID initiation and higher hostility levels in our models, though the statistical significance is mixed. Second, the president's belief about the *nature of the political universe* has a negative relationship with MID initiation and hostility levels (when the president sees others in the political universe as friendlier and more cooperative, he is less likely to escalate a situation), though in our models only once did this variable approach significance.[8] In general, this means that the president's views of other actors, positive or negative, may have an effect on dyadic conflict behavior.

We also investigated whether these psychological characteristics might matter more (or less) when the president is dealing with a target whose regime is also democratic. Generally speaking, the results do not indicate that joint democracy matters much, though a couple of models had significant and interesting effects. The coefficient for the interaction between *self-confidence* and *joint democracy* was positive (and significant in half the models), which indicates that if the United States escalated a situation with another democracy, it was more likely that the president scored higher on self-confidence. Remembering that escalations with other democracies are rare, this means bucking the cultural-situational norm; it takes a president who believes in himself highly to do so. A similar pattern can be seen in interaction between *control over historical development* and *joint democracy*. The norm is the United States is not to escalate in these situations, but if the United States did so, it took a president who firmly believed that he was largely in control.

Overall, the results here support the argument that we should include psychological variables in our scientific examination of international conflict behavior. This is the case even though the research project here investigated a "hardcase" question regarding the psychological effects on conflict; there are reasons to think that psychology may matter less in a set of US dyads than in a broader set of conflict cases. The vast majority of dyads in our sample were ones where the United States had a large preponderance of power, and, as our results show, the probability of conflict escalation when there is such a large disparity is very low.

Both potential initiator and potential target know when there is such an imbalance, so the target is likely to make concessions before a devastating escalation can take place. Does that mean that power level trumps the effect of psychology, and therefore the latter is not needed? Absolutely not. First, we control for power level, and it is highly significant, yet our psychological variables typically mattered in our models. Second, we fully expect that psychological characteristics will matter much more in a sample of cases where power levels are not so disparate.

In this chapter, we have investigated our new data set, the PsyCL, demonstrated some patterns in the data on US presidents that support some construct validity, and tested data in a hardcase analysis of US dyads. We believe that PsyCL will be an important and useful breakthrough, not only for those who are interested in the effects of psychology on foreign policy behavior, but also for any scholar who is interested in studying conflict using scientific methods. The data set will continue to grow over time and include actors from around the world and from the last 200 years of international politics, meaning it will have data for almost any conflict research project in that time period. Moreover, the data set is structured so that adding psychological variables to any project will be fairly easy and straightforward, no matter what the unit of analysis is.

In the end, therefore, we conclude that leaders do matter. Leaving them out of our best models is theoretically incorrect, and, as the data here demonstrate, it is also empirically incorrect, resulting in underspecified models. PsyCL will certainly not be the last word in data on psychological characteristics, and it is certainly not a panacea or an explain-all set of variables. Indeed, there is much work to be done. Nonetheless, it does represent a critically important breakthrough in political psychology and the scientific research on international conflict.

# Notes

1. The data set is publicly available at this website: http://psycldataset.com/.
2. It should be noted that there is a structural similarity between BACE and control over historical development (P-4). Both variables attempt to capture similar concepts albeit using different methods and operationalizations.
3. Significance is at the 5% level. Each z-score is calculated using the following equation: $z = ((x - \mu)/\sigma)$. Negative values represent significantly lower scores than the average, while positive values indicate significantly higher scores than the average.
4. For more in-depth reading on how Wilson's need for power influenced his decision making during the Versailles debate, see Walker (1995).
5. Supporting the idea that these two variables tap into a similar underlying psychological phenomenon is the fact that they are highly (and negatively) correlated. As a result, we run separate models for each of them, as seen in our results section below.
6. As anticipated, these three variables are all highly (and positively) correlated with each other. Our models below, therefore, only include one of them at a time.
7. Note that this a rare occurrence, as indicated by the significant and negative result for our control variable joint democracy; it is much less likely that the United States will initiate a MID in a dyad where both members are democracies.
8. Not presented here, but providing some support for our hypotheses in this area is the fact that bivariate models explaining MID initiation and hostility level were highly significant for both *distrust* and *nature of the political universe*.

# References

Bremer, S. 1992. Dangerous dyads: Conditions affecting the likelihood of interstate war, 1816–1965. *Journal of Conflict Resolution* 36: 309–341.

Brown, J. 1993. Self-esteem and self-evaluations: Feeling is believing. In *Psychological perspectives on the self: The self in social perspective*, ed. J. Suls, 27–58. Mahwah, NJ: Lawrence Erlbaum Associates.

Bueno De Mesquita, B., J. Morrow, R. M. Siverson. 1999. An institutional explanation of the democratic peace. *American Political Science Review* 93: 791–807.

Correlates of War Project. 2011. State system membership list, v2011. Online, http://correlatesofwar.org.

Cottam, R. W. 1977. *Foreign policy motivation: A general theory and a case study.* Pittsburgh, PA: University of Pittsburgh Press.

De Dreu, C. 1995. Coercive power and concession making in bilateral negotiation. *Psychometrika* 39: 648–670.

Ferris, D. L., D. Brown, D. Heller. 2009. Organizational supports and workplace deviance: The mediating role of organization-based self-esteem. *Organizational Behavior and Human Decision Processes* 108: 279–286.

Freud, S., W. C. Bullitt. 1999. *Woodrow Wilson: A psychological study.* Piscataway, NJ: Transaction Publishers.

George, A. L. 1969. The operational code: A neglected approach to the study of political leaders and decision making. *International Studies Quarterly* 13: 190–222.

George, A. L., J. L. George. 1964. *Woodrow Wilson and Colonel House: A personality study*. New York, NY: Dover Publications.

George, A. L., J. L. George. 1998. *Presidential personality and performance*. Boulder, CO: Westview Press.

Ghosn, F., G. Palmer, S. Bremer. 2004. The MID3 data set, 1993–2001: Procedures, coding rules, and description. *Conflict Management and Peace Science* 21: 133–154.

Gochman, C. S., Z. Maoz. 1984. Militarized interstate disputes, 1816–1976. *Journal of Conflict Resolution* 28: 585–615.

Hermann, M. 1980. Explaining foreign policy behavior using the personal characteristics of political leaders. *International Studies Quarterly* 24: 7–46.

Hermann, M. 1999. *Assessing leadership style: A trait analysis*. Slingerlands, NY: Social Science Automation, Inc. https://socialscience.net/docs/LTA.pdf.

Hermann, M. 2003. Assessing leadership style: Trait analysis. In *The psychological assessment of political leaders*, ed. J. Post, 178–212. Ann Arbor, MI: University of Michigan Press.

Hermann, M., T. W. Milburn. 1977. *A psychological examination of political leaders*. New York, NY: Free Press.

Holsti, O. 1967. Cognitive dynamics and images of the enemy. *Journal of International Affairs* 21: 16–39.

Holsti, O. 1970. The operational code approach to the study of political leaders. *Canadian Journal of Political Science* 3: 123–157.

Johnson, L. 1977. Operational codes and the prediction of leadership behavior: Senator Frank Church at midcareer. In *A psychological examination of political leaders*, ed. M. Hermann. New York, NY: Free Press.

Jones, D. M., S. Bremer, J. D. Singer. 1996. Militarized Interstate Disputes, 1816–1992: Rationale, coding rules, and empirical patterns. *Conflict Management and Peace Science* 15: 163–213.

Korman, A. 1970. Toward a hypothesis of work behavior. *Journal of Applied Psychology* 54: 31–41.

Lasswell, H. D. 1930. *Psychopathology and politics*. Chicago, IL: University of Chicago Press.

Leites, N. 1951. *The operational code of the politburo*. New York, NY: McGraw-Hill.

Lemke, D., W. Reed. 2001. The relevance of politically relevant dyads. *Journal of Conflict Resolution* 45: 126–144.

Maoz, Z., B. Russett. 1993. Normative and structural causes of democratic peace, 1946–1986. *American Political Science Review* 87: 624–638.

McLellan, D. 1971. The operational code approach to the study of political leaders: Dean Acheson's philosophical and instrumental beliefs. *Canadian Journal of Political Science* 4: 52–75.

Palmer, G., V. D'Orazio, M. Kenwick. 2015. The MID4 dataset, 2002–2010: Procedures, coding rules, and description. *Conflict Management and Peace Science* 32: 222–242.

Post, J. M. 1983. Woodrow Wilson re-examined: The mind-body controversy Redux and other disputations. *Political Psychology* 4: 289–306.

Russett, B., J. O'Neal. 2001. *Triangulating the peace: Democracy, trade, and international organizations*. New York, NY: Norton & Company.

Stuart, D., H. Starr. 1981. The 'inherent bad faith model' reconsidered: Dulles, Kennedy, and Kissinger. *Political Psychology* 3: 1–33.

Tajfel, H., J. Turner. 2001. An integrative theory of intergroup conflict. In *Intergroup relations: Key readings (key readings in social psychology)*, 1st Edition, eds. M. Hogg, D. Abrams, 94–109. Hove: Psychology Press.

Walker, S. G. 1977. The interface between beliefs and behavior: Henry Kissinger's operational code and the Vietnam War. *Journal of Conflict Resolution* 21: 129–168.

Walker, S. G. 1995. Psychodynamic processes and framing effects in foreign policy decision-making: Woodrow Wilson's operational code. *Political Psychology* 16: 697–717.

Walker, S. G., L. Falkowski. 1984. The operational codes of U.S. Presidents and secretaries of state: Motivational foundations and behavioral consequences. *Political Psychology* 5: 237–266.

Walker, S. G., M. Schafer, M. Young. 1998. Systemic procedures for Operational Code Analysis: Measuring and modeling Jimmy Carter's operational code. *International Studies Quarterly* 42: 175–190.

Walker, S. G., M. Schafer. 2007. Theodore Roosevelt and Woodrow Wilson as cultural icons of US foreign policy. *Political Psychology* 28: 747–776.

Weede, E. 1976. Overwhelming preponderance as a pacifying condition among contiguous Asian dyads, 1950–1969. *Journal of Conflict Resolution* 20: 395–411.

Weinstein, E. A. 2014. *Woodrow Wilson: A medical and psychological biography. Supplementary volume to the papers of Woodrow Wilson*. Princeton, NJ: Princeton University Press.

Weintraub, W. 1986. Personality profiles of American presidents as revealed in their public statements: The presidential news conferences of Jimmy Carter and Ronald Reagan. *Political Psychology* 7: 285–295.

# 9 Operational Code Beliefs and Threat Perceptions by US Presidents

*Collin J. Kazazis*

## Introduction

The primary focus in this chapter is to examine the effect that threat perception has on the decision to use, or not use, military force. In international relations, the topic that has always received maximum attention and research has been the area of war and other uses of military force. War at a basic level is devastating to the international system. It can lead to a massive loss of life, the breakup and change of territorial lines, and it can disrupt normal flows of trade and people. While a large literature is dedicated to the actual fighting of wars, there is also a large amount of research into determining why countries choose to go to war. These explanations range across realist perspectives, political psychology, the security dilemma, and others (Midlarsky 2011).

One of the more interesting explanations for why countries choose to go to war is threat perception (Holsti, North, and Brody 1968; Jervis 1976; Lebow 1981). This explanation has been in the literature for many years and has had multiple hypotheses as to how threat perception operates. Threat perception is the amount that a leader perceives another country's military strength and intent of action to be threatening to their own territory or strategic interests. While this may seem straightforward, it has been difficult to find a reliable measure, or variable, for threat perception. For that reason, this present study will investigate a way to quantify threat perception in the hopes that a reliable measure can be applied to future cases. Before proceeding to the specifics of this study, it is necessary to further introduce the concept of threat perception, as well as a few concepts from other aspects of political psychology.

## Literature Review

It is important to understand the development of threat perception in the literature. Threat perception can take on many different meanings depending on how it is defined. While earlier studies have dealt with objective measures of threat, later studies have shifted the focus back to perception. This review will look at several different studies to understand how the concept of threat perception has changed over time. While threat perception was not formally studied until the 1900s, there are several instances in history where threat perception has been discussed. The first study of threat perception is often linked to the Greek Historian Thucydides, who examined the Peloponnesian War that took place between Sparta and Athens.

As Thucydides (1976, 49) examined the conflict, he noted, "what made war inevitable was the growth of Athenian power and the fear which this caused in Sparta". The important parts of this statement for threat perception is the identification of an opposing power and the emotional response this caused. Sparta perceived an increasing threat from Athens, whether correct or not, and responded with an action they deemed appropriate. In a more recent analysis, Allison (2017) examined the "Thucydides Trap" emerging between China and the United States. His analysis substitutes China for Athens and the United States for Sparta in the quote from Thucydides regarding the increase in the probability of war between a rising power and its rival. Overall, Thucydides introduced an aspect of decision-making that was previously not widely considered in terms of the study of war.

The next early study of threat perception comes from Machiavelli and his work, *The Prince*. Throughout his work, Machiavelli stresses the importance of material factors, such as wealth and military strength, in assessing the strength of a country. By this standard, a leader must always be aware of situations that may threaten his or her own wealth, military strength, or interests. Additionally, he argues that leaders should always be prepared for war and pursue any opportunity that may bring monetary gains (Machiavelli 1532/1981). Machiavelli stressed the importance of objective factors and was primarily concerned with preserving and increasing a state's power at any cost.

The first major work in the study of threat perception in the modern era was done by Singer (1958). In his work, Singer examined the ways in which certain actions can be seen as threatening to other countries. By looking at several case studies, Singer was able to identify a working formula for threat perception as the product of estimated capability and estimated intent. While the first part of the formula is objective, the second part relies on how an action will be perceived. This perception mainly relies on image theory (Boulding 1956) as a military move by an ally may be seen as mutual defense, while a similar military move by an enemy may be seen as an indication for an upcoming attack. Although there were some limitations as his study relied on case studies, Singer's study was important in creating and continuing the conversation about threat perception and war. He was also responsible for the subsequent creation of the Correlates of War (COW) project, which is still the main dataset for analyzing the origins of war in the post-1814 international system (Singer 1972).

Pruitt (1965) focused his study of threat perception on the initial "predispositions" that a leader may hold of another country. From these predispositions, leaders are able to understand the actions of another more clearly. From there, Pruitt argues that there is "evidence of intent" that can be studied in order to understand threat perception more clearly. The "evidence of intent" involves capability (amount of arms that a state may possess), actions, statements, and conditions faced by other nations (Pruitt 1965). Though this provides an expanded view of Singer's focus on threat perception, it still has the problem of actually identifying the process of what causes a leader to experience threat perception.

Cohen (1978, 1979) argues that threat perception is a two-step process consisting of observation and appraisal. The first step is objective and involves the basic components of the action that has just happened. The second part is the subject meaning that is added to the news that informs a person of the intent of the action. The important addition to this understanding of threat perception is that it introduces the presence of active thought within a person (Cohen 1978, 1979). However, this study focuses more on defining actions that can be seen as threatening cues rather than the internal processes of a person's perception. Put another way, the units of measure are actions rather than psychological concepts. This gap was fulfilled by Jervis (1976) who reviewed the psychological literature to identify various information-processing mechanisms identified by psychologists that generate misperceptions, such as environmental stressors, motivated biases, and cognitive heuristics.

The study of threat perception subsequently branched out into multiple areas as it became used as a medium in the explanation of other phenomena. While image theory was mentioned earlier with Singer's study, another area where threat perception was used is the study of the security dilemma (Herz 1951). This concept was employed by Jervis (1978), who argued in the context of nuclear deterrence theory that a state's need to maintain a balance of power means that any imbalance created by an increase in arms in another state must be met with an increase in your own state. The end result of such an occurrence is that both states are captured in an arms race as a conflict spiral (Jervis 1976), which greatly increases the likelihood of an eventual outbreak of conflict. Threat perception plays a role in the dilemma, as it is possible that a leader may misperceive the amount that an opposing side increases their military or the actual intention for the military buildup. This important distinction can greatly impact the cycle of the security dilemma and can increase the severity of the cycle (Glaser 1997; He 2012).

Finally, emotion is another area of research where threat perception by elites can play a big role. The main emotion that has been examined is fear and the effect that it plays on threat perception (Page 1931). In multiple cases, it has been shown that fear of an outside state can lead to a heightened sense of threat perception. This, in turn, leads to a subscription to harsher policies to deal with the possibility of a threat (Riek, Mania, and Gaertner 2006; Stein 2013; Dunwoody and McFarland 2018; Obaidi et al. 2018; Semenova and Winter 2019).

There is also a growing group of recent studies that examine the existence of threat perception among the general public. This is often encapsulated within studies that examine views of Islam and terrorism. These studies utilize surveys targeted at people in the general population of a country to understand their attitudes and feelings toward other groups. They also focus on the distinction between realistic threats (territory and resources) and symbolic threats (beliefs and values), as the target of a threat may alter a person's reaction to it (Riek et al. 2006; Obaidi et al. 2018). Additionally, there is some research to suggest that a person's level of religiosity may affect their threat perception as they view certain events (Hampton 2013).

While it may be interesting to view current levels of threat perception in the general public to understand the support of authoritarian policies, it is important to understand that these people are not directly involved in the decision-making process. Furthermore, it is hard to determine the actual psychological levels of threat perception from a survey where people may alter their true answers to please the examiner. The main point to take away from a review of the threat perception literature is that most studies do not actually study threat perception as it is often conceptualized. Studies will either focus on public opinion or on structural variables that are removed from the leader making the decision.

Therefore, threat perception is often studied through proxy variables that do not actually measure threat perception as a psychological process attributed directly to a leader. In spite of this shortcoming, there are still several important things to consider in this review. The first is that threat perception deals with hostile views of opposing countries. Threat perception also involves an understanding that the opposing country will generally impede on a state's strategic interests. Finally, there is a sense that leaders will often view threatening actions as outside of their own immediate control. Considering these aspects, this study will attempt to introduce a variable that measures threat perception within leaders.

## Profiling Leaders: Leadership Trait Analysis and Operational Code

The following analysis will examine threat perception through the lens of political psychology. Methods from two research programs in political psychology will inform and guide the analysis. The first of these methods is from the Leadership Trait Analysis (LTA) research program, which was developed by Hermann (1977, 2003). Within LTA, there are seven psychological characteristics that are used to provide a description of a leader's psychology. The seven characteristics are need for power, distrust, in-group bias, conceptual complexity, belief in the ability to control events, self-confidence, and task orientation. These characteristics span the personality traits, motives, and cognitions of a leader to get a full image of that leader's style of leadership.

The other methods employed in this paper are from the research program in operational code analysis (OCA). OCA was developed by Leites (1951) and then further developed by George (1969). This research program deals with a leader's beliefs about himself (instrumental beliefs) and the nature of the political universe (philosophical beliefs). In sum, there are ten questions identified by George (1969), which delineate the belief system of a leader. By examining these beliefs, we are able to understand how a leader makes a decision by identifying how they will diagnose a political problem and prescribe the best strategies to overcome the problem (George 1969, 1979; Walker 1990; Walker and Schafer 2010).

Although defining these methods seems straightforward, implementing them can be difficult as leaders often cannot be reached to take a personality and cognitive examination. To get around this problem, both methods use verbal analysis of public statements by the leaders 'at a distance,' in order to glean psychological characteristics. By analyzing the use of certain words and other verbal constructions, it is possible to understand their core personal characteristics. The operational code program uses a method known as the Verbs in Context System (VICS), which was developed by Walker, Schafer, and Young (1998) to access their beliefs. The LTA program focuses on key nouns, verbs, and phrases to ascertain the personality characteristics of a leader (Hermann 1983, 2003). Since verbal material is going to be used, it is important to consider which kind of speech acts will be sources.

There are two types of speech acts: spontaneous and prepared. Prepared speeches are those that are written in advance and then presented more or less verbatim at the time of delivery; they are often organized in part by a speechwriter. On the other hand, spontaneous speech acts are given with little to no preparation and are typically found in interview and other question-answer formats. For the purposes of this study, both spontaneous and prepared speeches will be considered for the leaders involved. While there is the question of whether speeches by speechwriters truly represent the leader, it can be argued that speechwriters are hired to write speeches that are typical of the leader for which they are writing. Additionally, there have been studies that have shown there is little difference between the results of spontaneous and prepared speeches (Rosati 2000; Schafer and Crichlow 2010). Therefore, this study will use both prepared and spontaneous speeches for the analysis of threat perception.

## Research Design

The goal in this study is to examine the effect that threat perception has on the decision to use military force in a given situation. Rather than utilizing situational variables for threat perception, this study will use certain beliefs in a leader's operational code as a composite index to measure threat perception. This approach will access the cognitive psychology of the leader in the decision-making process. Specifically, OCA allows us to examine a leader's way of thinking as it relates to him/herself and the international system.

## Threat Perception

Since threat perception relies on the perception of outside threats, the index will consist of several indexes from the philosophical beliefs in the leader's operational code. The Nature of the Political Universe (P-1) measures a leader's beliefs regarding the essential nature of political life, whether it be hostile or friendly (George 1969). The P-1 scale ranges from −1 to +1, with hostile beliefs existing on the lower end of the scale and friendly beliefs existing on the upper end (Walker, Schafer, and Young 2003). A leader who views the world as hostile is likely to experience a higher level of threat perception. Conversely, a leader who views the world as friendly is likely to experience a lower level of threat perception. Thus, greater threat perception will be related to the lower end of the P-1 scale, while lesser threat perception will be related to the upper end.

The next belief that will be included in the variable for threat perception is the Prospects for Realizing Goals (P-2). The P-2 scale indicates the leader's expectations (optimistic/pessimistic) for realizing stated goals or objectives and ranges from −1 to +1, with pessimism relating to the lower end of the scale and optimism relating to the upper end of the scale (Walker et al. 2003). A leader who experiences a great amount of threat perception is likely to believe that their strategic goals are going to be harder to obtain. On the other hand, a leader who does not experience a great level of threat perception may believe that it will be easier to achieve goals without the interference of other countries. Thus, greater threat perception will be related to the lower end of the P-2 scale, while lesser threat perception will be related to the upper end.

The final belief that will be included in the index for threat perception is Control over Historical Development (P-4). The P-4 scale indicates a leader's perceived control over events, i.e., whether a leader believes he or she has a higher or lower sense of control over political events. This belief is scaled from 0 to +1, with low control over political events relating to the lower end of the scale, and high control over political events to the upper end of the scale (Walker et al. 2003). Since leaders who score on the lower end believe that they have little control over the flow of political events, a leader is likely to see threats as outside of his or her control. Thus, a leader is likely to have a heightened sense of threat perception. Conversely, a leader who scores on the upper end believes that he or she has high control over the flow of political events. Though a leader may be faced with various threats, he or she will understand these threats and have a firm grasp on how to control future developments. Therefore, greater threat perception will be related to the lower end of the P-4 scale, while lesser threat perception will be related to the upper end of the P-4 scale.

In order to create the composite index for threat perception, the three measures of beliefs from OCA will need to be combined. To ensure that there is consistency of interpretation among the various scales, each individual score will first be standardized against an overall mean. Once the scores are standardized, they will be added together to create one number that represents the level of threat perception experienced by the leader. Finally, the combined score will be multiplied by −1. The reason for this last operation is based on the way that the operational code scales are set up in relation to this study. Since the lower end of the three scales are related to greater threat perception, this final operation will ensure that higher numbers on the combined score relate to a greater level of threat perception. The individual measures will be pulled from the Psychological Characteristics of Leaders (PsyCL) dataset (see Chapter 8 in this volume) and will be based on speech analysis of both spontaneous and prepared speech acts given by the leaders selected.

### *Threat Perception Sources*

With the threat perception index created, I am interested in understanding the psychological causes of threat perception. Are there deeper psychological factors that predispose a person's level of threat perception? Are they rooted in personality characteristics that are central to a person's identity? In order to assess the relationship between personality characteristics and threat perception, Margaret Hermann's LTA inventory contains three characteristics that will be assessed: need for power, distrust, and in-group bias.

Need for power is one of the three main motivations identified by Winter (1973), which influence political behavior. This psychological characteristic denotes a leader's need to establish and maintain their own power and sense of control over events (Hermann 1983). Since leaders with a high need for power would want to exert their dominance over situations, it is likely that they will be more sensitive to situations that would threaten their dominance. Thus, the hypothesis for this relationship can be described as

> *H1*: A leader with a higher need for power will likely experience a higher level of threat perception.

Distrust is another important psychological characteristic from the LTA inventory. Distrust deals with suspicion and doubt regarding others' intentions and actions (Hermann, 1983). As distrustful leaders can be more inclined to see others' actions as suspect, the relationship to threat perception can be described as

*H2*: A leader with a higher level of distrust will likely experience a greater level of threat perception.

Finally, in-group bias is another important psychological characteristic to consider from the LTA inventory. In-group bias denotes the level that a leader will hold his own group in higher regard than everyone else (Hermann 2003). This claim can be built upon economic, cultural, or military reasons and usually results in the desire to make decisions that benefit the group. As such, the relationship between in-group bias and threat perception can be described as

*H3*: A leader with a higher level of in-group bias will likely experience a higher level of threat perception.

### *Threat Perception Effects*

After establishing the psychological characteristics that influence threat perception, the rest of the study will examine the effects that threat perception has on the use of force. In terms of the use of force, the dependent variable comes from Meernik's Use of Force dataset (2004) that examines the US decision to use, or not use, military force in a given situation. Rather than focus on cases where military force was absolutely required or absolutely not required, this dataset focuses on cases in which the leader has the opportunity to use military force. The use of military force is coded as a dummy variable with 1 being the use of force and 0 being no use of force.

In his dataset Meernik was interested in examining the effect on US uses of force of several situational variables, such as presidential approval ratings, economic aid to the targeted country, inflation, and relative power. The dataset ranges from 1948 to 1998 and includes 605 individual cases that were identified as situations that created an opportunity for a leader to use military force. The criteria for determining if there is an opportunity to use force are defined by Ostrom and Job (1986) as possessing one of the following five distinctions:

1 The threat is made to the territorial security of the United States, its allies, or proxies.
2 There is a danger to US citizens, diplomats, military personnel, or US assets.
3 The situation would result in the advancement of ideologies opposed to the United States.
4 The situation would result in a loss of US influence in a region.
5 The situation involved an interstate dispute or general disruption that could lead to many deaths or threaten the stability of a region.

The unit of analysis for detecting the effects of threat perception will be based on each opportunity to use force identified by the Meernik dataset. Each row of the Meernik dataset designates the year and month of the opportunity to use force. To ensure that the study captures the psychology of the president while avoiding endogeneity with the case, the operational code beliefs are taken from the speeches that a president gave 4–6 months before the decision was made. For instance, if a leader had an opportunity to use military force in April of 1957, the operational code beliefs will be extracted from speeches from October to December of 1956. Based on these selection criteria, the actual number of cases used for this study is 555. The main hypothesis regarding the effect of threat perception is

> *H4*: The higher the level of the threat perception, the more likely the leader will use military force.

To further test this hypothesis, three control variables are included to account for rival common explanations in international relations for the use of force. All three controls are a part of Meernik's (2004) dataset. The first control variable is US power as measured by the Correlates of War Composite Indicator of National Capability (CINC) variable. This variable measures several aspects of power such as total population, iron and steel production, military expenditure, and personnel, which all contribute to a country's share of global power. It is expected that a country with a greater share of global power will be likely to exercise that power in multiple situations. Thus, a high CINC score should correlate with a higher probability of the use of force.

The next control variable is presidential popularity as measured by an annual average of presidential approval ratings. A president who is unpopular may be incentivized to use force as a distraction from his administration. Thus, lower approval ratings should correlate with more use of force. Finally, the last control variable is economic violence against the United States. This categorical variable tracks whether a threat is made against US economic interests. It is expected that a threat made against the economic interests of the United States would incentivize the use of force to protect this vital area (Meernik 2004).

## Results

The following results will be reported in two separate sections that reflect the two main models tested by the hypotheses. The first section will look at the ability of psychological characteristics to predispose the level of threat perception a leader may experience. The second section will examine the way in which threat perception may play a role in a leader's decision to use force when given the opportunity. Before moving on to the models, it is important to ensure that the threat perception variable is properly constructed. Is there evidence to support the inclusion of the three operational code beliefs that make up threat perception? In order to make this assessment, I ran a Cronbach's alpha test to determine if there was enough internal consistency among the three Operational Code measures used for the threat perception variable. The result from this test can be seen in Table 9.4 in the Appendix. This test resulted in an alpha of 0.7536, which is greater than the traditional cut-off of 0.70. Although it is possible to improve this score by eliminating one of the operational code variables, these three variables cover more dynamic aspects that make up threat perception.

### Model 1: LTA and Threat Perception

The first part of the analysis is from a least squares regression consisting of all three of the LTA variables discussed earlier. As a review, the hypotheses for this model are that an increase in need for power, in-group bias, and distrust will lead to an increase in threat perception. Before running this regression, a Pearson correlation analysis was done to make sure that there were no two variables that correlated highly. The results of this check can be seen in Table 9.5 in the Appendix. While there are significant correlations, none of the correlations are large enough to bring concern about using all three of the variables in the regression.

The results of the regression are in Table 9.1. In terms of the overall model, the global F test is significant. Thus, there is evidence that the level of threat perception is reliant upon deeper psychological characteristics. With the overall model significant, the next step is to examine the individual variables. To begin, the need for power parameter estimate is significant. However, the direction of the parameter estimate is opposite to what was expected. As the scales for need for power, in-group bias, and distrust range from 0 to 1, the parameters are explained here in terms of .1 unit increases. Therefore, for every 0.1 unit increase in the need for power, the level of threat perception decreases by 1.484. Put another way, a higher need for power leads to a lower level of threat perception. This inverse relationship is contrary to the hypothesized expectation; possible reasons for this result are discussed later in the conclusion of this paper.

The parameter for in-group bias is close to significance at an alpha level of 0.10. Even though this result is not significant, the parameter is in

*Table 9.1* Results of the Regression Model for LTA Characteristics and Threat Perception

| Variable | Estimate | $p$ |
|---|---|---|
| Need for power | $-14.8444^{***}$ (4.45) | 0.0009 |
| In-group bias | $5.669+$ (3.5572) | 0.1116 |
| Distrust | $27.796^{***}$ (2.2956) | <0.0001 |

*Key:* $+ p < 0.2$, $^* p < 0.1$, $^{**} p < 0.05$, $^{***} p < 0.01$.

$R^2 = 0.2491$, F-value $= 60.93^{***}$, Standard Error in parentheses.

the direction that was expected. For every 0.1 unit increase in in-group bias, threat perception increases by 0.567. Therefore, a higher level of in-group bias leads to a higher level of threat perception. Finally, the parameter for distrust is in the direction that was expected and is highly significant. For every 0.1 unit increase in distrust, threat perception will increase by 2.78. This means that a higher level of distrust leads to a higher level of threat perception.

Finally, it is important to consider the goodness-of-fit of this model. The $R^2$ value for this regression is 0.2491, which means that approximately 24.9% of the variation in the threat perception variable can be explained by the three LTA variables. Though this is just one measure for goodness-of-fit, this result suggests that need for power, distrust, and in-group bias do have a large role in determining the level of threat perception when compared with the typical 10% benchmark used in other studies (Falk and Miller 1992). Overall, there is evidence that the new threat perception variable is rooted in psychological characteristics: higher levels of in-group bias and distrust seem to relate positively with threat perception, while need for power has a negative relationship with threat perception.

### Model 2: Threat Perception and the Use of Force

Now that the origins of threat perception have been investigated, the rest of this analysis will examine threat perception as an explanatory variable for the use of force. Does a higher level of threat perception increase the chances that a leader will use force? The following analysis looks first at threat perception as the only independent variable. By doing so, the effect of threat perception can be isolated and examined. The next step includes several control variables to investigate the effects of threat perception while controlling for other common explanations of the use of force.

Since the use of force is a categorical variable, a probit model is utilized. While there are many differences between regular regression and probit, the main thing to note is the interpretation of the parameter estimate. Rather than representing an increase or decrease in the dependent variable, the parameter estimates in probit models represent an increase or decrease in the z-score based on a normal curve. This result then translates into the probability that an event will occur when considering the value of the independent variable. If the parameter in a model is +1.0, this would then correspond to a z-score of 1.0. Referencing a normal curve, we can then say that there is an 84% chance that the outcome will occur based on the value of the independent variable.

To begin, the results of the first model with threat perception as the only independent variable are shown in Table 9.2. With a p-value of 0.052 at an alpha level of 0.10, there is evidence to support my hypothesis. According to the parameter estimate, a 1 unit increase in threat perception increases

*Table 9.2* Probit Model for Threat Perception and the Use of Force

| Variable | Estimate | p |
|---|---|---|
| Threat perception | 0.0435* (0.0224) | 0.0523 |

*Key:* $+ p < 0.2,$ $^* p < 0.1,$ $^{**} p < 0.05,$ $^{***} p < 0.01.$

$c = 0.554$, Standard Error in Parentheses.

the z-score by 0.0435. Put another way, when threat perception is 1, the likelihood of the use of force is 51.57%. When threat perception is −1, the likelihood of the use of force is 48.43%. In addition to the parameter estimate, it is important to consider how often this model will accurately predict the correct response. For that reason, I use the c-value as it gives a percentage related to the number of times that the model works correctly or matches up with the actual response.

For instance, the model is correct if a higher value corresponds to the use of force. On the other hand, the model also works if a lower value corresponds to no use of force. The c-model takes all the cases where the model works properly and divides them by the total number of cases. For this model, the c-value is 0.554. This means that the model will predict the correct response 55.4% of the time, which is slightly better than random 50–50 selection. Thus, this model shows that threat perception does have a role in the decision to use force. A higher level of threat perception makes the use of force more likely.

While threat perception has been shown to be a significant predictor of the use of force on its own, it is important to consider it in terms of other variables from the field of international relations that can be important in determining the use of force. For this purpose, the control variables that will be tested are US power, president popularity, and economic violence. Before running this model, it is important to make sure that there is no possibility of threat perception being closely tied to any of the other variables in the model. As the new variable for threat perception should be different from previous measures of threat perception, it is important to make sure the variables in the model are not correlated in any major way.

The results of the Pearson correlation check can be seen in Table 9.6 in Appendix. While there is some significance between threat perception and US power, the relationship is not large enough to warrant any caution. Other than threat perception, the main relationship that could be concerning is the significant correlation between US power and presidential popularity. Although it is significant, the relationship is again not very strong. Thus, it is acceptable to use these variables in the same model without the possibility of an independent variable affecting another independent variable.

*Table 9.3* Probit Model for Threat Perception and Control Variables for the Use of Force

| Variable | Estimate | p | %Change in Predicted Probabilities |
|---|---|---|---|
| Threat perception | 0.0525** (0.0299) | 0.0217 | 16.93 |
| US power | −1.5458+ (1.1033) | 0.1612 | −10.41% |
| Presidential popularity | 0.00835* (0.00438) | 0.0567 | 14.37 |
| Economic violence | 0.7583** (0.2413) | 0.0017 | 15.62 |

*Key:*  $+ p < 0.2$, $^* p < 0.1$, $^{**} p < 0.05$, $^{***} p < 0.01$.

$c = 0.606$, Standard Error in Parentheses.

The results of the second model can be seen in Table 9.3. Overall, there is evidence that threat perception is a significant predictor of the use of force. A higher level of threat perception makes the use of force more likely. The threat perception variable is significant at the 0.05 alpha level. Based on the estimate, a 1-unit increase in threat perception will lead to a 0.0525 increase in the z-score. This means that an increase in threat perception will increase the likelihood of a president using force in a given situation, similar to the previous result. Though not the main interest of this study, presidential popularity and economic violence are also significant predictors of the use of force.

For presidential popularity, a greater average annual approval rating leads to an increase in the likelihood of the use of force, which is opposite of the diversionary effect that was predicted. Though this may be contradictory, there is further evidence from James and Oneal (1991) that would suggest that an increase in presidential popularity would increase the likelihood of the use of force. A possible reason may be that a president who is popular may feel that he has the support necessary to explore different opportunities by using force. The presence of economic violence also increases the likelihood of the use of force. This result is expected, as an economic interest that is threatened is likely to bring a swift response. Finally, the CINC variable, as represented by power, is not significant and did not go in the expected direction. Although it is not significant, the estimate suggests that a high CINC score will relate to a lower likelihood of the use of force.

As with the previous model, another key area to consider with this model is how well it predicts actual behavior. Again, this check will rely on the c-value, which is listed in Table 9.3. The c-value indicates the percentage of cases where the model accurately predicts the response. For this model, 60.6% of the cases are predicted correctly, which is better than the previous model. This increase is the result of the inclusion of more variables, which allow for a better prediction model. Thus, this model is worthwhile as it is better at predicting the correct response than random 50–50 selection.

Though it is important to make sure that the model is a good fit for predicting behavior, it is important to be sure that threat perception is actually making a meaningful difference in the likelihood of using force. To understand this effect, a predicted probabilities check on the threat perception variable can help visualize how a change in the variable affects the probability of using force while holding the other variables constant. Figure 9.1 shows the result of this check with threat perception ranging from its minimum value to its maximum value. When threat perception is at its minimum, there is a 70.21% chance that the leader will use force. When threat perception is at its maximum, there is an 87.14% chance that the leader will use force. This means that there is a 16.93% increase in the chance of the use of force as the threat perception changes from its minimum to its maximum.

In order to judge how much of a change in probability this is, I also ran the same check with the other variables in the model. The result of this check can also be seen in Figure 9.1, which shows the percent change. A more detailed analysis is also in Tables 9.7–9.10, which are in the Appendix. When presidential popularity changes from its minimum to its maximum, there is a 14.37% increase in the probability to use force. When economic violence changes from its minimum to its maximum, there is a 15.62% increase in the probability to use force. Finally, when US power changes from its minimum to maximum, there is a 10.41% decrease in the probability to use force. Thus, threat perception is able to

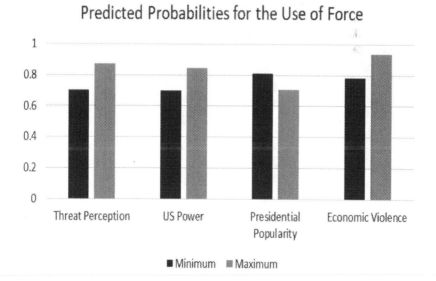

*Figure 9.1* Graph of the Predicted Probabilities for All Variables, Ranging from Their Minimum to Their Maximum

increase the likelihood of the use of force at a greater degree than competing explanations for the use of force.

## Conclusion

The main objective was to investigate the effect of threat perception on the use of force. After a review of the various types of proxies for threat perception, it became apparent that there was not a single variable that actually measured threat perception as a psychological variable. While situational factors should certainly be considered, none of the previous measures of threat perception were built with reference to threat perception as a psychological concept. For that reason, this project also had as an objective to create a new index of threat perception. This new variable was derived from three measures of operational code beliefs to reflect active cognitions that a leader holds in terms of his world view. With the creation of this new index, the following analysis split into two parts.

The first part investigated the effect of other psychological variables on threat perception, essentially asking if certain other psychological characteristics predisposed a leader to a higher level of threat perception. Did the need for power, in-group bias, and distrust affect the level of threat perception? These variables represent deeper personality traits that appear to be at the heart of threat perception. The results were mixed for these variables. Distrust was the most significant variable and followed the hypothesized direction: a higher level of distrust would lead to a higher level of threat perception. In-group bias was found to be close to significance and in the same direction as distrust: a higher level of in-group bias would lead to a higher level of threat perception.

While the previous two variables operated in the hypothesized direction, need for power acted in a different way. Although it was significant, a higher need for power correlated with a lower level of threat perception. This result was surprising and has prompted a consideration of why this variable would operate in the way it did. According to Hermann (2003):

> Need for power indicates a concern for establishing, maintaining, or restoring one's power or, in other words, the desire to control, influence, or have an impact on other persons or groups. It is coded by instances when the speaker (1) proposes or engages in a strong, forceful action such as an assault or attack, a verbal threat, an accusation, or a reprimand; (2) gives advice or assistance when it is not solicited; (3) attempts to regulate the behavior of another person or group; (4) tries to persuade, bribe, or argue with someone else so long as the concern is not to reach agreement or avoid disagreement; (5) endeavors to impress or gain fame with

an action; and (6) is concerned with his or her reputation or position (Hermann 2003, 190).

From this definition, we can see that need for power does not translate only to aggression. While aggression is certainly a part of it, need for power is made up of other actions that are utilized to establish and maintain one's power.

An extension of these actions would be that these leaders are adept at negotiation and understanding how to obtain stated goals through multiple methods. Because of these skills, leaders with a high need for power may be able to approach threatening situations in a different way. Rather than go immediately to the use of force, leaders with a high need for power may find different ways to manipulate a situation to fit their own goals for maintaining power. In addition, their ability to negotiate effectively could allow these leaders to work out peaceful solutions rather than the alternative.

Moreover, there may be other factors at work here. While only three LTA characteristics were examined in this study, there is an additional characteristic that is closely related to need for power and helps determine leadership style. This characteristic is belief in the ability to control events. As the name suggests, this characteristic reflects a leader's belief that he or she is able to control the situation as it unfolds. Hermann (2003) has noted a few patterns of leadership style that depend on how these two variables interact. If belief in the ability to control events is lower than need for power, the leader should be able to implement effective strategies to maintain power. On the other hand, if belief in the ability to control events is higher than the need for power, the leader would want to control everything but would be unable to do it effectively. The latter scenario is of interest for this study as a leader who is unable to control situations effectively may be more likely to use force (Hermann 2003, 188). A follow-up study can look at the relationship between these two characteristics and the role that they play in threat perception.

The second part tested the new threat perception variable's ability to explain the use of force. Did an increase in the level of threat perception increase the likelihood that a leader will opt to use force in a given situation? On the whole, this proposition was supported in the analysis. On its own, threat perception was a significant predictor of the use of force. This result was then further supported when control variables were added to the model. In the end, the predicted probabilities showed that when threat perception went from its minimum to its maximum, the chance of the use of force increased by nearly 17%.

While this present study of threat perception is concluded, there remain many opportunities for the advancement of threat perception and political psychology. There can be further investigations into what different psychological characteristics affect threat perception.

Belief in the ability to control events was mentioned earlier, but there are more factors. A leader low in cognitive complexity (sees the world as black and white, rather than gray) may be more inclined toward the use of force rather than seeking out other solutions (Hermann 2003). Need for affiliation may play a role as a leader high in this motive would most likely opt for more peaceful resolution rather than the use of force (Winter 2003). By looking at more characteristics, we can then determine which ones are crucial in the development of threat perception.

There are also many future avenues of research using threat perception as an explanatory variable in comparative and international politics. Going back to the study of war, it may be possible to improve on the current results by shortening the dead time period between the time the opportunity to use force is open and when the collection of speeches occurs. Through shortening this period, it will be possible to bring the measure of threat perception more in tune with what is occurring. Threat perception can also be used in studies of civil wars and in other research areas. Some domestic and international examples include examining a US president's relations with Congress or analyzing trade relations and alliance formation between countries.

## Appendix: Additional Tables

*Table 9.4* Cronbach's Alpha Result for Threat Perception Variable

| Cronbach Coefficient Alpha | | | |
|---|---|---|---|
| *Variables* | | *Alpha* | |
| Raw | | 0.753604 | |
| Standardized | | 0.744569 | |

| *Deleted Variable* | *Raw Variables* | | *Standardized Variables* | |
|---|---|---|---|---|
| | *Correlation with Total* | *Alpha* | *Correlation with Total* | *Correlation with Total* |
| P-1 | 0.834364 | 0.382982 | 0.767745 | 0.412423 |
| P-2 | 0.829488 | 0.389131 | 0.7114 | 0.486877 |
| P-4 | 0.303942 | 0.914542 | 0.298575 | 0.945638 |

*Table 9.5* Pearson Correlations for LTA Variables

| | *Need for Power* | *In-Group Bias* | *Distrust* |
|---|---|---|---|
| Need for power | 1 | 0.11907 (0.005) | −0.15834 (0.0002) |
| In-group bias | 0.11907 (0.005) | 1 | 0.0987 (0.02) |
| Distrust | −0.15834 (0.0002) | 0.0987 (0.02) | 1 |

Prob > |r| under H0: Rho = 0 in parentheses.

*Table 9.6* Pearson Correlations for Threat Perception and Control Variables

|  | Threat Perception | Presidential Popularity | Economic Violence | US power |
|---|---|---|---|---|
| Threat perception | 1 | −0.04813 (0.2576) | −0.04263 (0.3161) | 0.08795 (0.0383) |
| Presidential popularity | −0.04813 (0.2576) | 1 | −0.00651 (0.8784) | 0.16629 (<0.0001) |
| Economic violence | −0.04263 (0.3161) | −0.00651 (0.8784) | 1 | −0.0955 (0.0245) |
| US power | 0.08795 (0.0383) | 0.16629 (<0.0001) | −0.0955 (0.0245) | 1 |

Prob > lrl under H0: Rho = 0 in parentheses.

*Table 9.7* Predicted Probabilities for Threat Perception, Ranging from −4.76 to +6.73. All Other Variables Held Constant at Their Mean Values

| Contrast | Estimate | Standard Error | Confidence Limits | |
|---|---|---|---|---|
| Minimum | 0.7021 | 0.0902 | 0.5082 | 0.8509 |
| Maximum | 0.8714 | 0.0613 | 0.7126 | 0.9559 |

*Table 9.8* Predicted Probabilities for Presidential Popularity, Ranging from 24 to 82. All Other Variables Held Constant at Their Mean Values

| Contrast | Estimate | Standard Error | Confidence Limits | |
|---|---|---|---|---|
| Minimum | 0.699 | 0.0961 | 0.4923 | 0.8560 |
| Maximum | 0.8427 | 0.0648 | 0.6836 | 0.9375 |

*Table 9.9* Predicted Probabilities for US power, Ranging from 0.1355 to 0.3536. All Other Variables Held Constant at Their Mean Values

| Contrast | Estimate | Standard Error | Confidence Limits | |
|---|---|---|---|---|
| Minimum | 0.8108 | 0.0674 | 0.6527 | 0.9145 |
| Maximum | 0.7067 | 0.1030 | 0.4829 | 0.8708 |

*Table 9.10* Predicted Probabilities for Economic Violence, Ranging from 0 to 1. All Other Variables Held Constant at Their Mean Values

| Contrast | Estimate | Standard Error | Confidence Limits | |
|---|---|---|---|---|
| Minimum | 0.7815 | 0.0711 | 0.6197 | 0.8944 |
| Maximum | 0.9377 | 0.0588 | 0.7244 | 0.9933 |

# References

Allison, G. 2017. *Destined for war: Can America and China escape Thucydides' trap?* Boston, MA: Houghton-Mifflin.

Boulding, K. 1956. *The image.* Ann Arbor, MI: University of Michigan Press.

Cohen, R. 1978. Threat perception in international crisis. *Political Science Quarterly* 93(1): 93–107.

Cohen, R. 1979. *Threat perception in international crisis.* Madison, WI: University of Wisconsin Press.

Dunwoody, P. T., S. G. McFarland. 2018. Support for anti-Muslim policies: The role of political traits and threat perception. *Political Psychology* 39(1): 89–106.

Falk, R. F., N. B. Miller. 1992. *A primer for soft modeling.* Akron, OH: University of Akron Press.

George, A. L. 1969. The operational code: A neglected approach to the study of political leaders and decision-making. *International Studies Quarterly* 13(2): 190–222.

George, A. L. 1979. The causal nexus between beliefs and behavior. In *Psychological models in international politics*, ed. L. Falkowski, 95–124. Boulder, CO: Westview.

Glaser, C. L. 1997. The security dilemma revisited. *World Politics* 50(1): 171–201.

Hampton, M. 2013. *A thorn in transatlantic relations: American and European perceptions of threat and security.* New York, NY: Palgrave MacMillan.

He, K. 2012. Undermining adversaries: Unipolarity, threat perception, and negative balancing strategies after the Cold War. *Security Studies* 21(2): 154–191.

Hermann, M. G. 1977. *A psychological examination of political leaders.* New York, NY: Free Press.

Hermann, M. G. 1983. *Handbook for assessing personal characteristics and foreign policy orientations of political leaders.* Columbus, OH: Mershon Center.

Hermann, M. G. 2003. Assessing leadership style: Trait analysis. In *The psychological assessment of political leaders*, ed. J. M. Post, 178–214. Ann Arbor, MI: University of Michigan Press.

Herz, J. 1951. *Political realism and political idealism.* Chicago, IL: University of Chicago Press.

Holsti, O., R. North, R. Brody. 1968. Perception and action in the 1914 crisis. In *Quantitative international politics*, ed. J. D. Singer, 123–158. New York, NY: Free Press.

James, P., J. R. Oneal. 1991. The influence of domestic and international politics on the president's use of force. *Journal of Conflict Resolution* 35(2): 307–332.

Jervis, R. 1976. *Perception and misperception in international politics.* Princeton, NJ: Princeton University Press.

Jervis, R.. 1978. Cooperation under the security dilemma. *World Politics* 30(2): 167–214.

Lebow, R. 1981. *Between peace and war: The nature of international crisis.* Baltimore, MD: Johns Hopkins University Press.

Leites, N. 1951. *The operational code of the politburo.* New York, NY: McGraw-Hill.

Machiavelli, N. 1981. *The Prince (G. Bull, trans.).* London: Penguin Books. (Original Work Published 1532).

Meernik, J. D. 2004. *The political use of military force in US foreign policy.* Burlington, VT: Ashgate.

Midlarsky, M. 2011. *Handbook of war studies.* Vol. I. New York, NY: Routledge.

Obaidi, M., J. R. Kunst, N. Kteily, L. Thomsen, J. Sidanius. 2018. Living under threat: Mutual threat perception drives anti-Muslim and anti-Western hostility in the age of terrorism. *European Journal of Social Psychology* 48(5): 567–584.

Ostrom, C. W., B. L. Job. 1986. The president and the political use of force. *American Political Science Review*, 80(2): 541–566.

Page, K. 1931. *National defense: A study of the origins, results and prevention of war.* New York, NY: Farrar and Rinehart.

Pruitt, D. G. 1965. Definition of the Situation as a Determinant of *International Action. In International Behavior*, ed. H. G. Kelman, 393–432. New York: Holt, Rinehart and Winston.

Riek, B. M., E. W. Mania, S. L. Gaertner. 2006. Intergroup threat and outgroup attitudes: A meta-analytic review. *Personality and Social Psychology Review* 10(4): 336–353.

Rosati, J. A. 2000. The power of human cognition in the study of world politics. *International Studies Review* 2(3): 45–75.

Schafer, M., S. Crichlow. 2010. *Groupthink versus high-quality decision making in international relations.* New York, NY: Columbia University Press.

Semenova, E., D. G. Winter. 2019. Soviet and German implicit perception of mutual threat, 1939-1941. *Peace and Conflict: Journal of Peace Psychology* 25(1): 72–85.

Singer, J. D. 1958. Threat-perception and the armament-tension dilemma. *Journal of Conflict Resolution* 2(1): 90–105.

Singer, J. D. 1972. The "correlates of war" project. *World Politics* 24: 243–270.

Stein, J. G. 2013. Threat perception in international relations. In *The Oxford handbook of political psychology*, eds. L. Huddy, D. O. Sears, J. S. Levy, 364–394. Oxford: Oxford University Press.

Thucydides. 1976. *The history of the peloponnesian war* (M. I. Finley, Ed.; R. Warner, Trans.). Harmondsworth: Penguin.

Walker, S. 1990. The evolution of operational code analysis. *Political Psychology* 11: 403–418.

Walker, S., M. Schafer 2010. Operational code theory. In *The International studies encyclopedia*, ed. R. Denemark, 5492–5514. Vol. VIII. London: Wiley-Blackwell.

Walker, S. G., M. Schafer, M. Young. 1998. Systematic procedures for operational code analysis: Measuring and modeling Jimmy Carter's operational code. *International Studies Quarterly* 42: 175–190.

Walker, S. G., M. Schafer, M. Young. 2003. Profiling the operational codes of political leaders. In *The psychological assessment of political leaders*, ed. J. M. Post, 215–245. Ann Arbor, MI: University of Michigan Press.

Winter, D. G. 1973. *The Power Motive*. New York: Free Press

Winter, D. G. 2003. Assessing leaders' personalities: A historical survey of academic research studies. In *The psychological assessment of political leaders*, ed. J. M. Post, 11–38. Ann Arbor, MI: University of Michigan Press.

# 10 Presidential Personalities and Operational Codes

## Learning Effects and Midterm Congressional Election Results

*Joshua E. Lambert, Mark Schafer,*
*Stephen G. Walker and Collin Kazazis*

## Introduction

In this chapter, we investigate answers for two research questions raised by different domains of inquiry in the study of the US presidency: can and do presidents "learn" while in office? Do the psychological characteristics of presidents have an effect on how their party does during the president's first midterm Congressional elections? One question addresses a psychological phenomenon associated with elite politics regarding the occupant of the office of US president, while the other engages with a sociological phenomenon associated with mass politics regarding the collective behavior of US electoral institutions. The broader puzzle that links them is whether there is an important relationship between the two phenomena, namely, do the learning patterns of US presidents influence the outcomes of US midterm elections?

To solve this puzzle, we first examine the learning patterns of 36 US presidents during their first 2 years in office, ranging from James Monroe (1817–1818) to Barack Obama (2009–2010).[1] Our focus is on the learning patterns exhibited by these chief executives and the effect of their psychological characteristics, including learning, on electoral gains or losses. Our main hypothesis is that learning that demonstrates flexibility and adjustment will be associated with lower levels of electoral losses.

The theoretical thinking behind this hypothesis is the premise from democratic theory that the process of interaction between the US president and American voters is marked by holding the president accountable to the voters (Thorson 1962). If a president does not exhibit learning in office, s/he is more likely to make domestic or foreign policy mistakes, which are subsequently recognized as fiascos (public mistakes) by the electorate whose votes in the midterms then express their dissatisfaction with them (Tuchman 1984; Walker and Malici 2011; see also Brummer 2016). A variant on this argument is that by the midterm elections, US presidents have served beyond the "honeymoon" period of their initial term in office. Thus, some degree of "buyer's remorse" has inevitably emerged in US public opinion regarding presidential performance regardless of whether fiascos have occurred.

The issue is whether the president can minimize the electoral effects of this voter dissatisfaction by learning to adapt to an evolving political environment and survive to serve a second term (Alt, Bueno de Mesquita, and Rose 2011). Previous research has attempted to explain this variance in electoral outcomes with constructs such as "surge and decline" (Campbell 1966), "referendum" (Tufte 1975), and "balancing" (Alesina and Rosenthal 1995). None of these studies investigate the psychology of the president and are skewed more toward a focus on mass politics rather than elite politics. We also know that the presidency comes with a steep learning curve, as many presidents have acknowledged (Etheredge 1985; Burke and Greenstein 1991).

## Conceptualizations of Learning

While there is some previous research that investigates the learning effects of "shocks" on leader psychology in the domain of world politics (Walker et al. 1984; Walker, Schafer, and Young 1998; Schafer and Glasser 2000; Leng 2000; Malici 2011; Marfleet and Simpson 2011; Renshon 2011; Robison 2011; Walker and Malici 2011; Walker, Schafer, and Marfleet 2012, Walker 2013), we are primarily interested in general patterns of learning on presidential psychology, even absent environmental "shocks," during the first 2 years in office. We employ the master beliefs in the operational code construct to detect learning in the form of significant changes in a leader's core beliefs regarding the friendly or hostile nature of the political universe (P-1), the best strategy of cooperation or conflict for protecting and achieving political values (I-1), and the level of control (high or low) over historical development (P-4). If these beliefs change significantly from Year 1 to Year 2 for our sample of US presidents, then we shall infer that significant presidential learning has occurred.

The metrics for identifying operational code beliefs and election results follow the same internal logic. The operational code beliefs are measured annually by calculating the net balance between a president's friendly and hostile attributions to Others in the political universe (P-1), the net balance between a president's cooperation and conflict attributions to Self (I-1) in the political universe, and the net balance between the total number of these attributions attributed to Self and Others in the political universe (P-4). These attributions are retrieved from each leader's public statements during each year by coding the transitive verbs attributing actions either to Self or Others. The election results are measured by calculating the net balance between seats gained by the president's party and the opposition. The sources and formulas for calculating these measures are in the Appendix of this chapter.

Our conceptualization of learning follows the approach by Breslauer and Tetlock (1991), who argue that learning is "a function of the extent to which core beliefs or goals have changed" (Breslauer and Tetlock 1991, 10). More specifically, "Unless core beliefs and goals change, learning has not occurred but only adaptation. Learning in this sense requires at least a criterion for identifying core beliefs and goals, plus it implies a need for a criterion that defines when significant change has occurred in these beliefs" (Walker, Schafer, and Marfleet 2012, 115). The master beliefs in the operational code construct, measured during a president's first year, meet the criterion for identifying core beliefs and goals, while the second year's beliefs allow us to measure the extent of change in the beliefs.

Since learning is a significant change in goals and beliefs, it is indicated when the president's beliefs have moved in the opposite direction from the baseline of Year 1; therefore, a president who is prone dogmatically to conflict in Year 1 has learned when he becomes less conflictual in Year 2. Existing beliefs are "strengthened" when a dogmatically conflictual president becomes more conflictual; they are "weakened" when a dogmatically conflictual president becomes less conflictual (and the same is true for a dogmatically cooperative president). While beliefs also change when they are strengthened, we conceptualize significant learning here as occurring when they are weakened. This conceptualization of learning leads to two main hypotheses regarding learning effects and midterm outcomes as follows:

> *H1*: The greater the degree of significant learning regarding P-1 Nature of the Political Universe, the better is the outcome of the midterm election for the president's party.
>
> *H2*: The greater the degree of significant learning regarding I-1 Approach to Strategy, the better is the outcome of the midterm election for the president's party.

Support for our two hypotheses may depend as well on the influence of extra-cognitive (personality or environmental) variables on election results. We probe for their influence by including them as control variables in our models of learning effects on election results. We also explore their influence directly on changes in the operational code beliefs of the US presidents. We investigate these possibilities by running regression models with changes in the levels (scale values) from Year 1 to Year 2 of P-1, I-1, and P-4 as dependent variables. The independent variables in these models are the initial levels (scale values) of these three cognitive variables in Year 1 as well as personality and political environment variables.

The personality and environmental variables may qualify the existence and strength of the relationship between the levels of the cognitive independent variables and the changes in the learning dependent variables. The personality variables are retrieved from the public statements of the US presidents for Year 1 and Year 2, while the environmental variables are collected from different census sources of economic and security variables for the United States. The list of these variables and the formulas for calculating their values are in the Appendix.

## Levels of Learning and Their Origins

The learning variables in these regression models specify one kind of learning by US presidents. Learning theorists distinguish between social learning as behavioral changes in response to a stimulus and experiential learning as cognitive changes in response to processing old or new information (Levy 1994). Operational code analysis focuses on experiential learning as changes in key beliefs (P-1, I-1, P-4) in a leader's operational code, which specify different levels of learning (simple, diagnostic, and complex). A change in instrumental beliefs (I-1) prescribes a simple change in strategies of cooperation or conflict, while a change in philosophical beliefs (P-1) tracks diagnostic changes in the nature of the political universe as friendly or hostile, and changes in both the I-1 and P-1 can interact in complex ways to relocate the leader's strategic power position (P-4) as weaker or stronger in the political universe (Walker, Schafer, and Young 1998; Walker, Schafer, and Marfleet 2012, 113–118, 132–138).

The personality and environment variables include independent variables that define the context within which cognition, learning, and election outcomes occur over time. The interior context is defined by the personality variables, while the exterior context is defined by the environment variables. Collectively, three mechanisms define the processes that relate these variables within our models of cognition, learning, and elections. The process of *object appraisal* identifies beliefs about Self and Others in the environment. The process of *externalization and ego defense* identifies personality traits about the self. The process of *mediation of self-other relations* manages social relations between the Self and Others in the environment (Smith 1968).

Changes in the key operational code beliefs (P-1, I-1, P-4) are the learning effects of these three processes. A *cognitive* psychological explanation for these changes in beliefs is tested by analyzing whether these changes from Year 1 to Year 2 are related to the initial values for these beliefs in Year 1. An *extra-cognitive*, psychological explanation is tested by analyzing whether learning is related to the personality traits that define a president's leadership style: Distrust, In-group Bias, Need for Power, Task Orientation, Belief in Ability to Control Events, Self-confidence, and Cognitive Complexity. An *environmental* explanation is tested by analyzing whether learning is related to changes in the gross domestic product (GDP) of the US economy, the number of militarized interstate disputes (MIDs) in the international system for Year 2, and the composite index of national capability (CINC) that measures the US share of global power. The sources and indices for these variables are in the Appendix.

The potential relationships among these three sets of independent variables and changes in the three dependent variables (P-1, I-1, P-4) make rival or complementary models of learning. If the cognitive hypotheses about an inverse relationship between the values for P-1, I-1, and P-4 and their changes from Year 1 to Year 2 are supported, then those results will support an information-processing theory of learning, in which new information is recognized and the president revises his operational code to take account of it (Walker, Schafer, and Young 1998; Renshon 2011; Suedfeld, Guttieri, and Tetlock 2003; Walker, Schafer, and Marfleet 2012). If personality traits instead of operational code beliefs influence changes in P-1, I-1, and P-4, then personality traits that define his leadership style may block cognitive learning based on information and act to change beliefs based instead on the requirements of ego defense or mediation of Self-Other relations emanating from the leader's imagination regarding how a leader should act (Etheredge 1985; Post 2003; Renshon 2003; Winter 2003).

Finally, environmental characteristics may be more influential than either cognitive or extra-cognitive psychological characteristics. A structural change in the US power position in world politics or stimuli from the domestic or international environment may constrain or incentivize the president (1) to adapt his behavior while maintaining and strengthening his beliefs (social learning) or (2) to weaken his core beliefs as well (experiential learning) from Year 1 to Year 2. We investigate below each of these sets of possibilities regarding the sources and types of learning by the group of 36 US presidents from Monroe to Obama and then turn to an analysis of the effects of learning, personality, and environmental variables on midterm congressional election results.

## Data Analysis: Learning Effects

We begin by addressing our initial research question: do the psychological characteristics of presidents affect their learning patterns in office? In the following analysis, we run regression models for each of the Operational Code Analysis (OCA)-change dependent variables with Year-1 values of different Leadership Trait Analysis (LTA) variables on the independent side. A president's initial psychological characteristics may affect his learning as indicated by changes at Year 2 in his cognitive beliefs, so we also include as an independent variable the president's Year-1 OCA value for the corresponding OCA-change variable.

For example, in the P-1 models, with change in P-1 as the dependent variable, we include the president's Year-1 value for P-1 as an independent variable in all the models. This allows us to assess whether presidents are more likely to strengthen initial cognitive views (in which case the coefficient would be positive) or adjust their initial cognitive views in the opposite direction (in which case the coefficient would be negative). We also include three situational control variables that may affect changes in the president's cognitive beliefs: change in GDP, the number of militarized international disputes (MIDs) in the system that year, and the CINC (an indicator of the United States' share of global power). The results are presented in the next three tables.

In Table 10.1, the dependent variable is the president's change in P-1 from Year 1 to Year 2. Each column is a different regression model that includes one of the LTA variables. Each model also includes the president's Year-1 value for P-1 as an independent variable, and the three control variables. The most powerful result in the table is that the president's Year-1 score for P-1 is a strong predictor of the president's change in P-1 in the negative direction. This means that presidents incline to change their views of other actors in the system in a direction opposite the one they had when they started as president; those who viewed others as more cooperative tended to view others less cooperatively by Year 2, and those who viewed others as hostile tended to see them as less hostile over time.

This pattern is consistent across all seven models, regardless of the other psychological characteristics in the model, and the variable is significant in all the seven models. It appears that presidents come into office with set views about others in the political universe, and then, as their experience with others develops, they adjust their views and moderate them. If a president sees enemies everywhere when taking office, he tends to learn that others are not so bad; if a president initially views others in highly cooperative terms, he tends to learn that others may be more problematic.

For the remaining psychological variables in the models, only Conceptual Complexity is significant. The coefficient for Complexity is positive, meaning that the higher a president's complexity is, the more his views of others will change in a positive direction; more complex presidents tend to learn that others are more cooperative than they initially thought, whereas lower complexity presidents tend to see others as more hostile over time. The linear relationships between Conceptual Complexity and P-1 learning, and initial P-1 and P-1 learning are illustrated in Figure 10.1.

Of the three situational variables, CINC is the most prominent. The coefficient is significant in two of the models and is positive in all the seven models, indicating that when the United States' power is higher, the president shifts his views of others in a more cooperative direction. Change in GDP has a positive coefficient in all the models but does not approach significance. The number of MIDs in the system tends to have a negative effect on the president's P-1 score, but it is not significant in any model.

*Table 10.1* Presidential Learning: P-1

| | Dependent Variable: P-1 Learning | | | | | | |
|---|---|---|---|---|---|---|---|
| | (1) | (2) | (3) | (4) | (5) | (6) | (7) |
| Belief in Ability to Control Events | 0.02 (0.28) | | | | | | |
| Conceptual Complexity | | 0.942*** (0.334) | | | | | |
| Distrust | | | 0.325 (0.27) | | | | |
| In-group Bias | | | | -0.146 (0.698) | | | |
| Need for Power | | | | | -0.53 (0.387) | | |
| Self-confidence | | | | | | -0.205 (0.221) | |
| Task Orientation | | | | | | | -0.0 (0.346) |
| P-1 | -0.591*** (0.2) | -0.529*** (0.178) | -0.505** (0.206) | -0.594*** (0.199) | -0.597*** (0.193) | -0.584*** (0.196) | -0.589*** (0.2) |
| CINC Score | 0.453 (0.277) | 0.678** (0.258) | 0.358 (0.281) | 0.447 (0.278) | 0.427 (0.269) | 0.534* (0.285) | 0.455 (0.288) |
| GDP Change | 0.005 (0.011) | 0.004 (0.01) | 0.002 (0.011) | 0.004 (0.011) | 0.004 (0.011) | 0.006 (0.011) | 0.005 (0.011) |
| Number of MIDs | -0.013 (0.023) | -0.025 (0.018) | 0.006 (0.025) | -0.013 (0.02) | -0.014 (0.019) | -0.003 (0.022) | -0.012 (0.025) |
| Constant | 0.159 (0.133) | -0.41* (0.232) | 0.064 (0.148) | 0.191 (0.187) | 0.314* (0.166) | 0.196 (0.13) | 0.162 (0.265) |
| Observations | 36.0 | 36.0 | 36.0 | 36.0 | 36.0 | 36.0 | 36.0 |
| $R^2$ | 0.304 | 0.45 | 0.336 | 0.305 | 0.345 | 0.323 | 0.304 |
| Adjusted $R^2$ | 0.188 | 0.358 | 0.225 | 0.189 | 0.236 | 0.211 | 0.188 |
| Residual Std. Error | 0.09 | 0.08 | 0.088 | 0.09 | 0.087 | 0.088 | 0.09 |
| F Statistic | 2.62** | 4.899*** | 3.034** | 2.631** | 3.158** | 2.867** | 2.619** |

*Note:* $^*p < 0.1$; $^{**}p < 0.05$; $^{***}p < 0.01$.

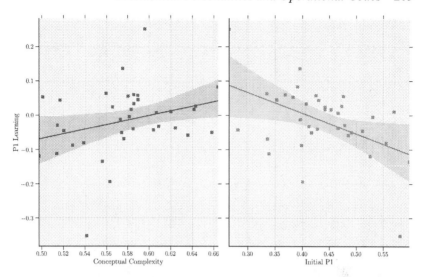

*Figure 10.1* Presidential Learning P-1: Conceptual Complexity and Initial P-1

Turning to the president's views of his own cooperative vs. conflictual policies (I-1), we see similar patterns in Table 10.2. The predominant variable in the model is the president's score on I-1 in Year 1 of his presidency, and again the pattern shows that presidents learn by moderating their initial position in the opposite direction. In this case, the negative coefficient for I-1 is even greater than it was in the previous models: for every unit increase or decrease in the president's initial I-1 score, the resulting I-1 score changes in the opposite direction by .8 on average.

Presidents who come to office with notably conflictual strategies learn to be more cooperative; those who come to office as more of an idealist tend to become more of a realist regarding the exercise of power in world politics.

Of the other psychological variables in the models, only Task Focus is significant: presidents with higher Task Focus scores tend to become more cooperative by their second year. Figure 10.2 illustrates the effect of the president's initial I-1 score and Task Orientation on I-1 learning.

The number of MIDs in the system also has an effect on the president's learning in terms of his tactics and strategies. The MIDs coefficient is consistently negative and is statistically significant in most of the models: the more MIDs in the system that year, the more conflictual the president's beliefs become regarding his policy patterns. Changes in GDP and CINC have consistent positive coefficients but do not approach significance.

The third set of models is shown in Table 10.3, which have the president's view of his control over events (P-4) as the dependent variable. In these models, the Year-1 value for P-4 is not statistically significant. It is

*Table 10.2* Presidential Learning: I-1

| | Dependent Variable: I-1 Learning | | | | | | |
|---|---|---|---|---|---|---|---|
| | (1) | (2) | (3) | (4) | (5) | (6) | (7) |
| Belief in Ability to Control Events | -0.403 (0.381) | | | | | | |
| Conceptual Complexity | | 0.336 (0.508) | | | | | |
| Distrust | | | -0.283 (0.349) | | | | |
| In-group Bias | | | | -0.939 (0.929) | | | |
| Need for Power | | | | | -0.18 (0.584) | | |
| Self-confidence | | | | | | -0.088 (0.309) | |
| Task Orientation | | | | | | | 0.9* (0.446) |
| I-1 | -0.846*** (0.179) | -0.817*** (0.177) | -0.794*** (0.175) | -0.811*** (0.174) | -0.822*** (0.191) | -0.81*** (0.18) | -0.864*** (0.169) |
| CINC Score | 0.391 (0.37) | 0.434 (0.392) | 0.446 (0.388) | 0.31 (0.371) | 0.349 (0.375) | 0.389 (0.395) | 0.151 (0.366) |
| GDP Change | 0.01 (0.015) | 0.009 (0.015) | 0.012 (0.015) | 0.005 (0.015) | 0.009 (0.015) | 0.01 (0.015) | 0.004 (0.014) |
| Number of MIDs | -0.049 (0.031) | -0.069** (0.029) | -0.081** (0.035) | -0.068** (0.028) | -0.066** (0.029) | -0.06* (0.031) | -0.025 (0.033) |
| Constant | 0.6*** (0.204) | 0.31 (0.33) | 0.545*** (0.19) | 0.675*** (0.253) | 0.56* (0.281) | 0.516** (0.197) | -0.043 (0.315) |
| Observations | 36.0 | 36.0 | 36.0 | 36.0 | 36.0 | 36.0 | 36.0 |
| R$^2$ | 0.43 | 0.417 | 0.421 | 0.428 | 0.411 | 0.41 | 0.479 |
| Adjusted R$^2$ | 0.335 | 0.32 | 0.325 | 0.333 | 0.312 | 0.312 | 0.393 |
| Residual Std. Error | 0.12 | 0.121 | 0.12 | 0.12 | 0.122 | 0.122 | 0.114 |
| F Statistic | 4.527*** | 4.297*** | 4.371*** | 4.494*** | 4.181*** | 4.177*** | 5.527*** |

*Note:* * $p < 0.1$; ** $p < 0.05$; *** $p < 0.01$.

Table 10.3 Presidential Learning: P-4

| | | | Dependent Variable: P-1 Learning | | | | |
|---|---|---|---|---|---|---|---|
| | (1) | (2) | (3) | (4) | (5) | (6) | (7) |
| Belief in Ability to Control Events | 0.049 (0.093) | | | | | | |
| Conceptual Complexity | | 0.285*** (0.101) | | | | | |
| Distrust | | | 0.014 (0.081) | | | | |
| In-group Bias | | | | -0.448** (0.194) | | | |
| Need for Power | | | | | -0.029 (0.126) | | |
| Self-confidence | | | | | | -0.023 (0.068) | |
| Task Orientation | | | | | | | -0.072 (0.102) |
| P-4 | -0.135 (0.14) | -0.159 (0.113) | -0.094 (0.131) | -0.053 (0.117) | -0.11 (0.132) | -0.091 (0.128) | -0.108 (0.125) |
| CINC Score | 0.023 (0.082) | 0.091 (0.076) | 0.023 (0.086) | 0.007 (0.076) | 0.026 (0.083) | 0.037 (0.086) | 0.045 (0.085) |
| GDP Change | 0.002 (0.003) | 0.001 (0.003) | 0.002 (0.003) | -0.0 (0.003) | 0.002 (0.003) | 0.002 (0.003) | 0.002 (0.003) |
| Number of MIDs | 0.012 (0.012) | 0.013 (0.011) | 0.011 (0.012) | 0.005 (0.011) | 0.012 (0.012) | 0.011 (0.012) | 0.008 (0.013) |
| Constant | -0.039 (0.033) | -0.196*** (0.064) | -0.033 (0.033) | 0.052 (0.045) | -0.022 (0.046) | -0.026 (0.032) | 0.016 (0.072) |
| Observations | 36.0 | 36.0 | 36.0 | 36.0 | 36.0 | 36.0 | 36.0 |
| $R^2$ | 0.059 | 0.25 | 0.051 | 0.193 | 0.052 | 0.053 | 0.065 |
| Adjusted $R^2$ | -0.098 | 0.125 | -0.107 | 0.059 | -0.107 | -0.104 | -0.09 |
| Residual Std. Error | 0.027 | 0.024 | 0.027 | 0.025 | 0.027 | 0.027 | 0.027 |
| F Statistic | 0.374 | 2.002 | 0.321 | 1.435 | 0.326 | 0.338 | 0.419 |

*Note:* $^*p < 0.1$; $^{**}p < 0.05$; $^{***}p < 0.01$.

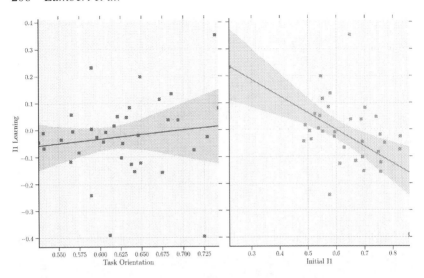

*Figure 10.2* Presidential Learning I-1: Task Orientation and Initial I-1

not the case that a president's preexisting sense of control predicts the change in his sense of control by Year 2. Two of the other psychological variables are significant, however. Conceptual Complexity is positive and highly significant. This indicates that higher complexity presidents are more likely to believe that their level of control is higher by the end of Year 2 than it was in the first year of their presidency. In addition, In-group Bias is significant, with a negative coefficient. This means that a president with a higher level of In-group Bias is more likely to sense themselves as having less control by Year 2. These relationships are visualized in Figure 10.3. None of the situational control variables are significant in these models.

Taken together, the models in the previous tables tell us a good bit about the effect of the president's psychology on his learning while in office. The higher a president's level of Conceptual Complexity, the more positively he will see other actors in the world, and the more control he will see himself having. The more Task focused the president is, the more his beliefs in cooperative strategies will increase. And the higher the president's level of In-group Bias, the lower his sense of control will be. However, by far the biggest predictor of learning in terms of conflict vs. cooperation is the president's own baseline on the P-1 and I-1 variables. Presidents whose views of the political universe (P-1) are friendlier to begin with learn to shift to less friendly views; those whose views are prone to hostility tend to shift toward less hostility.

The same pattern holds for presidential beliefs about strategies of cooperation and conflict (I-1). Presidents with more cooperative strategies shift toward less cooperation over time, while presidents with more

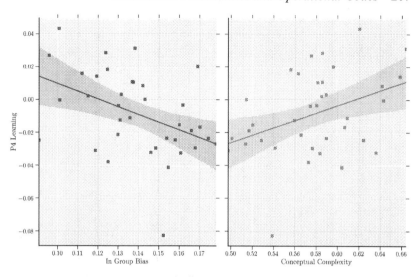

*Figure 10.3* Presidential Learning P-4: In-group Bias and Conceptual Complexity

conflictual strategies shift toward less conflict. These results are rather remarkable but perhaps not that surprising. Prior to taking office as president, these individuals are candidates, and the role of a candidate is very different from that of governing. The candidate must take strong and clear positions and then advocate and defend those positions vigorously; he must convince voters that he is right. Wishy-washy, equivocating candidates are hardly inspiring to voters.

Once the campaigning is done and the election has been won, however, then the governing must begin. And of course, no one is ever right about everything all the time, though a candidate rarely if ever says that about himself. Nonetheless, with governing comes reality testing; those strong ideals that are carefully articulated and defended during the campaign do not seem to hold up perfectly under the variety of governing circumstances associated with reality. Most presidents learn and change, and that means moving away from their more strident positions. Reagan and George W. Bush learned over time to soften their prototypical realism; Carter and Obama learned that the Russians and others could be quite hostile and dangerous.

Our study thus far has not investigated whether these learning trends continue into later stages of the presidency. That work must be saved for another day. But it is important to reiterate that even after 1 year in office, presidents do show patterns of changes in their beliefs; presidents do learn and learn quickly. While not all presidents learn and change their cognitive beliefs the same way, of course, we have clear evidence here that, probabilistically speaking, their preexisting psychological characteristics are fairly good predictors of presidents' patterns of learning over time.

## Data Analysis: Midterm Election Outcomes

We turn now to the results of our second substantive research question: do the psychological characteristics of presidents affect their electoral success, specifically in terms of their first midterm elections? Building on the research just reported, we also ask how the level of learning in a president affects the midterm results. Which presidents have more success with midterm elections: those who change key operational code beliefs or those who continue with their preexisting belief systems supported by extra-cognitive personality traits?

While it is true that the party of the president typically loses seats in Congress during midterm elections, there is great variance in the level of seat changes. Though the president is not on the ballot himself for the midterm election, research has indicated that voters' perceptions of the president may have an important impact on midterm results (Abramowitz 1985; Cohen 2019; King 2020). We speculate that several of the president's leadership traits (LTA) may be signifiers for voters and may influence the election's outcome. Specifically, we include in our analysis the following LTA variables: Belief in Ability to Control Events, Conceptual Complexity, In-group Bias, Need for Power, and Task (vs. Relationship) Focus. We also speculate that changes in the president's psychology may also influence the election. For example, if a president's Task Focus changes in the direction of more Relationship Focus, it may be appealing to voters who appreciate the move toward empathy.[2] So we also investigate change versions (from Year 1 to Year 2) of the LTA variables.

Building from our interest in learning, we also investigate variables marking change in the cognitive beliefs of the operational code. Recall that we conceive of changes in beliefs here as whether the president "strengthened" his original beliefs – meaning his beliefs went further in the direction of his initial disposition or "weakened" his original beliefs – meaning his beliefs changed in the opposite direction of his initial disposition. Note that strengthening and weakening can be from either a conflict-oriented original position or a cooperative one; if a president is first cooperative, and becomes more so, then his beliefs have strengthened; if a president is initially conflictual, and become more conflictual, he, too, has strengthened his beliefs.

To operationalize this pattern, we computed the mean scores of the US presidents on I-1 and P-1, then, based on the president's position above or below the mean, we calculated how much the president moved in the same direction (strengthened) or in the opposite direction (weakened). As discussed earlier, our general hypothesis with this variable is that those who show flexibility in learning by moving in the opposite direction of their initial beliefs are more likely to appeal to voters and will do better in the midterm elections. We operationalize midterm election results as the net gain (or loss) of seats in the US House of Representatives by the president's party.

Our models include two situational control variables that may also affect how the president's party does in the midterms: change in GDP and number of militarized interstate disputes (level three or higher) in the international system. Because we have so many possible independent variables and a fairly small n (36), we were not able to include all variables in one model. As a result, we have run many different versions of models, looking for patterns and identifying the most important variables. In Table 10.4, we present two models, one that best represents the patterns we found (column 1), and the other that includes one version (recall that there are two versions of each psychological variable) of all the variables we investigated (column 2).

In the first model, we see that four of the psychological variables have a statistically significant effect on how the president's party does in the midterm elections; three of those are LTA variables. Presidents who

*Table 10.4* Presidential Influence on Midterms

| | Dependent Variable: Midterm Results | |
|---|---|---|
| | *(1)* | *(2)* |
| Belief in Ability to Control Events | | 62.053 |
| | | (91.752) |
| Δ Conceptual Complexity | 387.234** | 401.345** |
| | (146.791) | (150.101) |
| In-group Bias | 295.257* | 314.818** |
| | (144.871) | (153.133) |
| I-1 Δ Strength | −116.09*** | −108.027*** |
| | (31.483) | (33.945) |
| Need for Power | | −93.894 |
| | | (129.055) |
| Δ Task Orientation | −205.081* | −209.74* |
| | (111.115) | (114.45) |
| Δ GDP | 1.359 | 2.672 |
| | (3.253) | (3.656) |
| Number of MIDs | 0.335 | −0.081 |
| | (0.485) | (0.713) |
| Constant | −87.181** | −87.061 |
| | (33.02) | (52.981) |
| Observations | 36.0 | 36.0 |
| $R^2$ | 0.456 | 0.475 |
| Adjusted $R^2$ | 0.343 | 0.32 |
| Residual Std. Error | 22.7(df = 29.0) | 23.099(df = 27.0) |
| F Statistic | 4.046***(df = 6.0; 29.0) | 3.056**(df = 8.0; 27.0) |

*Note:* *p < 0.1; **p < 0.05; ***p < 0.01.

increase their level of Conceptual Complexity are more likely to have better midterm election results; voters appear to notice and appreciate presidents who become more complex. Those presidents with higher levels of In-group Bias perform better in the midterms; appeals to the in-group, such as nationalism, appear to work to enhance the president's party in the elections. And presidents who change to become less Task Focused (meaning they become more Relationship Focused) tend to be rewarded in the midterms with better results. The patterns associated with these three variables were generally consistent in the models we investigated both in terms of direction and statistical significance.

The fourth psychological variable in our model is one that measures the president's strengthening or weakening beliefs about his own conflict vs. cooperation strategies and tactics (I-1 Strength). Interestingly, in all of the models we tested where we included this variable, it was virtually always significant and always the most important variable. The negative coefficient demonstrates that presidents who adjust and adapt their views by shifting their beliefs in the opposite direction ("weakening" their initial beliefs) are likely to do better in the midterm elections. Those who "strengthen" their beliefs, i.e., go further in the original direction of their beliefs (either cooperative or conflictual) are likely to do worse in the midterm elections.

The same general pattern showed for the P-1 version of this learning variable (though here we show only the I-1 versions of the models): presidents who shifted and changed their views of others in the opposite direction from their original position tended to do better in the midterm election; however, the I-1 version was typically the more statistically significant of the two. It appears that voters are quite sensitive to and appreciate those presidents who learn and show the ability to change in light of complex circumstances; voters tend not to appreciate those presidents who stay the course or become even more strident with their beliefs. Both the two control variables in the model have positive coefficients as we would anticipate, but neither one approaches significance.

Figure 10.4 illustrates the relationships between two of these psychological variables – I-1 Strength and change in Conceptual Complexity – and midterm performance. As leaders become more conceptually complex, their party has fewer losses in the midterm, and those who become more ingrained in their strategies (I-1 Strength) did worse in the midterm. Interestingly, almost all of those presidents who strengthened in I-1 (above 0) saw a loss of greater than 30 seats in the house.

The second model in Table 10.4 includes the remaining two LTA variables that we anticipated might also affect midterm election results, thus presenting a more fully specified model. However, in the various models we tested, these two variables typically did not have any notable effect on the dependent variable. The sign for Belief in Ability to Control Events is positive, as anticipated, indicating that presidents with a higher control orientation will do better in midterm elections, but the variable is not

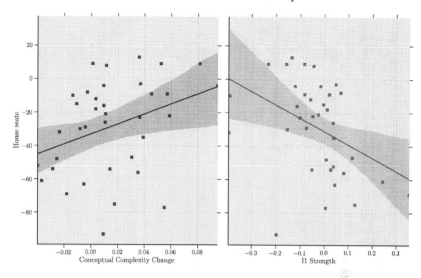

*Figure 10.4* Midterm Outcomes: Conceptual Complexity Change and I-1 Strength

significant. Need for Power in this model actually has a negative coefficient, opposite the one we anticipated, but it also is not significant. As can be seen, Conceptual Complexity Change, In-group Bias, and Task/Relationship Change are all significant or approaching significance in the same direction as in the previous model. And, as before, the dominant variable in the model is I-1 Strength, with a negative coefficient indicating again that those presidents who shift their cooperative vs. conflictual policy preferences in the opposite direction are more likely to have electoral success in the Congressional midterm elections. Neither GDP Change nor MIDs is significant in the larger model.

Not included in the models presented here is the president's approval level. Effective polling that produces approval data did not start until well into the 20th century, so including those data with the president as the unit of analysis significantly reduces the n and therefore reduces our ability to assess the role of the psychology of the president. However, we did run models with approval in them, and, as anticipated, the president's approval level is a good predictor of midterm outcomes. Even with the small n, several of the patterns with the psychological variables held up, especially the ones marking the president's experiential learning.

The clear message in these results is that the president's psychology matters for midterm elections. It appears that voters are sensitive to the psychological characteristics of the president and particularly to changes in the president's personality and beliefs. Voters prefer a president who shifts in the direction of more complexity, who demonstrates higher levels of In-group Bias, who becomes more relationship focused, and who adjusts and shifts away from his initial views on cooperation or conflict. These patterns support the inference that the American public prefers pragmatists over crusaders as presidents. They prefer presidents who follow pragmatic strategies and refuse to get locked into a losing strategy of either conflict or cooperation over the zeal of extreme realists or idealists, respectively, who pursue crusader strategies of unconditional conflict or cooperation that result in foreign policy mistakes (Osgood 1953; Stoessinger 1979; Walker and Malici 2011). An extension of this logic to encompass the leaders and publics of democracies would partly explain the democratic peace phenomenon; democracies do not fight (especially one another) because of the pragmatic operational codes of their leaders (Schafer and Walker 2006; see also Schafer and Walker 2001; Schafer, Young, and Walker 2002).

## Conclusion

Discussions among presidential scholars about the research agenda for presidential decision-making reveals a division of opinion between studies of the "personal" and the "institutional" presidencies (Neustadt 1960; Burke 2000, 1–24; Cameron 2000, 106–110; Preston 2001, 253–254; Walker 2009, 550).

> Personal presidency scholars tend to emphasize that the identity of the president is indispensable to explain the characteristics of decisions and actions that fall under the general category of leadership style... Institutional presidency scholars often substitute a general model of rational choice for the idiosyncratic traits of the president in their models of presidential decision making, arguing that the context of the decision influences choices within the White House especially in the domestic political arena" (Walker 2009, 550; see also Neustadt 1960; Cameron 2000; Greenstein 2004; De figueiredo, Jacobi, and Weingast 2006).

How do the results of our analysis of US presidents address this argument among presidential scholars?

We found evidence to support both approaches to presidential decision-making, which is manifested by our focus on presidential learning as an important aspect of the decision-making process. The operational code construct as our baseline model for making presidential decisions identified three belief-based processes, diagnosis, prescription, and learning, in which a US president diagnoses the political universe as friendly or hostile (P-1) and prescribes cooperation or conflict as the best strategy for realizing goals (I-1) while assessing the ability to control historical development (P-4) as relatively low or high. Learning is conceptualized in this context as the process of changing one or more of these three key beliefs about the exercise of power between the United States and others in the political universe.

These belief-based processes in our analysis clearly focus on the "personal" presidency, i.e., on cognitive personal characteristics of the US president that generate continuity and change in presidential decisions. However, we modeled their operation initially as a "bounded rationality" process regarding the exercise of power (George 1969; Simon 1985), which is generally consistent with a focus on the "institutional" presidency. We also introduced extra-cognitive characteristics of the leader's personality, which may enhance or impede rational decision-making and found that Cognitive Complexity, Task Focus, and In-group Bias are personality traits that varied across presidents and influenced the process of learning (belief change) regarding the diagnosis (P-1) of how others exercise power or the prescription (I-1) of how the self should exercise power in the political universe. Two environmental characteristics also significantly influenced belief change: the US power position in global politics (CINC) influences the direction of change in a president's belief regarding the nature of the political universe (P-1), while the frequency of militarized disputes in global politics (MIDs) influences the direction of change in the president's belief in the best approach to strategy (I-1).

Collectively, the significance of the two learning variables (changes in P-1 and I-1), the three personality variables (Cognitive Complexity, Task Focus, In-group Bias), and the two environmental variables (CINC and MIDs) suggest that a Goldilocks solution be pursued by presidential scholars, i.e., "a research agenda for studying presidential decision making be organized so as to exploit a potential alliance of psychological and rational choice models" in studies of presidential decision-making (Walker 2009, 569; see also Bueno De Mesquita and McDermott 2004). What does this conclusion portend for the operational code research program? It appears that operational code analysis is already positioned to act as a construct to link rational choice and psychological models of decision-making, as George (1969) implied in naming "bounded rationality" as its core concept.

An assessment of our results within the context of the operational code research program suggests that they both reinforce and qualify findings generated by previous operational code studies of US presidents. These studies report that presidential learning occurs in response to exogenous shocks (Walker, Schafer, and Young 1998; Marfleet and Simpson 2011; Renshon 2011; Walker, Schafer, and Marfleet 2012). Changes in P-1 are more likely to be statistically significant than changes in I-1, while changes in P-4 are relatively rare. Cumulative learning in the form of incremental change over time in the absence of a shock (a crisis or a change in power position) is relatively unlikely (Renshon 2011; Robison 2011). Malici (2011) reported that almost no instances of statistically significant, experiential learning occurred following the end of the cold war for the P-1, I-1, and P-4 beliefs of Fidel Castro and Kim Il Sung, respectively, as leaders of Cuba and North Korea.

Almost all of these studies except for Feng (2005, 2007), Malici (2011), Walker, Schafer, and Marfleet (2012), Walker (2013) focus on US cases during short-time intervals. These exceptions also employ simple, diagnostic, and complex conceptualizations of learning that measure learning as changes in the Verbs in Context System (VICS) indices for the key P-1, I-1, and P-4 beliefs. In the presence of shocks, e.g., military confrontations or the end of the cold war, significant changes in P-1 were most frequent and greater in range than changes in I-1, while changes in P-4 were relatively rare.

In contrast, we have reported cumulative learning by US presidents over a short period of time in office in the form of a change in direction for P-1 and I-1 without the presence of an external shock. A change in the US power position and the presence of more frequent militarized disputes were also associated with learning in the form of changes in the I-1 and P-1 beliefs of the 36 US presidents in our study. We investigated systematically as well the influence of personality traits on learning, which previous operational code studies have largely ignored, and then linked learning with electoral outcomes.

Placing the operational code mechanisms of diagnosis, prescription, and learning by the personal presidency within the context of the institutions of American government raises some broader questions about the conduct of US foreign policy: can governments learn? Can governments avoid or fix foreign policy mistakes? Are the mechanisms of a leader's operational code constrained and even selected by the presidency's institutional setting as an environmental niche within which the leader makes decisions? These issues are addressed in our study by linking a US president's operational code beliefs with the outcomes of midterm congressional elections. Are the operational code beliefs and decisions of a US president influenced by a version of the electoral imperative faced by congressional leaders (Mayhew 1974; Fenno 1978)?

We suggest the link that we report between a president's learning pattern and midterm election gains or losses is a manifestation of the logic of political survival identified by Bueno De Mesquita et al. (2003) and obeyed by congressional representatives as reported by Mayhew (1974) and Fenno (1978). Bueno De Mesquita et al. (2003, 8) suggest that "every leader faces the challenge of how to hold onto his or her job. The politics behind survival is...the essence of politics." The challenge is not always defined by the outcomes of elections, as in the United States. In autocratic regimes, a "selectorate" or coalition of influentials inside and outside the government reward or punish by retaining or dismissing a leader from office (Bueno De Mesquita et al. 2003, 9–12). This perspective on learning puts the process in a new context, namely, as a mechanism that helps a leader to avoid making political mistakes, i.e., making decisions that threaten the leader's political survival.

Finally, recall that our main finding is that there is an inverse relationship between the direction of belief change (strengthening [+] vs. weakening beliefs [–]) and the direction of midterm election outcomes. This relationship suggests the possibility that there may be more to political "learning" than a passive pattern of belief change in response to electoral imperatives. There may be an active pattern of belief change in which a leader sends a signal to the electorate about his/her beliefs that is designed to ensure electoral success (Robison 2011, 192–193). This signaling process may extend as well to targets in the foreign as well as the domestic political environment in the form of changes in foreign policy beliefs that emphasize different mixes of the exercise of positive and negative sanctions toward partners and rivals.

A prominent example of this possibility is the "New Thinking" doctrine adopted by Gorbachev in Soviet foreign policy toward the United States designed to end the cold war between the superpowers (Malici 2008). The signals embedded in this doctrine represented changes in the P-1 and I-1 beliefs of Russia's operational code away from extreme conflict and toward cooperation. In turn, the P-1 and I-1 beliefs of US leaders changed, as they learned lessons about the nature of the political universe and the best approach to strategy in dealing with the USSR (Malici 2006). An example of the opposite pattern of shifting toward conflict and away from cooperation is the America First doctrine of the Trump Administration directed toward NATO countries (Walker, He, and Feng 2019; see also Walker, Schafer, and Smith 2019). The level of learning represented in these two examples is *complex learning*, which we do not address in this chapter. We shall conclude by suggesting that future operational code studies of learning may want to focus more attention on the dynamics of complex learning.

Complex learning has been investigated in a few other operational code studies (Feng 2007; Walker and Schafer 2007; Marfleet and Simpson 2011; Walker and Schafer 2011). The two most recent studies (Walker 2013; Malici and Walker 2017) employ VICS learning indices for the key P-1, I-1, and P-4 beliefs so as to define a change in the roles of Self and Other as Ego and Alter in a role dyad. The VICS indices within the context of role theory become metrics that define a change in the complex of beliefs that diagnose a change in the respective roles of friend, partner, rival, or enemy attributed to Alter by a change in P-1 and prescribe a change in these same roles attributed to Ego by a change in I-1. In turn, the specification of these roles may be conditioned by a change in the P-4 index, which indicates the symmetrical or asymmetrical distribution in the exercise of power between them. These efforts anchor the origins of foreign policy roles in the operational codes of a state's leaders and thereby link binary role theory with operational code analysis (Walker, Malici, and Schafer 2011, 246–266; Malici and Walker 2017).

## Notes

1. William Henry Harrison, Zachary Taylor, and James Garfield all served less than 2 years total in office and are, therefore, excluded from this analysis. Grover Cleveland served as both the 20th and the 22nd president, but we are looking only at first terms in office, so his second administration is excluded. While we have some verbal material for the first four US presidents, (Washington, Adams, Jefferson, and Madison), there is not enough to construct meaningful psychological indexes. The data in this chapter

come from the PsyCL data set, which is publicly available at the following website: http://psycldataset.com/. More information on PsyCL can be found in Chapter 8 of this book.

2. Bill Clinton's famous line in his 1992 campaign against President George H.W. Bush comes to mind here, "I feel your pain."

# References

Abramowitz, A. I. 1985. Economic conditions, presidential popularity, and voting behavior in midterm congressional elections. *The Journal of Politics* 47(1): 31–43.

Alesina, A., H. Rosenthal. 1995. *Partisan politics, divided government, and the economy*. Cambridge: Cambridge University Press.

Alt, J., E. Bueno de Mesquita, S. Rose. 2011. Disentangling accountability and competence in elections: Evidence from U.S. term limits. *The Journal of Politics* 73(1): 171–186.

Bolt, J., J. L. Van Zanden. 2014. The Madison Project: Collaborative research on historical national accounts. *The Economic History Review* 67(3): 627–651.

Breslauer, G., P. Tetlock. 1991. Introduction. In *Learning in U.S. and Soviet foreign policy*, eds. G. Breslauer, P. Tetlock, 3–19. Boulder, CO: Westview.

Brummer, K. 2016. Fiasco prime ministers: Leaders beliefs and personality traits as possible causes of policy fiascos. *Journal of European Public Policy* 23(5): 702–717.

Bueno De Mesquita, B., R. McDermott. 2004. Crossing no man's land. *Political Psychology* 25: 275–287.

Bueno De Mesquita, B., A. Smith, R. Siverson, J. Morrow. 2003. *The logic of political survival*. Cambridge, MA: MIT Press.

Burke, J. 2000. *The institutional presidency*. 2nd Edition. Baltimore, MD: Johns Hopkins University Press.

Burke, J., F. Greenstein. 1991. *How presidents test reality*. New York, NY: Russell Sage Foundation.

Cameron, C. 2000. *Veto bargaining*. Cambridge: Cambridge University Press.

Campbell, A. 1966. Surge and decline: A study of electoral change. In *Elections and the political order*, eds. A. Campbell, P. Converse, W. Miller, D. Stokes. New York, NY: Wiley.

Cohen, J. E. 2019. Polls and elections: Presidential referendum effects in the 2018 midterm election: An initial analysis. *Presidential Studies Quarterly* 49(3): 669–683.

De Figueiredo, R., T. Jacobi, B. Weingast. 2006. The new separation of power approach to American politics. In *The Oxford handbook of political economy*, eds. B. Weingast, D. Wittman. New York, NY: Oxford University Press.

Etheredge, L. 1985. *Can governments learn?* New York, NY: Pergamon.

Feng, H. 2005. The operational code of Mao Zedong. *Security Studies* 14: 637–662.

Feng, H. 2007. *Chinese strategic culture and foreign policy decision-making*. New York, NY: Routledge.

Fenno, R. 1978. *Home style: House members in their districts*. Glenview, IL: Scott, Foresman & Company.

George, A. 1969. The operational code. *International Studies Quarterly* 13(2): 190–222.

Greenstein, F. 2004. *The presidential difference*. 2nd Edition. Princeton, NJ: Princeton University Press.

Hermann, M. 1999. *Assessing leadership style: A trait analysis*. Slingerlands, NY: Social Science Automation, Inc. https://socialscience.net/docs/LTA.pdf.

Hermann, M. 2003. Assessing leadership style: Trait analysis. In *The psychological assessment of political leaders*, ed. J. Post, 178–214. Ann Arbor, MI: University of Michigan Press.

King, J. D. 2020. Bill Clinton, republican strategy, and the 1994 elections: How midterms become referenda on the president. *American Review of Politics* 37(1): 76–99.

Leng, R. 2000. *Bargaining and learning in recurrent crises*. Ann Arbor, MI: University of Michigan Press.

Levy, J. 1994. Learning and foreign policy. *International Organization* 48(2): 279–312.

Malici, A. 2006. Reagan and Gorbachev: Altercasting at the end of the Cold War. In *Beliefs and political leadership in world politics*, eds. M. Schafer, S. Walker, 127–150. New York, NY: Palgrave.

Malici, A. 2008. *When leaders learn and when they don't*. Albany, NY: SUNY Press.

Malici, A. 2011. Learning to resist or resisting to learn? The operational codes of Fidel Castro and Kim Il Sung. In *Rethinking foreign policy analysis*, eds. S. Walker, A. Malici, M. Schafer, 153–168. New York, NY: Routledge.

Malici, A., S. Walker. 2017. *Role theory and role conflict in U.S.-Iran relations*. New York, NY: Routledge.

Marfleet, G., H. Simpson. 2011. Cognitive responses by U.S. presidents to foreign policy crises. In *Rethinking foreign policy analysis*, eds. S. Walker, A. Malici, M. Schafer, 205–220. New York, NY: Routledge.

Mayhew, D. 1974. *Congress: The electoral connection*. New Haven, CT: Yale University Press.

Neustadt, R. 1960. *Presidential power*. New York, NY: Macmillan.

Osgood, R. 1953. *Ideals and self-interest in America's foreign relations*. Chicago, IL: University of Chicago Press.

Palmer, G., V. D'Orazio, M. R. Kenwick, R. W. McManus. 2019. Updating the militarized interstate dispute data: A response to Gibler, Miller, and Little. *International Studies Quarterly* 64(2): 469–475.

Post, J. 2003. Assessing leaders at a distance: The political personality profile. In *The psychological assessment of political leaders*, ed. J. Post, 69–104. Ann Arbor, MI: University of Michigan Press.

Preston, T. 2001. *The president and his inner circle*. New York, NY: Columbia University Press.

Ragsdale, L. 1998. *Vital statistics on the presidency: Washington to Clinton*. CQ Press.

Renshon, J. 2011. Stability and change in belief systems: The operational code of George W. Bush from governor to second-term president. In *Rethinking foreign policy analysis*, eds. S. G. Walker, A. Malici, M. Schafer, 169–188. New York, NY: Routledge.

Renshon, S. 2003. Psychoanalytic assessments of character and performance in presidents and candidates. In *The psychological assessment of political leaders*, ed. J. Post, 105–136. Ann Arbor, MI: University of Michigan Press.

Robison, S. 2011. Experiential learning by U.S. presidents. In *Rethinking foreign policy analysis*, eds. S. G. Walker, A. Malici, M. Schafer, 189–204. New York, NY: Routledge.

Schafer, M., A. Glasser. 2000. Sadat takes control: A quantitative analysis of Sadat's operational code before and after the October War of 1973. *The Political Psychologist* 5: 10–16.

Schafer, M., S. Walker. 2001. Political leadership and the democratic peace: The operational code of prime minister Tony Blair. In *Profiling political leaders*, eds. O. Feldman, L. Valenty, 21–36. Westport, CT: Praeger.

Schafer, M., M. Young, S. Walker. 2002. U.S. presidents as conflict managers: The operational codes of George H.W. Bush and Bill Clinton. In *Political leadership for the new century*, eds. L. Valenty, O. Feldman, 51–64. Westport, CT: Praeger.

Schafer, M., S. Walker. 2006. Democratic leaders and the democratic peace. *International Studies Quarterly* 50(3): 561–584.

Simon, H. 1985. Human nature in politics. *American Political Science Review* 79(2): 293–204.

Singer, J. D. 1987. Reconstructing the correlates of war dataset on material capabilities of states, 1816-1985. *International Interaction* 14: 115–132.

Smith, M. B. 1968. A map for the analysis of personality and politics. *Journal of Social Issues* 24(July): 15–28.

Stoessinger, J. 1979. *Crusaders and pragmatists: Movers of modern American foreign policy*. New York, NY: W.W. Norton.

Suedfeld, P., K. Guttieri, P. Tetlock. 2003. Assessing integrative complexity at a distance. In *The psychological assessment of political leaders*, ed. J. Post, 246–270. Ann Arbor, MI: University of Michigan Press.

Thorson, T. 1962. *The logic of democracy*. New York, NY: Holt, Rinehart, & Winston.

Tufte, E. R. 1975. Determinants of the outcomes of midterm congressional elections. *American Political Science Review* 69(3): 812–826.

Tuchman, B. 1984. *The march of folly*. New York, NY: Random House.

Walker, S. 2009. The psychology of presidential decision making. In *The Oxford handbook of the American presidency*, eds. G. Edwards III, W. Howell, 550–574. New York, NY: Oxford University Press.

Walker, S. 2013. *Role theory and the cognitive architecture of British appeasement decisions*. New York, NY: Routledge.

Walker, S. G., A. Malici, and M. Schafer. 2011. *Rethinking foreign policy analysis*. New York: Routledge.

Walker, S., A. Malici. 2011. *U.S. presidents and foreign policy mistakes*. Stanford, CA: Stanford University Press.

Walker, S., M. Schafer. 2007. Theodore Roosevelt and Woodrow Wilson as cultural icons of U.S. foreign policy. *Political Psychology* 28: 747–776.

Walker, S. G. and M. Schafer. 2010. Operational code theory: Beliefs and foreign policy decisions. In *The international studies encyclopedia*, Vol. VIII, ed. R. Denemark, 5492–5514. Chichester, UK: Wiley-Blackwell.

Walker, S., M. Schafer. 2011. Dueling with dictators: Explaining the strategic interaction patterns of U.S. presidents and rogue leaders. In *Rethinking foreign policy analysis*, eds. S. Walker, A. Malici, M. Schafer, 223–244. New York, NY: Routledge.

Walker, S., M. Schafer, G. Smith. 2019. The operational codes of Donald Trump and Hillary Clinton. In *The Oxford handbook of behavioral political science*, eds. A. Mintz, L. Terris, on-line version. New York, NY: Oxford University Press.

Walker, S., K. He, H. Feng. 2019. Binary role theory and the evolution of world politics. Presented at the annual meeting of the International Studies Association meeting, Toronto, Canada, March 27–30.

Walker, S., M. Schafer, G. Marfleet. 2012. The British strategy of appeasement: Why Britain persisted in the face of negative feedback. In *When things go wrong*, ed. C. Hermann, 111–141. New York, NY: Routledge.

Walker, S., M. Schafer, M. Young. 1998. Systematic procedures for operational code analysis. *International Studies Quarterly* 42: 173–188.

Walker, S., M. Schafer, M. Young. 2003. Profiling the operational codes of political leaders. In *The psychological assessment of political leaders*, ed. J. Post, 215–245. Ann Arbor, MI: University of Michigan Press.

Walker, S., D. Bohlin, R. Boos, D. Cownie, H. Nakajima, T. Willson. 1984. Evidence of learning and risk orientation during international crises: The Munich and Polish cases. *British Journal of Political Science* 14: 33–51.

Winter, D. 2003. Measuring the motives of political actors at a distance. In *The psychological assessment of political leaders*, ed. J. Post, 153–177. Ann Arbor, MI: University of Michigan Press.

## Appendix: Variables and Indices for Personalities and Operational Codes of US Presidents

| Cognitive Variables[a] | Index |
|---|---|
| P-1 | O: $[(Co - Cf)/(Co + Cf)]$ |
| I-1 | S: $[(Co - Cf)/(Co + Cf)]$ |
| P-4 | HC: $[(S: (Co + Cf)]/[S: (Co + Cf) + O: (Co + Cf)]$ |
| P-1$\Delta$ | P-1 Year 2 minus P-1 Year 1 |
| I-1$\Delta$ | I-1 Year 2 minus I-1 Year 1 |
| P-4$\Delta$ | P-4 Year 2 minus P-4 Year 1 |

| Personality Variables[b] | Index |
|---|---|
| CC | % High Cognitive Complexity Words |
| Distrust | % Suspicious References |
| IGB | % Positive In-Group References |
| Power | % Self-References regarding exercise of power |
| Task | % Task-Reference Words |
| BACE | % Self-References Responsible for Actions or Plans |
| SC | % Use of First-Person Pronouns (I, me, we, us) |

| Environmental Variables[c] | Index |
|---|---|
| CINC | National Military Capabilities Ratio (COW) |
| GDP | Gross domestic product per capita |
| MIDs | Militarized Interstate Disputes (Hostility level 3 or higher) |
| House Seats | The number of house seats won/lost by the president's party |

[a]*Source:* Walker and Schafer (2010). P-1: Nature of Political Universe; I-1: Approach to Strategy; P-4: Historical Control; P-1$\Delta$: Year 2 minus Year 1; I-1$\Delta$: Year 2 minus Year 1; P-4$\Delta$ Year 2 minus Year 1; O: Other; S: Self; Co: Cooperation; Cf: Conflict; HC: Historical Control.
[b]*Source:* Hermann (1999, 2003). CC: Cognitive Complexity; IGB: In-group Bias; BACE: Belief in Ability to Control Events. The indices for the personality variables are percentages of relevant words or phrases as references to Self or Others.
[c]*Sources:* National Military Capabilities Ratio (COW) (Singer 1987 v.5.0); GDP: Gross domestic product per capita (Bolt and Van Zanden. 2014); MID: Militarized Interstate Disputes Data (Palmer et al. 2019, v4.3); House Seats – the number of house seats won/lost by the president's party (Ragsdale 1998).

# 11 US Presidential Belief Systems and the Evolution of Peace in the International System

*Stephen G. Walker, Mark Schafer, Gary E. Smith, and Collin J. Kazazis*

## Introduction

A recent study of the international system since 1900 shows a shift in direction from conflict toward cooperation in the dyadic relations between states in the second half of the 20th century (Goertz, Diehl, and Balas 2016, 201–206). The authors attribute the shift to three factors: a decline in territorial disputes; the emergence of norms against the use of violence for both conquest and secession as mechanisms for settling such disputes; and their replacement with norms of peaceful means and mutual consent in the form of mediation, arbitration, and adjudication as mechanisms for settling disputes. "The net result is that while territorial disagreements persist, they are less frequent than in previous eras, they are increasingly dealt with in a peaceful fashion, and outcomes are more peaceful and stable than those 'resolved' by military means" (Goertz et al. 2016, 206).

Two prominent roles assigned to the office of the US president are chief diplomat and commander-in-chief, which charge the occupant of the office with the responsibility for managing cooperation and conflict by the United States in the conduct of foreign relations. In this chapter we examine whether the shifts in the patterns of conflict and cooperation at the systemic level in world politics since 1945 are reflected at the agent level in the operational codes of US presidents. If so, we would expect that their instrumental operational code beliefs regarding the utility of different means for conducting US foreign relations should shift from conflict (the use of threats and punishments) toward cooperation (the use of promises and rewards). This change should accompany a shift in their philosophical operational code beliefs from mutual conflict to mutual cooperation regarding the nature of US dyadic relations in the political universe.

We are interested in the dynamic interactions of these historical patterns, because they may well exhibit three other patterns than the one identified by Goertz et al. (2016) at the systemic level of analysis. One possibility is that US dyadic relations do not exhibit the shift from conflict to cooperation after 1945. A second possibility is that the shift did occur, but it was not emulated by either the philosophical or the instrumental beliefs of US presidents. A third possibility is that a shift in beliefs also occurred; however, the changes were asymmetrical, i.e., one type of belief "mirrored" the shift while the other type of belief "steered" the shift in the opposite direction. The mirroring possibility relegates beliefs to a passive role in a socialization process represented by a shift in the norms of conduct in world politics that preceded a shift in the beliefs of US presidents. The steering possibility assigns beliefs an active role in a socialization process wherein a shift in the beliefs of US presidents preceded or resisted a change in the norms of conduct in world politics.

The theoretical significance of these different possibilities is that they represent different types of leadership by US presidents in the conduct of foreign relations. A pattern of passive leadership is one in which the president is a patient of socialization processes that shape the US operational code beliefs so that they mirror the norms of the international system. A pattern of active leadership is one in which a US president is an agent of socialization processes in which US operational code beliefs shape the norms of the international system (Walker 2017). It is likely that one of these modes of presidential leadership is more likely to occur, depending on the interaction between the external stimuli from the international environment and the internal dispositions emanating from the White House regarding the exercise of power in US foreign relations (Walker 2009).

We expect that the external stimuli will vary by historical period and take the form of either more conflictual or more cooperative norms before and after World War II, respectively, governing relations between dyads in the international system. We expect that the internal dispositions will vary, depending on leadership traits attributed to the president's leadership style, which reflects the personalities of the leader and his advisors as they interact to express the operational code beliefs of the US government regarding conflict or cooperation as norms in foreign relations. If these internal beliefs and external norms are consonant, it may be because external norms trumped internal personality traits in shaping operational code beliefs. If there is dissonance between presidential leadership style and systemic norms, it is more likely that dyadic relations between the United States and the other members of the international system may deviate from the norms of the international system.

We hypothesize that the outcome of a clash between these external and internal sources of norms governing the conduct of US dyadic relations may be reflected in the instrumental and philosophical beliefs of the US president's operational code. These beliefs as well as evidence of leadership traits associated with the personalities of US presidents and their advisors are to be found in the public speeches and interviews of US leaders. The Psychological Characteristics of Leaders (PsyCL) data set

(Schafer et al. 2016) has coded presidential speeches and interviews for the occupants of the oval office from 1900 to 2006, which corresponds to the time frame covered for dyadic relations in the international system by Goertz et al.'s (2016) Evolution of Peace data set. Automated content analysis systems can retrieve personality traits and beliefs attributed to the speaker from these documents, in order to construct the speaker's leadership style and operational code.

## Mapping the Personality and Political Nexus

The connections between individual-level characteristics and the political relations between nation-states raise the question of whether leaders matter in the domain of world politics. It is an instance of more fundamental questions about whether and how (1) the actions and (2) the personality traits of leaders make a difference in politics. Greenstein (1969) distinguishes between action and actor dispensability to address these questions. Action dispensability focuses on whether the decisions of states and the ensuing relations between them are attributable to the actions of leaders. The answer to this question rests on the power of the leader to control what is decided, which depends on a leader's strategic location in the decision-making process and a state's strategic location in the international system. Actor dispensability refers to whether a leader's personality is necessary or sufficient to explain the decisions of a state, i.e., whether individual differences in leaders make a difference in what is decided and what follows (Greenstein 1969; Walker 1982).

In the US government, the president's dual roles as chief diplomat and commander-in-chief locate him in a position of preeminence unless he chooses to delegate the power to make foreign policy decisions to others in his cabinet or the US Constitution imposes a check on some decisions, e.g., the power to fund foreign and defense expenditures or make the decision to declare war. The impact of a president's personality on US foreign policy decisions depends partly on presidential power to decide (a necessary condition) and partly on whether the leader's personality traits shape the decision (a sufficient condition) rather than situational constraints or incentives that over-rule individual differences in presidential personalities. A more complex possibility is when the confluence of personality and situational variables reenforces the influence of personality traits (Greenstein 1969; Hermann 1974; Holsti 1976).

Smith (1968) mapped the mechanisms and paths for linking the impact of personality on political decisions while leaving open what specific traits are likely the sources of a leader's decisions. Hermann (2003) has identified several traits that influence leadership style in processing information from the environment and making political decisions. George (1969, 1979) and others (Holsti 1976; Walker 1983) have advanced the argument that a leader's belief system both reflects and mediates the impact of personality traits on a leader's decisions. Beliefs are acquired as information from interaction with the environment while at the same time they may also reflect the motivational impact of unconscious desires and fears, such as the needs for power, affiliation, and achievement (Winter 2003), which bias the reception or processing of information from the environment. In turn, these motivated biases may stem from underlying personality traits, such as distrust, conceptual complexity, in-group bias, and self-confidence (Hermann 2003).

Decisions in this account are a "bounded rationality" process limited by both cognitive and extra-cognitive constraints on a leader's ability to process information (George 1969, 1979; Holsti 1976, 1977: Simon 1985; Gigerenzer and Selten 2001). We take this approach in modeling the decisions of US presidents by identifying beliefs, motivations, and personality traits to specify the mechanisms and organize the paths that represent the calculus for making US foreign policy decisions. We conceptualize this calculus as the "operational code" of beliefs about the exercise of power expressed by US presidents, which we postulate are emergent properties as the product of the interaction between a psychological model of *internal traits* emanating from the president and an ecological model of *external norms* emanating from the international environment. We suspect that *instrumental beliefs* about the exercise of US power reflect primarily the influence of internal traits while *philosophical beliefs* about the exercise of power by other states manifest the influence of external norms. These two sets of beliefs define collectively the calculus or operational code for making presidential decisions regarding US foreign relations (; see also ).

A representation of these two models specifying the psychological and ecological variables for analysis in this chapter is in Figure 11.1. The dyadic political behavior in this figure are the enactment of the political roles of friends, partners, rivals, or enemies as the product of interactions between variables in the two models of personality and situational norms. In turn, the origins of personality and situational norms, respectively, are the immediate biographical environment for the development of personality and the remote events in international history that shaped current norms in the international system. ) also anticipated the direct influence of international historical norms on the biographies of leaders (shown but not analyzed in this model), and he suggested the likely presence of feedback over time (neither shown nor analyzed in Figure 11.1) from political behavior to the evolution over time of the immediate situation, personality processes and dispositions, and the historical situation.

The ecological model in Figure 11.1 is populated by variables from Goertz et al.'s (2017) analysis of the evolution of the international system between 1900 and 2006. We connect them with the macro- and meso-arrows. The psychological model specifies the personality processes and dispositions of interest to us identified by ) and Winter (2003) in our analysis of US presidents and foreign policy behavior and connects

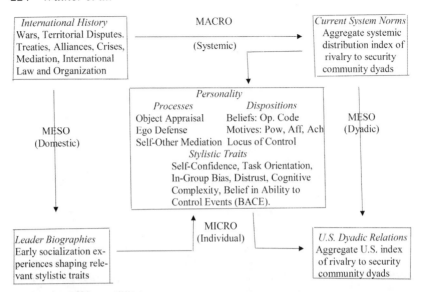

*Figure 11.1* Psychological and Ecological Models of the Operational Codes of US Presidents

Variable Sources:  Smith (1968); Hermann (2003); Goertz et al. (2017)

them with the micro arrows in Figure 11.1. The two sets of arrows specify two models for understanding the evolution of US foreign relations between 1900 and 2006. One is an ecological analysis of environmental influences while the other is a psychological analysis of US foreign policy dynamics. The points where the two paths converge indicate that the two models may complement one another for periods in which presidential personality traits and environmental systemic norms as mechanisms generate or reinforce conflict or cooperation as a particular kind of dyadic political behavior. They may also diverge in their prescriptions for conflict or cooperation behavior for the United States in conducting foreign relations.

One of the models is relatively simple while the other is more complex. The ecological systemic model in Figure 11.1 has a macroscopic focus on systems-level phenomena represented by the arrow connecting remote historical events with current systemic norms indexed by the distribution of dyadic relations from rivalries to security communities. Goertz et al. (2017) assume that macro-level interstate relations and processes at least supervene and at most constrain the distribution of meso-level (US-dyad relations) and micro-level (personality) processes emanating from the social environment and shaping the political behavior that sustains the evolution of peace at the systemic level of analysis. At least, "macro-level regularities must 'supervene'—come from and rely ontologically for their existence—on micro-level phenomena; however, …. macro-level phenomena need not be reduced to micro-level conditions in a causal explanation and...[at most]... can stand alone as a causal explanation" (Walker, Malici, and Schafer 2011, 27).

The psychological model in Figure 11.1 is more complex and addresses how meso- and micro-levels of analysis explain as well as inform ontologically the regularities of international relations at the macro-level of analysis. The outline of this explanation is represented by the arrows connecting the biographies of individuals with the personalities and behaviors of agents for states in the international system. We theorize and test a model at the individual-level of analysis for the US case in which the president of the United States is the focal actor as an agent through which his personality traits and/or those of his advisors shape US dyadic relations (Walker, Malici, and Schafer 2011; Walker 2013; Malici and Walker 2017). In this account the personality processes of ego defense, object appraisal, and mediation of self-other relations at the micro-level of analysis generate motivations and beliefs from personality traits and sustain them as emergent properties that influence US political behavior of conflict and cooperation in dyadic relations (Smith 1968; Hermann 2003; Winter 2003; Walker 2009).

The following five biographical propositions from operational code theory state how the social environment in Figure 11.1 generates the operational code beliefs of individuals as an expression of their personalities in the domain of politics regarding the exercise of social power (see also Walker and Falkowski 1985; Levy 1994; Walker 1995; Walker and Schafer 2010). They state how relevant stylistic personality traits (cognitive, temperamental, and behavioral) interact with one another and with life situations and socialization experiences to shape the motivational foundations of a leader's operational code beliefs regarding the exercise of power by self and others in the political universe (Walker, 1983; Walker, Malici, and Schafer 2011, 54–55):

> *Prop. 1*: As a result of childhood and early adult socialization experiences in family and society, an individual acquires the dominant motives in his personality prior to adopting a political belief system.
>
> *Prop. 2*: An individual tends to adopt a political belief system that is compatible with his/her constellation of the needs for power, affiliation, and achievement.
>
> *Prop. 3*: Although an individual's belief system may develop a consistency that is independent from random fluctuations in immediate personal needs, the activation of these beliefs by environmental stimuli may arouse personal needs embedded in the belief system as the individual uses the various elements of his belief system to interpret a decision-making situation.
>
> *Prop. 4*: Once aroused, these motives may contribute to the cognitive rigidity of an individual's beliefs and account for the intensity of cognitive dissonance and behavioral intransigence in the face of new information or other stimuli from the environment.

*Prop. 5*: Conversely, vivid stimuli or changes in context, respectively, may lead to behavioral change in the form of social learning or structural adaptation and even cognitive change in the form of experiential learning (changes in beliefs).

These propositions are consistent with a general biosocial model of the development of personality from biological genetic sources that interact with societal cultural norms to transform the nuclear self represented by the individual's biological endowment of genes into a social self represented by the interaction of the individual's emergent personality traits and cognitive beliefs with cultural memes in a process of biological and social coevolution (Dawkins 2006, 2008; Tang 2013, 2017; Mitchell 2009). The depiction of this developmental model for operational code beliefs and behavioral patterns as memes of the social self, generated by the processes of ego defense, object appraisal, and mediation of self-other relations in the nuclear self, is shown in the grid of key operational code beliefs and corresponding operational code types (A,B,C,DEF) constructed from them represented in Figure 11.2.

Figure 11.2 is a flat version of a topological map of personality structure with the needs for affiliation, power, and achievement in bold font as the bottom level (floor) of motivational foundations constituting the nuclear self from personality traits (Winter 2003; Kohut 1971). A layer of operational code types in bold font is the socio-cognitive in structure that emerges one level up from the floor. At the top level (apex) of the map in upper case font are strategic behavioral patterns of cooperation and conflict (passive, balanced, active) and leadership style (erratic, pragmatic, dogmatic), which emerge from the motivational and cognitive layers of the personality and mediate relations between the social self and others. The strategies of political behavior may escalate or de-escalate over time between passive and active levels of cooperation or conflict, and a leadership style can employ tactics that shift between cooperation and conflict, e.g., more erratically between appeasing and bluffing, pragmatically between rewarding and punishing on the basis of reciprocity, or more dogmatically between bullying and exploiting (Marfleet and Walker 2006; Walker, Malici, and Schafer 2011, 44–80).

This schematic vertical model in Figure 11.2 of the interface between beliefs and political behavior identifies four general types of operational codes characterized by different motivational profiles and configurations of the key operational code beliefs regarding the strategic direction of cooperation or conflict by self (I-1) and others (P-1), and the locus of historical control (P-4) between them. Beliefs about tactics in Figure 11.2 (appease/bluff, reward/compel, deter/punish, and exploit/bully) plus beliefs (not shown in this figure) regarding utility of means, risk orientation, predictability of the future, and the role of chance describe how each of these operational code types is constituted in more detail (Walker, Schafer, and Young 2003; Schafer and Walker 2006, 2007; Walker and Schafer 2010).

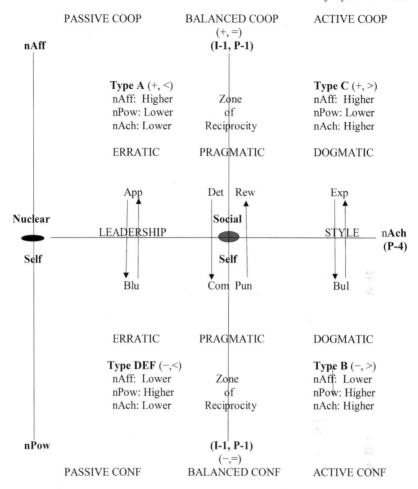

*Figure 11.2* Motivational Foundations of Beliefs for Operational Code Types

Sources: (Holsti (1977); Walker (1983); Walker and Falkowski (1985); Walker, Malici, and Schafer (2011); Walker (2013); Malici and Walker (2017). Motivations: nAff = need for affiliation; nPow = need for power; nAch = need for achievement. Tactics: App = Appease; Blu = Bluff; Rew = Reward; Com = Compel; Det = Deter; Pun = Punishment; Exp = Exploit; Bul = Bully. Behavior: Coop = Cooperation; Conf = Conflict.

The processes of personality development in Figure 11.2 originate in the interactions among genes that shape such personality traits as distrust, self-confidence, in-group bias, task orientation, cognitive complexity, belief in ability to control events, and need for power, which are aroused from an individual's interaction in a social environment as indicated in Figure 11.1. The following propositions articulate the links in Figure 11.2 between the needs for affiliation, power, and achievement as motivations generated from personality traits and the social environment that lead an individual to adopt key operational code beliefs regarding strategies of cooperation or conflict in the exercise of power.

*Proposition 1:* Variations in the motivational profiles of individuals generate the acquisition of different operational codes (beliefs about the exercise of social power) across leaders in political situations.

*Proposition 2:* The greater the leader's need for affiliation, the greater the individual's propensity to choose cooperation strategies in the exercise of social power.

*Proposition 3:* The greater the leader's need for power, the greater the individual's propensity to choose conflict strategies in the exercise of social power.

*Proposition 4:* The greater the individual's need for achievement, the greater the individual's resolve in the propensity to choose strategies of conflict or cooperation.

*Proposition 5:* These propensities are reflected in the cognitive beliefs about the exercise of social power as words or deeds in the form of cooperative political behavior (statements of support, promises, rewards) or conflict behavior (statements of opposition, threats, punishments).

In sum, the "operational code" is á psychocultural construct that identifies the cognitive and motivational dimensions of a leader's personality that are particularly relevant for understanding the exercise of power by a particular leader or by individuals who share or at least express the same operational code beliefs as the decision unit for a particular state. In the US case, the president through his public statements expresses the operational code of the US government as the focal actor for making US foreign policy decisions. The contents of his public statements contain the beliefs governing the exercise of US power in foreign relations, which he may believe himself or at least has come to adopt as the calculus for US foreign policy decisions (Walker, Schafer, and Beieler 2016).

The operational code beliefs regarding self's strategic orientation (I-1) and historical control (P-4) are the key beliefs that collectively define the strategies that the United States enacts; the corresponding key beliefs regarding the nature of the political universe (P-1) and the control over historical development by others (P-4) define the strategies of cooperation or conflict that the United States attributes to others in the political universe. The aggregation and evolution of these beliefs as emergent properties transforms individual beliefs at micro levels of spatial and temporal levels of analysis to operational code types attributed to states at the meso-level of analysis (Walker, Malici, and Schafer 2011; Walker 2013; Walker, Schafer, and Beieler 2016; Malici and Walker 2017).

## Hypotheses and Research Design

The psychological and ecological models in Figure 11.1 may be viewed and analyzed as rival or complementary non-recursive models. We shall examine them from both perspectives to see whether one or both fit the data for the US cases. We infer the following hypotheses regarding the dependent variables of US presidents' operational code beliefs (OCA) and US dyad behavior (USD) from the propositions in the Leadership Trait Analysis (LTA) and International Systemic Norms (ISN) models.

- LTA/OCA model: cognitive hypotheses

    *H-1:* The greater the US president's need for power (nPow), the less cooperation-oriented/more conflict-oriented is the president's approach to strategy (I-1) as a process of ego defense.

    *H-2:* The greater the US president's need for power (nPow), the less friendly/more hostile is the president's view of the political universe (P-1) as a process of object appraisal.

    *H-3:* The greater the US president's need for affiliation, the more cooperation-oriented/less conflict-oriented is the president's approach to strategy (I-1) as a process of ego defense.

    *H-4:* The greater the US president's need for affiliation, the more friendly/less hostile is the president's view of the political universe (P-1) as a process of object appraisal.

    *H-5:* The greater the US president's need for achievement, the greater is the value of the president's resolve to exert historical control (P-4) as a process of mediation between self and other.

- ISN/OCA model: cognitive hypotheses

    *H-6:* The less cooperation-oriented/more conflict oriented the systemic norms are, the more conflict-oriented is a US president's approach to strategy (I-1) as a process of experiential learning.

    *H-7:* The less cooperation-oriented/more conflict oriented are the systemic norms, the less friendly/more hostile is a US president's view of the political universe (P-1) as a process of experiential learning.

    *H-8:* The greater the absolute value of the orientation toward conflict or cooperation in systemic norms, the greater is the value of a US president's resolve to exert historical control (P-4) as a process of experiential learning.

- OCA/USD model: behavioral hypotheses.
- If the US president's operational code beliefs exert *steering effects* on the evolution of US dyadic relations, then

    *H-9:* The more cooperation-oriented/less conflict-oriented is the US president's I-1 belief, the more cooperation-oriented/less conflict-oriented is US dyadic behavior.

    *H-10:* The more friendly/less hostile is the US president's P-1 belief, the more cooperation-oriented/less conflict-oriented is US dyadic behavior.

    *H-11:* The greater the US president's P-4 belief, the greater the absolute value of US dyadic behavior.

- ISN/USD model: behavioral hypothesis.
- If international systemic norms of conflict or cooperation exert *learning effects* on US behavior in dyadic relations, then

  *H-12:* The more cooperation-oriented/less conflict-oriented are international systemic norms, the greater is US cooperation behavior in dyadic relations with other states as a process of social learning.

To test these hypotheses, we constructed a data set with the US country-year as the unit of analysis. The sample coincides with ) data set and covers the years from 1900 to 2006. All psychological variables were derived using standard at-a-distance methods that content analyze verbal material from each US president. We used all the verbal material spoken by each president in our data set, including both spontaneous comments and prepared speeches, and coded these for each year in the sample. LTA variables (nPow, nAff, and nAch) were coded using Margaret Hermann's constructs (Hermann 1999). While Hermann's scheme includes nPow, we needed to conceptualize proxy variables for the other two. For nAff, we used the inverse of Hermann's "Task" variable. Hermann (1999) conceptualizes that variable as follows: high scores indicate a person who focuses on getting things done (task-orientation), while low scores indicate a person who focuses on people and relationships, things that are consistent with general conceptions of nAff. For the proxy nAch, we use Hermann's variable Belief in Ability to Control Events, with the idea that those who see themselves as being in control are oriented toward high levels of achievement. Each of these variables ranges from 0 to 1.

For the OCA variables (I-1, P-1, and P-4), we used the system outlined in Schafer and Walker (2006). Both I-1 and P-1 are essentially indicators of conflict levels in a speaker's verbal material. I-1 captures the speaker's beliefs on the utility of self's conflict vs. cooperation strategies, whereas P-1 captures the speaker's beliefs about others' actions in terms of conflict and cooperation. I-1 and P-1 can range from −1 to +1. P-4 is an indicator of self's beliefs about the locus of control; higher scores indicate that self sees self (as opposed to others) as taking more action in the world; it can range from 0 to 1.

Our variable for International Systemic Norms (ISN) is operationalized using a very similar weighting process as found in operational code research, i.e. we created a weighted scale based upon the coding categories found in Goertz et al (2016). They code the behavior of all politically relevant dyads into five different ordinal categories: severe rivalry, lesser rivalry, negative peace, warm peace, and security community. They then compute percentages of dyads in each of the five categories for each of their temporal periods. We convert these scores to an additive scale by weighting each category respectively: −2, −1, 0, +1, and +2, then summing the results and dividing it by two so that it has a theoretical range of −1 to +1. This gives us a weighted average of the conflict vs. cooperative dyadic behavior across the system for each period. It coincides very nicely with Goertz et al.'s interpretation of their data showing that since 1900 the norms in the international system have evolved to become less violent and conflictual and more cooperative and peaceful.

We used the same weighting procedure to derive our variable on US Dyad Behavior (USD). From the Goertz et al. data set, we extracted all dyads that included the US We aggregated these to our unit of analysis, the year, calculated percentages of US dyads in each of the five categories, weighted them the same as above, and summed the results. This gives a weighted average of conflict vs. cooperative behavior per year for all dyads involving the US It ranges from −1 to +1. We also examine its absolute value (abs) in one of our hypotheses linking the historical control beliefs variable (P-4) and US dyadic behavior.

We also include two control variables that are common in conflict research: US annual GDP growth and US annual score on the Composite Index of National Capability (CINC). GDP growth may coincide with conflict in terms of a leader's beliefs (OCA dependent variables) or a state's behavior (USD dependent variable); as GDP falls, the actor may be inclined to divert attention away from the problem or pursue expansionist or interventionist policies to compensate. The US CINC score is the US's relative share of the world's collective power assessed across several measures[1] (Singer et al 1972). Essentially an indicator of national power, CINC is a proxy for the power position of the US in the international system, which changes significantly between 1900 and 2006 and may coincide with more assertive foreign policies.

## Results

Our hypotheses pertain to several different independent variables that explain five different dependent variables (I-1, P-1, P-4, USD, and (abs) USD). Therefore, we present the results in the following five tables, one for each dependent variable. All tests are conducted with OLS models with panel-corrected fixed effects. The fixed effects control for unobserved unit ("panel") heterogeneity by creating a dummy for each president.

The first dependent variable we investigate is the op. code belief I-1: the subject's views on the utility of self's cooperative vs. conflictual strategies. What factors affect the way the president thinks about the value of using friendlier vs. more assertive policies? We hypothesize about three factors, two pertaining to the president's own personality: nPow (H-1) and nAff (H-3), and one pertaining to the behavioral norms found across the international system, ISN (H-6). Table 11.1 presents two models that investigate these hypotheses. The first model includes only our hypothesized explanatory variables, while the second adds our two control variables (GDP and CINC).

*Table 11.1* Motives and System Norms Explaining I-1

| Variables | Full Sample | Full Sample |
|---|---|---|
| nPwr (H-1) | −1.152** | −0.985* |
| | (0.423) | (0.415) |
| nAff (H-3) | −0.576* | −0.474+ |
| | (0.241) | (0.242) |
| Int Sys Norms (H-6) | −0.337 | −0.690 |
| | (0.734) | (0.731) |
| CINC | | −0.755** |
| | | (0.280) |
| GDP growth | | 0.000120 |
| | | (0.00448) |
| Constant | 0.484* | 0.617** |
| | (0.210) | (0.216) |
| Observations | 107 | 107 |
| R-squared | 0.160 | 0.228 |
| Number of presidents | 19 | 19 |

Standard errors in parentheses.

*** $p < 0.001$, ** $p < 0.01$, * $p < 0.05$, + $p < 0.10$.

We hypothesized that a president's nPow would have a negative effect on his belief about the cooperative strategies, and indeed that hypothesis is supported in both models in Table 11.1. Presidents with higher scores on nPow tend to have lower scores on I-1. Presidents with a high need for power are more likely to believe in less cooperative strategies than those presidents with a lower need for power. We do not, however, find support for our hypothesis regarding nAff. While the variable is significant in the model without controls, and approaches significance in the full model, the sign of the coefficient is in the opposite direction of the one anticipated in our hypothesis. This means that presidents who have a higher need for affiliation tend to believe that a more conflictual strategy is better, a nonintuitive result that we discuss a bit more below.

Table 11.1 also shows that the norms in the international system did not affect presidents' beliefs about different strategies. In fact, the sign is opposite than the one expected (as the system norms became friendlier, president's beliefs about strategies became less friendly), but in neither model does the variable approach significance. Regarding the two control variables, while GDP is not significant in explaining I-1, CINC is. As the US share of global power increased, a president's beliefs about self's strategies became more conflictual: presidents seem to believe that a stronger United States could be a more belligerent United States.

Table 11.2 presents the results of the tests for the same set of independent variables, this time on the dependent variable P-1, presidential beliefs about the cooperative vs. conflictual nature of other actors in the political universe. Here the directional effects are the same as above, though only

*Table 11.2* Motives and System Norms Explaining P-1

| Variables | Full Sample | Full Sample |
|---|---|---|
| nPwr (H-2) | −0.503 | −0.374 |
| | (0.362) | (0.356) |
| nAff (H-4) | −0.286 | −0.227 |
| | (0.206) | (0.208) |
| Int Sys Norms (H-7) | −0.168 | −0.499 |
| | (0.628) | (0.628) |
| CINC | | −0.593* |
| | | (0.241) |
| GDP growth | | 0.00220 |
| | | (0.00385) |
| Constant | 0.351+ | 0.433* |
| | (0.180) | (0.186) |
| Observations | 107 | 107 |
| R-squared | 0.053 | 0.123 |
| Number of presidents | 19 | 19 |

Standard errors in parentheses.

*** $p < 0.001$, ** $p < 0.01$, * $p < 0.05$, + $p < 0.10$.

CINC is significant in either model: as the US share of power increases, presidents tend to believe the world is more conflictual. The international norms (H-7) do not have an effect on presidents' beliefs about others' conflict orientations. Once again, the sign is in the wrong direction, though the variable does not approach significance. Higher nPow (H-2) correlates with more conflictual views of the world as anticipated, though the variable is not significant. Once again, we see the unexpected direction of the nAff variable (H-4): more people and relationship-oriented presidents tend to see the world as more conflictual, though again the variable is not significant.

While the significant effect for nAff in Table 11.1 and the (non-significant) direction of the variable in Table 11.2 are certainly not intuitive, there may be either an empirical or a theoretical explanation (or both). On the empirical side, it may simply be that the inverse of Hermann's Task variable is not a good proxy for nAff; it may be that low scores on Task simply indicate those who are not task oriented, as opposed to those who are people oriented. On the theoretical front, we turn to an explanation of nAff offered by Winter (1993, 2003). He notes laboratory research where subjects with high nAff acted erratically and more hostile in some situations than expected (Winter 2003). Winter (1993) argues that this may be the case particularly when someone friendly to the subject engaged in less-than-friendly behavior or even when the subject was simply dealing with strangers rather than friends (Winter 2003, 157). Says Winter, "Hell hath no fury like an affiliation motivated person scorned" (Winter 1993, 114).

Thinking about this insight and US presidents, though American power, influence, and friendships were growing rapidly, there were also many

*Table 11.3* nAch and System Norms Explaining P-4

| Variables | Full Sample | Full Sample |
|---|---|---|
| nAch (H-5) | 0.0511 | 0.0516 |
|  | (0.0830) | (0.0831) |
| (absl)Int Sys Norms (H-8) | 0.0445 | 0.120 |
|  | (0.200) | (0.205) |
| CINC |  | −0.0854 |
|  |  | (0.0677) |
| GDP growth |  | 0.00116 |
|  |  | (0.00110) |
| Constant | 0.192$^{***}$ | 0.195$^{***}$ |
|  | (0.0425) | (0.0435) |
| Observations | 107 | 107 |
| R-squared | 0.005 | 0.037 |
| Number of presidents | 19 | 19 |

Standard errors in parentheses.

abs=Absolute value.

$^{***}$ $p < 0.001$, $^{**}$$p < 0.01$, $^{*}$$p < 0.05$, +p < 0.10.

periods where a rising United States faced harsh criticism, much of it coming from close friends. These include such periods as US isolationism in the 1930s, the Vietnam War in the 1960s, Reagan's SDI announcement and his INF buildup in Europe during the 1980s, and George W. Bush's steel tariffs and war in Iraq after 9/11. Though exploring these period effects is beyond the scope of the present paper, criticism from friends may indeed influence the unusual direction of the nAff variable in our study.

In Table 11.3, we investigate variables that may affect a president's resolve to exert control over historical events (P-4). We hypothesized above that this resolve may be affected by a president's nAch (H-5) or by the absolute value of the international system norms (H-8). The logic for the latter variable is that as a president sees more extreme behavior (in either direction) as the prevailing norm in the international system, it will cause the president to determine to be even more engaged in global events. However, as seen in Table 11.3, none of the variables are significant in either model. The directions for both our key explanatory variables are in the anticipated direction: higher nAch and more extreme behavioral norms are positively correlated with the resolve to control historical development by presidents, but neither one approaches significance. Additionally, both control variables are not significant as well.

In the end, we are most interested in explaining the behavior of dyads involving the United States. Our hypotheses offer two broad sets of possibilities: (1) that US dyadic behavior will be affected by the operational code beliefs of presidents (steering effects) and (2) that US dyadic behavior will be affected by prevailing norms in the international system (learning effects). Table 11.4 presents results of some of these hypothesis tests.

*Table 11.4* Op. Code Beliefs and System Norms Explaining US Dyad Behavior

| Variables | Full Sample | Full Sample |
|---|---|---|
| I-1 (H-9) | 0.02995 | 0.03385 |
| | (0.0331) | (0.03450) |
| P-1 (H-10) | 0.159*** | 0.168*** |
| | (0.0408) | (0.04191) |
| Int Sys Norms (H-12) | 0.0197 | 0.0970 |
| | (0.2271) | (0.2351) |
| CINC | | 0.05826 |
| | | (0.09618) |
| GDP growth | | −0.00168 |
| | | (0.0014) |
| Constant | −0.176*** | −0.182*** |
| | (3.047) | (0.0396) |
| Observations | 107 | 107 |
| R-squared | 0.194 | 0.211 |
| Number of presidents | 19 | 19 |

Standard errors in parentheses.

\*\*\* $p < 0.001$, \*\*$p < 0.01$, \*$p < 0.05$, +$p < 0.10$.

The most important finding in Table 11.4 is that presidential beliefs about the nature of others in the political world (P-1) have a significant, positive effect on the behavior of dyads involving the US In other words, as US presidents see others in the world in more cooperative terms, the behavior of their dyads is likely to be more peaceful. This provides strong support for the general idea that leader psychology impacts conflict and cooperation behavior of the leader's state, and for the specific idea that the beliefs of US presidents have steering effects on foreign policy behaviors. This finding is strong and significant even when controlling for systemic norms, the level of US power, and GDP growth.

Regarding presidents' beliefs about their own strategies (I-1), the direction of the effect is also positive (beliefs about more cooperative strategies coincide with more cooperative dyad behavior), but the variable is not significant in either model. Likewise, our tests for the effect of international system norms are not significant. It is not the case that US dyad behavior tends to follow the prevailing patterns of the international system, thus providing no support for our hypothesis about social learning effects on behavior.

Our final table investigates our hypothesis that as presidential resolve to control events (P-4) goes up, we expect to see more extreme behavior (in either direction) in US dyads, as reflected in the absolute value for the dependent variable of US dyad behavior. The results in Table 11.5 show that although the direction of the coefficient is as anticipated, P-4 is not significant in either model. Only CINC approaches significance, which provides an interesting finding: as the US power position in global

*Table 11.5* P-4 Explaining (abs)US Dyad Behavior

| Variables | Full Sample | Full Sample |
|---|---|---|
| P-4 (H-11) | 0.147 | 0.169 |
| | (0.142) | (0.143) |
| CINC | | 0.166+ |
| | | (0.0886) |
| GDP growth | | 0.0010 |
| | | (0.0014) |
| Constant | 0.0664* | 0.0250 |
| | (0.031) | (0.0378) |
| Observations | 107 | 107 |
| R-squared | 0.012 | 0.056 |
| Number of presidents | 19 | 19 |

Standard errors in parentheses.

*** $p < 0.001$, ** $p < 0.01$, * $p < 0.05$, + $p < 0.10$

politics increases, US dyads tend to demonstrate more extreme cooperative and conflictual behavior.

## Conclusion

In this paper we have investigated the relative contributions of systemic
norms and presidential belief systems as sources of US dyadic behavior
in foreign relations between 1900 and 2006. The investigation is an initial
attempt to broaden and deepen the spatial and temporal scope of the
operational code research program. Spatially, the research design locates
the origins of US operational code beliefs in the personality structures of
US presidents and also in the structure of the international environment
in which they make foreign policy decisions. Temporally, the analysis follows the impact of these potential sources of presidential beliefs in the
short run on strategies of cooperation and conflict by the United States
in its bilateral relations and identifies changes in both beliefs and behavior in the long run as the power position of the United States evolves in
the international system.

The results show statistically significant relationships between presidential personality structure and operational code beliefs in the hypothesized directions with one exception. The link between a president's needs
for power (nPow) and affiliation (nAff) with I-1 beliefs regarding strategies of cooperation vs. conflict are both significant; however, the relationship between nAff and I-1 is in the opposite direction than hypothesized.[2]
Our analysis also showed a statistically significant relationship in the
hypothesized direction between a president's belief about the nature of
the political universe (P-1) and US dyadic behavior.

In contrast, none of the relationships between an international systemic structure with norms favoring cooperation vs. conflict and either

presidential beliefs or US dyadic behavior were significant with one exception. While systemic norms were not linked to beliefs or behavior, there was a significant link between the US power position (CINC) in the structure of the international system and presidential beliefs about strategy (I-1) and the political universe (P-1). As the US power position increased, presidential beliefs about strategy (I-1) and the political universe (P-1), respectively, shifted from cooperative and friendly to more conflictual and hostile. However, there was no statistically significant, direct relationship between the US power position (CINC) and US dyadic behavior (USD).

These results address the following research questions that we posed at the beginning of this chapter.

- Does the systemic-level generalization hold for US dyadic relations regarding the evolution of dyadic relations away from conflict toward cooperation since 1900 (Goertz, et al. 2016)? The answer is "no." There is no significant relationship between (1) general systemic norms favoring either cooperation or conflict, (2) systemic norms manifested in US-Nth country dyads, or (3) the US global power position and (4) patterns favoring cooperation or conflict in US-Nth country dyads.
- Is the general evolutionary pattern in the international system of dyadic relations shifting away from conflict toward cooperation reflected in the presidential operational code beliefs regarding strategies of cooperation or conflict and the friendly or hostile nature of the political universe? The answer is again "no." The opposite temporal pattern is manifested by the significant inverse relationship between an increase in the US power position (CINC) and a shift toward less friendly/more hostile beliefs about the nature of the political universe (P-1).

While US dyadic behavior (USD) did not adapt and bend to international systemic norms (ISN) and was not affected directly by its power position (CINC) or growth in domestic product (GDP), it was affected by US presidential beliefs regarding the nature of the political universe (P-1). This relationship between a micro-level variable (belief in a less friendly/more hostile political universe) and less friendly/more hostile US dyadic behavior is a robust result ($p < 0.001$ in Table 11.4) after controlling for both macro-level (INS/CINC) and meso-level (GDP) variables that do not have significant direct effects on the US dyadic behavior variable (USD). It is joined by results in Table 11.1 supporting the importance of a psychological explanation as well for the origins of presidential beliefs regarding strategy. There is a robust relationship ($p < 0.05$) in this table between a president's need for power (nPow) and his belief (I-1) in a less cooperation-oriented/more conflict-oriented approach to strategy after controlling for the CINC systemic variable's significant relationship ($p < 0.01$) with this presidential belief.

Should the null results regarding the impact of INS, CINC, and GDP variables on USD behavior combined with these robust results in the predicted directions on US dyadic behavior (USD) be viewed as falsifying the systems analysis of Goertz et al. regarding the evolution of peace in the international system? The answer is probably "no." We have likely just demonstrated an instance of the "ecological fallacy," in which one risks failure when generalizing results from a higher or macro-level of analysis (the international system) to a lower or micro level of analysis (an agent in the international system). However, this awareness still begs the question: how do macro patterns emerge that supervene (depend on) micro patterns? One solution is the idea of "tipping points," in which a pattern among units in a system shifts incrementally by accretion or suddenly from an external shock to one aggregate pattern from another over time (Wendt 1999, 264; Schelling 1978, 99–102).

These possibilities may apply to both social and biological systems as part of the general theory of evolution pioneered by Charles Darwin in the biological sciences. The early flaws identified by critics who vilified social Darwinism have since been addressed by neo-Darwinian theorists and advocates of a coevolutionary argument, which synthesize genetic-based and culture-based models of biological and societal evolution over time (Hodgson and Knudsen 2010; Dennett 2017). The synthesis allows for both the steering effects of genes as inherited biological traits to explain personality differences and behavior across individuals and for the learning effects of memes as socialized cultural norms based on environmental differences to explain aggregate behavior as a general evolutionary theory of coevolution (Dennett 2017; Tang 2017; Wright 2000).

The Darwinian concepts of adaptation and fit remain integral to an emerging evolutionary synthesis across the biological and social sciences. Living organisms and societies "adapt" to their environment with different degrees of "fit" as complex adaptive systems (Axelrod 1984; Axelrod and Cohen 1999; Tang 2013; McDermott, Lopez, and Hatemi 2016) by exhibiting "adaptive rationality" (Gigenzer and Selten 2001). The concept of adaptive or ecological rationality refers to an explicit recognition of the necessity of taking into account both the psychological dispositions and limitations of the decision-maker (bounded rationality) and the ecological constraints of the environment (substantive rationality) in understanding how and why a decision is made on rational grounds (Simon 1985; Selten 2001; Walker, Schafer, and Smith 2019).

This biosocial approach is the basis for our research design in this chapter. Our analysis of the operational codes of US presidents suggests that the United States has occupied an ecological niche in the form of an evolving power position in the international system. The personality traits of US leaders were a "good enough" fit with the environment for the United States to survive in dyadic relations with other states. The cognitive beliefs regarding self steered US dyadic relations, and they were caused by extra-cognitive sources emanating from the personalities of US presidents and their advisors. At the same time, environmental influences in the form of increases in the power position (niche) of the United States in the international system exerted structural adaptation effects by at least permitting US dyadic conflict behavior and by stimulating experiential learning effects on presidential beliefs regarding a hostile political universe in response to change in the US power position. This evolutionary argument is also consistent with the statistically significant, inverse relationships of nPow and nAff with both presidential beliefs and US dyadic behavior.

## Notes

1. This score is an index of six key indicators: military expenditure, military personnel, energy consumption, iron and steel production, urban population, and total population.
2. The direction of the relationship between nAff and P-1 is also the same, though that relationship is not statistically significant.

## References

Axelrod, R. 1984. *The evolution of cooperation*. New York, NY: Basic Books.

Axelrod, R., M. Cohen. 1999. *Harnessing complexity*. New York, NY: Free Press.

Dawkins, R. 2006. *The selfish gene*. New York, NY: Oxford University Press.

Dawkins, R. 2008. *The extended phenotype*. New York, NY: Oxford University Press.

Dennett, D. 2017. *From bacteria to Bach and back: The evolution of minds*. New York, NY: W.W. Norton.

George, A. 1969. The operational code. *International Studies Quarterly* 1: 190–222.

George, A. 1979. The causal nexus of beliefs and behavior. In *Psychological model in international politics*, ed. L. Falkowski, 95–124. Boulder, CO: Westview Press.

Gigerenzer, G., R. Selten. 2001. *Bounded rationality*. Cambridge, MA: MIT Press.

Goertz, G., P. Diehl, A. Balas. 2016. *The puzzle of peace*. New York, NY: Oxford University Press.

Greenstein, F. 1969. *Personality and politics*. Chicago, IL: Markham Pub. Co.

Hermann, M. 1974. Leader personality and foreign policy behavior. In *Comparing foreign policies*, ed. J. Rosenau, 201–234. New York, NY: John Wiley.

Hermann, M. 1999. *Assessing leadership style: A trait analysis*. Hilliard, Ohio: Social Science Automation, Inc.

Hermann, M. 2003. Assessing leadership style: Trait analysis. In *The psychological assessment of political leaders*, ed. J. Post, 178–212. Ann Arbor, MI: University of Michigan Press.

Hodgson, G., T. Knudsen. 2010. *Darwin's conjecture: The search for general principles of social and economic evolution*. Chicago, IL: University of Chicago Press.

Holsti, O. 1976. Foreign policy formation viewed cognitively" In *The structure of decision*, ed. R. Axelrod, 18–54. Princeton, NJ: Princeton University Press.

Holsti, O. 1977. The 'operational code' as an approach to the analysis of belief systems." In *Final report to the national science foundation*. Grant SOC 75-14368. Duke University.

Kohut, H. 1971. *The analysis of the self.* New York, NY: International Universities Press.

Leites, N. 1951. *The operational code of the politburo.* New York, NY: McGraw-Hill.

Levy, J. 1994. Learning and foreign policy. *International Organization* 48: 279–312.

Malici, A., S. Walker. 2017. *Role theory and role conflict in U.S.-Iran relations.* New York, NY: Routledge.

Marfleet, B. G., S. G. Walker. 2006. A world of beliefs. In *Beliefs and leadership in world politics,* eds. M. Schafer, S. G. Walker, 53–73. New York, NY: Palgrave Macmillan.

McDermott, R., A. Lopez, P. Hatemi. 2016. An evolutionary approach to political leadership. *Security Studies* 25: 677–698.

Mitchell, M. 2009. *Complexity: A guided tour.* New York, NY: Oxford University Press.

Schafer, M., S. G. Walker. 2006. *Beliefs and leadership in world politics.* New York, NY: Palgrave Macmillan.

Schafer, M., S. G. Walker. 2007. Theodore Roosevelt and Woodrow Wilson as cultural icons of U.S. Foreign policy. *Political Psychology* 28: 747–776.

Schafer, M., S. G. Walker, C. Besaw, G. E. Smith. 2016. Psychological correlates and U.S. Conflict behavior: Introducing a new data set. In *Presented at the annual meeting of the International society of political psychology,* Warsaw, Poland, July 13–16.

Schelling, T. 1978. *Micromotives and macrobehavior.* New York, NY: W.W. Norton.

Selten, R. 2001. What is bounded rationality? In *Bounded rationality,* eds. G. Gigerenzer, R. Selten. Cambridge, MA: MIT University Press.

Simon, H. 1985. Human nature in politics. *American Political Science Review* 79: 293–304.

Singer, J. D., S. Bremer, J. Stuckey. 1972. Capability distribution, uncertainty, and major power, 1820-1965. In *Peace, war, and numbers,* ed. B. Russett, 19–48. Beverly Hills, CA: Sage Publications.

Smith, M. B. 1968. A map for the study of personality and politics. *Journal of Social Issues,* 24: 15–28. Reprinted in *A sourcebook for the study of personality and politics,* edited by F. Greenstein, M. Lerner. Chicago, IL: Markham.

Tang, S. 2013. *Social evolution of international politics.* New York, NY: Oxford University Press.

Tang, S. 2017. Toward generalized evolutionism: Beyond 'generalized Darwinism' and its critics. *Journal of Economic Issues* 51: 588–612.

Walker, S. 1982. Psychological explanations of international politics: Problems of aggregation, measurement, and theory construction. In *Biopolitics, political psychology, & international politics,* eds. G. Hopple, L. Falkowski, 114–150. New York, NY: St. Martin's Press.

Walker, S. G. 1983. The motivational foundations of political belief systems: A re-analysis of the operational code construct. *International Studies Quarterly* 27: 179–202.

Walker, S. G. 1995. Psychodynamic processes and framing effects in foreign policy decision-making: Woodrow Wilson's operational code. *Political Psychology* 16: 697–718.

Walker, S. G. 2009. The psychology of presidential decision making. In *The Oxford handbook of the American presidency,* eds. G. Edwards III, W. Howell, 550–576. Oxford, UK: Oxford University Press.

Walker, S. G. 2013. *Role theory and the cognitive architecture of British appeasement decisions.* New York, NY: Routledge.

Walker, S. G. 2017. Role theory and levels of change in world politics: When do leaders make a difference? In *Presented at the Annual Meeting of the International Studies Association*, Baltimore, MD, February 22–26.

Walker, S. G., L. Falkowski. 1985. The operational codes of U.S. Presidents and secretaries of State: Motivational foundations and behavioral consequences. *Political Psychology* 5: 237–266.

Walker, S. G., M. Schafer. 2010. Operational code theory: Beliefs and foreign policy decisions. In *The international studies encyclopedia*, Vol. VIII, ed. R. Denemark, 5492–5514. Chichester, UK: Wiley-Blackwell.

Walker, S., A. Malici. 2011. U.S. presidents and foreign policy mistakes. Stanford, CA: Stanford University Press.

Walker, S. G., A. Malici, M. Schafer. 2011. *Rethinking foreign policy analysis*. New York, NY: Routledge.

Walker, S. G., M. Schafer, J. Beieler. 2016. Belief systems and Foreign policy roles: Role contestation in U.S. Foreign policy decisions. In *Domestic role contestation, foreign policy, and international relations*, eds. C. Cantir, J. Kaarbo, 122–149. New York, NY: Routledge.

Walker, S. G., M. Schafer, G. E. Smith. Forthcoming, 2019. The operational codes of Donald Trump and Hillary Clinton. In *The Oxford handbook of behavioral political science*, edited by A. Mintz, L. Terris. New York, NY: Oxford University Press.

Walker, S. G., M. Schafer, M. Young. 2003. Profiling the operational codes of political leaders. In *The psychological assessment of political leaders*, ed. J. M. Post, 215–245. Ann Arbor, MI: University of Michigan Press.

Wendt, A. 1999. *Social theory of international politics*. Cambridge: Cambridge University Press.

Winter, D. G. 1993. Personality and leadership in the Gulf war. In *The political psychology of the Gulf war: Leaders, publics, and the process*, ed. S. A. Renshon, 107–117. Pittsburg, PA: University of Pittsburg Press.

Winter, D. G. 2003. Measuring the motives of political actors at a distance. In *The psychological assessment of political leaders*, ed. J. M. Post, 137–153. Ann Arbor, MI: University of Michigan Press.

Wright, R. 2000. *Nonzero*. New York, NY: Random House Viking Books.

# Part IV
# Computational Models of Foreign Policy Roles

# 12 Binary Role Theory and the Evolution of Cooperation in World Politics

*Stephen G. Walker, Kai He, and Huiyun Feng*

## Introduction

In this chapter, we address two important general questions about world politics. First, how do the actions of states as a whole combine to generate the emergent properties of world order? Second, how can leaders as agents guide the evolution of cooperation as an emergent property of world order? Our approach to these puzzles is a bit paradoxical, as it proceeds in two seemingly contradictory steps. In step one, we propose an agent-based model that would seem to violate the system-level focus of the questions. However, we solve the paradox in step two by showing how agent-based actions generate the emergent properties of interest in interaction with other environmental features at the level of the international system. This upward shift in the level of analysis in our model entails the central systemic process of interest to us, namely, "order transition," which we specify theoretically with binary role theory and then illuminate empirically with the analysis of three agent-based cases of order transition between key pairs of states in world politics.

Our strategy of inquiry is an application of complex adaptive systems analysis in the social sciences, an interdisciplinary research program that uses agent-based modeling methods to generate systems of agents whose features resemble complex systems found in the natural and life sciences (Axelrod 1984; Gell-Mann 1994; Axelrod and Cohen 1999; Jervis 1997; Miller and Page 2007; Mitchell 2009). Our assumption is that this particular approach to understanding the origins, the duration, and the transformation or destruction of complex natural systems may shed some light on how to understand more deeply the complex dynamics of order transition in social systems between states in world politics. This approach is congenial with the conceptualization of international order as a set of emergent properties from the interactions among agents (state and non-state actors) about issues across multiple dimensions, e.g., military, economic, and diplomatic, which may vary in number and variety over time and make international order a dynamic construct entailing order transition as a process that varies spatially across regions and temporally over time (Johnston 2019, 22–25).[1]

Axelrod and Cohen (1999, 7, italics and bold removed) summarize the characteristics of complex adaptive systems analysis as follows: "When a system contains agents or populations that seek to adapt, we will use the term complex adaptive system." An agent is an element in a system that can act "more or less purposefully" as a strategy that can vary and copy other strategies in interactions with other agents in a process of selection (changing strategies) that results in adaptation, that is, "improvement according to some measure of success" (Axelrod and Cohen 1999, 4–7). Complex adaptive systems analysis addresses the normative question: "In a world where many players are all adapting to each other and where the emerging future is extremely hard to predict, what actions should you take" (Axelrod and Cohen 1999, xi)?

The distinctive feature of this approach is to focus on the two-way interactions between agents (A) and environment (E), i.e., $\{A \leftrightarrow E\}$ rather than focusing primarily on the one-way actions of each on the other, i.e., $\{A \rightarrow E\}$ or $\{A \leftarrow E\}$. The two-way interaction emphasis is the defining feature of complex adaptive systems analysis, because a system is defined abstractly as the interdependent interactions of elements (agents) that define a system in an environment, which generates effects as emergent properties (Jervis 1997). The effects of the system of interest in our case are the norms-based, power-based, and rule-based features that define order or disorder at regional and global levels in the international system of world politics.

Perhaps the most well-known example of complex adaptive systems analysis in political science is Robert Axelrod's analysis of the prisoner's dilemma game, in which he asks an agent-based question to get a system-level answer: which strategy by players as agents in the prisoner's dilemma game is the optimum strategy for winning the game as a systemic outcome (Axelrod 1984; Mitchell 2009, 213–224)? In this case, the process of two-way interactions defined by the strategies (actions) of the players is the immediate mechanism that generates the emergent property (outcome) of interest in a social system (the game).

The prisoner's dilemma game also illustrates one of the methods associated with complex adaptive systems analysis, computational modeling, which is to use rules to represent the internal logic of the system of interest that is the game in this instance. "The rules of play of a game describe the possible choices of the players at each stage of play" (Brams 1994, 226). These rules are computations (definite procedures) that describe the game (Mitchell 2009, 56–64). In turn, the game may model (represent) the operation of a system of interest in the real world, such as describing how states compute strategies (make rule-based choices), which generate different outcomes as emergent properties of order in a regional or global system.

We shall employ computational models of strategic interaction from game theory to describe and explain the emergence of different levels and dimensions of international order in an abstract international system, in order to isolate and identify the logic associated with the mechanisms of order transition in a relatively simple international system. Our expectation is that this modeling effort can illuminate the menu of choices available to agents such as Russia, China, NATO, and the United States who are members of a more complex system of interest in the real world. In turn, these insights may help us to understand the dynamics of the current international order and the menu of possible transitions to a future international order available to policy makers at regional and global levels of the international system.

## Strategic Interaction Games as Complex Adaptive Systems

Figure 12.1 depicts the general logic that informs complex adaptive systems analysis, including game theory models (Gell-Mann 1994, 16–27). It shows three levels of analysis (inputs, processes, and outputs) that connect agents, mechanisms, and emergent systemic properties in the prisoner's dilemma game as an example. Inputs at the agent level of analysis specify preferences for different outputs by each player. These preferences provide information for each player to compute strategies of action toward one another. Interactions between the players at the process level of analysis are governed by rules of play defining the mechanisms that generate outputs of the system. The outputs at the systemic level of analysis are the outcomes of strategic interactions between the players and (if the players are states) constitute the logic of order in their international relations. Collectively, the players, their strategic interactions, and outcomes constitute a complex adaptive system, in which the whole system is greater than the sum of its parts. Its outputs are emergent properties that represent various features of international order and are attributed to the whole system and not to its parts (agents).

The example of the prisoner's dilemma game in Figure 12.1 is a model of the simplest possible international system, i.e., a social system with only two states as agents. The processes in this system are also relatively simple, i.e., the computations of choices by each agent are based upon their respective preference rankings regarding the possible outputs that define the order between them as final outcomes. The rules that govern the computation of choices of cooperation or conflict as a strategy by the players include: (1) a rationality rule that each player computes choices leading to a preferred outcome, based on the player's goals and the assumption that the other player also follows the rationality rule; (2) an order of play rule that specifies whether the players make simultaneous or alternate choices leading to the final outcome; and (3) a termination rule that addresses whether the game is repeated (played again) upon

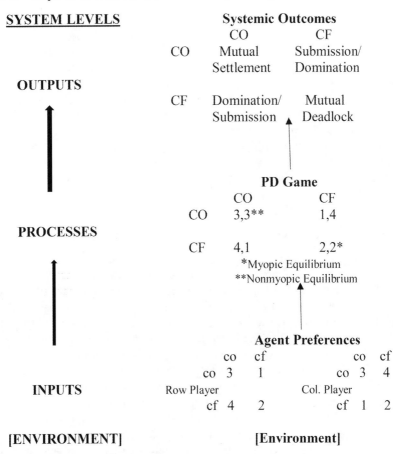

*Figure 12.1* The Prisoner's Dilemma Game as a Complex Adaptive System***

***CO is cooperation; CF is conflict. CO,CO outcome is mutual settlement; CO,CF outcome is row player submits/column player dominates; CF,CF outcome is mutual deadlock; CF,CO outcome is row player dominates/column player submits. Agent preferences of players for outcomes are ranked from (4) the highest to (1) the lowest and entered into the cells of the prisoner's dilemma game as row, column separated by a comma. The possible final outcomes for the PD game are either mutual settlement or mutual deadlock, depending on the rules of play and whether the game is played repeatedly or only once (Brams 1994, 218)

reaching the final outcome. Bracketed at the bottom of the figure is the context of background conditions that define the environment in which the system operates.

The environment of a system is the source of inputs for the system of interest, identifying who the agents are in this system, their goals, and the power relations among them. The environment that gives the prisoner's dilemma game its name identifies two prisoners as the agents whose goals are to get the minimum punishment regarding crimes with which they have been charged. The prisoners have the power either to cooperate with one another by staying silent or to conflict with one another by testifying as witnesses against each other. Their respective choices interact and are interdependent, making them agents in a dyadic system in which the system effects of their choices decide their fates: if both stay silent, they receive a lighter sentence; if both testify, they receive a heavier sentence; if one stays silent while one testifies, the sentence is heavier for the one who stays silent and lighter for the one who testifies (Mitchell 2009, 213).

Applying the rationality rule in this environment, each prisoner ranks their preferences for the possible outcomes in order to receive the lightest sentence, which are identified as inputs in Figure 12.1 and ranked from the highest to the lowest as follows: (4) Self (row player) testifies while Other (column player) remains silent as a CF,CO outcome; (3) both Self and Other remain silent as a CO,CO outcome; (2) both Self and Other testify as a CF,CF outcome; (1) Self remains silent, while Other testifies as a CO,CF outcome. Since the environment in this case also constrains the prisoners from pre-play communication, the order of play rule is that they must simultaneously choose either cooperation (CO) or conflict (CF). The termination rule for this situation is that the game is not repeated, i.e., their choices generate the end of the game. Conforming to these rules and environmental conditions, both players will choose conflict (CF) and a final outcome of (2,2), in which they not only avoid their lowest ranked preference (1) but also are denied their two higher ranked preferences (4 and 3).

## International Order Transition

How does the prisoner's dilemma game as an example of complex adaptive systems analysis illustrate how to understand order transition in the international system? It shows by example how to construct a particular kind of order transition model in a social system. Its rules and processes are applicable to states as well as prisoners, because the agents and systems in both instances are constituted by human beings as social systems. The mechanisms for the game matrix at the process level of analysis in Figure 12.1 can also be specified to describe the operation of mechanisms at the process level of regional or global international systems. We assume that it is fruitful to represent those systems as complex adaptive systems that have the same rules of operation as the game of prisoner's dilemma. We infer from this assumption that the strategic interaction processes of international order transition have the same internal logic as games like prisoner's dilemma.

A picture of regional or global international relations that emerges from this example at the agent level of analysis is a "one-agent/many games" model (Miller and Page 2007, 192), in which a state as an agent might play a prisoner's dilemma game with one state, a chicken game with another state; or a stag hunt game with a third state. The possible number of different $2 \times 2$ (two players with two choices) ordinal games is 78 (Rapoport and Guyer 1976; Stein 1990; Brams 1994). All of the games in our model share the same basic rules specified by Brams (1994) regarding rationality, order of play, and termination as the prisoner's dilemma example; however, their respective preference rankings for the cells in the game matrix differ along with the contextual stories in world politics that illustrate their application to a particular situation rather than being variations in the prisoner's dilemma story.[2]

To make this model of the international system even more complex, each of the states with which an agent plays a game may also play one another. Moreover, the goals that inform each player's strategy toward the other may be influenced by their respective strategies toward other states. We can simplify this aspect of the model by stipulating that we are interested in all of these strategies only insofar as they have the effect of maintaining the existing order or revising the status quo, i.e., do they support the current international order or not? We can further simplify our order transition model by distinguishing families of strategies by their highest ranked preference for a final outcome in our $2 \times 2$ game. The different strategies for the row player and their respective highest ranked outcomes are appease (CO,CO), bandwagon (CO,CF), balance (CF,CF), and bully (CF,CO) strategies (Waltz 1979; Schweller 1994); their respective locations in the four cells of the $2 \times 2$ game matrix are shown in Figure 12.2.

| **Appease\*** | | | | | | | **Bandwagon\*** | | |
|---|---|---|---|---|---|---|---|---|---|
| (<) | (=) | (>) | | | | | (<) | (=) | (>) |
| 4 3 | 4 2 | 4 2 | | | | | 3 4 | 2 4 | 2 4 |
| 2 1 | 1 3 | 3 1 | | | | | 1 2 | 1 3 | 3 1 |
| **4 3** | **4 1** | **4 1** | | **Column** | | | **3 4** | **1 4** | **1 4** |
| **2 1** | **2 3** | **3 2** | | CO | CF | | **2 1** | **2 3** | **3 2** |
| **Partner** | | | CO | Appease | Bandwagon | | **Friend** | | |
| | | | Row | | | | | | |
| **Bully\*** | | | CF | Bully | Balance | | **Balance\*** | | |
| (<) | (=) | (>) | | **2 x 2 Game Matrix** | | | (<) | (=) | (>) |
| 2 3 | 3 2 | 1 2 | | | | | 2 3 | 3 2 | 1 2 |
| 4 1 | 4 1 | 4 3 | | | | | 1 4 | 1 4 | 3 4 |
| 1 3 | 3 1 | 2 1 | | | | | 1 3 | 3 1 | 2 1 |
| 4 2 | 4 2 | 4 3 | | | | | 2 4 | 2 4 | 3 4 |
| **Enemy** | | | | | | | **Rival** | | |

*Figure 12.2* Families of Cooperation and Conflict Strategies Mediated by Power and Interests

*Ranked outcome preferences (4 = highest to 1 = lowest) for row player under three conditions of power (<, =, >) and secondary or vital interests. Ranked preferences for column player mirror the same logic

Binary role theory identifies each family of strategies in Figure 12.2 as different ways of enacting roles by agents in world politics.[3] The appease strategy enacts the role of partner, which ranks settlement (CO,CO) as its highest ranked outcome. The bandwagon strategy enacts the role of friend associated with submission (CO,CF) as its highest ranked outcome. The balance strategy enacts the role of rival and deadlock (CF,CF) as the highest ranked outcome. The bully strategy represents the enactment of the enemy role with domination (CF,CO) as the highest ranked outcome. The intersection of different strategies constitutes a game, in which each agent enacts a role in a role set with row as Ego and column as Alter (Malici and Walker 2017).

The appease strategy has an empirical record as a strategy associated with Britain's strategy of cooperation against the Axis states in the 1930s (Walker 2013). The bully strategy has an empirical record as a strategy of conflict followed by the three Axis powers (Japan, Italy, and Germany) toward Britain in the 1930s (Schweller 1998). An example of the bandwagon strategy of cooperation is Italy's alignment with Germany and Austria in the Triple Alliance prior to World War I, hedging against this alignment by staying neutral with the outbreak of war in 1914, and finally joining the Triple Entente of Britain, France, and Russia in the war against Germany and Austria in 1915 (Albrecht-Carrié 1958; Schweller 1998). The formation of the Triple Entente to counter the Triple Alliance is an example of the balance strategy of conflict pursued by Britain, France, and Russia (Hartmann 1983).

A simple conceptualization of each strategy within the context of a $2 \times 2$ game theory model with a repeated rule of play is to distinguish them as either dominant (bandwagon and bully) strategies or contingent (appease and balance) strategies. Bandwagoning is a dominant strategy of cooperation specified by the rule, "always choose cooperation" while bullying is a dominant strategy of conflict specified by the rule, "always choose conflict." Appeasement is a contingent strategy of cooperation specified by the rule, "always reciprocate cooperation" while balancing is a contingent strategy of conflict specified by the rule, "always reciprocate conflict." However, the application of these rules is mediated by the power and interest relations between the players, as shown by differences in ranked preferences within the families in Figure 12.2.

All four families of strategies in Figure 12.2 have subtypes defined by the rank order of the remaining preferences in the $2 \times 2$ game. These rankings are conditioned by environmental conditions identified by analysts who employ liberal, realist, and constructivist IR theories in their respective analyses of foreign policy strategies. Realists emphasize the international power distribution among states; liberals emphasize the distribution of domestic national interests among states; and constructivists focus on the distribution of cultural identities. The Western schools of international relations theory have their approximate echoes in the Confucian harmony (liberal), Legalistic norms (constructivist), and Parabellum conflict (realist) traditions of Chinese strategic thought that emerged during the Warring States Period (463–222 BC). These schools of thought collectively articulate the variety of parallel ideational environments or strategic cultures in the West and China, respectively, regarding how states as agents view the logic of international order (Feng 2007, 17–35).

These parallel ideas in Western and Chinese strategic culture lead us to postulate that embedded in them are a common set of games specified by ranked preferences for the different outcomes of settlement (CO,CO), alignment, (CO,CF), deadlock (CF,CF), domination (CF,CO) and corresponding appeasement, bandwagoning, balancing, and bullying strategies that generate order in regional and world politics. A corollary to this premise is the theorem that regional and global order transition is defined as a process of role transition. We shall not test this aggregated system-level theorem empirically, but we do specify it explicitly here for discussion and illustration. We also note it has been examined implicitly by previous empirical research (Johnston 1995a, 1995b; Feng 2007; Malici and Walker 2017; He 2018).

## Modeling International Order Transition

As noted earlier, each of the states with which an agent plays a game may also play one another. Moreover, the goals that inform each player's strategy toward the other may be influenced by their respective strategies toward other states. However, we simplified this aspect of the model by stipulating that we are interested in all of these strategies only insofar as they have the effect of maintaining the existing order or revising the status quo, i.e., do they support the current international order or not? These assumptions now allow us to specify four prototypical games that represent the dimensions of security, economic, diplomatic, and political relations between pairs of states, which operate potentially at three levels of international order: (1) the power-based level of material capabilities; (2) the rule-based level of social institutions; and (3) the norms-based level of cultural ideas (Wendt 1999, 246–312).

Our main hypothesis is that each of these dimensions is characterized by a separate family of games in Figure 12.2 and subsequently represented in Figure 12.3 as governed by a different principle of international order. Wendt (1999) identifies Hobbesian, Lockean, and Kantian strategic cultures of anarchy as sources of different types of international order. They are drawn from the Western cultural traditions in political philosophy that inform the realist (Hobbesian), liberal (Lockean), and constructivist (Kantian) schools of international relations theory. We have added a Rousseauvian strategic culture in Figure 12.3, which represents a fourth cultural tradition between the Lockean and Kantian strategic cultures (Waltz 1959; Skyrms 2004).

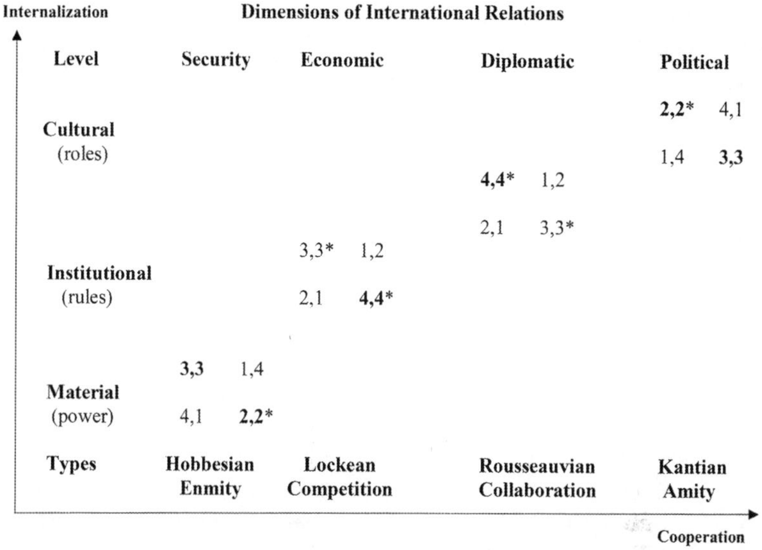

Internalization               **Dimensions of International Relations**

| Level | Security | Economic | Diplomatic | Political |
|---|---|---|---|---|
| Cultural (roles) | | | | **2,2**\*   4,1 |
| | | | | 1,4   **3,3** |
| | | | **4,4**\*   1,2 | |
| | | | 2,1   **3,3**\* | |
| Institutional (rules) | | **3,3**\*   1,2 | | |
| | | 2,1   **4,4**\* | | |
| Material (power) | 3,3   1,4 | | | |
| | 4,1   **2,2**\* | | | |
| Types | Hobbesian Enmity | Lockean Competition | Rousseauvian Collaboration | Kantian Amity |

Cooperation →

*Figure 12.3* Prototypical Games in Different Types of International Order

Sources: Brams (1994); Wendt (1999, 246–312); Skyrms (2004). Games assume equal power relations between players. Nash myopic equilibria are asterisked. Brams nonmyopic equilibrium solutions are in bold

Wendt is careful to distinguish between two dimensions in the process of international order transition: a horizontal dimension in the direction of greater cooperation represented by the sequence of enemy, rival, and friend roles as modal roles in a culture of anarchy; a vertical dimension in the direction of greater internalization represented by the ascending sequence of force, cost, and legitimacy as the basis for the modal role in a culture of anarchy (Wendt 1999, 251–258). He argues that Ego (row player) can internalize a role at three levels, depending on whether its transmission by cues from Alter (column player) is based on the exercise of different forms of social power. The highest level of internalization over the long term is based on the exercise of appeals to moral authority by Alter on behalf of the legitimacy of a role; the use of promises or threats regarding material rewards or punishments can induce a calculation by Ego in the middle term to accept a role so long as the benefits outweigh the costs; the exercise of rewards and punishments by Alter can be effective in the short term to enforce the enactment of a role.

Wendt privileges the cultural level of internalized norms on the vertical axis in Figure 12.3 under the condition of anarchy and argues that *roles* internalized at this level inform compliance at the institutional level of *rules* and submission at the material level of *power*. That is, "anarchy is what states make of it," (Wendt 1999, 246–312). The deep structure of anarchy, therefore, is culture defined as shared beliefs specified as roles.

Institutions have rules that reflect roles directing their enactment along different dimensions of order regarding the security, economic, diplomatic, and political interests of states as agents. States are socialized by different processes of interaction into these institutions, and their roles are also mediated by their respective power positions in the international system of interest.

In sum, states evolve and learn to be historical members of a particular regional or global system governed by rules and roles mediated by material capabilities and the exercise of social power. The history of international relations under anarchy is marked by processes of natural and cultural selection in the form of imitation and complex social learning, enhanced or constrained by environmental conditions of interdependence, common fate, homogeneity, and self-restraint. The Hobbesian, Lockean, Rousseauvian, and Kantian orders, along with their respective prototypical games, are possible outcomes of these processes and conditions. They have occurred at different points in the emergence and evolution of human societies as different patterns of international order (Wendt 1999, 313–369; Walker 2004).

During the past 3000 years, the number of independent political units in the world has declined from about 600,000 to about 200 and evolved collectively from a Hobbesian cultural order in a Lockean direction (Wendt 1999, 323). Wendt suggests that a Hobbesian cultural order of enmity was the initial normative order characterizing relations among primitive tribes, eventually succeeded by a Lockean normative order of rivalry in the form of the Westphalian states system that the European Great Powers expanded around the globe, followed by the partial emergence of a Kantian order of amity in Western Europe after World War II. The respective governing roles for agents in these different forms of state systems as societies are enemies, rivals, and friends. To this list, we have inserted the governing role of partner in a Rousseauvian order of collaboration between the rival and friend roles in Figure 12.3 (Skyrms 2004; see also Nowak and Highfield 2011).

This multistage interpretation of cultural evolution is supported generally by a quantitative empirical analysis of the evolution of peace in the international system over approximately the past 100 years by Goertz, Diehl, and Balas (2016; see also Wohlforth et al. 2007; Kaufman, Little, and Wohlforth 2007; Tang 2015). Goertz, Diehl, and Balas (2016) distinguish a five-position peace scale of dyadic state relationships spanning the 20th century up to 2006. The scale has two main dimensions extending in two directions from a position of negative (cold) peace (absence of war) either toward lesser and severe rivalries or toward positive (warm) peace and security communities. The operational definitions of these dyadic relations are based on the presence or absence of war plans between dyad members and the presence or absence of plausible counterfactual war scenarios between dyad members.

Specifically (1) severe rivalry is defined by war plans and frequent military conflicts; (2) lesser rivalry is defined by war plans and isolated military conflicts; (3) negative peace is defined by war plans but no military conflicts; (4) warm peace is defined by no war plans or plausible war scenarios; and (5) security community is defined by joint war planning against third parties and no plausible war scenarios (Goertz, Diehl, and Balas 2016, 27). The modal scale position for the aggregation of global dyadic relations corresponds roughly in the 20th century to a Lockean stage of negative peace. The percentage of dyads in the modal category of negative peace ranged from approximately 70 to 85% across 5-year intervals for the entire period. There are more deviations toward lesser rivalries and severe rivalries for the first 75 years versus more deviations in the direction of warm peace or security communities among dyads in the last 30 years, especially following the end of the cold war (Goertz, Diehl, and Balas 2016, 60–63).

This picture of the global system in an initial state of negative peace trending slightly toward a current state of positive peace suggests that international order evolves over time, punctuated by major events like the two world wars or the end of the cold war in the 20th century (Goertz, Diehl, and Balas 2016, 56–72). Such events are global in their scope and offer opportunities for reaching tipping points in the logic of international order between dyads, within regions, and across the globe in the form of changes in modal roles and institutional rules mediated by power relations. Similar events with regional or global reach, such as major wars, domestic revolutions, economic collapse, technological development, or ecological disaster, are other potential sources of discontinuity in social relations, which may generate or permit changes in the roles, rules, and power relations that will govern international order in the future.

However, leadership from key agents in a regional or global system is also important in generating, maintaining, or revising international order. Wendt's account of how international order emerges and evolves over time and across regions emphasizes culture (shared ideas) as the distinctive engine of order in a social system – it is shared ideas that shape what states make of anarchy by specifying roles for states and rules for the institutions of international order. Whose ideas are most influential is mediated by power relations and socialization processes, which take the form of the exercise of social power in strategic interactions between and among states as agents in a complex adaptive social system. Wendt (1999, 326–335) identifies the socialization processes of alter-casting and role-taking from role theory to model the emergence of enemy, rival, or friend roles as the modal role defining a Hobbesian, Lockean, or Kantian culture of anarchy. We extend this logic to include a Rousseauvian culture with a modal role of partner.

Leadership and power enter the international order equation as more powerful states socialize each other as well as weaker states. For example, one state as Ego casts the other state as Alter into one of these roles. Ego and Alter exchange cues as the exercise of social power in a process of role-taking with words (support/oppose, promise/threaten) or deeds (reward/punish). These exchanges may converge relatively easily as a process of role location with the exchange of appeals, promises, and rewards in a mutual definition of the situation as an outcome between them as they adopt either identical or complementary roles. Or a role conflict between them may occur, in which their roles do not converge without the exercise of social power to resolve it in the form of strategies of employing force, raising costs, or denying legitimacy to one another with the exchange of denials, threats, and punishments (Wendt 1999; Thies 2013; Baldwin 2016; see also Walker 1992; Malici and Walker 2017).

Wendt focuses primarily on the first definition of the situation in which Ego and Alter adopt identical roles of enemy, rival, or friend, while we expand his analysis here to include definitions of the situation with complementary and conflicting roles generating the outcome. Our repertoire of roles also extends the logic of Wendt's cultures of anarchy to include the role of partner and expands the four roles into the families of role sets in Figure 12.4 that share a common role identity enacted by Ego under different environmental conditions as role demands, including the role identity enacted by Alter (Thies 2013; Malici and Walker 2017). The enactment of a particular role can vary, depending on whether Ego and Alter are equal (=) or unequal (≠) in power and enact symmetrical or asymmetrical roles of cooperation (+) or conflict (–).These possibilities are modeled in Figure 12.4 as 2 × 2 games along with examples of how members of different role sets may evolve into identical or complementary role dyads with different outcomes as emergent properties of international order.

In Figure 12.4's first symmetrical role game with equal power relations, the enemy role associated with the Hobbesian culture of anarchy is the prisoner's dilemma game analyzed earlier in this chapter. Ego and Alter both prefer a dominant (unconditional) conflict strategy of bully and rank domination as their highest final outcome. The Lockean culture of anarchy postulates a game in which both players with equal power prefer a contingent conflict strategy of balance and rank deadlock as their highest final outcome. The social structure of these two cultures of anarchy represented in their games is consistent with the insights about balancing strategies from Western IR theory's offensive and defensive realist schools, respectively, and from Parabellum realist thought in Chinese philosophy (Waltz 1979; Wendt 1999; Mearsheimer 2001; Feng 2007, 17–35).

The Rousseauvian culture of anarchy postulates a collaboration game with equal power relations in which both players prefer a contingent (conditional) appeasement strategy and rank settlement as their highest final outcome. The Kantian culture of anarchy specifies a game with

## SYMMETRICAL CULTURAL ROLES

| | Enemies | | Rivals | | Partners | | Friends | |
|---|---|---|---|---|---|---|---|---|
| | Alter | | Alter | | Alter | | Alter | |
| (G32) | CO | CF | CO | CF | CO | CF | (G32) | <u>CO</u> CF |
| CO | **3,3** | 1,4 | CO 3,3 | 1,2 | CO 4,4 | 1,2 | <u>CO</u> | **2,2** 4,1 |
| Ego | | | Ego | | Ego | | Ego | |
| <u>CF</u> | 4,1 | **2,2** | CF 2,1 | **4,4** | CF 2,1 | 3,3 | CF | 1,4 **3,3** |
| | Hobbes | | Locke | | Rousseau | | Kant | |
| | (−,=) | | (−,=) | | (+,=) | | (+,=) | |

## COMPLEMENTARY CULTURAL ROLES

| | Enemies | | Rivals | | Partners | | Friends | |
|---|---|---|---|---|---|---|---|---|
| | Alter (<) | | Alter (<) | | Alter (<) | | Alter (<) | |
| (G16) | CO | CF | CO | <u>CF</u> | <u>CO</u> | CF | (G16) | <u>CO</u> CF |
| CO | 2,1 | 1,4 | CO 2,1 | 1,2 | CO 4,4 | 1,2 | CO 2,3 | 4,1 |
| Ego (>) | | | Ego (>) | | Ego (>) | | Ego (>) | |
| <u>CF</u> | **4,3** | 3,2 | <u>CF</u> 3,3 | **4,4** | CF 3,3 | 2,1 | CF **3,4** | 1,2 |
| | Hobbes | | Locke | | Rousseau | | Kant | |
| | (−,≠) | | (−,≠) | | (+,≠) | | (+,≠) | |

*Figure 12.4* Roles in Different Cultures of Anarchy Mediated by Power Relations*

*Nash equilibria are asterisked; Brams equilibria are in bold. Dominant strategies are underlined. Game numbers are from Brams (1994, 215–219). Strategies are conflict (−) or cooperation (+). Power relations are equal (=) or unequal (≠), i.e., one player is stronger (>) or weaker (<) than the other player

equal power relations, in which both players prefer a dominant strategy of bandwagoning and rank alignment with each other as their highest final outcome. The international order of these two cultures of anarchy is generally consistent with the insights of liberalism and constructivism in Western IR theory (Wendt 1999) and insights from Confucian and Legalist thought in Chinese philosophy (Feng 2007).

Under rules of repeated play and pre-play communication (Brams 1994), in which each player alternates moves and can communicate credible threat power to punish defection, there is an incentive in three of the four games to reciprocate cooperation as a contingent or a dominant strategy. The partial exception is the Lockean game in which a balancing strategy of choosing a conflict strategy by one player cannot be deterred by a credible threat from the other player, because both players have deadlock as their highest ranked outcome.

The same four roles, enemy, rival, partner, and friend, for Ego and Alter are also modeled in Figure 12.4 with unequal power relations between them. In the enemies game with Ego (>) stronger than Alter (<), Ego's dominant bullying strategy against Alter's contingent bullying strategy leads to a (4,3) outcome of submission to Ego by Alter. Both Ego (>) and

Alter (<) have dominant conflict strategies of balancing (≠) that lead to a mutual deadlock (4,4) outcome in the rivals game. In the partners game with unequal (≠) power relations, Alter (<) as the weaker player has a dominant appeasement strategy of cooperation against Ego's contingent appeasement strategy, which leads to a (4,4) outcome of mutual cooperation with the stronger Ego (>).

In the friends game with unequal (≠) power relations, Alter (<) as the weaker player has a dominant cooperation strategy of bandwagoning (+), which leads to a submission outcome (3,4) with Ego (>) as the stronger player. In contrast to the equal (=) power games, there is at least one player with a dominant strategy in all four of the unequal (≠) power games, which prevents the second player from reciprocating a cooperation move by the first player and reduces the incentives for a final outcome of mutual cooperation (CO,CO) except in the partners game. How do cultures of anarchy transition from one cultural order to another?

We suggest that certain states as agents in an international system are better able to lead the way toward mutual cooperation as a final outcome by socializing other states in their relations with them. These possibilities are illustrated by the alter-casting patterns in Figure 12.5. Each agent in these dyads is enacting an alter-casting role toward the other agent, and the roles are neither symmetrical (identical) nor complementary (with two exceptions) in defining the situation between them.[4] These agents are experiencing bilateral role conflict, in which each agent enacts a role that is not symmetrical or does not complement the role expectations of the other agent.

For example, in the first dyad in Figure 12.5 Ego enacts a rival role, while Alter enacts an enemy role. The two roles do not match one another, and if they do not change their respective roles, they will complete their strategic interactions at a final outcome of either (3,3) mutual cooperation or (4,2) mutual conflict, which are outcomes associated, respectively, with partner and rival roles. Both of these outcomes are also final outcomes for the symmetrical enemy/enemy game in Figure 12.4; however, the mutual cooperation outcome is accessible from more cells as initial states of play in the rival/enemy game in Figure 12.5 between players with equal power relations.

When a rival plays against an enemy in Figure 12.5, Ego as the rival player is able to achieve its two highest ranked preferences (4 and 3) compared to Alter's lower ranked preferences (3 and 2) as the enemy player and final outcomes of (4,2) deadlock or (3,3) settlement for the rival/enemy game compared to outcomes of (3,3) settlement and (2,2) deadlock for the enemy/enemy game of equal power relations. The implication of this analysis is that an international order of rivals is superior, i.e., more evolutionarily fit (Nowak and Highfield 2011), in achieving their highest ranked goals over an international order of enemies or a mixed order of enemy/rival dyads.[5]

## EQUAL POWER RELATIONS

|        | **Enemy** |       |        | **Enemy** |     |          | **Enemy** |         |
|--------|-----------|-------|--------|-----------|-----|----------|-----------|---------|
| (G49)  | CO        | <u>CF</u> | (G27) | CO   | <u>CF</u> |    | CO   | <u>CF</u> |
| CO     | **3,3**   | 1,4   | CO     | **4,3**   | 1,4 | <u>CO</u> | 2,3     | **4,4** |
| **Rival** |        |       | **Partner** |      |     | **Friend** |        |         |
| CF     | 2,1       | **4,2** | CF   | 2,1       | 3,2 | CF       | 1,1       | 3,2     |

|        | **Rival** |       |        | **Rival** |       |         | **Partner** |       |
|--------|-----------|-------|--------|-----------|-------|---------|-------------|-------|
| (G51)  | CO        | CF    | (G46)  | CO        | CF    | (G56)   | CO          | CF    |
| CO     | **4,3**   | 1,2   | CO     | 1,3       | **4,2** | <u>CO</u> | **2,4**   | 4,2   |
| **Partner** |      |       | **Friend** |       |       | **Friend** |          |       |
| CF     | 2,1       | **3,4** | CF   | 2,1       | **3,4** | CF      | 1,1         | **3,3** |

## UNEQUAL POWER RELATIONS

|        | **Enemy (<)** |       |        | **Enemy (<)** |       |        | **Enemy (<)** |       |
|--------|---------------|-------|--------|---------------|-------|--------|---------------|-------|
| (G40)  | CO            | CF    | (G23)  | CO            | CF    |        | CO            | CF    |
| CO     | 2,1           | 1,4   | CO     | 4,1           | 1,4   | CO     | 2,1           | **4,4** |
| **Rival (>)** |        |       | **Partner (>)** |      |       | **Friend (>)** |        |       |
| <u>CF</u> | **3,3**    | **4,2** | CF   | **3,3**       | 2,2   | CF     | **3,3**       | 1,2   |

|        | **Rival (<)** |       |        | **Rival (<)** |       |        | **Partner (<)** |       |
|--------|---------------|-------|--------|---------------|-------|--------|-----------------|-------|
| (G53)  | CO            | CF    | (G44)  | CO            | CF    | (G41)  | <u>CO</u>       | CF    |
| CO     | **4,3**       | 1,1   | CO     | **2,3**       | 4,1   | CO     | **2,4**         | 4,2   |
| **Partner (>)** |      |       | **Friend (>)** |      |       | **Friend (>)** |        |       |
| CF     | 3,2           | **2,4** | CF   | **3,2**       | 1,4   | CF     | **3,3**         | 1,1   |

*Figure 12.5* Role Conflict Games Mediated by Power Relations*

*Final outcomes are in bold; dominant strategies are underlined. Nash equilibria are asterisked. Brams equilibria are in bold. Game numbers are from Brams (1994, 215–219)

Similar comparisons of other mixed role sets with equal or unequal power relations indicate that a partner role trumps an enemy role with a (4,3) mutual cooperation final outcome in the partner/enemy game and holds its own against a rival role with final outcomes of (4,3) mutual cooperation and (3,4) deadlock in the partner/rival game. The same pattern basically holds for the two games when the partner player is stronger than the rival one. Finally, a friend player is unable to reach a stable outcome of mutual cooperation in Figure 12.5 against either an enemy or a rival player with one exception, namely, when the friend player is stronger than the rival player. But mutual cooperation is a stable final outcome in a friend/partner game from some initial states of play with either equal (=) or unequal (≠) power relations between them.

The results from these game simulations support the inference that it is possible for dyads to transition via the mechanisms of alter-casting and role-taking in a sequence from enemies to rivals to partners to friends, which was theoretically postulated by Wendt (1999) and reported empirically from the historical record at the global systems level by Goertz, Diehl, and Balas (2016). It is also logically implausible to leapfrog from enemy or rival orders to mutual cooperation with a friend strategy unless unequal power relations favor the player with the friend strategy. Is there any evidence from the historical record at the agent level of analysis to support the operation of alter-casting and role-taking as order transition mechanisms? Three recent historical cases appear to offer evidence as natural quasi-experiments to support the logic of the theoretical models and the results of their game simulations. They also highlight the importance of leadership by agents in understanding the evolution of international order.

## Leadership and International Order Transition

The first case is the Gorbachev phenomenon of "new thinking" at the end of the cold war. His "new thinking" doctrine of common security in international politics represents a systematic effort by the leader of the Soviet Union to change its role from enemy or rival to partner or friend in dyadic relations with the United States. Gorbachev's unilateral initiatives can be understood to be an alter-casting strategy of cues to evoke a role-taking process by the United States to convert its counter-role identity from enemy or rival to partner or friend. The process of role transition toward mutual cooperation was successful in the short run, as President Reagan took the cues seriously after some hesitation and accelerated the end of the cold war between the two superpowers (Malici 2006, 2008).

Malici (2008) identifies the strategies of Russia and the United States in Figure 12.6 between 1985 and 1989 as shifting from the enactment of mutual enemy roles in the cold war game to the enactment of partner and enemy roles, respectively, in a transition game in 1986, and then culminating in the enactment of mutual partner roles by 1989. A role conflict analysis of each game shows that the strategies of each player prescribe different final outcomes from three of the four cells (RCF = .75) in the transition game, which is the manifestation of role conflict over outcomes between Russia and the United States as Gorbachev attempted to redefine the situation from the cold war game of mutual enemies to the post-cold war game of mutual partners. His strategy of alter-casting also

## GAME ANALYSIS

|  | USA (− =) | |  |  | USA (−,=) | |  |  | USA (+,=) | |
|---|---|---|---|---|---|---|---|---|---|---|
| (G32) | CO | CF | | (G27) | CO | CF | |  | CO | CF |
|  | CO 3,3 | 1,4 | |  | CO **4,3** | 1,4 | |  | CO "**4,4**"* | 1,2 |
| RUS (−, =) | | | | RUS (+,=) | | | | RUS (+,=) | | |
|  | CF 4,1 | "**2,2**"* | |  | CF 2,1 | "3,2"* | |  | CF 2,1 | 3,3* |

|  |  |  |
|---|---|---|
| **Cold War Game** | **Transition Game** | **Post-CW Game** |
| RUS: Enemy; USA: Enemy | RUS: Partner; USA: Enemy | RUS: Partner; USA: Partner |
| (0/0, 1,2/2,3/3); (0/0, 1/1,2,3/2) | (0,3/0 & 1,2/2); (0,2/0, 1/1 & 3/2) | (0,1,2,3/0); (0,1,2,3/0) |
| RUS: [0111]; USA: [0111] | RUS: [0110]; USA: [0101] | RUS: [0100]; USA: [0001] |

**Game Cell**

| 0 | 1 |
|---|---|
| 3 | 2 |

**Numbers**

## ROLE CONFLICT ANALYSIS

| **Cold War Game** | **Transition Game** | **Post-CW Game** |
|---|---|---|
| RUS: (0223) Enemy | RUS: (0220) Partner | RUS: (0000) Partner |
| USA: (0122) Enemy | USA: (0102) Enemy | USA: (0000) Partner |
| RCF = .50 | RCF = .75 | RCF = .00 |
| RUS: [0111] Enemy | RUS: [0110] Partner | RUS: [0100] Partner |
| USA: [0111] Enemy | USA: [0101] Enemy | USA: [0001] Partner |
| RCF = .00 | RCF = .50 | RCF = .50 |

*Figure 12.6* Role Transition Dynamics between Russia and the United States*

*RUS: Russia; USA: United States of America. Game sources: Malici (2008). Initial state is in quotes; final state is underlined. Nash equilibria are asterisked. Bram equilibria are in bold. RUS, USA preferences are ranked from 4 (highest) to 1 (lowest) in each cell. Cells are numbered from upper left to lower left clockwise in parentheses, and initial and final states for each cell are separated by a slash mark. Algorithms for each player's strategies are in brackets with zero as "choose cooperate" and one as "choose conflict" from each cell. RCF: role conflict index or 1 minus C where C = degree of congruence between roles regarding final outcome in parentheses or next move in brackets by each player from each cell

created role conflict regarding next moves from two of the four cells in their game [RCF = .50] by enacting a strategy of conditional cooperation. The shift in Russian strategy signaled the United States to reciprocate by shifting from a dominant strategy of conflict to a conditional strategy of cooperation, which eventually resulted in the post-cold war game in Figure 12.6 and the symmetrical roles of mutual partners for Russia and the United States (see Malici 2008, 47–83).

The second case is the Trump phenomenon in Figure 12.7 of "making America great again" as an example of role reversal by President Trump's signaling a desire to change the US role as Ego from friend back to partner in its security relations with European NATO allies and to change the US role in economic relations and institutions from partner back to rival by threatening to withdraw from NAFTA or actually scuttling the Trans Pacific Partnership. It remains to be seen whether Trump's alter-casting

**GAME ANALYSIS**

| NATO (+ =) | | | NATO (−,=) | | | Ally (+,=) | | |
|---|---|---|---|---|---|---|---|---|
| (G32) | CO | CF | (G56) | CO | CF | (G51) | CO | CF |
| CO | "**2,2**"* | 4,1 | CO | **4,2**\* | 1,1 | CO | "**3,4**"* | 1,2 |
| USA (+, =) | | | USA (+,=) | | | USA (+,=) | | |
| CF | 1,4 | **3,3** | CF | 2,4 | "3,3" | CF | 2,1 | **4,3**\* |

| NATO Game | Transition Game | Post-NATO Game |
|---|---|---|
| USA: Friend; NATO: Friend | USA: Partner; NATO: Friend | USA: Rival; Ally: Partner |
| (0,3/0;1/1; 2/2); (0,1/0; 2/2; 3/3) | (0,2,3/0;1/2); (1/0; 0,2/2;3/3) | (1,3/0 & 0,2/2); (0,2/0 & 1,3/2) |
| USA: [0010]; NATO: [0010] | USA: [0100]; NATO: [1010] | USA: [1110]; Ally: [0001] |

Game Cell

| 0 | 1 |
|---|---|
| 3 | 2 |

**Numbers**

**ROLE CONFLICT ANALYSIS**

| NATO Game | Transition Game | Post-NATO Game |
|---|---|---|
| USA:    (0120) Friend | USA:   (0200) Partner | USA: (2020) Rival |
| NATO: (0023) Friend | NATO: (2023) Friend | Ally: (0202) Partner |
| RCF = .50 | RCF = 1.0 | RCF = 1.0 |
| USA:   [0010] Friend | USA:   [0100] Partner | USA: [1110] Rival |
| NATO: [0010] Friend | NATO: [1010] Friend | Ally: [0001] Partner |
| RCF = .00 | RCF = .75 | RCF = 1.0 |

*Figure 12.7* Role Reversal Dynamics between the United States and NATO**

**RUS: Russia; USA: United States of America. Initial state is in quotes; final state is underlined. Nash equilibria are asterisked. Bram equilibria are in bold. USA, Ally preferences are ranked from 4 (highest) to 1 (lowest) in each cell. Cells are numbered clockwise from upper left to lower left in parentheses, and the initial states and final states for each cell are separated by a slash mark. The algorithms for each player's strategies are in brackets with zero as "choose cooperate" and one as "choose conflict" from each cell. RCF: role conflict index is 1 minus C where C = degree of congruence between roles regarding final outcome or next move by each player from each cell

strategies will succeed in prompting a role-taking process by US military allies and economic partners leading to a role reversal from friend to partner in military relations or partner to rival in economic relations.

Figure 12.7 shows a possible role reversal process and increase to high role conflict over both outcomes (RCF = 1.0) and next moves (RCF = 1.0), in which the United States engages in alter-casting the roles of the United States and NATO from a mutual friends game based on a shared dominant strategy of unconditional cooperation to an occasional allies game between a rival and an ally oscillating between cooperation and conflict (Walker, Schafer, and Smith 2019). The intervening transition game in Figure 12.7 is marked by the shift from a friend to a partner role by the United States and a shift in US strategy to conditional cooperation with higher role conflict regarding both outcomes (RCF = 1.0) and next moves (RCF = .75).

The third case is "China's rise" as an emerging regional power with global reach, which has preoccupied scholars and policy makers especially since the end of the cold war and the breakup of the Soviet Union. China is one of the BRICS powers (Brazil, Russia, India, China, and South Africa) who have emerged to challenge international order in different regions. Thies and Nieman (2017, 117) employ role theory in a comparative analysis of the BRICS powers and ask in China's case whether it is emerging as a "responsible stakeholder or revisionist great power" in the post-cold war era. This question addresses the phenomenon of role evolution, in which states as agents adopt a new power position in world politics and thereby undergo a change in social identity by virtue of changing their master role in the system of world politics, e.g., evolving from a small to a middle power or from a middle to a great power (Thies 2013; Thies and Nieman 2017; see also Larson and Shevchenko 2019; Pu 2019).

Is China's evolving master role generating auxiliary dyadic roles in a revisionist direction, which reflect changes in China's material capabilities and may guide major foreign policy reorientations and changes in conflict behavior? Thies and Nieman (2017) test two general hypotheses to answer these questions. One is a structural materialist version of the Thucydides trap hypothesis (Allison 2017) consistent with power transition theory and neorealist theory. The other one is a foreign policy hypothesis consistent with complex adaptive systems analysis and role theory (Thies and Nieman 2017, 38. Italics omitted):

> *H1*: Increases in a BRICS state's relative material power are directly and positively correlated with the adoption of revisionist NRCs [national role conceptions] and increases in militarized and economically conflictual behavior as a result of interstate competition (structural materialist hypothesis).
>
> *H2*: Domestic political processes within BRICS states alongside socialization pressure from great powers mediate changes in relative material power, leading to more deliberate changes in NRCs [national role conceptions] and militarized and economically conflictual behavior (foreign policy hypothesis).

The authors reject H1 and find support for H2 after undertaking a qualitative historical and quantitative statistical analysis of China's NRCs and conflict behavior extending from 1870 to 2007, which covers much of the same period as Goertz, Diehl, and Balas's (2016) evolution of peace analysis in the international system (Thies and Nieman 2017, 117–118):

> Our qualitative and quantitative analyses find decreasing radicalization in China's identity and remarkable continuity in conflict behavior across time. While individual national role conceptions (NRCs) may come and go, the balance of the role set reflecting Chinese

identity has become more peaceful and less revisionist. Our statistical analysis of Chinese militarized and economic conflict behavior shows no structural breaks, indicating little change in the factors that produce conflict behavior over modern Chinese history. Overall, we find little evidence in words or deeds, identity or conflict behavior that lends credence to the notion of a China threat.

They conclude (p. 133) that "China will continue to view its identity as a responsible great power that engages in infrequent militarized disputes in its home region, but a dramatic shift in foreign policy orientation or conflict behavior is unlikely. Efforts to involve China in the expansion of trade agreements may also result in less militarized conflict."

However, the recent Trump phenomenon of role reversal from partner to rival has placed Sino-American economic relations at greater risk of mutual conflict. As China's power position in world politics has evolved from a regional power to a great power, it has the capacity to enact any of the four roles (friend, partner, rival, or enemy) with greater resolve and transition more easily from one role to another in dealing with both its neighbors and the United States. It is possible that Trump's potential shift from partner to rival may lead to a shift in Sino-American relations from partners to rivals or even enemies. These possibilities are displayed in Figure 12.8 for relations between China and the United States.

In the partners game, mutual cooperation (4,4) is both a myopic (Nash) equilibrium and a nonmyopic (Brams) equilibrium. That is, neither player can choose "move" from (4,4) without immediately resulting in a worse outcome in an adjacent cell or subsequently cycling back to (4,4) as the final outcome from any other cell in the matrix. In this "no-conflict" game, both players will also choose "move" from any other cell as an initial state toward (4,4) mutual cooperation as a final state. Therefore, the risk of mutual conflict is minimized, while mutual cooperation is maximized between the players. The risk of exploitation by one player over the other one is also lowered although cycling can still occur (Brams 1994).

## CHINA-USA GAMES

| | USA | | USA | | USA | | USA | | USA | |
|---|---|---|---|---|---|---|---|---|---|---|
| | CO | CF | CO | CF | CO | CF | CO | CF | CO | CF |
| CO | 4,4* | 1,2 | 4,3* | 1,2 | 3,3* | 1,2 | 3,3 | 1,4 | 3,3 | 1,4 |
| **CHN** | | | | | | | | | | |
| CF | 2,1 | 3.3* | 2,1 | 3,4* | 2,1 | 4,4* | 2,1 | 4,2* | 4,1 | 2,2* |
| | Partners (+,=) | | Transition | | Rivals (−,=) | | Transition | | Enemies | |
| CHN: | (0,1,2,3/0) | | (0,2/0 & 1,3/2) | | (0,1,2,3/2) | | (0,1,2/2 & 3/0) | | (0/0;1,2/2;3/3) | |
| USA: | (0,1,2,3/0) | | (1,3/0 & 0,2/2) | | (0,1,2,3/2) | | (0,2/0;1/1:3/2) | | (0/0;1/1;2,3/2) | |
| CHN: | (0000) [0100] | | (0202) [0100] | | (2222) [1110] | | (2220) [1110] | | (0223) [0111] | |
| USA: | (0000) [0001] | | (2020) [1011] | | (2222) [1011] | | (0102) [0101] | | (0122) [0111] | |
| RCF: | .00 | .50 | 1.0 | 1.0 | .00 | .50 | 1.0 | .75 | .50 | .00 |

*Figure 12.8* Role Reversal Dynamics between the United States and China

In the transition game, the United States has shifted to Trump's preferred role as a rival, which opens up the possibility that mutual conflict (3,4) as well as mutual cooperation (4,3) are final outcomes as nonmyopic (Brams) equilibria. These features raise the risk of a mutual conflict outcome while not ruling out a mutual cooperation outcome so long as China is willing to deal with the relative uncertainty of each outcome. Mutual cooperation in this game is an outcome with an untrustworthy and inherently unstable partner; China cannot deter a US defection from (4,3) nor can Trump deter defection by China from (3,4). This instability and the increased uncertainty arising from high role conflict (RCF = 1.0) between Ego and Alter over final outcomes from each cell and also high role conflict (RCF = 1.0) over next moves from each cell provide incentives for China to shift from a partner to a rival role if Beijing cannot persuade Washington to return to a partner role.

In the rivals game, mutual conflict (4,4) as a stable final outcome is both a Nash and a Brams equilibrium, trading off the risk of mutual conflict as the price for reducing the uncertainty associated with high role conflict (1.0/1.0) over outcomes and next moves in the transition game to the relative stability and lower role conflict (.00/.50) over both outcomes and next moves of the rivals game, which resembles relations between the Soviet Union and the United States during parts of the Cold War. However, this stability requires both players to maintain the balance of resolve between them and impedes mutual cooperation. The relative stability of this game can be transformed by one player shifting its role either to partner or enemy.

Shifting to a partner role results in the high role conflict (1.0/1.0) in the transition game positioned between the partners and rival games in Figure 12.8. Shifting to an enemy role by one player generates the transition game with high role conflict (1.0/.75) positioned between the partners and enemies games in Figure 12.8. This change in strategy by one player creates a path from (4,2) deadlock to (3,3) settlement as a nonmyopic equilibrium; however, both players would need to exercise credible deterrent threats to maintain (3,3) as a final outcome in repeated plays of this game. A shift to an enemy strategy by either player also risks imitation by the other player and the emergence of prisoner's dilemma as an enemies game in Figure 12.8 where mutual cooperation (3,3) as an equilibrium is unattainable logically from any other cell by either player.

## Conclusion: Agents as Role Models for International Order Transition

United States-China relations today are defined by the intersection of the "China's rise phenomenon" and the "Trump phenomenon." Some Chinese scholars have labeled United States-China competition as a "structural contradiction," which means that it originates from the international structure as a result of China's rise and the United States decline. Graham Allison (2017) has called this competition between the United States and China a "Thucydides trap" and suggests that a war is more likely to take place when a rising power like China challenges a ruling power or the hegemon – the United States – in the international system. In this view, the Trump phenomenon only exacerbates a structural conflict between the two states.

However, Wendt's analysis of international order suggests that this realist argument is unwarranted for three reasons. The two states share a common fate regarding security relations: nuclear weapons and mutual assured deterrence have made a large-scale war too costly to bear for both the United States and China. Their interdependent economic relations make militarized conflict unlikely between them. The Westphalian cultural norm of sovereignty in the current international order also ensures survival in the form of territorial integrity for most states, especially for great powers (Wendt 1999, 343–366).

The real threat to the security of the two states and to regional and global order is a lack of cultural homogeneity regarding the internalization of norms and their institutional expression beyond the norms of sovereignty and the territorial nation-state that govern a culture of rivals rather than partners. In both the Gorbachev and Trump cases, success should depend theoretically on the degree of internalization by Alter's role-taking response to a new role engendered by Ego's alter-casting initiative. Negative (cold) peace rather than positive (warm) peace will likely define the situation for Sino-American relations in the absence of the internalization of mutual partner roles and their enactment within shared institutions at regional and global levels of the international system.

Wendt's constructivist solution to the security problem is to emphasize the mechanisms of alter-casting and role-taking associated with role theory to achieve a normative level of internalization necessary for the robust use of soft power. States can lead effectively and increase their soft power by being role models, i.e., leading by example and making leadership important. However, it does not mean that all components of foreign policy can become elements of soft power. In an anarchical international system, states are still self-regarding, unitary actors. In order to get others' respect and admiration, a state needs to exercise self-restraint and do what others are not able or willing, but anxious and desire to do. Nye's (2008, 18–19) definition of a leader is someone who helps a group create and achieve shared goals – leadership is not just who you are but what you do.

The effective exercise of soft power with leadership means solving common problems through fostering cooperation among states. The common problems in world politics include some traditional ones, such as war and interstate disputes, as well as nontraditional ones, e.g., poverty, climate change, and pandemics. Cooperation is by no means easy for self-regarding states under anarchy. In theory, there are two obstacles for cooperation. One is the distributional problem and the other is the commitment problem. While the distributional problem refers to relative gains vs. absolute gains for states, the commitment problem arises because states may cheat one another even after reaching an agreement (Fearon 1998).

To sum up, the path to a regional or global international order based on soft power in the future lies in the roles that states model and their strategies for exercising social power in the enactment of those roles. We have attempted to demonstrate both theoretically and empirically that different roles are associated with different forms of social power and different degrees of internalization. An enemy role is enacted with a dominant conflict strategy of bullying and hard power; a friend role is enacted with a dominant cooperation strategy of bandwagoning and soft power. The roles of partner and rival are enacted with the contingent strategies of appeasement or balancing, respectively, based on reciprocal promises of rewards or threats of punishments. Order transition involves changing modal roles and strategies to generate socialization processes of alter-casting and role-taking to resolve role conflicts between dyads. Simulating dyadic games between agents with different roles can identify particular patterns of strategic interaction to guide the evolution of international order toward mutual cooperation as a final outcome.

## Notes

1. Johnston (2019) takes an inductive approach to analyzing the dimensions of international order, identifying eight issue areas (constitutive, military, political development, social development, trade, financial, environmental, information), which make the political universe a "world of many orders." Our approach is a deductive approach that employs game theory models of the roles and rules that specify the principles of order within and across issue areas, which may vary among agents across regions and eras as social systems (Wright 2000; Nowak 2011; Walker and Malici 2011, 239–262; Malici and Walker 2017; see also Tang 2015).
2. An example is the stag hunt story that accompanies a $2 \times 2$ game in which the players rank mutual cooperation highest instead of domination. The narrative for this game has the players with a choice to cooperate and together kill a stag in the bush or defect and kill a rabbit that appears at their feet. This story illustrates the dilemma of deciding whether "a bird (rabbit) in hand is worth two in the bush," i.e., should a player cooperate to pursue and share a greater collective good that also has a smaller chance of success or choose to defect and not share a lesser individual good with a better chance of success (see Waltz 1959; Skyrms 2004).
3. Binary role theory is a theory of uncertainty reduction in social relations in which agents exchange binary cues of cooperation or conflict to define the actual social relations between them as the enactment of four possible roles: friend, partner, rival, or enemy (Malici and Walker 2017). The enactment of these roles is modeled by the rules of strategic rationality in sequential game theory (Brams 1994), as mediated by the possible distributions of power and interests between them shown in Figure12.2. The roles specify each agent's ranking of the four outcomes in the $2 \times 2$ game in Figure 12.2 and the agent's corresponding strategy associated with the roles of partner (appease), friend (bandwagon), rival (balance),

or enemy (bully). The intersection of these strategies defines the social relations between the agents as they enact their respective roles according to the rules of Brams' sequential game theory.

4. The friend-enemy role dyads are not symmetrical, i.e., the friend role is not identical to the enemy role; however, they are complementary, i.e., both prefer CO,CF as the highest ranked outcome. So the two roles do not conflict.
5. The degree of fit here refers empirically to the achievement of benefits in the form of higher ranked outcomes, while the degree of fit refers normatively to the achievement of mutual cooperation. In the context of game theory, the first definition of fit is a Pareto-superior equilibrium (an outcome that is higher ranked for both players than the initial state), which may or may not also be an outcome of mutual cooperation, e.g., (4,4) is a Pareto-superior outcome compared to (3,3) for both players even when (4,4) is an outcome of mutual conflict for the game.

# References

Albrecht-Carrié, R. 1958. *A diplomatic history of Europe since the Congress of Vienna*. New York, NY: Harper & Row.

Allison, G. 2017. *Destined for war: Can America and China escape Thucydides's trap?* Boston, MA: Houghton-Mifflin.

Axelrod, R. 1984. *The evolution of cooperation*. New York, NY: Basic Books.

Axelrod, R., M. Cohen. 1999. *Harnessing complexity*. New York, NY: Free Press.

Baldwin, D. 2016. *Power and international relations*. Princeton, NJ: Princeton University Press.

Brams, S. 1994. *Theory of moves*. Cambridge: Cambridge University Press.

Fearon, J. 1998. Bargaining, enforcement, and international cooperation. *International Organization* 52: 269–305.

Feng, H. 2007. *Chinese strategic culture and foreign policy decision-making*. New York, NY: Routledge.

Gell-Mann, M. 1994. *The quark and the jaguar*. New York, NY: Henry Holt.

Goertz, G., P. Diehl, A. Balas. 2016. *The puzzle of peace*. New York, NY: Oxford University Press.

Hartmann, F. 1983. *The relations of nations*. 6th Edition. New York, NY: Macmillan.

He, K. 2018. Role conceptions, order transition and institutional balancing in the Asia-Pacific: A New theoretical framework. *Australian Journal of International Affairs* 72: 92–109.

Jervis, R. 1997. *System effects*. Princeton, NJ: Princeton University Press.

Johnston, A. 1995a. *Cultural realism: Strategic culture and grand strategy in Chinese history*. Princeton, NJ: Princeton University Press.

Johnston, A. 1995b. Thinking about strategic culture. *International Security* 19: 32–64.

Johnston, A. 2019. China in a world of orders. *International Security* 44(2): 9–60.

Kaufman, S., R. Little, W. Wohlforth. 2007. *The balance of power in world history*. New York, NY: Palgrave Macmillan.

Larson, D., A. Shevchenko. 2019. *Quest for status: Chinese and Russian foreign policy*. New Haven, CT: Yale University Press.

Malici, A. 2006. Reagan and Gorbachev: Altercasting at the end of the cold war. In *Beliefs and leadership in world politics*, eds. M. Schafer, and S. Walker, 127–150. New York, NY: Palgrave Macmillan.

Malici, A. 2008. *When leaders learn and when they don't*. Albany, NY: SUNY Press.

Malici, A., S. Walker. 2017. *Role theory and role conflict in U.S.-Iran relations.* New York, NY: Routledge.

Mearsheimer, J. 2001. *The tragedy of great power politics.* New York, NY: W.W. Norton.

Miller, J., S. Page. 2007. *Complex adaptive systems.* Princeton, NJ: Princeton University Press.

Mitchell, M. 2009. *Complexity: A guided tour.* New York, NY: Oxford University Press.

Nowak, M., R. Highfield. 2011. *Super cooperators.* New York, NY: Free Press.

Nye, J. 2008. *The powers to lead.* Reprint Edition. New York, NY: Oxford University Press.

Pu, X. 2019. *Rebranding China: Contested status signaling in the changing global order.* Stanford, CA: Stanford University Press.

Rapoport, A., M. Guyer. 1976. *The 2 x 2 game.* Ann Arbor, MI: University of Michigan Press.

Schweller, R. 1994. Bandwagoning for profit. *International Security* 19: 72–107.

Schweller, R. 1998. *Deadly imbalances.* New York, NY: Columbia University Press.

Skyrms, B. 2004. *The stag hunt and the evolution of social structure.* Cambridge: Cambridge University Press.

Stein, A. 1990. *Why nations cooperate.* Ithaca, NY: Cornell University Press.

Tang, S. 2015. *The social evolution of international politics.* Oxford: Oxford University Press.

Thies, C. 2013. *The United States, Israel, and the search for international order.* New York, NY: Routledge.

Thies, C., M. Nieman. 2017. *Rising powers and foreign policy revisionism.* Ann Arbor, MI: University of Michigan Press.

Walker, S. 1992. Symbolic interactionism and international politics. In *Contending dramas,* eds. M. Cottam, C. Shih, 19–38. New York, NY: Praeger.

Walker, S. 2004. Role identities and the operational codes of political leaders. In *Advances in political psychology,* ed. M. Hermann, 71–106. Vol. 1. London, UK: Elsevier.

Walker, S. 2013. *Role theory and the cognitive architecture of British appeasement decisions.* New York, NY: Routledge.

Walker, S. .Malici, A. 2011. *U.S. presidents and foreign policy mistakes.* Stanford, CA: Stanford University Press.

Walker, S., M. Schafer, G. Smith. 2019. The operational codes of Hillary Clinton and Donald Trump. In *The Oxford handbook of behavioral political science,* eds. A. Mintz, L. Tennis. New York, NY: Oxford University Press.

Waltz, K. 1959. *Man, the state, and war.* New York, NY: Columbia University Press.

Waltz, K. 1979. *Theory of international politics.* Reading, MA: Addison-Wesley.

Wendt, A. 1999. *Social theory of international politics.* Cambridge: Cambridge University Press.

Wohlforth, W., R. Little, S. Kaufman, D. Kang, C. Jones, V. Tin-Bor Hui, A. Eckstein, D. Deudney, W. Brenner. 2007. Testing balance-of-power theory in world history. *European Journal of International Relations* 13: 155–185.

Wright, R. 2000. *Nonzero.* New York, NY: Random House Vintage Books.

# 13 Binary Role Theory and the Operational Code Analysis of Grand Strategies

## Can Balancing Work?

*B. Gregory Marfleet and Stephen G. Walker*

**Introduction**

Research on the dynamics of historical international systems reveals a striking finding. Balancing behavior is relatively rare as the modal behavior of states and often fails to prevent systemic hegemony by a predominant state. A research team of several experts on various regional and historical international systems employed data covering approximately 10,000 system-years and reported the conservative estimate that 40–45% of their observations appear to have been hegemonic or unipolar configurations of power (Wohlforth et al. 2007, 180, n. 4). Their subsequent intensive case studies of eight international systems covering over 2000 years of world politics outside of the European international system support these statistical results and suggest why balancing behavior is relatively rare and often unsuccessful (Kaufman, Little, and Wohlforth 2007).

The authors infer that other causal mechanisms in foreign policy decision-making act as "systemic impediments to balancing even if one accepts the assumptions of balance of power theory" (Wohlforth et al. 2007, 158). Among these other mechanisms, they include impeding external balancing (forming alliances) due to the "free-riding" phenomenon associated with the logic of collective action in economic theory; impeding internal balancing (rearming) due to "institutional lags" associated with internal costs in allocating resources for guns rather than butter; impeding both forms of balancing due to psychological obstacles in processing information by individuals and groups, which leads to "pervasive uncertainty ex ante concerning the identity and severity of the hegemonic threat that would exacerbate the other system- and unit-level barriers to balancing" (Wohlforth et al. 2007, 158). These barriers to balancing against hegemony appear to be overcome in their case studies when there is system expansion, i.e., new members enter the system of interest, and when the administrative capacities of the potential or putative hegemon are not sufficient to sustain expansion of its power and the domination of others (Wohlforth et al. 2007, 158–159; see also Kaufman, Little, and Wohlforth 2007, 1–20).

In the context of a long view of history provided by these analyses, therefore, the pervasive reliance on balance of power theory by realists to explain world politics becomes parochial at best and perhaps susceptible to entailment as a theory by the rival causal mechanisms identified above at the agent level of analysis. The application of balance of power theory by realists to explain the dynamics of the European international system may be warranted, but its application to other geographical regions and historical eras is problematic.

More generally, the scope conditions of balance of power theory appear to need qualification in light of these results (Eilstrup-Sangiovanni 2009; Wohlforth et al. 2009). Classical realists and structural neorealists may contest this conclusion (Vasquez and Elman 2003). Neoclassical realists may be more comfortable in accepting this critique (Lobell, Ripsman, and Taliafarro 2009). The latter emphasize that the logic of balance of power theory is always qualified by the operation of agent-level mechanisms that can either facilitate or impede systemic cues and imperatives to balance against potential hegemons.

Agent-level theorists of information processing and decision-making within institutions and by leaders have long contended that the barriers to balancing identified by Wohlforth et al. (2007) call into question the power of realist models to explain the microfoundations of foreign policy decisions and their systemic outcomes. In particular, both rational choice theories and psychological theories are sensitive to the problem of uncertainty in its various forms, as decision makers make choices under varying conditions of imperfect or incomplete information compounded by limited capacities and opportunities to process existing and available information (Steinbrunner 1974; Jervis 1976; Vertzberger 1990; Lake and Powell 1999; Walker 2002; Lau 2003; Bueno de Mesquita and McDermott 2004; Schafer and Crichlow 2010).

Viewed in this perspective, the quintessential political problem becomes reducing uncertainty and managing complexity in world politics (Cioffi-Revilla 1998; see also Jervis 1997; Kydd 2005; Walker, Malici, and Schafer 2011). In order to understand how and why balancing as a systemic phenomenon is a relatively rare solution to this problem and why it often fails to prevent hegemonic or unipolar domination by one agent in the system, agent-level theorists argue that it is necessary to analyze the microfoundations of the decisions that generate these systemic-level patterns and outcomes. We also adopt that position in this chapter as our point of departure for the investigation of this problem.

Our approach combines features of rational choice and psychological models within an elastic analytical framework from the operational code analysis research program, which permits aggregation from agent-level decisions to system-level outcomes. The central theory in this analytical alliance is binary role theory, because its defining mechanism of role location is the process of reducing uncertainty and managing complexity in social systems. While it is possible in principle to apply role theory to larger ensembles of world politics, we shall limit its application to dyads as the simplest level of systemic outcomes in order to focus more closely on the logic of decisions by individual agents (Walker 2011a, 2011b, 2013; see also Walker and Malici 2011).

## Binary Role Theory and Balance of Power Theory

As the name implies, binary role theory conceptualizes the complexity of human behavior as reducible to the logic of binary choices to maintain or change behavior. Its assumptions include at least two agents, Self and Other, who as Ego and Alter enact a role and counter-role. Together they constitute a role set or social dyad as a social system either in the context of an environment or as a subsystem in the context of a larger social system (Holsti 1970; Walker 1987; Walker, Malici, and Schafer 2011). The binary choices in this version of role theory are to maintain the behavior associated with a given role or change this behavior in either an escalatory or a de-escalatory direction.

These changes are plotted within quadrants of a political field instantiated by the interaction of Ego and Alter, in which the behaviors are conceptualized as various forms of the exercise of power (Walker 2011a). The exercise of power is a binary construction in the form of either positive (+) sanctions or negative (−) sanctions, and the distribution of power between Ego and Alter is a binary construction in the form of a symmetrical (=) or asymmetrical (≠) distribution. Binary role theory identifies the exercise of power as role enactment while the distribution of power is a role demand (constraint) on the enactment of a role or counter-role (Walker 2011a).

Within the context of binary role theory, therefore, the balance of power can either refer to the strategic exercise of power as a characteristic of agents or the distribution of power between them as a systemic feature. Wohlforth et al. (2007) employ both referents of the concept in their critique of balance of power theory and their analyses of the balance of power as a strategy and a constraint. They contend that in their analyses of various historical and regional international systems, a balance of power strategy is relatively rare and often fails to prevent the balance of power distribution in these systems from taking and maintaining a hegemonic (one agent dominates) or a unipolar (one agent has over 50% of the power) distribution.

In our analysis, we focus on both features in the simplest form of such a system, namely, a two-member social system in which each agent can adopt a balancing strategy as its role or not, and the distribution of power may or may not lead to domination (hegemony) by one agent over the other member of the role set. The actual analysis takes the form of computer simulations of the strategic interactions between dyads that identify different binary roles and counter-roles in constituting and evolving their respective role sets (Marfleet and Walker 2006). In the simulations, the role sets may (1) have accurate two-sided information about the strategy of Ego and Alter or (2) one or both may have inaccurate information about the other's strategic orientation for Self and strategic view of Other.

According to realist balance of power theory, the condition of anarchy and the distribution of power between Ego and Alter should act as systemic constraints and be the basis for selecting a strategy (Wohlforth et al. 2007; Waltz 1979). The latter systemic constraint is also recognized as a role demand within the context of binary role theory. Bandwagoning and appeasement are strategies of Cooperation (+) in which either submission (Ego, Alter = CO, CF) or settlement (Ego, Alter = CO, CO), respectively, are the highest ranked outcomes. Balancing and hegemonic strategies as Conflict (−) strategies prefer either deadlock (Ego, Alter = CF, CF) or domination (Ego, Alter = CF, CO), respectively, as the highest ranked outcome.

The specification of a complete strategy in the form of ranking all four outcomes also depends partly on another constraint in realist theory, namely, the interests at stake for each agent. This additional role demand affects the form of a complete Cooperation or Conflict strategy, depending upon whether secondary or vital interests are the stakes. The form of a complete strategy is specified by the ranking of the other three outcomes given settlement, deadlock, domination, or submission is the top-ranked outcome. A sample of relevant possibilities for ranking outcomes is shown for Ego in Figure 13.1, as derived from realist assumptions about the impact of power and interests on foreign policy strategies (Walker, Malici, and Schafer 2011, 37–39, 286). Alter (preferences not shown) has the same eight choices of possible strategies as the ones shown for Ego in this figure, which are also specified by the same external focal points of power and interests summarized in the following eight propositions. These propositions collectively expand the logic of the realist aphorism that "the strong do what they can, and the weak suffer what they must" (Thucydides 1910, 5.89.1).

Once an agent selects either a strategy of Cooperation or Conflict, two factors constrain the ranking of realistic outcomes: the distribution of power and the agent's interests at stake. Both the distributions of power and interests are external focal points of information either already available to both agents in a strategic dyad or learned during the exchange of cues in the form of initial acts of cooperation or conflict toward each other within a game of strategic interaction (Snyder and Diesing 1977; Walker 2011a).

| | Cooperation Strategies | | | | Conflict Strategies | | | |
|---|---|---|---|---|---|---|---|---|
| | **Bandwagon** | | **Appease** | | **Balance** | | **Hegemony** | |
| | Alter | Alter | Alter | Alter | Alter | Alter | Alter | Alter |
| | CO CF | CO CF | CO CF | CO CF | CO CF | CO CF | CO CF | CO CF |
| CO | 3 4 | 2 4 | 4 3 | 4 1 | 3 2 | 2 1 | 3 1 | 2 1 |
| Ego | | | | | | | | |
| CF | 1 2 | 1 3 | 1 2 | 2 3 | 1 4 | 3 4 | 4 2 | 4 3 |
| NI: | Sec | Vit | Sec | Vit | Sec | Vit | Sec | Vit |
| Pow: | Ego < Alter | | Ego = Alter | | Ego = Alter | | Ego > Alter | |

*Bandwagoning Asymmetrical Power Proposition 1.1*: If agent A has secondary interests at stake and is weaker (<) than the other agent B in a dyad, then A may enact a bandwagoner role with a strategy of submission > settlement > deadlock > domination.

*Bandwagoning Asymmetrical Proposition 1.2*: If agent A has vital interests at stake and is weaker (<) than the other agent B in a dyad, then A may enact a bandwagoner role with a strategy of submission >deadlock > settlement > domination.

*Appeasement Equal Power Proposition 2.1*: If agent A has secondary interests at stake and is equal (=) to the other agent B in a dyad, then A may enact an appeaser role with a strategy of settlement> submission > deadlock > domination.

*Appeasement Equal Power Proposition 2.2*: If agent A has vital interests at stake and is equal (=) to the other agent B in a dyad, then A may enact an appeaser role with a strategy of settlement > deadlock > domination >submission.

*Balancing Equal Power Proposition 3.1*: If agent A has secondary interests at stake and is equal (=) to the other agent B in a dyad, then A may enact a balancer role with a strategy of deadlock > settlement > submission > domination.

*Balancing Equal Power Proposition 3.2*: If agent A has vital interests at stake and is equal (=) than the other agent B in a dyad, then A may enact a balancer role with a strategy of deadlock > settlement > domination >submission.

*Hegemonic Asymmetrical Power Proposition 4.1*: If agent A has secondary interests at stake and is stronger (>) than the other agent B in a dyad, then A may enact a hegemon's role with a strategy of domination > settlement > deadlock > submission.

*Hegemonic Asymmetrical Power Proposition 4.2*: If agent A has vital interests at stake and is stronger (>) than the other agent B in a dyad, then A may enact a hegemon's role with a strategy of domination > deadlock > settlement > submission.

*Figure 13.1* Grand Strategies and Inferred Preferences from Power and Interest Distributions

CO = Cooperation; CF = Conflict. Power (Pow) Distributions: Equal (=); Less Than (<); Greater Than (>). National Interests (NI) for Ego: Sec = Secondary; Vit = Vital. Preference rankings 4 (highest)...1 (lowest) are for Ego (row player) only (Walker and Marfleet 2012).

A completely specified strategy for Ego or Alter depends upon the distribution of power and interests plus the corresponding strategic orientations and outcome preference rankings for both Ego and Alter. This information may be symmetrical or asymmetrical for both players in a given game, i.e., each player may have accurate or inaccurate information about the power, interests, and preferences of both players.

In classical game theory, the two-sided information assumption of symmetry (both players with complete and accurate information)

permits each player to calculate a common solution for the game based on simultaneous decisions to construct a "final" state or outcome of the game, in which neither player has an incentive to continue the game. The rules for calculating decisions and outcomes are specified by the rules of play as well as the intersection of the preference rankings for the different outcomes by both players. If the rules of play allow for alternating moves by each player and/or repeated play of the same game, then the rules for optimizing outcomes increase in complexity for these sequential games (Brams 1994). If the two-sided information assumption is relaxed so that one or both players have imperfect information, then the outcomes of the games become more problematic to calculate, as each player may be playing a different subjective game based on their respective beliefs (Maoz and Astorino 1992; Schafer and Walker 2006; Walker, Malici, and Schafer 2011).

Missing from the realist models of power and interests in Figure 13.1 is any specification for the preference rankings for Ego when its highest ranked goal is domination and the power distribution is either symmetrical or favors Alter. Also omitted is a proper specification of the preference rankings for Ego when its highest ranked goal is settlement and the power distribution is asymmetrical and favors Ego. The possible logical solutions for these omissions and others are in Figure 13.2, which contains all of the possible combinations of preference-rankings across the dimensions of power and interests. This matrix identifies families of grand strategies that collectively form an entropy matrix of all possible states as roles between Ego and Alter formed by the logical intersections of strategies within and across each family within the constraints imposed by the logical rules of noncontradiction and transitivity plus the assumptions of both dominant or contingent strategies for Ego and Alter within each family of strategies (Walker 2013, 37).

The logically possible role and counter-role dyads in Figure 13.2 represent a formal model that integrates key variables from three traditions of general International Relations theory as a type of grand strategic role orientation theory in Figure 13.3, which we call a PIN model after its key variables of Power (P), Identity (I), and National (N) interests. This triad of variables in Figure 13.3 interacts to construct different rankings for the preferences in Figure 13.2 in complex ways that do not give primacy to any one of the three variables, depending on the particular combinations of values that each takes in relation to the others. Power can take a symmetrical (=) equal value or an asymmetrical ($\neq$) value of greater than (>) or less than (<) equal value. Identity can take either a cooperation (+) or conflict (–) value. National interests can take a secondary (s) or vital (v) value (see Walker 2011a; 2013, 39).

Foreign policy changes (changes in Grand Strategic Orientation or GSO) can be both spatial and temporal, i.e., strategies change from dyad to dyad (spatially) and over time for the same dyad (temporally). Sources

**Role Enactment Strategies**

| | Appeasement Strategies | Bandwagoning Strategies |
|---|---|---|
| | Settle>Submit>Deadlock>Dominate (s,<) | Submit>Settle>Deadlock>Dominate (s,<) |
| | Settle>Submit>Dominate>Deadlock (v,<) | Submit>Settle>Dominate>Deadlock (v,<) |
| **Cooperation (+)** | Settle>Deadlock>Submit>Dominate (s,=) | Submit>Deadlock>Settle>Dominate (s,=) |
| **Roles** | Settle> Deadlock> Dominate >Submit (v,=) | Submit> Deadlock >Dominate>Settle (v,=) |
| | Settle>Dominate>Submit> Deadlock (s,>) | Submit> Dominate>Settle> Deadlock (s,>) |
| | Settle>Dominate>Deadlock>Submit (v,>) | Submit>Dominate>Deadlock>Settle (v.>) |

**Partner Roles**                    **Friend Roles**

**Role Enactment Strategies**

| | Hegemonic Strategies | Balancing Strategies |
|---|---|---|
| | Dominate>Submit>Settle>Deadlock (s,<) | Deadlock>Submit>Settle>Dominate (s,<) |
| | Dominate>Submit>Deadlock>Settle (v,<) | Deadlock>Submit>Dominate>Settle (v,<) |
| **Conflict (−)** | Dominate>Settle>Submit>Deadlock (s,=) | Deadlock>Settle>Submit>Dominate (s,=) |
| **Roles** | Dominate>Settle>Deadlock>Submit (v,=) | Deadlock>Settle>Dominate>Submit (v,=) |
| | Dominate>Deadlock>Submit>Settle (s,>) | Deadlock>Dominate>Submit>Settle (s,>) |
| | Dominate>Deadlock>Settle>Submit (v,>) | Deadlock>Dominate>Settle>Submit (v,>) |

**Enemy Roles**                    **Rival Roles**

*Figure 13.2* Families of Binary Role Enactment Strategies

Sources: Walker (2007); Walker, Malici, and Schafer (2011). S = Secondary interests; V = Vital interests. Mathematical Symbols: Greater than (>), Equal to (=), Less than (<); Cooperation Role (+), Conflict Role (−)

of change include changes in identity (change in CO+ or CF−) for Ego or Alter, changes in interests (change in v or s) by Ego or Alter, and changes in power position (= or ≠) by Ego or Alter across dyads or over time. It is possible to start from any one of these theoretical perspectives and reach the configurations of ranked preferences in Figure 13.2 by introducing different scope conditions for specifying the PIN model's dynamics. A grand strategy research program within this theoretical context would ideally involve mapping how many dyads are in a state's role set and how many different strategies are pursued by a state, depending on the distributions of identities, interests, and power that define each dyad.

However, in this chapter, we address only the substantive problem of how different role dyads intersect with different strategies while paying particular attention to balancing strategies. We are interested in the

## PIN Models of Roles and Grand Strategies

**ALTER**

| | COOP | CONF |
|---|---|---|
| **COOP** | Partners (Appease) | Friends (Bandwagon) |
| **CONF** | Enemies (Hegemonic) | Rivals (Balance) |

**EGO**

P

GSO

I          N

**Families of Roles & Grand Strategies**
Appease = liberal cooperative security orientation
Bandwagon = small state security orientation
Hegemonic = offensive realist security orientation
Balance = defensive realist security orientation

**Elements of Grand Strategic Orientations**
P = Power politics orientation (realism)
I  = Identity politics orientation (constructivism)
N = Interest politics orientation (liberalism)

### Theoretical Assumptions Regarding Grand Strategic Orientations (GSOs)

1. Constructivist IR Theory says that GSOs are a function of identities (I), which can define which national interests (N) are ignored or highlighted and make power (P) less relevant, i.e., "Anarchy is what states make of it." GSO = I→N→P (Wendt 1999).

2. Liberal IR Theory says that GSOs are a function of national interests (N), which determine the range of relevant identities (I); then identities (I) specify the exercise of   power (P).  GSO = N→I→P (Moravcik 2003).

3. Realist IR Theory says that GSOs are a function of power (P) that permits a range of interests (N), which then specifies identities (I).  GSO = P→N→I (Waltz 1979).

4. Binary Role Theory says that knowledge of Alter's GSO over time can influence Ego's GSO selection between a Cooperation (+) Role or a Conflict (−) Role with different strategic orientations (Malici and Walker 2017).

5. PIN Models of Binary Role Theory specify families of grand strategies for Ego that can vary, depending on Alter's strategy.  PIN models specify what strategic role orientations for Ego and Alter emerge from the interaction among Power, Identity, and National interests while Binary Role Theory specifies the interactions and outcomes between Ego and Alter as a role and counter-role dyad with different configurations of Power, Identity and National interests (Walker 2011a, 2013).

*Figure 13.3* Elements and Theoretical Sources of Roles and Grand Strategies

Sources:  Walker (2007, 2011a, 2011b, 2013; Malici and Walker 2017)

question of whether balancing strategies for Ego are more effective as a GSO than other strategic orientations (i.e., result in greater payoffs or better than expected results) when confronted with an Alter, the GSO of which is known while only limited information regarding power or interests is available. As Figure 13.2 shows, there are six possible PIN configurations for each grand strategy and each could conceivably interact with any other GSO/PIN-based Alter (including ones that mirror their own preferences). In order to compare balancing strategy performance with the other three, we are presented with $24^2$ (576) possible dyadic pairs.

The number 576 differs from the typical number of $2 \times 2$ ordinal games identified by various taxonomies. The most well-known taxonomy is in Guyer and Rapoport (1966) who identified 78 strategically distinct games based on nested solutions. The number 576 represents the exhaustive list of $2 \times 2$ bi-matrices which could strictly be reduced by a factor of 4 if row and columns could be swapped (to 144) and further reduced in half if row and column players were considered interchangeable. For a discussion, see Goforth and Robinson (2005). Neither of these assumptions is warranted or attractive for our purposes, since we do differentiate between the behaviors suggested by the binary choices (cooperate or conflict) and likewise differentiate between row and column player conceptually as initiator and target. Nevertheless, we should anticipate evidence of symmetry in our results. To explore our entire set of dyads, we employ computational simulation methods.

## Simulation Methods

We begin our analysis with the assumption that agents operate under the belief that they are aware of the GSO of their opponent but may not know the distributions of power and interests for the other member of their dyad. Consequently, they must make assumptions about the specifics of the dyadic arrangement imputing factors and deducing attendant payoffs to define the subjective game that they anticipate playing. This expected game serves as the basis for a set of appropriate responses to moves and countermoves in future interactions.

For example, if one player has adopted a hegemonic GSO, it might be natural to assume that the opponent is weaker and likely to bandwagon (and vice versa since this is one of the symmetrical pairings). However, the assumptions about power may or may not be accurate. An opponent's identity could lead it to adopt any of the other GSOs regardless of power in the dyad in question. For each of these dyadic pairings, the intersection of interests (secondary and vital) additionally differentiates four possible game situations (SS, SV, VS, VV). Combined, the six strategies and four interest pairings delineate 24 possible subjective games.

Figures 13.4 and 13.5 depict some examples of these arrangements showing PIN-derived strategy, power, and interest pairings as game matrices. The figures include illustrations of subjective games for pairs of GSO, including some where cooperative players interact with cooperative opponents and others with noncooperative ones. Of course, space precludes the complete depiction of all of the possible pairings. The payoffs in these figures reflect the rank order of outcomes implied by the logic of the propositions outlined in Figures 13.1 and 13.2. Below each strategic form game, several rows of information indicate the expected outcome of the game and the strategies that each player would use.

**a. Realist Asymmetrical Power Arrangements: Hegemon (Ego) versus Bandwagon (Alter)**

|  |  | Alter (g37) |  | Alter |  | Alter(g36) |  | Alter |  |
|---|---|---|---|---|---|---|---|---|---|
|  |  | CO | CF | CO | CF | CO | CF | CO | CF |
|  | CO | 4,3* | 1,1 | 4,3* | 1,2 | 2,3 | 1,1 | 2,3 | 1,2 |
| Ego | CF | 3,4 | 2,2 | 3,4 | 2,1 | 4,4* | 3,2 | 4,4* | 3,1 |
|  | NI | Sec | Sec | Vit | Sec | Sec | Vit | Vit | Vit |
|  | Pow | Ego > Alter |  | Ego > Alter |  | Ego > Alter |  | Ego > Alter |  |
|  | TOM | (0,1,2 /0) & (3/3) |  | (0,1,2/0 & (3/3) |  | (0,1,2,3/3) |  | (0,1,2,3/3) |  |
|  | Mme | HESG |  | HEVG |  | HESG |  | HEVG |  |
|  |  | [0000 0111 | | [0000 0111 | | [1111 1111 | | [1111 1111 | |
|  |  | 0000 0001] | | 0000 0001] | | 1111 0001] | | 1111 0001] | |
|  | MMa | BWSL |  | BWSL |  | BWVL |  | BWVL |  |
|  |  | [0100 0000 | | [0100 0000 | | [1100 0000 | | [1100 0000 | |
|  |  | 0000 0000] | | 0000 0000] | | 0000 0000] | | 0000 0000] | |

**b. Realist Symmetrical Power Arrangements: Balance vs. Balance**

|  |  | Alter |  | Alter |  | Alter |  | Alter |  |
|---|---|---|---|---|---|---|---|---|---|
|  |  | CO | CF | CO | CF | CO | CF | CO | CF |
|  | CO | 3,3* | 2,1 | 3,3* | 2,2 | 3,3* | 1,1 | 3,3* | 1,2 |
| Ego | CF | 1,2 | 4,4* | 1,1 | 4,4* | 2,2 | 4,4* | 2,1 | 4,4* |
|  | NI | Sec | Sec | Sec | Vit | Vit | Sec | Vit | Vit |
|  | Pow | Ego = Alter |  | Ego = Alter |  | Ego = Alter |  | Ego = Alter |  |
|  | TOM | (0,1,2,3/2) |  | (0,1,2,3/2) |  | (0,1,2,3/2) |  | (0,1,2,3/2) |  |
|  | MMe | BLSE |  | BLSE |  | BLVE |  | BLVE |  |
|  |  | [1110 1111 | | [1110 1111 | | [1110 1111 | | [1110 1111 | |
|  |  | 0000 1111] | | 0000 1111] | | 0000 1111] | | 0000 1111] | |
|  | MMa | BLSE |  | BLVE |  | BLSE |  | BLVE |  |
|  |  | [1110 0000 | | [1110 0000 | | [1110 0000 | | [1110 0000 | |
|  |  | 1111 1111] | | 1111 1111] | | 1111 1111] | | 1111 1111] | |

*Figure 13.4* Possible PIN Models for Asymmetrical and Symmetrical Power Games

CO = Cooperation; CF = Conflict. Power (Pow) Distributions: Equal (=); Less Than (<); Greater Than (>). National Interests (NI) for Ego, Alter: Sec = Secondary; Vit = Vital. Preference Rankings: 4 (highest)...1 (lowest). Nash equilibria are asterisked and Brams' TOM equilibria are in bold. Dominant strategies are underlined. G-numbers for the two conflict games are from Brams (1994: 215–219). The TOM row indicates expected game outcome quadrant (O) using Brams' Theory of Moves solutions given beginning quadrant (Q) expressed as (Q,{Q, Q, Q}/O). MMe and MMa indicate the Moore machine codes for the Ego (row) and Alter (column) player, respectively, (0 = Cooperate and 1 = Conflict). The binary values indicate the player's move response while in that respective quadrant for each of four possible scenarios of prior moves used to reach this quadrant. Underlined values in the Moore machine indicate "unexpected" positions (impossible game situations given strict TOM rules of play). For each strategy (S), separate Moore machine codes for the case for S(Ego) and S(Alter) must be generated these are designated by the e or a character at the end of the strategy name

To explore the play sequence and anticipated outcomes of these strategic games, we apply Brams' Theory of Moves (TOM). Unlike Nash equilibrium solutions that require participants to simultaneously select a strategy given only information about the opponent's preferences, Brams' TOM solutions incorporate the history of prior interaction or knowledge

**a.   Similarly Cooperative Opponents: Appease vs. Appease**

|  |  | Alter |  |  | Alter |  |  | Alter |  |  | Alter |  |
|---|---|---|---|---|---|---|---|---|---|---|---|---|
|  |  | CO | CF |  | CO | CF |  | CO | CF |  | CO | CF |
|  | CO | 4,4* | 2,1 |  | 4,4* | 2,2 |  | 4,4* | 1,1 |  | 4,4* | 1,2 |
| Ego | CF | 1,2 | 3,3* |  | 1,1 | 3,3* |  | 2,2 | 3,3* |  | 2,1 | 3,3* |

|  | Game 1 | Game 2 | Game 3 | Game 4 |
|---|---|---|---|---|
| NI | Sec  Sec | Sec  Vit | Vit  Sec | Vit  Vit |
| Pow | **Ego = Alter** | **Ego = Alter** | **Ego = Alter** | **Ego = Alter** |
| TOM | *(0,1,2,3,/0)* | *(0,1,2,3,/0)* | *(0,1,2,3,/0)* | *(0,1,2,3,/0)* |
| MMe | APSE<br>[0000 1111<br>0000 0001] | APSE<br>[0000 1111<br>0000 0001] | APVE<br>[0000 1111<br>0000 0001] | APVE<br>[0000 1111<br>0000 0001] |
| MMa | APSE<br>[0000 0000<br>1111 0001] | APVE<br>[0000 0000<br>1111 0001] | APSE<br>[0000 0000<br>1111 0001] | APVE<br>[0000 0000<br>1111 0001] |

**b.   Equal, Dissimilar Opponents: Appease vs. Balance**

|  |  | Alter |  |  | Alter |  |  | Alter |  |  | Alter |  |
|---|---|---|---|---|---|---|---|---|---|---|---|---|
|  |  | CO | CF |  | CO | CF |  | CO | CF |  | CO | CF |
|  | CO | 4,3* | 2,1 |  | 4,3* | 2,2 |  | 4,3* | 1,1 |  | 4,3* | 1,2 |
| Ego | CF | 1,2 | **3,4*** |  | 1,1 | **3,4*** |  | 2,2 | **3,4*** |  | 2,1 | **3,4*** |

|  | Game 1 | Game 2 | Game 3 | Game 4 |
|---|---|---|---|---|
| NI | Sec  Sec | Sec  Vit | Vit  Sec | Vit  Vit |
| Pow | **Ego = Alter** | **Ego = Alter** | **Ego = Alter** | **Ego = Alter** |
| TOM | *(0,1/2) & (2,3/0)* | *(0,1/2) & (2,3/0)* | *(0,1/2) & (2,3/0)* | *(0,1/2) & (2,3/0)* |
| MMR | APSE<br>[0000 0111<br>1000 0001] | APSE<br>[0000 0111<br>1000 0001] | APVE<br>[0000 0111<br>1000 0001] | APVE<br>[0000 0111<br>1000 0001] |
| MMC | BLSE<br>[1110 1000<br>1111 1111] | BLVE<br>[1110 1000<br>1111 1111] | BLSE<br>[1110 1000<br>1111 1111] | BLVE<br>[1110 1000<br>1111 1111] |

*Figure 13.5* Possible PIN Models for Symmetrical Power Games

CO = Cooperation; CF = Conflict. Power (Pow) Distributions: Equal (=); Less Than (<); Greater Than (>). National Interests (NI) for Ego, Alter: Sec = Secondary; Vit = Vital. Preference Rankings: 4 (highest)...1 (lowest). Nash equilibria are asterisked and Brams' equilibria are in bold. Dominant strategies are underlined. G-numbers for the two conflict games are from Brams (1994: 215–219). The TOM row indicates expected game outcomes using Brams' Theory of Moves solutions given beginning quadrant (Q) expressed as (Q,{Q, Q, Q}/O). MMe and MMa indicate the Moore machine codes for the Ego (row) and Alter (column) player, respectively, (0 = Cooperate and 1 = Conflict). The bit values indicate the player's move response while in a respective quadrant for each of four possible scenarios of prior moves used to reach this quadrant [0 1 2 3]. Underlined values in the Moore machine indicate "unexpected" Positions (Impossible Situations Following Strict TOM rules of play). For each strategy (S), separate Moore machine codes for the case for S(Ego) and S(Alter) must be generated, which are designated by the e or a character at the end of the strategy name – all of these are not shown

of some starting position and allow for sequential choice in response to the opposition's current "move." While the TOM approach is not without its detractors (Stone 2001), it remains attractive to international relations scholars because of its ability to incorporate power, reflect the sequential action of historical episodes, and provide solutions as nonmyopic equilibria without resorting to iterated game play (Brams 2001).

For purposes of the simulation, it would certainly be possible to establish a fixed, ordinal 2 × 2 payoff matrix and then instantiate adaptive agents who, through competition and selection, would eventually display nonmyopic strategic behavior (see Axelrod 1997, 2006). Bednar and Page (2007) have demonstrated that it may be possible to extend this adaptive model to a situation with more than a single fixed ordinal game (they use pairs of two games). However, even if we assumed status as initiator or move order was irrelevant (and could reduce the combinations by half), we would still be presented with 288 possible games. In this context, rather than develop adaptive or evolutionary dynamics, we opted to use simple but sophisticated agents with strategies deduced via TOM.

Solving a game using TOM requires adherence to a set of rules of play. Paraphrased they are (1) the game begins in some quadrant of the normal form depiction (the initial state), (2) the initiating player has the option of staying at the initial state or changing strategy to move to a new quadrant, (3) the responding player can likewise move, (4) players will not move from a state unless it will lead (eventually) to a more preferred outcome (backward induction), (5) these response opportunities alternate until the player whose turn it is move chooses not to move, or (6) play returns to the initial state. In this last situation, since the outcome of the game is an unending cycle, it is assumed that rational players would not repeat their actions interminably (presuming there are some nonzero costs to moving that are not explicitly modeled).

Two caveats to these rules are as follows: first, that should the initiating player choose not to move on the opening round, the opponent may "take precedence" and override the player that attempted to stay thereby initiating the game and, second, backtracking is not allowed and any move that would return the game to a previously occupied quadrant results in termination (Brams 1994, 21–28). The act of determining which of the sometimes-many, TOM-identified, "non-myopic equilibria" (NMEs) that will emerge as the solution for any particular game depends on the initial state of the game: the starting quadrant.

Figures 13.4 and 13.5 depict all of the potential NMEs for each game by highlighting the payoffs for those quadrants in bold type. Nash solutions are also indicated for comparison. Below each game is a list of starting quadrants and associated NME outcomes in italic text. For example, *(0, 2, 3/0) & (1/1)* indicates that for games that start in quadrant 0, 2, or 3, the expected final quadrant is 0 while for those that start in quadrant 1, the outcome is quadrant 1. The identification of these equilibria provides two important pieces of information about a subjective game. First, they indicate the outcome (final quadrant) that an actor anticipates a game to end in given a starting state. Second, the act of solving the games using TOM rules to arrive at these quadrants suggests the pattern of actions or moves that an agent would employ in response to starting a dyadic exchange in a particular quadrant.

Below the row of TOM outcome predictions, the two rows titled MMe and MMa depict the pattern of moves associated with the players that generate these expected outcomes. MM stands, in this case, for Moore machine (the "e" and "a" for Ego and Alter, respectively). The sets of 0s and 1s amount to the digital DNA sequence or operational code of a finite computational agent. Moore machines are means to represent simple automata that are commonly used in agent-based modeling environments. Each agent possesses a set of conditional states (S1, S2...Sn) with associated behaviors and transition rules that govern the shift from one state to another (Hopcroft and Ullman 1979). The numbers in brackets for each of the MMs in the figures define these states and movement propensities. At each state, the machine provides the information needed for the agent to act in the given situation and to direct the agent to its next state (which could be any other state in its repertoire).

Digit lists (or bit strings), such as those in Figures 13.4 and 13.5, are a common way to depict finite computational automata. Lists of 0s and 1s representing cooperate (CO) and conflict (CF) moves in a game-theoretic setting have an extensive history. Miller (1996), for example, uses this approach to explore iterated prisoner's dilemma games. He notes that the well-known reciprocating strategy Tit-For-Tat can be depicted using a simple two-state, two-rule automaton. Moore machines with limited states and rules (to which new ones cannot be added or removed) are called finite-state automata.

The 16-bit strings provided in the figures and which correspond to our subjective games are able to generate significantly more complicated behavior than a two-state, two-rule agent. Because we employ TOM solutions to define the agent's expectations and movement repertoires, it seems sensible to consider the position of the game (the quadrant) as the basic "state" condition for our automata. For each of the four quadrants, agents are also provided with a list of four possible behaviors, which correspond to the number of moves that have already transpired in the current history of this dyadic interaction. We limited the move history to four since no more than four moves can occur in a $2 \times 2$ game before the players have cycled back to the starting position. According to TOM, a return to the starting quadrant terminates the game. Importantly, the 16-bit strings define the entire "state space" (all state-move conditions) of the $2 \times 2$ strategic form game geometry according to TOM.

To understand how these automata work, consider the example of the Bandwagon player (BW) who perceives they are in a lesser power position (L) and with secondary interests (S) or BWSL in Figure 13.4a pitted against what that player perceives to be a Hegemon player with great power also with secondary interests (HESG). The agent has an MMe of [0100 0000 0000 0000]. The first four numbers define the CO, CF choices the player will make when in quadrant 0, the second four define these choices in quadrant 1, etc. for a given move count. The large number of 0s in this bit-string indicates that the player will choose to cooperate in almost every situation. If this player starts the game with the first move, he will choose 0 (CO) regardless of quadrant.

However, if the player finds himself in quadrant 0 and one move has already occurred, he will perform his single conflictual act by choosing to play CF and moving the game to quadrant 3. In this case, the agent is relying on the logic of TOM. Through backward induction, he has determined that the game must have started in Q1 and will end there. (He knows this because he has been asked to move in Q0 with one move already having been played). By moving the game to Q3, he can expect the column player to act rationally and shift to Q2. In Q2, with three moves having been made, he can play CO and terminate the game at Q1 (due to cycling). This happens to be his preferred outcome; one which could only be reached in these circumstances. Figure 13.6 provides a graphical depiction of the states and moves sequence associated with this Moore machine (Miller and Page 2007, 178–194).

In each of these dyadic pairings, our simulations follow the rules of play for the *TOM* developed by Brams (1994; see also Marfleet and Walker 2006). Because the nature of the TOM solutions can vary dramatically based upon starting position, we have explored four separate games with each one starting in a different quadrant. Beginning with Ego (the row player), each agent was sequentially prompted for a move (CO or CF) given the current quadrant occupied and the current move count

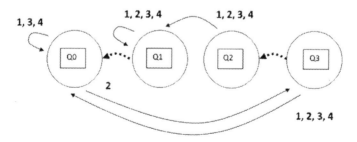

*Figure 13.6* Moore Machine Example Diagram for Bandwagon(BWSL) versus Hegemon (HESG)

Numbers in bold indicate move situation (first, second, etc.). Solid arrows indicate a move to new quadrant. Dashed arrows indicate the expected opponent moves based on TOM solutions given quadrant position and payoff. In the example provided the left, most dashed move is impossible as a 5th move if Q1 was the starting quadrant

| Subjective Game for HESG as Ego (row) | | | Objective Game | | | Subjective Game for BLVL as Alter (column) | | |
|---|---|---|---|---|---|---|---|---|
| | | | | CO | CF | | | |
| | CO | CF | CO | **4,3** | 1,1 | | CO | CF |
| CO | **4,3** | 1,1 | CF | 3,2 | **2,4** | CO | 3,3 | 1,1 |
| CF | 3,4 | 2,2 | | | | CF | 2,2 | **4,4** |

*Figure 13.7* An Example of the Intersection of Subjective Games

HESG player expects Q0 or Q3 outcome (bold) based on expectations of a BWSL opponent. BLVE player expects Q2 outcome (bold) based on BLVE opponent. The objective game reflects the blended payoffs of Ego and Alter but this structure is not known by either player. The objective game depicts the actual simulation outcomes (bold) based on the Moore machine–based play of each player (0, 3/2) & (1, 2/0). Two equilibrium points at Q0 and Q2 are identified

(counts were reset to zero for each new starting quadrant). The paired actors each executed their behavioral programs in accordance with the moves derived from its subjective game regardless. In each instance, neither player was informed of the actual game being played, which would be considered the "objective game" as defined by a fully informed third party with knowledge of each player's payoff structure. Figure 13.7 depicts how two subjective games interact to create a third, but unknown objective environment.

As noted above, the combinations of grand strategies and levels of national interest hypothetically allow for 576 possible subjective games. The matrix formed by this array is a 24-by-24 set of intersecting subjective games. Furthermore, since each of these intersections has one of four possible starting initial states, the total number of simulated games in our analysis could be as high as $24 \times 24 \times 4$ or 2304 games. To explore the question of how successful a balancing strategy is against other strategies and to identify the conditions under which it succeeds or fails compared to the other PIN alternatives of appeasement, bandwagoning, and hegemonic strategies, we simulate the possible interaction patterns and outcomes between all of the possible combinations of players. Because of the nature of these pairings, in some cases, agents will be pitted against symmetrically mirrored opponents (BWSL vs. HESG, or BLSE vs. BLSE, for example). Mostly, however, they will encounter players playing an unharmonious subjective game.

For each step of the simulation, one of the 24 PIN-identified GSOs with power and interest values was chosen to represent the Row Player in an upcoming encounter. To generate a TOM-based Moore machine for that player an "Expected Opponent" was selected based on information that could include knowing (1) only the opponents GSO, (2) GSO and Power, (3) GSO and Vital, or (4) GSO and Secondary interest orientation (a total of four information conditions). A particular opponent was then randomly selected across the unknowns. For example, if an

1. Establish initial set of players with payoffs
2. Set information rules
3. For each GSO (BWSL, BWVL …. HEVG):
    a. Select an Actual Opponent (AO)
    b. Given known information (P? V? S?) supplement with random selection to identify an Expected Opponent (EO).
    c. Resolve TOM solution to games based on GSO – EO preferences
    d. Remember play sequence strings [01001....]
    e. Record expected outcome (quadrant) for each starting quadrant with EO
    f. Complete steps b to d for AO also
    g. For each of 4 starting quadrants
        i. Solve the GSO-AO game using TOM solutions
        ii. Record outcome score and quadrants for that GSO-AO pair
    h. Repeat steps a to g 100 times
4. Report data for all possible 576 dyadic pairings
5. Return to step 1 and repeat for remaining information environments

*Figure 13.8* Basic Model Sequence

Appease GSO with equal power and vital interests (APVE) knew that it would encounter a Hegemon (and knew nothing more than the opponent's broad role category of HE, i.e., nothing about power or interests), then it would prepare by choosing an expected (HE) opponent randomly from among the three power conditions (Less than, Equal to, or Greater than itself) and National interest options (Vital or Secondary). Because of this random element, the results of the simulations are not strictly determined.

Having selected an expected opponent, the Row Player resolves its TOM solution for their interaction, which would serve as the behavior repertoire for a contest with the "Actual Opponent" (also a randomly chosen HE player in this case). The Actual Opponent (or Column Player) was similarly prepared. Row Player and Column player were then interacted 4 times (once for each possible starting quadrant) and the outcomes recorded. This sequence was repeated 100 times for each GSO and the entire simulation re-initialized under new information rules. A complete simulation therefore generated the outcomes of 24 × 24 × 100 × 4 or 230,400 games. An outline of the steps in these procedures is in Figure 13.8.

## Results

Table 13.1 provides summary statistics drawn from the same data as the grayscale heat maps in the Appendix. Scores for this table were aggregated by broad GSO grouping rather than by the specific dyads. A more fine-grained result is shown in those grayscale heat maps in the Appendix. All scores were generated following the basic simulation sequence outlined in Figure 13.8. For each of the 100 interactions per GSO pairing in a simulation, the individual game payoffs (integer values from 1 to 4) were recorded and compared with the expected payoff that the GSO would have received from the expected opponent used to generate the TOM move solution ($P_{diff} = P_{actual} - P_{expected}$) with positive values representing better than expected performance and negative scores arising from a poorer than expected payoff.

In addition to this difference, raw total scores were also summed across all interactions. Rather than report the score values themselves (the magnitude of which would be dependent on the number of iterations used per simulation), we report the relative performance using standardized scores with mean and variance values from the population of all GSOs across all simulations (N = 230,400 game outcomes). The reported scores represent the z-score values (standard deviation differences) from the population means. Scores above two represent significant differences at the 95% confidence level. We also report the mean payoffs for each GSO grouping (BW, BL, AP, HE) in Table 13.1.

The table reveals several patterns. Balancing strategies perform well overall in three of the four information conditions. The results in the first three columns of Table 13.1 show that the balancing approach consistently generated higher performance scores than bandwagoning or hegemonic strategies, which underperformed relative to expectations. Both balancing and appeasement strategies significantly overperformed relative to expectations with the balancing scores being consistently higher than the appeasement scores in three of the four information conditions.

In absolute payoff terms, the balancing approach also performed well. The results in the last four columns of Table 13.1 show that the balancing scores were significantly higher than the bandwagoning and hegemonic scores in absolute payoff terms but not significantly different than scores for the appeasement strategies in three of the four information conditions. The exceptions to this pattern are notable. In situations where opponents have vital interests at stake, the balancing approach performed poorly and was eclipsed by the appeasement strategy in terms of both absolute performance and performance relative to expectations. This result is almost entirely the result of a devastatingly poor performance versus Hegemon GSOs as revealed by the dark swath of gray shown on the right side of Figure 13.12 heat map in the Appendix.

To some degree, this deficit was offset by the balancing GSO's success in the secondary interest domain where it was the only strategy to yield results both above expectations and with the highest absolute scores. Again, the heat map figure bears out this pattern, showing generally very light grayscale regions in Figure 13.14 in the Appendix where payoffs versus Hegemon players are depicted. Taken together,

Table 13.1 Relative (Actual – Expected) and Absolute Payoffs for Grand Strategies Under Four Information Conditions

| Strategy | Mean Relative[a] Payoff (Standardized) | Mean Relative[a] Payoff per Interaction | Significant Relative[a] Payoff Difference between Strategy and Balancing (t-Test, p 0.05) | Mean Absolute Payoff (Standardized) | Mean Absolute Payoff | Mean Absolute Payoff per Interaction | Significant Absolute Difference between Strategy and Balancing (t-Test, p 0.05) |
|---|---|---|---|---|---|---|---|
| *Players with GSO Information Only* | | | | | | | |
| Bandwagon | -0.207 | -0.153 | Yes | -0.085 | 1278.285 | 3.196 | Yes |
| Appease | 0.174 | -0.039 | Yes | 0.085 | 1317.021 | 3.293 | No |
| Balance | 0.197 | -0.032 | n/a | 0.066 | 1312.569 | 3.281 | n/a |
| Hegemon | -0.164 | -0.14 | Yes | -0.066 | 1282.729 | 3.207 | Yes |
| *Players with GSO and Power Information* | | | | | | | |
| Bandwagon | -0.167 | -0.173 | Yes | -0.08 | 1283.882 | 3.21 | Yes |
| Appease | 0.131 | -0.037 | Yes | 0.076 | 1319.889 | 3.3 | No |
| Balance | 0.154 | -0.026 | n/a | 0.047 | 1313.097 | 3.283 | n/a |
| Hegemon | -0.118 | -0.151 | Yes | -0.044 | 1292.174 | 3.23 | Yes |
| *Players with GSO and Vital Interest Information* | | | | | | | |
| Bandwagon | -0.522 | -0.274 | Yes | -0.101 | 1273.618 | 3.184 | Yes |
| Appease | 0.456 | 0.07 | Yes | 0.091 | 1318.111 | 3.295 | Yes |
| Balance | -0.135 | -0.138 | n/a | 0.045 | 1307.313 | 3.268 | n/a |
| Hegemon | 0.201 | -0.02 | Yes | -0.035 | 1288.826 | 3.222 | Yes |
| *Players with GSO and Secondary Interest Information* | | | | | | | |
| Bandwagon | 0.19 | -0.032 | Yes | -0.06 | 1284.569 | 3.211 | Yes |
| Appease | -0.198 | -0.164 | Yes | 0.065 | 1313.278 | 3.283 | No |
| Balance | 0.483 | 0.068 | n/a | 0.078 | 1316.271 | 3.291 | n/a |
| Hegemon | -0.475 | -0.259 | Yes | -0.084 | 1279.09 | 3.198 | Yes |

Note:

a    Relative in this case means relative to expectations set through play with expected opponent. Relative performance compared to other GSO can be inferred by comparisons in this table.

the results suggest a pitfall for balancing strategies with regard to hegemonic powers. Failure to gauge whether secondary or vital interests are at stake can strongly affect the results of a dyadic exchange between these GSOs.

The grayscale heat maps in the Appendix reveal a number of patterns regarding dyadic pairings. On the macroscale, a general (but far from perfect) pattern of symmetry seems apparent based on the natural pairings of GSOs. Bandwagoners tend to perform well when paired with Hegemons, likewise for Appeasers with other Appeasers and Balancers with other Balancers. More relevant to our focus on balancing, all of the heat maps display the strong performance that balancers seem to enjoy when matched with other balancers. This holds across the figures in terms of both absolute performance and performance relative to expectations. Interestingly, the same holds true for some of the competing GSOs, particularly the Appease GSO. The explanation for this pattern is that both players rank the same outcome highest.

However, the performance of these pairings does seem to vary under different information conditions. For example, the bottom left and top right corners of the heat maps in the Appendix indicate the results of the Bandwagon and Hegemon player interactions. These figures depicting relative payoffs show substantial amounts of darker shading (indicating results below expectations) while the figures with absolute payoffs show generally lighter (and therefore higher) absolute payoffs. These results suggest that the dyad performs comparatively well but perhaps not at a satisfying level for the actors involved.

## Conclusion

At the outset of this study, we reiterated questions concerning the empirical frequency and effectiveness of balancing strategies raised by prior research in the field. Using the core international relations concepts of power, national interests, and identity – drawn from realist, liberal, and constructivist theory – we developed the PIN model as a logical system of preference orderings that represent the full range of possible GSOs for dyadic actors in the global system. Then we compared the performance of these GSOs through simulations. The results are consistent with, and provide explanatory backing for, the findings of Wohlforth et al. (2007) that balancing behavior is relatively rare as the modal behavior of states and that it often fails to prevent systemic hegemony by a predominant state.

Our modeling suggests that, despite its overall success, balancing performs poorly when (systemic) dyadic conditions are most intense – when vital interests are at stake. Analysis of the foundations of this pattern reveals that the main failing of balancing strategies is evinced in dyadic pairings against states pursuing hegemonic strategies. If history suggests that balancing approaches seem inadequate to prevent hegemonic or unipolar systems from emerging, it may well result from patterns of dyadic domination by hegemons advancing vital interests.

The tradeoff for balancing's weakness – its strong performance in secondary interest environments where defending the status quo is tenable – seems insufficient compensation for its shortcomings. Our results show that in three of the four information-poor environments, balancing strategies perform no better than appeasement strategies, which is actually the superior strategy in the fourth information-poor environment of high-intensity, vital interest circumstances. The relative historical rarity of balancing reported by Wohlforth et al. (2007), therefore, appears to be explicable when alternative strategies exist that are its equal under most conditions and are better under the worst circumstances.

Of course, the results of this study may be limited by our focus on dyadic exchanges and on the round-robin-tournament style of our dyadic pairings. Things might turn out differently in a more complicated environment. For example, we might find that balancing agents thrive if we take the interacting group only one step further toward triads (Maoz et al 2007). Alternatively, we could abandon the tournament style of model, where every pair is matched once, in favor of a representative population of simulated agents who are seeded into the system according to their empirical frequency in some historical context, e.g., simulating the GSO arrangements of pre–World War I Europe (Axelrod and Bennett 2007). In a world where hegemons are rare, or third parties matter, balancers might dominate.

## Appendix: Grayscale Maps of Simulation Results

Figures 13.9–13.16 depict Row Player GSO dyadic performance across the range of information conditions using heat maps. The grayscale heat maps depict performance relative to expected outcomes and absolute performance based on the average total payoff accumulated through all simulations conducted under the information rules. The names of the GSOs extend in the following order along the left side and top row of each heat map: bandwagoning, appeasement, balancing, and hegemony. For Figures 13.9, 13.11, 13.13, and 13.15, lighter shaded cells indicate that the Row Player's relative score (outcomes compared to expectations) were above the population average. Darker cells indicate below-average values. For Figures 13.10, 13.12, 13.14, and 13.16, the heat maps display absolute performance compared to the population mean. Again, scores were standardized and dark or light shading indicates performances above or below the mean. Numerical values representing standardized z-scores appear at the bottom right of each cell.

*Figure 13.9* Heat Map for Interactions with GSO Information Only and Standardized Actual versus Expected Payoffs

Darker = lower and lighter = higher than anticipated differences for Ego

*Figure 13.10* Heat Map for Interactions with GSO Information Only, Standardized Actual Payoffs

Darker = lower and lighter = higher absolute results for Ego

*Figure 13.11* Heat Map for Interactions w. GSO & Power Information, Standardized
     Actual versus Expected Payoff

Darker = lower and lighter = higher than anticipated differences for Ego

*Figure 13.12* Heat Map for Interactions With GSO and Power Information, Standardized Actual Payoffs

Darker = lower and lighter = higher absolute results for Ego

*Figure 13.13*  Heat Map for Interactions with GSO and Vital Interest Information, Standardized Actual versus Expected Payoffs

Darker = lower and lighter = higher than anticipated differences for Ego

*Figure 13.14* Heat Map for Interactions with GSO and Vital Interest Information, Standardized Actual Payoffs

Darker = lower and lighter = higher absolute results for Ego

*Figure 13.15* Heat Map for Interactions with GSO and Secondary Interest
   Information, Standardized Actual versus Expected Payoffs

Darker = lower and lighter = higher than anticipated differences for Ego

*Figure 13.16* Heat Map for Interactions with GSO and Secondary Interest Information, Standardized Actual Payoffs

Darker = lower and lighter = higher absolute results for Ego

# References

Axelrod, R. 2006. *The evolution of cooperation*. Rev. Edition. New York, NY: Basic Books.

Axelrod, R. and S. Bennett. 2007. A landscape theory of aggregation. *British Journal of Political Science* 23: 211–233.

Axelrod, R. 1997. *The complexity of cooperation: Agent-based models of competition and collaboration*. Princeton, NJ: Princeton University Press.

Bednar, J., S. Page. 2007. Can game(s) theory explain culture? The emergence of cultural behavior within multiple games. *Rationality and Society* 19(1): 65–97.

Brams, S. 1994. *Theory of moves*. Cambridge: Cambridge University Press.

Brams, S. 2001. Response to Randall Stone: Heresy or scientific progress. *Journal of Conflict Resolution* 45(2): 245–254.

Bueno de Mesquita, B., R. McDermott. 2004. Crossing no man's land. *Political Psychology* 25: 275–287.

Cioffi-Revilla, C. 1998. *Politics and uncertainty*. Cambridge: Cambridge University Press.

Eilstrup-Sangiovanni, M. 2009. The end of balance-of-power theory? *European Journal of International Relations* 15: 347–380.

Goforth, D., D. Robinson. 2005. *Topology of 2×2 games*. New York, NY: Routledge.

Holsti, K. 1970. National role conceptions in the study of foreign policy. *International Studies Quarterly* 14: 233–309.

Hopcroft, J., J. Ullman. 1979. *An introduction to automata theory, languages and computation*. Reading: Addison-Wesley.

Jervis, R. 1976. *Perception and misperception in international politics*. Princeton, NJ: Princeton University Press.

Jervis, R. 1997. *System effects*. Princeton, NJ: Princeton University Press.

Kaufman, S., R. Little, W. Wohlforth. 2007. *The balance of power in world history*. New York, NY: Palgrave Macmillan.

Kydd, A. 2005. *Trust and mistrust in international relations*. Princeton, NJ: Princeton University Press.

Lake, D., R. Powell. 1999. *Strategic choice and international relations*. Princeton, NJ: Princeton University Press.

Lau, R. 2003. Models of decision-making. In *Oxford handbook of political psychology*, eds. D. Sears, L. Huddy, R. Jervis, 19–59. New York, NY: Oxford University Press.

Lobell, S., N. Ripsman, J. Taliaferro. 2009. *Neoclassical realism, the state, and foreign policy*. Cambridge: Cambridge University Press.

Malici, A., S. Walker. 2017. *Role theory and role conflict in U.S.-Iran relations*. New York, NY: Routledge.

Maoz, Z., A. Astorino. 1992. Waging war, waging peace: Decision making and bargaining in the Arab-Israeli conflict, 1970–1973. *International Studies Quarterly* 36: 373–399.

Maoz, Z., L. Terris, R. Kuperman, I. Talmud. 2007. What is the enemy of my enemy? Causes and consequences of imbalanced international relations, 1816–2001. *The Journal of Politics* 69: 100–115.

Marfleet, B. G., S. Walker. 2006. A world of beliefs: In *Beliefs and leadership in world politics: Methods and applications of operational code analysis*, eds. M. Schafer, S. Walker, 53–76. New York, NY: Palgrave Macmillan.

Miller, J. 1996. The coevolution of automata in the repeated prisoner's dilemma. *Journal of Economic Behavior and Organization* 29: 87–112.

Miller, J., S. Page. 2007. *Complex adaptive systems*. Princeton, NJ: Princeton University Press.

Guyer, M., A. Rapoport. 1966. A taxonomy of 2 × 2 games. *General Systems* 11: 203–214.

Schafer, M., S. Crichlow. 2010. *Groupthink vs. high-quality decision making in international relations*. New York, NY: Columbia University Press.

Snyder, G. and P. Diesing. 1977. *Conflict among nations*. Princeton, NJ: Princeton University Press.

Stone, R. 2001. The use and abuse of game theory in international relations: The theory of moves. *Journal of Conflict Resolution* 45(2): 216–244.

Steinbrunner, J. 1974. *The cybernetic theory of decision*. Princeton, NJ: Princeton University Press.

Thucydides. 1910. *The Peloponnesian wars*, trans. R. Crawley. London: J. Dent. New York, NY: E.P. Dutton.

Vasquez, J., C. Elman. 2003. *Realism and the balancing of power*. Upper Saddle River, NJ: Prentice-Hall.

Vertzberger, Y. 1990. *The world in their minds*. Stanford: Stanford University Press.

Walker, S. 1987. *Role Theory and Foreign Policy Analysis*. Durham, NC: Duke University Press.

Walker, S. 2002. Beliefs and foreign policy analysis in the new millennium. In *Conflict, security, foreign policy, and international political economy*, eds. M. Brecher, F. Harvey, 56–71. Ann Arbor, MI: University of Michigan Press.

Walker, S. 2007. Generalizing about security strategies in the Baltic sea region. In *Power Disparity, Identity, and Cooperative Security in the Politics of the Baltic Region*, ed. O. Knudsen, 149-176. Burlington, VT: Ashgate.

Walker, S. 2011a. Binary role theory: Reducing uncertainty and managing complexity in foreign policy analysis. In *Rethinking foreign policy analysis*, eds. S. Walker, A. Malici, M. Schafer, 245–266. New York, NY: Routledge.

Walker, S. 2011b. The integration of foreign policy analysis and international relations. In *Rethinking foreign policy analysis*, eds. S. Walker, A. Malici, M. Schafer, 267–282. New York, NY: Routledge.

Walker, S. 2013. *Role theory and the cognitive architecture of British appeasement decisions*. New York, NY: Routledge.

Walker, S., A. Malici. 2011. *U.S. Presidents and foreign policy mistakes*. Stanford: Stanford University Press.

Walker, S., B. G. Marfleet. 2012. Binary role theory and grand strategies." Presented at the Annual Meeting of the International Studies Association Meeting, San Diego, CA.

Walker, S., A. Malici, M. Schafer. 2011. *Rethinking foreign policy analysis*. New York, NY: Routledge.

Waltz, K. 1979. Theory of international politics. Reading, MA: Addison-Wesley.

Wohlforth, W., R. Little, S. Kaufman, D. Kang, C. Jones, V. Tin-Bor Hui, A. Eckstein, D. Deudney, W. Brenner. 2007. Testing balance-of-power theory in world history. *European Journal of International Relations* 13: 155–185.

Wohlforth, W., R. Little, S. Kaufman, D. Kang, C. Jones, V. Tin-Bor Hui, A. Eckstein, D. Deudney, W. Brenner. 2009. The comedy of errors? A reply to Mette Eilstrup-Sangiovanni. *European Journal of International Relations* 15: 381–388.

# 14 Operational Code Analysis

## A Method for Measuring Strategic Culture

*Seyed Hamidreza Serri*

## Introduction

International politics involves high-stake games with multiple historical, economic, cultural, societal, military, and psychological variables that interact with each other at all levels of analysis. When game theory was introduced to bring some order to this complexity, improve decision-making, and reduce mistakes, Snyder (1977) criticized game theory as too general and abstract, arguing that one should also include the strategic cultures of actors. Johnston (1995) subsequently argued that any strategic culture should have a Central paradigm and an Operational paradigm. The Central paradigm has assertions about the nature of the adversary, the role of war in human life, and the usefulness of force. The Operational paradigm shows actors' ranked preferences for strategic options. Johnston also suggested that, ideally, strategic cultures should be extracted across time and actors. To achieve this goal, he identified two content analysis methods for discerning strategic cultures: cognitive mapping and symbol analysis.

In this chapter, I argue that the combination of targeted Operational Code Analysis and the Theory of Inferences about Preferences (TIP) provides a capable and agile alternative for extracting paradigms in strategic cultures (Schafer and Walker 2006; Walker, Malici, and Schafer 2011). Operational Code Analysis has specific indices for the nature of the world and the usefulness of cooperative and conflictual means. On the other hand, TIP extracts agents' ranked preferences for political outcomes. Using the rules of sequential game theory, the combination of operational code analysis and TIP also provides the necessary tools to extract an actor's subjective games for Self and Other across time and space. The case study in this chapter applies these methods to map the strategic cultures of Iran and the United States and their impact on US-Iran relations based on media coverage of Iran's nuclear program between 1989 and 2018.

## Strategic Culture

In research for the RAND Corporation, Snyder (1977) investigated the Soviet Union's possible reactions to a limited nuclear war. He criticized game theory's assumption that weapons of mass destruction dictate their logic and that a generic reasonable man understands the principles of nuclear deterrence (Schelling 1958). He argued that a culture-free game theory alone was not enough to predict the actions of the Soviet Union. According to Snyder, the United States and the Soviet Union had different approaches to nuclear wars, because organizational socialization and past experiences created unique perspectives for actors. To elaborate this difference between the United States and the Soviet Union, Snyder introduced the concept of strategic culture and defined it as "the body of attitudes and beliefs that guides and circumscribes thought on strategic questions, influences the way strategic issues are formulated, and sets the vocabulary and conceptual parameters of strategic debate." According to Snyder, strategic culture is the "sum total of ideas, conditioned emotional responses, and patterns of habitual behavior that members of a national strategic community have acquired through instruction or imitation and share with each other..." (Snyder 1977, 8–9).

After the introduction of strategic culture, the concept attracted the attention of many scholars. Johnston divides this scholarship into three generations (1995, 36–43). During the early 1980s, the first generation inspired by Snyder tried to explain the difference between the Soviet and American nuclear strategies based on macro-level factors such as geography, historical experiences, and political culture. Like Snyder, Gray (1981) believed that the United States and the Soviet Union did not have the same nuclear strategies. He argued that the decision-makers in the United States are constrained by a unique strategic culture that acts as a milieu for strategic and defense-related decisions and discussions. He also went further and claimed that the American strategic culture, which is part of the American national style, can not only explain past decisions but also predict US behavior.

Gray defined strategic culture as "modes of thought and action with respect to force, derives from the perception of the national historical experience, aspiration for self-characterization... and from all of the many distinctively American experiences... that characterize an American citizen" (Gray 1981, 22). American military experience from the Seven Years' War through to 1945 yielded some dominant national beliefs. First, the United States believes that it only fights wars for good causes. Second, Americans believe that they could reach any goals that they try for. Third, Americans think that they have unlimited power. And fourth, Americans believe that they could overwhelm any enemy with their power. Gray concluded that because of this strategic culture, the United States has had difficulty thinking strategically about nuclear wars (Gray 1981).

In another first-generation study, David Jones discussed how strategic culture takes shape. He argued that strategic culture impacts all levels of decision-making, even the tactical level. Three types of factors shape strategic culture. At the highest level (macro-level), strategic culture is shaped by history, geography, and cultural factors. In the middle level (societal level), political structure, and economic factors shape the strategic culture. And at the lowest level (micro-level) are organizational cultures and civil-military relations (Johnston 1995, 37). Starting in the mid-1980s, the second generation of strategic culture studies focused on the relationship between strategic culture and behavior.

According to the second generation of scholarship, the primary function of strategic culture is not shaping the behavior but providing cultural justification for states' actions. Strategic culture defines the boundaries of the legitimate use of violence, which serve interests that are not always mentioned in the declaratory policies. A strategic culture enables discourses that support those interests and silences the ones that do not. While there might be seemingly different strategic cultures, they all support the same interests in reality. For instance, the United States and the Soviet Union's seemingly different strategic cultures were designed to support their hegemonic interests (Johnston 1995, 39).

The third generation of strategic culture, which emerged in the 1990s, focused on cases where structural-materialist notions of interest could not explain a particular strategic choice. For instance, Johnston studied Chinese strategic culture. He argued that China has two strategic cultures. One Chinese strategic culture supports a cooperative approach in dealing with external threats. The other assumes that conflict is an endemic part of the interactions among states. Therefore, the use or threat of violence is the appropriate approach in dealing with threats. According to Johnston, the second Chinese strategic culture is the dominant one (Johnston 1998).

Beyond Johnston's three generations of strategic culture, a fourth generation is recently taking shape. While Snyder spoke about subcultures in his 1977 research, it was not until recently that scholars have focused on the study of strategic subcultures. The fourth-generation scholars argue that strategic culture consists of subcultures that compete with each other for hegemony among the custodians of a strategic culture. As a result, the fourth generation argues that there are ranges of strategic cultures and not one. Libel's (2016) study of changes in Israeli strategic culture is an example of the fourth generation of scholarship. He tried to answer when, how, and why Israeli security policies shifted from the early 1980s to 2014 (Libel 2016).

Despite all the interest in strategic culture, there is no agreement on strategic culture's definition, desired function, scope, sources, custodians, and methodology. However, this ambiguity should not discourage scholarship and research because (1) strategic culture is a relatively new concept in security studies, and (2) this ambiguity is not particular to strategic culture, as many concepts in politics and international relations suffer from this lack of clarity (Haglund 2004). To address these problems, Johnston (1995, 45) argues that an appropriate definition of strategic culture should be falsifiable (or at least distinguishes strategic culture variables from non-strategic culture variables) and provide empirical predictions that can be compared to other models.

Further, it should have "empirical referents (e.g., symbols and ranked preferences) which can be observed in strategic culture objects (e.g., texts, documents, doctrines); and its evolution (even dissolution) over time can be traced, as long as the [sic] one can observe whether successive generations of decision-makers are socialized in and share the basic precepts of the strategic culture." Strategic culture should also be able to provide "specific predictions about strategic choice" (Johnston 1995, 49). To achieve these goals, Johnston argues that any strategic culture should have a Central paradigm and an Operational paradigm.

The Central paradigm of strategic culture is about (1) "nature of the adversary"; (2) the "orderliness of the strategic environment"; (3) the "role of war in human affairs" and whether war is an aberration or inevitable; and (4) "efficacy of the use of force." The Central paradigm of the strategic culture is the result of historical experiences, and its primary function is to reduce "uncertainty about the strategic environment." The second part of strategic culture, the Operational paradigm, clarifies ranked preferences for strategic options. This feature is where strategic culture affects behavioral choices (Johnston 1995, 46–49). However, Gray (1999) argues that Johnston's approach to strategic culture has several errors.

According to Gray, Johnston is wrong to assume that a proper theory of strategic culture should distinguish culture from behavior. He treats strategic culture "as being 'out there' as a rich and distilled source of influence which might 'cause' behaviour." Gray, on the other hand, prefers to "regard strategic culture as being in good measure socially constructed by both people and institutions, which proceed to behave to some degree culturally." Strategic culture does not cause behavior; instead, it provides context for understanding actors' behavior and works as a guide to strategic action. Gray's main criticism is that Johnston reduces strategic culture to what can be observed in actors' behavior. Gray argues that Germans are Germans even if the theory does not fit their behavior: "In their strategic behaviour, Germans cannot help but behave except under the constraints of Germanic strategic culture, even when they are unable to adhere strictly to the dominant ideas and preferences of their strategic culture" (Gray 1999, 50–52).

## Operational Code Analysis

Despite the philosophical differences between Gray and Johnston, both would agree that the strategic culture scholarship would be a more robust research program if it finds more specific patterns. Neither of them would disregard specific and nuanced observations of actors. When it comes to theoretical specificity, Johnston's articulation of strategic culture specifies having a Central paradigm and an Operational paradigm to be specific and, therefore, analytically useful. The question is, how can one discern these two paradigms in a strategic culture? Johnston suggests the two content analysis methods of cognitive mapping and symbol analysis. However, targeted operational code analysis employing the TIP provides a capable and agile alternative for extracting the paradigms of strategic culture.

Schafer and Walker (2006) talk about the origins of operational code analysis, its central questions, and methodologies. The main goal of operational code analysis, invented by Leites (1951, 1953), was to show how beliefs shape actors' views of the world and their strategy. Strategic culture seeks to know how historical experiences and organizational identities affect an actor's use of force. George's questions for operational code analysis can illustrate the connection between the two research programs. Answers to the first set of philosophical (P) questions reveal an actor's beliefs about the strategic environment and the second set of instrumental (I) questions identify beliefs about how agents prefer to act in a strategic environment (George 1969, 201–216):

Philosophical Questions

P-1: What is the "essential" nature of political life? Is the political universe essentially one of harmony or conflict? What is the fundamental character of one's political opponents?

P-2: What are the prospects for the eventual realization of one's fundamental political values and aspirations? Can one be optimistic, or must one be pessimistic on this score; and in what respects the one and/or the other?

P-3: Is the political future predictable? In what sense and to what extent?

P-4: How much "control" or "mastery" can one have over historical development? What is one's role in "moving" and "shaping" history in the desired direction?

P-5: What is the role of "chance" in human affairs and in historical development?

Instrumental Questions

I-1: What is the best approach for selecting goals or objectives for political action?

I-2: How are the goals of action pursued most effectively?

I-3: How are the risks of political action calculated, controlled, and accepted?

I-4: What is the best "timing" of action to advance one's interest?

I-5: What is the utility and role of different means for advancing one's interest?

One can choose qualitative or quantitative methods to answer these questions. The method in this chapter uses the automated quantitative method of Verbs in Context System (VICS), which was introduced by Walker, Schafer, and Young (1998). VICS answers George's questions by using a computer software program (Profiler Plus) and a dictionary of transitive verbs describing the exercise of social power to extract those verbs attributed to Self and Other from a text (Young 2001; Schafer and Walker 2006).

Johnston argued that any strategic culture should have Central and Operational paradigms. The Central paradigm shows the orderliness of the strategic environment, the role of war in human affairs, and whether war is an aberration or inevitable. It also should clarify what actors think about the nature of the adversary and the efficacy of the use of force. As the operational code indices indicate, there are specific counterparts for each of the sections in Johnston's Central paradigm. The I-1, I-2, and I-4a beliefs address *the role of war* in human affairs. The I-1 index shows the overall direction of the actors' strategy and whether they are inclined to adopt conflictual or cooperative strategies. The I-2 index shows the tactical preferences of actors regarding levels of cooperative and conflictual behavior. The I-4a index measures how flexible actors are in their choice of cooperative and conflictual tactics. The flexibility of tactics can show whether conflict is an aberration or inevitable from an actor's perspective. Less flexible, conflictual tactics indicate that actors look at conflict as inevitable. On the other hand, flexible conflictual tactics indicate that actors look at conflict as an aberration and are open to choosing nonconflictual tactics to advance their interests.

The P-1 index can show the actor's perception of *the nature of the adversary*. This is especially true when one uses targeted operational code analysis. General operational code analysis answers the philosophical questions by considering all non-self Others. Targeted operational code analysis reflects attributes of a particular Other in answering P questions. For instance, the US P-1 index scores for the case study in this chapter show how the United States thinks about the nature of Iran's actions toward the United States. Similarly, Iran's P-1 indices present Iranian perceptions about the nature of the US actions toward Iran.

The last segment of Johnston's Central paradigm, *the efficacy of force*, can be shown via operational code I-5 indices. The I-5 indices present the utility of means in each strategic culture. In contrast to other studies in strategic culture, the operational code does not only show the inclination for conflictual and cooperative means. The I-5 indices show an actor's inclination for ranges of actions with different intensities. There are three categories for cooperative actions: Appeal/Support (+1), Promise (+2), and Reward (+3), with reward having the highest cooperative intensity and Appeal/Support having the lowest. The conflictual indices are the utility of Oppose/Resist (–1), Threaten (–2), and Punish (–3), which also range from the lowest to the highest intensity of conflict.[1]

### Theory of Inferences about Preferences (TIP)

Johnston also argues that any strategic culture should show the ranked preferences of actors for strategic options. TIP extracts the ranked preferences of Self and Other from operational code beliefs (Schafer and Walker 2006). It assumes that any actor can choose from four possible outcomes in interactions with others: Submit, Settle, Deadlock, and Dominate. The first two outcomes (Submit, Settle) are cooperative outcomes with Submit being the most cooperative. Deadlock and Dominate are conflictual outcomes, with Dominate being the most conflictual. TIP extracts the preferences for these conflictual and cooperative outcomes based on three sets of variables.

The first category of variables maps the relative cooperative and conflictual tendencies of Self and Other using (I-1, P-4a) and (P-1, P-4b) pairs of beliefs. The (I-1, P-4a) pair locates the Self's and (P-1, P-4b) locates the Other's preferences for a cooperation or conflict strategy. To standardize these four indices, their deviation from a norming group is calculated: $zI-1$, $zP-4a$ (zP4Self), $zP-1$, and $zP-4b$ (zP4Other). Next, TIP considers the power distribution (symmetrical or asymmetrical) between Self and Other. The third set of variables is the importance of the issue (vital or secondary interests) to Self and Other. Together these three sets of variables create 24 possible rankings for the four outcomes of Submit, Settle, Dominate, and Deadlock. These 24 possible rankings can be grouped into four families of roles based on their highest ranking preference for Submit, Settle, Deadlock, or Dominate as an outcome of the strategic interactions between Self and Other (Malici and Walker 2017).

If an actor as Ego sees its role as a Friend of the Other as Alter, then it chooses Submit {E,A: +,–} as its highest ranked outcome. Even in the face of negative actions by Alter, Ego as a Friend will still cooperate. A Friend follows the Bandwagoning strategy. If Ego sees itself as a Partner of the Alter, then it chooses Settle {E,A: +,+} as its highest ranked outcome. A Partner reciprocates cooperation with the cooperation and follows the strategy of Appeasement. If Ego defines the role of Rival for itself, then it chooses Deadlock {E,A: –, –} as its highest ranked option. An actor with the Rival role answers conflict with conflict and follows a Balancing strategy. If an actor defines an Ego-Alter relationship based on enmity, then Domination {E,A: –, +} will be its highest ranked option. An actor with the Enemy role answers cooperation with conflict and follows a hegemonic strategy (Malici and Walker 2017).

After selecting the most preferred outcome, an actor ranks the second, third, and fourth preferred strategies based on its power and whether its vital interests or its secondary interests are at stake. The convention is to treat one standard deviation from the norming group as the threshold for determining whether an actor's strategy ($zI-1$) and view of nature of the other ($zP-1$) is very cooperative or very conflictual. The same standard is used for historical control by Self (zP-4a) and historical control by Other (zP-4b). The literature treats the power of actors as equal when the indices for control of history (zP-4a, zP-4b) are within one standard deviation of the norming group. Therefore, a level of control (zP-4a, zP-4b) of –.8 deviation and +.8 deviation are treated as similar, and the power of the actors as equal.

In this chapter, I argue that, considering the level of sensitivity of VICS, the direction of deviations of zP-4a and zP-4b as less or equal to 1 or bigger or equal to –1 presents valuable information for identifying aspects of strategic culture. Therefore, instead of the three power levels of Weak, Equal, and Strong that the operational code literature uses, this chapter employs as descriptors the four power levels of Very Weak, Weak, Strong, and Very Strong. For instance, in the operational code literature, the power roles of a Friend can be described as a Weak Friend, Equal Friend, or Strong Friend. In this chapter the descriptors of the power roles for a Friend are Very Weak Friend, Weak Friend, Strong Friend, and Very Strong Friend. The naming conventions in this chapter, however, do not change the subsequent use of the ranked preferences specified by TIP for inferring the ranked preferences for the different outcomes associated with the original three levels (Weak, Equal, Strong) of each power role (Friend, Partner, Rival, Enemy).

## Measuring Strategic Cultures

For three reasons, I chose the news coverage of Iran's nuclear program as the data for extracting United States and Iran's strategic cultures toward each other: (1) it focused on a critical issue in Iran-US relations; (2) because of the availability of data; and (3) in this chapter it is an assumption that discussions in the media are extensions of debates in official remarks, white papers, and publications by think tanks. In turn, these debates reflect important aspects of the Central and Operational paradigms of US and Iranian strategic culture. The data in this chapter are from all the available news coverage from 1989 through the first 2 months of 2018 in the LexisNexis database about Iran's nuclear program.

All the news with the term "Iran nuclear program" in the headline or the first paragraph was chosen. In all, a total of 34,450 pieces of news were gathered. The sentences with transitive verbs were extracted using the Profiler Plus software. A total of 698,515 iterations of transitive verbs were identified and coded by the software. The subjects and objects referring to Iran and the United States were grouped under the two labels of Iran and USA. For instance, the words, *Iran, Tehran, Ahmadinejad,* and *Khatami* were all grouped under the general heading of *Iran.* The words *United States, Washington, White House, Obama, and Trump* were tagged as *USA.* Finally, only sentences with Iran as their subjects and their objects as USA or sentences with USA as their subjects and Iran as their objects were selected, which yielded a total of 5994 sentences for analysis.

In the next step, the publications of countries that have been closely involved in the Iran nuclear issue were identified: Iran, Israel, China, Russia, and the USA. The rest of the publications were grouped under the three sources of the Arab World,[2] the G77,[3] and the West.[4] In the final step, and because of the scarcity of the gathered transitive verbs between 1989 and 2002, all the sentences that were produced between 1989 and 2002 were grouped under the 2002 year. VICS indices were calculated for Iran and the USA in multiple groupings of actors, years, US administrations and Iranian governments between 2002 to 2018, and by most frequent publishers in the United States and Iran.

In calculating the VICS indices for Iran's strategic culture, transitive verbs of sentences were considered in which Iran was the subject of the sentence, and the USA was the object of that sentence. For the US strategic culture, transitive verbs of sentences were considered in which the USA was the subject of the sentence, and Iran was the object of that sentence. To increase the accuracy of calculations, only those groupings that could produce at least six iterations of transitive verbs for Self, six iterations of transitive verbs for Other, and at least 15 iterations of transitive verbs in total were selected. After calculating VICS indices for each grouping, the deviation from a norming group was calculated.

The norming group refers to the averages of VICS indices for 255 speech acts by world leaders from different regions and historical eras (Schafer and Walker 2006, 170, n.13). After calculating deviations in key VICS indices from the norming group, roles, strategies, and rankings of preferred outcomes were extracted according to the TIP conventions. *My main hypothesis is that key operational code beliefs address the Central and Operational paradigms of the U.S. and Iranian strategic cultures, which are exhibited in their relations with each other regarding the nuclear issue between them.* I examine below whether the Central and Operational paradigms showed consistency over time by years, over administrations, and across news agencies as sources.[5]

## The Strategic Culture of the United States

### *Central Paradigm of the US Strategic Culture*

Table 14.1, where the United States is the Self, shows the overall Central paradigm of the US strategic culture aggregated for the entire period under investigation (2002–2018) from the perspectives of the USA, Iran, the Arab World, China, G77, Israel, Russia, and the West. The P-1 index from the US publications in bold font shows how the United States perceived Iranian actions toward the USA. This index was calculated based on the

*Table 14.1* Overall Central Paradigm of the US Strategic Culture

| Publication | Self | Other | I1 | I2 | I4a | I5ap | I5pr | I5re | I5op | I5th | I5pu | P1 |
|---|---|---|---|---|---|---|---|---|---|---|---|---|
| Arab World | US | Iran | −.06 | −.11 | .94 | .33 | .04 | .10 | .26 | .05 | .22 | −.50 |
| China | US | Iran | −.15 | −.16 | .85 | .23 | .04 | .15 | .21 | .06 | .30 | −.33 |
| G77 | US | Iran | −.08 | −.13 | .92 | .28 | .07 | .10 | .20 | .09 | .25 | −.29 |
| **Iran** | **US** | **Iran** | **.06** | **−.07** | **.94** | **.40** | **.04** | **.09** | **.20** | **.05** | **.22** | **−.19** |
| Israel | US | Iran | .10 | .02 | .90 | .28 | .12 | .15 | .19 | .09 | .18 | −.28 |
| Russia | US | Iran | −.52 | −.40 | .48 | .10 | .05 | .10 | .24 | .14 | .38 | −.20 |
| **USA** | **US** | **Iran** | **−.09** | **−.14** | **.91** | **.34** | **.05** | **.07** | **.25** | **.06** | **.23** | **−.16** |
| West | US | Iran | −.25 | −.23 | .75 | .25 | .06 | .07 | .25 | .11 | .27 | −.43 |

utterances of transitive verbs in which Iran was the subject of the sentence, and the United States was the object. As the P-1 index for the USA shows, the United States perceived Iran as an adversary with a conflictual strategy toward the USA. The news sources in the rest of the actors, including Iran, also agreed with the United States that the direction of the strategy of Iran toward the USA was conflictual. The highest level of the conflictual strategy was assigned to Iran by the Arab World and by the West.

The USA Instrumental (I) indices were calculated based on the utterances of transitive verbs in which the United States was the subject of the sentence, and Iran was the object. When it comes to the role of war in human affairs, the USA I-1 index in bold font shows that the overall direction of the strategy of the USA toward Iran was conflictual. Except for Iran (also in bold font) and Israel, the other actors agreed that the US strategy toward Iran was more conflictual than cooperative. The West and Russia expressed the highest degree of conflictual strategy for the United States. Regarding the intensity of tactics (I-2), the US VICS index in bold font also shows that US tactics were conflictual. The other actors, except for Israel, agreed that US tactics toward Iran were conflictual. The I-4a index for the USA in bold font shows that the United States exhibited flexibility in its conflictual tactics toward Iran. This means that from the perspective of the USA, conflict with Iran was not inevitable. Except for Russia, the rest of the actors also agreed that US tactics toward Iran were flexible.

The I-5 indices for the USA in bold font present the overall utility of means in dealing with Iran. As Table 14.1 shows, the three means with the highest utility for the USA in dealing with Iran were Appeal, Oppose, and Punish, with Appeal having the highest utility. According to the West, Russia, and China, the means with the highest utility for the USA in dealing with Iran was punishment. Compared to other actors, Israel had the most different view about the utility of means for the USA in dealing with Iran, assigning a higher utility for Promise and a lower utility for Punishment to the United States. The US utility of means scores in bold font from Iranian news sources very track closely with the scores from US news sources.

**Temporal Consistency**

Table 14.2 presents the Central paradigm of the US strategic culture toward Iran disaggregated over the years. As this table shows, in the majority of the years, the United States perceived Iranian actions toward the USA as hostile (P-1 index). In some years, such as 2018, 2003, 2011, 2012, 2010, 2008, and 2017, the perception of the hostility of Iran's actions was high to very high. As the I-1 index shows, the overall direction of the US strategy toward Iran was negative. In some years, such as 2003, 2008, 2002, 2007, 2012, and 2018, the US direction of strategy toward Iran was very conflictual.

Regarding the intensity of tactics (I-2), the US tactics were conflictual in all years, except 2016. The index for the flexibility of tactics (I-4a) shows that in the majority of the years, the United States' tactics toward Iran were flexible. This means that in the majority of the years and from the perspective of the United States, conflict with Iran was not inevitable. The years in which conflict was more certain were 2003, 2008, 2002, 2012, and 2018. The I-5 indices show the utility of cooperative and conflictual means for the United States in dealing with Iran. Over the years, the United States found the highest utility in Appeal, Oppose, and Punish. The highest level of Appeal was in 2014, 2017, and 2013. Oppose had the highest utility for the United States in 2003, 2002, and 2018. And Punish had the highest utility in 2008, 2012, 2011, 2010, and 2014.

### Consistency across Administrations

Strategic culture scholarship from the beginning discussed the presence of subcultures in each strategic culture. Subcultures are a result of

*Table 14.2* Central Paradigm of the US Strategic Culture by Years

| Publication | Year | Self | Other | I1 | I2 | I3 | I4a | I4b | I5ap | I5pr | I5re | I5op | I5th | I5pu | P1 |
|---|---|---|---|---|---|---|---|---|---|---|---|---|---|---|---|
| USA | 2002 | US | Iran | −.47 | −.18 | .34 | .53 | .21 | .21 | .00 | .05 | .63 | .05 | .05 | .00 |
| USA | 2003 | US | Iran | −.83 | −.39 | .52 | .17 | .33 | .08 | .00 | .00 | .75 | .00 | .17 | −.78 |
| USA | 2006 | US | Iran | −.09 | −.15 | .10 | .91 | .45 | .37 | .05 | .04 | .25 | .11 | .19 | −.23 |
| USA | 2007 | US | Iran | −.40 | −.30 | .08 | .60 | .72 | .20 | .02 | .08 | .30 | .12 | .28 | .05 |
| USA | 2008 | US | Iran | −.57 | −.49 | .14 | .43 | .76 | .22 | .00 | .00 | .27 | .14 | .38 | −.26 |
| USA | 2009 | US | Iran | −.10 | −.11 | .05 | .90 | .58 | .29 | .06 | .10 | .24 | .11 | .19 | .29 |
| USA | 2010 | US | Iran | −.18 | −.23 | .09 | .82 | .76 | .27 | .09 | .05 | .22 | .04 | .33 | −.33 |
| USA | 2011 | US | Iran | −.33 | −.33 | .15 | .67 | .67 | .29 | .05 | .00 | .31 | .02 | .33 | −.38 |
| USA | 2012 | US | Iran | −.48 | −.40 | .10 | .52 | .74 | .20 | .03 | .03 | .28 | .12 | .34 | −.33 |
| USA | 2013 | US | Iran | −.01 | −.15 | .13 | .99 | .57 | .41 | .06 | .03 | .20 | .05 | .25 | .00 |
| USA | 2014 | US | Iran | .22 | −.07 | .22 | .78 | .69 | .50 | .07 | .05 | .09 | .01 | .30 | .29 |
| USA | 2015 | US | Iran | −.02 | −.08 | .07 | .98 | .57 | .33 | .07 | .09 | .25 | .06 | .20 | −.05 |
| USA | 2016 | US | Iran | .22 | .07 | .10 | .78 | .71 | .38 | .06 | .16 | .18 | .02 | .19 | −.06 |
| USA | 2017 | US | Iran | .01 | −.06 | .16 | .99 | .51 | .42 | .01 | .08 | .29 | .03 | .17 | −.27 |
| USA | 2018 | US | Iran | −.40 | −.23 | .18 | .60 | .70 | .20 | .00 | .10 | .45 | .00 | .25 | −.80 |

*Table 14.3* Central Paradigm of the US Strategic Culture across Administrations

| Publication | Year | Self | Other | I1 | I2 | I4a | I5ap | I5pr | I5re | I5op | I5th | I5pu | P1 |
|---|---|---|---|---|---|---|---|---|---|---|---|---|---|
| Iran | Bush | US | Iran | −.13 | −.14 | .87 | .29 | .05 | .09 | .27 | .07 | .22 | −.11 |
| Iran | Obama | US | Iran | .05 | −.08 | .95 | .39 | .04 | .10 | .18 | .07 | .23 | −.15 |
| Iran | Trump | US | Iran | .17 | −.02 | .83 | .48 | .03 | .08 | .20 | .01 | .20 | −.38 |
| USA | Bush | US | Iran | −.30 | −.24 | .70 | .27 | .03 | .04 | .34 | .11 | .21 | −.25 |
| USA | Obama | US | Iran | −.06 | −.14 | .94 | .34 | .06 | .07 | .22 | .06 | .25 | −.09 |
| USA | Trump | US | Iran | −.02 | −.08 | .98 | .40 | .01 | .08 | .30 | .02 | .18 | −.37 |

factors such as organizational socialization, generational experiences, and educational backgrounds. For instance, different think tanks or organizations in a bureaucracy might have different approaches to the issues related to the use of force. The question is whether Republican and Democrat administrations had different strategic cultures toward Iran. According to Table 14.3, all three US administrations perceived Iran as a hostile counterpart (P-1 indices). Iran was perceived as the most hostile during the Trump Administration and the least hostile during the Obama Administration.

As Table 14.3 shows, the direction of the US strategy (I-1) was conflictual under the three administrations. When it comes to the intensity of tactics (I-2), all three administrations expressed a preference for conflictual tactics toward Iran. The high I-4a indices during Obama and Trump show that these two administrations were flexible in their conflictual tactics toward Iran. The Bush Administration, on the other hand, had less flexibility. This means that during the Bush Administration, conflict with Iran was more likely. During the Bush and Trump Administrations, the three means with the highest utility were Oppose, Appeal, and Punish. During the Obama Administration, which signed Iran nuclear deal in 2015, both Iranian and American news agencies agreed that the three means with the highest utility for the Obama Administrations were Appeal, Punish, and Oppose.

### Consistency across Media Outlets

Do different American news media organizations represent different US strategic cultures regarding Iran? To answer this question the three most frequent US news outlets in the data, the *New York Times, Washington Post,* and *Christian Science Publishing Society (CSPS)* were selected. The verbs for other news agencies were grouped under *Others* category. Iranian news outlets were grouped under the four categories of *Conservative,*[6] *Reformist,*[7] *Governmental,*[8] and *Others.*

As Table 14.4 shows, three of the four American newsgroups perceived the Iranian actions toward the United States as hostile (P-1). The *Washington Post* assigned the highest level of hostility of actions to Iran.

*Table 14.4* Central Paradigm of the US Strategic Culture across Media Outlets

| Publication | News Agency | Self | Other | I1 | I2 | I4a | I5ap | I5pr | I5re | I5op | I5th | I5pu | P1 |
|---|---|---|---|---|---|---|---|---|---|---|---|---|---|
| Iran | Conservative | US | Iran | -.01 | -.10 | .99 | .35 | .04 | .11 | .20 | .06 | .25 | -.16 |
| Iran | Government | US | Iran | .09 | -.06 | .91 | .43 | .03 | .08 | .20 | .04 | .21 | -.23 |
| Iran | Others | US | Iran | .01 | -.09 | .99 | .36 | .04 | .10 | .20 | .06 | .23 | -.19 |
| Iran | Reformist | US | Iran | .06 | -.04 | .94 | .33 | .05 | .15 | .16 | .08 | .22 | -.09 |
| USA | CSPS | US | Iran | -.17 | -.19 | .83 | .28 | .04 | .09 | .23 | .08 | .27 | .33 |
| USA | NYT | US | Iran | -.07 | -.11 | .93 | .34 | .05 | .07 | .28 | .06 | .20 | -.23 |
| USA | Others | US | Iran | -.09 | -.15 | .91 | .35 | .05 | .06 | .24 | .06 | .24 | -.15 |
| USA | WP | US | Iran | -.10 | -.13 | .90 | .31 | .07 | .07 | .28 | .04 | .23 | -.35 |

Compared to the other three groups of American news agencies, the publications by the *Christian Science Publishing Society* presented a very friendly picture of Iran. The four groups of Iranian news agencies also expressed that Iran's actions toward the United States were hostile. The highest level of hostility was expressed by Iranian official news outlets, and the lowest level was expressed by the Reformist news sources.

All four groups of the US news agencies perceived the US strategy toward Iran as conflictual (I-1). Compared to American news outlets, the Iranian news agencies assigned a more cooperative strategy to the United States. Regarding the intensity of tactics (I-2), all four American news outlets assigned conflictual tactics to the United States. The Iranian news agencies agreed with their American counterparts that the US tactical approach toward Iran was conflictual. Both American and Iranian news agencies believed that US tactics toward Iran were also flexible (I-4a). This means that they did not perceive US conflict with Iran as inevitable. According to the Iranian and American news outlets, the means with the highest utility (I-5) for the United States were Appeal, Oppose, and Punish. It is noteworthy that compared to the American news agencies, the Iranian news outlets assigned more utility for Reward for the United States. Among the Iranian news agencies, the Reformist news outlets attributed the highest utility for Reward to the United States.

### Operational Paradigm

The Operational paradigm of a strategic culture presents actors' ranked preferences for strategic options. Using (zI1, zP4Self) and (zP1, zP4Other) pairs and based on the TIP presented in Figure 14.1, this section will extract the ranked outcome preferences in the US strategic culture regarding strategic options. The United States will have a choice between the two cooperation options of Submission and Settlement and the two conflict options of Deadlock and Domination. The Submit option is the highest level of cooperation, and the Dominate option is the highest conflictual option.

| Very Weak Friend | Weak Friend [I-1] | Strong Friend [P-1] | Very Strong Friend |
|---|---|---|---|
| Bandwagon<br>Submit<br>s: Submit>Settle>Deadlock>Dominate<br>v: Submit>Settle>Dominate>Deadlock | Bandwagon<br>Submit<br>s: Submit>Deadlock>Settle>Dominate<br>v: Submit>Deadlock>Dominate>Settle | Bandwagon<br>Submit<br>s: Submit>Deadlock>Settle>Dominate<br>v: Submit>Deadlock>Dominate>Settle | Bandwagon<br>Submit<br>s: Submit>Dominate>Settle>Deadlock<br>v: Submit>Dominate>Deadlock>Settle |

| Very Weak Partner | Weak Partner [+1] | Strong Partner [+1] | Very Strong Partner |
|---|---|---|---|
| Appeasement<br>Settle<br>s: Settle>Submit>Deadlock>Dominate<br>v: Settle>Submit>Dominate>Deadlock<br>P4a | Appeasement<br>Settle<br>s: Settle>Deadlock>Submit>Dominate<br>v: Settle>Deadlock>Dominate>Submit<br>-1 | Appeasement<br>Settle<br>s: Settle>Deadlock>Submit>Dominate<br>v: Settle>Deadlock>Dominate>Submit<br>+1 | Appeasement<br>Settle<br>s: Settle>Dominate>Submit>Deadlock<br>v: Settle>Dominate>Deadlock>Submit<br>P4a |

| Very Weak Rival | Weak Rival [-1] | Strong Rival [+1] | Very Strong Rival |
|---|---|---|---|
| P4b<br>Balancing<br>Deadlock<br>s: Deadlock>Submit>Settle>Dominate<br>v: Deadlock>Submit>Dominate>Settle | Balancing<br>Deadlock<br>s: Deadlock>Settle>Submit>Dominate<br>v: Deadlock>Settle>Dominate>Submit | Balancing<br>Deadlock<br>s: Deadlock>Settle>Submit>Dominate<br>v: Deadlock>Settle>Dominate>Submit<br>-1 | Balancing<br>Deadlock<br>s: Deadlock>Dominate>Submit>Settle<br>v: Deadlock>Dominate>Settle>Submit<br>P4b |

| Very Weak Enemy | Weak Enemy [I-1] | Strong Enemy [P-1] | Very Strong Enemy |
|---|---|---|---|
| Hegemony<br>Dominate<br>s: Dominate>Submit>Settle>Deadlock<br>v: Dominate>Submit>Deadlock>Settle | Hegemony<br>Dominate<br>s: Dominate>Settle>Submit>Deadlock<br>v: Dominate>Settle>Deadlock>Submit | Hegemony<br>Dominate<br>s: Dominate>Settle>Submit>Deadlock<br>v: Dominate>Settle>Deadlock>Submit | Hegemony<br>Dominate<br>s: Dominate>Deadlock>Submit>Settle<br>v: Dominate>Deadlock>Settle>Submit<br>P-1 |

*Figure 14.1* Modified Theory of Inferences about Preferences (TIP). "s" Stands for Secondary Interests, and "v" Stands for Vital Interests. The +1 and −1 Numbers along the Vertical and Horizontal Axes Mark Grids with Roles that are More than One Standard Deviation from the Norming Group Scores for I-1/P-1 or P4a/P4b

Table 14.5 presents the US power role and preferred rankings of strategies in dealing with Iran.[9] This table was created using the deviation of US I-1 and P4Self indices from a norming group.[10] As Table 14.5 shows, the power role that the United States assigned to itself in dealing with Iran was Very Strong Enemy. China, G77, Russia, and the West agreed with the United States that its role toward Iran was the role of a Very Strong Enemy. On the other hand, Iran, Israel, and the Arab World assigned the role of Very Strong Rival to the United States. Both of these roles are conflictual roles. There was no dispute about the power of the United States, and all actors, including Iran, agreed that the US was a very strong actor.

According to TIP in Figure 14.1, actors' ranked preferences for options depend on the type of interests they pursue. When it comes to vital interests, the United States most preferred strategies were Dominate, Deadlock, Settle, and Submit. In dealing with secondary interests, the United States ranked preferences were Dominate, Deadlock, Submit, and Settle. As mentioned, China, G77, Russia, and the West agreed with the United States regarding its most preferred strategies. However, according to Iran, Israel, and the Arab World, the United States most preferred options were Deadlock, Dominate, Settle, Submit for vital interests and Deadlock, Dominate, Submit, Settle for secondary interests. Regardless of the actor or interests, the two most preferred outcomes for the United States in dealing with Iran were Dominate and Deadlock, which points to a conflictual strategic culture toward Iran.

### Temporal Consistency

Table 14.6 shows the US power roles and ranking of preferred options in dealing with Iran over the years. In all the years of this study, the United States saw itself as a very strong actor when it dealt with Iran. As this table shows, over the years, the United States had two conflictual power roles toward Iran. In most of the years, the United States assigned the power role of Very Strong Enemy to itself. The second power role that the United States assigned to itself was the power role of Very Strong Rival. For these two roles, the two highest ranked strategies are Dominate and Deadlock.

### Consistency across Administrations

Table 14.7 presents the US power roles and ranked preferences for strategies based on presidential administrations. As this table shows, the United States adopted the power role of Very Strong Enemy during the Bush Administration. On the other hand, during the Obama Administration and the first 14 months of Trump Administration, the USA assigned the power role of Very Strong Rival to itself. Iran also

*Table 14.5* Overall Operational Paradigm of the United States

| Publication | Self | Other | $zI1$ | $zP4Self$ | Self, Power, Role | Self, s, Ranking of Outcomes | Self, v, Ranking of Outcomes |
|---|---|---|---|---|---|---|---|
| Arab World | US | Iran | -.96 | 4.78 | Very Strong Rival | Deadlock>Dominate>Submit>Settle | Deadlock>Dominate>Settle>Submit |
| China | US | Iran | -1.25 | 3.63 | Very Strong Enemy | Dominate>Deadlock>Submit>Settle | Dominate>Deadlock>Settle>Submit |
| G77 | US | Iran | -1.03 | 4.59 | Very Strong Enemy | Dominate>Deadlock>Submit>Settle | Dominate>Deadlock>Settle>Submit |
| **Iran** | **US** | **Iran** | **-.61** | **3.70** | **Very Strong Rival** | **Deadlock>Dominate>Submit>Settle** | **Deadlock>Dominate>Settle>Submit** |
| Israel | US | Iran | -.48 | 4.68 | Very Strong Rival | Deadlock>Dominate>Submit>Settle | Deadlock>Dominate>Settle>Submit |
| Russia | US | Iran | -2.42 | 3.76 | Very Strong Enemy | Dominate>Deadlock>Submit>Settle | Dominate>Deadlock>Settle>Submit |
| **USA** | **US** | **Iran** | **-1.07** | **4.70** | **Very Strong Enemy** | **Dominate>Deadlock>Submit>Settle** | **Dominate>Deadlock>Settle>Submit** |
| West | US | Iran | -1.57 | 4.63 | Very Strong Enemy | Dominate>Deadlock>Submit>Settle | Dominate>Deadlock>Settle>Submit |

*Table 14.6* Operational Paradigm of the US Strategic Culture over the Years

| Publication | Year | Self | Other | zI1 | zP4Self | Self, Power, Role | Self, s, Ranking of Outcomes | Self, v, Ranking of Outcomes |
| --- | --- | --- | --- | --- | --- | --- | --- | --- |
| USA | 2002 | US | Iran | −2.26 | 3.97 | Very Strong Enemy | Dominate>Deadlock>Submit>Settle | Dominate>Deadlock>Settle>Submit |
| USA | 2003 | US | Iran | −3.38 | 2.90 | Very Strong Enemy | Dominate>Deadlock>Submit>Settle | Dominate>Deadlock>Settle>Submit |
| USA | 2006 | US | Iran | −1.08 | 4.54 | Very Strong Enemy | Dominate>Deadlock>Submit>Settle | Dominate>Deadlock>Settle>Submit |
| USA | 2007 | US | Iran | −2.03 | 4.14 | Very Strong Enemy | Dominate>Deadlock>Submit>Settle | Dominate>Deadlock>Settle>Submit |
| USA | 2008 | US | Iran | −2.55 | 3.62 | Very Strong Enemy | Dominate>Deadlock>Submit>Settle | Dominate>Deadlock>Settle>Submit |
| USA | 2009 | US | Iran | −1.08 | 4.62 | Very Strong Enemy | Dominate>Deadlock>Submit>Settle | Dominate>Deadlock>Settle>Submit |
| USA | 2010 | US | Iran | −1.33 | 5.01 | Very Strong Enemy | Dominate>Deadlock>Submit>Settle | Dominate>Deadlock>Settle>Submit |
| USA | 2011 | US | Iran | −1.82 | 4.45 | Very Strong Enemy | Dominate>Deadlock>Submit>Settle | Dominate>Deadlock>Settle>Submit |
| USA | 2012 | US | Iran | −2.28 | 4.55 | Very Strong Enemy | Dominate>Deadlock>Submit>Settle | Dominate>Deadlock>Settle>Submit |
| USA | 2013 | US | Iran | −.80 | 4.77 | Very Strong Rival | Deadlock>Dominate>Submit>Settle | Deadlock>Dominate>Settle>Submit |
| USA | 2014 | US | Iran | −.10 | 5.41 | Very Strong Rival | Deadlock>Dominate>Submit>Settle | Deadlock>Dominate>Settle>Submit |
| USA | 2015 | US | Iran | −.84 | 4.80 | Very Strong Rival | Deadlock>Dominate>Submit>Settle | Deadlock>Dominate>Settle>Submit |
| USA | 2016 | US | Iran | −.10 | 4.37 | Very Strong Rival | Deadlock>Dominate>Submit>Settle | Deadlock>Dominate>Settle>Submit |
| USA | 2017 | US | Iran | −.74 | 5.03 | Very Strong Rival | Deadlock>Dominate>Submit>Settle | Deadlock>Dominate>Settle>Submit |
| USA | 2018 | US | Iran | −2.03 | 3.67 | Very Strong Enemy | Dominate>Deadlock>Submit>Settle | Dominate>Deadlock>Settle>Submit |

Table 14.7 Operational Paradigm of the US Strategic Culture under Bush, Obama, and Trump

| Publication | Year | Self | Other | zI1 | zP4Self | Self, Power, Role | Self, s, Ranking of Outcomes | Self, v, Ranking of Outcomes |
|---|---|---|---|---|---|---|---|---|
| Iran | Bush | US | Iran | –1.18 | 3.43 | Very Strong Enemy | Dominate>Deadlock>Submit>Settle | Dominate>Deadlock>Settle>Submit |
| Iran | Obama | US | Iran | –.62 | 3.56 | Very Strong Rival | Deadlock>Dominate>Submit>Settle | Deadlock>Dominate>Settle>Submit |
| Iran | Trump | US | Iran | –.24 | 4.19 | Very Strong Rival | Deadlock>Dominate>Submit>Settle | Deadlock>Dominate>Settle>Submit |
| USA | Bush | US | Iran | –1.73 | 4.26 | Very Strong Enemy | Dominate>Deadlock>Submit>Settle | Dominate>Deadlock>Settle>Submit |
| USA | Obama | US | Iran | –.96 | 4.77 | Very Strong Rival | Deadlock>Dominate>Submit>Settle | Deadlock>Dominate>Settle>Submit |
| USA | Trump | US | Iran | –.85 | 4.89 | Very Strong Rival | Deadlock>Dominate>Submit>Settle | Deadlock>Dominate>Settle>Submit |

assigned to the United States the power role of Very Strong Enemy during the Bush Administration and the power role of Very Strong Rival during the Obama and Trump Administrations.

### Consistency across Media Outlets

Table 14.8 presents the power roles that the American and Iranian news agencies assigned to the United States. As this table shows, all four American news outlets agreed that the US power role toward Iran was Very Strong Enemy. Interestingly, Iranian news agencies assigned a less conflictual power role to the United States. All four groups of Iranian news outlets assigned the power role of Very Strong Rival to the United States. While both of these roles are conflictual roles, the US news agencies talked about the US conflictual actions toward Iran more than the Iranian news outlets.

### Summary of US Strategic Culture

According to Johnston (1995), the Central paradigm of a strategic culture is about the orderliness of the strategic environment and reduces uncertainty about the strategic environment. The findings from the preceding analysis showed that the United States perceived the nature of Other, Iran, as hostile and adopted conflictual strategies and tactics in dealing with Iran. The means with the highest utility for the United States were Appeal, Oppose, and Punish. However, the conflictual tactics toward Iran were mainly flexible, showing that the US conflict with Iran was not inevitable. The results showed that the other actors, including Iran, were in overall agreement with the United States over its strategic culture's Central paradigm toward Iran. It was also shown that the US strategic culture toward Iran was to a very good degree, consistent over time, over administrations, and news agencies.

The analysis of the Operational paradigm in US strategic culture revealed its preferred strategies in dealing with Iran. In dealing with Iran, the United States assigned only two conflictual power roles to itself, Very Strong Enemy, and Very Strong Rival. Other actors, including Iran, also assigned these two conflictual roles to the United States. As a result of these two power roles, the United States had two sets of preferred strategies. When considering its vital interests, the United States' most ranked strategies were Dominate and Deadlock. When dealing with secondary interests, the highest ranked preferences for the United States were Deadlock and Dominate. Even in the years (2014, 2015, 2016) surrounding the Iran nuclear deal, the United States' most preferred strategies did not change to Settlement. The United States never assigned cooperative roles to itself when it dealt with Iran. This lack of change in role assignment indicates that the Iran nuclear deal was a single roll of the dice

Table 14.8 Operational Paradigm of the US Strategic Culture Based on Media Outlet

| Publication | News Agency | Self | Other | $zI1$ | $zP4Self$ | Self, Power, Role | Self, s, Ranking of Outcomes | Self, v, Ranking of Outcomes |
|---|---|---|---|---|---|---|---|---|
| Iran | Conservative | USA | Iran | -.80 | 3.50 | Very Strong Rival | Deadlock>Dominate>Submit>Settle | Deadlock>Dominate>Settle>Submit |
| Iran | Government | USA | Iran | -.49 | 3.90 | Very Strong Rival | Deadlock>Dominate>Submit>Settle | Deadlock>Dominate>Settle>Submit |
| Iran | Others | USA | Iran | -.74 | 3.31 | Very Strong Rival | Deadlock>Dominate>Submit>Settle | Deadlock>Dominate>Settle>Submit |
| Iran | Reformist | USA | Iran | -.60 | 3.53 | Very Strong Rival | Deadlock>Dominate>Submit>Settle | Deadlock>Dominate>Settle>Submit |
| US | CSPS | USA | Iran | -1.30 | 4.59 | Very Strong Enemy | Dominate>Deadlock>Submit>Settle | Dominate>Deadlock>Settle>Submit |
| US | NYT | USA | Iran | -1.01 | 4.90 | Very Strong Enemy | Dominate>Deadlock>Submit>Settle | Dominate>Deadlock>Settle>Submit |
| US | Others | USA | Iran | -1.05 | 4.75 | Very Strong Enemy | Dominate>Deadlock>Submit>Settle | Dominate>Deadlock>Settle>Submit |
| US | WP | USA | Iran | -1.11 | 4.18 | Very Strong Enemy | Dominate>Deadlock>Submit>Settle | Dominate>Deadlock>Settle>Submit |

(Parsi 2013) and did not represent a change in the US strategic culture regarding Iran.

## The Strategic Culture of Iran

### *Central Paradigm*

The overall Central paradigms of Iran's strategic culture toward the United States from Iran's perspective and other actors are presented in Table 14.9. The P-1 index shows that Iran in bold font did not evaluate the US actions as hostile. This index was calculated based on the utterances of transitive verbs in which the United States was the subject of the sentence, and Iran was the object. Except for Israel, other actors (including the United States in bold font) saw US actions toward Iran as conflictual. Iran's Instrumental (I) indices were calculated based on the utterances of transitive verbs in which Iran was the subject of the sentence, and the United States was the object.

When it comes to the role of war in human affairs, Iran's I-1 index in bold font shows that the overall direction of Iran's strategy toward the United States was conflictual. All other actors, including the United States, also agreed that the strategy of Iran toward the United States was conflictual. Iran and other actors also agreed that Iranian tactics toward the United States were conflictual. Iran's I-4a index in bold font shows that Iran was flexible in its tactics toward the United States and was open to cooperation. Except for the Arab World and the West, other actors agreed that Iran's conflictual tactics toward the United States were flexible.

The I-5 indices present the overall utility of means for Iran in dealing with the United States. As Tables 14.1 and 14.9 indicate, there are a couple of differences between Iran and the United States when it comes to the utility of means. As the US Central paradigm showed, the United States gave the highest utility to Appeal. Iran, in contrast, gave the highest utility to Oppose. Except for Russia and Israel, all other actors

*Table 14.9* Overall Central Paradigm of Iran's Strategic Culture

| Publication | Self | Other | I1 | I2 | I4a | I5ap | I5pr | I5re | I5op | I5th | I5pu | P1 |
|---|---|---|---|---|---|---|---|---|---|---|---|---|
| Arab World | Iran | US | −.50 | −.23 | .50 | .18 | .00 | .07 | .57 | .03 | .15 | −.06 |
| China | Iran | US | −.33 | −.07 | .67 | .17 | .00 | .17 | .50 | .13 | .04 | −.15 |
| G77 | Iran | US | −.29 | −.10 | .71 | .19 | .01 | .15 | .43 | .09 | .12 | −.08 |
| **Iran** | **Iran** | **US** | **−.19** | **−.09** | **.81** | **.31** | **.02** | **.08** | **.42** | **.09** | **.08** | **.06** |
| Israel | Iran | US | −.28 | −.26 | .72 | .31 | .02 | .03 | .26 | .17 | .21 | .10 |
| Russia | Iran | US | −.20 | −.23 | .80 | .30 | .10 | .00 | .20 | .20 | .20 | −.52 |
| **USA** | **Iran** | **US** | **−.16** | **−.09** | **.84** | **.26** | **.03** | **.13** | **.33** | **.10** | **.15** | **−.09** |
| West | Iran | US | −.43 | −.25 | .57 | .21 | .02 | .06 | .43 | .12 | .16 | −.25 |

(including the United States) also think that Oppose had a higher utility for Iran than Appeal. Another difference is that Iran did not show much utility for Punish, which might reflect Iran's weaker position. All other countries, including the USA, also agreed that Punish did not have much utility for Iran. Iran mainly opposed and rarely punished.

## Temporal Consistency

Table 14.10 presents the Central paradigm of Iran's strategic culture toward the United States over the years. As the P-1 index shows, Iran had a mixed perception of US actions. Half of the time, Iran assessed US actions as cooperative and half of the time as conflictual. As the I-1 index reveals, the overall direction of Iran's strategy toward the United States was conflictual. In some years, such as 2018, 2011, 2012, 2017, and 2002, Iran's direction of strategy toward the United States was very conflictual. The I-2 index shows that in the majority of the years, Iran's tactics toward the United States were conflictual as well. The I-4a index shows that in the majority of the times, Iran's tactics were flexible. Like the USA, Iran did not see their conflict as inevitable. However, in 2018 and 2011, Iran showed little flexibility in its conflictual strategy toward the United States. This means that Iran saw conflict with the United States as likely in those years. The I-5 indices show the utility of cooperative and conflictual means for Iran in dealing with the United States. The means with the highest utility for Iran were Oppose and Appeal. In contrast to the United States, Punish never had high utility for Iran, which might show Iran's general weakness compared to the United States.

## Consistency across Governments

Table 14.11 presents the Central paradigm of Iran's strategic culture toward the United States under the three governments of Khatami, Ahmadinejad, and Rouhani. While the P-1 index for Iran shows that the United States did not enact hostile actions during the Ahmadinejad and Rouhani governments, the United States described its actions during the Ahmadinejad governments as hostile. Iran's I-1 and I-2 indices show that all three Iranian governments adopted conflictual strategies and tactics toward the United States with Khatami's government adopting the most conflictual approach. During Ahmadinejad's government, Iran showed the most flexibility and, therefore, most inclination to change course and adopt a cooperative approach. The I-4a index shows that the Khatami government was the least flexible one.

As the I-1, I-2, and I-4a indices by the US news agencies confirm, the US media were in general agreements with their Iranian counterparts on Iran's direction of strategy, and intensity and flexibility of tactics toward the United States during the three governments of Iran. When it comes

*Table 14.10* Central Paradigm of Iran's Strategic Culture over the Years

| Publication | Year | Self | Other | I1 | I2 | I3 | I4a | I4b | I5ap | I5pr | I5re | I5op | I5th | I5pu | P1 |
|---|---|---|---|---|---|---|---|---|---|---|---|---|---|---|---|
| Iran | 2002 | Iran | US | -.33 | -.14 | .17 | .67 | .17 | .25 | .00 | .08 | .42 | .25 | .00 | .25 |
| Iran | 2006 | Iran | US | .02 | .02 | .14 | .98 | .40 | .38 | .00 | .13 | .33 | .09 | .07 | -.09 |
| Iran | 2007 | Iran | US | -.10 | -.12 | .21 | .90 | .30 | .40 | .05 | .00 | .40 | .00 | .15 | -.29 |
| Iran | 2008 | Iran | US | -.08 | -.15 | .16 | .92 | .46 | .38 | .08 | .00 | .31 | .00 | .23 | -.04 |
| Iran | 2009 | Iran | US | .24 | .05 | .30 | .76 | .29 | .57 | .00 | .05 | .29 | .10 | .10 | .39 |
| Iran | 2010 | Iran | US | .20 | -.03 | .30 | .80 | .20 | .60 | .00 | .00 | .20 | .10 | .10 | -.22 |
| Iran | 2011 | Iran | US | -.83 | -.42 | .38 | .17 | .33 | .08 | .05 | .00 | .67 | .08 | .17 | .37 |
| Iran | 2012 | Iran | US | -.52 | -.16 | .37 | .48 | .10 | .14 | .03 | .05 | .67 | .10 | .00 | -.26 |
| Iran | 2013 | Iran | US | .00 | -.04 | .30 | 1.00 | .15 | .48 | .00 | .00 | .43 | .00 | .08 | .17 |
| Iran | 2014 | Iran | US | -.12 | .00 | .07 | .88 | .74 | .19 | .04 | .25 | .31 | .13 | .12 | .13 |
| Iran | 2015 | Iran | US | -.20 | -.10 | .15 | .80 | .29 | .30 | .00 | .06 | .43 | .09 | .09 | -.06 |
| Iran | 2016 | Iran | US | -.12 | -.09 | .20 | .88 | .24 | .40 | .00 | .04 | .40 | .08 | .08 | .04 |
| Iran | 2017 | Iran | US | -.31 | -.13 | .20 | .69 | .21 | .28 | .00 | .07 | .48 | .14 | .03 | .22 |
| Iran | 2018 | Iran | US | -.85 | -.31 | .67 | .15 | .00 | .08 | .00 | .00 | .85 | .08 | .00 | -.13 |

*Table 14.11* Central Paradigm of Iran's Strategic Culture under Khatami, Ahmadinejad, and Rouhani

| Publication | Year | Self | Other | I1 | I2 | I4a | I5ap | I5pr | I5re | I5op | I5th | I5pu | P1 |
|---|---|---|---|---|---|---|---|---|---|---|---|---|---|
| Iran | Ahmadinejad | Iran | US | −.09 | −.07 | .91 | .39 | .02 | .04 | .41 | .04 | .09 | .00 |
| Iran | Khatami | Iran | US | −.50 | −.27 | .50 | .19 | .00 | .06 | .44 | .19 | .13 | −.04 |
| Iran | Rouhani | Iran | US | −.24 | −.09 | .76 | .26 | .01 | .11 | .43 | .11 | .07 | .09 |
| USA | Ahmadinejad | Iran | US | −.16 | −.09 | .84 | .29 | .03 | .11 | .37 | .09 | .13 | −.22 |
| USA | Khatami | Iran | US | −.48 | −.23 | .52 | .11 | .00 | .15 | .41 | .15 | .19 | −40 |
| USA | Rouhani | Iran | US | −.11 | −.08 | .89 | .26 | .03 | .15 | .27 | .11 | .18 | .04 |

to the utility of means, in all the three governments the two means with the highest utility for Iran were Oppose and Appeal. Also, in all the three governments Oppose had a higher utility for Iran than Appeal. Iran showed the highest utility for Punish during Khatami's government. The US I-5 indices for Iran show that the United States had a similar view about Iran's utility of the means. The United States also agreed with Iran that the Khatami's government assigned the highest utility for Punish.

### Consistency across Media Outlets

Did Iranian news agencies differ regarding the Central paradigm of Iran's strategic culture toward the United States? To answer this question Iranian news outlets were grouped under four categories of Conservative, Reformist, Government, and Others. The P-1 indices in Table 14.12 show that except for the conservative outlets with a slightly conflictual view of the US actions, the other three groups of the Iranian news media generally evaluated US actions toward Iran as cooperative. However, all of the US news outlets agreed that the US actions toward Iran were hostile. The I-1 and I-2 indices show that Iran's direction of strategy and intensity of tactics toward the United States were conflictual from the perspective of the Iranian news outlets. The I-4a indices show that Iran was flexible in its tactics, and therefore, did not see the conflict with the United States

*Table 14.12* Central Paradigm of Iran's Strategic Culture Based on Media Outlets

| Publication | News Agency | Self | Other | I1 | I2 | I4a | I5ap | I5pr | I5re | I5op | I5th | I5pu | P1 |
|---|---|---|---|---|---|---|---|---|---|---|---|---|---|
| Iran | Conservative | Iran | USA | −.16 | −.11 | .84 | .35 | .03 | .04 | .39 | .08 | .11 | −.01 |
| Iran | Government | Iran | USA | −.23 | −.06 | .77 | .27 | .00 | .11 | .46 | .10 | .05 | .09 |
| Iran | Others | Iran | USA | −.19 | −.13 | .81 | .31 | .02 | .07 | .36 | .10 | .14 | .01 |
| Iran | Reformist | Iran | USA | −.09 | −.09 | .91 | .39 | .02 | .04 | .37 | .07 | .11 | .06 |
| USA | CSPS | Iran | USA | .33 | .18 | .67 | .45 | .02 | .19 | .24 | .00 | .10 | −.17 |
| USA | NYT | Iran | USA | −.23 | −.12 | .77 | .26 | .00 | .13 | .38 | .10 | .14 | −.07 |
| USA | Others | Iran | USA | −.15 | −.10 | .85 | .26 | .03 | .14 | .28 | .13 | .16 | −.09 |
| USA | WP | Iran | USA | −.35 | −.18 | .65 | .18 | .06 | .08 | .44 | .06 | .18 | −.10 |

as inevitable. Except for CSPS, the other American news agencies agreed with the Iranian news outlets on Iran's strategy, the intensity of tactics, and flexibility toward the United States. The CSPS group assigned a very cooperative strategy and tactics to Iran and a conflictual strategy to the United States.

The I-5 indices show that from the perspectives of all of the Iranian news outlets, the two means with the highest utility for Iran were Oppose and Appeal. Except for the Reformist news outlets, the other three Iranian news agencies agreed that the utility of Oppose was higher for Iran than the utility of Appeal in dealing with the United States. The American news agencies also agreed that the two means with the highest utility for Iran were Oppose and Appeal. Except for CSPS, the other three American news agencies agreed that in dealing with the USA, Iran assigned more utility to Oppose than Appeal.

### Operational Paradigm

An examination of Iran's Operational paradigm in Table 14.13 shows the ranked preferences for strategic options and Iran's power role in dealing with the United States. As this table shows, Iran assigned the power role of a Strong Enemy to itself. When it comes to vital interests, Iran's ranked preferences were Dominate, Settle, Deadlock, and Submit. In achieving or protecting secondary interests, Iran's ranked options were Dominate, Settle, Submit, and Deadlock. All other actors also agreed that Iran's role toward the United States was the role of Enemy. However, they disagreed on the level of power of Iran. China assigned the power role of Very Strong Enemy to Iran. While G77, Russia, and the West assigned the power role of Strong Enemy to Iran, the USA, the Arab World, and Israel assigned the power role of Weak Enemy to Iran.

### Temporal Consistency

Table 14.14 presents the Operational paradigm of Iran's strategic culture over the years. As this table shows, over the years and in dealing with the USA, Iran assigned the two conflictual roles of Enemy and Rival to itself. Also, Iran's perception of its power fluctuated from Strong to Very Strong. Iran's first-ranked options in dealing with the United States, regardless of the intensity of interest, were Dominate and Deadlock. Regardless of the intensity of interest, Iran's most frequent second-ranked option was Settle.

### Consistency across Governments

Table 14.15 presents the Operational paradigm of Iran's strategic culture toward the USA during the three governments of Khatami,

*Table 14.13* Overall Operational Paradigm of Iran's Strategic Culture

| Publication | Self | Other | $zI1$ | $zP4Self$ | Self, Power, Role | Self, s, Ranking of Outcomes | Self, v, Ranking of Outcomes |
|---|---|---|---|---|---|---|---|
| Arab World | Iran | US | -2.34 | -.13 | Weak Enemy | Dominate>Settle>Submit>Deadlock | Dominate>Settle>Deadlock>Submit |
| China | Iran | US | -1.82 | 1.01 | Very Strong Enemy | Dominate>Deadlock>Submit>Settle | Dominate>Deadlock>Settle>Submit |
| G77 | Iran | US | -1.67 | .06 | Strong Enemy | Dominate>Settle>Submit>Deadlock | Dominate>Settle>Deadlock>Submit |
| **Iran** | **Iran** | **US** | **-1.37** | **.95** | **Strong Enemy** | **Dominate>Settle>Submit>Deadlock** | **Dominate>Settle>Deadlock>Submit** |
| Israel | Iran | US | -1.64 | -.04 | Weak Enemy | Dominate>Settle>Submit>Deadlock | Dominate>Settle>Deadlock>Submit |
| Russia | Iran | US | -1.41 | .89 | Strong Enemy | Dominate>Settle>Submit>Deadlock | Dominate>Settle>Deadlock>Submit |
| **USA** | **Iran** | **US** | **-1.27** | **-.05** | **Weak Enemy** | **Dominate>Settle>Submit>Deadlock** | **Dominate>Settle>Deadlock>Submit** |
| West | Iran | US | -2.12 | .02 | Strong Enemy | Dominate>Settle>Submit>Deadlock | Dominate>Settle>Deadlock>Submit |

*Table 14.14* Operational Paradigm of Iran's Strategic Culture toward the United States Over the Years

| Publication | Year | Self | Other | zI1 | zP4 | Self, Power, Role | Self, s, Ranking of Outcomes | Self, v, Ranking of Outcomes |
|---|---|---|---|---|---|---|---|---|
| Iran | 2002 | Iran | US | -1.82 | 1.75 | Very Strong Enemy | Dominate>Deadlock>Submit>Settle | Dominate>Deadlock>Settle>Submit |
| Iran | 2006 | Iran | US | -.71 | 1.56 | Very Strong Rival | Deadlock>Dominate>Submit>Settle | Deadlock>Dominate>Settle>Submit |
| Iran | 2007 | Iran | US | -1.09 | .77 | Strong Enemy | Dominate>Settle>Submit>Deadlock | Dominate>Settle>Deadlock>Submit |
| Iran | 2008 | Iran | US | -1.02 | .91 | Strong Enemy | Dominate>Settle>Submit>Deadlock | Dominate>Settle>Deadlock>Submit |
| Iran | 2009 | Iran | US | -.04 | 2.14 | Very Strong Rival | Deadlock>Dominate>Submit>Settle | Dominate>Dominate>Settle>Submit |
| Iran | 2010 | Iran | US | -.16 | .73 | Strong Rival | Deadlock>Settle>Submit>Dominate | Deadlock>Dominate>Settle>Submit |
| Iran | 2011 | Iran | US | -3.38 | 1.41 | Very Strong Enemy | Dominate>Deadlock>Submit>Settle | Dominate>Deadlock>Settle>Submit |
| Iran | 2012 | Iran | US | -2.42 | 1.31 | Very Strong Enemy | Dominate>Deadlock>Submit>Settle | Dominate>Deadlock>Settle>Submit |
| Iran | 2013 | Iran | US | -.78 | .45 | Strong Rival | Deadlock>Settle>Submit>Dominate | Deadlock>Settle>Dominate>Submit |
| Iran | 2014 | Iran | US | -1.15 | 1.76 | Very Strong Enemy | Dominate>Deadlock>Submit>Settle | Dominate>Deadlock>Settle>Submit |
| Iran | 2015 | Iran | US | -1.41 | .80 | Strong Enemy | Dominate>Settle>Submit>Deadlock | Dominate>Settle>Deadlock>Submit |
| Iran | 2016 | Iran | US | -1.16 | 1.05 | Very Strong Enemy | Dominate>Deadlock>Submit>Settle | Dominate>Deadlock>Settle>Submit |
| Iran | 2017 | Iran | US | -1.75 | .49 | Strong Enemy | Dominate>Settle>Submit>Deadlock | Dominate>Settle>Deadlock>Submit |
| Iran | 2018 | Iran | US | -3.42 | .30 | Strong Enemy | Dominate>Settle>Submit>Deadlock | Dominate>Settle>Deadlock>Submit |

Table 14.15 Operational Paradigm of Iran's Strategic Culture under Khatami, Ahmadinejad, and Rouhani

| Publication | Year | Self | Other | $zI1$ | $zP4Self$ | Self, Power, Role | Self, s, Ranking of Outcomes | Self, v, Ranking of Outcomes |
|---|---|---|---|---|---|---|---|---|
| Iran | Ahmadinejad | Iran | US | -1.06 | 1.06 | Very Strong Enemy | Dominate>Deadlock>Submit>Settle | Dominate>Deadlock>Settle>Submit |
| Iran | Khatami | Iran | US | -2.34 | 1.29 | Very Strong Enemy | Dominate>Deadlock>Submit>Settle | Dominate>Deadlock>Settle>Submit |
| Iran | Rouhani | Iran | US | -1.53 | .85 | Strong Enemy | Dominate>Settle>Submit>Deadlock | Dominate>Settle>Deadlock>Submit |
| USA | Ahmadinejad | Iran | US | -1.28 | .07 | Strong Enemy | Dominate>Settle>Submit>Deadlock | Dominate>Settle>Deadlock>Submit |
| USA | Khatami | Iran | US | -2.28 | .32 | Strong Enemy | Dominate>Settle>Submit>Deadlock | Dominate>Settle>Deadlock>Submit |
| USA | Rouhani | Iran | US | -1.13 | -.18 | Weak Enemy | Dominate>Settle>Submit>Deadlock | Dominate>Settle>Deadlock>Submit |

Ahmadinejad, and Rouhani. As this table shows, Iran assigned the role of Enemy to itself in all three governments. However, during the Khatami and Ahmadinejad governments, Iran assigned the power level of Very Strong to itself, and during the Rouhani government, it assigned the power level of Strong. The United States also assigned the role of Enemy to Iran during the three Iranian governments. During the Khatami and Ahmadinejad periods, the USA assigned the power level of Strong to Iran. During Rouhani's tenure, it assigned the power level of Weak. Therefore, both Iran and the United States assigned a weaker level of power to Iran during the Rouhani Administration. This difference in the assigned levels of power might be due to the different styles of the governments. It might also be an indication of the impact of sanctions on Iran.

### Consistency across Media Outlets

Table 14.16 examines whether the Operational paradigm of Iran's strategic culture toward the United States differed across news agencies in Iran. As this table indicates, all four Iranian news outlets assigned the role of Enemy to Iran. Except for governmental news agencies, the other agencies assigned the power level of Very Strong to Iran. The majority of the US news agencies agreed with their Iranian counterparts that Iran's role toward the United States was the role of Enemy. The only exception was the *CSPS*, which assigned the role of Partner to Iran. The US news outlets did not have a similar view of Iran's power level. The *New York Times* and Others assigned the power level of Weak to Iran. The *Washington Post* and *CSPS*, on the other hand, assigned the power level of Strong to Iran.

### Summary of Iran's Strategic Culture

Iran's Central paradigm revealed a strategic culture that did not have a very hostile view of the United States indicated by the P-1 indices. In contrast, the United States described US actions toward Iran as hostile. While explaining this anomaly requires a separate study, one hypothesis could be advanced using the Gramscian concept of hegemony. According to Gramsci, hegemony exists when those who are ruled accept the legitimacy of the actions by rulers (Gramsci and Buttigieg 2011). Iran's relatively positive view of the US actions toward Iran could manifest acceptance by Iran of US hegemony.

The Central paradigm of Iran's strategic culture toward the United States shows a strategic culture that does not have a clear definition of the Other and therefore indicates a strategic culture that has not shaped yet. When it comes to strategy and tactics, Iran showed different levels of cooperation and conflict across the years. When it comes to the utility of means, the means with the highest utility for Iran were Oppose

Table 14.16 Operational Paradigm of Iran's Strategic Culture Based on News Agencies

| Publication | News Agency | Self | Other | zI1 | zP4Self | Self, Power, Role | Self, s, Ranking of Outcomes | Self, v, Ranking of Outcomes |
|---|---|---|---|---|---|---|---|---|
| Iran | Conservative | Iran | USA | −1.28 | 1.15 | Very Strong Enemy | Dominate>Deadlock>Submit> Settle | Dominate>Deadlock>Settle> Submit |
| Iran | Government | Iran | USA | −1.49 | .75 | Strong Enemy | Dominate>Settle>Submit> Deadlock | Dominate>Settle>Deadlock> Submit |
| Iran | Others | Iran | USA | −1.38 | 1.34 | Very Strong Enemy | Dominate>Deadlock>Submit> Settle | Dominate>Deadlock>Settle> Submit |
| Iran | Reformist | Iran | USA | −1.05 | 1.12 | Very Strong Enemy | Dominate>Deadlock>Submit> Settle | Dominate>Deadlock>Settle> Submit |
| US | CSPS | Iran | USA | .26 | .06 | Strong Partner | Settle>Deadlock>Submit> Dominate | Settle>Deadlock>Dominate> Submit |
| US | NYT | Iran | USA | −1.51 | −.25 | Weak Enemy | Dominate>Settle>Submit> Deadlock | Dominate>Settle>Deadlock> Submit |
| US | Others | Iran | USA | −1.26 | −.10 | Weak Enemy | Dominate>Settle>Submit> Deadlock | Dominate>Settle>Deadlock> Submit |
| US | WP | Iran | USA | −1.88 | .46 | Strong Enemy | Dominate>Settle>Submit> Deadlock | Dominate>Settle>Deadlock> Submit |

and Appeal. Over the years and dealing with the USA, Iran did not find much utility for Punish. This might be the result of Iran's inferior power position or Iran's tendency to resort to less conflictual means. Iran's Operational paradigm, overall, was consistent across time, governments, and news outlets. Iran's Operational paradigm mainly assigned the role of Enemy to Iran. In contrast to the USA, Iran did not have a firm view of its power level. While Iran's most ranked options in dealing with the United States were Dominate and Deadlock, Iran considered Settle as its second option during several years.

## Conclusion

Actors act differently toward Others based on the level of positive and negative identifications assigned to one another (Wendt 1999). Their strategies toward friends, partners, rivals, and enemies are different. Therefore, actors do not have one monolithic strategic culture. Depending on their level of positive and negative identification with Others, and the roles they define for themselves, actors activate the norms of different strategic cultures. Furthermore, actors act differently based on their level of power. Facing a stronger or weaker adversary, actors adopt different strategies to survive and reach their goals. Therefore, strategic cultures should be tailored and targeted based on the relative power of actors. Lastly, actors pursue different strategies to protect their vital and secondary interests. They tend to resist or use force when it comes to their vital interests, and they tend to submit or cooperate when it comes to their secondary interests. Therefore, strategic culture should be issue-specific as well.

In this chapter, I have argued that actors can have two general strategic cultures: one is for cooperative roles and the other for conflictual roles. Based on the intensity of cooperative and conflictual roles, these two general strategic cultures have two subgroups. Within the cooperative strategic culture are strategic cultures for friends and partners. On the other hand, the conflictual strategic cultures are divided into strategic cultures of rivals and enemies. By considering the relative power of Self (Very weak, Weak, Strong, Very Strong) and importance of the issues at stake (vital, secondary), these four strategic cultures create the 32 subcategories of strategic culture associated with binary role theory in Figure 14.1 (Malici and Walker 2017).

To extract a targeted strategic culture that considers an actor's role toward a specific other, their relative power, and the importance of the issues at stake, the analysis in this chapter has employed a combination of operational code analysis methods and game theory models (Schafer and Walker 2006; Walker, Malici, and Schafer 2011). This combination of methodological tools can extract the Central and Operational paradigms of the Self's strategic culture and Self's perception of the Other's strategic culture. By extracting Self and Other's ranked strategies, the complex

| Game: 23143142 Very Strong Enemy (vital interest) v.s. Weak Enemy (secondary interest) First Choice: 4 Second Choice: 3 Third Choice: 2 Fourth Choice: 1 | | U.S. Perception of Other (Iran) Iran's Role towards U.S.: Weak Enemy Iran's Ranked Preferences for its Secondary Interests: **Dominate>Settle>Submit>Deadlock** | |
|---|---|---|---|
| | | Cooperation by Iran | Conflict by Iran |
| **U.S. Perception of Self (U.S.)** U.S. Role towards Iran: Very Strong Enemy U.S. Ranked Preferences for its Vital Interests: **Dominate>Deadlock>Settle>Submit** | **Cooperation by U.S.** | Slot 0 → Settlement by US - Settlement by Iran Third Choice - Second Choice 2 - 3 23 | Slot 1 → Submit by U.S. - Dominate by Iran Fourth Choice - First Choice 1 - 4 14 |
| | **Conflict by U.S.** | Slot 3 Dominate by U.S. - Submit by Iran First Choice - Third Choice 4 - 2 42 | ← Slot 2 Deadlock by U.S. - Deadlock by Iran Second Choice - Fourth Choice 3 - 1 31 |

*Figure 14.2* Modeling US-Iran Interactions from the Perspective of the United States

system of strategic actions between Self and Other can be modeled via sequential games. Figure 14.2 presents a 2 × 2 game that is created based on the American news agencies' perceptions of the ranked preferences for the United States (Self) and Iran (Other). When the United States and Iran both choose cooperation, their strategies are Settle. When they both choose conflict, their strategies are Deadlock. When one side chooses cooperation and the other conflict, then their respective strategies are Submit and Dominate.

A strategic culture extracted by the combination of the operational code analysis and TIP reveals Self and Other's ranked preference for Settle, Submit, Deadlock, and Dominate from best to worst. TIP extracts the ranking of the above four states for both vital and secondary interests. As a result, four sets of subjective games can be extracted for any dyad of actors. For instance, from the perspective of the United States, the US interaction with Iran can be modeled via the following four games: when they both consider Iran's nuclear program as their vital interests (US-vital, Iran-vital), when both consider Iran's nuclear program as their secondary interests (US-secondary, Iran-secondary), when the United States assess that Iran's nuclear program impacts its vital interests and Iran ranks it as its secondary interest (US-vital, Iran-secondary), and when the United States considers it as a secondary interest and Iran as a vital interest (US-secondary, Iran-vital).

To find the solutions for these four games, I use Brams' Theory of Moves. What distinguishes Brams' Theory of Moves from traditional game theory is that according to Brams, actors can change their starting and stopping states. Actors decide about these moves via thinking ahead and considering the consequences of their moves and Other's countermoves. As a result of changing starting and stopping states, sequential games can have what he calls non-myopic equilibrium (NME). Some games have one, some two, and some three non-myopic equilibria (Brams 1994).

Table 14.17 presents the solutions for the subjective games between Iran and the United States from the perspectives of Iran, the United States, the Arab World, China, Israel, Russia, and the West.[11]

As this table reveals, all of the games had only one non-myopic (NME) solution that is also the Nash equilibrium. It also shows that because of the type of strategic cultures that Iran and the United States have shown toward each other, a win-win solution of the settlement was not among the solutions. As this table shows, both Iran and the United States agree that if they consider the Iran nuclear issue as their vital interests, then they will both adopt the strategy of Deadlock. If they consider it as their secondary interests, then the best strategy for the United States is Dominate and for Iran is Submit. Iran and the United States also agree that if Iran sees the nuclear issue as its vital interest and the United States as its secondary interest, the best strategy for both is Deadlock. And finally, Iran and the United States agree that if Iran considers its nuclear program as its secondary interest and the United States as its vital interest, the best strategy for the United States is Dominate and for Iran Submit. Except for China, all other actors presented the same solutions for the four subjective games between Iran and the United States.

The results provide potential insights to policymakers of both countries for achieving different outcomes for their interactions. In the last four decades, there has never been a lasting relationship of mutual cooperation between Iran and the United States, which reflects the lack of a game with a stable settlement solution in the strategic cultures governing relations between the two states. Because of Iran's inferior power position, Iran has not been able to force the United States into a submission outcome, i.e., there is no non-myopic solution of domination for Iran. On the other hand, the United States has had the power to force Iran to submit, but to do so, it has to make Iran consider the disputed issues as its secondary interests.

When it comes to Iran's nuclear program, the main US goal is to make Iran submit to US demands, which is the dismantlement of Iran's nuclear program. To achieve this goal, the United States has needed to change the cost and benefit calculations of Iran and influence Iran in such a way that Iran considers its nuclear program as a secondary issue. As Table 14.17 presents, if Iran ranks the nuclear issue as a vital interest, the United States cannot achieve its goal of making Iran submit. The USA has tried to change Iran's calculations via threatening military actions and imposing extreme sanctions; however, it has not been successful. US policymakers apparently believe that if they pressure Iran enough, Iran will eventually reevaluate its interests and choose survival over its nuclear program. However, for three reasons, the United States has not succeeded in changing Iran's calculations.

First, because of its destructive power and its drastic impact on states' survival, the nuclear issue is usually ranked among a state's vital interests.

*Table 14.17* Subjective Games between Iran and the United States

| Publication | Self | Other | Self Power, Role | Other Power, Role | Self S: Secondary O: Secondary | Self S: Secondary O: Vital | Self S: Vital O: Secondary | Self S: Vital O: Vital | Other S: Secondary O: Secondary | Other S: Secondary O: Vital | Other S: Vital O: Secondary | Other S: Vital O: Vital |
|---|---|---|---|---|---|---|---|---|---|---|---|---|
| Arab World | Iran | US | Weak Enemy | Very Strong Rival | G: 31231442 NME: Submit | G: 32231441 NME: Submit | G: 31132442 NME: Deadlock | G: 32132441 NME: Deadlock | G: 31231442 NME: Dominate | G: 32231441 NME: Dominate | G: 31132442 NME: Deadlock | G: 32132441 NME: Deadlock |
| China | Iran | US | Very Strong Enemy | Very Strong Enemy | G: 11243342 NME: Deadlock | G: 12243341 NME: Deadlock | G: 21143342 NME: Deadlock | G: 22143341 NME: Deadlock | G: 11243342 NME: Deadlock | G: 12243341 NME: Deadlock | G: 21143342 NME: Deadlock | G: 22143341 NME: Deadlock |
| G77 | Iran | US | Strong Enemy | Very Strong Enemy | G: 31241342 NME: Submit | G: 32241341 NME: Submit | G: 31142342 NME: Deadlock | G: 32142341 NME: Deadlock | G: 31241342 NME: Dominate | G: 32241341 NME: Dominate | G: 31142342 NME: Deadlock | G: 32142341 NME: Deadlock |
| **Iran** | **Iran** | **US** | **Strong Enemy** | **Very Strong Rival** | **G: 31231442 NME: Submit** | **G: 32231441 NME: Submit** | **G: 31132442 NME: Deadlock** | **G: 32132441 NME: Deadlock** | **G: 31231442 NME: Dominate** | **G: 32231441 NME: Dominate** | **G: 31132442 NME: Deadlock** | **G: 32132441 NME: Deadlock** |
| Israel | Iran | US | Weak Enemy | Very Strong Rival | G: 31231442 NME: Submit | G: 32231441 NME: Submit | G: 31132442 NME: Deadlock | G: 32132441 NME: Deadlock | G: 31231442 NME: Dominate | G: 32231441 NME: Dominate | G: 31132442 NME: Deadlock | G: 32132441 NME: Deadlock |
| Russia | Iran | US | Strong Enemy | Very Strong Enemy | G: 31241342 NME: Submit | G: 32241341 NME: Submit | G: 31142342 NME: Deadlock | G: 32142341 NME: Deadlock | G: 31241342 NME: Dominate | G: 32241341 NME: Dominate | G: 31142342 NME: Deadlock | G: 32142341 NME: Deadlock |

(Continued)

*Table 14.17* Subjective Games between Iran and the United States (Continued)

| Publication | Self | Other | Self Power, Role | Other Power, Role | Self S: Secondary O: Secondary | Self S: Secondary O: Vital | Self S: Vital O: Secondary | Self S: Vital O: Vital | Other S: Secondary O: Secondary | Other S: Secondary O: Vital | Other S: Vital O: Secondary | Other S: Vital O: Vital |
|---|---|---|---|---|---|---|---|---|---|---|---|---|
| USA | Iran | US | Weak Enemy | Very Strong Enemy | G: 31241342 NME: Submit | G: 32241341 NME: Submit | G: 31142342 NME: Deadlock | G: 32142341 NME: Deadlock | G: 31241342 NME: Dominate | G: 32241341 NME: Dominate | G: 31142342 NME: Deadlock | G: 32142341 NME: Deadlock |
| West | Iran | US | Strong Enemy | Very Strong Enemy | G: 31241342 NME: Submit | G: 32241341 NME: Submit | G: 31142342 NME: Deadlock | G: 32142341 NME: Deadlock | G: 31241342 NME: Dominate | G: 32241341 NME: Dominate | G: 31142342 NME: Deadlock | G: 32142341 NME: Deadlock |
| Arab World | US | Iran | Very Strong Rival | Weak Enemy | G: 13244132 NME: Dominate | G: 13244231 NME: Deadlock | G: 23144132 NME: Dominate | G: 23144231 NME: Deadlock | G: 13244132 NME: Submit | G: 13244231 NME: Deadlock | G: 23144132 NME: Submit | G: 23144231 NME: Deadlock |
| China | US | Iran | Very Strong Enemy | Very Strong Enemy | G: 11243342 NME: Deadlock | G: 12243341 NME: Deadlock | G: 21143342 NME: Deadlock | G: 22143341 NME: Deadlock | G: 11243342 NME: Deadlock | G: 12243341 NME: Deadlock | G: 21143342 NME: Deadlock | G: 22143341 NME: Deadlock |
| G77 | US | Iran | Very Strong Enemy | Strong Enemy | G: 13243142 NME: Dominate | G: 13243241 NME: Deadlock | G: 23143142 NME: Dominate | G: 23143241 NME: Deadlock | G: 13243142 NME: Submit | G: 13243241 NME: Deadlock | G: 23143142 NME: Submit | G: 23143241 NME: Deadlock |
| Iran | US | Iran | Very Strong Rival | Strong Enemy | G: 13244132 NME: Dominate | G: 13244231 NME: Deadlock | G: 23144132 NME: Dominate | G: 23144231 NME: Deadlock | G: 13244132 NME: Submit | G: 13244231 NME: Submit | G: 23144132 NME: Submit | G: 23144231 NME: Deadlock |

| | S | O | Self | Other | | | | | | | | |
|---|---|---|---|---|---|---|---|---|---|---|---|---|
| Israel | US | Iran | Very Strong Rival | Weak Enemy | G: 13244132 NME: Dominate | G: 13244231 NME: Deadlock | G: 23144132 NME: Dominate | G: 23144231 NME: Deadlock | G: 13244132 NME: Submit | G: 13244231 NME: Deadlock | G: 23144132 NME: Submit | G: 23144231 NME: Deadlock |
| Russia | US | Iran | Very Strong Enemy | Strong Enemy | G: 13243142 NME: Dominate | G: 13243241 NME: Deadlock | G: 23143142 NME: Dominate | G: 23143241 NME: Deadlock | G: 13243142 NME: Submit | G: 13243241 NME: Deadlock | G: 23143142 NME: Submit | G: 23143241 NME: Deadlock |
| **USA** | **Iran** | | **Very Strong Enemy** | **Weak Enemy** | **G: 13243142 NME: Dominate** | **G: 13243241 NME: Deadlock** | **G: 23143142 NME: Dominate** | **G: 23143241 NME: Deadlock** | **G: 13243142 NME: Submit** | **G: 13243241 NME: Deadlock** | **G: 23143142 NME: Submit** | **G: 23143241 NME: Deadlock** |
| West | US | Iran | Very Strong Enemy | Strong Enemy | G: 13243142 NME: Dominate | G: 13243241 NME: Deadlock | G: 23143142 NME: Dominate | G: 23143241 NME: Deadlock | G: 13243142 NME: Submit | G: 13243241 NME: Deadlock | G: 23143142 NME: Submit | G: 23143241 NME: Deadlock |

*Abbreviations*: G: Game; S: Self; O: Other; NME: non-myopic equilibrium.

This is true for great powers, such as the United States, and the middle powers such as Iran and North Korea. Because of their overall weakness in conventional weaponry and facing enormous conventional powers of the great powers, the middle powers, including Iran, look at nuclear technology as a power equalizer. The more the United States puts pressure on Iran, the more Iran recognizes nuclear technology as necessary.

Second, Iran is surrounded by nuclear countries. As of May 2020, Israel has 90, Pakistan 160, and Russia 6370 nuclear weapons. The United States, which has 5800 nuclear weapons, surrounds Iran from Afghanistan, the Persian Gulf, and Iraq (Kristensen and Korda 2020). While Turkey is a non-nuclear country, it is a NATO member and, as a result, enjoys nuclear protection. Saudi Arabia also has US protection at least when it comes to Iran. Iran is the only power in that region that does not have nuclear weapons or protection.

Third, the US campaign to put pressure on Iran is not restricted to the nuclear issue. The United States expresses concerns about almost every aspect of Iran's domestic and foreign policies. It has imposed all kinds of sanctions from human rights, to terrorism, to nuclear issues. With every new sanction, Iran becomes more convinced that the main US goal is overthrowing Iran's regime and not the nuclear issue. Hence, nuclear technology becomes more important for Iran to survive. Iran's most significant submission to US demands happened when the Obama Administration sent the message to Iran that it was looking for better relations with Iran and was not after regime change.

In sum, through mild desecuritization tactics, like the meetings between John Kerry and Javad Zarif or Obama's phone call to Rouhani, the Obama Administration was able to exert enough influence to induce Iran to define the nuclear issue as a secondary interest. The mild desecuritization approach by the Obama Administration resulted in Iran's submission in JCPOA in 2015.[12] However, the Trump Administration's subsequent withdrawal from JCPOA in 2018 and its maximum pressure campaign has made it very difficult for Iran to consider its nuclear program as a secondary interest.

## Notes

1. I5ap: I-5 Appeal; I5pr: I-5 Promise; I5re: I-5 Reward; I5op: I-5 Oppose; I5th: I-5 Threaten; and I5pu: I-5 Punish.
2. Bahrain, Egypt, Iraq, Jordan, Kuwait, Lebanon, Libya, Oman, Qatar, Saudi, Arabia, Sudan, Syria, UAE.
3. Afghanistan, Algeria, Brazil, India, Indonesia, Kenya, Malaysia, Nepal, North Korea, Pakistan, Philippines, Singapore, South Africa, Sri Lanka, Thailand, Zimbabwe.
4. Canada, Cyprus, Czech Republic, France, Germany, Hungary, Ireland, Italy, Japan, Malta, New Zealand, Norway, South Korea Spain, Switzerland, United Kingdom.

5. Omitted from this analysis as less relevant to the Central and Operational paradigms in the strategic cultures of Iran and the United States are I-3, I-4b, P-2, P-3, and P-5 indices.
6. Some of the most frequent Conservative news sources were: Fars News, Javan, Jomhuri ye Eslami, Kayhan, Mehr News Agency, Resalat, and Tehran Times.
7. Some of the most frequent Reformist news sourced were Aaftab e Yazd, E'temad, Kargozaran, Mardom Salari, Sharq Newspaper, and Siyasat e Ruz.
8. Some of the most frequent governmental news sources were Al Alam, IRIB, IRNA News Agency, and Jaam e Jam.
9. s: Secondary Interests; v: Vital Interests.
10. In this study, a targeted operational code analysis study, the norming group's mean and standard deviation for P-1 (mean = .25, std = .32), was used for both I-1 and P-1. The reason behind this decision is that in the norming group, the I-1 index is mainly calculated using transitive verbs for pronouns, and the P-1 index is primarily based on transitive verbs for nouns. However, in this study, both I-1 and P-1 indices are extracted mainly based on transitive verbs for nouns. In this study, the norming group's mean and standard deviation for P-4a Self (mean = .21, std = .12) were used for both P-4a Self and P-4b Other. The reason behind this decision is that in general operational code analysis, the P-4a Self represents the attributes of one (single or collective) actor, and P-4b Other reveals the attributes of a general Other with multiple actors. In this study, however, Other does not represent multiple actors and is either Iran or the USA.
11. G: Game; NME: Non-Myopic Equilibrium; O: Other; S:Self.
12. Securitization happens when an "issue is presented as an existential threat, requiring emergency measures and justifying actions outside the normal bounds of political procedure" (Buzan, Waever, and de Wilde 2013, 24). Conversely, desecuritization refers to "the shifting of issues out of emergency mode and into the normal bargaining processes of the political sphere" (Buzan, Waever, and de Wilde 2013, 4).

# References

Brams, S. 1994. *Theory of moves*. Cambridge: Cambridge University Press.

Buzan, B., O. Waever, J. de Wilde. 2013. *Security a new framework for analysis*. Boulder, CO: Lynne Rienner.

George, A. 1969. The operational code: A neglected approach to the study of political leaders and decision-making. *International Studies Quarterly* 13(2): 190–222.

Gramsci, A., J. Buttigieg. 2011. *Prison notebooks*. New York, NY: Columbia University Press.

Gray, C. 1981. National style in strategy: The American example. *International Security* 6(2): 21–47.

Gray, C. 1999. Strategic culture as context: The first generation of theory strikes back. *Review of International Studies 25 (Print)*, 49–69.

Haglund, D. 2004. What good is strategic culture? A modest defence of an immodest concept. *International Journal* 59(3): 479–502.

Johnston, A. 1995. Thinking about strategic culture. *International Security* 19(4): 32–64.

Johnston, A. 1998. *Cultural realism: Strategic culture and grand strategy in Chinese history*. Princeton, NJ: Princeton University Press.

Kristensen, H., M. Korda. 2020. Estimated global nuclear warhead inventories. *Federation of American Scientists.* Last modified May 2020. https://fas.org/wp-content/uploads/2020/04/ WarheadInventories2020-1.jpg.

Leites, N. 1951. *The operational code of the Politburo.* New York, NY: McGraw-Hill.

Leites, N. 1953. *A study of Bolshevism.* Glencoe: Free Press.

Libel, T. 2016. Explaining the security paradigm shift: Strategic culture, epistemic communities, and Israel's changing national security policy. *Defence Studies* 16(2): 137–156.

Malici, A., S. Walker. 2017. *Role theory and role conflict in US-Iran relations.* New York, NY: Routledge.

Parsi, T. 2013. *A single roll of the dice: Obama's diplomacy with Iran.* New Haven, CT: Yale University Press.

Schafer, M., S. Walker. Eds. 2006. *Beliefs and leadership in world politics.* New York, NY: Palgrave.

Schelling, T. 1958. *Re-interpretation of the solution concept for non-cooperative games.* Santa Monica, CA: RAND.

Snyder, J. 1977. *The Soviet strategic culture: Implications for limited nuclear operations.* Santa Monica, CA: RAND.

Walker, S., A. Malici, M. Schafer. 2011. *Rethinking foreign policy analysis: States, leaders, and the microfoundations of behavioral international relations.* New York, NY: Routledge.

Walker, S., M. Schafer, M. Young. 1998. Systematic procedures for operational code analysis. *International Studies Quarterly* 42: 175–190.

Wendt, A. 1999. *Social theory of international politics.* Cambridge: Cambridge University Press.

Young, M. 2001. Building world views with profiler+. In *Progress in communication sciences,* ed. M. West, 17–32. Vol. 17. Westport, CT: Ablex Publishing.

# 15 An Operational Code Analysis of Foreign Policy Roles in US-Iran Strategic Dyads

*Stephen G. Walker and Akan Malici*

## Introduction

In the summer of 2015, the United States and Iran signed the Joint Comprehensive Plan of Action (JCPOA). It was a major achievement and good for both sides. The United States could be certain that Iran's nuclear program would be exclusively peaceful, while Iran would benefit from the lifting of United States and international sanctions. In January, 2017, President Trump succeeded President Obama, and the days of rapprochement were numbered. Trump's belligerent rhetoric and his cancelation of the JCPOA led to mutual escalation between the United States and Iran, which came to an acutely dangerous point in early January, 2020. When the United States assassinated the top Iranian Commander Qassem Soleimani while he was on a visit in Iraq, the two countries came to the brink of war before ultimately standing down after an Iranian retaliation in the form of missile strikes on a US military base.

While the immediate causes for this escalation lie in Trump's 2018 withdrawal from the JCPOA, the ultimate reasons lie back much further in history. In this chapter, we employ the Verbs in Context System (VICS) of content analysis to identify the strategies of cooperation and conflict that mark crucial historical episodes in the relations between the United States and Iran. By *crucial historical episodes*, we mean time periods of interactions between states that appear to be so fundamental that they have the potential to (re)define the roles and corresponding relations between them (Malici and Walker 2017, 4). These time windows and turning points are often conceptualized as military crises or diplomatic opportunities, in which relations between states present a threat of moving from cooperation to military conflict, or conversely, an opportunity to shift from conflict to cooperation (Hermann 1972; Snyder and Diesing 1977; Brecher and Wilkenfeld 2000; Walker 2002).

Three such turning points in US-Iran relations are Iran's oil nationalization and coup crisis (1950–1953), the Iranian revolution and hostage crisis (1978–1981), and the US-Iran diplomatic rapprochement and detente period (1997–2002). The first two cases are periods in which

Iran's relations with the United States oscillated toward conflict before returning to cooperation between 1950 and 1953 and then shifted decisively from cooperation to conflict between 1978 and 1981. The final case was a period of rapprochement from conflict toward cooperation before returning to conflict between 1997 and 2002. The immediate origins of these crises in US-Iran relations were changes in the leadership inside at least one of the members of this role dyad: the rise of Mossadegh in Iran and Eisenhower's election in the United States in the first case; the exile of the Shah and the return of the Ayatollah Khomeini to Iran in the second case; the election of Mohammad Khatami as the Iranian president in the third case. The expansion of the Cold War into the Middle East, the Iranian revolution, and the 9/11 terrorist attack, respectively, provided the different background conditions that either constrained or fueled the efforts of the new leaders in reshaping US-Iran relations.

While acknowledging that the identities of these leaders and background conditions are important in describing and explaining the interactions between Iran and the United States during these historical periods, we focus primarily on describing and explaining the effects of these interactions in defining Iran-US relations. We first identify different possible patterns of relations between the two states and then examine the macro-processes that define the transition from one pattern of relations to another over time, i.e., from cooperation to conflict or from conflict to cooperation. We describe these patterns and processes as exchanges of *cues*, i.e., the performance of particular sequences of social acts in the form of words or deeds to communicate information between Iran and the United States. We measure these cues with VICS indices from the operational code construct to identify these patterns and specify them as the enactment by Iran and the United States of *roles* that define their international relations within the context of binary role theory (BRT) as a social theory of world politics (Malici and Walker 2017).

## Cognitive and Social Operational Codes

Previous operational code studies have focused primarily on individual leaders, although the focus of the first operational code analysis (OCA) was the Soviet Politburo as the executive committee of the Communist Party in the Soviet Union (Leites 1951). The bridge between the two focal points was Lenin's domination of the politburo by the force of his personality and his beliefs about the exercise of power that constituted his operational code. In turn, the politburo's operational code became the operational code of the Soviet government, because the politburo was the immediate source of the Soviet state's decisions about the exercise of power in world politics. OCA specifies that different beliefs shape behavior into different patterns regarding the exercise of social power and that the beliefs of political leaders are the ones that shape the patterned behavior of states. If this theoretical premise is true, then these social behavior patterns are potentially valid markers of an agent's underlying operational code beliefs.

If beliefs and behavior are congruent, i.e., do match up, then this link means that beliefs are the cognitive dimension and behaviors are the social dimension of an agent's operational code. In this context, larger aggregations of individuals, such as small groups, bureaucracies, and states, can have social operational codes defined by their patterns of behavior. These patterns may be the expression of the beliefs of a leader (such as Lenin) or the products of interactions among members of a larger decision unit populated by different individuals with different beliefs who debate, negotiate, or fight and thereby generate the patterns of behavior that become the decision unit's social operational code. In this account, macro-level regularities "supervene—come from and rely ontologically for their existence—on micro-level phenomena" (Walker, Malici, and Schafer 2011, 27).

The macro-level regularities are the behavioral patterns of the larger decision unit, e.g., the state, in world politics. The microlevel phenomena are the social processes of interaction among a decision unit's members and the cognitive processes of bounded rationality associated with the operational code beliefs of individuals within the decision unit. It is possible to argue that so long as the microlevel processes are acknowledged as sources, the macro-level processes need not be reduced to these antecedents to construct a valid explanation of their consequents. Instead, the consequents of microlevel processes as internal patterns of state behavior become the causal antecedents of macro-level processes as external interaction patterns at higher levels of analysis (the dyad, triad, or larger ensembles of states), which explain the relations that emerge from these interactions. This logic thereby extends the scope of OCA from the explanation of actions by individuals to the explanation of actions by states and ultimately to the interactions and outcomes between them in world politics. OCA in this account becomes a potential explanation for patterns of cooperation and conflict at the systemic level of international relations as well as for decisions at the agent level of foreign policy analysis (Walker, Malici, and Schafer 2011; Walker 2013; Malici and Walker 2017).

What are the macro-level patterns of state behaviors that define a state's social operational code and which are realized causally in multiple ways via different microlevel processes from the cognitive operational codes of individuals that constitute larger decision units (single groups or coalitions of groups) inside states? The patterns of state behavior specified by the operational code construct are the various ways of exercising social power by one state to influence the behavior of other agents in world politics. They include strategies, tactics, and different means of exercising social power, defined as the exercise of positive (+) or negative

## Spatial &Temporal Levels of Aggregation

| Roles (E,A): | Friend | Partner | | Rival | Enemy |
|---|---|---|---|---|---|
| | (+, −) | (+,+) | | (−, −) | (−, +) |
| Strategies: | Bandwagon | Appease | | Balance | Bully |

| Tactics: | Deeds | | Words | Words | | Deeds |
|---|---|---|---|---|---|---|
| | +3 | +2 | +1 | −1 | −2 | −3 |
| Sanctions: | Reward | Promise | Appeal/Support | Oppose/Resist | Threaten | Punish |

*Figure 15.1*  Hierarchical Levels in the Exercise of Social Power by Ego and Alter

(−)sanctions (Walker, Malici, and Schafer 2011; Walker and Malici 2011; Baldwin 1989; Dahl 1957).

The VICS indices of OCA identify and distinguish among these different modalities of social power as related hierarchically to one another. The different ways to exercise positive and negative sanctions are the building blocks for tactical and strategic exercises of social power at higher levels of spatial and temporal aggregation. The hierarchy formed by these different levels of aggregation in the exercise of power appears in Figure 15.1. This figure shows that different kinds of positive and negative sanctions scale at different levels of intensity from +3 to −3 and aggregate from words to deeds in either a cooperative (+) or conflictual (−) direction over time in relations between Ego and Alter in a role dyad (E,A): (1) as bandwagon strategies leading to a submission (+, −) outcome; (2) as appeasement strategies leading to a mutual cooperation (+, +) outcome; (3) as balancing strategies leading to a mutual conflict (−,−) outcome; and (4) as bullying strategies leading to a domination (−, +) outcome. In turn, these different strategies are behavioral markers of different roles (friend, partner, rival, or enemy) selected and enacted between Ego and Alter (Walker 2013; Malici and Walker 2017).

VICS identifies the exercise of social power attributed to a leader, group, or coalition by examining the behavior of an agent as "text actions" recorded by first-party speakers in the public statements of agents or in event chronologies written by third parties who may retrieve and record them by direct observation or from the archival texts of direct observers (Walker, Malici, and Schafer 2011, 26–37). The recording unit for these actions is the text (hence "text actions") of written words that record the exercise of social power attributed to the agent or others. The written words include the transitive verbs employed in the text to describe the exercise of social power and the nouns or pronouns that identify the subjects exhibiting this behavior in the political universe.

VICS has a dictionary of transitive verbs that describe the exercise of social power as one of the six positive or negative sanctions in Figure 15.1. It employs Profiler Plus, which is a language-parsing software program that identifies the parts of speech in a text, including subjects and transitive verbs. It counts the frequencies of each type of transitive verb from the VICS sanctions dictionary and also notes the tense (past, present, or future) of these verbs attributed to different agents in a public statement or a third-party chronology (Young 2001). The VICS indices are calculated from these observations to describe the *balance* (+ vs. –), *scale* (+3 to –3), and *intensity* (average scale value) of cooperation (+) and conflict (–) attributed to different agents identified as subjects in the text.

Various combinations of these indices represent the exercise of social power at various levels (roles, strategies, tactics, and moves) as first-party mental events in the minds of the agents if the source is a public statement by an agent and as third-party social events in the relations between agents if the source is a third-party chronology. The vocabulary and grammar of the language system employed in each kind of text is the medium that contains and transmits this information for the analysis of world politics by both participants and observers (Walker, Schafer, and Young 1998; Schafer and Walker 2006; Walker, Malici, and Schafer 2011). In our analysis of US-Iran relations, we shall employ third-party texts to retrieve and record the social operational codes of the two states as they enact different roles and pursue different strategies and tactics of role enactment during the three crucial historical episodes that represent turning points or important inflections in their international relations.

## Turning Points in US-Iran Relations: Three Crucial Historical Episodes[1]

We suggest that there were at least three crucial historical episodes between Iran and the United States since World War II. The first crucial episode occurred during the oil nationalization crisis and the subsequent coup to oust the Iranian government from 1950 to 1953. The second episode occurred during the Iranian revolution and the subsequent hostage crisis with the United States from 1978 to 1981. A third crucial episode was the diplomatic rapprochement and detente efforts initiated by Iranian leader Mohammed Khatami from 1997 until President George W. Bush branded Iran as a member of an Axis-of-Evil in his 2002 State of the Union speech. In the following summaries, we elaborate briefly on each episode.

### First Crucial Historical Episode

Prior to the Second World War, Iran had for many generations suffered from Russian and British imperial machinations and exploitations. The country's autocratic monarchs were often complicit with these efforts and thus an additional hindrance to the people's ambition for national progress and self-realization. A new popular movement would eventually arise in 1906, however, and its effects would come to be known as the Constitutional Revolution (Afary 1996; Martin 1989). The revolution was to have three main objectives: the establishment of an accountable and responsive government, the creation of a decent socioeconomic order, and the assertion of national sovereignty (Azimi 2008, 29; Katouzian 2000, 18). While the revolution led to the establishment of a constitution and the Majlis (parliament), it ultimately failed to govern. Autocratic leaders would continue asserting themselves and so would European imperialists.

It was not until the 1940s that constitutional and parliamentary forces were able to reemerge in Iran and relegate the Shah, Mohammed Reza, to a secondary role. In this movement, one person stood out: Mohammad Mossadegh. He and other supporters would soon establish the National Front, and Mossadegh would subsequently become prime minister. With this new political elite, the demand for a new Iranian role of independence grew ever stronger. However, the AIOC continued to stand in the way of this new role, and one of the National Front's concrete ambitions was thus the nationalization of the oil industry (Galpern 2009, 87; Ramazani 1975, 181). As long as the AIOC owned Iran's single most important modern industry, effectively controlling not only its provinces but continuously attempting to control all of Iranian politics, a truly sovereign and democratic government could not emerge (Katouzian 2004, 6).

For Mossadegh and his collaborators, the AIOC as an agent of British imperialism would have to be eliminated from the Iranian landscape, and this goal would define the forthcoming conflict over Iran's relations with Britain. In a statement to the Majlis-appointed special commission on November 6, 1950, Mossadegh demanded, "that the oil industry of Iran be declared as nationalized throughout all parts of the country without exception, namely, all operations for exploration, extraction and exploitation shall be in the hands of the government" (Ramazani 1975, 192). Nationalization was accomplished on May 2, 1951.

This demand was unacceptable to the British who had reaped almost all of the oil benefits for decades. Mossadegh, the National Front, and the nationalism they represented were a serious danger to British interests in the Middle East, and the Iranian prime minister had to be removed from political power. The British were able to convince the American leadership that ridding Iran of Mossadegh would also be in the national interest of the United States, and thus the Central Intelligence Agency (CIA) masterminded and executed a coup to overthrow a democratically elected government. The story of the coup itself has been told many times, and its contours are surprisingly simple. Per Mohammad Reza Shah's order, Mossadegh was to be dismissed. CIA-paid mercenary mobs would counter potential National Front supporters, and complicit military officers would take over critical command posts and proclaim marital law.

The US-favored General Zahedi would be the new prime minister. Generous US support would continue, and the institutional basis for a dictatorship would be established (Cottam 1988, 106–107). With the aid of the United States, Mohammad Reza Shah assumed a new position of authority and reestablished traditional authoritarian rule. His policies would benefit US interests, and so he could count on American support for his repressive rule. Once again, the Iranian people were disappointed in their quest for a new role of independence for Iran. This shift from democracy to autocracy with a coup facilitated by the CIA is our first crucial historical episode.

### Second Crucial Historical Episode

The run-up to the second crucial historical episode begins in the imme-diate aftermath of the 1953 coup. It quickly became clear that the United States was replacing Britain as Iran's new patron. Iran remained in the role of a client, but the country was to take on additional attributes as laid out in Eisenhower's New Look strategy (Gasiorowski 1991, 93). The new US doctrine built on Truman's emphasis on Soviet containment, but it also recognized the costliness of American ground troops stationed overseas. Establishing or strengthening client states in spheres of Soviet influence was to serve US interests in more efficient ways. Tying sympa-thetic Western states in a formal political and economic alliance offered further organizational and operational benefits. Thus, the goal was to transform Iran "from a weak nation traditionally seeking a 'neutralist' position in world affairs into an anti-Communist asset" (U.S. National Security Council, 1955). No doubt, Iran was of crucial importance to American geopolitical goals and strategies. The Shah, in the words of President Lyndon Johnson was a "good guy" who was a defender of American interests in the Persian Gulf region (Bill 1988, 155–56).

By 1977, the Iranian populace's aversion against the Shah and the United States began to crest, and there was a predisposition for revo-lution (Bill 1988, 216; Cottam 1979, 5, 10; Ledeen and Lewis 1981, 97). The leader of the emerging movement was Ayatollah Khomeini, a con-servative cleric who had openly opposed the Shah and his oppressive reign since the 1960s. Khomeini was forced into exile from where he continued to position himself as a champion for Iranian independence. A central theme of his movement was the effort to strike a mortal blow at "American imperialism" (Ledeen and Lewis 1981, 107, 141; Bill 1988, 239). As the people's energy culminated in a revolution, the Shah was compelled to leave the country and Khomeini returned. Arriving from Paris at Teheran's Mehrabad airport on February 1, 1979, Khomeini (1981, 252–253) declared, "Our triumph will come when all forms of for-eign control have been brought to an end ...."

In the fall of that year, there was a serious escalation between the United States and Iran. On November 4th, a group of young men, call-ing themselves the "Students Following the Line of the Imam," stormed the American Embassy and took 66 diplomats and staffers as hostages. Among the demands were the return of the Shah to Iran for trial, a US apology for the 1953 coup, and the release of Iran's frozen assets in the United States (Bowden 2006, 548–551). A few were soon released, but 52 Americans were held for 444 days until January 20, 1981. When the revolution was over, the role relationship between the US and Iran had changed. The United States had not only lost an allied client but also gained an adversary. This transition is our second crucial historical episode.

### Third Crucial Historical Episode

In the 1980s, the enmity between the United States and Iran deepened further, as the United States supported Saddam Hussein in his war against Iran. In the mid-1990s, however, there would be a window of opportunity to redefine the relationship. It came with the election of Mohammad Khatami to the Iranian presidency. Khatami was a new type of leader, one that Western leaders did not anticipate and who spoke the language of conciliation.

Early in 1999, President Clinton responded to Khatami's appeals and endorsed cultural exchange, or "track two diplomacy," as it came to be called. Then came the horrific attacks of 9/11. Iran allowed the use of its airspace and port facilities for American military operations in Afghanistan and agreed to rescue downed US pilots. It also provided intelligence and detailed maps of bombing targets. Iran also facilitated an alliance with the Northern Alliance, which quickly proved a central ally on the ground in the defeat of the Taliban (Shakibi 2010, 213; Leverett and Leverett 2013, 76). This period of détente is our third crucial historical episode.

However, influential hawks and neo-conservatives in the Bush administration made sure that a lasting rapprochement would not come to pass. Their "ferocious" opposition rendered the Bush Administration unwilling to seize the "perfect opportunity" and remake the US-Iran role relationship (Slavin 2007, 196; Hunter 2010, 59; Leverett and Leverett 2013, 295–296). Instead, the opposite happened. In his State of the Union Address on January 29, 2002, President Bush branded Iran, along with Iraq and North Korea, as an "Axis-of-Evil." In the years to come, relations worsened significantly and improved only with the second term of the Obama Administration and the conclusion of the Joint Comprehensive Plan of Action (JCPOA) regarding Iran's nuclear energy program in July, 2015.

Finally, the US-Iran role relationship worsened again with the accession of the Donald Trump Administration in January, 2017. Trump's 2018 withdrawal from the nuclear proliferation agreement compelled a mutual escalation in US-Iran relations, which brought the two countries to the brink of war in 2019. To understand the current situation between the

United States and Iran, we conclude that one must understand the evolution of the relationship and the three crucial historical episodes as signposts in this evolution. It was these three historical junctures that shaped US-Iranian relations in fundamental ways and contributed significantly to the situation that the United States and the entire world face today in the Persian Gulf.

## Turning Points in US-Iran Relations: An Operational Code Analysis

The words in the preceding narratives of the three crucial historical episodes in US-Iran relations are from a language system (English), which is one medium of communication for transmitting and receiving information about each case. Our narrative of each case is both a sample and a summary of its history. In contrast, OCA employs mathematics and statistics to communicate information about the three cases. An OCA of US-Iran relations with the VICS of content analysis translates words in the language used by leaders and outside observers into symbols and algorithms, which communicate the "state of mind" of each agent's cognitive operational code and the "state of play" in the social operational code inferred from the interactions between the two agents.

The principles of sequential game theory use these binary symbols to represent the exchange of positive or negative sanctions between two agents as players in a game with rules of play in the form of alternating moves as the exercise of positive or negative sanctions. These games are extracted and identified from the chronologies of outside observers or inferred from the public statements of the players. They are the basis for revealing spatial and temporal patterns in the relations between the players (Walker, Schafer, and Young 1998; Brams 1994, 2002; Walker 2002, 2013; Walker and Schafer 2010). The rules for solving these games are outlined in the Appendix.

The VICS content analysis software program contains a dictionary of transitive verbs, which can be retrieved and coded by a language parser program (Profiler Plus) from a text that is stored as a digital file, e.g., a word file containing a public speech or interview emanating from government or media sources. A partial example of the contents retrieved by VICS from a particular text is in Figure 15.2. This example shows the binary information retrieved from a source and attributed either to Self or Other. The +s and −s represent the transitive verbs of cooperation (+) or conflict (−) in the source that are also in the VICS dictionary and identify the exercise of social power as a social act of reward (+3), promise (+2), support/appeal (+1) or oppose/resist (−1), threaten (−2), or punish (−3).

The information about intensity and type (word or deed) is omitted in this example, while each verb is shown as simply the exercise of a positive (+) or negative (−) sanction by Self or Other. The formulas for calculating

**Self:** $- - - - - + - - - - - + + + + + + - - - - - - - - - - - - - - - - - + - - - - -$ (n = 38)
    # of +'s = 8 (Cooperation)
    # of −'s = 30 (Conflict)
**I-1 (Self)**: [S(Coop) − S(Conf)] / [S(Coop) + S(Conf)]
    I-1= (8 − 30)/(8 + 30) = −.58

**Other:** $- + - - + + - + - - - - + + + + - + - - - - - - - - - - + - + - + + - - - +$ (n = 38)
    # of +'s = 14 Cooperation
    # of −'s = 24 Conflict
**P-1 (Other)**: [O(Coop) − O(Conf)] / [O(Coop) + O(Conf)]
    P-1 = (14 − 24) / (14 + 24) = −.26

**P-4a (Self)**: [(S / S + O) − O / (S + O)] = [38 / (38 + 38) − 38 / (38 + 38)] = .00
**P-4b (Other)**: [(O / S + O) − S / (S + O)] = [ 38 / (38 + 38) − 38 / (38 + 38)] = .00
**P-4d (P-4a minus P-4b)**: [.00 − .00] = .00

*Figure 15.2* The Calculation of VICS Indices for Key Operational Code Beliefs[*]

[*]S: Self; O: Other. I-1: Approach to Strategy; P-1: Political Universe; P-4 Historical Control

the percentages that are the basis for the VICS indices of these three operational code beliefs are straightforward. Each VICS index is the net difference between the percentage of positive sanctions (+'s) and negative sanctions (−'s) or the difference in the percentage of total sanctions exercised by Self and Other. The calculations of VICS indices for the three master beliefs (I-1) Strategic Orientation, (P-1) Nature of Political Universe, (P-4) Historical Control) are also shown in Figure 15.2.

They show that Self's I-1 index reveals a greater percentage of negative than positive sanctions attributed to Self (I-1 = −.58); the VICS index for Other shows a greater percentage of negative than positive sanctions is also attributed to Other (P-1 = −.26). The indices for the locus of historical control beliefs regarding the exercise of positive and negative sanctions are (P-4a = .00, P-4b = .00), which indicate that the percentages of total sanctions are evenly distributed between Self and Other (P-4d = .00).

The analysis of the text in Figure 15.2 could be of an imaginary public statement expressing the *cognitive* operational code of an imaginary public official. In fact, it is neither an imaginary nor an official statement. It is actually a chronology of Iran (Self) and the United Kingdom (Other) relations between 1950 and 1953, which represents an analytical summary of the *social* operational codes governing Iran and the United Kingdom, respectively, during the oil nationalization crisis that constitutes the first crucial historical episode. It is inferred from the exchange of cues (words and deeds) between Iran and Britain from March, 1951 to August, 1953; the cues were extracted from the *Washington Post* archives for this period (Malici and Walker 2017, Appendix 3: 196–206). It is a third-party, social account based on the actual conduct of Iran and Britain rather than a first-party, cognitive account based on the beliefs extracted from public statements by either state's leaders.

The VICS processes these information sources by screening, coding, and organizing the language in the texts, thereby making the transitive verbs into data for constructing VICS indices and doing an OCA (Young 2001). Depending on the information in the source, the results of the OCA represent the interactions between Self and Other with different degrees of precision. The results provide frequency counts of different types of transitive verbs, which can be coded, counted, and calculated to construct the balance and distribution between different types of verbs and between Self and Other, thereby providing a *spatial* map of the cognitive or social events attributed to Self and Other. However, missing from this inventory is the *temporal* order in which they occurred. There is no time line of dates to organize the chronology of events beyond their sequential order within the text and the grammatical (past, present, future) tense of the verbs (Schafer and Walker 2006).

Therefore, the valences (+ or − signs) attributed to Self and Other are simply building blocks for aggregation as VICS indices, which do not necessarily represent the temporal sequence in which cognitive or social events regarding the exercise of power actually occurred.

However, the information from the VICS indices is subject to temporal analysis if it is possible to order the events in question on a timeline. Fortunately, the temporal order of *social* events reported between Iran (Self) and Britain (Other) in Figure 15.2 is also available from the *Post* (see Malici and Walker 2017, Appendix 3: 196–206). We can test the temporal predictions of game theory models of role enactment derived from BRT and compare predictions from these models regarding the sequence of moves between Self and Other as Ego and Alter with the sequence of moves by Iran and Britain when the events in Figure 15.2 are organized by date on a time line.

## The First Crucial Historical Episode: The Oil Nationalization Crisis (1950–1953)

### *Binary Role Theory Analysis*

The 76 events for this crisis in Figure 15.2 are ordered temporally by date in the first half of Table 15.1 and partitioned into 19 strategic interaction episodes (SIEs) of four consecutive alternating events as moves exchanged between Self and Other per episode. Each SIE is a sequence of events that models a strategic interaction game between Self (Iran) and Other (Britain). The model for each SIE game is expressed as binary algorithms in the form of a bracketed series of zeros and ones and then compared to the binary algorithms for the BRT games predicted by different historical analyses of Iran-UK relations (Malici and Walker 2017, 87–92).

Systematic comparisons in Table 15.1a of the SIE algorithms for the 19 SIE's in the historical chronology with the algorithms for BRT's Weak

*Table 15.1a* Iran-Britain and Iran-US Binary Role Games, 1950–1953[a]

| | Weak Rival-Strong Rival BRT Game | | | | |
|---|---|---|---|---|---|
| Games | Iran | Britain | Games | Iran | Britain |
| Pred. | [1110] | [1011] | Pred. | [1110] | [1011] |
| Act. | [1110] | [1011] | Act. | [1110] | [1011] |
| **E#1.** | **C = 1.0** | **C = 1.0** | **E#11.** | **C = 1.0** | **C = 1.0** |
| Pred. | [1110] | [1011] | Pred. | [1110] | [1011] |
| Act. | [1110] | [1011] | Act. | [1110] | [1011] |
| **E#2.** | **C = 1.0** | **C = 1.0** | **E#12.** | **C = 1.0** | **C = 1.0** |
| Pred. | [1110] | [1011] | Pred. | [1110] | [1011] |
| Act. | [1110] | [0001] | Act. | [1110] | [1011] |
| **E#3.** | **C = 1.0** | **C = .50** | **E#13.** | **C = 1.0** | **C = 1.0** |
| Pred. | [1110] | [1011] | Pred. | [1110] | [1011] |
| Act. | [1110] | [1011] | Act. | [1110] | [1011] |
| **E#4.** | **C = 1.0** | **C = 1.0** | **E#14.** | **C = 1.0** | **C = 1.0** |
| Pred. | [1110] | [1011] | Pred. | [1110] | [1011] |
| Act. | [1110] | [1011] | Act. | [1111] | [0011] |
| **E#5.** | **C = 1.0** | **C = 1.0** | **E#15.** | **C = .75** | **C = .75** |
| Pred. | [1110] | [1011] | Pred. | [1110] | [1011] |
| Act. | [1010] | [1111] | Act. | [1111] | [0011] |
| **E#6.** | **C = .75** | **C = .75** | **E#16.** | **C = .75** | **C = .75** |
| Pred. | [1110] | [1011] | Pred. | [1110] | [1011] |
| Act. | [0100] | [0001] | Act. | [0101] | [0000] |
| **E#7.** | **C = .50** | **C = .50** | **E#17.** | **C = .25** | **C = .25** |
| Pred. | [1110] | [1011] | Pred. | [1110] | [1011] |
| Act. | [0100] | [0001] | Act. | [1110] | [1011] |
| **E#8.** | **C = .50** | **C = .50** | **E#18.** | **C = 1.0** | **C = 1.0** |
| Pred. | [1110] | [1011] | Pred. | [1110] | [1011] |
| Act. | [0110] | [1111] | Act. | [1110] | [1011] |
| **E#9.** | **C = .75** | **C = .75.** | **E#19.** | **C = 1.0** | **C = 1.0** |
| Pred. | [1110] | [1011] | $\Sigma$1–19 | 16.25 | 15.75 |
| Act. | [1110] | [1011] | **Mean** | **.86** | **.83** |
| **E#10.** | **C = 1.0** | **C = 1.0** | **$\Sigma$Mean** | | **.85** |

[a]*Note:* Pred. is predicted algorithm and Act. is actual algorithm. E# is episode number. Data source: Malici and Walker (2017).

*Table 15.1b* Iran-Britain and Iran-US Binary Role Games, 1950–1953[a]

| Games | Iran | United States | Games | Iran | United States |
|-------|------|---------------|-------|------|---------------|
| | | *Partner-Partner BRT Game* | | | |
| Pred. | [0100] | [0001] | Pred. | [0100 | [0001] |
| Act. | [1110] | [0000] | Act. | [0101] | [0000] |
| **E#1.** | **C = .50** | **C = .75** | **E#7.** | **C = .75** | **C = .75** |
| Pred. | [0100] | [0001] | Pred. | [0100 | [0001] |
| Act. | [0100] | [0001] | Act. | [0110] | [1111] |
| **E#2.** | **C = 1.0** | **C = 1.0** | **E#8.** | **C = .75** | **C = .25** |
| Pred. | [0100] | [0001] | Pred. | [0100 | [0001] |
| Act. | [0100] | [0001] | Act. | [1101] | [1000] |
| **E#3.** | **C = 1.0** | **C = 1.0** | **E#9.** | **C = .50** | **C = .50** |
| Pred. | [0100] | [0001] | Pred. | [0100 | [0001] |
| Act. | [0100] | [0001] | Act. | [1101] | [1000] |
| **E#4.** | **C = 1.0** | **C = 1.0** | **E#10.** | **C = .25** | **C = .50** |
| Pred. | [0100] | [0001] | Pred. | [0100 | [0001] |
| Act. | [0100] | [0001] | Act. | [0100] | [0001] |
| **E#5.** | **C = 1.0** | **C = 1.0** | **E#11.** | **C = .1.0** | **C = 1.0** |
| Pred. | [0100] | [0001] | Pred. | [0100 | [0001] |
| Act. | [0110] | [0000] | Act. | [1111] | [0011] |
| **E#6.** | **C = .50** | **C = .75** | **E#12.** | **C = .25** | **C = .75** |
| Σ1–6 | 5.00 | 5.50 | Σ7–12 | 3.50 | 3.75 |
| **Mean** | **.83** | **.92** | **Mean** | **.58** | **.63** |
| **ΣMean** | | **.88** | **ΣMean** | | **.61** |

| | | *Summary Analysis* | | | |
|-------|------|---------------|-------|------|---------------|
| Games | Iran | Britain | Games | Iran | United States |
| Σ1–19 | 16.25 | 15.75 | Σ1–12 | 8.50 | 9.25 |
| **Mean** | **.86** | **.83** | **Mean C** | **.71** | **.77** |
| **ΣMean** | | **.85** | **ΣMean** | | **.74** |

[a]*Note:* Pred. is predicted algorithm and Act. is actual algorithm. E# is episode number. Data source: Malici and Walker (2017).

Rival-Strong Rival game reveals the degree of congruence or fit between them. The degree of congruence (C-score) is calculated as the percent agreement between the Iran algorithms for each model and the UK algorithms for each model. These percentages are then summed and divided by the number of episodes to get the mean (average) degree of congruence or "fit" between the social operational code model from BRT and the actual game models of the 19 SIEs (Malici and Walker 2017, 86–92).[2] The underlying logic of the algorithms and the calculation of the fit between the predicted and actual games is explained and illustrated in the Appendix.

The results in Table 15.1a show the fit for each episode by comparing the algorithms for the BRT model with the algorithms for each episode and calculating the congruence (C) between them. The results from the BRT analysis following Episode #19 show that the BRT model's overall results (Mean C = .85) clearly exceeds the (C ≥ .70) threshold. The fit between the predictions of the two models for Iran (Mean C = .86) and Britain (Mean C = .83) are both very good (C ≥ .70) and are also very close to one another. The fit for individual episodes is also impressive, falling below (C = .70) for both agents in only three episodes (E#7, #8, and #17). A similar analysis of Iran-US relations in the second half of Table 15.1 during the same crisis shows a relatively good fit between the BRT's Partner-Partner model and Iran-US relations for the 12 SIEs between March, 1951 and August, 1953.

The summary analysis in Table 15.1b shows a ΣMean C = .71 for Iran and .77 for United States plus a ΣMean C of .74 for the collective Iran-US role dyad. However, Iran shifts its strategies from cooperation in the first six episodes to conflict in the final six, which decreases the fit between the BRT's Partner-Partner role model for Iran from ΣMean C = .83 for the first six episodes to ΣMean C = .58 for the last six. The same shift in strategies occurs for the United States, which decreases the fit for the United States from .92 to .63. The ΣMean C for the role dyad consequently decreases from C = .88 in the first six episodes to C = .61 in the last six. The congruence for the Partner role is greater than .70 for both Iran and the United States in the first set and lower for both agents in the last set of episodes. The fit with the Partner role is better in both sets of episodes for the United States (C = .92 and .63) than for Iran (C = .83 and .58).

The 13th and final episode (not shown in Table 15.1) in Iran-US relations was marked by the enactment of a Rebel (Weak Rival) role by Iran and a Rival role by the United States. It accompanied a change in Iran's leadership from Mohammad Mossadegh as Prime Minister to Mohammad Reza as the Shah via a coup led by the CIA against the Mossadegh government, which installed a Client-Patron role dyad as the norm to govern relations between the Shah's new government and the Eisenhower Administration in the United States. The games that model

|  | USA | |  | USA | |  | USA | |  | USA | |
|---|---|---|---|---|---|---|---|---|---|---|---|
|  | CO+ | CF− |  | CO+ | CF− |  | CO+ | CF− |  | CO+ | CF− |
| CO+ | **4,4** | 2,3 | CO+ | 2,4 | "1,2" | CO+ | 1,3 | 3,1 | CO+ | "**3,4**" | 4,3 |
| **IRAN** | | | **IRAN** | | | **IRAN** | | | **IRAN** | | |
| CF− | "1,1" | 3,2 | CF− | 4,1 | **3,3** | CF− | 2,2 | "**4,4**" | CF− | 1,1 | 2,2 |

| E#11 | E#12 | E#13 | Post-Coup |
|---|---|---|---|
| **Partner-Patron Game** | **Hegemon-Partner Game** | **Rebel-Rival Game** | **Client-Patron Game** |
| Role Dyad {+ + + −} | Role Dyad: {− + − −} | Role Dyad: {− − + +} | Role Dyad: {+ + + +} |
| IRA: Reward (+ + +) | IRA: Bully (− + −) | IRA: Bluff (− − +) | IRA: Reward (+ + +) |
| (0,1,2,3/0 [0100] | (0,1,2/2 & 3/3) [1111] | (0,1,2,3/2) [1110] | (0,2,3/0 &1/1) [0000] |
| USA: Exploit (+ + −) | USA: Deter (+ − −) | USA: Compel (− + +) | USA: Reward (+ + +) |
| (0,1,2,3/0) [0001] | (1,2,3/2 & 0/0) [0011] | (0,1,2,3/2) [1011] | (0,2,3/0 & 1,1) [0101] |

*Figure 15.3* Final Three Strategic Interaction Episodes and Postcoup Iran-USA
Game*

*Nonmyopic equilibrium solutions are in bold. Initial states are in quotation marks and outcomes are underlined. Each player's preferences for the four outcomes of each game are ranked from (4) highest to (1) lowest in each cell separated by a comma with the row player's ranking entered on the left side and the column player's ranking entered on the right side of the comma

the final three episodes (#11, #12, #13) preceding the coup plus the likely postcoup game are analyzed in Figure 15.3 (Malici and Walker 2017, 80, 98–99). These games are not congruent with a Partner-Partner game with the exception of the Partner-Patron (Strong Partner) game in Episode #11. None of the other episodes are congruent with the Partner-Partner game dating back until SIE#5, which marks when Britain and Iran appealed to US President Truman to mediate their dispute over Iranian oil and British oil concessions.

## Operational Code Analysis

A social OCA of the moves selected by Iran and Britain in this crisis can provide additional information on *how* each player enacted its respective roles toward one another. VICS indices reveal the (I-1) strategic balance (+ or −), the (I-2) tactical intensity (+1.0 to −1.0) of cooperation or conflict behavior, the (I-3) variation in risk orientation (.00 risk-averse to 1.0 risk-acceptant), the shift propensities (.00 low to 1.0 high flexibility) between (I-4a) cooperation vs. conflict and (I-4b) words vs. deeds, and the percentages (.00 low to 1.0 high) of different positive and negative sanctions by each protagonist on the I-5 scale (+3 to −3) of moves. This information reveals the respective centers of gravity between Iran and the United States regarding these characteristics. The indices can also be aggregated for the role dyad and compared across crises to assess the relative intensity, volatility, and predictability of these confrontations between Iran and Britain or the United States as turning points in world politics. The formulas for these VICS indices are shown in Table 15.2.

*Table 15.2* Verbs In Context System (VICS) Indices for Social Operational Codes

| | Elements | Index* | Interpretation |
|---|---|---|---|
| I-1. | APPROACH TO GOALS (Direction of Strategy) | % Positive minus % Negative Transitive Self-Attributions | +1.0 high cooperation to −1.0 high conflict |
| I-2. | PURSUIT OF GOALS (Intensity of Tactics) | Mean Intensity of Transitive Self-Attributions divided by 3 | +1.0 high cooperation to −1.0 high conflict |
| I-3. | RISK ORIENTATION** (Predictability of Tactics) | 1 minus Index of Qualitative Variation for Self-Attributions | 1.0 risk acceptant to .0 risk averse |
| I-4. | TIMING OF ACTION (Flexibility of Tactics) | 1 minus Absolute Value [% X minus % Y Self-Attributions] | 1.0 high to .0 low shift propensity be-tween Coop and Conf or Words and Deeds. |
| | a. Coop vs. Conf. Tactics | Where X = Coop and Y = Conf | |
| | b. Word vs. Deed Tactics | Where X = Word and Y = Deed | |
| I-5. | UTILITY OF MEANS (Exercise of Power) | Percentages of Self-Attributions for Power Categories a. through f. | +1.0 very frequent to .0 infrequent |

a. Reward. b. Promise. c. Appeal/Support. d. Oppose/Resist. e. Threaten. f. Punish.

*Indices vary between 0 and 1.0 except for I-1 and I-2, which vary between −1.0 and +1.0. I-2 is divided by 3 to standardize the range (Walker, Schafer, and Young 1998).

**"The Index of Qualitative Variation (IQV) for I-3 is a ratio of the number of different pairs of observations in a distribution to the maximum possible number of different pairs for a distribution with the same N [number of cases] and the same number of variable classifications" (Watson and McGaw 1980, 88). The IQV formula for calculating the results for the I-3 risk orientation scores here is IQV Index = $K(100\%^2 − \Sigma Pct^2/100\%^2)(K-1)$ where K = 6 (the number of I-5 categories a. through f.) and $\Sigma Pct^2$ is the sum of each percentage (a. through f.) of the I-5 scores (see also Crossman 2020).

The results for the OCA of the foreign policy roles enacted by Iran and Britain during the oil nationalization crisis are shown in Table 15.3. While both Iran and Britain pursued conflict strategies that matched their respective Rival roles, Iran's strategy (I-1) was more consistently conflictual (−.58 vs. −.26). The intensity of Iran's tactics (I-2) was also more conflictual (−.34 vs. −.15) and more risk-acceptant (I-3) regarding the escalation of conflict (.08 vs. .03) than Britain with lower propensities to shift between conflict and cooperation (I-4a = .41 vs. .74) and greater propensities, respectively, to use threats (I-5e = .342 vs. .184) and punishments (I-5f = .211 vs. .184) than Britain.

The United Kingdom primarily managed the risk of escalation in this crisis with its higher propensity to shift between conflict and cooperation.

*Table 15.3* Social Operational Codes for Iran-UK and Iran-US Dyads, 1950–1953[a]

| Index | Iran | United Kingdom | Dyad | Iran | United States | Dyad |
|---|---|---|---|---|---|---|
| I-1. Strategy | −.58 | −.26 | −.42 | +.15 | +.62 | +.38 |
| I-2. Tactics | −.34 | −.15 | −.26 | +.10 | +.31 | +.21 |
| I-3. Risk | .08 | .03 | .04 | .05 | .26 | .14 |
| I-4. Timing[b] | .41/.63 | .74/.68 | .58/.66 | .85/.62 | .38/.70 | .53/.60 |
| I-5. Sanctions | | | | | | |
| a. Reward | .105 | .158 | .132 | .192 | .269 | .231 |
| b. Promise | .026 | .053 | .039 | .077 | .000 | .038 |
| c. Support | .079 | .158 | .118 | .308 | .538 | .423 |
| d. Oppose | .237 | .263 | .250 | .230 | .038 | .135 |
| e. Threaten | .342 | .184 | .263 | .077 | .077 | .077 |
| f. Punish | .211 | .184 | .197 | .115 | .077 | .096 |

[a]Data source: Malici and Walker (2017).
[b]Flexibility of tactics: coop vs. conf./words vs. deeds.

Both Iran and Britain also managed the risk of escalation with similar propensities to shift between words and deeds (I-4b. = .63 and .68) in the exercise of their respective tactics and strategies. The aggregate operational code profile for the Iran-UK role dyad in Table 15.3 is marked by relatively high conflict strategies (I-1 = −.42), relatively low conflict tactics (I-2 = −.26), a very risk-averse orientation (I-3 = .04), and robust shift propensities (I-4) to shift between conflict or cooperation (.58) and words or deeds (.66). The collective propensity to use threats (I-5e) was greater (.263) than the propensity to use punishments (.197) in this crucial historical episode.

Britain and the United States pursued cooperation strategies in Table 15.3 consistent with their respective Partner roles, although the US strategy (I-1) was more consistently cooperative (+.62 vs. +.15). The intensity of US tactics (I-2) was also three times more cooperative (+.31 vs. +.10) and five times more risk-acceptant (I-3) regarding domination by Iran (.26 vs. .05) with a much lower propensity than Iran to shift between conflict and cooperation (I-4a = .38 vs. .85) Both Iran and the United States managed the risk of escalation with similar propensities to shift between words and deeds (I-4b. = .62 and .70) in the exercise of their respective tactics and strategies. Finally, the operational code profile for the Iran-US role dyad is marked by relatively robust cooperation strategies (I-1 = +.38), relatively moderate cooperation tactics (I-2 = +.21), a somewhat risk-averse orientation (I-3 = .14), and robust shift propensities (I-4) to shift between conflict or cooperation (.53) and words or deeds (.60). The collective propensity to use positive sanctions (I-5) was over twice as high (.692) as the propensity to use negative sanctions (.308) in this crucial historical episode.

## The Second Crucial Historical Episode: The Revolution and Hostage Crisis (1978–1981)

The Iran-US game in Figure 15.3 following the CIA-led coup to replace the Mossadegh government with autocratic rule by the Shah in August, 1953 assigns a Client role to Iran and a Patron role to the United States. It has two nonmyopic (NME) equilibrium solutions. The (3,4) solution of mutual cooperation (+ +) is the equilibrium solution from each cell as the initial state except for the upper right cell when (4,3) Iranian submission and US domination (+–) is the solution as well as the initial state. These outcomes reflect the power asymmetry between Iran and the United States, in which Iran's choice as a Client is to choose cooperation (+) no matter whether the US choice as a Patron is cooperation (+) or conflict (–).

The United States thereby replaced Britain as the dominant external power in the Middle East during the Cold War and became the focus of Iran's resentment against foreign influence in their domestic affairs via the US exploitation of Iran as a junior diplomatic partner and military ally. The political opposition to the Shah's government and to the US presence in Iran was led by the Ayatollah Khomeini. He returned in February, 1979 from political exile in Paris following the Shah's ouster by revolutionary forces at the end of 1978 and departure later in 1979 from the country to seek medical treatment for cancer. When students stormed the US Embassy in early November, 1979 and demanded the Shah's return from the United States for trial in Iran, relations between Washington and the new government in Tehran deteriorated rapidly (Malici and Walker 2017).

### Binary Role Theory Analysis

The analysis of the dynamics between Washington and Tehran in Table 15.4 indicates that Iran and the United States engaged in a pattern of role enactment as mutual Rivals from the seizure of hostages by Iranian students

*Table 15.4* Summary Analysis of Iran-US Rival-Rival Role Games, 1978–1981[a]

| Games | Iran | United States | Games | Iran | United States | Games | Iran | United States |
|---|---|---|---|---|---|---|---|---|
| Σ1–10 | 6.50 | 6.00 | Σ11–20 | 8.00 | 8.25 | Σ21–30 | 7.25 | 7.00 |
| **Mean** | **.65** | **.60** | **Mean** | **.80** | **.83** | **Mean** | **.73** | **.70** |
| ΣC1–5 | 3.00 | 2.50 | Σ11–15 | 4.00 | 4.00 | Σ21–25 | 3.25 | 4.00 |
| **Mean** | **.60** | **.50** | **Mean** | **.80** | **.80** | **Mean** | **.65** | **.80** |
| ΣC6–10 | 3.50 | 3.50 | Σ16–20 | 4.00 | 4.25 | Σ26–30 | 4.00 | 3.00 |
| **Mean** | **.70** | **.70** | **Mean** | **.80** | **.85** | **Mean** | **.80** | **.60** |
| ΣMean 1–10 | | .63 | ΣMean 11–20 | | .83 | ΣMean 21–30 | | .70 |

[a]Data source: Malici and Walker (2017).

in November, 1979 until their attempted rescue by US commando forces failed in April, 1980. The boundary episodes for this 1978–1981 period in Table 15.4 are Episode #5 and Episode #20. Between these boundaries, the prediction algorithms of the Rival-Rival model consistently fit the roles enacted by each member of the dyad with congruence scores averaging well above (C ≥ .70) for this period with both Iran matching their actual behavior to the model's predictions. In contrast, there is a poor fit between the predictions of the model and the strategies of the agents during the first five episodes (E#1–E#5) with low Mean congruence scores for Iran (C = .60) and the United States (C = .50). The fit for the final ten episodes (E#21–E#30) is volatile but still has a ∑Mean C = .70 score. The entire sequence of games is in the Appendix.

## *Operational Code Analysis*

An OCA in Table 15.5 of the moves selected by Iran and the United States in the hostage crisis provides additional insights into how each player enacted their respective Rival roles toward one another. The VICS indices for the hostage crisis in Table 15.5 reveal that their conflict strategies (I-1) were very similar (−.24 vs. −.20). The intensity of their tactics (I-2) was also very close (−.23 and −.22) with virtually the same risk-averse orientation (I-3) regarding the escalation of conflict (.06 and .05). Their propensities to shift between conflict and cooperation (I-4a) displayed the same symmetry (.76 and .80), as did their shift propensities between words and deeds (.44 and .50). The symmetry pattern extends to their use

*Table 15.5* Social Operational Codes for Iran-US Dyads, 1978–1981[a]

| Index | 1978–1981 Revolution/Hostage Crisis | | |
| --- | --- | --- | --- |
| | *Iran* | *United States* | *Dyad* |
| I-1. Strategy | −.24 | −.20 | −.26 |
| I-2. Tactics | −.23 | −.22 | −.23 |
| I-3. Risk[b] | .06 | .05 | .05 |
| I-4. Timing[c] | .76/.44 | .80/.50 | .74/.46 |
| I-5. Sanctions | | | |
| a. Reward | .100 | .117 | .108 |
| b. Promise | .067 | .067 | .067 |
| c. Support | .217 | .217 | .217 |
| d. Oppose | .350 | .317 | .333 |
| e. Threaten | .150 | .150 | .150 |
| f. Punish | .117 | .133 | .125 |

[a]Data source: Malici and Walker (2017).
[b]IQV Index = K(100%$^2$ − ∑Pct$^2$/100%$^2$ (K−1) where K = 6 (the number of I-5 categories a. through f.) and ∑Pct$^2$ is the sum of each percentage (a. through f.) of I-5 scores.
[c]Flexibility of tactics: coop vs. conf./words vs. deeds.

of positive and negative sanctions (I-5) in Table 15.5, which is consistent with the enactment of a Rival role by each agent with reciprocity strategies of contingent conflict.

The collective operational code profile for the Iran-US role dyad in this crisis period mirrors these symmetrical patterns regarding the direction of strategy (I-1), the intensity of tactics (I-2), risk orientation (I-3), and the management of risk (I-4a and I-4b). This crisis is marked by moderate conflict strategies (–.26) and tactics (–.23), a very risk-averse orientation (I-3 = .05), a very robust flexibility (I-4) to shift between conflict or cooperation (.74) and a lower propensity to shift between words or deeds (.46). The collective propensity to use words (.77) as positive or negative sanctions (I-5) was three times greater than the propensity to use deeds (.23) in this crucial historical episode, a pattern exhibited by both Iran (.78 vs. .22) and the United States (.75 vs. 25). Following the failure of the US attempt to rescue American hostages held by Iran in April, 1980, the two protagonists were able to negotiate their release with the signing of the Algiers Accord in January, 1981, which ended the crisis. The timing of the agreement coincided with the ascendance of the Reagan Administration in Washington, DC.

## The Third Crucial Historical Episode:
## The Détente Period (1997–2002)

Although the Algiers Accord called for the end of US military and political intervention, directly or indirectly, in the domestic affairs of Iran, the new US Administration did not honor this pledge, and the two states remained Rivals for over a decade and a half until the beginning of the second term of the Clinton Administration (Malici and Walker 2017, 143–156). When President Khatami launched an attempt to relax tensions between Iran and the United States in 1998, the United States also responded with conciliatory moves. Both sides began to normalize relations with cultural exchange programs and new trade relations. When the United States was attacked by Al Qaeda terrorists on September 11, 2001, the cooperation between Washington and Tehran to find and defeat Al Qaeda in Afghanistan extended to diplomatic and military coordination between them. However, this trend toward rapprochement and the normalization of relations between Iran and the United States was arrested by the ascendance of the Bush Administration in 2001.

### *Binary Role Theory Analysis*

An analysis of Iran-US relations in Table 15.6 during the détente period shows a relatively good fit between the BRT's Partner-Partner model and Iran-US relations for the 13 SIEs between August, 1997 and January, 2002 (Mean C = .69 for Iran and .73 for United States) and a ∑Mean C of .71 for

*Table 15.6* Comparisons of Binary Role Models for Détente Period, 1997–2002[a]

|  | Rival-Rival Model | | Partner-Partner Model | | Axis-of-Evil Model | |
| --- | --- | --- | --- | --- | --- | --- |
| Games | Iran | United States | Iran | United States | Iran | United States |
| ∑C1–6 | 4.25 | 3.75 | 4.25 | 4.75 | 1.75 | 3.75 |
| Mean | .71 | .63 | .71 | .79 | .29 | .63 |
| ∑C7–13 | 4.75 | 4.25 | 4.75 | 4.75 | 2.00 | 3.00 |
| Mean | .68 | .61 | .68 | .68 | .29 | .43 |
| ∑C1–13 | 9.00 | 8.00 | 9.00 | 9.50 | 3.75 | 6.75 |
| Mean | .69 | .62 | .69 | .73 | .29 | .52 |
| ∑Mean 1–13 | .66 | | .71 | | .41 | |

[a]Data source: Malici and Walker (2017).

the joint Iran-US role dyad. Iran and the United States shift their respective strategies from cooperation in the first six episodes toward conflict in the final seven episodes, however, which decreases the fit between the BRT's Partner-Partner role model to ∑Mean C = .68 for the last seven episodes. The decreased fit for the Partner-Partner role is accompanied by a change from the Clinton Administration to the Bush Administration in Washington, DC, which culminates in the "Axis-of-Evil" passage in President Bush's State of the Union address in January, 2002. The 13th and final SIE in Table 15.6 includes this declaration, which redefines relations between Iran and the United States.

The three games in Figure 15.4 include the two models of Iran-US relations bracketing the 1997–2002 time period associated with the Partner-Partner détente model in Table 15.5. Compared to the fit for the Partner-Partner model (∑Mean C = .71), the Rival-Rival conflict model of Iran-US relations prior to 1997 associated with Khomeini is a poor fit (∑Mean C = .66), as is the "Axis-of-Evil" model after 2002 (∑Mean C = .41), for the 13 SIEs between 1997 and 2002.

The "Axis-of-Evil" game in Figure 15.4, which was implied by President Bush in his State of the Union address, is a mutual Enemies game with

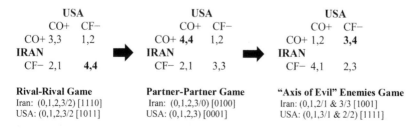

*Figure 15.4* Role Transition Models in Iran-US Relations, 1997–2002*

*Nonmyopic equilibrium solutions are in bold. Arrows show the time sequence between 1997 and 2002. CO+: Cooperation; CF–: Conflict

Iran enacting a Rebel (Weak Enemy) role as a rogue state and the United States enacting a Hegemon (Strong Enemy) role as an anti-terrorist state. A comparison of the relative fit of these models with the data in Table 15.5 demarcates the détente period as clearly an aborted departure from the Iran-US rivalry that preceded it and the deterioration in Iran-US relations that followed it.

### Operational Code Analysis

A comparison of the operational code profiles for Iran and the United States during the rivalry and détente periods reenforces the contrasts depicted by the transition from a Rival-Rival to a Partner-Partner game while qualifying the durability of the transition. Iran's (I-1) strategy in Table 15.5 de-escalated from a conditional strategy of conflict (−.24) in the hostage crisis to a marginal strategy (I-1) of conflict (−.08) in Table 15.7 and from relatively intense (I-2) conflict tactics (−.23) to mixed tactics (±.00) of conflict and cooperation with a very high shift propensity (I-4a) between cooperation and conflict (.92). The high shift propensity between cooperation and conflict was not accompanied by a high propensity (I-4b) to shift between words and deeds (.30), reflecting that the Iranian shifts between cooperation and conflict were primarily limited to words in the form of diplomatic statements of support (I-5c = .308) or opposition (I-5d = .462).

*Table 15.7* Social Operational Codes for Iran-US Dyads, 1997–2002[a]

| Index | 1997–2002 Détente Period | | |
| | *Iran* | *United States* | *Dyad* |
| --- | --- | --- | --- |
| I-1. Strategy | −.08 | +.23 | +.08 |
| I-2. Tactics | +.00 | +.27 | +.13 |
| I-3. Risk[b] | .19 | .15 | .15 |
| I-4. Timing[c] | .92/.30 | .77/.70 | .92/.50 |
| I-5. Sanctions | | | |
| a. Reward | .077 | .308 | .192 |
| b. Promise | .077 | .038 | .058 |
| c. Support | .308 | .269 | .288 |
| d. Oppose | .462 | .346 | .404 |
| e. Threaten | .000 | .000 | .000 |
| f. Punish | .077 | .038 | .058 |

[a]Data source: Malici and Walker (2017).
[b]Risk IQV Index = $K(100\%^2 - \sum Pct^2/100\%^2 (K-1)$ where K = 6 (the number of I-5 categories a. through f.) and $\sum Pct^2$ is the sum of each percentage (a. through f.) of I-5 scores.
[c]Timing index is flexibility of tactics: coop vs. conf. and words vs. deeds.

The US strategy (I-1) shows a much more pronounced transition from a strategy of conditional conflict (–.20) to conditional cooperation (+.23) and tactics (I-2) exhibiting decidedly more cooperation (–.22 vs. +.27) while retaining a relatively high shift propensity (I-4a) between cooperation and conflict (.80 vs .77) and a higher shift propensity (I-4b) between words and deeds than Iran in both the rivalry period (.50 vs. .44) and the détente period (.70 vs. .30). The risk orientations of both Iran and the United States shifted from very risk-averse (.06 and .05) to modestly risk-acceptant (.19 and .15) orientations across the rivalry and détente periods. Finally, the collective operational code profile for the Iran-US role dyad during the détente period is marked by marginal strategies of cooperation (I-1 = +.08), relatively low conflict tactics (I-2 = +.13), a modestly risk-acceptant orientation (I-3 = .15), and a much greater shift propensity (I-4) between conflict or cooperation (.92) than between words and deeds (.50). Also notable is the lack of credible threats (I-5e) overtly exchanged between Iran and the United States (Walker and Hoagland 1979; Walker 1982).

## Conclusion

In this chapter, we have employed the metrics and methods of OCA and the concepts and models of BRT to do an analysis of the foreign policy roles enacted during three crucial historical episodes in US-Iran relations (Malici and Walker 2017). The analyses in these case studies illustrate how an alliance between OCA and role theory can yield results that complement one another across spatial and temporal levels of analysis and bridge the gap between foreign policy analysis and the analysis of international relations between the United States and Iran. They provide a "proof-of-concept" test in support of an agent-based research design to generate system-level results.

The methodological expansion of the operational code from a cognitive to a social construct links the interior world of mental events in the minds of agents with the exterior world of social events in world politics. They are both complex adaptive systems that share strategies, tactics, and moves as isomorphic phenomena constituting both the dimensions of beliefs as cognitive systems and the elements of roles as social systems. The formal theoretical bridge uniting cognitive and social OCA is BRT in this chapter. Its concepts provide the spatial and temporal scope necessary to expand the analysis of foreign policy decisions in space and time to encompass interactions between states as agents as well as decisions by them. The next step in future research would seem to be "scaling up" from one role dyad to multiple sets of role dyads in regional systems over longer periods of time.

## Methodological Appendix: Game Theory
## Models of Role Enactment Patterns

BRT employs mathematical models from sequential game theory (Brams 1994) to represent the exchange of cues between two agents (Ego and Alter) as a process of role location. A $2 \times 2$ game is inferred from the consecutive exchange of four alternating cues between Ego and Alter. It is represented as a matrix formed by two rows and two columns (hence a $2 \times 2$ game). Each cell in the matrix represents the intersection of different pairs of choices by the players. In BRT, the players are Ego (row) and Alter (column) with the two choices being cooperation (CO+) and conflict (CF−). The four cells represent the intersection of these choices made by the two players, which define the possible outcomes of the game as the following social power relations between them: CO+,CO− (mutual cooperation); CO+,CF− (submission by Ego and domination by Alter); CF−,CF− (mutual conflict); CF−,CO+ (domination by Ego and submission by Alter). The $2 \times 2$ game matrix employed by BRT to specify these possibilities is in Figure 15.5 (Walker and Malici 2011, 28–33).

The strategies for playing the game constructed by this matrix are for Ego and Alter to rank the four cells as outcomes from highest (4) to lowest (1) and to choose "stay" or "move" from each cell until both players choose "stay" and the game ends. Each player has two basic strategies: cooperation (+) or conflict (−) with two variants. A dominant strategy is "always choose cooperation" or "always choose conflict," while a conditional strategy is either "reciprocate cooperation or conflict" or "do not reciprocate cooperation or conflict." Examples of each kind of strategy are presented in Figure 15.6 (Walker, Malici, and Schafer 2011; see also Brams 1994).

The game in Figure 15.6 is an example of a game in which Self (the row player) has a dominant "always choose conflict" strategy regarding cooperation and conflict, while Other (the column player) has a conditional strategy of "reciprocate cooperation and conflict." If the rules of play are for each player to make alternating choices to "stay" or "move" from an "initial state" until both choose "stay," then depending on the "initial state" (cell) from which play begins in this game, the "final state" (solution) is (3,3) mutual cooperation (3,3) or mutual conflict (2,4).[3]

|  |  | Alter | |
|---|---|---|---|
|  |  | CO+ | CF− |
|  | CO+ | (+,+) | (+,−) |
| Ego |  |  |  |
|  | CF− | (−,+) | (−,−) |

*Figure 15.5* A $2 \times 2$ Game Matrix*

*CO+: Cooperate; CF−: Conflict

## Examples of Ego's Possible Strategies

**Dominant\*\***                                **Conditional\*\***

| | Alter + | Alter − | | | Alter + | Alter − |
|---|---|---|---|---|---|---|
| Ego + | 4 | 3 | | Ego + | 3 | 1 |
| Ego − | 2 | 1 | | Ego − | 4 | 2 |
| | Always Choose Cooperation | | | | Always Choose Conflict | |

| | Alter + | Alter − | | | Alter + | Alter − |
|---|---|---|---|---|---|---|
| Ego + | 3 | 1 | | Ego + | 3 | 2 |
| Ego − | 2 | 4 | | Ego − | 4 | 1 |
| | Reciprocate Coop & Conf | | | | Don't Reciprocate Coop & Conf | |

| | Alter + | Alter − | | | Alter + | Alter − | | | Alter + | Alter − |
|---|---|---|---|---|---|---|---|---|---|---|
| Ego + | 3 | 1 | | Ego + | **3,3** | 1,2 | | Ego + | 3 | 2 |
| Ego − | 4 | 2 | | Ego − | **4,1** | **2,4\*** | | Ego − | 1 | 4 |

| Ego's Strategy | (G49) Enemy-Rival Game* | Alter's Strategy |
|---|---|---|
| **Dominant** | Ego: (0/0,1/2,2/0,3/3) [0101] | **Conditional** |
| **Conflict** | Alter: (0/2,1/0,2/2,3/2) [1011] | **Reciprocity** |

*Figure 15.6* A 2 × 2 Game and Examples of Dominant and Conditional Strategies

*The game's identification number (G49) is taken from the taxonomy of 2 × 2 games in Brams (1994, 219). A Nash equilibrium solution is asterisked, while nonmyopic equilibrium (NME) solutions are in bold for the game. The numbers in parentheses separated by a slash below the game are its cells numbered from "0" the upper left cell clockwise to "3" the lower right cell. The slash separates an "initial state" cell from the "final state" cell for each player's strategy, e.g., 2/0 for Self reads "If initial state for Self is the lower right cell/ then the final state cell for Self is upper-left cell." The numbers in brackets are algorithms for "0" cooperate and "1" conflict choices made by Self and Other from each cell in the game matrix reading clockwise from the upper left cell to the lower left cell. **These examples of Ego's dominant strategy (always choose conflict) and Alter's conditional strategy (reciprocate cooperation and conflict) rank the outcomes from highest (4) to lowest (1) as payoffs in their respective strategies

Depending on the "initial state" (cell) in which play begins, the solution may also be either a Nash myopic equilibrium solution from which neither player can improve his/her payoff by moving to an adjacent cell, e.g., (2,4), or the solution may be a Brams nonmyopic equilibrium (NME), e.g., (3,3), from which "neither player, anticipating all rational moves and countermoves from the initial state, would have an incentive to depart unilaterally because the departure would eventually lead to a worse, or at least not a better, outcome" (Brams 1994, 224). In this game, the (2,4) outcome is both a Brams and a Nash equilibrium, while the (3,3) outcome is not a Nash equilibrium, because one player (Self) can improve its payoff by moving from "3" to "4" by choosing "move" to an adjacent cell rather than "stay" at (3,3).

The remaining information below the game in Figure 15.6 summarizes the enactment of the strategies of each player (Self or Other) against the other player from each cell as an "initial state" to a cell as a "final state" in the game matrix when the rules of play prescribe alternating choices by each player to "stay" or "move" from a given cell. Examination of the information in parentheses for each player reveals what the "final state" or solution to the game is depending on what cell is the "initial state" and which player has the next move. For example, if the "initial state" is the upper left cell and coded hypothetically as "0/0" for both players, then they will choose "stay" in the upper left cell coded as "0," thereby making this cell also the "final state" or nonmyopic (NME) equilibrium solution. In contrast, if the "initial state" is the upper left cell and coded instead as "0/2" for Other, then Other will choose "move" to the lower right cell coded as "2," while Self will choose "stay" at "0" from this cell (Marfleet and Walker 2006).[4]

The information in brackets specifies the binary choice (cooperation "0" or conflict "1") that each player will make from each cell in the game matrix. The locations of the four cells in brackets are read from left to right as from upper left cell clockwise to lower left cell. For example, the bracket for Self is [0101], which reads from left to right as follows: Self should choose cooperation "0" from the upper left, conflict "1" from the upper right, cooperation "0" from the lower right, and conflict "1" from the lower left cell. This information translates as choices to "stay" or "move," depending on whether Self's location is already in the predicted location. For example, Self will choose "stay" in the upper left cell, because cooperation "0" is already where Self is located. In contrast, Self will choose "move" from the upper right cell, because conflict "1" is not where Self is already located (Marfleet and Walker 2006).

BRT specifies that the enactment of a Friend role is a cooperation (+) strategy that ranks submission as the highest (4) outcome. The enactment of a Partner role is a cooperation (+) strategy that ranks mutual cooperation as the highest (4) outcome. The enactment of a Rival role is a conflict strategy that ranks mutual conflict as the highest (4) outcome. The enactment of an Enemy role is a conflict strategy that ranks domination as the highest (4) outcome. Ego's role for the game in Figure 15.6 is "Enemy," because Ego ranks domination (–,+) as the highest (4) outcome. Alter's role in this game is "Rival," because Alter ranks mutual conflict (–,–) as the highest (4) outcome. Conversely, any series of four alternating decisions to choose "stay" or "move" by Ego and Alter from an initial state can be interpreted by BRT as a game that enacts a pair of these four roles (Walker, Malici, and Schafer 2011; Walker 2013; Malici and Walker 2017).

The binary algorithms for the actual role games in this chapter enacted as SIEs between Iran and the United States during the Iranian revolution and hostage crisis period in Iran-US relations (1978–1981) are numbered in chronological order from E#1 through E #30 in Table 15.8. The predicted algorithms for the Rival-Rival game are also in Table 15.8. The

*Table 15.8* Iran-US Rival-Rival Binary Role Games in the Hostage Crisis, 1978–1981[a]

|  | Iran | United States |  | Iran | United States |  | Iran | United States |
|---|---|---|---|---|---|---|---|---|
| Pred. | I: [1110] | U: [1011] |  | I: [1110] | U: [1011] |  | I: [1110] | U: [1011] |
| Act. | I: [0100] | U: [0001] |  | I: [1110] | U: [1011] |  | I: [0100] | U: [1011] |
| **E#1.** | **C = .50** | **C = .50** | **E#11.** | **C = 1.0** | **C = 1.0** | **E#21.** | **C = .50** | **C = 1.0** |
| Pred. | I: [1110] | U: [1011] |  | I: [1110] | U: [1011] |  | I: [1110] | U: [1011] |
| Act. | I: [1101] | U: [1000] |  | I: [0110] | U: [1111] |  | I: [0101] | U: [1011] |
| **E#2.** | **C = .50** | **C = .50** | **E#12.** | **C = .75** | **C = .75** | **E#22.** | **C = .25** | **C = 1.0** |
| Pred. | I: [1110] | U: [1011] |  | I: [1110] | U: [1011] |  | I: [1110] | U: [1011] |
| Act. | I: [1101] | U: [1000] |  | I: [1110] | U: [1011] |  | I: [1101] | U: [1000] |
| **E#3.** | **C = .50** | **C = .50** | **E#13.** | **C = 1.0** | **C =1.0** | **E#23.** | **C = .50** | **C = .50** |
| Pred. | I: [1110] | U: [1011] |  | I: [1110] | U: [1011] |  | I: [1110] | U: [1011] |
| Act. | I: [1110] | U: [0001] |  | I: [1111] | U: [1010] |  | I: [1110] | U: [1011] |
| **E#4.** | **C = 1.0** | **C = .50** | **E#14.** | **C = .75** | **C = .75** | **E#24.** | **C = 1.0** | **C = 1.0** |
| Pred. | I: [1110] | U: [1011] |  | I: [1110] | U: [1011] |  | I: [1110] | U: [1011] |
| Act. | I: [0100] | U: [0001] |  | I: [0100] | U: [0001] |  | I: [1110] | U: [0001] |
| **E#5.** | **C = .50** | **C = .50** | **E#15.** | **C = .50** | **C = .50** | **E#25.** | **C = 1.0** | **C = .50** |
| Pred. | I: [1110] | U: [1011] |  | I: [1110] | U: [1011] |  | I: [1110] | U: [1011] |
| Act. | I: [1000] | U: [1101] |  | I: [1110] | U: [1011] |  | I: [0110] | U: [0000] |
| **E#6.** | **C = .50** | **C = .50** | **E#16.** | **C = 1.0** | **C = 1.0** | **E#26.** | **C = .75** | **C = .25** |
| Pred. | I: [1110] | U: [1011] |  | I: [1110] | U: [1011] |  | I: [1110] | U: [1011] |
| Act. | I: [0000] | U: [0101] |  | I: [0100] | U: [1011] |  | I: [1110] | U: [1011] |
| **E#7.** | **C = .25** | **C = .25** | **E#17.** | **C = .50** | **C = 1.0** | **E#27.** | **C = 1.0** | **C = 1.0** |
| Pred. | I: [1110] | U: [1011] |  | I: [1110] | U: [1011] |  | I: [1110] | U: [1011] |
| Act. | I: [1110] | U: [1011] |  | I: [1111] | U: [0111] |  | I: [1111] | U: [1010] |
| **E#8.** | **C = 1.0** | **C = 1.0** | **E#18.** | **C = .75** | **C = .50** | **E#28.** | **C = .75** | **C = .75** |
| Pred. | I: [1110] | U: [1011] |  | I: [1110] | U: [1011] |  | I: [1110] | U: [1011] |
| Act. | I: [0110] | U: [1111] |  | I: [1110] | U: [1011] |  | I: [1000] | U: [1101] |
| **E#9.** | **C = .75** | **C = .75** | **E#19.** | **C = 1.0** | **C = 1.0** | **E#29.** | **C = .50** | **C = .50** |
| Pred. | I: [1110] | U: [1011] |  | I: [1110] | U: [1011] |  | I: [1110] | U: [1011] |
| Act. | I: [1110] | U: [1011] |  | I: [0110] | U: [1111] |  | I: [0100] | U: [0001] |
| **E#10.** | **C = 1.0** | **C = 1.0** | **E#20.** | **C = .75** | **C = .75** | **E#30.** | **C = .50** | **C = .50** |

[a]*Note:* Pred. is predicted algorithm and Act. is actual algorithm. E# is episode number. I = Iran; U = US Data source: Malici and Walker (2017).

degree of Congruence (C) or match between the predicted Rival role algorithm and the actual algorithm for each episode (game) is calculated by comparing the cells of the two algorithms for Iran and the United States to see how frequently they match. For example, Iran's predicted and actual algorithms for E#1 match two out of four times or C = .50 for each algorithm.

The binary algorithms for the actual role games in this chapter enacted as SIEs between Iran and the United States during the Detente period in Iran-US relations (1997–2002) are numbered in chronological order from E#1 through E#13 in Table 15.9. These actual algorithms are compared to the predicted algorithms for three models of Iran-US relations during

*Table 15.9* Comparisons of Binary Role Models for Détente Period, 1997–2002[a]

|  | Rival-Rival Model | | Partner-Partner Model | | Axis-of-Evil Model | |
|---|---|---|---|---|---|---|
|  | *Iran* | *United States* | *Iran* | *United States* | *Iran* | *United States* |
| Pred. | I: [1110] | U: [1011] | I: [0100] | U: [0001] | I: [1001] | U: [1111] |
| Act. | I: [1110] | U: [1011] | I: [1110] | U: [1011] | I: [1110] | U: [1011] |
| **E#1.** | **C = 1.0** | **C = 1.0** | **C = .50** | **C = .50** | **C = .25** | **C = 1.0** |
| Pred. | I: [1110] | U: [1011] | I: [0100] | U: [0001] | I: [1001] | U: [1111] |
| Act. | I: [0100] | U: [0001] | I: [0100] | U: [0001] | I: [0100] | U: [0001] |
| **E#2.** | **C = .50** | **C = .50** | **C = 1.0** | **C = 1.0** | **C = .25** | **C =.50** |
| Pred. | I: [1110] | U: [1011] | I: [0100] | U: [0001] | I: [1001] | U: [1111] |
| Act. | I: [0100] | U: [0001] | I: [0100] | U: [0001] | I: [0100] | U: [0001] |
| **E#3.** | **C = .50** | **C = .50** | **C = 1.0** | **C = 1.0** | **C = .25** | **C = .50** |
| Pred. | I: [1110] | U: [1011] | I: [0100] | U: [0001] | I: [1001] | U: [1111] |
| Act. | I: [1111] | U: [1010] | I: [1111] | U: [1010] | I: [1111] | U: [1010] |
| **E#4.** | **C = .75** | **C = .75** | **C = .25** | **C = .25** | **C = .50** | **C = .75** |
| Pred. | I: [1110] | U: [1011] | I: [0100] | U: [0001] | I: [1001] | U: [1111] |
| Act. | I: [1110] | U: [0001] | I: [1110] | U: [0001] | I: [1110] | U: [0001] |
| **E#5.** | **C = 1.0** | **C = .50** | **C = .50** | **C = 1.0** | **C = .25** | **C = .50** |
| Pred. | I: [1110] | U: [1011] | I: [0100] | U: [0001] | I: [1001] | U: [1111] |
| Act. | I: [0100] | U: [0001] | I: [0100] | U: [0001] | I: [0100] | U: [0001] |
| **E#6.** | **C = .50** | **C = .50** | **C = 1.0** | **C = 1.0** | **C = .25** | **C = .50** |
| Pred. | I: [1110] | U: [1011] | I: [0100] | U: [0001] | I: [1001] | U: [1111] |
| Act. | I: [1101] | U: [1000] | I: [1101] | U: [1000] | I: [1101] | U: [1000] |
| **E#7.** | **C = .50** | **C = .50** | **C = .50** | **C = .50** | **C = .75** | **C = .25** |
| Pred. | I: [1110] | U: [1011] | I: [0100] | U: [0001] | I: [1001] | U: [1111] |
| Act. | I: [0100] | U: [0001] | I: [0100] | U: [0001] | I: [0100] | U: [0001] |
| **E#8.** | **C = .50** | **C = .50** | **C = 1.0** | **C = 1.0** | **C = .25** | **C = .25** |
| Pred. | I: [1110] | U: [1011] | I: [0100] | U: [0001] | I: [1001] | U: [1111] |
| Act. | I: [1111] | U: [0011] | I: [1111] | U: [0011] | I: [1111] | U: [0011] |
| **E#9.** | **C = .75** | **C = .75** | **C = .25** | **C = .75** | **C = .50** | **C = .50** |
| Pred. | I: [1110] | U: [1011] | I: [0100] | U: [0001] | I: [1001] | U: [1111] |
| Act. | I: [0100] | U: [0001] | I: [0100] | U: [0001] | I: [0100] | U: [0001] |
| **E#10.** | **C = .50** | **C = .50** | **C = 1.0** | **C = 1.0** | **C = .25** | **C = .25** |
| Pred. | I: [1110] | U: [1011] | I: [0100] | U: [0001] | I: [1001] | U: [1111] |
| Act. | I: [1110] | U: [1011] | I: [1110] | U: [1011] | I: [1110] | U: [1011] |
| **E#11.** | **C = 1.0** | **C = 1.0** | **C = .50** | **C = .50** | **C = .25** | **C = .75** |
| Pred. | I: [1110] | U: [1011] | I: [0100] | U: [0001] | I: [1001] | U: [1111] |
| Act. | I: [0110] | U: [0000] | I: [0110] | U: [0000] | I: [0110] | U: [0000] |
| **E#12.** | **C = .75** | **C = .25** | **C = .75** | **C = .75** | **C = .00** | **C = .00** |
| Pred. | I: [1110] | U: [1011] | I: [0100] | U: [0001] | I: [1001] | U: [1111] |
| Act. | I: [0110] | U: [1111] | I: [0110] | U: [1111] | I: [0110] | U: [1111] |
| **E#13.** | **C = .75** | **C = .75** | **C = .75** | **C = .25** | **C = .00** | **C = 1.0** |

[a]Note: Pred. is the predicted algorithm and Act. is the actual algorithm. E# is episode number. Data source: Malici and Walker (2017).

the Détente period: the Rival-Rival, Partner-Partner, and Axis-of-Evil games. The degree of Congruence (C) or match between the predicted role algorithm and the actual algorithm for each episode (game) reveals which model provides the best "fit" for each episode.

For example, the predicted and actual algorithms for Iran and the United States in E#1 are more congruent overall with the Rival-Rival model (C = 1.0 and 1.0) than for the Partner-Partner model (C = .50 and .50) or the Axis-of-Evil model (C = .25 and .1.0). It is also possible to do a more detailed analysis to see exactly where the predicted and actual models overlap or diverge in their predictions regarding whether each member of the dyad will choose "stay" or "move" from a given cell in a role game and whether the models agree with the actual decision by Iran or the United States to choose "stay" or "move."

For example, the Rival-Rival and the Axis-of-Evil models both predict that Iran will choose "move" from the upper left to the lower left cell of their respective games, i.e., will choose "1" (conflict), while the Partner-Partner model predicts that Iran will choose "stay" in the upper left cell, i.e., choose "0" (cooperation). The predictions of the Rival-Rival and Axis-of-Evil models for E#1 are correct: Iran chooses "1" (conflict); the prediction of the Partner-Partner model that Iran will choose "0" cooperation is not correct for E#1. The same predictions hold for the United States across the three models and in E#1 when the initial "state of play" is the upper left cell of each game.

## Notes

1. The narrative summaries in this section are slightly modified synopses from Malici and Walker (2017).
2. Four models were tested to assess the degree of fit between their predictions regarding the foreign policy roles of Iran and Britain: Rebel-Patron, Rebel-Hegemon, Partner-Partner, Rival-Rival, and Enemy-Partner. These roles were identified from a VICS analysis of first person, public statements by Iranian or American officials. The Rebel (Weak Rival)-Hegemon (Strong Rival) model provided the best fit (Mean C > .70) for Iran and Britain both across agents (Iran and Britain) and across the two halves (1–10 and 11–19) of the 19 SIEs (see Malici and Walker 2017, 87–92). The Rebel-Hegemon C-scores in Table 15.1 also correct minor calculation errors in Table 5.4 of Malici and Walker (2017, 91).
3. If the rules of play are for each player to choose simultaneously, then the "initial state" and "final state" are the same cell. Ego has a dominant strategy of "always choose conflict" so that the "final state" should be (2,4), which is the choice dictated for Alter who has a conditional strategy of "reciprocate cooperation and conflict."
4. "If it is rational for one player to move and one player not to move from the initial state, then the player who moves takes *precedence*: its move overrides the player who stays, so the outcome will be induced by the player who moves" (Brams 1994, 28. Italics are Brams).

## References

Afary, J. 1996. *The Iranian constitutional revolution, 1906-191*. New York, NY: Columbia University.

Azimi, F. 2008. *The quest for democracy in Iran*. Cambridge, MA: Harvard University Press.

Baldwin, D. 1989. *Paradoxes of power*. New York, NY: Blackwell.

Bill, J. 1988. *The eagle and the lion*. New Haven, CT: Yale University.

Bowden, M. 2006. *Guests of the Ayatollah*. New York, NY: Atlantic Monthly.

Brams, S. 1994. *Theory of moves*. Cambridge: Cambridge University.

Brams, S. 2002. Game theory in practice. In *Millennial reflections on international studies*, eds. M. Brecher, F. Harvey, 392–405. Ann Arbor, MI: University of Michigan.

Brecher, M., J. Wilkenfeld. 2000. *A study of crisis*. Ann Arbor, MI: University of Michigan.

Cottam, R. 1979. Goodbye to America's Shah. *Foreign Policy* 34: 3–14.

Cottam, R. 1988. *Iran and the United States*. Pittsburgh, PA: University of Pittsburgh Press.

Crossman, A. 2020. Index of qualitative variation. *Thoughtco* (February 11). Online at: thoughtco.com/index of qualitative variation-iqv-3026706.

Dahl, R. 1957. The concept of power. *Behavioral Science* 2: 201–215.

Galpern, S. 2009. *Money, oil and empire in the Middle East*. New York, NY: Cambridge University.

Gasiorowski, M. 1991. *U.S. foreign policy and the Shah*. Ithaca, NY: Cornell University.

Hermann, C. 1972. *International crises*. New York, NY: Free Press.

Hunter, S. 2010. *Iran's foreign policy in the post-Soviet Era*. Santa Barbara, CA: Praeger.

Indyk, M. 2009. *Innocent abroad*. New York, NY: Simon and Schuster.

Katouzian, H. 2000. *State and society in Iran*. New York, NY: I.B. Tauris.

Katouzian, H. 2004. Mossadegh's government in Iranian history. In *Mohammad Mossadegh and the 1953 coup in Iran*, eds. M. Gasiorowski, M. Byrne, 1–26. Syracuse, NY: Syracuse University Press.

Khomeini, R. 1981. *Islam and revolution*, trans. and ann. H. Algar, 27–166. Berkeley, CA: Mizan.

Ledeen, M., W. Lewis. 1981. *Debacle: The American failure in Iran*. New York, NY: Knopf.

Leverett, F., H. M. Leverett. 2013. *Going to Tehran*. New York, NY: Metropolitan Books.

Leites, N. 1951. *The operational code of the politburo*. New York, NY: McGraw-Hill.

Malici, A., S. Walker. 2017. *Role theory and role conflict in U.S.-Iran relations*. New York, NY: Routledge.

Marfleet, B. G., S. Walker. 2006. A world of beliefs: Modeling interactions among agents with different operational codes. In *Beliefs and leadership in world politics*, eds. M. Schafer, S. Walker, 53–76. New York, NY: Palgrave Macmillan.

Martin, V. 1989. *Islam and modernization*. Syracuse, NY: Syracuse University.

Ramazani, R. 1975. *Iran's foreign policy, 1941-1973*. Charlottesville, VA: University Press of Virginia.

Schafer, M., S. Walker. 2006. Operational code analysis at a distance: The verbs in context system of content analysis. In *Beliefs and leadership in world politics*, eds. M. Schafer, S. Walker, 25–52. New York, NY: Palgrave Macmillan.

Shakibi, Z. 2010. *Khatami and Gorbachev: Politics of change in the Islamic Republic of Iran and the USSR*. New York, NY: I.B. Tauris.

Slavin, B. 2007. *Bitter friends, bosom enemies*. New York, NY: St. Martin's.

Snyder, G., P. Diesing. 1977. *Conflict among nations*. Princeton, NJ: Princeton University.

U.S. National Security Council. 1955. U.S. Policy toward Iran, NSC 5504, January 15.

Walker, S. 1982. Bargaining over Berlin: A re-analysis of the first and second Berlin crises. *Journal of Politics* 44: 152–164.

Walker, S. 2013. *Role theory and the cognitive architecture of British appeasement decisions*. New York, NY: Routledge.

Walker, S. 2002. Beliefs and foreign policy analysis in the new millennium. In *Conflict, security, foreign policy, and international political economy*, eds. M. Brecher, and F. Harvey, 56–71. Ann Arbor, MI: University of Michigan.

Walker, S., S. Hoagland. 1979. Operational codes and crisis outcomes. In *Psychological models in international politics*, ed. L. Falkowski, 125–168. Boulder, CO: Westview.

Walker, S., A. Malici. 2011. *U.S. presidents and foreign policy mistakes*. Stanford, CA: Stanford University Press.

Walker, S., M. Schafer. 2010. Operational code theory. In *The international studies encyclopedia*, ed. R. Denmark, 5492–5514. Vol. VIII. Chichester: Wiley-Blackwell.

Walker, S., A. Malici, M. Schafer. 2011. *Rethinking foreign policy analysis*. New York, NY: Routledge.

Walker, S., M. Schafer, M. Young. 1998. Systematic procedures for operational code analysis. *International Studies Quarterly* 42: 173–189.

Watson, G., D. McGaw. 1980. *Statistical inquiry*. New York, NY: John Wiley.

Young, M. 2001. Building world views with Profiler+. In *Progress in communication sciences*, ed. M. West, 17–32. Vol. 17. Westport, CT: Ablex.

# Part V

# Beyond Beliefs in World Politics

# 16 Operational Codes and Foreign Policy Roles

## Conceptual Insights and Empirical Results

*Stephen G. Walker and Mark Schafer*

## Introduction

In this chapter, we assess the conceptual insights and empirical results of the operational code analysis (OCA) and foreign policy role studies in this volume with criteria identified as markers of progress in scientific research programs. Do these studies represent advances in the form of solving conceptual or empirical problems, expanding the scope of analysis into new domains of inquiry, and identifying new avenues of research (Lakatos 1970)? Can an alliance of OCA and role theory as a "theory complex" link the domestic and foreign domains of world politics (Laudan 1977)? Does an alliance also address the gap in foreign policy theory and practice between the academic and policy communities (George 1993)? Are conceptual and empirical anomalies resolved and conflicting theories reconciled across research programs in foreign policy analysis (FPA) and world politics (Lakatos 1970; Laudan 1977)? Are the solutions to these problems also consistent with the solutions to problems of evidence, inference, and conceptualization in psychological explanations of world politics (Greenstein 1987)? Do they represent significant progress for crossing Simon's bridge and linking the sciences of the mind and the social sciences (Lupia, McCubbins, Popkin 2000)?

Almost 15 years ago we stated, "Operational code analysis may make more contributions to foreign policy theory in the next decade than in the last decade" (Walker and Schafer 2006, 246). Specifically, (pp. 246–248) we anticipated progress by OCA along four paths: (1) as the core of a cognitivist research program that offers an agent-centered account of foreign policy and world politics; (2) as a method for system-level research programs to augment and enrich their structure-oriented explanations of world politics; (3) as an approach offering alternative or complementary accounts of strategic interactions between states at the dyadic level of analysis in world politics; (4) as an approach to identify non-linear processes and emerging properties of complex systems with agent-based simulations of strategic interactions.

In this chapter, we revisit these forecasts as well as the prospects for substantive, theoretical, and methodological progress in the operational code research program regarding the advancement of actor-specific, situation-generic, and abstract-theoretical knowledge of foreign policy and world politics (George 1993).

## Substantive Progress

The chapters in Part II, *The Operational Codes of World Leaders,* focus on the cognitive explanation offered by a leader's key operational code beliefs in an agent-centered account of foreign and domestic policy decisions regarding the exercise of power by specific leaders in autocratic (Putin) and democratic (Bush, Obama, Trump) political systems. This approach to *actor-specific knowledge* of political leaders is also used in this volume to augment or qualify system-level and structure-oriented explanations of various features of world politics, including variations in the beliefs of individual leaders (Kumaratunga in Sri Lanka, Morales in Bolivia, Al-Qaeda and ISIS leaders in the Middle East and North Africa) to account for the variations in civil violence in Sri Lanka, the international rivalry between Bolivia and Chile, and the organization and lethality of militant terrorist groups in the MENA region.

The chapters in Part III, *The Psychological Characteristics of US Presidents,* integrate models and methods from agent-centered and system-level research programs to focus on the decisions and actions of the United States as a key agent in 20th century world politics. This focus extends from the personality traits and operational code beliefs of US presidents through the economic and military power of the United States and the evolution of international norms over the course of the 20th century to analyze dyadic relations between the United States and other states between 1900 and the dawn of the 21st century. This effort yields *situation-generic knowledge* about the most powerful agent in world politics during military dispute situations (MIDS) and insights about linkages between presidential leadership patterns in the foreign policy domain and congressional electoral outcomes in the domestic policy domain. Generic patterns of learning and threat perception by US presidents as a group in the 20th century are also revealed along with their origins from variations in presidential personality traits.

The chapters in Part IV, *Computational Models of Foreign Policy Roles,* synthesize *abstract-theoretical knowledge* across different levels of aggregation and analysis in world politics. Their focus is on strategic interactions among dyads and evolutionary patterns over time among states in different regional and world systems. In particular, the link between key operational code beliefs about the nature of the political universe, the optimal strategies for exercising social power in the form of positive and negative sanctions, and control over historical development are linked to the emergence of the foreign policy roles of friend, partner, rival, and enemy in world politics. In turn, the interaction patterns between roles enacted by pairs of states as role dyads are examined to link their dynamics to the outcomes between them of mutual cooperation or mutual conflict and domination or submission. The strategies of appeasing, bandwagoning, balancing, or bullying are specified as different computational models for enacting different foreign policy roles measured by the metrics of operational code indices applied to data from computer simulations or historical case studies of interactions between states.

The conceptual insights, empirical metrics, and mathematical models of OCA as a research program are the methodological tools for "bridging the gap" (George 1993) in this volume between actor-specific, situation-generic, and theoretical-abstract knowledge about FPA and international relations (IR) as domains of scientific inquiry. The OCA research program's aggregation and synthesis of the personalities and beliefs of leaders and the roles of states with foreign policy strategies and dyadic relations between agents in world politics represents substantive progress in the integration of FPA and IR as fields of study in political science.

## Theoretical Progress

Have these substantive advances followed sound principles of theoretical and methodological progress in the natural and social sciences? If there has been progress, what is the quality of these contributions? There are various standards offered by different philosophers of science and practicing political scientists for assessing progress in a scientific research program (Kuhn 1962; Lakatos 1970; Laudan 1977; Elman and Elman 2003; Jackson 2011). Their criteria include "the generation of novel facts, the solution of conceptual and empirical problems... escaping the endogeneity trap and... [surviving]... severe testing" (Walker 2003, 274). The form that the employment of these criteria take can vary, but they share a common goal of deeper understanding and explanation via "the systematic application of a set of theories and concepts so as to produce a 'thoughtful ordering of empirical actuality'" (Jackson 2011, 20 citing Weber 1999), which is the distinguishing characteristic of science as a knowledge-production enterprise (Jackson 2011, 16–23). A conceptual framework's logical form or model can be represented as a temporal narrative, statistical array, or mathematical equation, and the fit with empirical contents can be with inductive, deductive, abductive or reflexive methods of inference (Jackson 2011).

Theoretical progress primarily involves strengthening and extending the analytical reach of the conceptual framework in a research program.

It can take the form of refining, extending, or replacing an existing conceptual framework. Over the past 15 years, the conceptual framework of the operational code research program has experienced all three forms of theoretical progress. The concept of an operational code has been refined from being simply a belief system that expresses a code of conduct in the exercise of social power to a multi-dimensional construct of philosophical beliefs about the political universe and instrumental beliefs about the utility of different kinds of social power manifested by different types of agents (individuals, groups, coalitions, and institutions). It has been extended as well to include an agent's pattern of cognitive beliefs about the exercise of power and an agent's pattern of actual social conduct in the exercise of social power.

If these theoretical amendments result in the discovery and corroboration of novel facts, then their succession marks theoretical progress (Lakatos 1970; Walker 2003). The empirical contents of operational code theory are represented by the chapters in this volume as a series of theoretical models focusing on cognitive and social phenomena. As a cognitive theory $(T_1)$, the model was expressed as the cognitive consistency between philosophical and instrumental beliefs and the congruence between the beliefs and decisions of agents. As a cognitive-motivational theory $(T_2)$ that incorporated personality as well as cognitive features, the model predicted novel facts about relationships between the exercise of social power and a leader's beliefs, motivations, and interpersonal style.

This progression from a cognitive to a motivational model occurred at the expense of the hierarchical relationship of cognitive consistency in $(T_1)$ between philosophical and instrumental beliefs. There emerged a dissonance pattern between types of beliefs and behavior and then a third operational code model of "hot" cognition $(T_3)$, which guided operational code research until the focus of the operational code research program expanded from the study of individual leaders to include the explicit analysis of states and dyads as units of analysis (Walker 2003; Walker and Schafer 2010). Today a fourth model of role enactment $(T_4)$ informs the application of metrics and mathematics from OCA as the mechanics for applying binary role theory to the political universe (Walker 2013; Malici and Walker 2017). While the succession of theoretical models and novel facts resembles the pattern of theoretical progress identified by Lakatos (1970), it adheres more closely to the criteria of theoretical progress identified by Laudan (1977):

> The multiple criteria for defining and detecting progress, i.e., the inflation of solved empirical and conceptual problems and the deflation of conceptual problems, capture important activities within the operational code research program. The solution of conceptual problems is largely ignored in a Lakatosian account of the program's trajectory.... More generally, there is less flexibility in the Lakatos account for simultaneously investing in several theories, dividing one's intellectual

labor across theories, and giving equal weight to the tasks of empirical and conceptual problem-solving (Walker 2003, 270–271).

There is also little evidence in the operational code research program to support Kuhn's (1962) thesis that scientific progress follows a revolutionary pattern rather than an evolutionary pattern. There has been no paradigm-shift characterized by a dramatic change in the program's theory and methods. There is instead a pattern of cooperation rather than competition and the evolution of a "theory complex" or alliance among models and methods at different levels of aggregation and analysis marking theoretical and methodological progress in OCA (Walker 2003, 274–276).

## Methodological Progress

Two criteria for assessing methodological progress include "escaping the endogeneity trap" and surviving "severe testing" (Walker 2003, 274; see also Dessler 2003; Keohane and Martin 2003). "Escaping the endogeneity trap requires that for beliefs to matter, they must be relatively independent of structural features of the decision-making environment and have a significant causal impact on decisions and outcomes" (Walker 2003, 274). This formulation of the endogeneity trap resembles the arguments advanced by political psychologists regarding the scope conditions for when the individual differences between leaders make a difference in political decisions and/or political outcomes (George 1969; Hermann 1974; Holsti 1976; Walker 1982; Greenstein 1987 [1969]). In this view, the cognitive and extra-cognitive personality traits of leaders compete with situational variables for influence over the exercise of power in politics.

The dispositional variables are more likely to be influential and perhaps indispensable in understanding and explaining decisions and outcomes when the environment is loosely structured and/or a leader is located in a strategic position in the decision-making process. In a loosely structured, uncertain environment where information is either very scarce or too plentiful to process prior to the point of decision, then who leads matters, e.g., in a crisis situation where a single leader or a small group makes decisions for war or peace under the stress of high stakes, surprise, and a short time to decide (Hermann 1972; Brecher and Wilkenfeld 1997).

Under such conditions, a decision maker's emotions and idiosyncratic biases may directly influence decisions by re-enforcing or substituting for unreliable information from the environment as the basis for making choices that turn out to be foreign policy mistakes (Greenstein 1987; Schafer and Crichlow 2010; Walker and Malici 2011). Under more favorable conditions where decision-making is made with more systematic and less ad hoc procedures and decision units, the influence of a leader's personality and beliefs may be exercised indirectly by the leader's control over the organization of the advisory system and who are advisors

(George 1980; Hermann and Preston 1994: Preston 2001; Schafer and Crichlow 2010; Winter 2003).

Escape from the endogeneity trap in the operational code research program is managed with the adoption of "bounded rationality" as a Goldilocks "just right" solution to the problem (Walker 2009). Both the dispositions of the agent (A) and conditions in the environment (E) influence decisions, actions, and outcomes regarding the exercise of power by their interaction (A $\leftrightarrow$ E). Moreover, both (A) and (E) as a system of interaction are agents in a *social* system and internalize both their relative personality traits as instrumental beliefs for ego defense and their respective environmental conditions as philosophical beliefs for object appraisal in their *cognitive* belief systems. Collectively, they mediate self-other relations by constructing through their interaction the map of a complex adaptive social system constituted from complex adaptive subsystems of beliefs and personality traits (Smith 1968). The complexity of their interactions is measured statistically by the VICS metrics of OCA applied to texts of mental and social events and modeled mathematically with the rules of games specified by binary role theory (Walker and Schafer 2010; Walker, Malici, and Schafer 2011; Walker 2013; Malici and Walker 2017).

This solution is entailed as well by Simon's (1957) concept of *bounded rationality*, in which "Policy makers may act rationally, but only within the context of their simplified subjective representations of reality" (Simon 1957; Tetlock 1998, 876; cited in Walker 2003, 255). It is also consistent with Hawking and Mlodinow's (2010, 42–46) position: "There is no picture- or theory-independent concept of reality. Instead we will adopt a view that we will call model-dependent realism: the idea that a physical theory or world picture is a model... and a set of rules that connect the elements of the model to observations.... According to model-dependent realism, it is pointless to ask whether a model is real, only whether it agrees with observation. If there are two models that both agree with observations... then one cannot say that one is more real than another" (cited in Walker 2013, 228, n. 18).

Jackson (2011, 197) identifies four kinds of models employed by IR theories, which are distinguished by their respective ontological and epistemological stances regarding whether their methodological commitments are (1) dualistic or monistic ontologically with respect to the relationship between knower and known; (2) phenomenological or transfactual epistemologically with respect to the relationship between knowledge and observation. The issue of whether the theoretical models in the OCA research program will survive "severe testing" becomes defined by these criteria for testing them as bounded rationality models (Jackson 2011, 196–201).

The bounded rationality models in the OCA research program take a monistic stance in which the knower and the known are both endogenous to the model. They take a phenomenalist stance regarding what is observable by assuming that internal dispositions and thoughts can be detected from external patterns of speech and actions that communicate information about personality traits and beliefs. The criteria for testing these kinds of models in the OCA research program are testing hypotheses with frequentist patterns of statistical association and inference and testing analytical narratives with sequentialist patterns of computational rules of congruence. The statistical tests address how frequently do patterns of beliefs and actions occur and how likely they have not occurred by chance. The analytical narrative tests address how closely the distribution pattern of beliefs or sequence of actions are congruent (match up) with the pattern of distribution or sequence in the analytical narrative (Walker, Schafer, and Young 1998, 2003; Schafer and Walker 2006; Walker, Malici, and Schafer 2011).

## Crossing Simon's Bridge: The Road Ahead

In this volume, we have compiled several previously unpublished studies from the OCA research program under the general rubric of "crossing Simon's bridge." Crossing Simon's bridge refers to bridging the sciences of the mind and the social sciences. The phrase articulates a unifying theme connecting the chapters in Parts II, III, and IV of the book, which move from a focus on the minds of individual political leaders in Part II to placing leaders in political situations in Part III, and examining the ensuing patterns of political actions and outcomes in Part IV. While we have not followed the same leaders along this path, we have employed a common set of analytical tools to mark the location and progress of different kinds of political agents across these levels of political aggregation and analysis. The tools are the models and metrics of OCA that bridge the gap between actor-specific knowledge of the personalities and beliefs of individual leaders, the situation-generic knowledge of political situations, and the abstract-theoretical knowledge of political systems.

These models and metrics provide a lexicon, a common language for detecting and analyzing the phenomena of beliefs, actions, and outcomes, which are the major ontological dimensions of the "intentional stance" in understanding and predicting human behavior as a competence theory (Dennett 1989; Jackson 2011). In contrast, the physical stance is a sub-personal performance theory, which emphasizes comprehension rather than competence. Employing the physical stance is to "predict the behavior of a system, determine its physical constitution (perhaps all the way down to the microphysical level) and the physical nature of the impingements upon it, and use your knowledge of the laws of physics to predict the outcome for any input" (Dennett 1989, 16). The design stance is a variant of the physical stance wherein "one ignores the actual (possibly messy) details of the physical constitution of an object, and, on the assumption that it has a certain design, predicts that it will behave as it is designed to behave under various circumstances" (Dennett 1989, 17).

Dennett (1989, 43–82) locates the intentional stance within three levels of psychological explanation: the folk psychology of ordinary language, the personal intentional system of social psychology, and the sub-personal performance system of cognitive psychology. Folk psychology refers to the explanations offered by lay persons (rather than scientists) when they use beliefs and desires as every day terms to explain human behavior while the intentional stance links those terms as an intentional system of bounded rationality. "Intentional system theory… is envisaged as a close kin of, and overlapping with, such already existing disciplines as decision theory and game theory, which are similarly abstract, normative, and couched in intentional language. It borrows the ordinary terms "belief" and "desire" but gives them a technical meaning within the theory" (Dennett 1989, 58). The physical stance's methodology employs instruments from the natural sciences applicable to studying the sub-personal characteristics of the human brain such as the trilogy of cognitions, emotions, and motivations associated with neuroscience (Ledoux 2002).

The intentional stance is for analyzing the personal and social levels of the human self, which we understand here in terms of the concept of bounded rationality and through access to the instruments of language and other forms of observing interpersonal communication. The building blocks for "crossing Simon's bridge" in the OCA research program are beliefs and desires as specified by the concept of bounded rationality in the domain of world politics. The internal boundaries of bounded rationality at the individual level of analysis are extracted from texts and text-actions as patterns of instrumental beliefs or sequential actions attributed to the self while the external boundaries are extracted from texts or text-actions as patterns of philosophical beliefs or sequential actions attributed to others. The corresponding boundaries at the state level of analysis are the patterns of role conceptions, role expectations, and role enactments attributed to the self as Ego and to others as Alters.

Greenstein (1987, 14–20) identifies three steps in aggregating a psychological explanation of personality and politics across individual and state levels of analysis to systemic outcomes: (1) single case studies of individual leaders; (2) typological studies to classify leaders; (3) aggregative analyses to contextualize the performance of types of leaders. He specifies two general strategies of bridging the gap between them: "building up from direct observation of small-scale political processes…. and working back from theoretical analyses of systems and their psychological requirements" (Greenstein 1987, 127–139; Greenstein and Lerner 1971). These building blocks and strategies of aggregation are reflected in the organization of this volume. The operational code beliefs of the individual leaders in Part II are analyzed as (1) single case studies and classified into (2) a typology of belief systems and motivational profiles developed by Holsti (1977) and refined by Walker (1983). Strategies of aggregative analyses (3) are followed in Parts III and IV to contextualize the performance patterns of different types of leaders or other focal actors (e.g., groups, coalitions, organizations, institutions, states).

The "building up" strategy of aggregation analysis is pursued in Part III from small-scale phenomena exhibited by individual leaders by aggregating to state-level phenomena in the form of performance patterns associated with the US presidency and the electoral system plus US dyadic behavioral patterns regarding militarized disputes and international norms. The disaggregation strategy of "working back" from theoretical analyses of systems to the psychological requirements of their leaders is followed in Part IV wherein different principles of international order represented by different combinations of foreign policy roles are identified for states as agents. Then the psychological requirements for the enactment of those roles are specified in the form of different types of social and cognitive operational codes.

The overall patterns of aggregation (building up) and disaggregation (working back) are both hierarchical and recursive, i.e., it is possible for subsystems to aggregate as the building blocks for a larger system and also to disaggregate from the larger system into the smaller subsystems. These patterns of composition and decomposition between parts and wholes have potential spatial and temporal dimensions, which fluctuate and reveal them as complex adaptive systems that persist or change as they adapt to their environments (Simon 1969; Gell-Mann 1994; Axelrod and Cohen 1999). At the state level of aggregation and analysis, dyads, triads, and larger ensembles of states aggregate *spatially* into even larger regional systems of world politics, which Buzan and Waever (2003) identify as security complexes. They also aggregate *temporally* into relations of amity, collaboration, discord, and enmity and their corresponding roles of friend, partner, rival, and enemy, which are the building blocks that define their relations.

These roles are identified by their respective strategies of unconditional cooperation (friend), conditional cooperation (partner), conditional conflict (rival), and unconditional conflict (enemy). Binary role theory specifies the models of interaction games between pairs of states who are members of a regional security complex, defined collectively by Buzan and Waever (2003, 491) as "a set of units whose major processes of securitization, desecuritization, or both are so interlinked that their security problems cannot reasonably be analyzed or resolved apart from one another" (see also Lake and Morgan 1997; Walker 2007). In these games, the players (Ego and Alter) exchange cues that signal their respective role identities and their transitions from one role to another over time. Searching for these patterns in regional systems of world politics along the following paths of inquiry are likely future trajectories in the operational code research program, as its scope expands from analysis of the cognitive operational codes of individual leaders to the analysis of the social operational codes of states, dyads, triads, and larger ensembles of agents and systems in world politics.

- One future path of inquiry is to expand the cognitive operational code profiles of individual leaders. The PsyCL data set presented in this volume is an expanding data resource for retrieving the personality traits and belief systems of both US and foreign leaders as the sources of foreign policy roles.
- A second future path of inquiry is either to collect event data sequences independently or from other scholars and analyze the role enactment patterns that emerge spatially and temporally to define relations among members of a domestic or regional security complex (see Goertz, Diehl, and Balas 2016; Walker, Schafer, and Beieler 2016).
- A third future path of inquiry is to compare the role conceptions and role expectations attributed to one another by pairs of predominant leaders or other focal actors whose public statements contain this cognitive information with the actual roles enacted between them as members of a domestic or regional security complex.

Data collection methods for these paths of inquiry are exemplified in Part II of this book. The information about role enactment and role selection from these sources may be analyzed either statistically with VICS metrics or computationally with formal TOM models. Prototypes of data analysis methods for statistical research designs are in Part III and for computational research designs in Part IV of this volume. Event data collections by other scholars offer opportunities to analyze the role enactment patterns of state-level actions and the social operational code profiles of states and institutions within states (Goertz, Diehl, and Balas 2016; Walker, Schafer, and Beieler 2016).

Finally, the evolution of OCA beyond the beliefs of individual leaders to focus on the social operational codes of larger decision units as focal actors also offers a fourth path of inquiry, which is to expand beyond the intentional stance and employ the design stance to do an OCA of artificial systems (Simon 1969). The social roles and corresponding strategies that constitute the games in binary role theory are artificial social systems of interaction that are subject to human design and simulation. Such games will also occur "naturally" as patterns of interaction between agents as the political universe "programs" itself the way that the physical universe does in the absence of intervention by human engineers (Lloyd 2006).

The building blocks for designing artificial systems of world politics are the roles specified as games by binary role theory. These roles perform the same function for building the social operational codes at the state level of analysis as beliefs do for building cognitive operational codes at the individual level of analysis. As building blocks for aggregations of behavioral patterns between and among states, roles can be deployed in a physical stance and fit Dennett's (1989,16) earlier description of the physical stance by substituting "social" or "psychology" for "physical" or "physics" as follows:

> If you want to predict the behavior of a [social] system, determine its [social] constitution (perhaps all the way down to the [microsocial] level) and the [social] nature of the impingements upon it, and use the knowledge of the laws of [psychology] to predict the outcome for any input (Dennett 1989, 16).

Investigating and designing these patterns and programs as complex artificial systems informed by binary role theory from a physical stance is a task for another day, which is already under way in the operational code research program (Walker no date). In the meantime, world leaders and other focal actors will continue to be analyzed in the operational code research program as the "programmers" of world politics from an intentional stance defined by binary role theory models and the metrics of OCA (Walker and Malici 2011; Dennett 2017; Malici and Walker 2017, 178–184; Walker 2007).

## References

Axelrod, R., M. Cohen. 1999. *Harnessing complexity*. New York, NY: Free Press.

Brecher, M., J. Wilkenfeld. 1997. *A study of crisis*. Ann Arbor, MI: University of Michigan Press.

Buzan, B., O. Waever. 2003. *Regions and powers: The structure of regional security*. Cambridge: Cambridge University Press.

Dennett, D. 1989. *The intentional stance*. Cambridge, MA: MIT Press.

Dennett, D. 2017. *From bacteria to Bach and back: The evolution of the human mind*. New York, NY: W.W. Norton.

Dessler, D. 2003. Explanation and scientific progress. In *Progress in international relations theory*, eds. C. Elman, M. Elman, 381–401. Cambridge, MA: MIT Press.

Elman, C., M. Elman. Eds. 2003. *Progress in international relations theory*. Cambridge, MA: MIT Press.

Gell-Mann, M. 1994. The Quark and the Jaguar. New York: Henry Holt and Company.

George, A. 1969. The 'operational code': A neglected approach to the study of political leaders and decision making. *International Studies Quarterly* 23: 190–222.

George, A. 1980. *Presidential decision making in foreign policy: The effective use of information and advice*. Boulder, CO: Westview.

George, A. 1993. *Bridging the gap: Theory and practice in foreign policy*. Washington, DC: United States Institute for Peace.

Goertz, G., P. Diehl, A. Balas. 2016. *The puzzle of peace*. New York, NY: Oxford University Press.

Greenstein, F. 1987. [1969]. *Personality and politics*. Princeton, NJ: Princeton University Press.

Greenstein, F., M. Lerner. 1971. *A source book for the study of personality and politics.* Chicago, IL: Markham.

Hawking, S., L. Mlodinow. 2010. *The grand design.* New York, NY: Bantam Books.

Hermann, C. 1972. *International crises.* New York, NY: Free Press.

Hermann, M. 1974. Leader personality and foreign policy behavior. In *Comparing foreign policies,* ed. J. Rosenau, 201–234. New York, NY: John Wiley.

Hermann, M., T. Preston. 1994. Presidents, advisors, and foreign policy. *Political Psychology* 15(1): 75–96.

Holsti, O. 1976. Foreign policy viewed cognitively. In *The structure of decision,* ed. R. Axelrod, 18–54. Princeton, NJ: Princeton University Press.

Holsti, O. 1977. *The 'operational code' as an approach to the analysis of beliefs systems.* Final Report to the National Science Foundation. Grant SOC 75-15368. Durham: Duke University.

Jackson, P. 2011. *The conduct of inquiry in international relations.* New York, NY: Routledge.

Keohane, R., L. Martin. 2003. Institutional theory as a research program. In *Progress in international relations theory,* eds. C. Elman, and M. Elman, 71–109. Cambridge, MA: MIT Press.

Kuhn, T. 1962. *The structure of scientific revolutions.* Chicago, IL: University of Chicago Press.

Lakatos, I. 1970. Falsification and the methodology of scientific research programmes. In *Criticism and the growth of knowledge,* 91–196. Cambridge: Cambridge University Press.

Lake, D., P. Morgan. Eds. 1997. *Regional orders: Building security in a new world.* University Park, PA: Pennsylvania State University Press.

Laudan, L. 1977. *Progress and its problems: Toward a theory of scientific growth.* Berkeley, CA: University of California Press.

Ledoux, J. 2002. *Synaptic self: How our brains become who we are.* New York, NY: Viking Press.

Lloyd, S. 2006. *Programming the universe.* New York, NY: Alfred Knopf.

Lupia, A., M. McCubbins, S. Popkin. Eds. 2000. *Elements of reason: Cognition, choice and the boundaries of rationality.* New York, NY: Cambridge University Press.

Malici, A., S. Walker. 2017. *Role theory and role conflict in U.S.-Iran relations.* New York, NY: Routledge.

Preston, T. 2001. *The president and his inner circle.* New York, NY: Columbia University Press.

Schafer, M., S. Walker. 2006. *Beliefs and leadership in world politics.* New York, NY: Palgrave.

Schafer, M., S. Crichlow. 2010. *Groupthink vs. high-quality decision making in international relations.* New York, NY: Columbia University Press.

Simon, H. 1957. *Models of man.* New York, NY: John Wiley.

Simon, H. 1969. *Sciences of the artificial.* Cambridge, MA: MIT Press.

Smith, M. B. 1968. A map for the analysis of personality and politics. *Journal of Social Issues* 24: 15–28.

Tetlock, P. 1998. Social psychology and world politics. In *Handbook of social psychology,* eds. D. Gilbert, S. Fiske, G. Lindzey, 869–912. New York, NY: McGraw-Hill.

Walker, S. 1982. Psychological explanations of international politics: Problems of aggregation, measurement, and theory construction. In *Biopolitics, political psychology, and international politics*, ed. G. Hopple. London: Francis Pinter.

Walker, S. 1983. The motivational foundations of political belief systems. *International Studies Quarterly 27*: 179–202.

Walker, S. 2003. Operational code analysis as a scientific research program: A cautionary tale. *Progress in international relations theory* eds. C. Elman and M. Elman, 245-276. Cambridge: MIT Press.

Walker, S. 2007. Generalizing about security strategies in the Baltic Sea region. In *Security strategies, power disparity, and identity*, ed. O. Knudsen, 149–176. Burlington, VT: Ashgate.

Walker, S. 2009. The psychology of presidential decision making. In *The Oxford handbook of the American presidency*, eds. G. Edwards, W. Howell, 550–576. New York, NY: Oxford University Press.

Walker, S. 2003. Operational code analysis as a scientific research program: A cautionary tale. In *Progress in international relations theory*, eds. C. Elman, M. Elman, 245–276. Cambridge, MA: MIT Press.

Walker, S. no date. *Thinking small: Binary role theory and the dynamics of world politics*. Unpublished manuscript.

Walker, S. 2013. *Role theory and the cognitive architecture of British appeasement decisions*. New York, NY: Routledge.

Walker, S. 2003. Operational code analysis as a scientific research program: A cautionary tale. *Progress in international relations theory* eds. C. Elman and M. Elman, 245-276. Cambridge: MIT Press.

Walker, S., M. Schafer. 2006. Structural international relations theories and the future of operational code analysis. In *Beliefs and leadership in world politics*, eds. M. Schafer and S. Walker, 237–248.

Walker, S., M. Schafer 2010. Operational code theory. In *The international studies encyclopedia*, ed. R. Denemark, 5492–5514. Chichester, UK: Wiley-Blackwell.

Walker, S., A. Malici. 2011. *U.S. presidents and foreign policy mistakes*. Stanford, CA: Stanford University Press.

Walker, S., A. Malici, M. Schafer. 2011. *Rethinking foreign policy analysis*. New York, NY: Routledge.

Walker, S., M. Schafer, M. Young. 1998. Systematic procedures for operational code analysis. *International Studies Quarterly 42*: 175–190.

Walker, S., M. Schafer, J. Beieler. 2016. Belief systems and foreign policy roles: Role contestation in U.S. foreign policy decisions. In *Domestic role contestation, foreign policy, and international relations*, eds. C. Cantir, and J. Kaarbo, 122–139. New York, NY: Routledge.

Weber, M. 1999. Die 'objektivitat' sozialwissenschaftlicher un sozialpolitischer erkenntnis. In *Gesammmelte aufsatze zur wiissenschaftslehre*, ed. E. Flitner, 146–214. Potsdam: Internet-Ausgabe, www.uni-potsdam.de/u/paed/Flitner/Flitner/Weber/.

Winter, D. 2003. Measuring the motives of political actors at a distance. In *The psychological assessment of political leaders*, ed. J. Post, 153–177. Ann Arbor, MI: University of Michigan Press.

# Index

Printed in the United States
by Baker & Taylor Publisher Services